SOCIAL INEQUALITY

Like past editions, this ninth edition of *Social Inequality: Forms, Causes, and Consequences* is a user-friendly introduction to the study of social inequality. This book conveys the pervasiveness and extensiveness of social inequality in the United States within a comparative context, to show how inequality occurs, how it affects all of us, and what is being done about it.

This edition benefits from a variety of changes that have significantly strengthened the text. The authors pay increased attention to disability, transgender issues, intersectionality, experiences of Muslims, Hispanic populations, and immigration. The ninth edition also includes content on the fall-out from the recession across various groups. The sections on global inequalities have been greatly updated, emphasizing comparative inequalities and the impact of the process of globalization on inequality internationally. The authors have also added material on several current social movements, including Occupy Wall Street, Black Lives Matter, and Marriage Equality.

Charles E. Hurst is Emeritus Professor of Sociology at the College of Wooster in Ohio. His work focuses on issues of social status, comparative poverty and inequality, and the uses of theory in understanding contemporary problems. Recently these interests also include studies of status in Amish communities in Ohio.

Heather M. Fitz Gibbon is a Professor of Sociology at the College of Wooster in Ohio. Her published research focuses on definitions of motherhood within the welfare system and on child care systems. She has also been an active community-based researcher, evaluating antipoverty and family literacy community programs.

Anne M. Nurse is a Professor of Sociology at the College of Wooster in Ohio. Author of two books and multiple articles on juvenile incarceration and its impact on families and communities, she is an expert on inequality and the criminal justice system. She also teaches courses in statistics, criminology, and research methods.

Social Inequality is clearly written, up to date, historically accurate, and comes with a host of resources which are very helpful for teaching this type of course which for some students is hard to conceptualize. Addressing new emerging social movements like the Black Lives Matter movement and the expansion of research on disability makes this new edition a valuable tool for teaching.

Sister Nancy DeCesare, *IHM, PhD, Professor of Human Services, Chestnut Hill College*

Many of my students are strong believers in "pulling yourself up by your own bootstraps" and that they can do and be whatever they want if they just want it enough and work hard enough so I'm always eager to have the textbook like *Social Inequality* help students become aware of structural factors in social stratification.

Mary Donaghy, *Associate Professor of Sociology, Arkansas State University*

Ninth Edition

Social Inequality

FORMS, CAUSES, AND CONSEQUENCES

Charles E. Hurst,
Heather M. Fitz Gibbon,
and Anne M. Nurse

Routledge
Taylor & Francis Group

NEW YORK AND LONDON

Reprint 2018

First published 2017
by Routledge
711 Third Avenue, New York, NY 10017

and by Routledge
2 Park Square, Milton Park, Abingdon, Oxon, OX14 4RN

Routledge is an imprint of the Taylor & Francis Group, an informa business

© 2017 Taylor & Francis

The right of Charles E. Hurst, Heather M. Fitz Gibbon, and Anne M. Nurse
to be identified as author of this work has been asserted by them in
accordance with sections 77 and 78 of the Copyright, Designs and
Patents Act 1988.

Library of Congress Cataloging-in-Publication Data
Names: Hurst, Charles E., author. | Fitz Gibbon, Heather M., author. |
Nurse, Anne, 1968- author.
Title: Social inequality: forms, causes, and consequences/by Charles E.
Hurst, Heather M. Fitz Gibbon, and Anne M. Nurse.
Description: 9th edition. | New York, NY: Routledge, 2016. | Includes
bibliographical references and index.
Identifiers: LCCN 2016005920 | ISBN 9781138688551 (hbk) |
ISBN 9781138688544 (pbk)
Subjects: LCSH: Equality–United States. | United States–Social
conditions.
Classification: LCC HN90.S6 H87 2016 | DDC 305.0973–dc23
LC record available at http://lccn.loc.gov/2016005920

ISBN: 978-0-815-36760-4 (pbk)
ISBN: 978-1-315-53685-9 (ebk)

Typeset in Times
by Sunrise Setting Ltd, Brixham, UK

Printed in India by Saurabh Printers Pvt. Ltd.

For sale in India, Pakistan, Nepal, Bhutan, Bangladesh and Sri Lanka only.

To Mary Ellen

CONTENTS

PART 2   General Explanations of Inequality

PART 3   Consequences of Social Inequality

PREFACE

It is fair to say that concerns about social inequality have dominated the news and the public consciousness over the past few years. Following the Great Recession of 2008–2010, the public has been increasingly aware of growing levels of economic inequality and pernicious inequalities surrounding issues of race, gender, sexuality, gender expression, and disability. Levels of economic inequality have never been higher in this country, and our awareness of these inequalities is far more heightened than in years past. While the economy has greatly recovered, most people remain insecure about their economic futures, and recovery has had a different impact on people depending on their economic class. Similarly, the past several years have seen a rise in social activism on a number of issues surrounding inequality, including racial inequality, gay rights, and class inequality. This edition highlights several social movements including Black Lives Matter, Occupy Wall Street, and the Marriage Equality movement.

Like past editions, this ninth edition of *Social Inequality: Forms, Causes, and Consequences* is intended as a user-friendly introduction to the study of social inequality. The assumptions on which it is based are the same as in previous editions: (1) inequality is multidimensional; (2) explanations of the various forms of inequality are necessary for any resolution of inequality's undesirable consequences; (3) demonstrating inequality's vast extent and forms provides motivation for understanding how it is to be explained; (4) couching a discussion of inequality in its broader historical, cultural, and international context provides a deeper understanding of the nature and role of inequality in society; and (5) an evenhanded approach covering the full range of perspectives and information on inequality is most appropriate, especially for students being exposed to this material for the first time. Our goal is to convey, as simply but as compellingly as we can, a sense of the pervasiveness and extensiveness of social inequality in the United States within a comparative context, to show how inequality can be explained, how it affects all of us, and what is being done about it.

This edition benefits from a variety of changes that, we believe, have significantly strengthened the text.

1. At the suggestion of reviewers, we have increased attention to issues of disability, an important but often neglected aspect of social inequality.
2. As the last edition was produced at the end of the Great Recession, this edition includes material addressing the fall-out from the recession across various groups.
3. We have greatly increased attention to the concerns and issues surrounding transgender people.
4. Throughout the text we have amplified discussions of intersectionality and provided additional examples of inequalities stemming from the intersections of various statuses. We have included a broader discussion of intersectionality in Chapter 10.
5. The chapters in Parts 1, 3, and 4 have been revised, often extensively, with up-to-date information and research so that readers can be made aware of the latest findings on inequality and its consequences.
6. In a number of chapters we have included a greater analysis of the experiences of Muslims and discrimination on the basis of religion, and increased attention to the lives of Hispanics. Similarly, we have expanded attention to issues of immigration.

7. The sections at the conclusion of each chapter addressing global inequalities have been greatly updated, emphasizing comparative inequalities and the impact of the process of globalization on inequality internationally.

8. Many new critical questions, photos, and Nutshell features have also been added.

9. Finally, we have added material on several current social movements, including Occupy Wall Street, Black Lives Matter, and Marriage Equality.

The ninth edition is divided into four major parts. *Part 1* examines the extent of economic, status, and political inequality in a general sense, as well as the impact of gender, sexual orientation, and race/ethnicity on economic status and political inequality. Specific updated theories on gender and racial/ethnic inequality are also presented in detail. *Part 2* covers in-depth discussions of general explanations of inequality. The classical arguments included are those of Marx, Weber, Durkheim, and Spencer, while the contemporary theories discussed include functionalist, social constructionist, reproduction, intersectionality, and labor market theories, along with explanations of inequality between nations. Rather than placing them at the beginning as other texts usually do, we have placed the theory chapters after discussions of the extent of inequality because we believe students will be more inclined to study theories once they realize how extensive inequality is in society. Though scholars often think deductively, students are more likely to start with their own lives, and see what is going on around them before becoming inquisitive about the causes of what is happening in society. The chapters in *Part 3* demonstrate how inequality affects our personal life chances in the forms of physical health and mental well-being as well as how it impacts society's crime rates, environmental inequities, social trust, and social movements. There is no question that inequality's effects are pervasive. Finally, *Part 4* addresses processes of change and stability in the structure of social inequality through discussions of social mobility and attainment, and the justice and legitimacy of inequality. The book concludes with a Glossary of many of the basic terms used in the text.

ACKNOWLEDGMENTS

Although any shortcomings in the book are our own responsibility, any improvements in this edition are due in large part to others. These include our friends and colleagues Christa Craven and Amyaz Moledina at the College of Wooster, plus our two outstanding research assistants, Dana Stamos and Grace Billiter. We would like to give special thanks to Michael G. Federspiel and Pamela J. Forman for their extremely helpful guidance on Chapter 7. The reviewers, Jana Sladkova, UMASS Lowell; Nancy DeCesare, Chestnut Hill College; Hephzibah V. Strmic-Pawl, Coastal Carolina University; Patricia Burke, UT Arlington; Mary Donaghy, Arkansas State University; Stephen Merino, University of Texas–Pan American; and Kendra Murphy, University of Memphis, provided many thoughtful suggestions for improvement of the text. We are grateful for all their detailed comments. Thanks also to Samantha Barbaro at Taylor and Francis for guiding us kindly and wisely through the publication process.

We would like readers to know that this book was originally written by Charles Hurst, and he was the sole author for the first eight editions. Two new authors have been added for this edition, but they can only be credited with building off the incredibly strong foundation Chuck created.

We are all indebted to our families for their support during this project. Chuck's wife, Mary Ellen Hurst, has been there for all nine editions of the book. From the Fitz Gibbon family we thank Stewart, Andrew, and Thomas (including Thomas' research assistance), and from the Nurse/Thompson family we are grateful to John, Alexander, Jacob, and Gabriel. In previous editions, Chuck said of Mary Ellen that "in an unequal world, she is without equal." We agree but think the expression applies equally well to both of them.

CHAPTER 1

An Introduction to the Study of Social Inequality

Inequality is the root of social evil.

POPE FRANCIS (1936–)

Cathy was working as an executive assistant when she was laid off after 15 years on the job. She feels lucky because she received a severance package and is eligible for unemployment insurance, but she knows the money will only last so long, and she needs to find another job quickly (Phillips 2015). Cathy joins millions of others who are worried about keeping afloat economically. For most people in the United States and globally, the last few years have been a time of economic pain.

While unemployment rates are much lower than they were during the financial crisis of 2008–2010, the number of individuals living in poverty remains at an all-time high (DeNavas-Walt and Proctor 2015). This is partly because 2014 marked the third consecutive year of stagnant annual median household income (U.S. Census Bureau 2015d). And as the ranks of the poor have swelled, the gap between the richest and poorest has continued to widen. In fact, a 2014 study indicates that the gap between middle and upper income households is the widest wealth gap on record (Fry and Kochhar 2014). All of these events have helped to foment greater feelings of economic insecurity among individuals and strengthened tendencies toward social fragmentation in society.

This is a book about social inequality in all its forms, and how it continuously affects not only social conditions in U.S. society but also our personal lives on the most intimate levels. While social inequality has been a topic of concern at least since the days of Aristotle, the international economic crisis of the last few years has crystallized and intensified its significance and the problems associated with it.

Of course, these problems weigh unevenly across the U.S. population. Individuals are affected more or less by them because of their economic position, ethnicity, race, sexuality, and gender. People also reside in places that vary in terms of culture, economic resources, and potentials. Together, a person's individual attributes and how these are interpreted, along with family background, and the political, social, and economic contexts in which people reside, affect their specific attitudes, orientation to life, and their chances for decent and satisfactory lives. Consider your own situation. Imagine that you had come from a family of noticeably different wealth or from a different region or nationality, or that you were of a different race or sex, or that you were disabled. How would your experiences, perceptions, and opportunities be different?

Inequality is present and affects us at all stages of our lives. Think of your own experiences. Even when young, we hear of people as being from a "bad neighborhood," as not being "our kind," as being "above" or "below" us. We hear epithets aimed at persons because of their race, ethnicity, gender, or sexual orientation. As youths, we notice that because of the way they dress, where they live, and who their parents are, some children are treated differently and have more or fewer opportunities than others. We are also smart enough to see that there are class differences associated with different neighborhood schools, and even churches. These economic differences show no sign of disappearing.

Economically, the gap between the top and the bottom has increased and class mobility has stagnated in the last few decades. The middle class has been particularly hard-hit. Analyses by newspapers such as the *Wall Street Journal* and the *New York Times* have publicized the growing inequality. "The portion of U.S. adults living in middle-income households fell to 50 percent in 2015 from 61 percent in 1971. The overall share of the upper-income tier increased to 21 percent from 14 percent, while the overall portion of lower-income households increased to 29 percent from 25 percent," writes Janet Adamy in the *Journal* (2015). Nicholas Bloom, a professor at Stanford who was quoted in the *Times*, agrees. He says, "This is a truly global phenomenon, and I don't know any serious economist who would deny inequality has gone up. The debate is over the magnitude, not the direction" (Schwartz 2016).

Census data confirm the extensive inequality. For example, in 2014, the Census Bureau classified almost 46.7 million people, or 14.8 percent of the U.S. population, as poor. Over 21 percent of children under 18 years of age lived in poverty. For a single person under 65 years old, this meant having an income below $12,316, and for a family of two adults and two children, having an income of no more than $24,008 (U.S. Census Bureau 2014c). In 2014, the median household income in the United States was $53,657—even less than what it was 15 years earlier. The highest-earning 20 percent of U.S. families earned 61.8 percent of all income in 2013 (DeSilver 2015). And the 2014 compensation of chief executive officers (CEOs) in the top 500 U.S. corporations was over 300 times that of the average worker (Mishel and Davis 2015).

The gap in income has been fueled by a combination of a growth in corporate profit and layoffs in the top 500 U.S. corporations. Comparing the period from 2010 to 2012 to the period from 2005 to 2007, we see that the percent of the country's GDP going to corporate profits increased, and the share of worker incomes decreased (Norris 2013). This earnings gap is one indicator of the increasing polarization of incomes in the United States. Since the financial crisis of 2008, "families at the bottom of the income distribution saw continued substantial declines in average real incomes between 2010 and 2013," whereas "families at the very top of the income distribution saw widespread economic gains" (Bricker et al. 2014). As we will see in the next chapter, wealth is even more highly polarized than income in the United States, with a small percentage controlling most of the resources. Indeed, economic inequality thrives in the United States.

Recent events have intensified the trend toward greater inequality. To further strengthen their economic positions, for example, an increasing number of companies have been able to successfully pass off their pension obligations to the federal government; consequently, workers will likely receive only a small proportion of their originally promised pensions. In 2014, the federal government approved further pension cuts to multiemployer plans (retirement plans that included a number of different employers) (Miller 2014). A number of cities have also cut their pension plans. Detroit took this step as part of a bankruptcy agreement. Walter Knall, a former city worker and father of three, now worries that he will not be able to pay for his children's education. He said, "It really hurts a lot because it was something that I was counting on and I thought I was supposedly guaranteed. I will fight to the very end" (Ferretti 2015).

Among those especially hard-hit have been blue-collar workers whose manufacturing plants have moved or shut down. In 2015, for example, over 1000 workers were laid off at United Steel. This happened, at least in part, because of imports of cheap Chinese steel. Isaiah Henderson is one of those laid-off workers. He successfully fought cancer only to find out that there was no job for him to go back to. "When times were good, it was an excellent place to work. Great pay, great benefits," Henderson said. "The last couple of years, it's just gone down. With the economy being the way it's been, there was nothing that could be done" (Gray 2015).

Despite the layoffs in the steel industry, the national unemployment rate has been decreasing since 2010. This is good news for many workers who suffered spells of unemployment during the financial downturn. At the same time, many of the available jobs today are part-time or have erratic schedules. This is problematic for people who need or want consistent full-time work. For example, Melody Pabon is having trouble supporting her child on her part-time salary. "I've been working at Zara, a women's clothing store in Manhattan, as a cashier and on the sales floor for about four years. I also just started school to become a medical assistant. I used to be scheduled to close the store a lot. On those nights I got home to Brooklyn after Mason, my four-year-old, was already asleep. I wanted to be able to spend time with him in the evening, so I asked for an earlier shift. But at my job, anyone who is not available 24/7 always seems to get their hours cut. And that is what happened to me. I went from working 35 hours to 25 over the course of a few weeks. That's almost a third of my paycheck" (National Women's Law Center 2015).

The injurious impact of inequality is not confined to the working class and poor, however. In recent years, as companies downsize to meet competition and maintain profits, the effects of social and economic forces pushing people into different economic circumstances have been increasingly felt by those in the white-collar ranks. In San Antonio, 39-year-old Denise Stoll was laid off from her job as a vice president of a technology group. Because she earned considerably more than her husband, the family is struggling. She is trying to make the best of it by enjoying time with her kids and "teaching them lessons about thrift" (Luo 2009). Unfortunately, Ms. Stoll's story is not unique. In the first quarter of 2015 alone, nearly 4 million workers applied for unemployment insurance (Office of Unemployment Insurance 2015).

The streamlining and downsizing of businesses have left millions of experienced, specialized workers with temporary part-time jobs or without jobs. Frequently, these workers and their families experience various problems that result from downward mobility. For example, Paul Bachmuth lost his job at an energy consulting company, and, as the months went by, tensions in his family grew. His 12-year-old daughter started having uncontrollable fits of anger, and his younger daughter began pulling out her hair. His marriage was under stress. Mr. Bachmuth said that his wife "kind of had something in the back of her mind that it was partly my fault I was laid off, maybe you're not a good enough worker" (Luo 2009).

At the same time that many people are experiencing downward mobility, advances in computer and information technologies have created opportunities for others to become phenomenally rich. Five years ago, nobody had heard of Evan Speigel. Yet in 2015, the 25-year-old creator of the application Snapchat was among the richest Americans, with wealth well in excess of a billion dollars (Wang 2015).

Certainly, individuals disagree on what causes people to wind up in the economic positions they are in. Erma Goulart, a 67-year-old retiree and widow with only a high school diploma, believes that she "worked hard for what I have" but feels that "[t]he rich get more benefits and tax breaks and the poor people don't." In contrast, Steve Schoneck, a 39-year-old college graduate and accounting official for a utility company, thinks that "[y]ou always have the opportunity to try and move forward financially.. . . Over all, I've achieved the American dream. I'm happy" (Scott and Leonhardt 2005, p. A16). These assessments suggest the different emphasis that people place on the relative roles of individual and extra-individual factors in explaining their class positions, and the fact that those who are less successful are less likely to be fully content with their positions.

SOME CONTROVERSIAL ISSUES OF SUBSTANCE

Inequality and its effects are all around us. Consider the impact of inequality one is likely to see during a lifetime involving differences in possessions, places, wealth, experiences, bodies, races, genders, and power. The extensiveness of such inequality is almost overwhelming. And yet, there is a great deal of controversy about social inequalities. Are social inequalities inevitable, especially in a capitalist society that stresses competition and individual success? Why do some people have more than others? Is this natural or unnatural? Do "you always have the opportunity to try" as Steve Schoneck suggests, and does "hard work" always pay off despite the odds against average people that Erma Goulart believes exist? Is inequality a *social* problem or an *individual* one? Is it desirable or not? Is inequality a source of divisiveness or a basis for integration in U.S. society? Are social *classes* really present in the United States, and, if so, are they the most important dimension of inequality in our society? Can equality in political power even exist if economic resources are distributed unequally? Or does the golden rule operate—those with the gold rule? Does the globalization in the world economy strengthen or weaken inequality? These are among the most intriguing and consequential questions that have been raised in the study of social inequality. We now examine some of these in more detail.

Is Inequality Inevitable?

Perhaps the most basic issue relates to the inevitability of inequality. It is important to clarify that reference is being made here to *institutionalized* rather than *individual* inequality (i.e., structured inequality between categories of individuals that are systematically created, reproduced, legitimated by sets of ideas, and relatively stable). We would not be studying this phenomenon if it was not a prominent feature of contemporary society with significant consequences. To ask whether it is inevitable is to address the origins of inequality (i.e., whether it is caused by natural or artificial factors). If social inequality is directly linked to conditions inherent in the nature of groups of individuals or society, then little might be expected to eliminate it. On the other hand, if such inequality arises because of the conscious, intentional, and freely willed actions of individuals or the structures they create in society, then perhaps it can be altered.

One side argues that inequality is always going to be present because of personal differences among individuals either in the form of basic differences in their own makeups or differences in the amount of effort they expend. A large majority of Americans would appear to agree. A recent poll, for example, found that 65 percent of Americans think that people can get ahead if they just work hard (Pew 2014b). In explaining his own success, Steve Schoneck believes he took advantage of the opportunities available to everyone and, as a result, was able to achieve the American dream. In his view, he had what it took to get ahead. If there is an open society and if people vary in their talents and motivations, then this would suggest that inequality is inevitable, a simple fact of society. "Some inequalities come about as a result of unavoidable biological inequalities of physical skill, mental capacity, and traits of personality," argued Cauthen (1987, p. 8) in his treatise on equality. Some early philosophers also argued that there are "natural" differences between individuals; in fact, some people still maintain that differences of this type separate the sexes, resulting in the inevitability of inequality. Aristotle took the position that "the male is by nature superior, the female, inferior; and the one rules, and the other is ruled" (in Kriesberg 1979, p. 12). These and other explanations of inequality will be discussed in detail later.

Other theorists have argued that inequality is inevitable because as long as certain kinds of tasks are more necessary for the survival of the society than others, and as long as those who are able to perform those tasks are rare, social inequality of rewards among individuals is needed to motivate the best people to perform the most difficult tasks. Under these conditions, the argument goes, inequality cannot be eradicated without endangering the society.

On the other side of the fence are those who argue that economic inequality is not inevitable and is largely the by-product of a system's structure and not the result of major differences in individual or group talents, characteristics, and motivations. Rousseau, for example, linked the origins of inequality to the creation of private property (Dahrendorf 1970, p. 10). It is the characteristics of the political economy and the firms and labor markets within it that are primary determinants of differences in income and wealth. Where a person works and in what industry have major effects on income. Certainly, the job changes resulting from downsizing would suggest this. Essentially, then, this argument states that it is not human nature and individual differences but rather structural conditions that determine where an individual winds up on the ladder of economic inequality. Discrimination is another of those conditions.

Clearly, Erma Goulart suspects that her situation may be at least partially determined by forces (e.g., tax policies) beyond her control. If the conditions that generate social inequality are artificial creations of human actions, then they can be changed, and economic inequality is not inevitable, nor is it necessarily beneficial for the society and all its members. We will examine this controversy more thoroughly in later chapters.

Is Inequality Desirable or Undesirable?

Some scholars think of inequality as a source of integration in society. The functionalist view, for example, which we will explore later, argues that inequality in rewards is a way of making sure that critical occupations are filled with the most qualified persons. That is, since rewards provide motivation to do certain tasks, the structure of inequality is really an incentive system that helps the whole society survive. Other analysts contend that economic and other kinds of inequality create divisiveness between the haves and the have-nots, men and women, minorities and majorities. This is in large part because these groups are not equally likely to believe that the system of inequality is fair. Nor do they agree that inequality works to the benefit of the entire society rather than only a few select groups. Because of this, inequality is more likely to instigate conflict than it is to strengthen cohesion between groups and in society in general.

A variety of studies have asked Americans how they feel about equality and inequality, and it is clear that they have mixed emotions. Americans are decidedly ambivalent about what should be done about social inequality. National studies of U.S. adults suggest that while Americans do not want equality for everyone and that some differences are needed to motivate people to work hard, they think the present degree of income and wealth inequality is too great and unfair and should be reduced (Norton and Ariely 2011). In a national poll conducted in 2015, 63 percent of respondents said that the current distribution of wealth and income was unfair (Newport 2015a). While Americans tend to believe in freedom and individual responsibility, they also feel that governmental help should be given when opportunities for some are blocked and when others need help because of disabilities.

In some ways, Americans are attracted to equality; in other ways, they view inequality as justified. Part of the problem here is that people think about different things when they think about inequality, and people feel differently about the various kinds of equality/inequality; thus, the meaning of equality/inequality is not self-evident. For example, Bryan Turner (1986) identified four basic kinds of equality: (1) equality of human beings—that is, the notion that basically we are all the same and equally worthy as persons; (2) equality of opportunity—the idea that access to valued ends is open to all; (3) equality of condition—that is, that all start from the same position; and (4) equality of results or outcome, or equality of income. The latter is the most radical of the four and the one most likely to incite controversy.

Americans feel quite differently about equality of opportunity than they do about equality of income, and groups feel differently about the fairness of the system. A national poll conducted by the Pew Research Center (2012) found that 70 percent of Americans feel that the government should adopt policies to enhance equality of opportunity but less than half support policies that directly redistribute income. This shows that they feel any fair distribution of goods should be based more on equality of *opportunity* rather than equality of *result*. We will examine the tangle of American beliefs about inequality and its fairness more fully in Chapter 15.

Are There Classes in the United States?

The economic differences that exist among families and among individuals can be easily recognized, but does that mean that social *classes* exist in the United States? There is much to discourage the belief in classes, including the traditional American value system, which stresses individualism, liberty, and the notion that all can get ahead if they work hard. It is inconsistent with these values to believe in or to have class inequalities in which a person's fate is largely determined by the group to which they belong. The value of equality—that we are all one people, that, underneath, U.S. citizens are all "common folk" without formal titles (e.g., duke, lord)—also helps to reinforce the basic notion that all Americans are equal and not members of different classes. To believe otherwise would be un-American.

In addition to some central U.S. values, other conditions moderate the belief in the existence of classes. First of all, a lack of agreement in the conceptualization of "class" makes it difficult for there to be agreement on the existence of classes. Second, in contrast to race and sex, there are far fewer reliable and clear-cut physical clues to class position. Walking down the street, it is much easier to tell accurately whether someone is Black or White and male or female than it is to tell what class they occupy. Class is often invisible, and therefore we seem to be less often confronted by it. People do not always wear their class positions on their sleeves, so to speak. Think about it: Can you reliably and accurately tell the class positions of your classmates simply by their appearance?

Third, this very invisibility makes it much easier to create and manipulate ideas about the existence of classes in society. It is much easier to say that classes simply do not exist. Finally, the increasing concern for privacy and personal security in U.S. society, which isolates people from each other, enhances the belief in the absence of classes. It is hard to recognize classes and the predicaments of others if we live in shells. Any individual differences in wealth would be viewed as a continuum along which all individuals and families could be located. Here, the image of a system of inequality is one of a tall but narrow ladder. Discrete, wide, separate class layers would not be a part of this perspective.

In fact, some social theorists have argued that the term *social class* has no relevance for the United States, at least in its Marxian definition. In this view, social classes, as unified class-conscious groups with their own lifestyles and political beliefs, do not apply to the United States, whereas they may still fully apply to European countries that have a tradition of class conflict, such as Italy or France. There may be differences in lifestyle and status between different occupational groups, but these differences are not thought to be class based. Much of the traditional research in the field of inequality, in fact, has focused on social lifestyle differences between groups rather than on economic-class differences. The focus of research is, of course, conditioned by the historical context in which it occurs, the cultural milieu, and the events of the times. As we shall see, this is clearly the case in research by Americans on social inequality in the United States.

One position, then, is that social classes as full-fledged antagonists do not characterize present-day U.S. society. A second view is that fairly distinct classes exist at the extremes of the inequality hierarchy but not in the middle, which is considered largely a mass of relatively indistinguishable categories of people. A third position is that distinct classes have always existed and continue to exist in the United States, and that class conflict, especially in the institutionalized form of union–management friction, continues to this day. Distinct disparities in the incomes of those in different occupational categories would appear to reinforce the notion that classes exist in the United States, and the increasing polarization of incomes and wealth might further crystallize the image of a class structure in the minds of individuals.

But even if classes do exist, does this mean that they are the most important dimension of social inequality in the United States? Certainly, there are other bases and forms of inequality that are important, such as those between the sexes and between races. Moreover, inequality not only can take an economic form, but also can appear in a social or political form. We will be examining all these forms in the next several chapters, beginning with those forms of inequality that appear more as *outcomes* (i.e., economic, status, political) and then moving on to those forms that can be viewed more as *bases* for those outcomes (i.e., gender, sexual orientation, race/ethnicity). As we will see, Max Weber conceived of each of the three outcomes above as aspects of the distribution of power in society. Power can take each of these forms, and how much power one has in these areas appears to be at least partially *based* on one's gender, sexual orientation, and race/ethnicity. Oftentimes, the latter three bases intersect in their impact or have compounding effects. The combination of being not only a woman but also Black rather than White, for example, can have distinct effects on how far one can get economically, socially, and/or politically. In several of the following chapters, we will have occasion to look at the impact of this "intersectionality" on inequality outcomes.

Can Capitalism and Democracy Coexist?

Do economic and political inequality necessarily go together? The *economic* system of **capitalism** has been linked to the *political* system of democracy in both a positive and a negative manner (Almond 1991). It has been viewed as a determinant as well as an enemy of democracy. Can capitalism and democracy effectively coexist? Pure capitalism demands that markets be open and free and that individuals be able to freely pursue their economic goals, competing with others within the broad framework of the legal system. Capitalism's ideal conditions assume *equality of opportunity,* regardless of sex, race, or any other category. Presumably, individual talents and motivations are the prime determinants of how far a person goes in the system. This is how many would explain the high executive salaries noted previously. For example, the cosmetic company Estée Lauder described its CEO compensation policy in a required yearly statement to its shareholders. It stated that its policy is created to "attract and retain high-quality people and to motivate them to achieve" (Melin 2015). A system like this presumably would result in the best people being in the highest positions, with the consequence being an efficiently run economy. But if this type of competitive capitalism operates in the United States, then economic inequality is unavoidable, since the talents and motivations of individuals and supply and demand for them vary. There is a potential for economic concentration under these circumstances, with a few having much while many have little. In his recent widely cited analysis of inequality, Piketty (2014) states that "[w]hen the rate of return on capital exceeds the group rate of output and income, as it did in the nineteenth century and seems quite likely to do again in the twenty-first, capitalism automatically generates arbitrary and unsustainable inequalities that radically undermine the meritocratic values on which democratic societies are based" (p. 1).

Alongside the U.S. capitalistic economic system exists a political democracy in which everyone is supposed to have a vote in the running of the government. "One person, one vote" is the rule. *Equality of result* is expected in the political arena in the sense that power should be equally distributed. The question is, Can equality of political power and inequality in economic standing coexist? Or does economic power lead to inordinate, unequal political power, thereby making a mockery of political equality? Can open economic capitalism and political democracy exist harmoniously alongside each other? John Adams, one of the Founding Fathers of the United States, expressed concern that "the balance of power in a society accompanies the balance of property and land. . . . If the multitude is possessed of the balance of real estate, the multitude will have the balance of power and, in that case, the multitude will take care of the liberty, virtue and interest of the multitude in all acts of government" (Adams 1969, pp. 376–377). Bryan Turner wrote, "Modern capitalism is fractured by the contradictory processes of inequality in the marketplace and political inequality at the level of state politics. There is an inevitable contradiction between economic class and the politics of citizenship" (1986, p. 24). How do individuals who lack economic resources react politically to this situation? Does the contradiction generate resistance? Is it possible to have a society that is both capitalistic and democratic? During the recent economic crisis, which exposed extensive fraud and inequality, government intrusion into market mechanisms suggested that capitalism and democracy are inherently antagonistic to each other. Conversely, the Supreme Court's 2010 decision to allow unfettered corporate funding to political campaigns would appear to open the door to greater political power for those who have the money.

Conservatives and liberals generally take different positions on each of the issues we have been discussing. Conservatives tend to praise the virtues of open capitalism and emphasize its benefits for the individual, rather than to see the internal contradictions between capitalism and democracy. Liberals, on the other hand, view unbridled capitalism as destructive of human beings and stress the linkage between economic and political power, seeing money as a contaminant of the political process. Conservatives also tend to view social inequality as inevitable, if not necessary and desirable, and perceive the United States as being largely classless, seeing the similarities among Americans as being more fundamental than the differences. In sharp contrast, liberals conclude that inequality is neither inevitable nor desirable, that the United States is a class society, and that basic social, economic, and political conditions create deep divisions within the population.

Does Globalization Reduce or Increase Inequality?

As a whole, U.S. society is increasingly susceptible to conditions and developments beyond its borders. Many of these are economic, but others are political, social, cultural, and sometimes even religious in nature. The weakening of national boundaries that attends globalization has allowed nations to trade, borrow, and transport goods and services more easily. At the same time, it has also meant a greater flow and interchange of currencies, peoples, and influence. As a worldwide force, has globalization had a positive or negative effect on inequality? As we will see later, some argue that free trade and exchange of ideas and technologies encourage the leveling out of differences and inequalities among nations, while others contend that open markets favor the powerful and are used by economic powers to strengthen and deepen their hold on global economic operations. The former argue that open exchange fosters the dissemination of technology and medicine to nations in need of help, leading to benefits such as the development of larger middle classes in places such as India and China. The latter allege more negative outcomes: Freedom and open borders advantage wealthy countries and disadvantage poorer ones. Transnational corporations and other international organizations can bypass restraints and regulations by individual countries, thereby weakening the power of national governments over them. The opening up of broader markets and labor supplies also gives corporations more leverage over local governments and workers.

Whatever its effects, the impact of globalization is not simply economic. Open exchanges among nations have political, social, and cultural consequences as well that affect the shape and character of national systems of inequality. Globalization's rapid expansion has made international relationships much more complicated and difficult to understand because of the vast differences in histories, traditions, and cultures that exist among partners in the world marketplace. The combination of open borders and a lack of full understanding of other countries and peoples can breed feelings of insecurity and encourage protectionist tendencies by national governments. Those in power can then feed worries about dangers like terrorism to push policies that help to maintain their power (Béland 2007). These policies often take the form of more restrictive immigration and trade policies. The inflow of immigrant workers with cultures and behaviors quite different from those of native or dominant populations increases the significance of status differences and inequality, and can inflame hostilities within the working class. Because it makes borders more permeable, globalization also breaks down a country's insulation from a multitude of problems originating in other nations. The increasingly dense network of relationships around the globe means that changes and conditions in one place can reverberate throughout the whole international system. Consequently, the full impact of globalization on the economic, status, and power balance *among* countries and economic, social, and political inequality *within* them has yet to be completely mapped out. But there appears to be little question that globalization's impact across the world, at least for the near future, will continue unabated.

ISSUES OF METHODOLOGY

In addition to the preceding substantive controversies, there are also important methodological issues that must be considered in the study of inequality, most of which you will encounter as you read through the following chapters.

How these questions are handled by scholars heavily affects the conclusions they draw about the nature and extent of social inequality. These issues frequently involve questions about definitions and measurement of concepts, levels of analysis, and the relative impacts of race, class, sexual orientation, and gender on individual lives.

Definitional Problems

One of the most fundamental questions involves the measurement of social class and poverty. As noted later, *social class* has been defined in different ways, using different indices. Some consider social classes simply as different categories of people in which individuals in the same category happen to have similar levels of education, income, and occupational **prestige**, whereas others view different classes and organized groups in conflict with each other. Still others focus on lifestyle as the critical factor that distinguishes social classes. These different definitions result in different measures of social-class position.

As in the case of social class, *poverty* has also been defined and measured in different ways. Some argue that being poor means more than not having money—it also means a lack of status and power. Even when money is used as the measure of poverty, there is disagreement about whether it should be gross or net income, whether it should include income from government programs, whether it should be current or long-term income, and so on. Currently, the federal government sets income thresholds to determine one's poverty, and uses gross income from all sources as the measure of a person's income. Other methodological issues arise when examining additional dimensions of social inequality. How to measure discrimination when discussing racial or gender inequality, how to measure the openness of a society using its mobility rates, how to measure political power, and how to gauge the comparability of situations when discussing how the degree of social inequality in the United States stacks up against that found in other countries—all are methodological issues of significance and difficulty.

Why are these differences in measurement and definition so professionally and practically important? Professionally, varying definitions and measures make comparability of results difficult and raise problems of communication among scholars supposedly studying the same phenomenon. Practically, these different perspectives are significant and involve heated discussion among politicians because how such things as openness, discrimination, poverty, and class are measured affects what kinds of policies they think should be pursued. For example, the measure of poverty affects how much poverty exists, how big a problem it is, and how much, if anything, needs to be done about it. Simply recognizing poverty as a social problem, in fact, is the result of some individuals or groups "making claims" about poverty's problematic nature and then using a particular style to convince others that it is a problem (Ibarra and Kitsuse 2003). Others may not see poverty as a social problem or may not be convinced by the styles used to demonstrate that poverty really is a social problem. The definition and measurement of poverty, therefore, is a political hot potato because so much rides on which approach is accepted at the time.

In addition to class and poverty, "race" is also a contested concept because while we have traditionally thought of it as designating innate and fixed biological differences between individuals, it has increasingly been shown to be a concept that has been *socially constructed* over time. Rather than an inherent quality of individuals, it is seen as a manufactured product, resulting from social conflict and power arrangements in society. Racial classifications and positions within them change as political, social, and other shifts occur in society. We will discuss the theory of racial formation more fully in Chapter 8.

With respect to the discussion of women, the trend in terminology has been to use the term *gender* rather than *sex* when discussing differences and inequalities between men and women. However, they mean different things. When we speak of a person's *sex,* we ordinarily are referring to the perceived biological status of *female* or *male generally* assigned at birth. *Gender,* however, denotes the definitions, assignments, and behaviors that different groups and cultures assign to the sexes, and these can vary across societies. These are definitions and assignments "built into" the roles and positions in the economy and other institutions, creating a gendered social structure (Lorber 2001). In other words, *gender* is a "cultural construct" (Caplan 1987).

As we will see, some have argued that *sex* is also a product of culture, which would give the usually biological term a decidedly cultural, that is, social scientific, interpretation. From the 1960s onward, many social scientists have embraced the above distinctions between sex and gender, and have even emphasized the term *gender* over *sex,* sometimes avoiding the latter term altogether. "Dropping sex and adopting gender buried biology," contends Dorothy Smith. "Although legitimate as a political move, it has left us with no way of recognizing just how biology enters into relations among women, men, and children. I think of my bodily experience, particularly as a mother, and I am powerfully aware of how biological fundamentals entered into that experience" (Smith 2009, p. 76). There are biological components to who we are as beings (e.g., menstruation, hormones); even how we react to them is largely a cultural phenomenon. While analytically separate, sex and **gender** almost always intersect.

Finally, the concept of *power* is also a fuzzy one. Power can exist in many forms and can be viewed on several levels. In the discussion of political inequality in Chapter 5, we will focus initially on power in decision-making processes in the *political institution.* It is not unusual for us to think of power solely as a property of the political or governmental realm. But power inequality can also exist in the employment relationships between men and women, bosses and workers, Blacks and Whites. Since work dominates the everyday lives of most adults, we will also examine power relationships in the work environment.

In addition to the definitional issues swirling around all these concepts, there is also a dilemma involving their interrelationship. Can one effectively separate the independent effects of race, class, sex, and gender on the individual? Although each is a distinct variable, all are inextricably intermixed in the lives of actual individuals.

Persons simultaneously occupy positions on each of these, and, in real life, they are deeply interconnected. We must recognize both their separateness and their interconnectedness when considering their roles in people's lives.

Levels of Analysis

The study of social inequality is concerned with both individuals and groups, personal positions as well as structural arrangements. Thus, analysis proceeds on several levels. For example, we are interested in how an individual's class-related characteristics affect the probability of that person being arrested, but we are also interested in how the structure of inequality itself affects the crime rate for the society as a whole. We are interested in the process by which individuals attain higher or lower status positions, but we are also interested in how class structures shift in society and how changes in occupational structures affect rates of social mobility. We will look not only at how an individual's race or sex affects their income but also at how institutionalized discrimination affects the overall structure of inequality between the races and sexes. Many of the chapters to follow take into account these important methodological issues.

ORGANIZATION OF THE BOOK

The text is divided into four major parts. Part One addresses the extent of inequality in its various forms. Chapters 2, 3, 4, and 5 focus on specific forms of inequality that concern resource *outcomes* (i.e., income/wealth, poverty, social status, and power) which are distributed unequally among individuals and groups in the United States. Inequalities related to gender, sexual orientation, gender identity and expression, and race, while viewed as specific forms of inequality in their own right, are also significant *bases* for inequalities in resource outcomes. They are addressed in Chapters 6, 7, and 8. Gender (including both gender identity and expression), sexual orientation, and race affect the distribution of wealth, status, and power in our society. Unlike some other

inequality texts, we have included a chapter on sexual orientation, gender identity, and gender expression because, as many recent examples of bullying, harassment, and discrimination in the United States indicate, it is a significant basis for social and economic inequality. Finally, to place the U.S. structure and dynamics of inequality within a broader framework, we briefly discuss the global context of U.S. inequality at the end of each of these chapters. The reader will then be able to see how the United States stands in relation to other nations.

Several of the chapters in Part One include *specific* causes of given forms of inequality. Part Two presents the major *general* explanations for social inequality, with Chapter 9 including discussions of Marx's, Weber's, Durkheim's, and Spencer's classical perspectives on inequality. Chapter 10 analyzes more contemporary explanations, ranging from functionalist theories, to social reproduction and constructionist theories, to intersectional theories of inequality.

Having discussed the extent and explanations of inequality in Parts One and Two, Part Three demonstrates the pervasive *consequences* of inequality for individuals and society. Physical and mental health, hunger, and homelessness are all subject to the influences of individual positions in the hierarchy of social inequality. These personal effects are the focus of Chapter 11. The long arm of inequality reaches far into personal and private worlds, but its effects also extend into the wider society as well. In Chapter 12, the effects of inequality on crime, environmental equity, social trust, and solidarity are explored. Specifically, the effects of socioeconomic position, race, and sex and gender on criminal justice are examined, ranging from the chances of being arrested to the likelihood of being given a long sentence. Street crimes, white-collar crimes, and hate crimes are each discussed. Inequality also has played a role in generating high crime rates, and raising questions about environmental justice. As we will see when examining the negative effects of inequality in a global context, the United States does not always fare well when compared to other rich industrial nations.

On a broader level, the labor, civil rights, and women's movements can be viewed as reactions to inequalities based on class, race, and gender, respectively, inequalities that are perceived as unjust. Chapter 13 surveys the history of these movements and their relationship to inequality.

Part Four of the book examines what has been happening to the system of inequality and how people feel about it. Chapter 14 asks whether there is a great deal of mobility in U.S. society. Do rags-to-riches stories provide a typical picture of the careers of most Americans? How does the United States compare with other countries in its rate of mobility? Is it more open than others? Have African Americans and women become more upwardly mobile in recent years? What determines how far up people go in the occupational hierarchy? Finally, Chapter 15 discusses the thorny issue of the equity of inequality. What do Americans think about their system's inequality? Is it fair or not? What do they think determines or *should* determine how far one gets in the system? These comprise some of the central questions addressed in Part Four.

Each chapter ends with a short set of questions and film suggestions, addressing some critical issues raised by the chapter. They are aimed at forcing you to come to grips with central problems in inequality, often by looking at inequality in your own life. *Web Connections* sections suggest various websites where you can get more information and which you can use as bases for course exercises. These should broaden and deepen your understanding of inequality. Many chapters also contain a brief *Nutshell* covering a topical issue from the popular press or a *Mini-Case* addressing a specific issue to be analyzed. Each issue is introduced to serve as a point of departure for classroom discussion. Finally, a *Glossary* of basic terms used in the text follows the last chapter.

The lines separating the social sciences are often vague, the result being that discussions in the book often will draw on the work of economists, anthropologists, as well as sociologists, and others. In addition, there is material from other countries. These inclusions, hopefully, result in a more thorough and well-rounded perspective on the structure and process of social inequality in the United States.

Critical Thinking

1. Try to think of a personal relationship you have with someone who is unequal to you in some way, and yet the inequality appears to have few negative effects on you or your relationship. What characteristics lessen the impact of the inequality in this relationship? Discuss some lessons from this relationship that might be used to diminish the negative effects of inequality in society as a whole.
2. Is social inequality a problem that demands the full attention of society, or is it merely a personal

problem of those living below the middle class? Explain your answer.
3. Is it possible for *equality* in political power to exist alongside economic *inequality*?
4. Gazing into your crystal ball, do you think the long-run impact of increasing relationships among peoples around the world will lead to a leveling of inequalities among them, or will it solidify or increase existing inequalities?

Web Connections

Several of the following chapters use information obtained from national polls, many of which are published on the Internet. The National Council on Public Polls suggests that among the questions you should consider before accepting poll results are the following: (1) Who sponsored and who conducted the poll? (2) Is the sample large enough and

representative of the whole population? (3) Were any important groups excluded from the poll? (4) Was the technique used in the interview likely to affect the answers received? (5) Was the wording of the questions neutral or biased in some way? (6) Are the survey results still valid or are they out-of-date? (Carr 2005).

PART 1

Extent and Forms of Social Inequality

CHAPTER 2

Class, Income, and Wealth

With the people, for the people, by the people. I crack up when I hear it;
I say, with the handful, for the handful, by the handful, cause
that's what really happens.

FANNIE LOU HAMER (1917–1977)

In the next several chapters, we will be considering several forms of inequality: economic, status, gender, sexuality, racial, and political. In this chapter, we examine economic inequality in the form of social class and income/wealth differences. Chapter 3 considers the extent of poverty and attempts to address it. We begin with economic inequality because other aspects of inequality are often strongly related to economic or class inequality in a society. As we will see in later chapters, economic position has a significant impact on the prestige, power, and life chances that individuals possess. Consequently, a discussion of social class and economic inequality is critical for a full understanding of other forms of inequality.

THE EVERYDAY REALITY OF CLASS

In general, Americans do not like to talk about **class.** "Class is not discussed or debated in public because class identity has been stripped from popular culture. The institutions that shape mass culture and define the parameters of public debate have avoided class issues. . . . [F]ormulating issues in terms of class is unacceptable, perhaps even un-American" (Mantsios 2004, p. 193). But their reluctance to discuss class does not mean that Americans do not think about it. The meaning of class for the public is rooted in their everyday experiences and relationships. Awareness of class differences begins early; even preschool children categorize individuals as rich or poor and make judgments about them on that basis (Horwitz, Shutts, and Olson 2014). By elementary school, children can reliably identify social class location, and they have definite ideas about behavioral and social differences between groups (Mistry et al. 2015).

Class structure is also a subjective reality for adults. When asked about it, people in the United States are much more likely to agree on and have clear images of the top and bottom of the class structure than they are of the middle classes, which are seen as more amorphous and heterogeneous. The perceived distinctiveness of the top, for example, is based not only on their wealth, but also on the social and cultural boundaries that are seen as separating them from those below. Because of their extraordinary wealth, those at the top of the economic hierarchy often take on notoriety or celebrity status (e.g., Bill Gates, the Kennedy family). Those who have "old wealth" are often very guarded about who is let into their group and who is not, which again identifies them as unique and different from those below them (Kendall 2002; Howard 2008). The popular image of the bottom is similarly clear, with that perception being dominated by stereotypes of individuals who are chronically on welfare, homeless, and often of minority status. The economic middle, in contrast, is seen as mainly made up of white-collar professionals, semiprofessionals, and highly paid blue-collar "aristocrats," that is, a loose collection of widely varying individuals not nearly as homogeneous in the public's eye as those at the top and bottom. Below them, the working class is often described as being composed of those in less-skilled, routine white-collar and blue-collar positions.

Most Americans feel at least fairly strongly that they belong to a particular class (Hout 2007). When asked to place themselves in the class structure, usually 80–90 percent of adults say that they are either "middle" or "working" class. In 2015, a survey by the Gallup Organization indicated that 51 percent of the adults interviewed considered themselves as "middle" or "upper-middle" class, while 33 percent classified themselves as "working" class. Only 1 percent thought they were "upper class," and 15 percent labeled themselves "lower" class (Newport 2015b).

But on other aspects of class structure, individuals vary in their perceptions. When asked in surveys to describe the nature of the class structure in the United States, individuals' images have differed depending on their own class positions. Historically, middle-class respondents have described the class structure more as a relatively smooth continuum with few major breaks between classes, while those in the working and lower classes have been more likely to see classes as discrete, distinct groups, and to perceive a smaller number of classes. A recent poll found that 73 percent of Blacks compared to only 40 percent of Whites believe that the United States is divided into the "haves" and "have-nots." However, both groups' percentages have grown over the last two decades corresponding to growth in the polarization of incomes and wealth (Pew 2011b). The survey also found that those in the lower classes are more likely than those in higher classes to believe there is a greater distance between the top and the bottom.

Criteria used to place individuals in a given class also vary, although we know that income, education, and occupation are all very important. Other variables that appear to be linked to subjective class include age, home ownership, and marriage (Hout 2007). Occupational positions that are seen as requiring mental ability or as having authority over others are generally classified as at least middle class rather than working class (Jackman and Jackman 1983). Class position itself affects what individuals think distinguishes persons in different class positions. For example, those in the working and lower classes are more likely to see the upper class as being distinguished by *money,* while those in the higher classes see their main distinction as deriving from their *lifestyle.* Indeed, individuals in the higher professions are significantly more likely than persons in other occupational statuses to engage in "highbrow" cultural activities (Gerhards, Hans, and Mutz 2012). With respect to other criteria, married men and women vary in how much they consider their separate incomes and educations when describing their class position. Married men and women, for example, agree that both the husband's and wife's incomes affect their class position equally, but they differ on whether their own as well as their spouse's educations help define their class position (Yamaguchi and Wang 2002). What all these research results suggest is that while Americans tend to agree on some broad ideas about U.S. class structure, there are also many ways in which their views vary, resulting in the absence of a single crystallized image of the U.S. class structure as a whole.

TWO VIEWS OF U.S. CLASS STRUCTURE

Mirroring popular disagreements are debates among scholars about the nature of the class structure in the United States. Some portrayals of class structure use sets of very diverse criteria, following closely a socioeconomic definition of class, whereas others try to be more faithful to Marxian criteria. Neither of these approaches is inherently better than the other, and each focuses on criteria that have been found to have separate effects on individuals' life conditions. Each approach attempts to identify meaningful breaks in the class system, and, as such, each is useful in characterizing different aspects of economic inequality. Consequently, rather than presenting only one model of the U.S. class structure, in the following sections we will examine both socioeconomic and Marxian images of the U.S. class system.

Class Structure as a Continuum

Traditionally, U.S. researchers have defined social class statistically in terms of occupational status, education, and/or income. Individuals or families that fall in the same category on these dimensions are then said to be in the same social class. Generally, persons receive a score based on their placement on these variables; in essence, social class is determined by a statistical score. Since these scores are continuous, with small differences in scores between individuals in adjacent positions, the class hierarchy is frequently viewed as a continuum where the boundaries between classes are not always clear and distinct. Classes may merge imperceptibly into one another and, as a result, boundary determination becomes an important problem.

Another characteristic of this approach is that the dimensions used to measure social class

are not all purely economic in nature. Occupational status is essentially a measure of the *prestige* of an occupation—that is, it reflects the subjective judgment of individuals about an occupation. Education is also a noneconomic phenomenon. The result is that this measure of social class is multidimensional in that it mixes economic with social dimensions of inequality. Consequently, this measure is often referred to as **socioeconomic status (SES)**.

Finally, this measure does not assume any kind of necessary relationship between the classes. There is no assumption, for example, that the upper and working classes are in conflict with each other. Classes are merely the result of scores on a series of socioeconomic dimensions. In sum, the traditional, more conservative measure in the United States assumes that the structure of social class, or socioeconomic status, is (1) a continuum of inequality between classes, (2) partly the result of subjective judgments as well as objective conditions, (3) multidimensional, and (4) nonconflictual in nature.

As an example of this approach to class, Gilbert (2014) defined social class as "groups of families, more or less equal in rank and differentiated from other families above or below them with regard to characteristics such as occupation, income, wealth and prestige" (p. 11). Using this definition, Gilbert proposed that the United States contains six major classes. A condensed version of his model is presented here. The percentage of households in each class is enclosed in parentheses.

1. *Capitalist Class (1%):* Graduates of high-ranking universities who are in top-level executive positions or are heirs who have an income average of $2 million mainly from assets.
2. *Upper Middle Class (14%):* Individuals with at least a college degree who are in higher professional or managerial positions or owners of medium-sized businesses who have incomes of about $150,000.
3. *Middle Class (30%):* Individuals who have high school degrees and maybe some college

who are in lower managerial or white-collar, or high-skilled, high-pay, blue-collar occupations who make about $70,000 a year.

4. *Working Class (30%):* Persons with high school degrees who are in lower-level white-collar (e.g., clerical, sales workers) or blue-collar positions (e.g., operatives) whose incomes are about $40,000 per year.

5. *Working Poor (13%):* Those with some high school who are service workers, or are in the lowest paid blue-collar and clerical positions who have average incomes of $22,000.

6. *Underclass (12%):* Individuals with at best some high school education who work part-time, are unemployed, or are on welfare, and who have incomes under $15,000.

In surveying different models of U.S. class structure that use several kinds of socioeconomic criteria, there are some remarkable *similarities* as well as differences among them. These models usually see the structure as being composed of five to seven classes, rather than as a dichotomy or trichotomy. Also, the proportion of the population said to be in each class in each model is very similar. Generally, the working and middle classes, in which the majority of the population is placed, are considered to be about equal in size, and the upper class is generally said to be around 1 percent. Then, depending on whether employed as well as unemployed are included in the lower class, its percentage can range from 10 to 25 percent.

Some of the most significant *differences* in traditional models center on the criteria used to place individuals in various classes. One notable difference lies in the distinctions made about the lower class. Some researchers simply include all those who are poor, while others draw a line between those who are poor but work and those who are chronically unemployed and poor for long periods of time. The term **underclass** came into popular use in the 1980s and 1990s to refer to the latter group. A number of critics have argued, however, that the term has come to have a pejorative and racialized meaning (Gans 1996; Wacquant 2007). In other words, the term is used to refer

symbolically to poor urban Blacks and it implies that poverty is solely the result of deviant behavior, rather than emphasizing structural roots. For this reason, we have chosen to use the term "severely disadvantaged" throughout this text except when we are discussing a model, such as Gilbert's, that uses the underclass term. There is some debate about the definition and actual size of the severely disadvantaged class. In 1987, a conference of experts agreed that the category contains, "poor people who live in a neighborhood or census tract with higher rates of unemployment, crime, and welfare dependency" (McFate 1987, p. 11). By this definition, the severely disadvantaged class would include 5–10 percent of the population.

Another difference among the models of class structure concerns the way they treat white-collar and blue-collar occupations. Traditionally, blue-collar work has been considered manual in nature, while white-collar work has been defined as nonmanual. Manual work was generally viewed as requiring primarily physical and routine rather than mental and intricate skills/tasks. Recently, however, the lines distinguishing the nature of blue-collar and white-collar jobs have become blurred. The routine nature of much low-level white-collar work has encouraged some analysts to place individuals who do this kind of work into the working class, and to place those who do complex, high-skilled, well-paying blue-collar work into the middle class. As technological change occurs, and some physical labor by humans is replaced by machines, the character of the working class changes correspondingly.

The question of the relative importance of the manual/nonmanual and level-of-complexity criteria is the subject of some debate and has become focused in the debate about the **proletarianization** of some white-collar work and the **embourgeoisement** of some blue-collar work. Briefly, the proletarianization argument states that a significant and increasing number of white-collar jobs are routine and boring, demand little skill, and involve little worker control. Qualitatively, this makes them no different from many blue-collar jobs. Some have described those who occupy those positions as a "new working class," especially as the economy advances and becomes more automated (Riahi-Belkaoui 2003). Generally, Marxists tend to view the U.S. class structure in a manner consistent with the proletarianization thesis.

In contrast, the embourgeoisement thesis proposes that complex, high-paying blue-collar jobs take on many of the sociocultural characteristics of the white-collar middle class. As society moves into a postindustrial phase and its labor force becomes more saturated with white-collar service positions, the size of the blue-collar workforce shrinks. Most people become middle class in their standards of living and lifestyles.

Examination of occupational shifts over the last 25 years suggests that changes have occurred throughout the economy, resulting in multiple trends. The expansion of high-tech jobs near the top of the occupational hierarchy has accompanied an increase in low-paying service jobs at the lower rungs of the occupational ladder. In between these extremes, the middle suffered the decline of unionized, high-paying manufacturing jobs (Autor 2010). The Department of Labor anticipates that between 2012 and 2022, growth will be highest in the broad professional and service occupations such as psychology and personal and home health care work (U.S. Bureau of Labor Statistics 2015a). If these shifts continue, they may signal a faster movement toward a more polarized occupational structure.

Class Structure as Antagonistic Categories

In contrast to the continuum approach, Marxian sociologists generally object to the mixing of economic, status, and other socioeconomic variables because they believe it dilutes what Marx considered to be the core economic meaning of social class. Marx believed class was basically an economic phenomenon and was defined by an individual's position in the social relations of production, by control over the physical means (property) and social means (labor power) of production. In other words, class is not defined by income or occupation but rather by ownership/control in the system of production. In this view, introducing other socioeconomic variables, such as prestige or occupational status, only distorts the meaning of social class. Thus, in the Marxian definition, class is much less multidimensional in nature. Moreover, the crucial differences between the social classes are qualitative in nature—that is, the class system is not a continuous hierarchy in which the lines between classes blur and classes merge into each other. Rather, the boundaries between the classes are discrete and clear. Finally, classes in this view are defined by the exploitation that exists between them and by the interconnection between the functions of each class. This means that a given class is defined by its relationship to another class. Workers are members of the working class, for example, *because* of the nature of their relationship to capital and capitalists. Different classes perform distinct but interrelated functions in capitalist society.

While some Marxists define class strictly in terms of structural position, others incorporate a social-psychological dimension into their conception, arguing that **class consciousness** or a shared sense of belongingness and organized opposition must also be present for *social* classes to be present—that is, individuals must identify with each other and understand their real relationship to other classes and act on that knowledge. Kraus, Piff, and Keltner (2011) stated flatly that the concept of class has both subjective and objective dimensions with the subjective element being a sense of unity that develops as a class emerges. "Social class reflects more than the material conditions of people's lives. Objective resources (e.g., income) shape cultural practices and behaviors that signal social class. These signals create cultural identities among upper- and lower-class individuals—identities that are rooted in subjective perceptions of social-class rank vis-à-vis others" (p. 246).

In this approach, people become a real *social* class when they acquire a common culture and political awareness. In addition to occupying the same location or position in relation to the means of production, then, people in the same social class "share the distinctive traditions common to their social position" (Szymanski 1978, 26). This common identity, especially when it involves awareness of common exploitation and engagement in class struggle, Marx suggested, is what welds an aggregate of people into a social class, or a "class-for-itself" (Carrier and Kalb 2015).

The existence of a class-for-itself means that it exists as a self-conscious group ready to advance its own interests. The strength of this kind of class consciousness among the working class in the United States has been moderate at best, and it pales in comparison to some European countries such as Sweden, France, and Italy. There have been specific instances when workers have banded together and fought corporations despite dangers to each worker's welfare (McCall 2008). But while evidence suggests that there is some consistency between class position and attitudes toward corporations and management, American workers as a whole have not acted on their beliefs in the political arena. The lower level of unionization and the absence of a working-class political party in the United States have slowed the development of class solidarity (Sernau 2006).

As we have seen, there is lack of agreement on the exact definition and measurement of social class even among Marxists. Marx never gave an explicit, clear-cut definition of class. He suggested various definitions and different numbers and types of social classes at different points in his writing. Nevertheless, his approach and that of contemporary Marxian analysts are clearly different from those discussed earlier who define class in broader socioeconomic terms. In sum, Marxists generally view classes as (1) discrete rather than continuous, (2) real rather than statistical creations, (3) economic in nature, and (4) conflict-ridden. In contrast, traditional conservative approaches define classes as existing along a continuous hierarchy, largely statistically created, and being multidimensional and relatively harmonious in their relationships.

Perhaps the most sophisticated attempt to analyze the class structure of the United States in Marxian terms comes from Erik Wright. Wright's characterization of U.S. class structure uses exploitation as the defining element (Wright and Cho 1992; Western and Wright 1994). Classes and class locations are distinguished by an individual's ability to exploit or be exploited on the basis of (1) property, (2) organizational authority, or (3) expertise or skill.

Combining these three criteria, Wright identified several class "locations" within this structure of class relationships. The most elemental distinction involves those who have property from those who do not (owners vs. nonowners). Among *owners,* Wright has separated capitalists who employ others (employers) from those who do not (petty bourgeoisie). Application of the other two criteria of class location, authority and expertise, results in distinctions among *employees,* which create a number of class locations. Considering the criterion of bureaucratic authority, there are those who have it and those who do not (managers and nonmanagers). Individuals are considered managers if they are involved in policy decisions and are in a position to impose sanctions on others. Employees also differ in level of skill or expertise, which is the third criterion of class position. There are (1) managers and professionals who are experts, (2) workers and managers who are not experts, and (3) semiprofessionals (such as those in technical jobs) who are in between. In this scheme, the owners might be considered the capitalist class, and the workers compose the working class. The remaining groups among employees (managers, professionals, semiprofessionals) might be viewed as the middle class because they have characteristics of both those above and below them. In a real sense, as Wright has put it, these employees occupy "contradictory" locations because not only are they exploited as employees but they also exploit other employees because of their authority and/or expertise assets. Frequently, this group of employees is referred to as a "new" middle class because of its relatively recent growth within capitalism. Figure 2.1 graphically depicts Wright's class structure.

The figure gives a rather static, broad view of the class structure and how persons might be located within it. But Wright has pointed out that class position also depends on the relationship a person has with others in their family—relationships that may link the individual to different classes. In other words, a person's own position is "mediated"

OWNERS (approximately 15 percent)
(are self-employed in the system of production)

includes

(1) employers, (2) petty bourgeoisie

EMPLOYEES IN CONTRADICTORY (MIDDLE) LOCATIONS
(approximately 45 percent)
(have expertise and/or authority but are not owners)

includes

(3) manager/experts, (4) other managers, (5) professionals, (6) semiprofessionals

WORKERS (approximately 40 percent)

includes

(7) those who are in nonowner/nonexpert/nonmanagerial positions

FIGURE 2.1   Wright's Class Structure

by the position of others. For example, two individuals may both be professionals, but one lives in a family made up primarily of workers while the other lives in a family in which all the adults are professionals. These varying sets of relationships connect each of these professionals to the class structure in different ways. The subjective meaning of social class and how they place themselves in the class structure may be different for college professors whose parents are working class, for example, than it is for professors who come from a fully professional family. One can easily see how the life experiences and lifestyles of these individuals would likely differ.

In addition, two individuals may be in the same class at a given time, but one is located on a clear and recognized career path that will take that person to a higher position (e.g., being on the "fast track" to an executive position at a corporation) while the other person is in a dead-end job. This "temporal" aspect of class position means that to define class location fully, one must take into account the span of the broader career trajectory in which the current position is embedded. The addition of the concepts of mediated and temporal class position makes Wright's characterization of class structure more complex as well as realistic.

Common to this Marxian conceptualization of social class is the idea that classes are tied together by relationships of exploitation. Like Wright, Sørensen (2000) suggested a measure of class that uses exploitation as its central characteristic. He defined *exploitation* in terms of the ownership or control of assets that produce returns or "rents" for the individual. "Rents are returns on assets that are in fixed supply because single owners of the asset to the market control the supply of those assets. ... I propose to define *exploitation class* as structural locations that provide rights to rent-producing assets" (p. 1525). Consequently, the class structure consists of classes who do or do not own such assets and that are fixed in an antagonistic relationship to each other. While Wright agreed with Sørensen on the importance of using exploitation to define class relationships and structure, recall that he believed the bases of exploitation and the nature of the relationships between exploiter and exploited are more complex than what is suggested by the concept of rent-producing assets.

Several critics have raised questions about Wright's measure of class position. Meiksins (1988) argued that it is not necessarily true that those with skills or credentials exploit those below them. This is an empirical issue and cannot simply be settled by conceptual fiat. Resnick and

Wolff (2003) have further suggested that the recent emphasis on basing a Marxian class model on the concept of exploitation has led to neglect in the use of another central concept in Marx's theory as a basis for class modeling, namely, "surplus value." Resnick and Wolff argue that classes of employees can be distinguished according to whether they (1) produce surplus, (2) appropriate (i.e., take) it, or (3) are given part of the distribution of the surplus that is produced. This would suggest that there are three main classes in a capitalist society like the United States. In a word, they view workers as *producing* the surplus, capitalists as *appropriating* it, and managers/supervisors as receiving *distributed* surplus because they provide the conditions under which workers produce surplus. Following Marx, Resnick and Wolff define workers as "productive" because they actually create the surplus, while capitalists, managers, and the like are classified as "unproductive." Resnick and Wolff do not contend that their class model is better than Wright's, but only that there are potentially several models, each of which taps a different part of social and economic reality and, therefore, helps us to understand some parts of class reality while ignoring others.

SOME GENERALIZATIONS   As you have seen, all analysts of U.S. class structure wrestle with recurrent issues of where to place given sets of individuals within the class structure. Most prominent among these issues are (1) whether to place lower white-collar positions (i.e., routine clerical, service, sales occupations) within the middle or working class; (2) whether to place high-level managers within the middle or upper class, or in a separate category such as the corporate class; (3) how and where to incorporate the rising number of "knowledge" workers or professionals within the class structure; and (4) whether to include the poor and/or unemployed among the working class or to consider them a separate lower class. As the nation's economy experiences downsizing and similar corporate moves, another increasingly relevant issue will be to figure out how temporary, floating, contingent workers, and new entrepreneurs fit into the U.S. class structure.

In reviewing both the multidimensional socioeconomic and Marxian models, a few generalizations may be made about U.S. class structure. *First*, there appears to be general agreement across all these models that the upper or capitalist class makes up only a very small percentage of the population, about 1 to 2 percent. *Second*, most of these schemes suggest that the working class comprises at least close to half of the population. *Third*, estimates of the lower class or severely disadvantaged class range from approximately 5 to 12 percent. *Finally*, most of these models place lower-level routine white-collar occupations in the working class rather than in the middle class. These scholarly assessments are broadly consistent with the popular perceptions of Americans discussed earlier.

If you were to consider each of these conceptualizations of social class, how would your perception of U.S. class structure change as you went from one to another? Certainly, the definition a person has of something affects what they see. This is no less true of class perceptions.

EMERGING ISSUES IN THE SHAPING OF THE U.S. CLASS STRUCTURE

The class structure of any society is shaped by the political, cultural, economic, and technological context in which it is embedded. *Politically,* changes in rules and resources governing labor–management conflict, including unionization of workers, affect class conditions and relationships. Government trade and immigration policies, poverty programs, tax laws, and restrictions on business help determine the size and composition of classes, the extent of income and wealth differences, and the channels for moving up and down the class ladder. *Culturally,* broad-based values about democracy, equality, and justice can serve to temper the extent of social inequality, whereas the presence of prejudice, stereotypes, and derogatory ideologies about different groups can perpetuate such inequality. Finally, *economic* and *technological* developments have become increasingly significant for the changing composition of classes and for shifts in the distribution of individuals among classes. These developments need to be emphasized.

In recent years, technological developments have sped the integration of national economies into a global network. What happens to steel-workers in Ohio, textile employees in North Carolina, and electronic-component workers across the country is directly tied to the international context within which the U.S. economy operates. The ties created among nations make each more vulnerable to economic and political shifts in other countries. Like a giant web, pressure on any part causes reverberations throughout the system. The growth of China and India as economic powers, political instability in the Middle East, economic changes in Russia, the economic union of European countries, and attempts by Latin American nations to better integrate their economies all have economic repercussions for the United States.

The demand for goods produced by U.S. employees fluctuates with economic and political changes in other countries. For example, the disappearance of almost 5.7 million U.S. manufacturing jobs between 1998 and 2013 was linked to a wide range of international issues. In the 1990s, as economic crises occurred in Asian markets, their currencies were devalued, prices of their goods dropped, and importation of these goods into the United States became more attractive (Scott 2015). Between 2009 and 2015, the United States complained numerous times that the Chinese government manipulated the value of its currency so as to make its exports more attractive, resulting in lower demand for U.S.-made goods. Trade deficits continue today, not only with China, but also with countries including Mexico, Germany, and Japan (U.S. Bureau of Labor Statistics 2015d).

Downsizing, lean production, and the exportation of jobs to cheaper foreign labor markets have been primary ways used by U.S. manufacturers to reduce costs and respond to foreign competition. *Successful* penetration of U.S. firms into foreign countries may mean higher profits for some, but it also spells lower incomes for many workers, white collar and blue collar alike. Higher unemployment means lower incomes for those affected, in part because it means lower pressures for increased wages. Not surprisingly, job loss and fear of job loss dampen appeals for wage increases, as does the weakness of U.S. labor's power (Volgy, Schwarz, and Imwalle 1996; Aaronson and Sullivan 1998). *Unsuccessful* foreign penetration by U.S. corporations, on the other hand, means fewer exports for U.S. firms, lower profits, and, very likely, lower stock prices. The latter means declines in the wealth of those who own these stocks. Thus, individuals throughout the entire class system are affected by international economic events, but not in the same ways.

Just as international events and conditions affect economic fortunes in the United States, so too do U.S. activities affect economic conditions in other countries. The deep economic crisis of 2008–2010 originated in the United States but had worldwide implications. American mortgage problems and falling house prices, for example, devalued stocks in markets in Europe and elsewhere. This, in turn, reduced the wealth of many average citizens. The very interconnectedness of nations means that problems in one of them, especially a dominant one like the United States, have severe repercussions for others.

Progress in the technology of communication networks and information systems, which has brought together individuals and organizations around the globe, has intensified the interconnectedness of the world economy. Technology also has repercussions for the occupational structure. Increased computer usage in all kinds of organizations has provided the impetus for increases in jobs for systems analysts, software programmers, and computer technicians. Between 2012 and 2022, for example, employment in information technologies is expected to grow by an average of 10.8 percent with especially notable growth for computer systems analysts (24.5 percent) and information security analysts (36.5 percent) (U.S. Bureau of Labor Statistics 2015a).

In addition to their effects on occupational distribution, advances in computer technology and the rapid growth of the Internet have also created greater possibilities for flexible work patterns and new forms of economic organizations. Because technology allows for the dispersion of workers

Photo 2.1 Abandoned factories such as those in the upper Midwest and Atlantic states are an indicator of the decline of U.S. manufacturing jobs in recent decades. Many of those jobs have moved abroad where cheaper labor and better corporate tax advantages are available. The jobs lost are often those that had been unionized and paid well, and provide one reason for the earnings gap in the United States.

© Atomasui/Shutterstock.

across space, even across countries, work groups are being formed in cyberspace, resulting in the creation of "virtual organizations" (Crandall and Wallace 1998). The Internet has opened up scores of opportunities for individuals who are adept at using it. New companies made possible by powerful computer technologies have arisen overnight, and their stocks have rocketed so suddenly that their youthful creators have become millionaires in a very short time. In 2013, a full quarter of the 400 richest people in the United States had made their money through technology (Carlyle 2013).

While technological change itself does not appear to explain the rise in wage inequality in recent decades (Mishel et al. 2012), variations across socioeconomic groups in technology usage do have an impact. Higher-status individuals are more likely than those in lower statuses to have access to information technologies (IT), own better IT equipment, and know how to use the Internet in ways that strengthen their economic standing (DiMaggio and Bonikowski 2008; Zillien and Hargittai 2009; Stern 2010). In 2015, a full 15 percent of Americans did not use the Internet. While a third of the non-users cited lack of interest, 31 percent said that it was "too difficult," and 19 percent said it was too expensive (Anderson and Perrin 2015). This **digital divide** forms another basis for economic inequality.

Employment and unemployment patterns are also being dramatically affected by computer technology and the Internet. For example, the **contingent** workforce (people who do not have a traditional employment arrangement but pick up jobs on a project or time-limited basis) has been expanding due to the Internet (see Mini-Case 2.1). The freedom from restrictions of space and time that the Internet provides also means that the line between home and work can easily become blurred. Employees can stay at home and still be employed in computer tasks. Workers who are interested in moving but wish to remain employees are not limited in their job searches by local newspaper advertisements. Conversely, because of new communication technologies, employers can hire qualified individuals who live in very diverse locations. Knowledge and skills in new computer technologies have become a critical avenue for success. These possibilities hold the potential to complicate the processes of status attainment and diversify the compositions of given classes.

Moreover, new technology has made corporations and their workers less loyal to each other. It has created employment for some, unemployment for others; higher profits for some, and lower incomes for others. All this means that some will benefit from the ongoing technological revolution while others will remain onlookers, lacking access to and/or participation in it.

INCOME AND WEALTH INEQUALITY IN THE UNITED STATES

Because social class has been first and foremost thought of as an economic phenomenon, it should not be surprising that "income" has frequently been used as a measure of class position. As such, its distribution can provide clues about the character of U.S. class structure and trends within it. *Money income,* as defined by the Census Bureau, includes money from virtually all sources, including wages or salaries, Social Security, welfare, pensions, and others. There are some advantages to using *total money income* when assessing the extent of economic inequality. In the first place, it is certainly more immediately quantifiable than many other measures, such as real estate. Second, income is highly valued in U.S. society and serves as a base on which people are evaluated by others. Third, income inequalities saturate and are reflected in a number of other economically related areas. Unemployment, inflation, farm and food prices, rent control, feminism, racism, and welfare are all areas that involve income-differential issues. In your own case, think about the number of ways that income is implicated in different areas of your life. Income, then, at least at first glance, would appear to be a more than adequate measure of economic inequality.

However, when interpreting income statistics, several limitations should be kept in mind. First, income is only a partial measure of a family's or individual's economic well-being. It does not include the value of stocks, real estate, or other noncash economic assets, and, second, if it is *current* income, it does not take into account the income trajectory an individual may be on if, for example, they are just beginning in a lucrative career. Third, some of the estimates of income are based on pooled findings from several government studies that are not always identical in methodology or measures of income. Finally, and most significantly, the U.S. Census Bureau contends that income is underreported, with some sources of income being more likely to be reported than others. Tax filers tend to underreport their incomes on tax forms, and not all persons who are required to file income tax returns do so (IRS 2012). The majority of underreported income is from businesses or self-employment because these are sources that are hard for the IRS to track (Tax Policy Center 2008). Related to this, high-income earners are more likely to underreport income than low-income earners (Johns and Slemrod 2010).

While income provides important information about people's life circumstances, wealth gives us a more complete measure of a family's economic power, since it consists of the value of all the family's assets minus its debts. Thus, wealth includes the value of homes, automobiles, businesses, savings, and investments. Even this measure, however, does not fully reflect the access of the wealthy to a greater number of economic tools that serve to enhance their economic opportunities and market situation. For example, ownership of a great deal of stock in a corporation that is interlocked or directly connected with other corporations may give an individual indirect influence over the economic behavior of the latter organizations. Like poverty, wealth has economic implications beyond the actual size of the holdings. Economic opportunities are at least in part a function of the economic tools a person has at their disposal.

Consensus about the methodology used to uncover the distribution of wealth does not exist to the degree that one would desire. Some of the difficulties associated with present methods are clear. First, information about wealth is difficult to obtain. Virtually all data about it come from various field surveys and administrative records. Often, individuals are hesitant to be interviewed, and this is especially true of the wealthy who, for several reasons, may be sensitive about their wealth. "As a rule," stated Allen (1987), who conducted an extensive analysis of the country's richest families, "the members of wealthy capitalist families refuse to divulge even the most rudimentary details of their wealth. . . . In order to maintain their anonymity, the members of corporate rich families typically refuse to disclose even basic biographical information about themselves" (pp. 26–27). What is requested of individuals in surveys and what is given are frequently not the same.

Social scientists, in general, have produced hundreds of studies of the poor and poverty, even the middle class, but good broad-based information about the wealthy and wealth concentration has always been and remains difficult to find. Another problem with wealth data is that personal items such as jewelry, antiques, and art are often undervalued. Finally, researchers use different units of analysis in discussing the distribution of wealth. Sometimes the unit used is the individual, while in others the family or consumer unit is the basis of analysis.

Income and Wealth in U.S. History

If ever there was a time when equality was present, it surely must have been when the United States was first being established. When this nation was forming politically, many citizens had left their European homelands because of oppression of one kind or another to escape to the "land of the free," where the streets were thought to be paved with gold. The Founding Fathers, using "the voice of justice," forged a document that not only enumerated the offenses committed against the then new American people but also demanded freedom and equality for all. While some, such as Alexander Hamilton and Thomas Jefferson, argued about whether the government should or should not take a strictly egalitarian form, many believed the period was an "era of the common man" (Pessen 1973). The Founders recognized the belief that "all men are created equal" and later devised a constitution that had among its objectives to "establish justice."

In his famous visit to the United States, Alexis de Tocqueville (1966) was surprised by the "equality of conditions" that seemed to prevail in the youthful country. And although he believed wealth was certainly present, no one group held a monopoly on it. Indeed, de Tocqueville believed that wealth moved about quite a bit in the country.

Recent studies have simply not borne out these beliefs. Social historians, poring over probate records, tax forms, and old census documents, have found a decidedly different America than one might have expected. Studies of wealth distribution in the early United States consistently point to the fact that wealth inequality was a clear and constant condition during this period. This was especially true for the period between the Revolution and the Civil War, a time in which inequality was on the rise.

Before the Revolution, however, the increases in inequality do not appear to have been as great or as consistent, but differences in wealth were quite noticeable. Studies in Philadelphia and Chester County, Pennsylvania; Boston and Salem, Massachusetts; and Hartford and rural Connecticut point not only to evident variations in wealth among people, but also in some cases to increasing differences as time passed (Pessen 1973). Income inequality also existed in the Colonies, but it was less pronounced than it was in England at the time. Notably, it was also lower than in the present-day U.S.

Uniform evidence about a trend toward increasing inequality before 1776 does not exist; but after 1776, the trend toward inequality is present everywhere. In his studies of cities in New England, the Middle Atlantic, the South, and the Midwest, Sturm (1977) found little support for the idea of the U.S. as egalitarian. Using probate data, he found distinct and increasing inequality in estate wealth for the period from 1800 to 1850. During this time, per capita holdings of the very wealthy went up about 60 percent (Sturm 1977). An examination by Pessen for this period in Brooklyn and Boston likewise confirms the general trend toward inequality. In Brooklyn in 1810, 1 percent of the population held 22 percent of the private wealth, and in 1840, 1 percent owned 42 percent (Pessen 1973, p. 36). Figures for Boston and New York echo these findings. Income data also tentatively suggest that inequality rose between 1774 and 1860, particularly in the South (Lindert and Williamson 2012).

Concentration of wealth in the nineteenth century appears to have peaked during the period from 1850 to 1870. Soltow (1975) found that while wealth inequality remained fairly constant during this period, it was also very high. Using census data on real and personal estate holdings among free adult males, he found that in 1860, the top 1 percent owned almost 30 percent and the top 10 percent owned about 73 percent of estate wealth, again demonstrating a strong degree of wealth concentration. During the period from 1850 to 1870, "there very definitely was an elite upper group in America in terms of control of economic resources" (Soltow 1975, p. 180). A small percentage had great wealth, but large numbers had little, if any. In 1850, over half of free adult males owned no land even though it was quite cheap. Nor did the situation change much in the years following 1850 (p. 175). Given the period, as one might expect, a person was more likely to be an owner of real estate if that person was native born, older, and a farmer (Soltow 1975). The main conclusion to be drawn from these data is that at least from the mid-eighteenth to the mid-nineteenth centuries, there was high and increasing

concentration of wealth in the U.S. Income concentration also increased but was less marked.

Estimates are that the richest 1 percent held about 30 percent of all wealth during the 1920s, although their wealth decreased to under 30 percent in the 1930–1950 period. By the late 1950s, however, their assets increased to almost 35 percent of all wealth (Keister and Moller 2000). During the first half of the 1970s, the proportion of wealth going to the top 1 percent declined, but then began to rise significantly during the late 1970s. To summarize, the data for income indicate that inequality rose from 1900 to 1930, then dropped dramatically after the Great Depression. It continued to decrease until the late 1970s (OECD 2014).

Income Inequality: Current Trends

Income data from 1980 to 2014 reveal high and increasing inequality. Table 2.1 summarizes information on how U.S. households were distributed among different income categories in 1980, 1990, 2000, 2010, and 2014. Presenting the data in these increments is useful because it can illustrate broad trends. At the same time, it hides variability within each period. For example, both the data from 2010 and from 2014 are

TABLE 2.1 Percentage Distribution of Households by Income Level: 1980–2014

Income*	1980	1990	2000	2010	2014
Under $15,000	13.6	12.4	10.4	12.4	12.6
$15,000–$24,999	11.5	10.8	10.1	11.5	11.0
$25,000–$34,999	11.2	9.9	9.8	10.4	10.1
$35,000–$49,999	15.3	14.9	13.5	13.3	13.1
$50,000–$74,999	21.5	20.0	18.0	17.1	17.0
$75,000–$99,999	13.1	13.2	13.1	12.2	11.5
$100,000–$149,999	9.9	12.2	14.3	13.0	13.4
$150,000–$199,999	2.5	3.8	5.7	5.3	5.7
$200,000 and above	1.3	2.9	5.0	4.8	5.6
Median Income	$47,658	$51,086	$57,724	$53,507	$53,657

* Measured in 2014 adjusted dollars.

Source: DeNavas-Walt, Carmen, and Bernadette D. Proctor. 2014. Income and Poverty in the United States: 2013. Current Population Reports. U.S. Census Bureau. https://www.census.gov.edgekey-staging.net/content/dam/Census/library/publications/2014/demo/p60-249.pdf.

affected by the "Great Recession," the worst economic downturn in the U.S. since the Depression. This important event is highlighted below.

Looking at the top line in the income distribution in Table 2.1, we see that the percentage of families with incomes below $15,000 has declined very slightly over the period (from 13.6 percent in 1980 to 12.6 percent in 2014). At the same time, the percentage of those with incomes of at least $100,000 rose far more dramatically (from 13.7 percent to 24.7 percent). The percentages of those in the $25,000–$74,999 categories have generally declined. While shifts in the top and bottom categories in this table may suggest that economic conditions have improved since 1980, we need to reserve judgment until we explore the matter further.

Research suggests income inequality has grown since the late 1970s, with the top 10 percent getting more than 90 percent of all the gains in income, thereby further distancing themselves from the rest of the population. The bottom 90 percent experienced declines during this period (Mishel et al. 2012; McCall and Percheski 2010). The extent of income concentration was higher in 2013 than it has been since the late 1920s. In 2012,

the mean household income of the top 20 percent was almost 16 times that of the poorest 20 percent. In contrast, 35 years ago it was 11 times as great (DeNavas-Walt, Proctor, and Smith 2010; Elwell 2014). Part of the explanation lies in the fact that an increasing proportion of the national income has gone to profits and capital, and less to wages and salaries (Mishel, Bernstein, and Allegretto 2007). Changes in tax policies, which favored high-income groups and high unemployment rates, have also contributed to the increase in income inequality (Mishel et al. 2012).

Figure 2.2 confirms the decline in income shares going to those below the top 20 percent. As the figure indicates, the percentage of all income going to the bottom and middle quintiles of the population has declined since 1980, while that going to the top 20 percent increased from 44.1 percent in 1980 to 51.2 percent in 2014. The top 5 percent alone received over 22 percent of all income in 2014.

Trends in the Gini ratio—which measures the extent of discrepancy between the *actual* distribution of income and a *hypothetical* situation in which each quintile of the population receives the

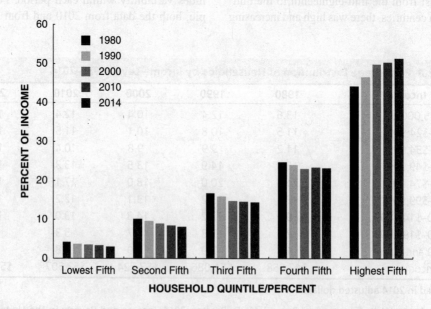

FIGURE 2.2   Percentage Share of Aggregate Income Received by Each Fifth of Households: 1980–2014

Source: U.S. Census Bureau, Table H-2, http://www.census.gov/hhes/www/income/data/historical/household.

same percentage of income—also indicate increasing concentration of income in the United States. The ratio has a possible value range of 0 to 1; 0 indicates complete equality, and 1 indicates complete inequality. In 1980, the ratio for households stood at 0.403; by 2014, it had risen to 0.48, the highest of any highly developed country in the world (U.S. Census Bureau 2014b, Table H-4).

One way in which income inequality shows up clearly is when comparisons are made between racial and **ethnic groups**. About 22 percent of Black and 15 percent of Hispanic households had incomes below $15,000 in 2014, compared to 10.4 percent of non-Hispanic White households. On the other end of the income scale, 28 percent of non-Hispanic White households had incomes of at least $100,000, compared to about 13 percent of Black and 15 percent of Hispanic households. Not surprisingly, the median incomes of households varied as well in 2014, ranging from $35,398 for Black to $42,491 for Hispanic to $60,256 for White non-Hispanic households (DeNavas-Walt and Proctor 2015).

Incomes also vary between family types. As might be expected, households with married-couple families are generally better off than those headed by only males or females, regardless of race. But as Figure 2.3 demonstrates, Blacks and Hispanics are worse off than non-Hispanic Whites in each type of family. Female-headed families have the lowest incomes within each racial and ethnic group. Overall, such families have less than half of the income of married-couple families.

The middle and lower classes are well aware of the recent declines in their economic fortunes. In 2014, 56 percent of Americans said that their income had fallen behind the cost of living and only 44 percent identified as middle class (down from 53 percent in 2008) (Pew 2014c). On average, about two-thirds of a family's income comes from employment earnings (not including business, farm, and self-employment), but the proportion is much greater for those in the middle class (Bricker et al. 2014). It should not be surprising, then, that the acceleration in income inequality since 1980 is due heavily to the increase in earnings inequality, especially between those in the top 10 percent and the rest of the working population. In 2013, the compensation of CEOs at top corporations was 331 times that of average workers. Those earnings differences partly reflect a polarizing increase in both high- and low-paying jobs alongside a decrease in middle-wage

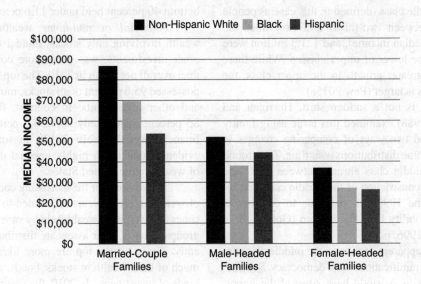

FIGURE 2.3   Median Incomes for Family Types by Race: 2014

Source: U.S. Census Bureau, Table F7, http://www.census.gov/hhes/www/income/data/historical/families.

positions (Autor, Katz, and Kearney 2008; Mouw and Kalleberg 2010).

Recent high unemployment rates, shifts in the occupational structure, declines in the power of unions, a lagging minimum wage, and globalization account for most of these changes (Mishel, Bernstein, and Allegretto 2007). Economic instability, resulting in the need for workers to change or find new jobs, also contributes to a stagnation or decline in their wages (Mouw and Kalleberg 2010). It is important to note that it is not only falling or stagnating wages that make life more difficult for the middle class. Between 2000 and 2012, the real prices of health care increased by 21 percent, child care by 24 percent, and higher education by 62 percent (Wednesday 2014). Increases in these basic expenses can cause real hardship for the middle class.

IS THE MIDDLE CLASS SHRINKING?

Regardless of how it is measured, most of the analyses on the middle class indicate a shrinking in the size and prosperity of the middle-income groups. In fact, for the first time in four decades, the middle class was declared to be in the minority in 2015. Specifically, 120.8 million people were in the middle class (defined in this case as people earning between two-thirds and two times the national median income), and 121.3 million were in either the lower or upper classes. While there has been greater growth in the upper class, the lower class is larger (Pew 2015e).

This is not a sudden shift. Horrigan and Haugen (1988) examined this issue using family income and two ways of comparing changes in family income distributions over time. They found that the middle class shrank between 1969 and 1986. The constriction of the middle class continued into the 1990s, in part due to declines in upward mobility from the bottom (Gottschalk in Bernstein 1996, p. 90).

The apparent decline of the middle class has significant ramifications for a democracy. Scholars as far back as Aristotle have stressed the importance of a large and prosperous middle class for the stability, cohesiveness, and productivity of a society

(Pressman 2007). Yet throughout the United States, the number of middle-class neighborhoods has declined, while poor and rich neighborhoods have grown (Galster, Cutsinger, and Booza 2006). Leicht and Fitzgerald put the matter bluntly: *"Middle-class prosperity in the late twentieth and early twenty-first centuries is an illusion"* (2006, p. 4, italics in original).

Wealth Inequality: Current Trends

Turning now to wealth, we see that in 2013, the median wealth or **net worth** of households, that is, the value of all their assets minus their debts, was over $80,000 (Fry and Kochhar 2014). Income and wealth is highly correlated: Upper-income Americans had 6.6 times the wealth of the middle income. This is the widest wealth gap in 30 years of record-keeping. The richest 20 percent had an average of $2.3 million in wealth, while the bottom 40 percent averaged only $2,200. Between 1983 and 2007, the number of households with wealth of at least $10 million increased six-fold, but the percentage of households with zero or negative wealth also rose from 16 to 19 percent. As Figure 2.4 shows, the wealthiest 20 percent owned over half of all wealth in 2013, while the bottom 40 percent held under 11.6 percent.

Financial or *non-home* wealth, that is, wealth involving only stocks, mutual funds, and other investments, was even more concentrated than overall net worth in 2010. The top 20 percent possessed 95.6 percent of all stocks, mutual funds, and other investments. In contrast, the bottom 80 percent owned only about 4.7 percent of all financial wealth (Wolff 2012). In sum, all the evidence indicates a highly unequal distribution of wealth in the United States.

The reasons for the increasing concentration of wealth in recent years are related to the differences in the types of wealth held by various income groups. That is, their assets are distributed differently. Those on the top are more likely to have much of their wealth in stocks, bonds, and related kinds of investments. In 2010, the vast majority of the wealth of the richest 1 percent was in stock, mutual funds, financial securities, or business

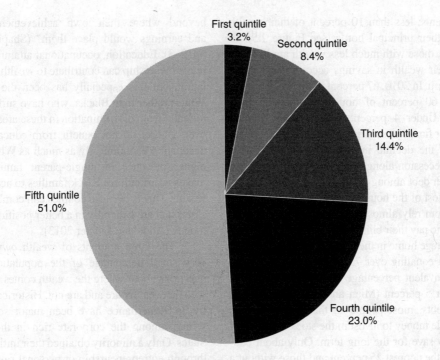

FIGURE 2.4 Distribution of Net Worth by Quintile: 2013

Source: http://www.statista.com/statistics/203247/shares-of-household-income-of-quintiles-in-the-us.

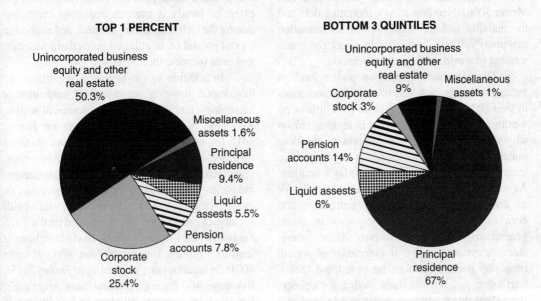

FIGURE 2.5 Distribution of Asset Types in Top 1 Percent and Bottom 3 Quintiles of Wealth: 2010

Source: Based on Edward N. Wolff, "The Asset Price Meltdown and the Wealth of the Middle Class." November 2012. Working Paper No. 18589, p. 55, Table 6. National Bureau of Economics Research.

investments; less than 10 percent of their wealth was in their principal home (see Figure 2.5). In contrast, those with much less wealth are likely to have their wealth in savings accounts and home ownership. In 2010, 67 percent of the wealth of the bottom 60 percent of households was in their homes. Under 4 percent was in stock, mutual funds, or financial securities (Wolff 2012). Consequently, the decline in home values during the Great Recession along with stagnant incomes led to greater debt among those in the middle class.

Most of the households in the middle and at the bottom rely almost completely on wages and salaries to pay their bills. Many are heavily in debt. The average home in the bottom quintile of wealth has debt equaling over 75 percent of their assets. The equivalent percentage for the top quintile is just over 5 percent (Mian and Sufi 2014). Given these debts, most people in the lower quintiles have little money to invest in the stock market; nor can they save for the long term. Only about one-third of the poorest 25 percent and those without a high school diploma save at all, compared to about three-quarters of the richest 10 percent and those with college degrees (Bucks, Kennickell, and Moore 2006). Needless to say, mounting debt and the inability to save make wealth accumulation extremely difficult, and directly affect the transmission of wealth to the next generation.

The constraints placed on poorer families mean that they are less able to provide inheritances to their children, leaving the latter with little or no wealth on which to build. This is another reason why wealth inequality is so important—its accumulation has direct implications for economic inequality among the children of today's families. As a basis for future economic status, wealth (or its absence) helps to stabilize, reproduce, and even exacerbate economic inequality in future generations (Oliver and Shapiro 2006). Inheritances contribute to the maintenance of wealth inequality over generations because these "head-start assets ... often include paying for college, substantial down-payment assistance in buying a first home, and other continuing parental financial assistance ... [This inherited wealth allows its recipients to live] economically and socially beyond where their own achievements, jobs, and earnings would place them" (Shapiro 2004, pp. 2–3). Education, occupational attainment, and home ownership can contribute to wealth accumulation, but this especially has been the case for Whites rather than Blacks, who have suffered historically from discrimination in these areas. Moreover, Blacks do not benefit from education and occupation economically as much as Whites. The higher presence of single-parent families also makes it difficult for Black families to accumulate wealth. This is because couples can combine their assets and are generally in a better position to save money (Addo and Lichter 2013).

The large amounts of wealth owned by a very small percentage of the population raises questions about where the wealth comes from and who the wealthy are and are not. Historically, family and inheritance have been major sources of wealth among the corporate rich in the United States. Only a minority obtained their initial wealth through entrepreneurship or personal saving. Gift and estate laws have done little to stem the flow of inherited wealth to subsequent generations. Wealth is kept in the family, and this is one reason why the extended family is such an important institution among the rich. The social, cultural, and economic capital passed on to children helps them maintain and even increase their wealth.

In addition to the historical importance of inheritance, however, technological innovation is becoming a much more prevalent source of wealth. About 60 percent of the individuals on *Forbes* 2015 list of the 400 richest Americans obtained their wealth in the service, food and beverage, manufacturing, media, technology, or investment industries. Many started their own businesses or are self-employed. Few achieved their vast wealth because of inheritance. To be included on the 2015 *Forbes*-richest list, one's wealth has to have been at least $1.7 billion. Together, the net worth of these 400 individuals totaled $1.34 trillion (*Forbes* 2015). But these 400 do not represent most Americans. For most, inheritance still plays an important role in laying a foundation for wealth accumulation.

What characteristics are related to the amount of wealth one has? Certainly race and

TABLE 2.2 Median Household Net Worth and Non-Home Wealth by Race and Hispanic Origin: 2011

	Median Net Worth	Median Non-Home Wealth
Non-Hispanic Whites	$110,500	$33,408
Non-Hispanic Blacks	$6,314	$2,124
Hispanics	$7,683	$4,010

Source: Mark Mather and Beth Jarosz, "The Demography of Inequality in the U.S." Population Reference Bureau. November 2014.

ethnicity are factors that are involved. As Table 2.2 demonstrates, Blacks and Hispanics generally have significantly less wealth than Whites. In 2011, the median net worth among non-Hispanic Whites was about 17.5 times that of non-Hispanic Blacks, and their median non-home wealth was about 14 times greater than Hispanics.

Wealth also varies by family type, with married-couple households possessing about three to four times the wealth of single-headed households. Among age groups, those in the 65–74 age bracket had the most net worth, and those under 35 the least. Finally, in 2011 the wealth of those with college degrees far exceeded that of less educated individuals (U.S. Census Bureau 2014d).

Income and Wealth during the Great Recession

At the end of 2007, the U.S. entered a deep recession. The causes of the crisis were complicated, but the housing market was an important driver. Starting in 2000, the housing market was artificially inflated due to speculation, low interest rates, and subprime mortgages (mortgages available to higher-risk borrowers; they often have low initial interest rates followed within 2 to 3 years by much higher variable rates). By 2006 many mortgage rates began to increase, causing people to fall behind on their mortgages and end up in foreclosure. High rates of foreclosures led to a decreased demand for housing and a decrease in prices as there were suddenly many houses on the market. Some homeowners found themselves underwater, meaning that their houses were worth less than they owed. Banks were

unwilling or unable to renegotiate mortgages, leaving homeowners with few options. Over 2.5 million Americans went into foreclosure between 2007 and 2009 alone. The housing crisis was devastating for many Americans, but particularly for the lower and middle classes because the bulk of their wealth was in their homes. Blacks and Latinos were hit particularly hard by the housing crisis—in part this was a result of higher levels of unemployment, but it was also due to discriminatory lending practices (see Chapter 8). Blacks had a foreclosure rate of 7.9 percent, Latinos 7.7 percent, and Whites 4.5 percent (Bocian, Li, and Ernst 2010). The bursting of the housing bubble set off a series of financial waves throughout the economy. Americans who were suddenly paying higher mortgages or who faced foreclosure cut back on their spending, leading to a reduction in hiring across most sectors of the economy.

Although not all economists agree, it appears that rising income inequality beginning in the 1980s may have been one factor linked to the Great Recession. Middle- and lower-class people's incomes stagnated, and it became impossible for them to maintain the lifestyle they were used to. To solve this problem, some turned to credit—credit made possible after bank deregulation in 1980. The extension of credit, including subprime mortgages, to lower- and middle-class people was supported by wealthy individuals and institutions looking for new financial investments (Maloney and Schumer 2010).

The Great Recession was linked to increases in both income and wealth inequality. The average American family lost 11.6 percent of their income between 2007 and 2009. The recovery of the bottom 99 percent of the income distribution has been slower than that of the upper 1 percent. By 2014 the bottom 99 percent had only regained 40 percent of the loss, with most of the gain happening in 2013 (Saez 2014). Looking at the effect of the recession on incomes in another way, we see that between 2008 and 2009 the income share of the bottom 20 percent of households decreased from 3.6 percent to 3.4 percent. Both the second and third quintiles also experienced losses, while the fourth saw its share of income remain stagnant. The top 20 percent of Americans gained all the lost income share of the lower quintiles, seeing increases in their share from 42.5 to 49.4 percent (Smeeding 2012).

In terms of wealth during the recession, one-quarter of American households lost more than 75 percent of their wealth, and a half lost more than 25 percent (Pfeffer, Danziger, and Schoeni 2013). While those with high wealth saw the greatest losses in absolute terms, the middle class lost the most in proportional terms. Because the least wealthy have few assets, they lost the least proportionally (Smeeding 2012).

What will be the long-term inequality effect of the Great Recession? As discussed above, the Great Depression of the 1930s was followed by decreasing levels of inequality in both income and wealth. The data available today suggest that the

recession will not have the same effect. In fact, inequality in both income and wealth has only increased since 2009. By 2010, the wealthiest people in this country had already recouped the losses they experienced during the Recession, while the middle class had not. This is largely because the financial sector recovered more quickly than the housing sector (Smeeding 2012).

The 1 Percent

The Occupy Wall Street Movement began in September of 2011 in New York. It turned into a loosely organized set of gatherings to protest inequality around the country. Its slogan, "We are the 99 percent," referred to the huge advantages held by the top 1 percent of wealth-holders in the United States. Looking at the 1 percent is a useful illustration of inequality in today's society. To be in the top 1 percent in income in 2012, a worker would have had to earn $291,000 (Guvenen, Kaplan, and Song 2014). Wealth data is much harder to come by, but an analysis with 2008–2010 data showed that to be in the top 1 percent of wealth, a household would have to hold $8.4 million (Gebeloff and Dewan 2012). There is overlap between the income and wealth groups: Half of those in the 1 percent income category also fall in the 1 percent wealth category.

MINI-CASE 2.1

Gig Economy

In recent years there has been considerable growth in the number of websites that offer services provided by individuals working as contractors. In most major cities, for example, consumers can use Uber and Lyft to find a ride in a private car. Airbnb allows people to rent out rooms in private homes. TaskRabbit provides a way to hire help for minor home renovation or cleaning or errand running. Consumers are attracted to these services because they are inexpensive. Under most conditions, for example, an Uber car is less expensive than a taxi (Silverstein 2014).

For workers, jobs in the gig economy can be attractive because they offer much more flexibility—and sometimes

higher hourly pay—than traditional jobs. Many workers also like not having a boss looking over their shoulders. The down side to these jobs is that they do not offer workers health or unemployment insurance. They also do not pay into Social Security or offer sick and vacation days. Most do not guarantee a minimum weekly wage. Because these types of jobs are relatively new, it is still not clear what the long-term impact will be on inequality. There have already been a number of lawsuits challenging the legality of hiring workers as contractors when they are working many hours a week. What do you think? Should gig economy workers be allowed to continue as contractors? ■

NUTSHELL 2.1   Sources of Wealth Measurement

The observations drawn about the extent of wealth inequality rely heavily on the work of economist Edward Wolff, who uses data from the Survey of Consumer Finances (SCF) conducted by the Federal Reserve Board since 1983. This data source yields a more accurate picture of wealth distribution because it uses a broader and more inclusive definition of net worth and a sample that includes a better representation of the wealthiest households. The SCF is the source used most often in investigations on wealth distribution (Keister and Moller 2000). Other surveys, such as the U.S. Bureau of the Census's Survey on Income and Program Participation (SIPP) and the Panel Survey of Income Dynamics (PSID), underrepresent the richest families and, therefore, significantly understate the wealth of the richest segments of society and the extent of wealth inequality in the United States. Consequently, Wolff contends that these two surveys "are probably useful for studying the wealth accumulation behavior of the middle class, but are not reliable for analyzing the behavior of the very rich" (Wolff 1998, p. 134). Moreover, since the sample used in the SCF is different from those of the two other surveys, so is the composition of the wealth found in its top 20 percent and bottom 80 percent.

Two of the important terms used by Wolff in his analyses are net worth and *financial wealth*. **Net worth** refers to "the current value of all marketable or" cash-convertible "assets less the current value of debts" (Wolff 1998, p. 133). It includes the value of housing, real estate, cash, savings, certificates of deposit, money market accounts, bonds, stocks, and equity in businesses and trust funds owned by the household. It also includes the cash value of retirement, life insurance, and pension plans. Wolff believes that this measure is important because it "reflects wealth as a store of value and therefore a source of potential consumption" (p. 133). Spilerman also views wealth for its potential "as a capitalized income stream" (2000, p. 500). Wolff goes on to say that, "I believe that this is the concept that best reflects the level of well-being associated with a family's holdings" (Wolff 2000, p. 3). In contrast to net worth, **financial wealth** is a narrower concept and is defined as one's net worth less the net equity in one's house. Financial wealth includes only those forms of wealth that are easily convertible to cash. Therefore, home equity is excluded because "it is somewhat difficult to liquidate one's housing wealth in the short term" (Wolff 1998, p. 133).

There is a good deal of variation among people in the top 1 percent. For example, different regions of the country have different thresholds for the 1 percent. At the same time, some generalizations can be made. The 1-percenters tend to be men, to live on one of the coasts, to be married and Protestant, and to report better-than-average health. Most are middle aged or older. Whites and Asians are overrepresented among the 1-percenters. Those who work tend to be in finance/insurance or health care, but a substantial percentage live off assets and inherited wealth (Dewan and Gebeloff 2012; Keister 2014; Guvenen, Kaplan, and Song 2014).

CONFRONTING ECONOMIC INEQUALITY

Although little attention has been given by policymakers to programs that directly address the reduction of social inequality, the federal income tax system and government transfers purportedly address the issue of distribution of economic resources among individuals in the United States.

The Effects of Taxes and Transfer Programs

The tax system is supposed to be "progressive"— that is, to lessen income differences between income strata by taxing higher-income groups at higher rates. To what extent does it accomplish this goal? Looking at Table 2.3, we find that inequality is greatest under "market income," which essentially is pretax income gained only from the market, and does not include income from government insurance and welfare programs. We can see that the degree of income inequality declines when the benefits from government programs are added to

TABLE 2.3 Average Household Income, Transfers, and Taxes, by Before-Tax Income Group, 2011 Dollars

	Lowest Quintile	Second Quintile	Middle Quintile	Fourth Quintile	Fifth Quintile	All Households
Market Income	15,500	29,600	49,800	83,300	234,700	80,600
Government Transfers	9,100	15,700	16,500	14,100	11,000	13,300
Before-Tax Income	24,600	45,300	66,400	97,500	245,700	93,900
Federal Taxes	500	3,200	7,400	14,800	57,500	16,600
After-Tax Income	24,100	42,100	59,000	82,600	88,200	77,300

Notes: Market income consists of labor income, business income, capital gains (profits realized from the sale of assets), capita income excluding capital gains, income received in retirement for past services, and other sources of income. Government transfers are cash payments and in-kind benefits from social insurance and other government assistance programs. Those transfers include payments and benefits from federal, state, and local governments. Before-tax income is market income plus government transfers. Federal taxes include individual income taxes, payroll taxes, corporate income taxes, and excise taxes. After-tax income is before-tax income minus federal taxes. Income groups are created by ranking households by before-tax income, adjusted for household size. Quintiles (fifths) contain equal numbers of people. For more detailed definitions of income, see the appendix.

Source: Congressional Budget Office. https://www.cbo.gov/sites/default/files/113th-congress-2013-2014/reports/49440-Distribution-of-Income-and-Taxes.pdf.

the income definition, as in "before-tax income." Inequality declines even further when taxes are taken into account, as in "after-tax income." These changes indicate the redistributive effects of both taxes and governmental assistance programs.

An important tax program with a substantial redistributive effect is the Earned Income Tax Credit (EITC). This program was set up to encourage employment by allowing low- and moderate-earning workers, especially those with children, to receive a tax credit. The credit is scaled depending on income and family size, with a phase-out starting at a certain income level. When a person receives a tax credit, it is first applied against their tax bill (for example, if they owe $1,000 in taxes and get a $1,500 EITC, they do not owe any taxes). In addition, any money left over after taxes is refunded to the worker (in the case just mentioned, the worker would receive a check for $500). A recent analysis suggests that the EITC pulls more children out of poverty than any other governmental form of assistance (Hoynes 2014).

When compared to other industrial countries, however, the effects of taxes and transfers in the United States on inequality and poverty are small. International studies reveal that U.S. programs were less effective than other developing countries in reducing inequality and poverty rates (OECD 2014). The direct effect of taxes on reducing economic inequality in the United States is minor, but they do have an indirect effect because they are used to fund government transfer programs, which have a greater impact on inequality. However, the regressive effect of sales and payroll taxes weakens any positive consequences that come from income taxes (Kenworthy 2009).

Part of the reason for the lower effect of taxes on reducing inequality over the last two decades has been a decline in the progressive nature of the federal tax system, fueled by a decrease in the number of tax brackets and cuts in tax rates for wealthy individuals. For example, most of the benefits from tax cuts in 2001 and 2003 went to the wealthiest 2 percent (Zuckerman 2006). In addition, over 14,000 tax loopholes were added that allowed many of the wealthy to reduce their tax payments (Sawhill 2008). Federal taxes do, however, remain progressive—to a point. Data from the

Internal Revenue Service indicate that in 2012 the tax rate for Americans increased along with earnings through the top 1 percent (who paid an average of 22.8 percent). Those in the very upper tiers of wealth (the top .01 and .001 percent), however, paid a lower rate (19.53 and 17.69, respectively) (Dungan 2015). This might help account for the finding that 52 percent of all Americans think that wealth should be distributed by taxing the wealthy more heavily (Newport 2015b).

Nevertheless, the wealthy provide most of the individual tax payments received by the Internal Revenue Service. In 2014, the top 20 percent were responsible for over 80 percent of federal tax revenue with the top 1 percent paying about 45 percent of the nation's income taxes (Saunders 2015). In 2011, as Mitt Romney highlighted in his presidential bid, almost half of all Americans paid no income tax; most of these were from low-income groups who receive federal tax credits, which cancel out their tax liability (Williams 2010). All this may suggest to some that the government is taking away from the rich more than from the poor, and indeed, the official tax rates are higher for those in higher income brackets. Four points should be kept in mind, however. *First*, a large number of non-tax payers are unemployed elderly people, and, of those who are not, a significant percent pay payroll taxes (Plumer 2012). *Secondly*, tax rates have declined most precipitously for the highest-income groups in the past two decades (Orr 2010). *Thirdly*, since most of the wealth of the wealthiest is in the form of stocks, a much higher percentage of the incomes of the wealthy derives from capital gains, which are taxed at a lower rate than earnings from employment. The latter is the principal source of income for those in the middle and working classes. Consequently, the *percentage* of their incomes that is paid in taxes by the wealthiest is generally lower than the percentage that is paid by those whose incomes are derived largely from job earnings. This suggests the *fourth* point, namely, that the higher *amount* paid by the wealthy is testament to the large size of their incomes. Conversely, the much smaller amounts of taxes contributed by those on the bottom give evidence to the meagerness of their incomes.

When considering the mild effect of *individual* federal income tax on income inequality, it should be noted that *corporate* taxes are not included, nor is the value of nonincome wealth. The proportion of total federal government revenue that comes from corporate taxes steadily declined throughout the twentieth century. By 2014, only 11 percent of Internal Revenue collections came from corporate taxes compared to 46 percent from individual income taxes (Center on Budget and Policy Priorities 2015b). Some of this decrease can be explained by the increasing use of special laws of incorporation that allow for taxation only on individual, rather than corporate, earnings. At the same time, according to the Government

Photo 2.2 Following the Great Recession, Occupy Wall Street demonstrations nationwide challenged the growing inequality between the top 1 percent economically and the rest of the population.

© lev radin/Shutterstock.

Accountability Office, in 2010 the corporate tax rate was 35 percent, but the average amount paid was only 16.8 percent—and some large and profitable corporations paid no tax at all (GAO 2013a). Increasingly, U.S. corporations have sought to incorporate parts of their businesses outside the United States in order to avoid payment of corporate taxes. As of 2015, such "inversions," as they are called, were legal under U.S. law, although the Treasury Department passed rules in 2014 intended to limit them. Locating elsewhere allows companies to benefit from advantageous tax and banking laws in the chosen countries (McKinnon and Paletta 2014). The Joint Commission on Taxation, a nonpartisan think tank, estimated that offshore accounts will cost about $20 billion in lost tax revenue over the next 10 years. While there is some controversy about that number, it is clear that offshore accounts have deep effects on tax revenue (Worstall 2014).

Just as corporations benefit from current law, so too do the wealthy benefit from the structure of estate tax laws. In 2014, $10.68 million of a married couple's estate was exempt from taxation. Thus, fewer than 2 of every 1,000 estates paid any taxes at all (Center on Budget and Policy Priorities 2015b). This encourages the **sedimentation** of wealth. Consequently, the inequality of economic resources is not reduced by either corporate or estate taxes, both of which allow the well-to-do to keep more of their wealth.

Other Suggestions Reducing Inequality

Taxes and transfers are only two of the programs that relate to the issue of economic inequality. Not surprisingly, many of the suggestions for alleviating poverty and reducing inequality focus on attempts to maximize incomes for those at the bottom. These include proposals to (1) raise the minimum wage, which has not kept up with inflation; (2) extend the Earned Income Tax Credit to different types of households; (3) provide more subsidies for higher education or simply make it free, at least for low-income people; (4) make the tax system more progressive; (5) mandate employers pay

into retirement accounts for workers; and even (5) encourage greater unionization (Wolff 2002; Danziger and Danziger 2006).

Several modern administrations have also considered proposals for a guaranteed annual income for all citizens that would replace many traditional welfare programs. One of the principal reasons these proposals failed during the Kennedy, Nixon, and Carter presidencies is that the guaranteed income, by applying to all citizens, lumped everyone together, thus violating a deep cultural belief in the distinction between deserving and undeserving individuals. This belief is part of what shapes the way policymakers frame their views on welfare (Steensland 2006).

Compared to citizens in other Western industrial countries, Americans in general also have a greater "taste for inequality" and a stronger belief that the market rather than the government should determine income (Crutchfield and Pettinicchio 2009; Birchfield 2012), both of which would also discourage acceptance of a guaranteed income for all. In addition, some argue that a guaranteed income would encourage an individual's dependence on the government and lead to a massive exodus from the workforce, thereby endangering the whole economy. Others say that a government program that offers access to health care, education, child care, and housing would be a more efficient and effective way than universal cash grants to reduce inequality (Bergmann 2006). On the positive side, others contend that a universal basic income would provide individuals with the opportunity to explore additional productive activities without having to worry unduly about wages. It may also help to equalize power between classes because it would make available to workers a source of income other than wages (Wright 2006). Passage of new income distribution proposals, of course, depends in part on the sympathies of government officials. Historically, the policies of conservative democratic governments tend to increase economic inequality, while those of liberal governments appear to reduce it (Bartels 2004; Brady and Leicht 2008).

One of the more controversial proposals to address broad-based inequality in the United States was put forward by Ackerman and Alstott (1999). Briefly, Ackerman and Alstott suggest that the most direct way to address economic inequality between individuals is to grant every young adult a "stake" so they can begin their adult lives on a more equal level. Specifically, they suggest a one-time stake of $80,000 for young adults to use as they wish to develop their futures. Individuals take responsibility for the success or failure of their choices, and in old age they would have an obligation to repay the stake if they are able to do so.

To fund the $80,000 stakes for beginning adults, a tax of 2 percent on all wealth would need to be levied. Ackerman and Alstott believe this is fair, since "every American has an obligation to contribute to a fair starting point for all" (p. 5). They stress that all citizens are in the American enterprise together, and thus we have to work together to reach a more just society. Existing programs of the welfare state have been too divisive, and we need a plan that will invigorate common values. Ackerman and Alstott say that a "stakeholder society" will accomplish that. Two objections raised against this proposal are that the tax required to fund it takes away wealth from those who have legitimately earned it, and that giving individuals a large stake essentially dampens any motivation to save and accrue assets through one's own efforts (Wright 2006).

Attempts at reform have frequently gotten hung up due to the difficulty of trying to balance conservative and liberal approaches, trying to be tough but compassionate at the same time. Suggestions aim to help those who need help but also to encourage individual responsibility. American values encourage us to be generous but also to realize that there is no "free lunch." Both society and the individual have obligations. "Any successful social policy must strike a balance between collective compassion and individual responsibility," wrote Christopher Jencks (1992, p. 87). Historically, the reform pendulum has swung between these two themes.

Recent federal suggestions have mirrored some of the preceding state efforts, but have also incorporated elements of compassion. For example, some argue that we should increase the amount of the EITC to low-income families and also widen eligibility. The Obama administration, for example, has proposed increasing the amount given to childless workers, a group that receives little under the current formulation of the program. In recent years, there have also been calls for requiring that employers contribute to mandated employee retirement accounts, with the expectation that it would reduce poverty among the elderly. Currently Social Security only replaces about 39 percent of the wages of a person retiring at age 65 (Miller 2015). Finally, in the 2016 presidential election, at least three candidates proposed plans that would drastically reduce college costs (Healy 2015).

All of these efforts reflect a concern for compassion, but many aspects of current policy also reflect a laissez-faire view of income distribution. The political paralysis that often exists because of opposition from powerful economic interests and competing perspectives among officeholders suggests that what may be needed to bring about real changes in economic inequality is a broad-based, grassroots social movement (Raphael 2009).

THE GLOBAL CONTEXT AND THE IMPACT OF GLOBALIZATION

The discussions of income and wealth discrepancies just presented document the extensiveness of economic inequality in the United States. To better evaluate the significance of these economic inequalities, we need to consider them in a broader context, even though this can be difficult. Cross-national comparisons of economic-inequality systems have always been hazardous because of variations in definitions, measures of economic status, units of analysis, and data-collection times. Nevertheless, some gross comparisons can be made.

When it comes to levels of income inequality, generally countries lower in living standards by UN measures have levels that exceed those in industrial nations. Included among the most unequal are many African nations. In fact, while there has been tremendous growth in some of the African economies, 6 of the 10 most unequal countries are located on the continent (African

Development Bank Group 2012). Other parts of the world struggle as well. For example, in Haiti, a country that has been battered by natural disasters and political problems, the richest 20 percent receive more than 64 percent of the total income (World Bank 2012).

In comparison with other rich industrial countries, however, the United States possesses the highest degree of income inequality. As Table 2.4 shows, individuals in the 90th percentile of the U.S. population had 2012 average incomes that were almost 18 times those of people in the 10th percentile. Confirming the high degree of inequality, the Gini coefficient of 0.40 for the United States was higher than that of any other rich industrial

TABLE 2.4 Income and Inequality among Households within Rich Industrial Countries, 2012

Country	Gini Coefficient	Top 10% vs. Bottom 10%
Australia	0.33	8.8
Austria	0.28	7
Belgium	0.27	5.9
Canada	0.32	8.6
Denmark	0.25	5.2
Finland	0.26	5.5
France	0.31	7.4
Germany	0.29	6.6
Greece	0.34	12.3
Ireland	0.3	7.4
Italy	0.33	11.4
Japan	0.34	10.7
Netherlands	0.28	6.6
New Zealand	0.33	8.2
Norway	0.25	6.2
Spain	0.34	11.7
Sweden	0.27	6.3
Switzerland	0.28	6.7
United Kingdom	0.35	10.5
United States	0.4	18.8

Source: http://www.oecd.org/social/in-it-together-why-less-inequality-benefits-all-9789264235120-en.htm.
Note: OECD calulates Gini differently from other organizations but it is useful for comparative purposes.

country in 2012. When compared to those in other industrial countries, U.S. individuals in the 90th percentile are further *above* and those in the 10th percentile are further *below* the median income in the United States than is the case in any other country.

As in the United States, wealth is even more unequally distributed between nations than income. North America, Europe, and well-to-do Asian-Pacific countries account for over two-thirds of the world's household wealth (Credit Suisse 2013). Estimates suggest that the richest 1 percent of people in the world own 48 percent of the wealth (up from 44 percent in 2009), while the bottom 80 percent own 5.5 percent (Hardoon 2015). Per capita wealth is lowest in countries located in central Africa and South Asia (Credit Suisse 2013). The wealthiest countries in terms of wealth per capita include Switzerland, Australia, and Norway. Looking at within-country wealth inequality, Russia ranks the highest with almost 85 percent of its wealth held by the top 10 percent. Other countries with notable levels of inequality include Turkey and Hong Kong. The United States ranks seventh (Credit Suisse 2013).

Given the widespread inequality among nations, coupled with the breakdown of national boundaries in the world economy, it is not surprising that the relationship between global economic inequality and globalization has become a hot topic of research. Does more extensive involvement of all nations in the world economy reduce the economic inequality between them? Is globalization a way out of world poverty? Has globalization reduced or exacerbated economic inequality within the United States? We need to address these questions.

Globalization itself has been defined in two basic ways, one which is narrowly economic and another which incorporates a variety of dimensions and is sometimes referred to as the "grand" theory of globalization. In this latter view, "Globalization refers to a multidimensional set of social processes that create, multiply, stretch, and intensify worldwide social interdependencies and exchanges while at the same time fostering in people a growing awareness of deepening connections between the local and the distant" (Myers Jr 2014, p. 45). A narrower conceptualization of globalization views it as a strictly economic phenomenon, involving the increase in direct investment, flow of workers, and free trade between countries. It is this definition that we will use in our assessment of globalization's impact on inequality among nations and within the United States.

There is no theoretical agreement over whether globalization has been a primarily positive or negative force in the world at large. The positive or "**neoliberal**" view envisions globalization as raising the average economic fortunes of all nations as members of a world community through the opening up of opportunities and sharing of skills and technologies (Taylor 2002). Globalization encourages internationalism and opens up all countries to the same set of market forces. Since the global marketplace is an open competitive arena, it creates pressures on countries to use their resources efficiently and to find a niche or specialty that puts them at a comparative advantage in the market. The supposed result is a reduction in poverty, a decline in inequality between nations, and, consequently, a wholesale breakdown in the dichotomies that have characterized the world (e.g., rich–poor, core–periphery, North–South; Wade 2004). In this view, globalization should also reduce economic inequality *within* countries because it is a win–win situation for everyone involved.

The critical view, in contrast, interprets globalization as a force that strengthens the opportunity for powerful nations to take advantage of more vulnerable and less powerful ones through the dismantling of traditional protections for the less wealthy and the consequent exploitation of their labor. Transnational corporations have weakened the power of labor and unions, intensifying competition between home-based and foreign labor. The deindustrialization accompanying globalization reduces the number of high-paying manufacturing jobs and pushes more workers into lower-paying service work (Alderson and Nielsen 2002). One result is a widening of economic inequality between skilled/educated and less skilled/uneducated workers within countries and between developed and underdeveloped nations (Maskin 2014). It is also possible that globalization leads to a "brain drain" as highly-skilled workers move from less-developed to more-developed countries (Docquier and Rapoport 2012). Poorer countries are more likely to subscribe to this critical view, because they believe that their countries enter the world economy with many disadvantages. Free trade is supposed to operate in the global marketplace, for example, but they know that wealthy nations often subsidize their farmers, putting farmers from poorer countries at a disadvantage.

A more nuanced view of globalization states that while globalization harmed less-developed countries in the 1970s, it has more recently hurt employees in developed countries through the exportation of work to lower-wage countries. It has been argued that the effect of globalization on **world inequality** may change as different stages in the world economy and international relationships develop. As globalization becomes initially established, inequality between nations grows, but in later stages the advantages of rich nations are slowed and inequality between nations declines (Krugman and Venables 1995).

So what is the answer: Has globalization had a positive, negative, or mixed impact on economic inequality? "On this very important question, responsible opinion tends towards diametrically opposing views" (Seshanna and Decornez 2003, p. 354). In a multicountry analysis, Otsubo (2015) found that the answer depends on a wide range of factors including location, time horizon, context, and the group in society to which a person belongs. The truth is, however, the jury is still out.

Since the early 1800s and up to the recent past, most world inequality has been due to economic inequality *between* nations (Goesling 2001). Economic inequality between nations grew significantly during the Industrial Revolution and the twentieth century at the same time that globalization was occurring. And some argue that globalization has continued to create more inequality and has either increased or had no effect on poverty in the world (Seshanna and Decornez 2003; Wade 2004; Kiely 2004). They find that direct investment in the world market is concentrated in the developed countries rather than evenly spread among all countries, resulting in a concentration rather than dispersion of capital.

Others disagree about the negative effects of globalization, contending that it actually reduces economic inequality between countries (Dollar and Kraay 2004; Firebaugh and Goesling 2004; Weede 2008). Countries that are most globalized are more likely to thrive economically. In their study of countries across the economic spectrum, for example, Firebaugh and Goesling (2004) found that, while still large, economic inequality between nations declined in the last part of the twentieth century "primarily because of [globalization's] role in the spread of industrial technology in Asia" (p. 285). Moreover, they anticipate that it will continue to decline because of industrialization and the fact that most of the growth in the working-age population will be in these poor nations. But even though its contribution has declined, economic inequality among countries still accounts for roughly two-thirds of world inequality (Firebaugh 2000; Goesling 2001).

In sum, there are conflicting findings on whether globalization has a positive or negative effect on economic inequality between countries. It has been suggested that among the main reasons for these disagreements are differences in methodology (Mills 2009). Earlier we alluded to the difficulties of finding comparable data and definitions in assessing inequality between nations. Those who argue that globalization has reduced inequality criticize the methodology, conceptualizations, and logic of those on the other side. For example, proponents say that critics of globalization define *technology* as meaning information/communications rather than industrial technology. While the former may indeed worsen between-nation inequality, the latter does not (Firebaugh and Goesling 2004). What dimensions of globalization are included in studies also makes a difference because some dimensions may be related to economic inequality in some countries while others are not. In their study of the EU-27 countries, for example, Asteriou, Dimelis, and Moudatsou (2014) found that open trade reduced inequality but that foreign direct investment increased inequality. Older research showed this to be the case in less-developed nations as well (Reuveny and Li 2003). On the other hand, the free flow of financial capital does not seem to affect income inequality.

Despite these variations, on the whole there seems to be much more agreement that globalization raises economic inequality within countries, including the United States (Alderson and Nielsen 2002; Firebaugh and Goesling 2004; Wade 2004; Weede 2008; Massey 2009; Ezcurra and Rodríguez-Pose 2013). Declining inequality in many industrialized nations has been replaced with increasing inequality. The "great U-turn" in income inequality within advanced nations is partially explained by globalization. In the global marketplace, countries that exercise fewer controls on the movement of capital experience greater earnings inequality as a result (Mahler 2004). Examining data from 16 industrial countries, Alderson and Nielsen (2002) found that while direct investment abroad has led to more capital for employers, it has also spurred a decline in high-paying jobs, a reduction in demand for low-skilled compared to high-skilled labor, and an increase in the number of immigrants who have varying levels of skills. These developments have widened the economic gaps within advanced countries. Mishel and others add that globalization has also reduced employment in traditionally high-paying manufacturing jobs, lessened investment in the U.S. manufacturing base, and reduced the price of many goods, thereby indirectly causing a decline in the average wages of U.S. workers. They also note that competition from foreign workers can cause U.S. employees to reluctantly accept wage reductions. Finally, the "offshoring" of many high-tech white-collar service jobs and competition in trade also appear to have had a depressing effect on the salaries of U.S. white-collar professionals (Mishel, Bernstein, and Allegretto 2007). "Whatever the causes," writes Robert Wade (2004) perhaps with some exaggeration, "the fact is that the United States is now back to the same level of inequality of income as in the decades before 1929, the era of the 'robber barons' and the Great Gatsby" (p. 578).

Summary

This chapter has analyzed economic inequality as a fundamental form of social inequality. Economic inequality was defined as including social-class, income, and wealth differences in the United States. Americans have complex views of the class structure itself and on what determines their places within it. Scholars as well vary in their depictions of it, usually seeing the class structure either as a socioeconomic continuum or as a set of more discrete classes. Despite these variations in class models, there are some general agreements on the proportions found in different classes. Disagreements about U.S. class structure include the question of the placement of lower-level white-collar workers, the issue of the shrinking middle class, and the question of proletarianization or embourgeoisement of the working class.

Discussing class structure is only one way to depict economic inequality. Describing the extent of income inequality is another. Such inequality has increased in recent years, with the top 20 percent receiving a greater proportion of total income and the bottom 80 percent a smaller proportion. These differences are in part manifested in the growth in wage inequality between CEOs and other workers. In recent years, this gap has been propelled by technological and globalization processes that affect unemployment and the bargaining position of labor on the worker side, and lower costs, better tax positions, and higher profits on the CEO/corporate side.

The increases in income inequality are overshadowed by even greater wealth inequality. Recent estimates show that the richest 1 percent own more wealth than the bottom 95 percent combined (Institute for Policy Studies 2015). As a broad measure of an individual's or family's economic position, wealth is a better indicator than income because it incorporates a broader range of assets that can affect economic inequality across generations. In sum, whether measured by social-class indicators, income, wage, or wealth distributions, economic inequality is extensive and appears to have grown since the early 1980s in the United States.

As in the United States, there are significant differences in economic inequality among nations. Generally, economic inequality is greater in poorer countries, although there are major variations among industrial nations. When compared to its industrial counterparts, the United States ranks at the top in terms of its income and wealth inequality.

Poverty rates provide an additional measure of economic inequality and another one on which the United States ranks unfavorably among industrial nations. And, as we will see in the next chapter, poverty in the U.S. shows no sign of abating.

Critical Thinking

1. Why do you think the United States fares poorly on measures of poverty and economic inequality when compared to other industrial nations?
2. Consider the jobs you have held. What factors do you think led to your being employed and affected the earnings you received?
3. Were you surprised by the extent of income and wealth inequality in the United States? Why or why not?
4. What do you think economic and technological conditions will be like 10 years from now? How will these affect your chances of moving up or down in wealth?

Web Connections

The U.S. Census Bureau regularly collects data on income and poverty in the United States. Go to their website at www.census.gov and click on "topics" and then "income and poverty." United for a Fair Economy is an independent, nonprofit organization interested in greater equality that also gathers information on wealth, earnings, and income distribution and their relationship to race and democracy. They also write reports on this information. Visit www.faireconomy.org. Do you think inequality undermines democracy?

Film Suggestions

People Like Us: Social Class in America (2001). A survey of the classes in the U.S. class structure and relationships between classes.

Masters of Deception: Social Class in American Pop Culture (2014). Examines how popular culture shapes our notions of social class in relation to a wide range of topics including consumerism, beauty, and romantic love.

The American Ruling Class (2005). A "dramatic documentary musical," this film explores the lives of two students, one rich and one not rich. The story is interwoven with interviews with prominent scholars on class.

CHAPTER 3

Poverty and Welfare

Poverty is a great enemy to human happiness; it certainly
destroys liberty, and it makes some virtues impracticable
and others extremely difficult.

SAMUEL JOHNSON (1709–1784)

The distribution of income and wealth discussed in the last chapter provides a portrait of economic inequality in the United States. Information about the extent and distribution of poverty within the population adds to that picture. The measurement of poverty, attitudes about welfare, and policies that are supposed to address poverty have all become contentious issues, in part, because of the popular image of the poor and because the welfare programs in which they participate are believed by many to be at odds with fundamental American values. The design of poverty policies is affected by the cognitive and emotional pictures that policymakers and the public have of the poor. Often these images are erroneous, and, consequently, the bases of programs and their potential for positive impact are weakened.

This chapter begins with an analysis of public perceptions and myths regarding the poor as they relate to core cultural values. It then presents federal statistics on the measurement and extent of poverty and who the poor actually are. From there, the chapter moves to a discussion of some major antipoverty programs, welfare reform, and the effectiveness of government programs. To provide a broader perspective, the chapter concludes with a summary of how the U.S. poverty rate and programs compare to those of other countries.

HISTORICAL ROOTS OF U.S. POVERTY PERSPECTIVE

Images that we have of the poor are bound up with our explanations for their poverty. Our deeper cultural values affect the theories of poverty that we find acceptable and color our perceptions of the poor. Most of the images of the poor and the causes of poverty that have dominated U.S. history have focused in one way or another on alleged weaknesses among the poor themselves. This focus on the individual's characteristics as the basic cause of poverty emerged in fourteenth-century Europe with the rise of industrialism, the emergence of the freed wage-laborer, and the growth of international commerce. The massive economic changes occurring on the Continent and in England during this period—in addition to famines, widespread diseases, and war—generated a large number of paupers and beggars. Something had to be done to deal with these individuals. At the same time, the process of industrialization demanded the ready availability of workers.

As the dominant source of relief and welfare moved progressively out of the hands of churches and private charities and into the hands of public institutions and officials, a clear distinction between the "deserving" and "undeserving" poor developed in the late fifteenth century. Pregnant women, seriously ill individuals, and the elderly were among those who were considered worthy of help. Individuals who could but did not work were considered undeserving of assistance. The principle of "less eligibility" prevailed—that is, the idea that any relief given not be great enough to discourage work. The amount of relief was not expected to be higher than the wages of the lowest worker in the community (Besley, Coate, and Guinnane 2004).

The Elizabethan Poor Law of 1601 distinguished among the "able-bodied poor," the "impotent poor," and "dependent children." The former were required to work; refusal to do so meant punishment, and nonpoor citizens were forbidden to aid them. Those classified as being "impotent"—such as the disabled, deaf, blind, elderly, and mothers with small children—were given either "in-door relief" (placed in an institution or almshouse) or "outdoor relief" (allowed to stay in their own homes but given food, clothing, or other needed goods). "Dependent children" who could not be supported by their families were farmed out as apprentices, taught trades, and expected to serve in this capacity until early adulthood (Abramovitz 2000). To be eligible for aid, a poor person was expected to be a stable member of the community and without family support.

The distinction between the deserving and undeserving poor found in the Elizabethan Poor Law became deeply ingrained in the approaches taken to the poor and welfare in Britain and the United States and have remained so to this day. In early America, poverty was becoming a serious problem. Before the Civil War, upheavals in the economy, sickness, immigration, and demographic changes generated large numbers of poor individuals. Specifically, the decline in the home manufacture of goods, unemployment, the rise of low-wage labor, the seasonality of much work, and crop failures were among the economic changes responsible for poverty. Growing population pressure on the land, the changing age structure of the population, and increasing immigration also led to increased poverty levels (Katz 1996).

Reaction to the problem of poverty in the United States was heavily influenced by the English approach. Relief was considered a public responsibility, to be locally administered and controlled; it was not to be given to those who had families who could support them, and those who could work were expected to do so (Katz 1996). Even then, however, many believed that any relief would discourage the motivation to work and weaken character. Efforts were made then, as now, to seek out and eliminate the "able-bodied" from the relief rolls. The Quincy Report, an 1821 Massachusetts study of poverty and welfare, made the by-now familiar distinction between the impotent poor and the able poor. The "poorhouse," an early attempt to take care of the poor, sought to (1) eliminate the undeserving from help by requiring work and banning alcohol for residents and (2) encourage children and the deserving able poor by stressing work education and discipline in the hopes that such treatment would set them on the path out of poverty. The goal was to transform the character and behavior of its residents (Katz 1996).

The poorhouses did not work out very well. The conflict in goals that plagues many current welfare programs was already present in the early poorhouse program. A concern for order, cost, routine, and custody overshadowed the initial goal of reforming the individuals in them. Many became rundown, and the care given became less than adequate. Officers of the poorhouses were often found to be guilty of graft. Inmates had greater and greater control over their behavior in the poorhouse; discipline was not enforced, nor was useful work found for most inmates (Katz 1996).

EXPLANATIONS AND RACIALIZATION OF POVERTY AND WELFARE

When debating how to structure poverty programs, policymakers generally frame arguments in terms of who is deserving and who is undeserving of governmental help (Yoo 2008; Guetzkow 2010). That is, they categorize poor individuals into different groups. How subgroups among the poor are classified and viewed depends on (1) the perceived cause of their poverty, (2) the composition of the subgroup, (3) whether they are believed to be on welfare, and (4) who is doing the categorizing. Frequently, the categorization of a group by the public depends heavily on whom or what they think is responsible for the group's poverty, and people vary in the explanations they accept. Some believe that most poverty is caused by an individual's own attitudes, behavior, and/or flaws. That is, they blame the individual. Others argue that poverty is caused by conditions beyond a person's control, such as economic recession or illness. Finally, some even attribute poverty to "divine intervention" (Brimeyer 2008; Robinson 2009). Most Americans subscribe to a mix of individualistic and structural views, but a majority lean in the direction of blaming the individual (Robinson 2009). Individuals who live in an area in which the majority of people are Republicans and most of the poor are Black, are most likely to believe the poor are destitute due to individual failings rather than structural problems and, thus, to view them as undeserving (Hopkins 2009). Generally, persons with less education, higher occupational status, and who are politically and religiously conservative are more likely to blame poverty on the poor themselves, while more liberal and highly educated individuals attribute poverty primarily to structural or situational causes (Robinson 2009).

Reaction to the poor also depends on the group to which they belong; some poor are thought of more positively than others. Generally, those on welfare are viewed as undeserving, while those who reject welfare but are homeless or are among the working poor are defined as deserving. Those on welfare are perceived as being "poor by choice," while others are thought to be "poor by circumstance" (Robinson 2009, p. 513). Individuals on welfare are seen as undeserving because they appear to violate the widespread and deeply held belief in the work ethic and to not take advantage of chances to move out of poverty. Surveys have consistently shown that the public views *poor* individuals positively while holding a negative view of *welfare* recipients (Henry, Reyna, and Weiner 2004). Welfare itself has been widely interpreted as discouraging work and fostering dependence on government even where employment opportunities for the poor are believed to exist (Allard 2009).

Negative portrayals of welfare by the media have helped to perpetuate opposition to welfare, especially in areas where high levels of racial prejudice and large numbers of Blacks are present (Dyck and Hussey 2008; Fullerton and Dixon 2009; Hopkins 2009). During discussions and design of the 1996 welfare reform in the United States, for example, the typical welfare mother was labeled by the media as being a lazy, immature person, often a teenager, who gave birth to multiple children and who was also an incompetent mother. This image helped to shape the requirements built into the Welfare Reform Act of 1996 (Kelly 2010). Negative mental depictions of groups during debates about who should be eligible were also operative. The presentation of immigrants as irresponsible and as coming to the United States solely to get public aid motivated politicians to make them ineligible for programs such as Supplemental Security Income (Yoo 2008).

Popular stereotypes about race are a major reason for the negative view of welfare and its beneficiaries. Poverty is believed to be a largely urban Black problem, and Blacks are thought by many to be lazy and responsible for their own lack of economic progress (Henry, Reyna, and Weiner 2004; Hanson and Zogby 2010). In other words, rather than seeing them as victims of discrimination, they are considered to be responsible for their own poverty. A primary explanation for the historically negative attitude toward welfare is that the public believes most of those on welfare are Black and, therefore, responsible for their poverty. Consequently, welfare recipients are believed to be undeserving of government aid. These racial attitudes have infiltrated popular feelings about poverty and undermine support for welfare programs (Masters, Lindhorst, and Meyers 2014). Programs are seen by many poor Whites as a "Black benefit" less available to poor Whites (Cleaveland 2008). In this way, welfare is racialized as being a Black program, which lowers its standing in the eyes of the public. Since those on welfare are viewed as being undeserving, this combination of seeing poverty and welfare as Black issues means that Blacks are viewed as undeserving of governmental aid. In sum, cultural values, racial stereotypes, and categorizations of the poor all combine to reinforce American attitudes about the poor and welfare. Certain values, particularly those concerning individual responsibility and work, are especially powerful in shaping our perceptions of the poor and how they should be treated.

CULTURAL VALUES AND THE POOR

Historically, perceptions of the poor have been conditioned by the cultural context. A number of U.S. values have had a significant impact on our views of the poor. Among the most central of these are (1) individualism/autonomy and (2) the belief in work, intertwined with its moral character.

Individualism/Independence

The quintessential image of the pioneer as someone who, when confronted by the rigors of frontier life, worked hard and took individual responsibility for their own fate, has been ingrained in the American psyche as what true Americans should be like. Despite the fact that most early Americans traveled and lived in groups, the idea of the rugged individual has held great appeal (Hirschfield 2015). Basic to this ideal image of the heroic American are several components:

1. This person is physically and psychologically independent; they need no help from others.

2. Individual achievement is sought despite difficult obstacles.
3. Achievement even under difficult circumstances means that anyone can succeed if they try hard enough.
4. Those who do not make it either lack the ability or are lazy and therefore immoral. In any case, they do not have what it takes to succeed.
5. The possibility of material gain is needed to motivate people (Dolgoff and Feldstein 2012).

These components suggest that being poor or rich is largely the result of a struggle in which the best win and the worst fail. Individuals who are poor either do not have the personal qualities necessary to succeed or do not put forth enough effort. Moreover, being poor and on welfare indicates dependency on others, and therefore flies in the face of the ideal that Americans should be independent.

The Enlightenment of the eighteenth century and Adam Smith's economic theories provided intellectual support for belief in the autonomous individual. It was believed that intelligent individuals, equipped with modern knowledge, could do almost anything for themselves as well as society. Smith's economic theories stressed a laissez-faire approach to economic affairs. Free individuals, unencumbered by governmental and other regulations, seeking their own goals, would create the most efficient and productive society. Governmental interference in the form of any aid was believed to violate the intricate processes of freely working, "natural systems." "The 'inefficient poor' like inefficient businesses, were to die off through natural selection" (Tropman 1989, p. 137).

The beliefs that individuals should be self-reliant, exercise self-restraint, and take responsibility for their own lives are still reflected today in polls that show a large majority of Americans favor policies that require work, impose time limitations on welfare benefits, and allow no increases in benefits when women on welfare have more children.

The Moral Character of Work

"God helps those who help themselves" goes the old saying. The belief that individuals are responsible for their own destinies can be traced back to religious doctrines consistent with a U.S. society that had a large frontier to be explored and conquered. One of these religious strands was Calvinism, which Miller has called "the most individualistic development out of the most individualistic wing of the most individualistic part of the Judeo-Christian heritage" (1977, p. 3). Calvinism is a puritanical religion that stresses the importance of the individual and their own work as an indication of whether they are among the "elected." Under this doctrine, work is considered crucial to a meaningful life. Idleness is not only a sin but a social evil as well. People who become poor do so because they lack character. Since they are not successful, it is a sign that they are not among God's elect. Calvin was even against individuals freely giving alms to those he considered idle and lazy (Dolgoff and Feldstein 2012).

Many early American religious practitioners subscribed to these beliefs. The American Puritan minister Cotton Mather (1663–1728) confirmed the religious significance of work in his exhortations about the importance of having "a calling." Every man should have an occupation through which he contributes to society, argued Mather, otherwise he cannot expect anything from society. "How can a man Reasonably look for the *Help of other men*, if he be not in some *Calling* Helpful to *other men*?" wrote the minister. When men do not put forth their efforts, what happens? "By *Slothfulness* men bring upon themselves . . . Poverty . . . Misery . . . all sorts of Confusion . . . On the other Side . . . a *Diligent* man is very rarely an *Indigent* man" (Rischin 1965, p. 24–28; emphasis in original). It is easy to see why those in positions of wealth and power might subscribe to these views, since they not only justify the wealth of those at the top but also locate the source of poverty in a lack of effort by the poor individual.

Although the explicitly religious character of many of these pronouncements has lessened, the hold of the essential ideas is still strong. To place the reason for economic success or failure on the individual is to exonerate society and others from being responsible for poverty, and, just as importantly, to isolate the poor from the rest of society and to foster a "them versus us" imagery among the population. The further perception, though inaccurate, of most of the poor as Black intensifies the belief that the poor are qualitatively different in character from the rest of the population. A recent study suggested that U.S. adults are more likely to view Blacks as more lazy than Hispanics or Whites (Embrick and Henricks 2013).

The work ethic is at the heart of the rationale for current welfare policies. The thrust is on getting able-bodied people to work outside the home so that they will not take advantage of welfare benefits. Only the deserving poor should receive help. The notion that those without jobs, especially during times of relative prosperity, are to blame for their own economic troubles goes back deep in our history. While perceptions of the poor as lazy and undeserving have lessened a bit during times of economic downturn, even in times of extreme economic stress such as the Great Depression, the poor were by and large characterized as immoral, and relief was seen as morally suspect (Katz 2013). Similarly, the economic stresses of the recent Great Recession resulted in an increase in anti-immigrant and anti-Hispanic attitudes (Ybarra, Sanchez, and Sanchez 2015).

The beliefs in individualism and the moral character of work influence present-day images of the poor and welfare. This is not to say that other values are not also implicated in current images. A sense of community and compassion (humanitarianism), the beliefs in achievement and success as upward mobility, and the belief that the family is supposed to play a crucial role in maintaining its members are all additional values that have helped to shape our perceptions of the poor and what is to be done about poverty. The focus here has been on individualism and the work ethic because, more often than not, these values have been most salient to and have informed the perceptions of those responsible for crafting welfare policies.

MYTHS ABOUT THE POOR

Values and beliefs often distort social reality because they suggest that most of the poor have characteristics that they, in fact, do not possess. These distortions matter, as recent research has demonstrated that how we see the poor and how we represent their plight have important consequences for support for public policy and the creation of new policy surrounding poverty (Rose and Baumgartner 2013; Santiago 2015). But as we look more closely, there is little evidence to support these distortions.

Increasingly, media portrayals have focused on the personal characteristics or failings of the poor, rather than on structural or societal issues (Santiago 2015). In media portrayals of the poor, they are often presented as lazy, as cheaters, and poverty is too often interpreted as a solely urban phenomenon (Rose and Baumgartner 2013). Blacks are often believed to make up the bulk of those who are poor and on welfare (Gilens 2003), whereas Hispanics are underrepresented in images and perceptions of the poor (van Doorn 2015). The reality is, however, that non-Hispanic Whites comprised 42.1 percent, while Blacks were 23 percent and Hispanics 28 percent of the poor population in 2014. Given their beliefs about work and their images about those on welfare, some people assume that the majority of those receiving aid are able-bodied, middle-aged men who are too lazy to work. In fact, 43 percent of the poor are either below 18 or over 64 years old. Of the remainder, roughly 16 percent of the nonaged poor have a disability of some sort, and 50 percent of poor families are headed by a female parent (DeNavas-Walt and Proctor 2015). Thus, the majority are not able-bodied, middle-aged men. Many in the recent poverty ranks are the "new poor," that is, individuals who have been laid off or made poor because of medical expenses, and who have never been poor before (Weissman 2013).

There are other misconceptions about the poor that reinforce the belief that they are undeserving. One is that they have a significantly greater number of children than the nonpoor. This is simply not the case. There is little difference in the average size of poor and nonpoor families. In 2014, the average size of U.S. families in general was 3.13, and that of poor families was 2.93 (Current Population Survey 2016). There is even some evidence that higher fertility rates are occurring among couples with high incomes and elite educations (Weeden et al. 2006). A 2011 survey by the Department of Labor found no difference in family size between those receiving public assistance and those not (Foster and Hawk 2013). Thus, the differences in household composition between those on and those not on "welfare" are not nearly as great as welfare stereotypes would suggest.

Nor is there any good evidence that poor mothers have children, including those outside of wedlock, to increase their benefits. The assumption that people have children to get more support from the government simply does not hold up when the evidence is examined (Morris and Williamson 1986). Increases in welfare benefits do not appear to have a significant impact on poor parents' decisions to have more children (Gensler 1997; Zavodny and Bitler 2010).

First, the vast majority of unmarried mothers on welfare have only one child, and rates of childbearing outside of wedlock tend to be lower in states with higher welfare benefits (Ellwood and Bane 1984; Bell 1987). Second, welfare benefits are quite low, making it uneconomical to have more children to receive more benefits. In 2014, for example, the average per-person monthly food stamp benefit was $125.01, and in 2010 the average monthly child support payment was $430 (U.S. Census Bureau 2012a). When comparing these benefits with the estimated $164,160 it took in 2013 for a lower-income, single-parent, two-child family to raise the younger child to age 18 (Lino and U.S. Department of Agriculture, Center for Nutrition Policy and Promotion 2014, p. 14), it becomes apparent that the economic incentive to have large numbers of children would be very low.

Another reason why many balk at giving the poor too many cash benefits is that they are perceived as wasting their money on frivolous purchases. However, evidence from the 2012 Consumer Expenditure Survey conducted by the U.S. Department of Labor suggests that the poor spend most of their incomes on basic needs. Table 3.1 compares the percentages and amounts of income spent on different items households in the poorest income quintile with the percentages spent by those in the richest income quintile.

Total expenditures for those in the lowest quintile are less than one-fourth of the top quintile ($22,154 vs. $99,368). In terms of how income is spent, 82 percent of the $22,154 in outlays is spent on housing, food, transportation, and utilities by the lowest-level households. An additional 8 percent is spent on health care. Significant for future quality of life, only 2 percent of the expenditures of the lowest-expenditure group is put aside for insurance and pensions. In contrast, while they spend more, in absolute terms, in each category, smaller *percentages* are spent by the richest quintile on housing, food, and health care. But these households spend eight times as much money as the lowest income group on insurance and pensions, providing them with a better foundation for a stable future.

Another perception of those on welfare is that they are usually guilty of fraud and cheating. But in fact, only an extremely small percentage cheat, and then, in almost all cases, only a small amount of money is involved. Estimates from 2009 to 2011, for example, suggest that fraud in the use of food stamps accounts for 1.3 cents of every dollar spent (Mantovani, Williams, and Pflieger 2013). More prevalent and more serious than cheating by recipients are the honest mistakes and errors made by public officials when determining eligibility for and level of public aid (Bell 1987). In addition, recent exposures of pervasive fraud by building contractors and others who profit from the government's housing program, extensive overcharging by contractors charged with cleaning up polluted areas, and fraudulent charges by health care providers and fictitious clinics strongly suggest that if fraud is a problem in poverty programs, the poor are not its primary source. In fact, 2010 estimates are that Medicare fraud alone (that is, fraud committed by medical professionals to get higher reimbursements) amounts to $60 billion a year (Weaver 2010).

When considering the deservedness of those who receive welfare and who they are, one should remember that many nonpoor people also receive governmental welfare, although one usually does not think of middle-class or wealthy persons or corporations as receiving such aid. For this reason, it has been called **phantom welfare** (Huff and

TABLE 3.1 Average Annual Expenditures and Percentages Spent in Major Categories for Lowest and Highest Income Quintiles: 2012

Major Spending Category	Lowest Income Quintile		Highest Income Quintile	
	Amount	Percentage	Amount	Percentage
Housing	$8,836	40%	$29,705	30%
Food	$3,502	16%	$11,334	11%
Transportation	$3,447	16%	$16,344	16%
Utilities	$2,177	10%	$5,330	5%
Health Care	$1,677	8%	$5,785	6%
Entertainment	$989	4%	$5,444	5%
Insurance and Pensions	$489	2%	$15,534	16%
Other Expenditures	$376	2%	$1,617	2%
Average Annual Expenditures	$22,154	100%	$99,368	100%

Source: Bureau of Labor Statistics, *Consumer Expenditures in 2012,* Report 1046, March 2014.

Johnson 1993) or more commonly "corporate welfare" as famously coined by Michael Harrington (1969). Direct cash and credit subsidies, tax exemptions and deductions, subsidized or reduced-cost services, and various trade restrictions are among the assistance programs provided to businesses. The recent multibillion dollar "bailout" or "rescue" of financial institutions by the federal government is among the latest examples of government support for the nonpoor.

Not only businesses but also nonpoor persons receive significant amounts of aid. Among the benefits to the middle class in the "fiscal welfare system" are tax deductions for mortgages and exemptions for parents of college students (Abramovitz 2001, p. 298). Despite the many governmental benefits that flow to the nonpoor, it is generally only the poor who are perceived as receiving "welfare" and often seen as undeserving of that aid. Yet, if the degree to which it is deserved is a measure of whether governmental benefits should go to a group, then the phantom welfare that is given to nonpoor individuals and organizations needs to be given more attention than it has received.

NUTSHELL 3.1   A Dark Side of Welfare Reform

While the 1996 welfare reforms reduced the number of individuals on welfare and pushed many into the labor force, it also created a variety of problems for those who had hoped to escape poverty. In her interviews with TANF recipients in West Virginia, Melissa Latimer found that many complained about the minimal government effort to bring jobs into the region and the lack of help in job placement. Availability of and access to relevant training was also a widespread issue. When seeking help, these residents also felt that they were treated poorly by human services workers:

> "These workers make you feel like a bum every time you apply for help."
> "They think you ain't much of nothing."
> "When a person signs up for help, they should not be made to feel like a failure."
> "[They should] quit putting employees in there that look down on more welfare people." (Latimer 2008, pp. 87, 95)

These findings are not unusual; the manner in which welfare recipients are treated has changed little as a result of welfare reform. The shadow of being considered "undeserving" still hangs over the poor who seek help. As Sandra Danziger recently put it: "[I]n the current cash welfare programs the poor are neither pitied nor entitled" (2010, p. 535). Some have to fight the image of being undeserving:

> "I have always worked and paid taxes."
> "I support my own children and I have health problems but I am determined."
> "I am doing my best." (Latimer 2008, pp. 88–89)

Older poor women, especially those who live in poor rural areas and seek help, often face unique problems because of their age and the generation in which they were raised:

> "People like us, we were taught to do for ourselves . . . be self-reliant. But there's too many people like me (seniors) that need help . . . even if they have to swallow their pride."
> "I need to be doctored up because I'm a swellin' from my arthritis. I cain't hardly walk. But I cain't get medication for it cause I ain't got the money."
> "Since I'm over 60, there's nobody out there's gonna hire me when they find out my age." (Henderson and Tickamyer 2008, pp. 160, 161, 163)

How do we change the culture of welfare so that no poor person is automatically stigmatized when they seek help?

Sources: Melissa Latimer, "A View from the Bottom: Former Welfare Recipients Evaluate the System," *Journal of Poverty* 12 (1): 77–101; Sandra K. Danziger, "The Decline of Cash Welfare and Implications for Social Policy and Poverty," *Annual Review of Sociology* 36: 523–545; Debra A. Henderson and Ann R. Tickamyer, "Lost in Appalachia: The Unexpected Impact of Welfare Reform on Older Women in Rural Communities," *Journal of Sociology & Social Welfare* 35: 153–171.

The Poor and Incentive to Work

Perhaps the most consequential perception of the poor involves their attachment to work and the work ethic. As mentioned earlier, the value of work is deeply ingrained in U.S. culture, as is the belief that most people can succeed if they try hard enough. These beliefs force us to raise some important questions about the poor. First, are people poor primarily because they do not work? Second, do the poor believe in the work ethic, or do they prefer not to work? With respect to the first question, census data indicate that a significant proportion of the poor work, many of them full-time. In 2014, 38.2 percent of poor individuals 18 years of age or older worked during the year, and almost one-third of these did so full-time, year-round. Yet they are still poor. Working 40 hours per week for 50 weeks during a year at the 2015 minimum wage of $7.25 would provide a household income of $14,500, only two-thirds of the amount needed to raise a family of four (two parents, two children) above the poverty level. Thirty-eight percent of all American workers made less than $20,000 in 2014, and 51 percent of all American workers made less than $30,000. Most would not expect the 38 percent of the poor who are under 18 or over 65 to work much, if at all. In addition, there are others who are genuinely disabled and unable to work, including military veterans. In 2012, more than 28 percent of adults aged 21–64 who are disabled lived in poverty (Majority Committee Staff Report 2014).

Low wages, in concert with a weak labor market, declining governmental supports, and increased income inequality are major factors behind the recent rise in poverty (Mishel, Bernstein, and Shierholz 2009). The level of wages is especially important because 80–90 percent of the incomes of poor families with one full-time worker come from wages. Even among single-parent families, a majority of income is derived from earnings (Stanczyk 2009).

The low-wage workforce is disproportionately composed of the most vulnerable groups in our society. In contrast to the rest of the labor force, women, members of minorities, youth, and workers with no more than high school educations are overrepresented among low-wage employees. Women who are single parents have been caught in a particularly difficult bind in the last 15 years because there remains societal pressure to both work *and* take care of their children. While both are likely to be desired by a single parent, as a young welfare mother put it, you can't have both at the same time (Hennessy 2009). Both are full-time. And yet to not do both of these is culturally unacceptable.

What these data indicate is that many poor individuals work, but despite their efforts and the difficulties they face, they remain poor. Because of the importance of earnings as a source of income for most families, it is important that programs be designed with work incentives in mind. Both the poor and the nonpoor respond to such incentives (Danziger, Haveman, and Plotnick 1986). Most Americans want to work. When asked if they would continue to work even if they did not need the money, 70 percent of American adults said that they would continue to work (GSS 2015). This includes those with disabilities: Nearly 70 percent of adults with disabilities strive to work (Kessler Foundation 2015). Interviews with poor single mothers confirm these general findings. Work "gives me a feeling of accomplishment"; it shows my children "a good example." "When I don't work, I feel useless like I'm wasting my life." "I don't want to live on welfare" (Hennessy 2009, pp. 566–567). These findings should not be surprising given that work is a hub around which many Americans' most cherished values revolve. Work is a major source of self-esteem and identity.

WHO ARE THE POOR?

This is not an easy question to answer because of continuing complaints and disagreements about how "poverty" should be officially measured. The federal poverty measure considers pretax income from all sources to determine one's income level. Consequently, it does not include the value of noncash benefits or the effect of taxes and tax credits on income. It also contains a household spending formula that is outdated. Alternative poverty measures that address these issues, such as those developed by the National Academy of Sciences, more often indicate that poverty levels are higher than suggested by the official measure (U.S. Census Bureau 2015b). However, because longitudinal governmental data on poverty are based on it, the official poverty measure will be used in the present discussion.

In contrast to the long-term movement toward greater income and wealth inequality, trends in official poverty rates have been more erratic since 1980, going up in the early 1980s before declining and then rising again in 1989. They began to decline again in 1993 and did so for the remainder of the decade before increasing again in 2001, and then more dramatically during the Great Recession of 2008–2010. In 2014, the poverty rate stood at 14.8 percent (46.7 million people), up from 11.3 percent (31.6 million) in 2000, but down from 2013 (U.S. Census Bureau 2015d).

Whether persons or families are defined as "poor" by the Census Bureau depends on whether their income falls below a given threshold. These thresholds vary by one's age, and family size and composition. For example, in 2015, individuals younger than 65 years were defined as poor if their total income fell below $12,316. On the other hand, a family of four with two parents and two children under 18 years of age had to have a gross income of under $24,008 to be classified as poor (U.S. Census Bureau 2014b).

Contradicting the stereotype, most of the poor are not Black. Non-Hispanic Whites account for 42.1 percent of the poor, compared to Black Americans, who make up 23 percent (U.S. Census Bureau 2014c). However, Table 3.2 shows that Hispanics and Blacks have poverty rates that are almost three times those of Whites. Hispanics have become an increasingly large part of the poverty population. In 1980, they composed only 12 percent of the poor population, in 1990, 18 percent, and in 2014, 28 percent. The increase can be linked to the increase in immigration of poor Hispanics during this period. The poverty rate for families with female householders is about five times that of married-couple families, and the poverty rate for children is noticeably higher than that for any other age group. In 2014, children under 18 had a 21.1 percent poverty rate, compared with the national poverty rate of 14.8 percent (U.S. Census Bureau 2015e). Children in families headed by a female are four times more likely to be poor than children living in families with a married couple. Their poverty rate is 39.8 percent (Eichner and Robbins 2015).

While a popular stereotype is that most poor live inside principal cities, 2014 data indicate that

TABLE 3.2 Poverty Rates by Race, Age, and Family Status: 1980–2014

	Poverty Rate (% in Poverty)				
	1980	**1990**	**2000**	**2010**	**2014**
All persons	13	13.5	11.3	15.1	14.8
Under 18 years old	18.3	20.6	16.2	22	21.1
18 to 64 years old	10.1	10.7	9.6	13.8	13.5
65 and older	15.7	12.2	9.9	8.9	10
Whites, non-Hispanics	9.1	8.8	7.4	9.9	10.1
Blacks	32.5	31.9	22.5	27.5	26.2
Hispanics	25.7	28.1	21.5	26.5	23.6
Married-couple families	6.2	5.7	4.7	6.2	6.2
Female-headed families	32.7	33.4	25.4	31.6	30.6
Male-headed families	11	12	11.3	15.8	15.7

Source: U.S. Census Bureau, *Income, Poverty and Health Insurance Coverage in the United States: 2015.*

a slight majority of the poor actually live outside major cities (DeNavas-Walt and Proctor 2015, p. 13). Geographically, poverty rates are higher in rural areas and in the core of central cities, and are higher in the South and West than in the Northeast or Midwest. Mississippi, Alabama, Arkansas, Kentucky, and Louisiana were among the states with 2013 poverty rates that were well above the national average. Mississippi had the highest poverty rate with 24 percent. In contrast, the rates in Alaska, Connecticut, Maryland, and New Hampshire were significantly lower than the national average (Bishaw and Fontenot 2014, p. 3). Despite expectations to the contrary, families in rural areas suffer more food insecurity than those in urban areas, particularly following the recession, as small grocery stores, often the only source of food within miles, have been closing. Without access to transportation, families in poverty struggle to meet their food needs (Piontak and Schulman 2014).

One group particularly hard hit by the recent Great Recession is the disabled, perhaps because those with disabilities are the "last hired" and "first fired," and economic downturns might add stress and exacerbate disabilities. During the recession, applications for disability benefits through Social Security Insurance reached an all-time high, as the recession resulted in a 9 percent decline in the presence of workers in the labor force (Kaye 2010).

Within the poor population, some people are poorer than others. Some have incomes that are very near the poverty threshold, whereas the incomes of others fall well below that poverty line. Two measures are used to indicate how far an individual's or family's income falls below their poverty threshold. One of these is a *ratio* that compares their actual income with their poverty threshold. A ratio of 1.00 indicates that their income is exactly the same as the threshold. A ratio below 1.00 is a measure of how far *below* poverty the person's or family's income falls; conversely, a ratio above 1.00 indicates how far their income is *above* the poverty threshold. In 2014, about 44.6 percent of poor families, or 20.8 million individuals, had incomes that were

Photo 3.1 It is common to associate poverty with the inner city, and indeed central cities have the highest poverty rates of any residential area. But rural poverty is also significantly higher than the national average. The poverty rate for those living outside metropolitan areas was 16.5 percent in 2014. Almost two-thirds of the poor live in the South and West. Rural states such as Alabama, Arkansas, Louisiana, and New Mexico have high poverty rates compared to others.

© Stephen Mcsweeny/Shutterstock.

less than half of the amount that the government uses to classify them as poor. In 2014, 6.8 million children lived in families with this level of income (Denavas-Walt and Proctor 2015, pp. 17, 18).

The second measure used to show the depth of poverty is the **income deficit**, which is the difference between a family's income and its poverty threshold. In 2014, the average poor family's income deficit was $10,137, which means that their income was actually $10,137 below their poverty threshold. Thus, they were not only poor, but *very* poor.

A particularly troubling trend in poverty rates in the United States is the growth in extreme poverty, or the number of families living on less than $2 per day per individual (Edin and Shaefer 2015). Families living at the poverty level survive on $8.50 per person per day; those in extreme poverty somehow manage to survive on far less. Since 1996 the number of families in extreme poverty has increased dramatically: Measuring just cash income, the number in extreme poverty has increased by 159 percent. Including both cash income and noncash benefits

such as food and housing assistance, the number has increased by over 50 percent, with 1.17 million children living in extreme poverty in 2011 (Shaefer and Edin 2014).

WELFARE REFORM AND CURRENT POVERTY PROGRAMS

Historically, there have been different kinds of attempts to address the problem of poverty. Some of the earliest were private and local in nature. There are still a large number of national and regional nongovernmental organizations that have as their major goal the reduction of poverty and the problems associated with it, such as homelessness and hunger. Among the most effective are Action Against Hunger USA, National Alliance to End Homelessness, Coalition for the Homeless, Action Aid International USA, Bread for the World Institute, and Second Harvest. Other programs involve different levels of governmental participation. Whether the government should fully carry the burden of

Photo 3.2 In January 2015, 564,708 people were homeless in the United States. Over 200,000 of these are people in families. Often people become homeless because of an unexpected economic crisis such as job loss or a health crisis. About 8 percent of homeless are veterans, and about 2 percent of homeless are chronically homeless (National Alliance to End Homelessness 2016).

© iStock.com/alptraum.

solving this problem, rather than private voluntary groups, has been a source of controversy.

Consequently, there are different perspectives on how extensive the government's programs should be. The most stringent view—the **residual**, or conservative, view—holds that social welfare aid should only be given to the poor when their families and their involvement in the private economy have not been able to lift them out of poverty. In this sense, welfare is to serve a "residual" function, coming in only after other more traditional, nongovernmental sources of help have been exhausted. As this function implies, social welfare expenditures and programs are expected to be kept to a minimum, and only those who demonstrate indisputably that they are in need are considered eligible for welfare help. Even then, benefits will be low and short term so as not to discourage work. Poverty is viewed as being caused primarily by individual defects and character flaws, rather than by wider social or cultural conditions. Under these circumstances, there is a social stigma for those seeking welfare. Up until the New Deal, this approach to welfare dominated the U.S. welfare system (Bell 1987), and it still maintains a strong grip.

The second view of social welfare—the **institutional**, or liberal, perspective—has basically the opposite characteristics from the residual approach. Specifically, it assumes that social welfare programs are an integral part of the institutional structure of modern society, and that like other institutions, they play a vital role in dealing with many of the problems generated by society's social structure and events, such as business cycles and aging, which are largely inevitable. The institutional approach is consistent with the situational and structural theories of poverty. Since poverty is largely beyond the control of most poor, people should be able to expect help without a stigma being attached to such aid. Beginning with the New Deal in the 1930s, an institutional element was formally introduced on a broad scale into the general income-maintenance system of the United States. The result is that the present system is largely a mixture of both approaches.

A third view of social welfare programs interprets them differently than either conservatives or liberals. Instead of being considered either an unnecessary burden on government or as an integral and humane part of it, this *pacifying* perspective interprets social welfare programs as a means of controlling the working class and the poor. Social welfare programs expand when there is rising unrest among these groups and contract when these groups are calm (Piven and Cloward 2012). This placating function of welfare is closely related to the uneven operation of the capitalist economy. Oversupplies of labor lead to increases in government-sponsored programs. At the same time, however, the work requirements and benefit levels of welfare programs are stringent enough to ensure the availability of a cheap labor force to employers.

Despite variations in the perspectives, flaws and complaints about public assistance programs instigated an effort to change the structure of welfare policy, and in 1996 the Congress passed a welfare-reform package. At first glance, changes brought about by the Personal Responsibility and Work Opportunity Reconciliation Act of 1996, as its title suggests, are based on many of the same assumptions of past programs: individual characteristics are responsible for poverty, policymakers have to get tough with those on welfare to save them, people need to be pushed off welfare into work, welfare creates dependency, and single mothers form the core of those on public assistance.

The 1996 welfare reform movement was based in part on the controversial belief that public-assistance programs have built-in work disincentives. Behind this belief is the conviction that "generous" benefit levels discourage recipients from seeking employment. However, this relationship is not as straightforward as it may appear, as it is affected by many variables including the health of the labor market, the nature of the incentive, and the demographics of the workers. For example, unemployment insurance is more likely to lengthen the return to work in a weak labor market than in a strong one. Thus, during the Great Recession, there was a small but statistically significant relationship between the level of unemployment benefits and length of unemployment (Farber and Valletta 2013). But studies have found no relationship between SNAP benefits (formerly known as the food stamp program) and employment rates (Moffitt 2015a). The Earned Income Tax credit has practically no impact on the work of married men, small negative effects on married women, but positive effects for single women; specifically, single women are more likely to enter the labor market in the presence of the EITC (Hoynes 2014).

A great deal of controversy similarly exists over whether public assistance fosters the disintegration of marriages and encourages non-marital childbirth (Murray 1984). Most studies have found no relationship between benefit levels, family dissolution, and non-marital childbirth (e.g., Kearney and Levine 2012; Ellwood and Summers 1986; Wilson 2012). Nor have higher state benefit levels been linked to increases in the number of female-headed households. In fact, the number of female-headed households grew even when benefit levels declined (O'Hare 1987). Some recent studies, however, suggest that policies such as family caps or two-parent rules for receiving benefits have slightly reduced single-parenthood (Moffitt, Phelan, and Winkler 2015), but others argue that this is due to the fact that single women with children simply left the welfare rolls, while remaining in poverty (Purtell, Gershoff, and Aber 2012). Changes in family composition are more closely tied to shifts in attitudes about families and divorce as well as to broader events in the economy. Family dissolution and reluctance to marry are related, for example, to the greater employment opportunities for women and perceived employability problems encountered by Black men (Edin and Kefalas 2011; Sawhill 1988).

The 1996 Act was designed to reform the welfare system through an emphasis on making welfare recipients less dependent on public aid by pressuring them to find and accept work in the marketplace, and an emphasis on reducing non-marital childbearing. Consistent with past policy on welfare recipients, the provisions of the law assume that those on welfare need to be pushed into work, and that, if given the chance, they would prefer to remain dependent on welfare. But in contrast to past legislation, it does not guarantee public aid to a poor person, thus it is not an entitlement. Among the Act's provisions are the following:

- Able-bodied adults are required to work after 2 years of aid or lose benefits.
- Aid is only available to families with children under 18.
- Aid is limited to 5 years over a person's lifetime, and only 24 consecutive months.
- Block grants are given to states that can devise their own programs (Aid to Families with Dependent Children [AFDC] is eliminated).
- Future legal immigrants are ineligible for benefits in their first 5 years.
- Spending on food stamps is lowered by about $24 billion over a 6-year period, and guarantees of cash assistance for children are eliminated.
- Medicaid coverage is continued for people on welfare and for 1 year after leaving it if they are working.
- Teenage mothers are encouraged to identify the fathers of their children, stay in school, and live at home with parents.

Proponents hailed the new package as a reflection of American values of traditional family, work, and independence, and as a way of forcing those on welfare to be "responsible." Critics claimed that it created few, if any, jobs in which welfare recipients could work and would push more than a million more children into poverty. In many ways, the new legislation appeared to have a number of the same flaws that plagued past policies.

President Clinton also signed into law an increase in the minimum wage to $5.15. Although many believe that good wages and earned income tax credits are a better way to remove people from poverty than welfare programs (Sykes et al. 2015), this wage increase alone did not raise most poor families out of poverty. If one worked full-time, 40 hours a week, 52 weeks a year, minimum wage earnings still totaled well below what was needed to raise an average poor family above the poverty line. Inadequacy has been a traditional weakness of American welfare programs, and, as suggested, some critics feared that more children would be thrown into poverty by the 1996 changes.

The block grants resulting from the welfare reforms of 1996 were aimed at giving states more leeway in shaping their own programs and encouraging individuals to reduce their assumed dependency on welfare by becoming employed as soon as possible. Consequently, by July 1997, every state had devised its own mixture of programs and requirements that fall within federal guidelines (National Governors' Association Center for Best Practices 1999). Some states impose lifetime limits of 60 months on assistance, while others have shorter limits. Some require individuals to be working before 2 years of aid are over, while others hold to the 2-year limit. Many states simply do not spend their allotted funds, and in recent years many states have cut back on core welfare services and have shifted expenditures to fill state budget holes (Schott, Pavetti, and Floyd 2015). States vary on how they treat interstate immigrants and drug felons. They also have different policies about transitional child care and the existence of caps on total assistance amounts.

A central feature of these reforms was the Temporary Assistance for Needy Families (TANF) program, which replaced AFDC. Thus, it is one of the more controversial dimensions of welfare reform. Individuals participating in TANF are required to seek employment. In the event individuals do not find jobs, they are given subsidized or community employment, or are required to enter a work-training program. The aim is to remove individuals from welfare rolls as soon as possible. After 2 years, they are on their own, and can only be in the program for a total of 5 years over their lifetimes. The programs of all the states emphasize self-sufficiency as a goal and impose time limitations beyond which individuals are no longer eligible for benefits.

One of the major changes that occurred with welfare reform was the shift from cash assistance to social service (noncash) assistance to the poor. The value of cash benefits for TANF is now 20 percent below their 1996 levels in most states (Floyd and Schott 2015). Before 1995, more than three-quarters of welfare was in the form of cash

assistance; since 1996, only one-third is in cash assistance (Allard 2009). This dispels a popular view of everyone on welfare receiving generous monthly checks. The focus on getting people to work was one source for the increased emphasis on social services.

A Profile of Some Major Programs

Current U.S. income-maintenance programs can be divided into two general parts: social insurance and public assistance. Both parts include cash and **in-kind benefits. Social insurance** is aimed at replacing income lost because of death, unemployment, disability, or retirement. Most of the social insurance programs were developed under the Social Security Act of 1935; they include old-age insurance, survivors' insurance, disability insurance, unemployment insurance, and, in many cases, workers' compensation. Medicare is also a social insurance program. These programs are financed by the insured through payroll taxes, by employers, and by the government. Eligibility for participation depends on the extent of a person's prior work history. As long as individuals satisfy certain basic requirements, they are automatically eligible for these programs. There is little stigma attached to participation in these programs because individuals are thought of as deserving of such benefits. These programs are most illustrative of the "institutional" perspective on welfare.

Public assistance programs, which have been more "residual" in terms of the assumptions built into them, are "means-tested" programs that aim at temporarily assisting poor individuals and families. These make up what most people think of as "welfare." The major programs included in the public assistance category are TANF, Supplemental Security Income (SSI), Supplemental Nutrition Assistance Program (SNAP), and Medicaid. SNAP was formally known as the Food Stamp Program. In addition to these programs, local general assistance and housing also are included in this category. Public assistance programs are financed by general revenues, and instead of individuals being automatic participants upon the satisfaction of basic requirements, persons wishing to receive welfare (i.e., public assistance) must prove that their income is low enough to justify their receiving aid. Thus, there tends to be more of a stigma attached to applying for and receiving welfare than is the case, for example, when one receives a Social Security check.

SOCIAL INSURANCE PROGRAMS Table 3.3 indicates the number of recipients and federal amounts for the major social insurance and public-assistance programs in 2012 and 2013. Social Security was and is by far the most expensive of the income-maintenance programs. In 2015, annual payments exceeded $870 billion, and the program served almost 59 million beneficiaries. Social Security provides monthly benefits to eligible retired and disabled workers, as well as to their spouses, children, and survivors. Retirement benefits make up most of these expenses. In 2015, the average monthly retirement benefit was $1,335.

Although most of the benefits from the Social Security retirement program go to nonpoor recipients, millions are protected from falling into poverty because of the program. Despite this benefit, Social Security has become a source of contention between younger and older generations. As its costs have gone up due to an aging population and a comparatively smaller base of workers to support it, younger workers resent the program's immediate cost to them and worry whether it will be able to support them when they retire. In addition to the retirement program, survivors' and disability insurance are also a part of Social Security. Under the first type, a worker's surviving dependents receive cash benefits. Disability insurance provides protection against the loss of family income resulting from a "breadwinner" being disabled. In 2015, about 15 percent of the total social security benefits was paid to disabled workers and their dependents.

TABLE 3.3 Number of Recipients and Federal Expenditures for Major Social Insurance and Public-Assistance Programs: 2014

Program	No. of recipients/ beneficiaries (in millions)	Benefits/ payments (in billions)
Social Insurance		
Social Security (total)	59.0	$848.2
Social Security (retirement)	41.9	$592.6
Social Security (survivors)	6.1	$114.0
Social Security (disabled)	10.9	$141.6
Medicare	54.0	$510.5
Public Assistance		
Supplementary Security Income	9.3	$54.7
Supplementary Nutrition Assistance	46.6[a]	$74.2
Temporary Assistance for Needy Families	3.5[a]	$14.0
Medicaid	65.0	$498.9

[a]Average number of monthly recipients.

Source: https://www.ssa.gov/news/press/basicfact.html
https://www.ssa.gov/oact/STATS/table4a5.html
http://www.acf.hhs.gov/sites/default/files/ofa/tanf_financial_data_fy_2014.pdf
http://www.fns.usda.gov/pd/supplemental-nutrition-assistance-program-snap
https://www.medicaid.gov/medicaid-chip-program-information/by-topics/financing-and-reimbursement/downloads/medicaid-actuarial-report-2014.pdf

In 1965, Medicare was added to the Social Security package. Its purpose is to provide hospital and medical insurance to people age 65 or older and those who are disabled but covered by Social Security. Payment under Medicare is made directly to the care provider. At the present time, Medicare does not pay for all medical services. For example, it does not cover custodial or routine dental care, nor does it pay for long-term nursing home care. The latter has been an issue of increasing concern, especially as the number of elderly increases. Medicare benefits totaled almost $632 billion in 2015 for its 55 million enrollees, compared with over $110 billion in 1990 (Kaiser Family Foundation 2015b).

PUBLIC ASSISTANCE PROGRAMS The programs that we have been discussing are largely based on the assumption that their beneficiaries have contributed both to the financial support of those programs and to society in general through their years of employment. Thus, the benefits are interpreted more as a right than as a handout; that is, they are viewed as deserved. In contrast, public assistance programs are controversial in large part because many of the recipients are seen as undeserving. It is with these programs that questions about fraud, laziness, and deservedness arise most often. Groups that traditionally have been the most vulnerable to poverty conditions are most likely to receive welfare. These include women, children, minorities, and the elderly.

Under the public-assistance umbrella are TANF, SNAP, Medicaid, and SSI programs (see Table 3.3). All of these programs are *means tested*; that is, individuals are required to prove that their level of need is such that they require help. Most of them involve at least two levels of government in their administration or funding. The federal government has given states wide latitude in determining eligibility criteria. The form of benefit also varies. The benefits from the TANF and SSI programs come in the form of cash assistance, while those from SNAP and Medicaid come in the form of in-kind benefits (e.g., checks are not sent to the beneficiaries; rather it is goods or services that are provided). Let us look briefly at each of these major programs.

Largely because of its cost and the controversy surrounding it, Aid to Families with Dependent Children (AFDC) was replaced in 1996 by Temporary Assistance for Needy Families (TANF). As its name suggests, the program provides cash assistance for poor families with children. In 2014, federal and state expenditures for TANF were $14 billion. While TANF's overall design was created by the federal government, the program's specific eligibility rules and administration are carried out by each state. Adult recipients are required to fulfill work requirements and to pass income eligibility tests. TANF heavily emphasizes the need to work and the amount of time over which a person can receive benefits.

Table 3.4 presents some of the basic characteristics of TANF participants. Contrary to the stereotype, the average TANF family tends to be fairly small, averaging fewer than two children. Most adult recipients are female, about one-third are White, another third Black, and about one-quarter are Hispanic. Over 35 percent have less than a high school education, and only 5.7 percent have more than a high school degree. Just under one-quarter are employed. Nearly 43.9 percent of the children in these families are under 6 years of age, and only 8.4 percent are older than 15.

Supplemental Security Income (SSI) is another cash-benefit welfare program aimed at people who are in financial need, and who are either 65 years of age or older, blind, or disabled. Implemented in 1974, it replaced federally reimbursed programs being run by the states to help the elderly, blind, and disabled. In 2014, over 8 million persons received federally administered SSI payments totaling $54 billion. Monthly payments ranged from $417.44 for the elderly to $547.15 for disabled persons and $542.13 for blind individuals (U.S. Social Security Administration 2014).

The Supplemental Nutrition Assistance Program (SNAP) is one of the major in-kind public assistance programs offered by the federal government. Although a food program operated during the period from 1939 to 1943, it was not reinstituted again until the early 1960s. Even though some experts would have preferred increases in cash benefits to a food program, the program has

TABLE 3.4 Characteristics of TANF Households and Recipients: 2013

Average number of persons in household	3
Average number of children per family	1.8

Adult Recipients	Percent
Sex	
Male	14
Female	86
Race/Ethnicity	
Hispanic	27.70
Non-Hispanic White	33.30
Black	33.10
Other	5.80
Education (number of years attained)	
Less than 10 years	8.60
10–11 years	27.40
12 years	56.40
More than high school	7.60
Citizenship Status	
U.S. citizen	93.10
Qualified alien	6.40
Employment Status	
Employed	22.60
Receiving earned income	20.10

Child Recipients	Percent
Less than 6 years old	43
6–11 years old	32.20
12–15 years old	16.40
16–19 years old	8.40

Source: U.S. Department of Health and Human Services, Administration for Children & Families, *Characteristics and Financial Circumstances of TANF; Recipients: Fiscal Year 2013 (2015).* Available at http://www.acf.hhs.gov/sites/default/files/ofa/tanf_characteristics_fy2013.pdf.

grown significantly since 2000. In 2014, about $76 billon in benefits were allotted, and there were over 46.5 million recipients. Still, in 2012 only 72 percent of those eligible signed up to receive

benefits (Center on Budget and Policy Priorities 2015a). SNAP participants tend to be among our most vulnerable citizens. In 2012 more than half of the participants were children or elderly. The average SNAP household contained 2.1 persons. Seventy-five percent of these households contained a disabled, child, or elderly person, and were likely to receive SSI or Social Security income. The average SNAP household had income from earnings that was slightly less than 60 percent of the poverty guideline (Gray and Eslami 2014). A profile of SNAP participants is provided in Table 3.5.

Medicaid is another in-kind program aimed at providing financial assistance to states to pay for the medical care of low-income adults and children under 138 percent of the federal poverty level ($16,245 for an individual in 2015). It is different from Medicare in a number of ways. First, it is a selective program, whereas Medicare is a nearly universal program. This means that applicants have to satisfy certain economic requirements before they can receive the service; that is, the program is

TABLE 3.5 Participants in Supplemental Nutrition Assistance Program: 2009

	Percentage of Participants
Children	44.80
Nondisabled adults, age 18–49, childless	19.90
Elderly adults	17.40
Disabled nonelderly person	20.30
Gross household income as percentage of poverty line:	
No Income	21.50
>0–50%	21.20
51–100%	40.20
101–130%	11.90
131%+	5.20

Source: U.S. Department of Agriculture, *Characteristics of Supplemental Nutrition Assistance Program, Households: Fiscal Year 2013* (2014). Available at http://www.fns.usda.gov/sites/default/files/ops/Characteristics2013.pdf.

means tested. In contrast, everyone in a particular age category is qualified to receive basic Medicare benefits, regardless of income. Second, Medicaid is a federal- and state-administered program, whereas Medicare is federally administered.

The Affordable Care Act, enacted in 2010, greatly expanded access and coverage of Medicaid and CHIP (Children's Health Insurance Program), though a Supreme Court ruling in 2012 allowed states to opt out of the Medicaid expansion. As of 2016, 19 states have opted out, leaving more than 3 million uninsured adults with a coverage gap (Garfield and Damico 2016). In 2014, federal expenditures for the roughly 64.9 million recipients who received Medicaid benefits for all services totaled almost $440 billion. Between the implementation of the Affordable Care Act and the open enrollment date of December 2014, Medicaid and CHIP enrollment increased by more than 10.7 million individuals (Paradise 2015).

There seems to be fairly widespread agreement that programs such as Medicare and Medicaid have made it possible for more people to get needed medical care. More people have used more health services than before the inception of these programs. Despite these salutary trends, however, problems still remain. Since the 1996 reform bill, the number of families getting cash benefits from public assistance programs has dropped significantly, but the number of participants in noncash programs such as Medicaid, food programs, and disability benefits has grown as problems in the economy have multiplied. Participation in the food stamp program approached record numbers in 2014 (Center on Budget and Policy Priorities 2015a). Variations between states in their coverage rules and the optional facilities/services available create inequalities among individuals who are equally in need of medical care.

AN ASSESSMENT OF THE REFORM ACT OF 1996

Given the controversial nature of the Personal Responsibility and Work Opportunity Reconciliation Act of 1996, it should not be surprising that there is similar disagreement about its effects on welfare recipients. The popular press has generally emphasized success criteria that show the Act to have had positive effects, and has downplayed criteria and evidence that suggest the Act's negative impacts (Schram and Soss 2001). Indeed, whether welfare reform is viewed as having been a success depends on how "success" is measured.

By some measures—number on welfare, employment, child poverty—there has been success. First, between 1996 and 2015, the number of welfare recipients fell by almost two-thirds, from 4.7 million to 1.7 million (Floyd and Schott 2015). The number of people on welfare is lower than it has been since 1969, and the percentage on cash assistance is the lowest it has ever been. Second, women who were on welfare have been pressed to end their dependency and enter the labor force in large numbers. Between 1996, the year of the reform legislation, and 2000, there was a 16 percent increase in work by single women, and a 35 percent increase among never-married women (Haskins 2015). Third, the child poverty rate fell from 20.5 percent in 1996 to 16.2 percent in 2000, although it increased to 21.1 percent in 2014 (U.S. Census Bureau 2014a). There was also a decline since 1996 in the rate of pregnancy among unwed teenagers (Lichter and Jayakody 2002).

Even for the above positive effects, however, there is debate about the role of welfare reform in creating them. The expansion of CHIP and the Earned Income Tax Credit in the early 1990s had significant impacts on employment and poverty rates (Haveman et al. 2015). More significantly, a strong economy at the time of legislation is also thought to have contributed heavily to reductions in welfare rolls and increased employment, resulting in reductions in child poverty (Haveman et al. 2015). The question is whether reform will have the same effect when the economy is not so robust. Greenberg and Bernstein (2004) provide an answer to the question, noting that between 2001 and 2004, the number of people on welfare fell at the same time that the poverty rate increased. It appears that welfare reform "generally performed well during the tightest labor market in 30 years [mid-to-late 1990s] but has been far less effective amid the slack labor market that has prevailed since the 2001 recession" (p. B2). The high unemployment rate during the 2008–2009 recession and the reluctance of employers to hire in 2010–2011 because of instability in the economy also placed greater pressure on welfare programs at a time when serious concerns about government spending were beginning to grow. TANF only modestly increased during the Great Recession, leaving many uncovered.

Welfare reform did create a "work-based safety net," but it was incomplete. While it did create a safety net for those poor families who could find jobs by increasing funding for poor working families and for families with disabled adults, this represented a shift away from single workers, the lowest income poor, and nondisabled (Center on Budget and Policy Priorities 2015c). "These redistributions likely reflect long-standing, and perhaps increasing, conceptualizations by U.S. society of which poor are deserving and which are not" (Moffitt 2015b, p. 729). TANF serves proportionally a much smaller percentage of the poor than did AFDC: Currently only 26 families per 100 in poverty received TANF, whereas in 1979 AFDC reached 82 families per 100 (Floyd and Schott 2015). The decrease in caseloads might be because of increases in other areas, such as the Earned Income Tax Credit, or, as some researchers argue, because potential recipients simply assume that support is not available to them (Edin and Shaefer 2015).

Other evidence on welfare reform's effects is also less positive. The 1996 Act has increased the inequalities in welfare programs between states. One consequence has been increased migration *out* of states with especially stringent welfare regulations, although the reasons for migration *into* particular states appear to be multiple and not fully understood (De Jong, Graefe, and Pierre 2005).

There have also been employment consequences. While many mothers who left welfare are employed, most are not working 40 hours per week consistently, many are in low-wage positions that do not offer many health or other benefits, and most are unlikely to move up into more stable positions with significantly higher pay. Only a minority will be in good jobs. Consequently, many of these new

workers have simply joined the ranks of the working poor, working for incomes that are often lower that those they had before leaving welfare (Cancian 2001; Lens 2002). As one scholar and former welfare participant put it: "If the goal of welfare reform was to get people off the welfare rolls, bravo. . . . If the goal was to reduce poverty and give people economic and job stability, it was not a success" (cited in Ohlemacher 2007, pp. A1, A3).

In her 3-year ethnographic study conducted among welfare families and at welfare offices, Sharon Hays (Hays 2003) found that 40 percent of the women and children who had gotten off welfare had *no* source of income, and of the remaining 60 percent, about half were still poor. Similarly, Cancian and Meyer's study of former welfare participants in Wisconsin (2004) found that while more than 50 percent have gotten out of poverty, they have not achieved economic independence, and continue to rely on noncash benefits from the government. Researchers speak to the growing number of "disconnected" individuals, those who are neither employed nor receiving welfare. Estimates are that between 20–25 percent of low-income, single mothers are disconnected (Loprest 2011).

Most of the employment is in metropolitan rather than rural areas, even though many of the latter areas have some of the highest poverty rates in the United States. In fact, there is evidence that, because of its urban bias, welfare reform may have actually worsened economic conditions among poor rural mothers. "Rural America . . . is too often forgotten in the welfare policy debates. Most predominately rural states provide low TANF benefits in comparison to generous urban states" (Lichter and Jayakody 2002). As a result, child care is often unaffordable and frequently costs more than the income brought in by the job. The availability of adequate child care centers, health services, and transportation continues to be a significant issue (Mammen, Dolan, and Seiling 2015).

The vast majority of welfare recipients who work little or do not work at all face a variety of difficulties that prevent them from entering the active labor force. These include educational and experience deficits as well as family issues like domestic violence and physical and mental problems (Butler et al. 2008; Danziger 2010). Low-income foster mothers, for example, are conflicted when faced with the policy demands to work as well as care for children who have been victims of abuse and neglect (Critelli and Schwam-Harris 2010).

A mismatch between the location of the poor and social service agencies created to help them also creates a barrier to moving out of poverty. Areas with high poverty rates have only half as many services readily available than areas with low poverty rates (Allard 2009). So the likelihood of a poor person getting the help needed is reduced.

At the present time, poor parents are caught in the gears of policies that make contradictory demands on them. For example, they are encouraged by welfare policies to work at the same time that their schools and their students are being monitored and expected to raise educational standards and performance. The more time poor parents spend working, the less time they have to help their children perform better in school. Parents need to work to support their families, but support for today is not the same as support for tomorrow. It is the degree of investment in their children's education that may very well affect the chances that the next generation will be out of poverty (Newman and Chin 2003).

These problems tend to fall disproportionately on young single mothers who have little education. Those most likely to be helped by welfare reform and to be early leavers are those who are most likely to find employment—that is, the able-bodied, better educated, skilled, and experienced. This leaves a core of less-educated, less-experienced, disabled individuals who are unlikely to be able to become self-sufficient and who find it difficult to move off welfare. It may be much more difficult to enforce TANF rules with this group (Moffitt 2015b).

The full consequences of the 1996 welfare reform legislation will probably not be known for a while. For reform to have a chance of being effective, all of the components needed to make recipients self-sufficient have to be in place. This requires solving the problems of child care, transportation, and training/education. It also demands addressing the broader issues of employment supply and sex discrimination in the workplace. At the present time, it appears that the reforms implemented in most states have not improved the lives of welfare recipients (Haveman et al. 2015).

The persistence of poverty has suggested to some that the poor may serve basic functions for the society, and particular nonpoor groups within it. Indeed, having an "undeserving" poor population serves many functions for the rest of us, including helping us feel superior, creating social work jobs, providing an accessible low-wage labor pool, and reinforcing dominant values (Gans 1995). By indicating these and other basic functions performed by the poor in U.S. society, Gans implied that poor people are not an isolated group who are poor because of their lack of integration into the mainstream of society, but rather are an integral part of the society. Alternative poverty programs that have been suggested vary in the extent to which their recommendations focus on the poor as a unique and separate group or as an integral and integrated part of the larger society. Those that stress the former tend to believe that the root causes of poverty lie in the flawed characters and characteristics of the poor themselves, whereas those in the latter camp are more likely to argue that societal structures and processes create a poor population.

Because of widespread stereotypes of those on welfare, including those that suggest welfare recipients are personally responsible for their condition, some have argued that broader-based policies and programs must be implemented to address problems the poor face. For more than a decade, William Julius Wilson (2012) has stressed that for any program to be fully accepted by the public it must be seen as benefiting everyone, not just particular groups. "I am convinced," wrote Wilson in 1987, "that, in the last few years of the twentieth century, the problems of the truly disadvantaged in the United States will have to be attacked primarily through universal programs that enjoy the support and commitment of a broad constituency" (p. 120). Most fundamentally, Wilson believes that racial, ethnic, and other groups need to de-emphasize how they are *different* from one another, and emphasize and act on the values, goals, and destinies that they have in *common*. Organized coalitions of different groups that focus on problems that they all share are more likely to be effective. Since we are all part of one society, economic events and inequality have implications for all of our lives.

U.S. POVERTY AND WELFARE IN COMPARATIVE PERSPECTIVE

When we look across the world, we find that some populations not only have much higher rates of poverty, but also have degrees of poverty that are significantly more abject than those found in the United States. The greatest numbers living in extreme poverty are in South Asia, Central and sub-Saharan Africa, and East Asia, respectively. India alone is estimated to have 27.8 percent of its population living in severe poverty. In Madagascar, Democratic Republic of the Congo, Nigeria, Mozambique, Zambia, Burundi, Liberia, and Rwanda over half the population live on $1.25 per day (United Nations Development Programme 2015, p. 229). When compared to other rich Western industrial nations, however, the United States does not fare as well. In 2013, the United States had the highest relative poverty rate: "The average poor child liv[es] in a home that makes 36 percent less than the relative poverty line." It also had the second greatest percentage of children in poverty, just above Romania (Fisher 2013). Additionally, "Americans are more likely to experience significant declines in their standard of living when they retire and to be relatively poor in old age than people in other advanced economies. . .," according to a 2014 analysis (Morrissey 2014). Finland, Norway, and Sweden had child poverty rates that were two and a half times lower than the U.S. rate—the United States ranks 20th out of 20 developed OECD countries for relative child poverty (UNICEF Innocenti Research Centre 2012). Combining life expectancy, expected years of schooling, mean years of schooling, and gross national income per capita into an index of quality of life called the Human Development Index (HDI), the United

Nations ranked the United States eighth (United Nations Development Programme 2015, p. 208). Clearly, the United States does not rate well in these comparisons of poverty levels.

Why might the United States have higher levels of poverty and inequality than most other rich democracies? Several factors are at play, including cultural values that discourage extensive government involvement in the lives of individuals, a market economy that emphasizes free exchange and competition and drives the society toward greater income inequality, and welfare policies that do not have a large impact on reducing poverty.

Societies with free, largely unregulated market economies tend to have higher degrees of economic inequality than other nations where governments are more actively involved in economic matters (Birchfield 2012). In the former, given an assumption of equal opportunity for all, the operation of an open market determines the outcome and distribution of goods and resources among the people. Let the chips fall where they may, so to speak.

In the abstract, Americans tend to subscribe to conservative values of small government, a free economy, and individual responsibility. But at the same time, evidence indicates they realize that problems may arise during the actual operation of society that demand government intervention on behalf of those who are victimized or trapped. While Americans are cool toward helping those whom they believe can help themselves (i.e., are undeserving), they tend to be generous toward those they believe are poor for reasons beyond their control (i.e., are deserving). Their feelings toward groups that are usually the focus of government assistance such as the poor and elderly are much warmer than those felt about the rich and big business, for example (Bartels 2008). Page and Jacobs' 2007 national survey revealed that most people support government assistance to the poor for their basic necessities (2009). The researchers refer to this seemingly contradictory mixture of beliefs as "conservative egalitarianism." One consequence of this ambivalent stance is that while the United States has some welfare programs, they tend not to be overly generous, and thus, do not drive down the poverty rate very much.

There appears to be little question that a generous welfare policy reduces poverty (Brady 2009). But compared to other industrial nations, the United States does not fare well. American welfare programs are less effective than those in Britain, for example, in reducing persistent poverty, speeding movement out of poverty, and alleviating the poverty problems associated with race (Worts, Sacker, and McDonough 2010). Our welfare benefits are the most meager of all Western democracies; the chances that a middle-aged adult will become poor are more than

16 times greater in the United States than in Denmark, which has the most generous welfare program (Smeeding 2005; Brady, Fullerton, and Cross 2009).

Some societies choose to devote more resources than others toward reducing poverty. As Timothy Smeeding put it: "We have more inequality and poverty than other nations because we choose to have more" (2005, p. 980). More inequality means that the richest groups in our society have moved further away from the middle class and poor. Their material interests are different, and they see little need for a generous welfare program (Smeeding 2005).

Summary

This chapter has discussed many of the assumptions and perceptions of the poor that provide an important part of the underpinnings for current welfare policy. Often, these perceptions are not consistent with government data on the actual poor population.

American attitudes about the poor are frequently ambivalent. Traditional values of individualism, independence, hard work, and material success encourage a negative attitude toward those who are not economically successful. At the same time, humanitarian and community values encourage people to take care of those who are less fortunate than themselves. Believing that virtually all people can make it if they try hard enough, but at the same time knowing from historical events such as the Depression, plant closings, and market declines that not everything about their economic fates is in their hands to control, has resulted in a somewhat bifurcated approach to poverty programs for the needy. There are elements of both a residual and institutional approach in this system.

Problems of inequity, inadequacy, and goal conflict have permeated public assistance programs for the poor. In addition, questions about how they affect work incentive, family composition, and effectiveness have also generated heated

debate. Alternative proposals attempt to grapple with the problems of adequacy, employment, work incentives, and so on. Many have suggested economic growth and full employment as the keys to the puzzle of poverty, as they would lead to greater self-sufficiency for everyone. Indeed, the Welfare Reform Act of 1996 focused on pushing individuals into the labor force.

Current programs fall into the broad categories of social insurance and public assistance. Social insurance programs such as Social Security retirement, disability, and Medicare insurance provide universal coverage with a minimum of stigma to a wide variety of individuals who fall into a particular demographic category. There is no means testing or demeaning administrative process suggesting that these recipients are receiving welfare. In the other category of public assistance are those who are poor but not elderly and/or disabled. Individuals with these characteristics—often women who head their own households, children, and members of minority groups—must provide proof that they are indigent. They must prove that they are deserving of nutrition assistance, Medicaid, and benefits from other programs.

Follow-up investigations on the effectiveness of the 1996 reforms are decidedly mixed in their results. In many cases, policies have deepened poverty, at least in the short run. More time is needed, however, to fully assess the full impact of the states' reforms. It is clear that, when compared to other industrial countries, the United States has higher poverty rates and its programs are less effective in reducing poverty.

As difficult as poverty may be to understand, we still have not confronted the even thornier issue of economic inequality. A focus on inequality unavoidably involves all of us, since we all live out our lives within its structure. If inequality continues to grow as it has in recent years, we may be forced to address this topic. The real question is whether poverty, let alone inequality, can be eliminated within a democratic capitalist society. This brings us back to some of the core questions with which we began this book.

If poverty is generated not merely by differences among individuals, but by conditions that are part of a capitalist economy, such as unemployment and the pressure for profit and lower wages, then a permanent solution, as Morris and Williamson (1986) suggested, is very unlikely unless fundamental changes in the political economy occur. Are inequality and poverty inevitable? Given the present social structure, the answer is probably yes. Are inequality and poverty desirable? It depends. Although it is a serious problem for those who must suffer with it, poverty appears to be functional for others. It helps maintain the attractiveness of low wages and menial jobs, especially when coupled with low benefits from

programs. At the same time, it provides employment for many middle-class professionals. As to the immediate future of inequality and poverty, the fact that income and wealth inequality has increased in recent years, despite the presence of income-maintenance programs, suggests that (1) we do not really consider inequality to be a major problem, (2) we do not really know what causes it to fluctuate, and/or (3) some find inequality beneficial.

Evidence strongly suggests that what happens in the economy has a major impact on both inequality and poverty. Instability in our globalized economy has generated greater unemployment and income insecurity. At the dawn of the twenty-first century, many organizations are streamlining and downsizing in an effort to maintain profits in the face of intensified domestic and foreign competition. While executives and shareholders frequently reap the economic benefits of these leaner and more efficient organizational structures, the attendant layoffs have led many in the middle class to fall near or into poverty. These shifts have also exacerbated the poor financial conditions of those already at the bottom and are also likely to cause further tensions among racial/ethnic groups and between the sexes. In sum, the rewards and punishments of recent economic changes are clearly and unequally divided. The combination of the economic trends and their varied effects on different groups, together with our reluctance to address the problem of inequality and to recognize its social roots, are not good omens.

Critical Thinking

1. In your opinion, what would be the determining factor in setting a poverty threshold? Why?
2. What can be done to separate the ideas of race and welfare in the minds of many people? How can we stop the racialization of welfare?
3. To what extent, and under what conditions, if any, is the federal government responsible for

reducing or eliminating poverty? Defend your answer.
4. Given what has been suggested in this chapter, what do you think should be the cornerstone features of any effective antipoverty plan?

Web Connections

The Economic Policy Institute is a nonprofit, research and analysis think tank that is dedicated to making the needs of low- and middle-income Americans heard in economic policy conversations. They specialize in many areas of research, including inequality and poverty. Visit their website at http://www.epi.org/research/inequality-and-poverty/.

Film Suggestions

28 Women (2005). Depicts the experiences of single mothers trying to create stable lives.

Tent City, USA (2012). This documentary shows Nashville's tent city that was created due to the most recent economic recession. The city could barely support one in five of the homeless population, so the homeless created their own city that they self-govern.

CHAPTER 4

Status Inequality

Superfluous wealth can buy superfluities only.

HENRY DAVID THOREAU (1817–1862)

Differences in *economic* resources are not the only kind of inequality. Frequently, inequality can take a *social* form that is not necessarily rooted in one's wealth or power. Social status is about having a particular lifestyle and set of social characteristics. It is about being viewed as a certain kind of person, as a member of a specific subgroup that has attached to it a definite degree of high or low prestige. The previous two chapters discussed the various types of *economic* inequality present in U.S. society. But the ranking system is more complicated than that, and experiences in everyday life tell us that invidious distinctions are made between individuals on grounds other than economics. It is not just the *amount* of wealth, but the *kind* and *source* of wealth as well as how it is *used* that are ranked. It is not just the amount of education, but the kind and place of education. It is not just the earnings of the occupation, but the kind of occupation it is. It is not just whether one is poor, but whether one is on welfare. If economic inequality is primarily about *quantities,* status inequality is about *qualities*.

People often are evaluated and ranked on the basis of their education, religion, possession of "culture," type of occupation, and even their speech patterns and clothing styles. Think about how students are evaluated by their peers. In addition to gender and race/ethnicity, fraternity/sorority membership, academic major, athletic status, the regions of the country they are from, and even the dormitories in which they live serve as criteria for status rankings. In each case, these function as systematic bases for high or low prestige.

Evidence presented in previous chapters supports the existence of *economic* classes, but there is no doubt that inequality includes *social* dimensions as well. More often than not, we notice these social distinctions in our contacts with others; that is, they become most salient when we interact with individuals whose characteristics and lifestyles differ from our own. Research suggests that we often rank people differently depending on those characteristics and lifestyles. Indeed, the term **social stratification** suggests that alongside economic inequality we have a system of status inequality, and often these two forms are intertwined with each other, as we shall see. Quite often, for example, an individual's economic position will affect his or her social position. But an individual's or group's social status need not be tied to either economic or political power. This requires that we examine social status as a separate form of ranking system. In this chapter, we will examine the nature of this status dimension of inequality.

THE THEORY OF SOCIAL STATUS

Social **status** refers to an individual's ranking with respect to some socially important characteristic; thus, some people are thought to be low in social status, while others are high on this scale. Max Weber, the great German sociologist, stressed the importance of distinguishing between (economic) class and (social) status inequality, even while he pointed out that they could be empirically related to each other, as when social status is dependent on *class* position. Weber viewed a person's *status situation* as "every typical component of the life fate of men that is determined by a specific, positive or negative *social estimation of honor.* This honor may be connected with any quality shared by a plurality" (Gerth and Mills 1962, p. 187). This means that status is ultimately a subjective assessment rendered by a community or another group. "Status is the sum of the evaluations that are 'located' in the minds of other people with whom one interacts" (Milner 2016, p. 39). This means that individuals are or are not given homage and respect because they possess or lack some characteristic the community considers honorable or dishonorable. That quality is social rather than economic in nature; for example, one's family name, the street where one lives, the kind and degree of education one possesses, or one's race or gender all may elicit such honor or dishonor. Weber argued that this "claim to positive or negative privilege with respect to social prestige" may be based on (1) a "mode of living," (2) "a formal process of education which may consist in empirical or rational training and the acquisition of the corresponding modes of life," and/or (3) "the prestige of birth, or of an occupation" (Weber 1964, p. 428).

Status groups that are ranked in a certain place on a community's social hierarchy are characterized by (1) a set of conventions and traditions, or lifestyle; (2) a tendency to marry within their own ranks; (3) an emphasis on interacting intimately—for example, eating only with others in the same group; (4) frequent monopolization of economic opportunities; and (5) emphasis on ownership of certain types of possessions rather than others (Weber 1964). All of these features reflect the tendency in status groups to establish and maintain the integrity of the boundaries that separate them from other groups. Wearing team jackets or particular types of clothes, associating with only particular kinds of people, and participating in an initiation process when becoming a member of a group are all signals that social status is operating.

Murray Milner Jr. (2016) explains that an individual's status within a group is dependent on conformity to the group's norms. These norms may involve expectations with respect to behavior (e.g., involvement in rituals), social relationships (e.g., friends and enemies), certain physical characteristics (e.g., beauty, race, gender), and use of appropriate symbols (e.g., dress, language). Since high status is coveted and in short supply, those at the top may change the norms or make them more complicated to maintain their position, making it more difficult for those below them to move up and displace them. One's own status is always at the expense of someone else's social position.

To be an accepted member of a status group, a person is expected to follow the normative lifestyle of the group and to have "restrictions on 'social' intercourse" (Weber 1964, p. 187). This means that the person is expected to associate intimately with only similar kinds of people. Consider what might happen when people in a distinct status group step out of line by violating the expected customs of the group. They might be confronted, ostracized, shunned, or punished in some other more physical way, and told in no uncertain terms what they need to do to get back in the good graces of their community or group. Because status groups are separated by social and cultural boundaries, the above efforts are made to maintain them. Continuous "boundary work" is needed to reinforce status distinctions between groups.

A group tries to set itself apart from other status groups, especially those that might contaminate the purity of the group. An extreme instance of this process exists when individuals of a particular status group agree to marry only among themselves (i.e., to practice endogamy) and to chastise or shun anyone who marries outside the group. In the past, high-status families in the United States exerted a great deal of pressure on children to marry people of their own social standing. This pressure has decreased somewhat, but research suggests that when a lower-status person "marries up," they never feel entirely comfortable in their new position (Streib 2015). After all, status honor rests on "distance and exclusiveness." In her study of upper-class women's involvement in voluntary associations, for example, Diana Kendall (2002) notes how carefully new applicants are screened and the elaborate application process that is involved before a new person is accepted as a member. To maintain the integrity and value of membership, applicants need to negotiate a complex application process. The extent and intensity of the application process is a direct indicator of the strength of the social boundary of a status group. The maintenance of a status group's cultural and social integrity requires continual vigilance of its boundaries with the outside. Not just anyone can be accepted.

It should not be surprising that to be accepted as a member of a particular status group requires possessing certain credentials. Many see credentialism as a major tool in the practice of exclusion (Brown 2001). Having the proper credentials might mean, for example, having a given license or educational degree, to be accepted into the "club." Because they help to control the labor supply, for example, requiring particular education credentials and/or licensing even enhances the earnings associated with an occupation (Weeden 2002).

"Exclusion" is a primary mechanism by which those in powerful status groups keep others from gaining power (Parkin 1979). Voluntary residential segregation in a secure gated community on the part of a high-status group might also be seen as an attempt at separation from people of lower status. Or men may attempt to keep their corporate positions exclusive by preventing women from moving to the top of the ladder. Even high-status 6-year-olds exclude lower-status children from their play (Fanger, Frankel, and Hazen 2012).

So far, we have seen that status groups (1) are associated with different estimations of social honor, (2) are based on a variety of socially relevant characteristics such as occupation or ethnicity, (3) tend toward closure—that is, maintenance of boundaries with outside groups, and (4) enforce adherence to their lifestyle and social interaction expectations. In addition, status groups tend to monopolize particular types of economic opportunities and acquisitions, while they discourage the possession of other kinds. For example, a status group whose honor or prestige is based on its class position may encourage its members to acquire fancy homes in particular neighborhoods, but it may be considered bad form to spend money acquiring a new bowling ball or a gaudy automobile. Under certain conditions, social status can become the primary form of social inequality. For example, social status becomes more significant when access to other forms of power is weak (Milner 2016). When people have little else to use as leverage in social situations, they use their own status conventions and goods as a means of controlling others or enhancing their social positions. George (2013), for example, has shown how the new occupation of "life coaches" have used credentials, professional experiences, and careful labeling to create a social status as a profession. Milner (2016) has demonstrated how teenagers use visibility on the Internet as a mechanism for the maintenance of status distinctions among their peers. It follows from these examples that status groups reflect the differential distribution of power within a community.

Weber argued that when social and economic conditions in a community are stable, stratification by status becomes dominant. Further, after status has been "lived in" for a while, status privileges can become legal privileges. In the United States, these conditions are frequently found in small towns where the same kin groups have lived for generations, where relationships are based on family name, and where social connections are important. Ironically, status also becomes salient when change threatens or tradition is in danger of being upset, as when politically or economically powerful newcomers come

Photo 4.1 Formal gates usually mark the entrances and exits of areas populated by status groups noted for their distinctive lifestyles and cultures. Geographic spatial separation between groups, whether on a playground, in a school lunch hall, in a corporate headquarters, or in a city, creates boundaries distinguishing groups in an area.

© Andy Z./Shutterstock.

to town (Milner 2016). The "old guard" may try to maintain their high position by stressing their social status in the community, for example, the fact that they have lived there all their lives and are leaders in the culture of the community.

When legalization of status privileges occurs, a society may be on the road toward a full-fledged caste system. According to Weber, the extreme of a caste system developing out of a status system happens only when the "underlying differences . . . are held to be 'ethnic'" in nature (Gerth and Mills 1962, p. 189). Race is a basis for deference/honor because "it is thought to represent the possession of some quality inherent in the ethnic aggregate and shared by all its members." This "essential quality" is "manifested in . . . external features such as colour, hair form, physiognomy and physique" (Shils 1970, p. 428). The existence of varying degrees of social distance among various **ethnic groups** in the United States provides ample evidence of such a ranking system. In this instance, distinctive ethnic status groups are converted into a set of hierarchically arranged groups, those on the

top thought to be the most pure and those on the bottom considered to be impure, contaminating, or even untouchable. What may trigger this conversion are the differences in the degree of ownership by these groups of other highly valued characteristics (e.g., education, religion) or commodities (e.g., wealth, technology; Berger and Fişek 2006). The "pariah" groups may be tolerated only because they may perform necessary but dishonorable, dirty, and onerous work. For example, lower castes may be the only groups ritualistically permitted to collect garbage or dead carcasses from the street. While these extreme forms of separation are not as evident in the United States, tendencies for groups to avoid groups of different statuses do exist.

Groups that are dishonored or low in status may attempt to usurp prestige by creating their own ranking system. This enhances their own social status often to the denigration of other groups. One example is provided by Lamont (2001) who found that working-class men use their own criteria to distinguish themselves as an honorable and distinct status group from those above and below them. Rather than wealth or political power, which would relegate them to a lower status, these men use moral criteria (being hardworking and responsible, having integrity, etc.) to separate themselves from others. These are the kinds of criteria that define the social and cultural boundaries which distinguish their own group from others, and they are the criteria that provide them with a higher social status in their own eyes.

When ranking does occur among status groups, *deference* is expected to be shown toward those in more prestigious or honored groups. The ways by which individuals greet and compliment others, as well as similar behaviors of homage, are examples of deferential behavior (Goffman 1959; Goffman 1967). For example, students are often concerned with how they should address faculty members: Should it be "Professor," "Doctor," "Mr./Ms.," or simply a first name? Some clearly feel uneasy using the latter form of address because they think it suggests a lack of respect or deference.

While those in lower statuses may show deference for those at the top, the latter can use their resources to present themselves in ways that elicit and justify such respect. They typically have the resources and motivation to appear impressive, and so manage situations to obtain the responses they desire. Through their *demeanor,* individuals of higher status can suggest that they are worthy of such deference. Demeanor is "that element of the individual's ceremonial behavior typically conveyed through deportment, dress, and bearing, which serves to express to those in his immediate presence that he is a person of certain desirable or undesirable qualities" (Goffman 1967, p. 77).

Deference behavior between individuals in differently ranked status groups can be based on a variety of criteria. A member of a group may be considered entitled to such behavior from others because of occupation, race or ethnicity, level and type of education, gender, lifestyle, political or corporate power, family name or kinship network, income, and amount and type of wealth. Service work on behalf of a community or society and formal titles also can serve as grounds for status

honor in some locations. All these factors are deference relevant because they are linked with basic values and/or issues in the society. A region or area can also be the basis of deference because it is thought to be associated with a particular lifestyle or occupational role (e.g., Appalachia with coal mining, Manhattan with the stock market), with the exercise of power in a society (e.g., Washington, D.C.), or with some other valued criterion (e.g., New England with quality education).

SPHERES OF STATUS IN THE UNITED STATES

As suggested earlier, the esteem in which a person is held in the United States can be related to a number of areas of life, for example, occupation, education, lifestyle, and wealth. Less noticed, but also arenas of status, are physical appearance and geographic place. Finally, race and gender are also factors that elicit status rankings.

Occupation

Occupational role, of course, is frequently associated with both social class and social status, but the most commonly used measures of occupational ranking tap the prestige/esteem dimension rather than the economic one. Occupation is a basis for deference and honor not only because of its association with valued goals (income, power, etc.) but also because there are lifestyles associated with particular roles—lifestyles that receive different degrees of honor. Plumbers and professors clearly are accorded different levels of honor because of what people associate with each of these occupations. Occupational status groups also are distinguished by the level and kinds of education and training that members undergo, as well as the types of behavior that characterize their occupations.

An interesting example of an occupational status group is professional musicians. Bensman (1972) and more recent researchers (see for example Dobson 2011) have argued that musicians form a "status community" in that they adhere to a particular and somewhat unique set of values that shapes their lifestyles. The institutions, behaviors, and practices that organize and constitute their lives, in turn, are based on those core values. Insiders are clearly separated from outsiders. There are regularized interactions and rituals that help keep the community cohesive. When musicians get together informally, they perform, discuss music, or attend concerts, all of which increase their allegiance to the community's values. In addition to having its own subcultural values, the music community is internally stratified according to a number of musically relevant criteria such as the instrument one plays and the skill with which it is played.

Generally, status communities based on occupation are among the most relevant for one's status. Over the years, there have been several attempts to rank occupations according to prestige or status. Early efforts to measure occupational status suffered from the fact that they generally were based on inadequate samples of respondents, were of a subjective nature, and contained prestige differences within the general occupational categories that were often almost as great as those between such categories.

Several attempts were later made to perfect an occupational status ranking, the most influential being the North-Hatt scale developed in the mid-1940s. It differed from earlier scales in that a much wider range of occupation types was considered, and it relied less on the creator's judgment of rankings. The first prestige rankings obtained were based on a 1947 survey of 2,920 individuals who were asked to classify the *general standing* of each of 90 occupations. No mention was made of prestige. The most frequently cited reasons for awarding a given occupation an excellent standing, in order of decreasing frequency, were that it paid well (18 percent), served humanity (16 percent), required a lot of previous training and investment (14 percent), and had a high level of prestige associated with it (14 percent). A replication of the study in 1963 yielded very similar rankings for the 88 distinct occupation types (Hodge, Siegel, and Rossi 1964).

However, the criterion considered most important in ranking the status of occupations appears to have changed along with the political and social climate. A 2014 national poll queried 2,537 adults about the degree of prestige they accorded 23 occupations. The list included a variety of blue-collar, white-collar, and service occupations in different institutional areas (Harris Polls 2014). It was clear that association with high earnings was not enough to give an occupation a high ranking. Real estate brokers and stockbrokers were at the bottom of the list. At the same time, a number of the occupations chosen as the most prestigious were those that served humanity (fireman, scientist, doctor, nurse).

Education

Like occupation, education is also considered an important and valuable dimension of one's life in the United States. Level of education is supposed to be related to the level of knowledge and skill one has in a particular field. In addition to that, however, education also prepares one for a particular status group and ensures the continuation of status groups. The type of education as well as the place where it is received are bases for prestige. A degree from an Ivy League school such as Yale or Harvard, or a small private school such as Amherst or Smith is quite prestigious compared to a degree from a local community college. The elitism and degree of selectivity associated with a school is linked to the level of prestige accorded to it. Think about the differences in the students you might know who graduate from each type of school. Schools like to pride themselves on the kinds of students they produce. Different types of schools instill different sets of values and outlooks in their students, thereby encouraging the development of different cultural groups.

The cultural/status effects of education have been analyzed in depth. Bourdieu (1977a) suggested that higher education helps to reproduce the class structure by functioning to reinforce the value and status differences between the classes. It does this by honoring the **cultural capital** held by those in the higher classes. This capital— which consists of a group's cultural values, experience, knowledge, and skills—is passed on from one generation to the next. In organizing itself around the linguistic and cultural competence of the upper classes, higher education ensures that members of the upper classes are successful in school. This legitimates the class inequality that results because, on the surface, it appears that the inequality is largely the result of individual performance in a meritocratic, open educational system. That is, the language used, the cultural knowledge expected for success in school, and the values and behaviors honored are those of the upper class. In the words of one interpreter, "The school serves as the trading post where socially valued cultural capital is parlayed into superior academic performance. Academic performance is then turned back into economic capital by the acquisition of superior jobs" (MacLeod 2008, p. 14). The experiences in school and in the workplace of those in the working and lower classes, coupled with the general outlook and specific attitudes they have acquired because of their class milieu, lead them to believe that they cannot succeed in school, thus lowering their aspirations to do so (MacLeod 2008). The result is stratification within the educational system, which then reinforces the class stratification in the wider society.

From early childhood, middle- and upper-class parents engage in what Annette Lareau (2003) has termed "concerted cultivation," the conscious preparation of their children in the skills and values they will need to be successful and to maintain their higher position in the social hierarchy. Or as Kendall describes it in her study of how upper-class women go about perpetuating their social-class positions, "Most elite parents strongly believe that, early on in their children's lives, the parents should start putting together all the right 'building blocks' that their children will need in order to take their own places in elite circles in which the parents live, and that the parents need to continue this process of social reproduction as the children grow into adulthood" (2002, p. 81). As several of the studies indicate, schools play a central role in the social reproduction of the class structure from top to bottom.

One of the principal functions of education is to prepare students for the cultural status groups they will enter after graduation (Collins 1971). In his biting satire at the beginning of the twentieth century, Thorstein Veblen (1953) observed that elite schools of higher learning had as their primary purpose "the preparation of the youth of the priestly and the leisure classes . . . for the consumption of goods, material and immaterial, according to a conventionally accepted, reputable scope and method" (p. 239). Similarly, the authors of an empirical study of elite prep schools found that, while the curriculum has become more global in the last two decades, it retains its distinctive emphasis on "high culture" with classes in classical languages, philosophy, and the arts (Cookson and Persell 2010). But they also observed, in sharp contrast to Veblen's emphasis on the nonfunctional learning of the "leisure" class, that the education is serious and geared toward preparing students for selective colleges and managerial careers.

Analysis of the history of U.S. schools supports the conclusion that they were developed to help the established upper class isolate and reaffirm its cultural characteristics. Initially, the founders hoped that these schools would help separate their cultural group from the new wealth developing in industry and from the increasing numbers of lower-class immigrants. This suggests again the strong impetus toward social closure among the old rich. But the need for financial support of these schools necessitated taking in some of the sons of individuals who had become recently wealthy from industrial, manufacturing, or other enterprises in the latter part of the nineteenth century (Levine 1980). These *nouveaux riches*, consequently, infiltrated the boarding schools even though the established patrician families winced because the former were often seen as lacking in manners and polish. One of these new-wealth parents, Phillip Armour, once described his occupation as converting "bristles, blood, and the inside and outside of pigs and bullocks into revenue" (Levine 1980, p. 83). This kind of comment is hardly the type that would have won over persons from the established old-wealth families.

While stressing the rigor and difficulty of attainment within them, studies of elite prep schools confirm the importance of cultural capital and the

Photo 4.2   Even the classical architecture and spacious, finely manicured grounds of prestigious prep schools conspire to create a feeling of tradition and specialness among their students.

Photo by Charles E. Hurst.

role of these schools in perpetuating the class system. A large part of the education for students in these status seminaries involves learning how to be proper members of their class. In his ethnography of an elite boarding school, Gaztambide-Fernandez (2009) points out that having economic resources is not enough—the school must teach "the symbolic materials and subjective dispositions that are required to demonstrate membership in particular status groups" (p. 11). Students must also learn to believe that their own privilege is legitimate. This is done both by "having individuals work hard enough so that they feel they can deserve what they have and keeping them separate from the rest of the world that doesn't share their assumptions about the highly unequal distribution of rewards" (Cookson and Persell 2010, p. 26).

Where elite schools strongly inculcate class consciousness, research indicates that public schools in working-class areas do the exact opposite—they discourage class consciousness and emphasize individuality and individual effort (Finn 2012). It is rare that the two worlds meet, as boarding school students are together 24 hours a day. The hothouse, intense, closed setting of the prep school helps to foster a "brick wall syndrome," a belief that exclusivity should be the norm and that there is nothing wrong with the separation of this group of students from those in the outside society (Kendall 2002).

For their students, elite prep schools also serve as a major linchpin between parental class position and obtaining positions of power in the wider society. These students tend to get into the better colleges and universities and, ultimately, to obtain positions of influence in the leading political, cultural, legal, and corporate institutions of society. Giving admission preferences at elite universities and colleges to the sons and daughters of alumni illustrates not only the passing on of social status between generations, but also high-status schools' tendencies toward exclusivity and boundary maintenance. **Legacy** preferences help schools maintain the integrity of their lifestyle, but they also violate values associated with equality of opportunity (Kahlenberg 2010).

Studies of prep school graduates reinforce the conclusion that these students believe they need to go on to the "right" universities, such as Harvard, Yale, or Princeton; beyond that, they have to get into the appropriate clubs and societies at these universities, and to do this a student has to come from the "right" boarding school. Getting into the right sorority or fraternity, especially one in which your parent was a member, is an important step in the process of class cultivation. Among the values and skills learned in these organizations are the importance of screening potential members, allegiance to your own kind of people, and the development of social networks that will be helpful in later years (Kendall 2002; Robbins 2004). Upon graduating from their universities, these students can take up their memberships in the most exclusive social clubs and become established in high-status Wall Street law or brokerage firms. This process, from the teen years through attainment of an occupation, helps ensure the exclusivity and survival of this high-status group.

School and Lifestyle

Status inequalities between groups can be found in a variety of school levels. Unambiguous categorization of individuals according to appearance, behaviors, values, and attitudes develops early in childhood. Social cliques and categories have been found even among elementary school children, as well as in junior and senior high schools. Attachment of a student to a social category or clique has real consequences in the school setting. Self-esteem and identity appear to be linked to the status of one's "crowd" in school (Brown and Lohr 1987; Adler and Adler 1998). If one is considered a member of a low-prestige crowd, it not only can affect one's self-esteem but also cause alterations in behavior. Sometimes this can have devastating effects, as was found recently in a survey of high school students in New York City. One third of the students who qualified for the subsidized lunch program chose not to take advantage of it. They would rather pay for lunch themselves, even though they cannot afford it, or go without eating at all. They fear losing status if

they are seen as poor (Fertig 2014). Such can be the power of status groups.

High schools have a hierarchical ranking system. Social clusters at different schools go by many names: jocks, burnouts, band geeks, preppies, trendies, skaters, nerds, rockers, goths, wannabees, freaks, punks. People with similar interests, backgrounds, or accomplishments join together to separate themselves from others and to solidify their identities and sense of membership at school. Belonging to a clique or category is a way of avoiding social isolation. It is also a means of ranking different kinds of individuals. From his own study of high schools, Milner (2016) suggests that the status ranking of cliques or groups in schools depends partly on their adherence to expectations regarding areas such as beauty, athletic ability, visibility on the Internet, clothes and style. Not all of these is necessarily linked to income or class position, again confirming the frequent noneconomic nature of social status.

Although membership can be unstable and rankings within each of them can shift, these social clusters have many of the properties of status groups (Cairns and Cairns 1994; Eder 1995; Adler and Adler 1998). As such, they represent a type of status inequality. Among these qualities is *group ranking* in terms of popularity and prestige at school. A second feature following from this involves explicit attempts to attract certain youths while keeping others out, that is, *attempts at maintaining boundaries* between insiders and outsiders. Being mean, bullying, picking on outsiders, and "putting them down" are techniques to keep outsiders at arm's length. Careful recruitment and monitoring of behavior and attitudes are common ways of ensuring insider loyalty once in a group (Brown 2011).

A third status feature of these groups is a *lifestyle* that is perceived to be distinctive. A large part of the unique lifestyles among student groupings is suggested by the clothing and adornments they wear. Students labeled as "emo" tend to wear dark clothes and have tattoos and piercings, whereas rockers wear band tee shirts and jeans. As part of the distinctive lifestyles, involvement in school activities, musical tastes, and language also systematically vary. Fourth, *exclusive places or locations* tend to be associated with different social clusters. Physical space takes on a *social* significance. Just like gangs controlling neighborhoods, given lunch tables are "owned" by clusters, as are places where students hang out. Finally, *stigmatization and avoidance of social contamination* is also found within these school groups. Because of recurrent jockeying for status within groups, individuals pick on each other and single out some for intense ostracism. Avoidance of outsiders antagonistic to the group is also expected. Paradoxically, meanness to others is a way of maintaining popularity in the group (Merten 1997).

Wealth and Class

Having a particular amount and type of *wealth* and/or *income* as reflected in one's class position can also be a basis for status if only because economic resources usually serve as a control on the kind of lifestyle one can afford. The right kind and level of consumption may gain one entrance into the upper class. The use of inherited wealth, family lineage, club membership, quality of education, and general lifestyle as criteria for membership into the established upper class helps maintain the exclusivity of that class. We have already seen how boarding schools function in this regard. Practicing endogamy within the class helps determine who can get into "Society." Maintaining a closed circle in the face of an ostensibly open democratic society demands that mechanisms be present to keep just anyone from getting into the circle.

Some believe that the United States contains a national urban upper class with its own tradition that is tightly knit and class conscious. This upper class has been buttressed historically by institutions that serve its members, such as boarding schools, select eastern universities and colleges, and the Episcopal Church (see for example, Domhoff 1971; Ostrander 1983). The upper class as a status group practices a particular kind of lifestyle with particular kinds of rules associated with it. Specifically, children are expected to be well-bred, with manners and a sense of their importance in society. Boarding schools are a principal source of this training, but family ties are also central. Keeping the family line intact and marrying the right kind of person are important. Marriages are not made as independently as might be the case in other social classes. But some restricted social activities, such as debutante balls and fox hunts, which once were prominent elements in the lifestyle of the upper class, have declined in recent years. Acceptable occupations include financier, lawyer, business executive, physician, art collector, museum director, and even architect. Living in an exclusive residence separate from middle class and other neighborhoods and maintaining a second summer home are also means by which separation from outsiders is preserved.

Upper-class families tend to be patriarchal, but even the female spouse may be a member of a private social club. Frequently, she is expected to be involved in charitable activities and other social events. There is a division of labor between the sexes in many of these families. Evidence suggests that members of this upper-status group are concerned with maintaining their separation from others, even in death. Their burial customs and sites tend to be different from those of people from the lower classes (Cassell, Salinas, and Winn 2005). A historical analysis of cemeteries in the United States noted the long-term attempts by the middle and upper classes to segregate themselves physically in burial sites from those of a more lowly status, and to freely use monuments and mausoleums to proclaim their status. In recent years, mausoleums and monuments have again increased in popularity. Today, well-off people can purchase "million dollar mausoleums" that will remind viewers of how much success was attained during one's lifetime (Chen 2013). As these characteristics indicate, "members of the upper class not only have *more,* they have *different*" (Domhoff 1971, p. 91).

Weber thought that status groups are ranked according to their patterns of consumption as manifested in their lifestyles (as cited in Gerth and Mills 1962, p. 193). Many possessions have a level of prestige that differs drastically with their actual monetary value. For example, consider the relative prestige of a new Chevy pickup and an older BMW, both of which may cost the same amount. It is not so much the economic value per se of the consumed goods that is important, but rather the fact that these goods, especially if owned by a higher-ranking status group, serve as symbols of worth and ability. It becomes a matter of self-respect and honor to conspicuously display such goods, not merely to "keep up with the Joneses" but to surpass them if possible (Veblen 1953).

VEBLEN'S THEORY OF THE LEISURE CLASS

The linkage of class position to status is most clearly seen in the arguments of Thorstein Veblen. His discussion of status applies most directly to the periods up to the early part of the twentieth century. Veblen contended that manual labor had become defined as dishonorable and undignified, not becoming to one who wished to be considered of high social status. On the other hand, he argued that nonproductive labor, such as that of being a business executive, increased the probability of owning great amounts of property, which in turn increased one's status honor. Owning property had become, in Veblen's view, the equivalent of possessing honor. In order to show this honor and property to others, one then had to engage in ostentatious displays of wealth and status, namely various forms of what he called "conspicuous consumption." This display served as a symbol of one's worth and ability.

Veblen argued that the modern leisure class of the industrial era engaged not only in conspicuous consumption and leisure but also in conspicuous waste. Women, for example, had become, in Veblen's view, not only the "property" of men but also an ornament with which men could display their wealth and power. Women took on a ceremonial function with the rise of the Industrial Revolution and were expected to avoid industrious, productive work. Rather, in their behavior and appearance, women were to symbolize the status of their husbands. In their attire, they were expected to be especially wasteful; that is, their dresses were to be nonfunctional material. "Special pains should be taken in the construction of women's dress, to impress upon the beholder the fact (often indeed a fiction) that the wearer does not and cannot habitually engage in useful work. . . . [It is] the woman's function in an especial degree to put in evidence her household's ability to pay" (Veblen 1953, p. 126).

We can summarize Veblen's ideas by indicating that he felt that people's worth and honor, in modern times, were linked to their ability to pay—that is, their wealth and possessions. The more a person can display such resources, the greater the respect attributed to them. This leads to an ostentatious show for others in a desire to impress and to a competition to outdo others in such display. Such display covers a wide range of possessions, even such things as better-groomed lawns, ownership of prize horses, and conspicuous dress. Everyone battles in this competition, according to Veblen, but the leisure/business class is most successful.

Since Veblen, there have been other analyses of the lifestyle of the upper class. Brooks (1979) argued that Veblen's ideas must be updated because the lower classes do not revere the upper class as in Veblen's day, nor is leisure strictly the province of the upper class today. More often, people engage in "parody display" of honored status symbols. Just as in a literary parody, people poke fun at possessions that, in the past, have commanded great respect. Brooks views this parody as the result of a mixture of admiration and ridicule by the lower classes. But still he finds that competitive display and conspicuous consumption are alive and well in U.S. society. Speech, clothing, and membership in exclusive clubs, for example, continue to be used in making invidious comparisons. Using beautiful women as ornamentation or as trophies also continues today.

Portrayals of the lifestyles and distinguishing traits of the social classes are not limited to the upper class. Widespread images of all the classes can be found in the media, and they carry consistent themes that suggest Americans' subjective views about each group. Kendall's study (2011) of newspaper and television characterizations of classes uncovered a variety of both positive and negative presentations for each class:

> *Upper Class:* just regular people who are generous, materialistic, and worthy of emulation, but also sometimes unhappy, unfulfilled, and deviant. Some media coverage portrays them as greedy and criminal, especially in the wake of the recent financial crises.
>
> *Middle Class:* people who should be the normative standard for the country and whose problems are frequently caused by those above and below them, but who often are in debt because of inability to pay for their lifestyle.
>
> *Working Class and Working Poor:* hardworking, unsung heroes, but also corrupt, bigoted, without taste or "class" who are unemployed or unhappy in their jobs.
>
> *Poor and Homeless:* victims of circumstance who deserve help but who too often do not help themselves, have deviant lifestyles, and are dependent on welfare.

Media images suggest that we think about social classes in paradoxical ways but recognize them as status groups with distinctive lifestyles. A recent study of the attitudes of the general public confirm this finding but also emphasize negative images of the upper class (Hahl and Zuckerman 2014). In experiments, people were suspicious of high-status actors and were more likely to see them as cold, calculating, and less authentic than low-status actors. Interestingly, people of all statuses harbored these same beliefs. This may be because people recognize that there are incentives to cheat and trample on other people to gain status. These possibilities throw into question high-status people's actions. To allay these suspicions, the researchers found that high-status people sometimes try to find ways to prove their sincerity, or they appropriate symbols of lower-status culture to signal their authenticity.

Physical Appearance and Status

Clearly, physical appearance is often a basis for social status. "In twentieth-century American society, physical beauty emerged as a resource, like wealth or talent" (Rubenstein 2001, p. 212). Apparently, the power of beauty as a resource is evident very early in life. A study found that parents give more attention and care to beautiful than to less attractive children (cited in Dowd 2005). Children also recognize and prefer attractive people (Principe and Langlois 2013). While beauty is a resource, it may also be used to reinforce gender inequality. Popular folk-tales that have been most often reproduced (e.g., Cinderella, Snow White) are those that stress the value of female rather than male beauty. This consistent encouragement to be beautiful may discourage women from pursuing roles, activities, or positions that will make them appear less attractive.

"'Beauty' is a currency system like the gold standard. Like any economy, it is determined by politics, and in the modern age in the West it is the last, best belief system that keeps male dominance intact" (Wolf 2002, p. 12). By encouraging women to spend a lot of time on how they look and act as they attempt to meet culturally enforced standards, the "beauty myth" weakens their ability to fully develop their mental, political, and economic potential (Wolf 2002). For men, women's entrapment in the beauty myth serves as a means of social control over women because it removes a source of potential competition (Baker-Sperry and Grauerholz 2003).

To further realize the importance of beauty, one need only look at the media to see how it is used to sell everything from automobile transmissions to cologne. Beauty implies that those who possess it have other mental and behavioral qualities that set them apart from less attractive individuals. For example, physically attractive people are seen as more trustworthy (Zhao et al. 2015). They also do better during their careers. Attractive employees earn more than less attractive workers and are promoted more rapidly (Hamermesh 2011; Rhode 2010). People who are rated as physically attractive also tend to have better psychological health and lower rates of depression (Datta Gupta, Etcoff, and Jaeger 2015). In criminal cases, defendants who are more physically attractive tend to be treated more leniently, especially in cases in which beauty is not relevant to the type of crime. When

NUTSHELL 4.1   Language as an Indicator of Status Group Membership

One of the ways that group insiders identify outsiders is through the use of terms and phrases that are unfamiliar to outsiders and that are associated with particular groups. Familiarity with a group's argot is a badge of social status, and unfamiliarity provides a group with a way of separating themselves from others, of maintaining a boundary. Consequently, a clue to an individual's status group membership can often be found in the language she or he uses. Sometimes the argots of these status groups are organized around ethnicity or race, and sometimes around specialized occupations. Below are some terms associated with the groups that are listed. See if you know the meaning of these terms.

Biker/Motorcyclist discourse:

A. darksiders
B. endo
C. jug huggers
D. Rolex riders
E. wrench

Corporate executive discourse:

A. disconnect
B. value-added
C. take-away message
D. value proposition
E. plugged in

Appalachian discourse:

A. airish
B. gaum
C. liketa
D. poke
E. sigogglin

Biker meanings: (a) people who replace the back tire of their motorcycle with an automobile tire; (b) a trick accomplished by riding the bike forward and applying the front brake to make the rear wheel lift off the ground; (c) after-market exhaust pipe that makes the bike louder; (d) middle- or upper-middle-class riders who have nice gear but mediocre or poor riding skills; (e) a person who is talented at working on motorcycles. *Sources:* William E. Thompson. *Hogs, Blogs, Leathers and Lattes* (2012).

Corporate meanings: (a) failure in communication; (b) something that adds value to a service or product; (c) the main point of a statement; (d) results a customer or client can anticipate from a service or product; (e) being in the know or an insider. *Source:* Candace Goforth, "'Plug in' to the Lingo." *Akron Beacon Journal,* February 27, 2006, p. D1.

Appalachian meanings: (a) chilly outside; (b) to clutter, make a mess; (c) almost, nearly; (d) a bag; (e) unusually crooked. *Source:* Maxwell Tani, *National Geographic Blogs,* 2014.

beauty is used as a weapon in a crime, however, more attractive individuals receive more severe punishments. "It is as if beauty is a gift, and its malevolent manipulation is condemned" (Rubenstein 2001, p. 215).

Research suggests that high school students who are overweight or obese are less likely than others to be chosen as friends (Crosnoe, Frank, and Mueller 2008). Obese persons are also less likely to be chosen as spouses (Rhode 2010). While both Black and White young women are conscious of their bodies, White women are particularly likely to have negative feelings about their body shape and weight (Greenwood and Dal Cin 2012). The widespread use by women of elective plastic surgery, liposuction, and cosmetics

that promise to make them look younger suggests the importance of appearance in their lives. In 2014, 15.6 million cosmetic surgeries were performed in the United States, 92 percent of them on women (American Society of Plastic Surgeons 2014). Eating disorders, such as bulimia and anorexia, are also attempts to make one look thinner and more attractive in present-day society.

Beauty, of course, is in the eyes of the beholder, but what the beholder sees and how it is interpreted are shaped by culture's values. Beauty is a social construction. The definitions of beauty and other status symbols vary among societies and over time within the same society. Whereas in East Asia the face is used as the criterion of beauty, in the United States it is the body in general that is used as a measure of beauty (Frith, Shaw, and Cheng 2005). Beauty standards can also vary among racial and ethnic groups within the same society (Webb et al. 2013). Such standards also change over time. The beauty of the human figure portrayed in a Rubens painting is not the same ideal of beauty seen today in the clothing ads of Victoria's Secret or Ralph Lauren.

Especially in open and democratic societies, the salience and ranking of status symbols wax and wane over time. In one year, having a particular characteristic or possession may result in great status honor or prestige, but a few years later, that same possession may be of little social importance, while another has ascended to a position of high prestige. It appears that the level of income inequality has an effect on the importance of status goods. A recent analysis of Google search terms (Walasek and Brown 2015) suggests that people are more interested in status symbols (such as designer clothing) in states with higher

levels of income inequality than in those with lower levels.

It is well established that one of the most often-used status symbols in urban settings concerns fashions in clothing. Veblen (1953) observed that at the turn of the twentieth century, clothing was particularly well suited to being a status symbol since "our apparel is always in evidence and affords an indication of our pecuniary standing to all observers at the first glance" (p. 119).

Undoubtedly, how we dress affects the attitudes and behavior of others toward us. "Clothing itself is the beginning and end of human display, touching on one side the skin of the person and reaching out on the other to announce to all what the person inside the skin is or wishes to be" (Brooks 1979, p. 201). Clothing takes on a moral character in that people assume that your dress indicates something about the kind of person you are. Hoodies are an interesting example of this because they take on multiple meanings depending on the wearer and the location in which they are

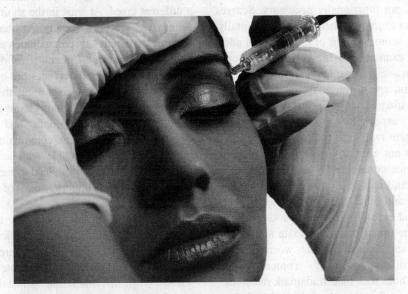

Photo 4.3 In the United States, physical beauty is a currency that can be cashed in for improved social status. The subjective importance placed on beauty is indicated by the more than 15.6 million cosmetic surgeries performed in the United States in 2014, according to the American Society of Plastic Surgeons. Over 90 percent of these surgeries were on women.

© Lucky Business/Shutterstock.

being worn. In the 1970s hoodies were associated with skaters, punk rock, and the nascent hip-hop movement (Wilson 2012). After Trayvon Martin, a 17-year-old unarmed black youth was killed while wearing a hoodie, it became a symbol of protest. In 2015, a legislator in Oklahoma proposed a law that would prohibit wearing them in public. While the legislator claimed that hoodies obscure people's face making it easier for them to commit crimes, critics charged that the bill was racially motivated since hoodies have become associated with Black youth (Stern 2015). Hoodies are also worn as a statement of casual cool by celebrities such as Mark Zuckerberg, the founder of Facebook.

Some research suggests that clothing frequently brings out status-related reactions. Alison Lurie (1987) suggested a number of ways in which clothing can be used to give an impression of high status. She labeled these as "conspicuous" addition, division, multiplication, and labeling. Conspicuous addition refers to the technique of layering clothes—that is, wearing several kinds of clothing over each other, even though it is not functionally necessary. Scarves and vests, for example, when worn ornamentally, would be a demonstration of conspicuous addition and an example of what Veblen called conspicuous waste. Conspicuous division and multiplication are different forms of the technique of wearing a wide variety of different types of clothing, especially for separate occasions. The point here is that, to indicate high status, a person does not want to wear the same piece of clothing twice consecutively and does want to wear different kinds of clothes for evening, dinner, casual, and other sorts of situations. Shoes provide good examples of conspicuous multiplication. Some urban youth associate status with the number and kinds of sneakers worn (Chertoff 2012). Similarly, well-off women collect Louboutin shoes with their trademark red soles.

Finally, a fourth form of clothing technique mentioned by Lurie, conspicuous labeling, is a way of ensuring that the knowledgeable would be able to distinguish the high-status piece of clothing from an imitation. Otherwise, a status crisis could occur for those who wish to use clothing as a status symbol, since several brand names of clothing may look virtually identical. Labeling on the outside, rather than the inside, of a garment is an obvious way of advertising your status to those around you. Interestingly, however, a recent study suggests that companies make brand markings on some items (such as sunglasses and handbags) more subtle on their most expensive items. The researchers believe that this is because high status "insiders" want to make it harder for lower-status others to copy their style. They also found that because other high-status people can recognize more subtle symbols, they are an effective way to communicate with insiders (Berger and Ward 2010).

Religion

Religion has been important across many cultures and time periods as a determinant of status. Today, recent violent incidents have sensitized more Americans to the religious division of Islam, Judaism, and Christianity, and have led to retributions of members of one religion against those who follow a different creed. At least in the short term, these actions and reactions solidify the boundaries that separate these religious communities as some individuals "look down on" members of different religions. The religious differences are often viewed with ethnic overtones, suggesting that Muslims, Christians, and other religious groups are made up of different *kinds* of people, and confirming Weber's belief that status communities are perceived as groups of people who are *inherently* different. This situation can lead to the reinvigoration of religion as an important basis of status honor or dishonor.

Religious tension is not new in America. Since Colonial times, both Catholics and Jews have been seen as inherently different—and as inferior—in comparison to the Protestant mainstream. While discrimination against these groups has decreased dramatically in the U.S., Jewish people are still subject to harassment and discrimination for their faith. In 2014, for example, a gunman killed three people at a Jewish community center and a retirement center in Kansas City. FBI records show that, in raw numbers, Jews are the targets of the most religious hate crime in the U.S. (Ingraham 2015). Perhaps because Catholics are Christians, they are seen as less "other" than Jews and are far less often the target of hate crime.

Today the religious group that is seen as most different from the majority are Muslims. Just under 1 percent of the U.S. adult population is Muslim (Lipka 2015). Muslims are an extremely diverse group—they are of many ethnicities, races, and backgrounds. The type of Islam they practice is diverse as well. Data on Muslims is hard to come by because the U.S. Census does not ask the religion of respondents. The Pew Foundation, however, conducted a large-scale study in 2011. They found that while only about 37 percent of Muslims in the U.S. are native born, a very high percentage (81 percent) of all Muslims are citizens. Muslims tend to have about the same rate of college education as the non-Muslim population but have a higher rate of people in poverty (45 percent reported an annual income of less than $30,000 compared to 36 percent of the U.S. population more generally). This wealth disparity emerged after the 2008 recession (Pew 2011b).

Muslims are one of the few groups who have seen hate crimes against them increase over the last 15 years. After the 9/11 attacks in 2001, the rate of hate crimes against people who were perceived to be Muslims increased fivefold (Ingraham 2015). In a 2011 survey, over a quarter of Muslims reported that people had acted suspicious of them in the last year. About 22 percent reported they had been called offensive names (Pew 2011a). On a more positive note, non-Muslims' knowledge about Islam and their levels of contact with Muslim people are increasing over time in the U.S. As we see with public opinion toward other minority groups, familiarity with a group is linked to more positive views (Pew 2009a). Continuing anti-Muslim sentiment, however, indicates that their position as a low-ranked status group may continue for some time.

Disability and Status

Disability, though a powerful contributor to inequality, presents a somewhat more complex case than other categories. This is because, "disability (in its mutability, its potential invisibility, its potential relation to temporality, and its sheer variety) is a particularly elusive element to introduce into any conjunctural analysis" (Berube 2006). There are many different types of disabilities—some permanent, some temporary, some that are invisible, some not. Disabilities may or may not have a severe impact on a person's ability to live independently, just as some disabilities can incur huge medical costs while others do not. A discussion of how disability relates to inequality is difficult for all these reasons but also because, as Berube points out, the lived experience of having a disability varies widely across categories of social class, sexuality, race, age, and gender.

At the same time that the term "disability" hides huge diversity, there are reasons to consider its members as a status group. First, being able-bodied is considered to be "normal," and any deviation from that state is seen as inferior (McRuer 2006). Disabled people face stigma and stereotyping—from images of them as sexual predators, to asexual, to violent, to childlike. Many disabled people are well aware of the stigma and their categorization as "other" (Jahoda et al. 2010). In other words, many recognize themselves as a group with common interests. Disabled people are sometimes kept out of mainstream institutions, and, when they do form romantic partnerships, it is often with other disabled people (Brown 1996).

Looking broadly at disability as a status group, we see that, on average, disabled people are more likely to be poor than their non-disabled peers. They are less likely to obtain higher degrees and have more difficulty accessing health services (APA 2016). Disabled women are four times more likely to be the victims of assault than nondisabled women (Martin et al. 2006). It is clear that disability status is directly related to a range of inequalities in our society.

Place and Status

Think for a moment of the United States as a large geographical grid on which different groups travel and reside in particular places. If you could see this grid from above, what would it look like?

Social patterns of enclaves, segregation, inclusion, and exclusion would become evident.

Historically, sociologists have not paid much attention to the role that the physical environment plays in our understanding of society's social structure. Indeed, the arrangement of space and the role of place have been neglected in the study of inequality. But space and place have increasingly been recognized as being related to social status (Lobao, Hooks, and Tickamyer 2007). Tyler and Cohen (2010) explored how space in organizations reflects the gendered power inequities in society. They also examined how women perform gender within those spaces. They found that women's spaces in organizations tend to be more constrained and more visible. This is similar to the finding of older work (Spain 1992), which found that women's workplaces are most often open spaces characterized by a lack of doors and walls (e.g., as in a secretarial pool), in sharp contrast to the privacy found in the closed-door higher-status jobs of men.

Where people live is also associated with their status lifestyles. Figure 4.1 illustrates, for example, that high concentrations of the upper class reside in New England, Florida, and California, whereas few upper class live in heartland states such as South Dakota, Iowa, Kansas, and Oklahoma, or the southeastern states including Louisiana and Alabama (Brown 2013). The United States has neighborhood clusters, many of which are clearly and intentionally connected with specific groups occupying different status levels. The elegant mansions of the so-called blue blood estates neighborhoods in places such as Beverly Hills and Scarsdale hold those at the top of the status ladder, while the public-assistance neighborhoods of West Philadelphia and Watts are disproportionately dwelling places of African American and single-parent families. Public housing has also become increasingly occupied by female-headed families, and contains disproportionate numbers of elderly, disabled people, and children (National Low Income Housing Coalition 2012). Throughout the status ladder are found neighborhoods known as "young suburbia," "middle America," "shotguns and pickups," and

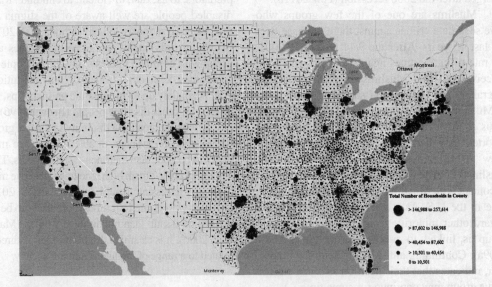

FIGURE 4.1 Affluent Neighborhoods

Source: www.arcgis.com. Portions of this image include intellectual property of ESRI and its licensors and are used herein under license. Copyright © April 29, 2015. All rights reserved.

The "Affluent Households" category includes those households in each county with a median income over $116,100 and a median net worth of $391,600.

(For further description, see http://downloads.esri.com/esri_content_doc/dbl/us/2014_Tapestry_LifeMode_Group_Summary_Tables.pdf.)

"new urban." Each of these has its own core values and lifestyle. That these distinct cultural pockets exist should not be surprising: "People seek compatible neighbors who share their family status, income, employment patterns and values" (Weiss 1988). If they have appropriate resources, the neighborhoods people choose to live in are those with residents whose political and cultural values are similar to their own (Bishop 2009).

We must not forget, however, that living in a particular community or neighborhood is not always the result of free choice. Resources and status help dictate where one lives. Constraint also enters the picture when people try to keep "undesirables" out of their neighborhoods through mortgage-loan practices, building restrictions, and zoning procedures. Increasingly, one can find new housing developments for the affluent and cultured that are surrounded by walls and maintained by armed guards at secured entrances. Often, these communities are planned and monitored by electronic surveillance devices, and constitute another, perhaps more blatant, form of segregated neighborhood.

As noted earlier in this chapter, Weber made a point of identifying exclusionary tactics as devices used by higher status groups to keep their position intact. Privacy and security, and, most important, seclusion from others, mark these "walled communities" (Atkinson and Smith 2012). Turf wars are perpetrated not only by those at the bottom of the status system but also by those at its pinnacle. The control of physical space is one reflection of status inequalities in our society.

On a broader scale, not only do neighborhoods and communities conjure up different perceptions and evaluations, but so do regions. There are stereotypes and lifestyles, for example, that have been attributed to Californians, New Englanders, the Old South, the New South, Midwesterners, and Appalachians. Regions can be and have been the basis for status grouping and ranking, even though the cultural, social, and sometimes even topographical homogeneity attributed to these set-apart places is usually mythical rather than factual. Nevertheless, some of these regions, perhaps most notably Appalachia, have been identified as constituting not only separate subcultures but also status groups that have been consciously

ranked as being low in prestige. Let us briefly explore Appalachia as an example of status based on region.

As a strip in the eastern part of the United States, Appalachia covers parts of 13 states, bordered on the north by southern New York state; on the south by parts of Mississippi, Alabama, and Georgia; on the west by the eastern sections of Kentucky and Tennessee; and on the east by the western portions of Pennsylvania, Virginia, and the Carolinas. It includes all of West Virginia. Most of the discussion of Appalachia as a subculture, however, is based on material from southern Appalachia (northern Georgia, Alabama, North and South Carolina, and parts of Tennessee and Virginia), whereas discussions of the coal industry focus on central Appalachia (Kentucky, West Virginia, southwestern Virginia, and eastern Tennessee).

Recent census analyses indicate that, while there are variations within Appalachian subregions, wages lag behind the national average. Appalachian per capita income is only about 82 percent that of non-Appalachian regions (Appalachian Regional Commission 2011). Part of the reason appears to be related to differences in the distribution of employment fields; the economic returns from mining and farming are significantly lower than those from services and manufacturing (Cardiff 1999). Central Appalachia, where most of the mining occurs, also happens to be the poorest segment of Appalachia (Baumann 2006). At the same time, it should be noted that Appalachians have made great gains in education over the last 30 years. In 2009 about the same percent of Appalachians and non-Appalachians over age 25 had a high school degree. There was a difference in college graduation, however, with 27 percent of all Americans and only 20 percent of Appalachians having a degree (Pollard and Jacobsen 2011).

Appalachia is often viewed as a region with different values from the mainstream. Individualism, a love of and dependence on family and an attachment to home, a belief in personal liberty and independence, fatalism and resignation, a belief in the essential equality of all individuals, a disdain for and suspicion of formal education, and the centrality of personal religion all have been characteristics frequently associated with Appalachians

Photo 4.4 The coal produced in Appalachia more often economically benefited absentee company owners than it did local residents, exacerbating wealth differences within the region. Railroads provided transportation for coal as well as the setting for many modest homes in places such as southwestern Virginia.

© Will Griffith/Shutterstock.

(e.g., Erikson 1976; Batteau 1984). Alongside the negative image of Appalachia as a stagnant and backward region, another more patronizing image exists. This interpretation fosters the view of Appalachia as an area of great natural beauty being despoiled by greedy economic interests. Unsullied nature and the rugged individualism of mountain men are integral components of this perspective of Appalachia as an innocent victim (Batteau 1984). In this view, the mountains take on a mystical, romantic quality. This is part of the region's appeal for tourists.

As was indicated earlier in this chapter, the social status given to another person or group is a subjective process, one in which the group is portrayed as having a specific lifestyle and set of beliefs that distinguish it from surrounding groups. A problem with such subcultural descriptions—especially of an area that has been said to be socially, culturally, and physically shut off from the rest of the country—is that they tend to become caricatures over time, ignoring internal differences within the region and changes that

have occurred in its relationship with other parts of the world. The fact is that despite the stereotypical view often taken of it, Appalachia is a region with varied resources, a differentiated geography, and people of varied ethnic backgrounds.

Subcultural characteristics also have been interpreted as the principal causes for the unusually high rates of poverty found in Appalachia. This constitutes a form of victim blaming, however, because evidence suggests that it has not been primarily subcultural values or isolation but rather the nature of a region's ties to the outside that have exacerbated and perpetuated the high poverty rate. Numerous scholars, many from the region, have labeled Appalachia as a rich land with poor people, poor because their resources have been exploited by outsiders (e.g., Gaventa 1984; Eller 1982).

The image of Appalachia as being composed of backward, fundamentalist, individualistic mountaineers has lowered the status prestige of this region for most Americans. How do the elements of this discussion of Appalachia relate to our earlier conclusion that status can be based on region? Let us review the core factors that determine status and status-group ranking. We noted that status honor/prestige is subjectively given by a community to another person or group. This perception, in turn, depends on the characteristics attributed to the person or group and on how valued these characteristics are in mainstream culture. Status honor can be based on (1) lifestyle, (2) extent of empirical-rational formal education, (3) family genealogy, and/or (4) occupation, according to Weber (1964). We also said that a distinct lifestyle and isolation from outsiders characterize status groups. Weber further argued that individuals in similar status situations tend to form cohesive communities. This cohesiveness is reaffirmed and maintained through intimate associations among themselves and by their wariness of and distance from outsiders. Status groups also are characterized by some uniqueness in their acquisitions; that is, their possessions may be exclusively associated with members of the group. Finally, higher-status groups try to avoid contaminating contact with lower-status groups, since they represent "impure" qualities and, in the extreme case, may be considered pariah groups.

The evidence we have reviewed strongly suggests that most Americans have a fairly coherent conception of Appalachians as a group and that they perceive them as having distinctive values and behaviors. Moreover, this subculture is more often than not portrayed in negative terms; that is, it is perceived as low status. The Appalachian subculture is thought to have a unique lifestyle, according to the traditional conception, that includes a denigration of formal education, a genealogy composed of so-called common folk, and traditional occupations that are usually blue collar or agricultural in nature. None of these characteristics enhances the status honor accorded Appalachians. The mountain people frequently have been portrayed as being physically, socially, and culturally isolated from the outside world, and conversely, as having close relationships among themselves, especially within families. The qualities assessed as different by the standards of the dominant culture lead to the ridicule and romanticism heaped upon mountaineers and "hillbillies" by outside urbanites. In correspondence with the

romantic view of mountain culture, some of the artifacts associated with this culture, such as musical styles and instruments, have been viewed as being unique and worthy of preservation, especially by intellectual outsiders. In sum, what exists in Appalachia is an interesting confluence of economic, colonial, and status factors that must be understood within their historical context. Most importantly, our traditional image of Appalachians, while not consistent with much empirical evidence, has encouraged us to label Appalachians as a separate status group with low prestige.

THE IMPORTANCE OF SOCIAL STATUS IN THE GLOBAL ARENA

Beyond the United States, social status distinctions are also found in other societies as well. A long-term project in Britain, for example, has uncovered status and lifestyle distinctions that provide evidence for defined stratification among status groups, and these distinctions are not reducible to economic class differences (Chan and Goldthorpe 2004). In other words, Weber's argument for the analytic separation between class and status is supported. These status groups are distinguished by differences in the breadth of their consumption of cultural activities (e.g., art, music). Members of the same status group also tend to carry out their intimate relationships with each other rather than with outsiders.

Inequality based on status group differences is widespread, and is not always reflected simply in taste differences. The violent conflicts that exist in many parts of the world also suggest the existence of status differences. Often these conflicts are rooted in religious differences, but they sometimes are grounded in prejudice and discrimination based on sexual orientation and ethnic membership. Violence between Christians and Muslims in parts of Africa and Central Europe, between Hindus and Muslims in South Asia, and between Jews, Muslims, and Christians in the Middle East are just a few of ongoing battles based on religion. Often, the dominant religious group oppresses the minority.

As the above examples illustrate, status inequality is a worldwide issue. But while research has been done on the relationships between globalization, on the one hand, and economic and political inequality on the other, virtually no research has been conducted on the potential impact of globalization on status inequality or status communities. In some ways, this is rather curious because globalization generally involves the movement and intermixing of people with different cultural, religious, political, and educational backgrounds. What we will do here is briefly suggest some possible relationships between globalization and the development of new bases of status resulting in the rise and fall of status communities within and between nations. So consider the following few paragraphs as food for thought.

It seems to us that increased immigration from Latin America and Asia, public discussions about various religious groups, and concerns about the global educational and digital divide are all seedbeds for the development of new status communities and the strengthening of nascent ones. Historically, adaptation by immigrants to the United States sometimes took the form of economic, social, and cultural enclaves. Within them, immigrants could maintain their distinct cultural ways of life, creating a sometimes voluntary and sometimes involuntary boundary between themselves and the larger society. Given the continuing controversy about the economic, educational, environmental, and other effects of immigration on U.S. society, and the conviction on the part of some that we ought to severely limit immigration and be more rigorous in our monitoring of recent immigrants, it may be that the boundaries between immigrant enclaves and the rest of society will become more solidified, reinforcing any tendencies toward exclusion and exclusivity now present. The result could be more stratification by status based on immigrant position, where immigrants are labeled and stigmatized. Might this not encourage them to turn inward to develop more fully their own communities to the neglect of ties with others? The immigrant–native divide may have political and economic implications as well.

There has also been discussion by international leaders about the "global digital divide" that separates developed from less developed nations. The gap is large: In the U.S., for example, about 80 percent of the population has a working computer in their household. Rates are much lower in places such as South Asia and sub-Saharan Africa (Pew 2015a). Access to the Internet is beginning to increase globally, however, as more people obtain smartphones. In a 2013 survey of people in 13 emerging nations, Pew found that, while smartphone ownership varied widely, a significant percentage of people in many developing countries have them. For example, 45 percent of people in Lebanon and 39 percent in Chile own a smartphone. This compares to 23 percent in Egypt and 15 percent in Brazil. The data from 2015 indicate that about 64 percent of Americans own a smartphone (Smith 2015). While photo taking and social networking are popular around the world, smartphones sometimes serve different purposes regionally. For example, in Kenya and Uganda, large percentages of people use them to make or receive payments (Pew 2014a).

Using an index that measures network infrastructure, usage of technology, and innovation, the World Economic Forum produces a ranking of countries. In 2014, the top technological countries were Finland and Singapore. The Unites States ranked seventh. Countries including India, Brazil, and China slipped somewhat in the rankings, most likely because of disparities in technological access in urban and rural areas (Bilbao-Osorio, Dutta, and Lanvin 2014). While this may change, the current situation conjures up an image of a world community in which some parts are left "out of the loop" about what is happening in the world and others are not. This again strengthens boundaries between different kinds of people, and since the rate of computer and other modern technology usage is correlated with other bases of inequality such as race, wealth, education, occupation, and gender, technological inequality further deepens and reinforces inequality along these axes. The "global e-lite" may form a new class or status group (Drori 2006). Do you think new status communities may develop as a result of globalization? Will the continuing infiltration of new values, styles, and technologies into countries create new social disparities where none have existed?

Summary

This chapter has addressed the topic of social status, a form of inequality that is analytically separate from economic inequality, even though it is frequently based on an individual's economic resources. Status also can be based on occupation, education, lifestyle, physical appearance, disability, religion, region, race, gender, and sexual orientation. The type of occupation one has, the kind of education one receives, the lifestyle one pursues, and the way one appears in public are each a badge of status. Each affects how others perceive us and how they treat us. Each also forms a basis for the groups with which we identify. In their extreme, status groups can be legally sanctioned where the boundaries separating insiders and outsiders are virtually impermeable. Veblen was acutely aware of the invidious comparisons that groups made with each other in the early 1900s, and these continue today. Even the labels attached to various places and regions of the country suggest that they have implications for social status. We examined Appalachia in some depth because differences in economic and political power and social status all converge in this region. By analyzing the region, one can see several forms of inequality at work all at once. In Chapters 6, 7, and 8, we will turn our attention to gender, sexual orientation, and race/ethnicity as additional bases of status ranking. Clearly, the groups involved in these areas elicit images of distinct lifestyles and concerns about contamination and purity. But before exploring these groups, we turn to the political dimension of inequality.

Critical Thinking

1. Discuss the new forms or bases of status developing in the United States. What are they, and how important are they? Will they replace status based on older grounds? Explain your answer.
2. How can individuals present themselves to others to indicate their membership in particular status groups?
3. On an everyday basis, how do students in junior high school and high school behave to maintain or enhance their social status among their peers? That is, how do they "do" status?
4. Does the formation of tightly knit status groups encourage fragmentation in the United States, or do they simply enrich and strengthen our diversity?

Web Connections

Appalachia has often been described in contradictory ways—as beautiful but ravaged, and as rich in resources but impoverished. The Appalachian Regional Commission's website will give you a better idea of trends in its population, employment, education, and poverty. Visit www.arc.gov.

Film Suggestions

Killing Us Softly 4 (2010). Explores media advertising of women.

CinemAbility (2013). Examines media representations of disabled people and analyzes the effects such representations have on the inclusion.

The Last Mountain (2011). A documentary about Appalachia and a social movement to stop a coal company's efforts to destroy the last remaining mountain in a community. The film also explores the health effects of coal mining on communities.

Born Rich (2003). Interviews with children born into wealthy families about what it is like to be born rich.

CHAPTER 5

Political Inequality

Where some people are very wealthy and others have nothing, the result will be either extreme democracy or absolute oligarchy, or despotism will come from either of those excesses.

ARISTOTLE (384–322 BCE)

The exercise of power and the experience of powerlessness are implicit in all the forms of inequality. The relationships between the wealthy and nonwealthy, men and women, gay and straight people, and Blacks and Whites are frequently mediated by the relative economic, social, and cultural power of these groups. Power also has a narrow political meaning as well, relating to the varied involvement and impact of individuals and groups in the national government. Power differentials shape the everyday work worlds of men and women as well. We will examine the political and work arenas of power, beginning with a discussion of images of political power structure in the United States then moving to a review of evidence that bears on those images.

PORTRAITS OF NATIONAL POWER STRUCTURE

The founding architects of the U.S. national government did not agree on how large or how strong it should be, nor did they consistently agree on whether everyone should have an equal influence on government. Washington and Adams, for example, believed in the need for a strong, centralized government, while Jefferson and Madison worried that such a government would move the country toward a European-style monarchy rather than a democracy.

Arguments on how widespread such power is have continued to this day. Basically, the debate boils down to one over the extent of inequality in political power. Most of these views can be listed under one of the following types: (1) pluralist, (2) power elite, or (3) ruling class. The principal issue on which these approaches differ is the degree to which they see power as being concentrated in the United States. After the summaries of these perspectives, a survey of the empirical evidence that bears on them will be presented.

The Pluralist View

Basically, this widely accepted position argues that there are a number of competing groups and organizations that hold much of the power in the country, but no one of these groups holds power all of the time. There is no central or **inner circle** that dominates or coordinates the connections between these groups, because each is relatively autonomous and self-interested. Each group pursues issues that are of narrow interest to its organization; in those areas it can have influence, but in others it has little or no power. Generally, social inequality is "noncumulative, i.e., most people have some power resources, and no single asset (such as money) confers excessive power" (Manley 1983, p. 369). Although there is some contact between organized groups, it tends to be inconsistent and deals with specific issues rather than broad orientations (Higley and Moore 1981). For example, conservative and liberal religious organizations may join together and have some power in their support of proposed policies revolving around rights of the unborn, but on other issues, they may differ or have no influence or interest. The shifting of power from group to group as issues fluctuate keeps power in a rough balance throughout the society. Individuals can exercise power in part by becoming members of these groups.

In sum, although the pluralist approach has spawned a number of specific theories, most share these four core ideas:

1. Power is shared rather than concentrated among a variety of groups and individuals.
2. These groups are relatively autonomous of each other and become politically active primarily when political policies are at issue that directly affect their narrow interests.
3. The average citizen can be politically influential through membership in these groups and through voices of responsible journalists and intellectuals.
4. The consequence of items 1 through 3 is that there really is no single, permanent

structure of power. Power is mercurial and its distribution is somewhat balanced by the existence of varied competing groups.

In these theories, one is given the impression of a society that is fundamentally based on *a broad system of values about which there is a widespread consensus*, even though the society is composed of a variety of groups with specific interests that may be different. In this society, each individual is rational and free, and interests are taken into account in one way or another by those organizations such as government or corporations that might be seen as having greater power. Power and powerlessness do not appear to be problems. The sharing of power actually helps the society to function.

For more than 50 years, **pluralism** has been roundly criticized (Mills 1956; Connolly 1969; Prewitt and Stone 1973). The central criticisms of pluralism frequently reflect skepticism about the reality of democracy in society today and are based on an analysis of current events on the political scene. First, the issues of concern to many people frequently are not dealt with by the government. In large part, this occurs either because these individuals are not in positions to make their interests known or because their interests are of less concern than those of people who hold positions of economic and social power and whose values are represented and reflected in the government (Connolly 1969; Prewitt and Stone 1973). Second, voluntary associations are no longer effective representatives of the average citizen, as they have themselves become oligarchic in nature. In addition, individuals in positions of organizational power do not represent the average membership. Most members of voluntary associations do not have access to power (Kariel in Connolly 1969, p. 16). Because of these critiques, some theorists propose a variant on majoritarian pluralism called "biased pluralism." In this theory, while there are various interest groups at play in politics, those aligned with corporations and economic elites tend to have more success

(Schlozman, Verba, and Brady 2012). Finally, many point to the "free rider" problem. This suggests that if there are many individuals who share an interest, but who are not in contact with one another, each will assume that the other will take responsibility for solving the problem, and therefore nobody will (Gilens and Page 2014).

The Power-Elite View

The idea of a **power elite** differs drastically from pluralist conceptions and Keller's concept of strategic elites, but it is not the same as the ruling-class concept, which we will discuss shortly. Perhaps the most famous U.S. power-elite theory was developed by C. Wright Mills (1956). Because Mills's portrayal of the power elite has drawn an inordinate amount of attention in the years since it was written, and because it represents a prime example of a theory in opposition to the pluralist position, it is presented here in detail. Mills's essential argument is that power is centralized in a power elite. According to Mills, certain historical changes have brought about the development of a power elite. As society has grown, institutions have become more complex, and national functions have become centralized in specific institutions—namely, economic, military, and political institutions. Mills contended that with historical changes, the tasks in top positions in each of these institutions have become so similar that it is now possible for those at the top to interchange positions. Consequently, in addition to centralization in institutions, there has been an increasing coalescence, so much so that *three* separate political, military, and corporate elites are now *one* power elite made up of individuals in the highest positions in an interconnected set of institutions. "By the power elite, we refer to those political, economic, and military circles which as an intricate set of overlapping cliques share decisions having at least national consequences" (p. 18). The nucleus of the power elite consists of those who hold high positions in more than one of the three major institutions, as well as those, such as prestigious lawyers and financiers, who serve to knit the three institutions together.

The persons within this structure have their power because of their positions. They do tend to come from the same kinds of economic, social, and educational backgrounds and do informally intermingle. Ultimately, however, it is their position that makes them powerful in national decision making.

Some may feel that Congress is part of the power elite, but Mills did not agree. Rather, he referred to Congress as a "semi-organized stalemate" made up of people who, since they have their eyes on reelection, are concerned largely with the fluctuating local issues of their constituencies back home. In other words, such groups as the farm bloc, labor unions, white-collar workers, and Congress really have little to do with decisions of national consequence. These groups, specifically Congress, make up a middle level of power in the United States. If the competition of groups in pluralism operates at all, it is at this level, as congressional members exchange favors, make compromises, and balance each other out. Mills (1956) further believed that the wealthy and political officers who are entrenched in local interests will not become nationally important. As he stated, "to remain merely local is to fail" (p. 39). Local society has, by and large, been swallowed up by the national system of power and prestige. This is in part due to increasing urbanization, increasing satellite status of smaller towns, improved transportation networks, and the Internet. Again, it has been changes in the structure of the society that have resulted in the appearance of a particular kind of power structure.

On the bottom of this pyramidal power structure are the large majority of people who are quickly developing into a **mass society**. Masses are characterized by the fact that they are always on the receiving end of opinions, cannot or do not effectively respond to opinions expressed in the mass media, and really have no outlet for effective action in society. Mass media, largely controlled by those on the top of the power structure, have only served to weaken communications between the top and the bottom of the structure. The media tell people what their experiences are or should be and stereotype them. Education only serves to help people "adjust" to a society that is extremely hierarchical in terms of power. Voluntary associations, although they may be viewed theoretically as a link between the individual and the people at the top, do not perform this function because as they have grown, the individuals in them feel less powerful. Power is distant and inaccessible to average members.

It should be pointed out that Mills was not saying that there is a conspiracy on the part of a small group of individuals to control political power in the United States. Rather, it has been a sequence of historical and structural events and changes, such as the growth in major institutions, that has led to the development of such a power structure. For example, the military is not powerful because it is conspiring against civilian populations, but it is in a position of power because the United States as a nation is now within an international military neighborhood, surrounded by allies and enemies. This means that what in the past may have been simply and purely political issues have now become largely military issues. Foreign aid is no longer just an economic or political issue but a military issue as well.

The *current* power elite is a relatively recent phenomenon that, in Mills's view, came into existence only after the New Deal in the 1940s and 1950s. Before that time, the power structure passed through several other epochs in which either no single institution or one of the three major institutions was dominant. Today, the hierarchy among these institutions is much less clear, and they are much more equal and intertwined.

Mills's power-elite theory has been criticized on several grounds, including the arguments that his terminology is vague and his selection of issues to test his theory is biased. He has also been faulted for choosing data that support his theory and ignoring contrary evidence. Third, some critics have attacked his conception of power as being too narrow in that it omits the role that moral and other kinds of authority may play in offsetting the power of an elite. His argument that power is based on position rather than actual decision making has also been contested, as has his contention that power only flows from the top down.

After Mills's death, the power of civil rights and the women's movement to influence policy confirmed the ability of those on the bottom to organize and have an impact. Finally, some have argued that Mills attributed too much independent power to the military and unions and too little to the Congress (Domhoff 2006; Weston 2010).

Despite these criticisms, Mills's analysis improved the quality of the debate about power differences (Prewitt and Stone 1973) and initiated a stream of research on national power structure. Moreover, recent headlines have substantiated his contention about the great power that corporate and political institutions have over average citizens (Winters and Page 2009).

The Ruling-Class View

As we have seen, Mills's description of the power structure is one in which a group of individuals in high positions in core institutions dominate, while those at the bottom comprise an unorganized, ineffectual mass. The bottom has little power and offers little active resistance. Rather, these individuals are manipulated and educated in a manner that makes them almost willing subordinates in the society. The **ruling-class** view similarly proposes that a small group has inordinate political power in the society and that there are important interconnections between economic and political institutions. However, aside from these similarities, the ruling-class model differs from the power-elite model in three ways:

1. Rather than stressing several types of institutions as being involved in the elite, the ruling-class view emphasizes the dominance of the economic institution and position within it.

2. The ruling-class model often views the bottom of the power structure as being more active and effectual as a working class. It can organize and bring about change in the society. In the case of the power-elite model, the mass is largely passive in response to its position, whereas in the ruling-class model the working class can be class conscious and

organized. Thus, the relationship between those on the top and those at the bottom is characterized more fully by conflict (Bottomore 2006).

3. The relationship between the upper class or bourgeoisie and political power is portrayed as being much tighter than is the case in Mills's power-elite theory in which the upper class and celebrities are more tangential to the political process. In Mills's view, it is strictly *institutional position*, not *personal wealth*, that leads to political power.

G. William Domhoff's argument that rich corporate owners constitute a "dominant class" that largely controls the political process is perhaps the best representation of a ruling-class theory of U.S. politics. Briefly, Domhoff (1998) contends that a cohesive power elite dominates federal governmental affairs, and it is composed of those members of the upper class whose wealth is heavily concentrated in corporate holdings and who actively become involved in corporate affairs and political policy making. Consequently, their power is based in both class position and corporate attachment. In addition, these individuals have similar backgrounds, often know each other, and have general political and economic interests in common. Because of the cohesiveness founded on these similarities, the upper class "is a *capitalist* class as well as a *social* class" (Domhoff 1998, p. 116, emphasis added). Although there may be internal disagreements over specific policies, there is broad agreement over the general direction that policy should take. The corporate-based elite dominates the political arena through its heavy influence on public opinion, participation in lobbying through its powerful interest groups, and involvement in policy formation through foundations, boardroom discussions, and various research groups.

In contrast to Mills's view of the power elite, Domhoff does not suggest there is a mass society without voice and in which no group but the elite can have any power of consequence. Rather, he notes that unions and different liberal groups frequently conflict with the corporate rich but that, generally, it is the latter group that sets

the parameters within which conflict occurs. Domhoff is quick to point out that, given the size, internal disagreements, and bases of the dominant class, his is not a conspiracy theory. Rather his argument focuses on providing evidence that there is "an upper class that is tightly interconnected with the corporate community . . . [and] that the social cohesion that develops among members of the upper class is another basis for the creation of policy agreements" (1998, p. 71). In sum, while Domhoff does recognize that there are other bases of power, they pale in comparison to the inordinate power exercised by those with massive economic resources. Clearly, the pouring of huge amounts of private money into the electoral process would seem to support his emphasis on economic power. In fact, a recent study of the empirical basis for theories of political inequality, including pluralism and elite theory, found that there is evidence that economic elites have "far more independent impact upon policy change than the preferences of average citizens do" and that the average citizens' influence on policy making is "near zero" (Gilens and Page 2014, p. 576).

DISTRIBUTION OF POLITICAL POWER

Each of the positions just discussed makes a different argument about political inequality on the national level in the United States. But the data that bear on them must be examined before conclusions can be drawn about the actual concentration and dispersion of political power. The degree of political power and political participation can be measured in a variety of ways, and each of these measures provides clues concerning the actual distribution of power.

Although some people feel they have little influence, perhaps they are wrong. One means by which to assess the potential political impact of a group is through its history of participation in the political process. A group obviously has to make its desires known if it is to have the possibility of gaining political power under the present system. "Party politicians are inclined to respond positively not to group *needs* but to group *demands*, and in political life as in economic life, *needs* do not become *marketable demands* until they are backed by 'buying power' or 'exchange power' because only then is it in the 'producer's' interest to respond" (Parenti 1970, p. 528; emphasis in original). Individuals and groups can make their demands known by participating in the political process through (1) voting, (2) holding political office, and/or (3) putting pressure in the form of lobbying and monetary support.

Voting

Voting is a frequently used measure of political participation. Voting turnouts for national elections in this country are well below the 80 percent turnouts found in other industrial democratic nations. This lower voting rate is somewhat surprising, given that evidence suggests Americans tend to be more politically aware than adults in other similar countries. The party system's lack of close connection with many other social groups, along with voluntary registration, has weakened participation in the U.S. political process (Powell 1986). A little over 38 percent of voting-age citizens did not vote in the 2012 presidential election (File 2013).

As Table 5.1 indicates, minorities and members of lower socioeconomic groups are generally less likely to vote than Whites or those with higher educations or incomes, though when controlling for factors such as education and income, Blacks have a higher political participation rate than Whites, Hispanics, or Asians (Logan, Darrah, and Oh 2012). The overrepresentation of lower socioeconomic individuals among nonvoters is exacerbated by the fact that organized efforts to get individuals to the polls focus on those who are most likely to vote anyway, that is, the affluent and more highly educated segments (Campbell 2007). Moreover, to the extent that individuals with higher incomes and educations vote for candidates and legislation that favor their positions, lower-ranking groups may suffer from the resulting political policies. Finally, poor and minority people are more likely to have felony records that, in some states, preclude them from voting. In 2014, 5.85 million

TABLE 5.1 Voting Rates among Citizens 18 and Older in the 2012 Presidential Election, by Selected Characteristics

	% Voting*
Sex	
Men	54
Women	59
Race and Hispanic Origin	
White, non-Hispanic	63
Black	62
Asian	31
Hispanic (any race)	32
Educational Attainment	
Less than high school graduate	38
High school graduate or GED	53
Some college or associate degree	64
Bachelor's degree	75
Advanced degree	81
Annual Family Income	
**Less than $20,000	48
$20,000–$29,999	59
$30,000–$39,999	58
$40,000–$49,999	63
$50,000–$74,999	68
***$75,000 and over	77
Employment Status	
Unemployed in labor force	52
****Employed in labor force	67

*All percentages rounded to nearest whole.
**Average of three income categories (under $10,000; $10,000–$14,999; $15,000–$19,999).
***Average of three income categories ($75,000–$99,999; $100,000–$149,999; $150,000 and over).

Source: U.S. Census Bureau, *Voting and Registration in the Election of November 2012—Detailed Tables.*

Americans were prevented from voting through these laws. This represents 1 in every 13 Blacks of voting age (Sentencing Project 2015b).

The power of class differences to influence voting and legislation, however, may apply primarily to White voters. Research based on exit polls of over 12,000 Black Los Angeles voters during the 1978–2000 elections suggests that race may make a difference. Among Blacks, middle-class votes appeared to align with lower-class Black sympathies (Hajnal 2007), and levels of racial empowerment and group consciousness affect voting rates (Logan, Darrah, and Oh 2012). In other words, among these voters race overrides the significance of class divisions when it comes to choosing candidates or voting for legislation. While Black voters are more likely to vote for Black candidates, however, the political party does matter. A study of 2010 elections showed that the presence of Black Democratic candidates increased Black voter turnout; the same was not true for Black Republican candidates (Fairdosi and Rogowski 2015). There is some concern, additionally, that younger Blacks view the political process differently than older Blacks, and may be less likely to vote or support the traditional agenda of the older generation (Bositis 2007).

The data for Hispanics in Table 5.1 has to be interpreted carefully as well since the data only include citizens and not all Hispanic adults. In 2013, 34 percent of Hispanics in the population were not citizens. The political impact of this ethnic group will no doubt increase as more become citizens. In fact, Hispanics have been increasingly courted by national candidates, in large part because they are expected to compose one-fourth of the U.S. population by 2050. Immigrant Hispanics, or those not born in the United States, are more likely to vote than any other group (Logan, Darrah, and Oh 2012). In addition, 74 percent of the Hispanic population is concentrated in just eight states, states that contain 80 percent of the electoral votes needed to win the presidency (Campo-Flores and Fineman 2005). Finally, religious and moral issues of the kind that have become prominent (e.g., abortion, gay marriage) complicate voting patterns for Hispanics, since although they tend to vote Democratic, many come from strong religious traditions emphasizing traditional family structures. In combination, these factors make Hispanics an increasingly important political constituency.

As voting data suggest, some groups are, at best, only minimally involved in the political process. Those who are totally inactive have disproportionate numbers from low-income and low-education backgrounds, whereas "complete activists" have an overrepresentation of high-status individuals in their ranks (Brady, Schlozman, and Verba 2015). The complete activists are individuals who participate in a variety of ways (voting, attending meetings, making campaign contributions, contacting officials, etc.). "Wealthier and better-educated citizens are more likely than the poor and less-educated to have clearly formulated and well-informed preferences, and significantly more likely to turn out to vote, to have direct contact with public officials, and to contribute money and energy to political campaigns" (Bartels 2008, p. 252). Business and professional groups continue to be politically involved, but tend to promote the interests of the affluent and educated (Skocpol 2007). There is also evidence to suggest that this inequality in political participation is perpetuated over generations through educational differences. Parents who are highly educated tend to be politically involved, provide a variety of politically relevant experiences to their children, and perhaps most significantly, maximize the chances of their children becoming highly educated themselves. "In turn, well-educated offspring are likely to ... have challenging and financially rewarding jobs, to develop civic skills and to receive requests for participation in non-political institutions, to be politically informed and interested, and so on. ... Most of the proximate causes of political participation have their roots, at least in part, in social class background" (Verba, Burns, and Schlozman 2003, p. 58). These differences in preparation and participation mean that "ordinary Americans speak in a whisper while the most advantaged roar" (quoted in Dionne 2004, p. B2).

Historically, the less advantaged have also been less organized and less powerful when attempting to influence the political system. While some organizations and movements advocating their interests have sprung up in recent years, other groups such as unions have declined in membership. Union members have higher rates of voting than nonmembers in similar occupations (Kerrissey

1980s and 1990s shows that the positions of wealthy constituents were much more likely to be considered by lawmakers than those of poorer constituents, and that those on the bottom were not likely to be considered at all (Bartels 2008).

While class position affects political participation, some have argued that, as a basis for political advocacy, class has been supplanted by "cultural" factors. Prominent issues such as gay marriage, abortion, medical malpractice, stem cell research, marijuana usage, and immigration incite groups that are not organized around *class* but around religious and other *cultural* dimensions. *Status*-based politics has moved into the foreground while *class*-based politics has receded. Michael Hechter (2004) observes, "[t]hat status politics may be gaining in recent times is suggested by the increasing political salience of ethnicity, religion, nationalism, gender, and sexual orientation" (p. 404). But while status-based issues may be increasing in prominence, especially within the upper class, economic issues still predominate in the minds of voters. Government spending and income-maintenance programs are more salient among voters than are topics such as abortion and gay marriage (Bartels 2008). The 2016 presidential election highlighted the continuing importance of economic issues such as income inequality, jobs, and taxes.

Photo 5.1 Although working-class families have been among the most openly patriotic and have generally contributed their members disproportionately to serving their country militarily, they are less likely to vote or occupy political positions than are those in higher classes.

Photo by Brendan R. Hurst.

and Schofer 2013), but the percentage of private-sector workers that are unionized is much smaller than that found among public-sector workers. When these conditions are combined with the fact that private-sector union members tend to have less education and lower wages than those in the public sector, the result is that the political power of the working class as expressed through voting is weakened, making political inequality between the classes greater (Rosenfeld 2010).

In addition to lower voting rates and less participation in political activities, weakness in the political power of the working and lower classes is further indicated by the lack of government responsiveness to the arguments of these classes. An analysis of data from the Senate in the

Holding Political Office

Holding political office is another and more substantial means by which to wield political power. White males dominate political positions at the federal level. In terms of absolute figures, the number of Black elected officials has gone up dramatically since 1970. In 2001, there were 9,101 Black elected officials, compared to 1,469 in 1970. But Blacks still compose only about 2 percent of all elected officials, even though they make up over 11 percent of the voting-age population. Under 1 percent of these positions are at the federal level. In the 114th House of Representatives, 48 of the 441 members, or about 10 percent, were Black, compared to 34 Hispanic, 11 Asian American, and two Native American members. The 114th Senate in 2015 had two Black members, compared with four Hispanics and one Asian American. At the same time, there was only one openly gay person in the Congress. In total, minorities made up about 21 percent of the House and 7 percent of the Senate in 2011.

Women in general are underrepresented in elected political positions. Eighty-eight (20 percent) of the 441 members of the 2015 House of Representatives were women; 20 (20 percent) of the members of the Senate were women (Manning 2015, p. 7). Although the first woman was elected to the House of Representatives in 1916, the influx of women into the Congress is a relatively recent phenomenon. Regular increases in the number of women serving in Congress began in the 1970s. About one-third of all the women ever to have served in Congress were members in 2006 (Palmer and Simon 2010).

Despite the increased movement of women into elected federal positions, gender stereotypes still create obstacles for them. Men have more often held leadership positions and have,

consequently, been thought to have stronger leadership qualities. Whereas men are viewed as being more forceful, sure of themselves, and knowledgeable, women are generally seen as being more compassionate, relational, and open to compromise. Stereotypes are also one of the reasons women are less likely than men to consider running for office (Dolan 2005; Palmer and Simon 2010; Carli and Eagly 2007). Counteracting these pressures has been the international women's movement, which has fostered an increase in participation by women in the political process (Paxton, Hughes, and Green 2006). Internationally, however, women still lag behind men in holding legislative positions. Worldwide in 2015, only 11 women served as heads of state and 13 served as heads of government, and only 22 percent of cabinet members were women. Moreover, in only a small number of countries do women compose more than 30 percent of members of parliament (United Nations 2015).

In addition to gender and race, socioeconomic status has also been tied to holding political

Photo 5.2 Women and minorities are underrepresented on Capitol Hill in Washington, D.C. In 2011, only 17 percent of the House of Representatives and 15 percent of Senate members were women. Racial and ethnic minorities composed 18 percent of the House and 4 percent of the Senate.

© Brandon Bourdages/Shutterstock.

office. Historically, most members of Congress not only have been White men, but also members of the middle or upper class, and a majority have been lawyers, bankers, or other businessmen (Matthews 1954). The Congress of 2015 was similarly composed; 93 of the 100 Senators were either lawyers and/or businesspeople, while only four were blue-collar workers. In the House of Representatives, 382 of the 435 members (87.8 percent) were in business or law; 29 (6.6 percent) were in blue-collar labor (Manning 2015, pp. 2–4). The overrepresentation of individuals from higher-status backgrounds has clearly continued in Congress.

The executive branch has also historically contained disproportionate numbers of higher-status individuals. Mintz (1975) and Freitag (1975) researched the class backgrounds of *all* cabinet officers during the period from 1897 to 1973 and found that there were strong ties to the upper class. A full 66 percent of these officers were from upper-class backgrounds, and 90 percent had occupied a top corporate position before or after being appointed or had upper-class origins. The particular political party that happened to be in power at the time did not make much difference (Mintz 1975). Freitag's analysis supports Mills's conclusion that there is a clear connection between corporate and political elites, and does not support Keller's and other pluralists' arguments about autonomous elites. His study, based on biographical information for all cabinet secretaries from McKinley to Nixon's first term, involving 358 cabinet positions, shows that *at least* 76 percent of cabinet members were tied to the corporate sector by being either corporate executives, officers, or corporate lawyers. Since President Truman's administration, this percent is even higher: 86 percent under Eisenhower, 77 percent under Kennedy, 86 percent under Johnson, and 96 percent under Nixon (Freitag 1975). Freitag concluded that the data do not prove that the corporate and governmental elite sectors are unified in terms of policies, but they do suggest that it is a "serious possibility" that the cabinet may be accountable to large corporations.

A predominance of individuals in cabinet positions with strong ties to business continued under the Reagan, Clinton, Bush, and Obama administrations. Those individuals most responsible for crafting U.S. global and economic policy strategies in all four administrations came to their positions predominantly from the sectors of finance and law, and once out of office, returned to the corporate world (Van Apeldoorn and De Graaff 2014). "These affiliations in many cases display a revolving door pattern indicating that the actors concerned are not just closely tied to but actually are themselves members of the corporate elite" (Van Apeldoorn and De Graaff 2014, p. 18).

Top federal officials are not likely to come from working-class or lower-class families. Presidents also tend to come from higher educational and occupational backgrounds, and certain ethnic backgrounds are overrepresented in these positions. For example, 34 of the first 44 presidents (Washington through Obama) had college degrees, and the vast majority of them received their educations at elite schools in the Northeast. Twenty-eight of them were lawyers by occupation.

For over two decades, Dye (2002) has documented the characteristics, backgrounds, and interconnections of the institutional elite in the United States. He included in his definition of elites all those who occupy positions of high authority in the governmental, media, educational, civic/cultural, military, financial, industrial, and legal institutions in the United States. Considering only the governmental elite—that is, those who occupy the top positions in the executive, legislative, and judicial branches—almost 75 percent have law or other advanced degrees. More than 40 percent are graduates of highly prestigious, private universities or colleges. Women and African Americans, as might be expected, are grossly underrepresented.

What is the meaning of these studies in terms of the perspectives on power presented earlier? If the essence of pluralism is the presence of a rough balance of power between constituencies with different interests, then these data clearly do not support the pluralist position. Some groups—most notably women, racial minorities, and working- or lower-class individuals—are seldom found in national-level offices of political power.

MINI-CASE 5.1

States' Rights versus the Federal Government

One of the main reasons for the Civil War was disagreement about the power of individual states versus the power of the central federal government. This issue has not disappeared. States often differ in their laws over fundamental issues such as gun control, Medicaid, and what constitutes a crime. As in the case of the criminalization of marijuana, sometimes these laws clash with federal law. For example, several states have legalized the sale of recreational marijuana, but it remains illegal at the federal level. Thus banks may not lend money or open an account for those selling marijuana, even in states where it is legal. As a result, from the point of view of the state, individuals may have certain rights, but not according to federal law. When, if ever, should state law take precedence over federal law? ◼

To the extent that these offices are a principal means by which to gain and exercise political power, and that incumbents reflect and work for their own interests, then some groups have much less power than others.

INTERLINKAGE OF ECONOMIC AND POLITICAL POWER

As noted in Chapter 1, there has been a longstanding concern for keeping economic power from contaminating the political arena and thereby keeping those who are wealthy from controlling the political process. A recent analysis of data from numerous advanced democratic nations, including the United States, demonstrates the significant relationship between economic inequality and political participation. Greater income inequality reduces interest in political issues, dampens political debate, and lowers voter participation among all citizens except the wealthy (Solt 2008). When compared to past active protests and mass movements against the political power of wealth, "the democratic urge to rein in the dangerous ambitions of privileged elites has grown frail" (Gerstle and Fraser 2005, p. 291). While presidential candidate Bernie Sanders enjoyed significant success in the early stages of the 2016 election in raising the national alarm about income inequality, it remains to be seen whether this issue will gain traction in the final vote. A number of factors limit the extent to which governmental policy can be focused on inequality. These include the great polarization of voters, the lack of voter participation, the influence of high-income campaign contributors, and the inability of political institutions, most notably Congress, to address these issues (Bonica et al. 2013).

Those who have higher incomes can maintain their interest and involvement in politics because they have an inordinate effect on the political process, shaping policies that fit their own interests rather than those of the majority: "Rarely have elites pioneered on the frontiers of democratic reform" (Gerstle and Fraser 2005, p. 287). This may be a partial explanation for the consistent relationship that has existed between socioeconomic status and voting. In the absence of effective power, the nonwealthy and uneducated may feel that the political process is out of their hands. These findings give credence to arguments going back to Aristotle, de Tocqueville, and others that contend there is a close tie between economic equality and political democracy. The studies discussed earlier in this chapter show that office incumbents are most likely to come from high social classes. This class connection raises additional questions about the relationship between economic and political power. First, are political action committees (PACs) and lobbying groups so influential in the political process as to suggest dominance by one social class? Does money buy elections and votes? Second, and perhaps most important, is the upper class in general and its ruling "power elite" as united as Domhoff suggests?

Candidate Selection and Campaign Funding

Running for a federal political office is extremely expensive. The 2012 presidential and congressional campaigns, during which $7 billion was spent, outdid the 2008 elections by $1.7 billion (Federal Election Commission 2014). The 2014 congressional elections cost an estimated $4 billion. Short of actual occupancy in a political office, another substantial manner in which an individual or organization can attempt to have political impact is through direct influence of officeholders. In the recent past, direct lobbying has been carried out by various groups with financial power. Since the 1960s, there has been a significant increase in the number and activity of interest groups, an increased centralization of their headquarters in Washington, D.C., a rise in the number of public-interest and single-issue interest groups, and more "formal penetration" on their part into governmental activities (Cigler and Loomis 2015). The number of PACs has spiraled upward in recent years, reaching 7,548

in 2015 (Federal Election Commission 2015). Basically, **political action committees (PACs)** are interest groups that receive money from individuals sympathetic to their cause(s), so they can affect a federal election.

PACs represent many different interest groups. Corporations, labor, assorted trade associations, and nonconnected specific-issues groups are among the organizations with PACs, and each follows different strategies. In 2013–2014, the top 10 PACs spent between $2.4 and $3.8 million each (Center for Responsive Politics 2015).

So-called super PACs developed in 2010 as a result of a Supreme Court decision on campaign financing. These groups can raise unlimited amounts of money from organizations and individuals and then spend unlimited amounts in support of specific issues or candidates. The most successful super PAC, American Crossroads, raised about $22 million by July 2010 for the fall congressional elections. But unlike PACs in general, super PACs cannot give funds directly to a candidate (Center for Responsive Politics 2010).

Contributions by PACs are part of the "soft money" candidates receive during their campaigns. Such funds also include money from individuals,

Photo 5.3 The Supreme Court ruling referred to as "Citizens United" highlighted the influence of large institutions such as corporations, unions, or lobbying groups in our election process.

© Susan Montgomery/Shutterstock.

unions, and corporations. Loopholes in federal legislation have fostered growth in the amount of soft money in political campaigns. More money has flooded into political campaigns because of recent Court rulings. The Supreme Court's 2010 decision in the *Citizens United v. Federal Election Commission* opened the door to unlimited spending by corporations and unions, arguing that these organizations have the same First Amendment rights to free speech as individuals. While they cannot give money directly to individual candidates, these organizations can use their own money to fund federal election campaigns that advocate issues and candidates that they prefer.

The concern over the influence of PACs is based on the assumption that, *as a monolithic group*, contributors disproportionately influence federal policies. But it should be kept in mind that these groups vary widely in their specific interests and are not monolithic in this sense. In fact, the proliferation of varying interest groups might be viewed as an indication of pluralism at work (Alexander 1992). At the same time, however, there is some question about whether the attention paid to *specific* interest groups will hinder the ability of governing officials to effectively address problems that affect the *general* interest of U.S. society (Cigler and Loomis 2015).

Regarding the issue of PACs and their impact, studies suggest that although PACs may increase an individual's access to given members of Congress, they do not systematically affect how these members vote. However, Senator Russell B. Long once said that "the distinction between a large campaign contribution and a bribe is almost a hairline's difference" (quoted in Stern 1988, p. 146). But in a research study on 20 labor-related issues in the U.S. House of Representatives, Jones and Keiser (1987) found that the amount of contributions from union-approved PACs was related to voting only on issues that had little media attention. In other words, the less visible the issue, the greater the effect of contributions on voting behavior.

An analysis of the judgments of policy historians demonstrates that PACs do influence legislation, and that a few interest groups such as the AFL-CIO and the National Association of Manufacturers regularly influence behavior (Grossmann 2012). The influence of PACs is particularly important on highly ideological issues, and it is likely that as our political parties become more ideologically polarized, parties will have a greater influence than PACs (Witko 2006). It is not through the amount of the PAC contribution itself, but through other mechanisms that economically powerful groups can influence voting patterns. Peoples and Gortari (2008) found that U.S. representatives who received funds from the same *business* groups voted in a similar manner, but did not vote in the same way if they received money from the same *labor* organizations. In a study of Ohio state legislators, Peoples (2008) discovered that contributions affect voting of lawmakers primarily when they are in the same party. The qualifications and varied results in these studies suggest that contributions may have an effect only under certain conditions. The conditions included and methods used in these studies differ, yielding different findings. An overview of current research studies on the relationship between monetary contributions and roll call voting found mixed results, with some studies suggesting that contributions have a major impact, while others find that they have little or no effect on public voting by congressional members (Hojnacki et al. 2012).

The impact of money on elections and voting continues as an issue largely because it pits those who are concerned about the corruption of politics against those who believe that everyone, including corporations and labor unions, should be allowed to spend their money as they wish. The recent Supreme Court ruling supporting First Amendment rights for corporations and other organizations served to bring this debate more fully into the public consciousness.

RULING-CLASS UNITY

Concerns about soft money and the power of PACs are related to suspicions that those with plentiful resources are unified and will exercise disproportionate control of the political process. Most of the data on elite cohesiveness for the past several decades indicated that the elite are broadly unified because of similarities in class

NUTSHELL 5.1   Money, Politics, and Justice

The infiltration of money into the political process has been an ongoing concern throughout U.S. history. Alexander Hamilton and John Jay, our first chief justice, believed that the people who own the country ought to run it, whereas Thomas Jefferson and Theodore Roosevelt argued against and tried to stem the tendency towards a plutocracy, that is, government by the wealthy. It should come as no surprise then that the issue of unlimited and unrestricted campaign contributions would be a hot-button topic that would rally opposing groups to loudly argue their positions.

On January 21, 2010, these positions intensified when the United States Supreme Court issued a ruling in the case of *Citizens United v. Federal Election Commission*, 130 S. Ct. 876 (2010). Briefly, the 5–4 majority opinion ruled that a section of the Bipartisan Campaign Reform Act (popularly known as the "McCain-Feingold Act"), which prohibited corporations and unions from spending money on media political ads during the final stages of campaigns, violated the First Amendment to the United States Constitution. Citing prior decisions which recognized that corporations have First Amendment rights, the Court concluded that the ban on such corporate spending was an impermissible ban on speech. The decision conflicted with laws in 24 states that banned corporations from using money from their general funds in campaigns. It also further polarized opinions. President Obama saw it as a victory for big companies and interest groups and a setback for ordinary Americans who have little leverage and little money.

The Supreme Court was clearly divided on the issue. Proponents viewed the decision as a victory for the First Amendment that in part says, "Congress shall make no law . . . abridging the freedom of speech." Even though corporations are not flesh-and-blood entities, under the law they have the same rights and responsibilities as persons. Consequently, being allowed to spend one's money the way one wants is one aspect of the individual's (or corporation's) right to free speech. "Political speech is 'indispensable to decision making in a democracy, and this is no less true because the speech comes from a corporation rather than an individual.'"

Citizens United, 130 S. Ct. at 904 (quoting *First Nat'l Bank v. Bellotti*, 435 U.S. 765, 777 [1978]; footnote omitted). Judges supporting the decision did not believe it would undermine public support for the government: "The appearance of influence or access, furthermore, will not cause the electorate to lose faith in our democracy." *Citizens United*, 130 S. Ct. at 910 (citing *Buckley v. Valeo*, 424 U.S. 1, 46, 96 S. Ct. 612 [1976]).

Opponents of the decision worried about the potential flood of money that may lead to the buying of government positions by those with the most wealth. Former Supreme Court Justice Stevens, dissenting from the majority decision in *Citizens United*, argued that giving corporations the same status as individuals was wrong, that corporations and individuals are not the same. "In the context of election to public office, the distinction between corporate and human speakers is significant. Although they make enormous contributions to our society, corporations are not actually members of it" (*Citizens United*, 130 S. Ct. at 930 [Stevens, J., dissenting]). He also contended that the decision overturns past rulings that limited corporate spending: "The majority's approach to corporate electioneering marks a dramatic break from our past. Congress has placed special limitations on campaign spending by corporations ever since the passage of the Tillman Act in 1907" (*Citizens United*, 130 S. Ct. at 930 [Stevens, J., dissenting]). Finally, Justice Stevens argued that lawmakers have a duty to guard against possibly negative effects of corporate spending in local and national elections. One of these effects, he feared, was a weakened stature for the Court: "The Court's ruling threatens to undermine the integrity of elected institutions across the Nation. The path it has taken to reach its outcome will, I fear, do damage to this institution" (*Citizens United*, 130 S. Ct. at 931 [Stevens, J., dissenting]).

The costs for state and federal elections have skyrocketed. These include spending for supreme court positions in the states' court systems, which more than doubled since the 1990s to $56.4 million in the 2011–2012 election cycle. The economic tug-of-war for these elections primarily involved powerful interest groups on the right and

(continued)

NUTSHELL 5.1 *(continued)*

left who sought to move the justice system in their direction. U.S. Supreme Court Justice Ruth Bader Ginsberg and former U.S. Justice Sandra Day O'Connor worry that this trend can erode the average American's belief in the fairness of the justice system and confirm the belief of those who feel that those with money rule. A central question, of course, is whether the election of a given state court judge means that he or she will always cast decisions favorable to the interests that heavily funded the election. The majority in the *Citizens United* decision apparently would not envision a problem here. "The fact that speakers may have influence over or access to elected officials does not mean that these officials are corrupt" (*Citizens United*, 130 S. Ct. at 910).

_____

Sources: Alicia Bannon and Lianna Reagan, "New Politics of Judicial Elections 2011-12," *Brennan Center for Justice*, October 23, 2013; Kristin Sullivan and Terrance Adams, "Summary of *Citizens United v. Federal Election Commission*, "*OLR Research Report* 2010-R-0124, March 2, 2010; Adam Liptak, "Justices, 5-4, Reject Corporate Spending Limit," *New York Times*, late edition, January 22, 2010, pp. A1 and A18; and *Citizens United v. Federal Election Commission*, 130 S. Ct. 876 (2010).

background, membership patterns on corporate boards, and political behavior (Chu and Davis 2015; Khan 2012).

Mills's and Domhoff's descriptions of the social backgrounds of the elite and the historical circumstances in which they rule suggest that they should be unified. Domhoff described their common membership in and interaction at exclusive clubs, attendance at elite schools, and frequent listing on the Social Register, while Mills described not only their social-psychological similarities but also the concentration and coalescence that occurred among the major institutions involved in the power elite. Domhoff detailed some evidence of intermarriages, unique schooling, and common leisure and social activities that point, he argued, to the existence of a cohesive upper class of which the public is conscious. Dye (2002) also concluded that there is general unity of opinion among the elite, even though there is some evidence of rising factionalism within it. And while there was an era of "high brow" culture, beginning particularly during the Gilded Age, when elites separated themselves from the masses by their cultural knowledge and associations (e.g., attendance at the opera, support of classical music and art), increasingly the elite embrace a variety of cultural forms. "Such omnivorousness could be because elites are more open or inclusive, or omnivorousness may be the new symbolic boundary that marks elites, like snobbishness of old" (Khan 2012, p. 368).

Further, Dye (2002) argued that a split has developed within the elite between those he labels the "sunbelt cowboys" and the "established yankees." As the labels suggest, the "cowboys" as a group are individualistic, conservative, and often from non-upper-class backgrounds. Their wealth has been recently acquired. In contrast, the "yankees" tend to be more liberal and have established family wealth. They have attended the best Ivy League schools and are also likely to have occupied high positions in prestigious corporate, financial, or legal institutions. Thus, as to the issue of how unified the elite or upper class is, it is important to indicate whether one is speaking of the *general* or *specific* level, in *ideal* or *real-situational* terms, and of *social background* or *behavioral* unity. In some ways, these groups appear unified and in others they do not; the results from attitudinal and positional studies on unity are clearly mixed, and one can find statistics to support both positions.

Like Domhoff, Dye, and others, Mizruchi has dissected the capitalist class and its unity in detail. His studies concern the interlocking connections between elites and the corporations they represent, and whether these connections lead to common political behaviors among corporations (Mizruchi and Bunting 1981; Mizruchi 1989;

Mizruchi and Stearns 2001). His 1981 research documented, for example, that among 456 Fortune 500 manufacturing firms, more than 70 percent had at least one officer who sat on a board of a financial institution. Similarly, in his 1989 research on political behavior among large American corporations, he found that the close geographical proximity of corporations in the same field and ties formed from individuals serving together on boards of directors of financial institutions led to similar corporate political contributions from their PACs.

In similar early research, Useem (1984) directly addressed the issue of the political unity of what he calls the "inner circle" of business, looking at whether members of this group act on behalf of their own separate corporations or on behalf of the capitalist class as a whole. Useem drew his information and conclusions from a wide variety of data sources, including personal interviews and documentary and survey data. The inner circle he described is a network of leaders from large corporations who serve as top officers at more than one firm, who are politically active, and who serve the interests of the capitalist class as a whole rather than the narrow immediate interests of their individual companies. To be a member of the inner circle, it helps to (1) have been successful in a major corporation, (2) have multiple directorships, (3) have occupied a senior position, (4) be a member of business associations, and (5) have been a consultant or advisor to government. Members of the inner circle are more often members of the upper class than are other business leaders—that is, they are richer, have attended elite prep schools, and are in the Social Register (Useem 1984, pp. 66–70). The circle's political style is to adopt a "posture of compromise" and accommodation rather than to be directly confrontational on any specific issue. Its interests are in the general protection of capitalism as a whole, not in the interests of specific companies.

Useem (1984) viewed capitalism in the United States as having moved from (1) "family capitalism" in which individual upper-class families dominated corporate ownership, through (2) "managerial capitalism" in which managers began to replace the dominance of upper-class owners around the turn of the twentieth century, to (3) "institutional capitalism" in which networks of intercorporate ties characterize the core of capitalism. The increasing control of corporations by their managers rather than owners and the increased concentration and interlocking in the corporate sector during this century have helped lay the basis for the development of this powerful circle.

Indeed, Dye's study (2002) of individuals in top institutional positions revealed that 6,000 individuals have formal control over 50 percent of the country's industrial, banking, communications, insurance, educational, legal, and cultural assets. The top 500 out of 5 million corporations control about 60 percent of all corporate assets. Twenty-five banks out of 12,000 possess over 50 percent of all banking assets in the United States, and 30 of the 2,000 insurance companies control over half of all insurance assets. Some 15 percent of the 7,314 institutional leaders studied by Dye occupied more than one top position (i.e., were interlockers), and a smaller percent held as many as six or more such positions. He viewed this "inner group" as cohesive for a number of reasons, and, like Useem, found that multiple corporate interlockers were more likely than single directors to participate in governmental and other major organizations. Inner-circle members play crucial political roles by directing nonprofit organizations, serving as political fund-raisers, endorsing candidates, giving larger campaign contributions, and influencing media content (Useem 1984, pp. 76–94).

This inner circle is much more politically active than business in general because its members occupy several important positions at once, which (1) creates cohesiveness among its members, (2) helps mobilize economic and other resources, and (3) provides a powerful platform from which to express political positions. Moreover, its members are also closely tied to the upper class, which increases the circle's influence (Useem 1984). In contrast to other research, Useem found that if members of the upper class are in the business elite, they are more likely than persons from other classes to get into the inner circle. In sum, characteristics of the U.S. political economy create opportunities for the interconnection of political and economic power.

Since 2000, however, researchers suggest the possible beginning of a fragmentation of the inner circle, as once tightly connected boards have become increasingly disconnected from one another (Chu and Davis 2015). As corporations have been under pressure to diversify their boards, and as the "inner circle" has been tainted by the controversies leading to the Great Recession, boards are composed of newcomers with fewer ties to other boards. This suggests that the corporate elite is less able to act in a coordinated manner, and that the individual shareholder has come to have much more power than the corporate board (Mizruchi 2013). This has resulted in a greater political polarization—where elites might have voted to further the interests of the corporation, votes are now more ideologically aligned. Ironically, this happens at a time when "social power and economic rewards have become increasingly concentrated in the hands of the few" (Khan 2012, p. 361).

A significant part of the reason for the tie between economic and political power lies in the interlocking between private and corporate wealth and political opportunity. It takes wealth, or at least access to wealth, to run a viable campaign for a major national political office. The connection between economic and political power may be deeper than this suggests, however, and may be based not on the characteristics of particular *individuals* but rather on the *structure and functioning* of the society.

The *structuralist* position suggests that given the structure of a capitalist society such as the United States, the government *must* act in a manner that supports the capitalist class and capitalism in general. This occurs regardless of the individuals who are in office. Political and economic institutions are so intertwined that the government, although it may be "relatively autonomous," is constrained to support and pass policies that maintain the capitalist economy. The state needs to provide a hospitable environment for investment and create a stable and smooth-running economy because it relies on the returns from the economy for its revenue. A stable economy also encourages political support for the government. In addition, the state provides programs (e.g., welfare, unemployment compensation) to deal with the fallout that comes from the operation of a capitalist system in which a relatively small number of corporations exercise inordinate influence. Inevitably, the state becomes involved in economic matters (Wilks 2013). During the 2008–2009 economic crisis, for example, the U.S. government provided hundreds of billions of dollars to large financial institutions—despite widespread public opposition—arguing that such support was needed to strengthen all aspects of the economy.

The preceding studies on campaign financing, holding office, and the capitalist economy indicate that both individuals and structural arrangements foster a relationship between economic and political power. Structural ties among institutions make it possible for some individuals to have access to positions of great power. According to some, however, one of the major problems with both these analyses is that they assume that all major policies are made within the government and, therefore, the focus of both approaches is on the state. In fact, it has been suggested, many major policies are created outside the government, principally by the actions of corporations. Industrial change, for example, to the extent that it can be considered a "policy," has largely been the result of actions by the private sector, not the government (Schwartz 1987).

POWER INEQUALITY IN THE WORK EXPERIENCE

The discussion so far should leave little doubt that, by a variety of measures, there is extensive inequality in power at the national level. The focus in this section will be on power differentials that are experienced by individuals in their everyday work world. Unfortunately, until recently, organization-level data have seldom been the focus for studies of inequality (Stainback, Tomaskovic-Devey, and Skaggs 2010). The power differences found in organizations are often related to central characteristics of organizations, as well as to society-wide issues of race, gender, and class. What exists and happens *outside* organizations often infiltrates and affects what happens *within* them. As we will see in Chapter 13, there have been social movements going on for decades based on class, race, and gender that are generally organized attempts to gain greater power in society. The historical conflict between labor and management, for example, was generally one over the relative power and control of each side. In addition, developments in technology have allowed contemporary corporations to expand their monitoring power and control over their employees. With cell phones, smartphones, e-mail, texting, and iPads, is it ever possible for a manager to escape from work? Technology has broken down the traditional divide between work and home, the public and private spheres.

The structures and traditions of organizations themselves affect the manner in which power is organized and exercised. Total institutions such as the military and strict religious orders, with their clear, fixed, and legitimate hierarchies and complete control over members, perhaps provide the best expression of the use of power in organizations. Power differentials in organizations can be maintained simply because of the inertia that exists in them (Stainback, Tomaskovic-Devey, and Skaggs 2010). The status quo can be comfortable and inviolate, while change can be threatening and disruptive. Older, smaller organizations with long-standing patrimonial traditions tend to rely upon factors such as age, kinship, and seniority rather than a formal hierarchy as bases for the exercise of power. Still other organizations rely on the charisma and normative power of their leaders to control their members.

Power itself can be situational, that is, it may be operative only in particular contexts (e.g., at work but not elsewhere), or it may be trans-situational, that is, apply regardless of the situation (e.g., as against a minority person). Power can also be derived from a number of sources. As the examples above suggest, sometimes power is based on one's formal position in an organization

(*legitimate* power). In other situations, power is based on one's knowledge (*expert* power), attractiveness (*referent* power), ability to reward (*reward* power), or ability to punish (*coercive* power) (French and Raven 1959). *Information* can also be a base of power (Raven 1965), as can connections or associations one has with others (*referred* power). In each of these cases, but for different reasons, one person is *dependent* on another, and can be constrained to act in a particular way despite his or her resistance. In their classic study of working-class employees, for example, Sennett and Cobb (1973) found that workers promoted greater independence for their children by encouraging college educations so that they could become professionals rather than manual workers; that is, they wanted their children to have autonomy in their jobs and be able to exercise greater control over their own lives.

The different bases of power conjure up some interesting scenarios about the relationship between power on the one hand, and race, class, and gender on the other. Men, for example, are thought to possess more expert and legitimate power than women, while women are believed to have more referent power, that is, their greater likeability gives them some leverage in relationships (Ragins and Winkel 2011). Individuals in lower-authority positions, administrative assistants for example, can exercise power through their control or possession of information. Professionals who have a specialized knowledge/experience can exercise power over higher-ranking individuals who are dependent on their expertise. Persons who appear threatening to others, for example, Black males, can exercise control over others with higher status based on their perceived power to coerce. These are just a few of the ways in which bases of power are linked to race, class, and gender in everyday life.

In addition, power relationships are shaped by people's mental biases and beliefs about individuals in other groups. Gender ideology, racism, and class distinctions are frequently implicated in the treatment employees receive from others, including their superiors. Internalized images about the fundamental traits of men versus women,

Blacks versus Whites, and professional versus working-class manual workers affect the way members of each group relate to individuals in the other group. Gender and racial stereotypes also have impacts on the kinds of positions for which candidates are deemed suitable, and on the relative power of individuals once they obtain positions in work organizations (Stainback, Tomaskovic-Devey, and Skaggs 2010). Whether a job requires "masculine" or "feminine" abilities, for example, can affect who is hired into the position (Gorman 2005; King and Cornwall 2007). In some cases, beliefs about a lower-status group can even allow a person in a lower position in the organization to dominate a superior, as when, for example, a male subordinate harasses a female supervisor (Rospenda, Richman, and Nawyn 1998). Thus, power at work and at home are often derived from the dominant society-wide ideologies and policies about gender, sexuality, race, and class.

Bullying is a good example of how cultural ideologies about women and minorities affect power in the workplace. *Bullying* refers to "*repeated* and *persistent negative* acts towards one or more *individual(s)*, which involve a *perceived power imbalance* and create a *hostile work environment*" (Salin 2003, pp. 1214–1215, italics in original). While supervisors, who have power because of their formal position, can and sometimes do bully subordinates, bullying can also occur between individuals who are formally equal in their work positions, but who differ in race, class, or gender. In other words, power imbalances between groups in the wider society can infiltrate the work setting. "Thus, for example, power differences associated with traditional gender roles and minority status may also affect bullying behavior, as it can be assumed that women and minorities are perceived to have less power and status" (Salin 2003, p. 1219). The differential status of individuals invites a greater probability of bullying. Employees who are women, lower-paid workers, or members of a minority group are more likely to be victims of bullying than their higher-status counterparts, as are temporary employees or those with little job security (Roscigno, Lopez, and Hodson 2009).

Conditions in the work environment, such as a poorly articulated organizational structure, a lack of accountability, and the absence of groups to protect the vulnerable also enhance the probability of bullying behavior (Roscigno, Lopez, and Hodson 2009). Power and bullying are likely to operate when serious competition exists and significant rewards are at stake. When a company is bought out or merges with another, it becomes apparent how dependent and how powerless employees are. It is often when the economic environment is changing or uncertain, when resources are limited or strained, or when the decision-making process is not fixed that many of the nonlegitimate forms of power cited above become most evident in an organization because battles over turf, position, and rewards become more prominent under these conditions. Battles for power in the workplace often bring racial, gender, and class ideologies and related discourses to the foreground.

Women and members of minority groups occupy positions of lower authority and greater dependence than White males. Individuals in these positions often complain about the lack of respect they receive (e.g., Johnson 2002). Minorities and women have less power than White men at work, in part because of less education and/or experience. But even if these deficiencies did not exist, women and minorities would still have difficulty gaining power because of racism and gender bias that could be used by White men to keep these groups out of power (Elliott and Smith 2004). Men not only are more likely to dominate positions of high authority, but also to screen potential colleagues so that individuals who are similar to them are admitted into those positions, while those who are dissimilar are screened out.

Central characteristics held by those in power become a basis for favorable evaluations, while opposite characteristics become a basis for unfavorable evaluations (DiTomaso, Post, and Parks-Yancy 2007). Individuals are more attracted to persons who are like themselves, and are, therefore, more likely to interpret the behaviors of those individuals in a positive manner while interpreting the behavior of dissimilar others in a more negative manner: People who are like us are successful because they work hard and are talented, whereas people who are not like us are successful because they are lucky or were given a break (Stainback, Tomaskovic-Devey, and Skaggs 2010). Because the duties of executive positions tend to be central to organizations, yet broad in scope, it is important to those already at the top that reliable (i.e., similar) persons be brought in when vacancies occur. The result is "homosocial reproduction" in which White men in high-level positions recruit other men similar to themselves (Kanter 1977a).

To move up the authority ladder, one needs a "cognitive map" of the social network at the organization and may have to be a "team player" as well. To be such a player, one has to appear to be similar to colleagues, subscribe to the dominant approach or ideology of the organization, and spend a lot of time at the office. All these qualities make other managers or executives feel comfortable with you (Jackall 1988). It is when people step out of line, violate traditional cultural expectations, or are believed to have a distinct outlook or lifestyle that difficulties arise for them. In their study of sexual harassment, for example, Uggen and Blackstone (2004) found that "women in supervisory positions and men who do more housework are likely to experience the behavioral harassment syndrome" (p. 83).

If a "token" or dissimilar person such as a woman or working-class or minority person does reach a high level in an organization, she or he will be under intense pressure to perform and conform to racial, class, or gender expectations. Research indicates that women, for example, face greater pressure and discrimination as they gain experience and move up the corporate ladder (Kanter 1977b; Carli 1999; Elliott and Smith 2004; Uggen and Blackstone 2004). In part, this is because they are viewed as outsiders to the males who dominate the positions, and because they are expected to conform to mainstream gender expectations about women at the same time that they are also expected to excel at their jobs. This often produces such a high degree of pressure that some women resign their positions. "A woman who

behaves in a competent and assertive manner is often less influential, particularly with men, because she lacks legitimacy. At the same time, when a woman does not exhibit exceptional ability, her competence is doubted by both genders and she is less able to influence women. These findings underscore the dilemma that women face in the workplace" (Carli 1999, p. 95).

Such pressure and the power used with it can be justified by gender, class, or racial ideologies, or by one's perception of the "target" of the pressure. Bruins (1999) theorizes that "the stronger the means of influence used by the agent [of power], the more the agent [e.g., White male] will tend toward making an internal attribution for the target's [e.g., minority, woman] compliance, in turn leading to a more negative evaluation of the target and a tendency to increase the social distance toward the target" (p. 10). In other words, claims about the basic inferiority or inadequacy of the target will be used as justifications as more force or power is exercised over the subordinate.

Durr and Wingfield's research (2011) on Black women professionals reveals the additional emotional labor that they must perform in the workplace to conform to racialized and gendered expectations. To combat the controlling ideologies and stereotypes as "angry Black women," they continually silence themselves and keep from speaking their minds, even though this behavior may limit their chances for promotion. "So, as they learn the verbal and body language of bureaucracy, they must negate values and styles of communication developed as a survival skill in their community" (p. 565). The result is that women needed to engage in more emotional labor to appear successful to colleagues.

The success or power one has at work affects power relationships at home. Traditionally, husbands' power at home has been tied to their ability to support their families through their occupations. Their work in the public sphere has generally meant, especially in past generations, that their wives' efforts were restricted to the private sphere of family. The balance of power and dependence has shifted as more women have entered the labor force and earn their own salaries. However, this does not always mean that their increased independence is accepted at home, because it violates traditional beliefs about appropriate gender roles. A study of U.S.-born Mexican Americans found that the more women earned outside the family and participated in decision making at home, the more spousal abuse they reported (Harris, Firestone, and Vega 2005).

POWER INEQUALITY IN A GLOBAL AND GLOBALIZING CONTEXT

We have noted above that power maneuvers and differences are most likely to become salient when economic conditions are in a state of flux, when one's employment and income are at stake. An unpredictable economy produces a sense of competition among its workers, workers who will use the tools at their disposal to maintain or attain scarce positions. Among these tools are cultural ideologies and policies that privilege some groups over others. Increasingly, the operation of national economies has become less predictable because of their involvement in the worldwide network of economies and states.

Over the last few decades, there has been extensive discussion about the structure of the world economic system, the shifting relationships among nations, and the effects of globalization on the relative power of nations in the international order. In broad terms, the world system is often described as consisting of interdependent core, semiperipheral, and peripheral countries. Each of these types tends to perform particular functions in the world system. Core nations are those that are wealthy, industrialized, and technologically advanced. They hold a privileged position in the world economic system because they possess an inordinate amount of the world's capital and also have strong, stable political systems. Peripheral nations, on the other hand, are described as poor, technologically deficient, generally "underdeveloped," and lacking in political stability. Semiperipheral countries occupy an intermediate position in the system. Because the poor and working classes in peripheral nations are primarily racial minorities and women, economic, political, and immigration relationships with core nations take on racial and gender overtones.

The global power of a nation partly depends upon the "**soft power**" it wields among its international neighbors. In contrast to the hard forms of power such as military or economic, a country's soft power is based upon the respect accorded its culture, values, and ideals by other nations. Historically, a significant source of the international influence of the U.S. has been due to its soft power.

For all of the twentieth century, the West, particularly the United States, dominated international politics and economics. In recent years, however, some parts of Asia, especially China, have strengthened their international economic position. In the next decade or two, China's productivity is expected to increase threefold. Its surging economic power and large population have also meant greater political leverage in the world system. With increasing openness in trade and foreign investment across the globe, China's progress suggests that a significant realignment in international power arrangements may be taking place.

Also part of the world's "new geography of power" are (a) transnational corporations that are beyond the full control of any given nation, (b) transnational legal institutions that regulate international economic relationships, and (c) the growth of electronic technology, which makes economic transactions possible independent of space. While these three developments may appear to reduce somewhat the regulatory power of sovereign states, they also mean that the state's role in the world political economy is changing (Sassen 2000). Evidence indicates that between 1960 and 2000, core nations have strengthened their global power position by increasing their ties to international nongovernmental organizations and creating new ones (Beckfield 2003).

Historically, the economic power and political power of a nation have been intertwined. International economic expansion generally leads to more political power, power which is then used to maintain economic dominance. But today, capital and national governments are bases of international political power that are more autonomous than in the past. As Hanagan puts it, "[i]n an age when capital can electronically flee continents in nanoseconds, can national states resist transnational markets? Despite the claims of distinguished scholars, most nations simply cannot" (2000, p. 83). The developments mentioned above also have implications for the sources, nature, and extent of immigration to be discussed in subsequent chapters, and the structure of economic inequality within nations.

Wider political input within a society promotes less economic inequality. The greater the percentage of individuals who vote and the more wages are determined on a national basis, the lower is earnings inequality. A survey of

84 studies found that democracy indirectly promotes economic growth by fostering increases in human capital, economic freedom, and political stability (Doucouliagos and Ulubaşoğlu 2008). Increased governmental spending on social programs such as education and health care also encourages greater income equality (Rudra 2004). Greater participation by women in national legislatures, in turn, increases the probability for higher spending in these areas (Bolzendahl and Brooks 2007). Taken together, the results of these studies strongly suggest that policies reached democratically are most likely to benefit all citizens rather than just a privileged segment. This again alerts us to the significance of the democracy–equality connection.

Summary

We began this chapter with a brief discussion on the importance and difficulty of conceptualizing power. We then moved to an analysis of pluralist, power-elite, and ruling-class views of the national power structure, and the data that bear on the validity of each.

There are clear relationships between socioeconomic position and voting, holding political office, and other forms of political participation. Those closer to the bottom of the class hierarchy are less likely than those in the middle and upper classes to vote, be elected to office, and be represented in powerful lobbying groups. Research indicates that those from higher socioeconomic levels, especially the upper class, are disproportionately represented in elite positions in a variety of institutional spheres. The tie between economic and political power, however, is more than just individual in nature; it is also structural. The fates of government and economy are linked—each needs the other. Consequently, a government in a society with a capitalist economy, for example, must support capitalism because its revenue and stability heavily depend on the smooth operation of that economy.

In addition to power differences at the national level, power inequality also exists in the workplace. Power has a variety of immediate sources within organizations but can also be rooted in broader cultural ideologies surrounding race, class, and/or gender. To some extent, power differentials are based in features of organizations themselves, including their traditions, the clarity and strength of their structure, and the presence or absence of positions to enforce accountability. They are also determined and maintained by broader ideologies and stereotypes regarding the characteristics of groups distinguished by race, sex, and social class.

Worldwide power differentials also exist between nations, as countries occupy different positions in the world's economic and political system. Throughout most of the twentieth century, the United States was a dominant political player. Transnational corporations and international nongovernmental organizations are part of a broader network that in many cases binds nations together but at the same time can benefit some more than others. Finally, the political structure within nations affects the degree of social inequality within them. Generally democratic characteristics lend themselves to less inequality.

Critical Thinking

1. Are information technology and the Internet creating new bases for power and domination? Is it the corporate rich who will claim these bases, or are new, powerful groups being created by these technological developments? Discuss your answer.
2. As globalization continues to open up nations to each other, do you think the soft power of a nation, that is, the respect for its culture, ideals, and values, will increasingly affect power arrangements between nations?
3. If the working and lower classes are underrepresented among those who vote, hold office, donate large sums of money to elections, and have effective lobbying power, how can we ensure representative or democratic government in the United States?
4. What features would you introduce into the design of an organization so that the chances of bullying and inappropriate use of power would be minimized?

Web Connections

The Center for Responsive Politics lists the amount of money spent on federal elections, along with the amounts given by major individual and organizational donors. The center also gives information on the political affiliations of these donors. Visit www.opensecrets.org. Another source, the Joint Center for Political and Economic Studies, presents summary information on Black elected officials at every level of government. Its information also allows you to compare rates for Black men and women as well as differences in rates between states. Where does your state stand on electing Blacks to office? Visit www.jointcenter.org.

Film Suggestions

Fourteen Women (2007). Explores the history of women in the Senate.

Legalize Democracy (2014). Critiques the current state of democracy in the U.S.

CHAPTER 6

Sex and Gender Inequality

*A woman can hardly ever choose . . . she is dependent
on what happens to her.*

GEORGE ELIOT (1819–1880)

Race and sex are ascribed statuses in the sense that there is a physical component to each of them. These physical components are given particular meanings within the context of a culture's values and beliefs, and a society's economic and political arrangements. What is immediately significant about race and sex, therefore, is not the physical differences in themselves, but the fact that these characteristics are socially defined and have meanings attached to them. These interpretations often result in races and sexes being hierarchically arranged and differentially treated in society. Both race and sex are "categorical inequalities" (Ridgeway 2011), meaning that a person's place-ment in one category or another can affect their access to societal resources. These categories become rigid, such that even though the biological realities of sex are far more complex than the binary we generally assume (Ainsworth 2015), we are placed in one category or another, and that placement has lifelong implications for our material, social, and psychological well-being.

Despite this categorization, though, not all women and men are in the same social and economic positions. Because the United States is a multicultural, multiracial society, the status of any of us is complicated by our race, class, gender identity, or sexuality, and these statuses inter-sect, creating a complex matrix of relationships and inequalities. Thus the position of a woman as well as the expectations of and interpretations associated with being a woman often depend on whether she is a member of a particular minority group or class.

In Chapter 8, we will pursue this matrix further with an analysis of racial inequality and demonstrate how race, gender, and economic inequality are intertwined. In this chapter, we will be surveying the forms and extent of gender inequality, as well as explanations for it. Though certainly, as we will see, our definitions of masculinity have led to inequalities for some men, our social system has primarily privileged men over women. As such, we begin with a brief overview of the historical condition of women in U.S. society.

THE STATUS OF WOMEN IN THE EARLY UNITED STATES

What has it meant to be a woman in the United States? Even though the three of us grew up in different decades, when each of us were children in the 1940s, 1960s, and 1970s, our parents had traditional arrangements—our mothers were primarily homemakers and our fathers "brought home the bacon." At various points in their lives, however, generally before and after having young children at home, our mothers did work for pay outside of the home. Throughout our nation's history, women have contributed to the economy while still maintaining a family.

In our own agricultural, preindustrial colonial society, women were directly involved in a variety of ways in production. On the one hand, their work contributed significantly to the prosperity of the society, but on the other hand, the nature of the labor was more often than not based on gender (Blau 1978; Marshall and Paulin 1987; Padavic and Reskin 2002). The cultural norms of that time, as well as for the periods that followed, dictated that first and foremost women should be good wives and mothers; but, in fact, women were involved in the economy and often had difficult lives. They were involved in raising stock, weaving, gardening, and even running businesses. While some women took over for their deceased or disabled husbands, most of the unmarried and widowed women went on the market as hired domestic workers (Marshall and Paulin 1987). Women in slavery were expected to work alongside men in fields and factories, with a much less distinct sexual division of labor (Padavic and Reskin 2002).

Although there is some debate about the actual diversity of employment undertaken by women during this period, they made valuable contributions to local economies, but were deprived of many of the political-legal, economic, and personal rights accorded men. They were attached to their families in a literal way, dependent on and subservient to their husbands or, in the case of slavery, to their owners (Collins 1998). A woman's identity was defined by her relationship to her husband and children. "The husband had the right to chastise his wife physically, and he had exclusive rights to any property she might have owned as a single woman, to her dower, and to any wages and property that might come to her while she was his wife. In short, like slave or servant women, married women whether rich or poor were legal non-entities" (Foner 1979, p. 11). Thus, the idealized life of the female as someone removed from the harsh realities of economic life was strongly inconsistent with the actual circumstances of her life. Of course even this ideal was never imagined for women of color, as this image of the protected "angel in the house" closely intersected with ideologies of race, class, and nation (Collins 1998).

Through their economic activities, women contributed to the development of the first significant *industrial* organizations in the United States. The first textile factories, built around 1800 in Rhode Island and Massachusetts, recruited unmarried women from the farms of New England. Despite the promises of a proper place to work, conditions at these early factories left much to be desired. Even at Lowell Corporation in Massachusetts, among the most famous early textile mills, women worked an average of 13 hours a day, 73 hours a week, including 8 hours on Saturday (Kessler-Harris 2003). Working conditions were stifling. Windows in the plant were nailed shut, and the air was periodically sprayed with water to keep it humid enough so that the cotton threads would not break (Eisler 1977). The Lowell Corporation paid women mill workers $1.85 to $3.00 per week, depending on their abilities, from which $1.25 was deducted for board. Female workers were paid only half of what men were paid, even though they made up approximately 75 percent of the workers at Lowell (Eisler 1977; Marshall and Paulin 1987).

Jobs in these early plants were also gender segregated. Men held all supervisory positions as well as jobs in the mill yard, watch force, and repair shop; women were restricted to particular jobs operating equipment such as the looms and dressing machines. The immediate reasons given for this segregation concerned differences in the skills developed and monopolized by men and women over the years, perceived physical strength and

Photo 6.1 Workers at the Lowell Textile Mill, circa 1870.

Center for Lowell History, University of Massachusetts Lowell Libraries.

dangers associated with various jobs, and the general cultural values prescribing particular roles for men and women (Dublin 1979). Men also were concerned about the entrance of women into the labor market because they felt that it would have a depressing effect on their wages. They fought to keep women out of the craft unions that later developed. Women held strikes in the 1830s and 1840s to protest reductions in wages, speedups in work pace, and increases in working hours (Dublin 1979).

Between the end of the Civil War and 1900, the percentage of females in the workforce increased (Hooks 1947, p. 34). In 1900, just over 20 percent (5 million) of all U.S. women 15 years of age and older were employed as breadwinners, but only 15 percent of White, native-born females

were, compared to 43 percent of Black females and 25 percent of White females with at least one foreign-born parent (U.S. Department of Commerce and Labor 1911, p. 262). Many young women 10–15 years of age also worked outside the home. In 1900, almost 6 percent of White, native-born females did so, compared to over 30 percent of non-White females 10–15 years old.

At the turn of the twentieth century, women made up a disproportionate number of workers in several occupations. For example, in 1900, they constituted 80–90 percent of all boarding and lodging housekeepers, servants, waiters, and paper box makers and over 90 percent of all housekeepers and stewards, nurses and midwives, dress makers, milliners, and seamstresses. Men, on the other hand, dominated agricultural, common labor, bookkeeping, clerk/copyist, watch- and shoemaker, printer, dye works, and photography positions (U.S. Census Office 1903; Plate 90). Perhaps surprisingly, women comprised over 70 percent of the teachers and professors in colleges and over 50 percent of teachers of music, and men made up the majority of artists and teachers of art (Plate 90). Black females, however, were more likely to be wage earners than either native- or foreign-born White females. Those who were "native White of native parents" dominated the higher status professions, with over 50 percent of college teachers and clergy and about 75 percent of lawyers and physicians coming from this group. In contrast, they made up less than 30 percent of those in servant, tailoring, laundering, and textile mill working positions (Plate 88).

GENDER AND CONTEMPORARY LABOR FORCE PARTICIPATION RATES

While there is a strong and continuing history of women working for pay outside the home, the labor force participation of both women and men is tied to gendered and racialized cultural norms about who can do what kind of work, social policy changes, and overall changes in the structure of our economy (see Figure 6.1). As discussed in Chapter 2, our economy is increasingly characterized by service work rather than manufacturing, part-time work, frequent job changes and temporary contracts, flexibility in hours, and team-based and project-based work (Williams 2013). These structural changes affect women differently depending on their education, age, citizenship status, and race.

Over the last several decades, the percentage of employed women in the civilian labor force has increased dramatically, while the percentage of men 16 years of age and older employed in the labor force has consistently declined. In 1973, for example, 42 percent of women 16 years of age and older were employed, compared to 57 percent in 2014. In contrast, the employment of men slid from 76 percent in 1973 to 69 percent in 2014 (U.S. Bureau of Labor Statistics 2014). In recent years, however, the labor force participation of women in the United States has lagged behind that of most other industrialized countries, due in part to weaker social policies in the United States that support women's labor participation (Blau and Kahn 2013).

In 2014, Asian, Black, Hispanic, and White women participated in the labor force at roughly equal rates, generally between 56 and 60 percent

(U.S. Bureau of Labor Statistics 2014). While educational and other **human capital** factors help account for slight differences between some groups, other elements such as cohort and cultural differences in the meaning of marriage as well as legal status also appear to be important, especially as immigration creates a more diverse population (Flippen 2014). For example, immigrant Latina women experience multiple impediments to work, including their position as low-skilled workers, belonging to a largely undocumented population, language barriers, gender, and pronounced work-family conflict (Flippen 2014).

Among the most important factors behind the increased participation of women in the labor force are the shift toward a service and information-based economy, increased possibilities for flexibility in work scheduling, lower marital stability, higher educational attainment, and a greater need for dual-earner families (Blau and Kahn 2013). The fastest growing employment sectors have been in areas dominated by women, such as health care and retail. While this provides opportunities for women, these jobs tend to be lower wage

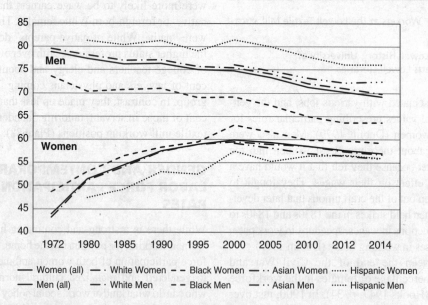

FIGURE 6.1 Labor Force Participation by Sex and Race, 1972–2014

Source: U.S. Bureau of Labor Statistics, Current Population Survey, 2014 annual averages, http://www.bls.gov/cps/cpsaat03.htm.

and part-time. For both men and women the number of hours worked declined during the recession of 2008, with men's hours declining at a faster rate. In 2014, 25.8 percent of women workers were part-time, compared to 12.7 percent of men; still, 66.1 percent of all part-time workers were women. These rates vary by race and ethnicity, however. While 26.9 percent of White women worked part-time in 2014, only 20.8 percent of Black women did so (U.S. Bureau of Labor Statistics 2014). While some of the decision to work part-time is due to issues involving work–family balance, more women than men cite economic reasons such as the inability to find full-time work for their choice to work part-time (U.S. Bureau of Labor Statistics 2014). And while many jobs offer greater flexibility in hours, this flexibility is more easily negotiated for those at the top of the pay scale than at the bottom (Gerstel and Clawson 2014).

In working- and lower-class families, the income brought into households by women is a necessity, and makes a major difference in the economic lives of families. In middle-class families, a college-educated wife is likely to work because her education allows her to receive a good salary. Forgoing the opportunity for employment by staying home would cost her family those earnings, so there is an incentive to work outside the home. This has been a primary reason why well-educated women enter the labor force (England 2010). One ironic consequence of highly educated spouses entering the labor force, however, is that the greater parity with her husband's earnings increases the earnings inequality between married-couple families (Schwartz 2010).

On average in 2012, married women accounted for 37.3 percent of their families' incomes. In 2012, married women who worked full-time earned a median weekly salary of $751, significantly higher than that of women who were single, divorced, separated, or widowed. Both the proportion of income that wives contribute and the proportion of wives who earn more than their working husbands have increased in the last few decades. In 2013, for example, over 29 percent of all working wives earned more than their working husbands (U.S. Bureau of Labor Statistics 2015c).

But the impact of wives' incomes on family economic status is not equally distributed across the income hierarchy. Rather, the contributions of wives are especially noticeable among lower-income families. Without their incomes, family incomes in the bottom 60 percent would suffer significantly. Wives' incomes make much less of an impact in families with the highest incomes. This suggests that were it not for wives' earnings in middle- and lower-income families, the degree of income inequality between families would be much higher than it is (Mishel, Bernstein, and Shierholz 2009).

The increase in hours worked by married women since the late 1970s, in turn, has intensified the struggle to balance home and work responsibilities. The related stresses are greater for women because of traditional gender-role expectations of women's responsibilities to families. Most employed married men and women agree that it is women who end up being most responsible for cooking, cleaning, shopping, and child care. If a child is ill, it is overwhelmingly employed mothers rather than fathers who are most likely to miss work because of it—in one survey, while 74 percent of employed mothers reported staying home with a sick child, only 40 percent of fathers did so. This is despite the fact that men are far more likely to have access to paid sick days (Smith and Schaefer 2012). After the birth of a child, when both parents are working full-time, the mother increases her labor at home by 2 hours a day, while the father increases his by only 40 minutes (Yavorsky, Kamp Dush, and Schoppe-Sullivan 2015). In the case of dual-career professional families, when the husband works increasingly longer hours (Cha and Weeden 2014), the chances of his wife quitting her job increase as well. In the reverse situation, however, the probability that the husband will quit his job does not go up. This increases the likelihood that the traditional gender roles of men at work and women at home will be reinforced (Cha 2010).

BALANCING WORK AND HOME

Women's contribution to housework does decrease a bit as they earn more, and the housework done by husbands' increases. Ironically, at the point where wives begin to earn more than their husbands, the latter also reduce their housework, suggesting an attempt by husbands to counter their income dependency on their wives by reinforcing traditional gender roles at home (Bittman et al. 2003; Evertsson and Nermo 2004). But the tendency for men to contribute more to household tasks when they earn less than their spouses appears to be related to how important a society considers the traditional masculine tasks of employment and high earnings. In cultures that rank paid work and high earnings as highly important in life, men who earn less than their spouses contribute less to household chores than comparable men in other societies. Men in the latter societies who are not breadwinners contribute significantly more to household work than do male breadwinners in those societies (Thébaud 2010). While women's time spent doing housework decreased greatly between 1965 and 2010 and men's increased greatly, on average wives do 1.7 times the housework of men, and married mothers do 1.9 times the housework of married fathers (Bianchi et al. 2012).

Due to their traditional role as caregivers, "women in the middle" are often expected not only to take care of their children but also an elderly parent as well. Opting for contingency or part-time employment, having fewer children, and choosing a nonstandard work schedule are some of the ways women juggle home and work responsibilities (Kelly et al. 2014). More often than not, it is mothers who make the compromise at work and who feel that they are not doing as well as they could in either the family or work spheres. Under these conditions, neither family life nor work is fully satisfying (Sandberg et al. 2013). This may be especially true for women who work in lower-status service jobs rather than for high-ranking professional women, whose businesses are more likely to make accommodations for their motherhood (Kantor 2006). Even the anticipation of parenting negatively affects the career aspirations of some women, as women are more likely to downgrade their career aspirations as they reflect on balancing work and family (Bass 2015). Until a better integration of home

and work conditions is reached, stress will remain high for the majority of employed mothers.

GENDER SEGREGATION IN OCCUPATIONS

Gender inequities involved in balancing home and employment comprise just one area of gender-based inequalities. Inequalities also extend to the kind of work that women and men perform. To identify occupational inequalities between women and men in their work experiences, however, it is important to examine how they are distributed (1) across broad occupational categories, (2) among detailed occupations, and (3) among specific occupations within specific organizational contexts. At each of these levels, from the broad to the very specific, there is evidence of gender segregation and inequality. This is despite the apparent liberalizing of attitudes about women's roles that attended women's increased entrance into the labor market over the last 40 years and the increasingly globalized workforce (Gauchat, Kelly, and Wallace 2012).

In spite of the increase in labor-force participation by women, occupational distinctions between the sexes remain within *broad occupational* groupings. Analysis of broad occupational categories suggests some recent decline in overall gender segregation, but declines in occupational gender segregation in private firms were more significant between the late 1960s and mid-1980s than they were later (Hegewisch and Liepmann 2013). Changes in the economy's industrial composition were a major reason for the decline, but the decrease in some traditionally male occupations such as agriculture, unskilled labor, and self-employment also contributed to those declines (Blau, Brummund, and Liu 2013). Declines in gender segregation were not uniform across the economy. The degree of gender segregation in firms varies, with larger companies in more concentrated industries having less gender segregation (Stainback and Tomaskovic-Devey 2012). The movement of women into management positions has been especially evident in the growing service sector (Stainback and Tomaskovic-Devey 2012).

Table 6.1 presents current information on the distribution of men and women over broad occupational categories. In general, women tend to be concentrated in white-collar and service occupations, while men are more spread out throughout the occupational spectrum. But among women, there are also significant variations. While White women are more likely than Black women to be managers or professionals, Black and Hispanic women are more likely to be found in service and blue-collar production positions.

The gendered nature of occupations extends to the intersection of gender and sexuality. A recent student of gay and lesbian workers found that gay men are more likely to be found in female-majority occupations, and lesbian women are more likely to work in male occupations (Tilcsik, Anteby, and Knight 2015). Even here, though, gender disparities exist. In the highly feminized occupation of fashion design, gay male designers are far more successful and valued than women designers, suggesting a sort of "glass runway" effect (Stokes 2015).

Although Table 6.1 indicates some gender differences in occupation, as we examine more *detailed occupational* categories, the nature and extent of occupational segregation become clearer. A decline in occupational segregation has occurred in broad occupational categories, largely because of shifts in technology and organizational structures. But despite these general improvements, women still are found disproportionately in particular kinds of occupations. For example, women have increasingly moved into the ranks of managerial and professional occupations, but they tend to be concentrated among gender-typed occupations, such as teaching and nursing, and hold only a small percentage of positions as computer specialists, scientists, and engineers. Similarly, a man and a woman may both be in sales, but the woman is much more likely to be in clothing sales, while the man is involved in the selling of stocks and bonds. Craft occupations (carpentry, electrical contracting) and occupations that produce goods rather than services are another group of occupations in which women continue to be significantly underrepresented (Cartwright, Edwards, and Wang

TABLE 6.1 Broad Occupational Distribution of Employed Persons 16 Years and Over, by Occupation and Sex: 2014

Occupation	Men	Women
Management, professional, and related	35%	42%
Service	14%	21%
Office and administrative support	6%	19%
Natural resources, construction, and maintenance	17%	1%
Production, transportation, and moving	18%	5.5%

Source: U.S. Bureau of Labor Statistics, 2015c.

2011). Initially moving into traditionally male occupations is easier than sustaining a growth in the percentage of women in those occupations. There appears to be resistance when the number of women grows too high (Krymkowski and Mintz 2008).

Despite small movement toward gender desegregation, many aspects of current occupational profiles are quite similar to those that existed in earlier years. In 1940, almost all of the servants, stenographers/secretaries, housekeepers, and nurses were women, and they comprised more than half of the teachers, apparel and accessories operators, waitresses, and bookkeepers. As far back as 1870, women dominated in servant, clothing, certain kinds of teaching, and nursing occupations (Hooks 1947, p. 52).

Table 6.2 suggests that this gender-typing has continued. As one glances over the lists, it is easy to see that the positions in which women dominate tend to be those that demand "feminine" or "motherly" characteristics. Being able to work directly with people and to take care of others are qualities that are required in these occupations. In contrast, the positions held mostly by men are characterized by a different set of qualities; they require manual labor or physical attributes, often contain an element of danger, involve work with a product rather than a person, and demand technical

TABLE 6.2 Broad Sample of Occupations in Which Women Represent at Least 90 Percent or Less Than 5 Percent of Employed Labor Force: 2014

Over 90%	Under 5%
Speech-language pathologists	Crane and tower operators
Preschool/kindergarten teachers	Roofers
Medical transcriptionists	Brickmasons
Dental assistants	Locomotive engineers
Child care workers	Highway maintenance workers
Hairdressers/hairstylists/cosmetologists	Pipelayers/plumbers/pipefitters
Secretaries and administrative assistants	Carpenters
Medical assistants	Boiler operators
Dietitians and nutritionists	Carpet, floor, and tile installers
Occupational therapists	Electricians
Nurse practitioners	Construction laborers
Receptionists and information clerks	Aircraft mechanics
Teacher assistants	Pest control workers
Medical records	Natural resources occupations

Source: U.S. Bureau of Labor Statistics, *Employment and Earnings,* January 2015, Table 11, at http://www.bls.gov/opub/ee.

or scientific skill. In essence, these two sets of occupations are distinguished by their "feminine" or "masculine" character. Why does this gender-typing continue? It is due to a combination of the devaluing of traditionally "female" positions and the continued belief that men and women have different qualities by nature and are, therefore, meant for different jobs. Both of these notions have stalled the movement of women into most "male" blue-collar occupations and the movement of men into "female" occupations (England 2010).

Many of the occupations dominated by women also do not have the protections afforded other positions. It was not until 2011, for example, that household workers were recognized by the International Labor Organization as being worthy of the same labor protections offered other workers (Boris and Fish 2014). Nannies and maids often suffer long hours, low pay, few legal protections, and physical harassment, and often these nannies or domestic workers are recent immigrants who fear deportation and thus are dependent on their employers for fair treatment (Parreñas 2015).

When we move on to examine particular occupations *within specific organizational contexts* in the private economy, occupational segregation is again magnified. Not only are women found among fewer occupations than men, but within the same occupation they are employed in different kinds of organizations and economic sectors, tend to have less authority and have different job titles, and make less money in their jobs than men do. While record numbers of women are entering the medical professions, for example, women are still far less likely to enter the more prestigious fields of surgery, anesthesiology, radiology, and pathology (Davis and Allison 2013). Just breaking into the authority hierarchy, especially at the lower ranks of management, appears to be very difficult for women regardless of their personal qualifications, resulting in significant gender differences in authority among employees (Baxter and Wright 2000). Currently only 4.4 percent of CEOs of the Fortune 500 are women, and fewer than 20 percent of seats on boards of directors are held by women (Catalyst 2015).

Though an increasing number of women have moved into professions that promise high levels of rewards, such as the legal profession, they still do not fare as well as men. The chances of promotion for women already employed in a corporate law firm are lower near the top of the organization (Gorman and Kmec 2009). A recent study of almost 800 lawyers found that even when background, training, experience, seniority, preferences, and personal values are taken into account, female lawyers are less likely than men to practice or become partners in lucrative firms. Women who choose to work fewer hours or leave a high-powered legal firm lower their chances of becoming highly paid partners. This is at least in part due to the fact that difficulties in balancing work and family demands have a negative effect for women (but not for men) on the probability that they will become partners (Hull and Nelson 2000). Women are more likely to work in public law rather than in private law firms, and those who work in firms dominated by men, such as elite firms, still suffer lower salaries (Dinovitzer and Hagan 2014).

Similarly, a study of nearly 700 MBA recipients demonstrated that gender stereotypes about women's commitment to work result in both fewer internal rewards and fewer opportunities for women to move up in their profession by changing firms (Merluzzi and Dobrev 2015). Some research even suggests that higher standards and expectations are placed on women in jobs, even when men and women are in the same positions (Catalyst 2007; Gorman and Kmec 2009).

Not only is it difficult for women to obtain positions of authority, which are usually dominated by men, but if they do get such a position, a variety of gender-related pressures make it hard for them to retain or want to stay in the position. The result is that women often move on to other less-prestigious, less-authoritative, and consequently, lower-earning positions in smaller firms. A result is continued gender segregation in occupations. Roth's study (2004b) of securities positions on Wall Street bears out the problems that women face in a male-dominated profession. These women were much more likely than men to leave their positions because of family pressures or outright discrimination. In performance ratings, women were not given the leeway that was allowed for men. Roth (2004a) also found that the belief that securities clients

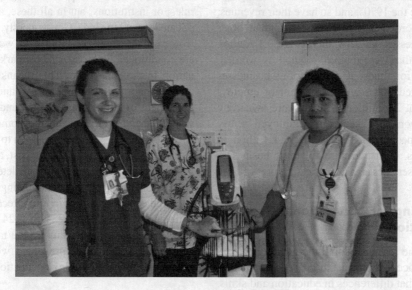

Photo 6.2 For salary and image reasons, men seldom seek out occupations that have been dominated by women. About 9 out of 10 individuals in nursing are women.

Photo by Brendan R. Hurst.

(who are primarily male) preferred to work with male employees further strengthened gender segregation in these occupations.

Women have been underrepresented in higher posts even in those institutions that have publicly indicated a concern for equality and fairness. In higher education, for example, women are more likely than men to be employed at less-prestigious institutions and at nonresearch universities. They are less likely to be found at the full-professor level or to be among the tenured faculty—in 2013, nearly 70 percent of full professors were male (National Center for Education Statistics 2015). Women are also much less likely to be found in the leadership positions of unions. Even in occupational areas where they dominate (e.g., elementary education and social work), they are not often found in the decision-making positions of principals or department heads. And, as Kanter's research (1977b) in corporations demonstrates, when women are put in unusual positions of authority, they are watched closely and under great pressure to perform because they are seen as "**tokens**."

Despite all the difficulties discussed above, or perhaps in part because of them, the number of businesses owned by women has increased significantly since the 1970s, and so have their revenues, growing more than 1.5 times faster than other small businesses. In 2014, there were 9.1 million businesses that were majority-owned by women, accounting for almost 30 percent of all businesses in the United States and 14 percent of employment. About 2.9 million of them were owned by minority women. These firms employed nearly 8 million people and had over $1.4 trillion in annual sales. Over two-thirds of these businesses were in the services area (American Express 2014).

Accounting for Occupational Gender Segregation

What are the reasons behind the gender segregation in the occupations just discussed? Some have suggested that differences in education and skills, experience, and career aspirations may account for women moving into particular kinds of jobs, but evidence suggests that individual factors such as these do not fully account for differences in

occupations and earnings between the sexes (e.g., Blau, Brummund, and Liu 2013; England 2010). Gender-role socialization appears to have affected choice of occupation (Cech 2013), but differences based on such socialization have declined in recent years. Those who argue that gender-role socialization is an important source of gender segregation also overestimate the incompatibility of home and employment responsibilities (Blau and Kahn 2013). Among mothers, valuing motherhood and achievement in work are positively related to each other (McQuillan et al. 2008).

One should keep in mind that the free choice of an occupation takes place within a gendered structure with particular characteristics. In a broad sense, employment is limited by shifts in the types of jobs on the market and by the supply of and demand for qualified workers. This context also includes cultural values into which both employers and employees have been socialized and a historical record, both of which encourage the employment of men and women into certain kinds of occupations. As Risman and Davis (2013) argue, "gender is deeply embedded as a basis for stratification not just in our personalities, our cultural rules, or institutions, but in all these, and in complicated ways" (p. 744). Consequently, the choices women make about jobs and their work at home are conditioned by broader labor-market discrimination in the first place. This means that labor-market opportunities affect the role and amount of time spent in home labor by men and women. If women spend more time in the home than men because of fewer opportunities open to them in the market, it seems questionable, at best, to argue that it is their free choice alone that determines the amount of time spent in accumulating the experience and education which in turn affect their occupational positions (Blau 1984, pp. 124–125).

The following are among the more prominent barriers that have prevented women from obtaining more well-paying occupations:

- Less access to training and apprenticeship programs
- Appointment to perceived gender-related tasks ("light" work)

- Nonbureaucratized, patrimonial relationships with males in authority positions
- Less access to information about job openings
- Less fully developed job and contact network
- Seniority systems that limit women
- Protective laws inhibiting women from pursuing certain positions and restricting the number of hours and time of day they could work
- Pressure on women to take on the bulk of family obligations
- Tendency for coworkers or clients to prefer employees of matching gender
- Stereotyping, discrimination, and the consequent crowding of women into certain kinds of positions
- Lack of internal mobility ladder for many so-called female occupations within organizations (i.e., dead-end or flat-career jobs; see Dencker 2008)
- Prevalence of informal recruitment practices

Several factors also appear to be at work that specifically limit the number of women in high-level supervisory or executive positions. First, the **social capital** of men and women is different. Because social relationships tend to be dominated by members of the same sex, women receive most of their information about job openings from other women. That is, since men dominate in top positions and tend to share information with other men, women do not have access to as much information as men about high-level positions (McDonald, Lin, and Ao 2009; Williams, Muller, and Kilanski 2012). Second, some organizations are more open to women because they have a "gender logic" that is supportive of qualities that have traditionally been associated with women, such as nurturing, providing personal attention, and so on (King and Cornwall 2007; Haveman and Beresford 2012). Other, less supportive organizations are imbued with logics that are more masculine in nature.

Third, the **human capital** of men and women differs, including educational attainment, job preferences, and work experience (Haveman and Beresford 2012). While overall women's educational experiences have equaled, and in recent years outpaced those of men, there remain differences in the types of degrees received by women. Women are still underrepresented in STEM fields and in fields requiring background in mathematics, areas increasingly important for those in management. For example, a recent study of MBAs indicated that women are less likely to major in finance, the field most represented by those in upper management. Women are also less likely to graduate with advanced degrees from the more prestigious institutions (Bertrand, Goldin, and Katz 2010). Job preferences of men and women are another element of human capital that explain inequalities. A recent study of college graduates found that individuals who saw themselves as more self-expressive, or caring, were more likely to enter fields dominated by women (Correll et al. 2014; Cech 2013). Finally, women continue to lag men in work experience, due to the range of experiences provided to them in the workplace and to gaps in their work histories due to motherhood. Women are often not given the broad range of work experiences provided to men, in part because managers question their commitment to the job (Hoobler, Lemmon, and Wayne 2014). Also, over the course of their career, women are likely to leave or be pushed out of career ladders demanding longer and longer hours, due to parenting pressures (Cha and Weeden 2014).

Finally, men are more likely than women to perceive support when in positions traditionally dominated by members of the opposite sex (Taylor 2010). Men who are in female-dominated positions like nursing or child care, for example, not only receive frequent support but also can ride a smooth "**glass escalator**" to higher positions in those fields. This is especially the case for White men (Wingfield 2009; Williams 2013). Each of the above elements are often affected by the race and class of the women involved, but all of these factors create conditions and mechanisms that make it difficult for women to assume positions of high authority.

Many of the barriers listed above occur at the job level within the contexts of work organizations.

It is, in part, within these concrete settings that gender inequality is reproduced. "All organizations have inequality regimes, defined as loosely interrelated practices, processes, actions, and meanings that result in and maintain class, gender, [sexuality] and racial inequalities within particular organizations" (Acker 2006, p. 443). Formally, these regimes cover a wide variety of interrelated areas including how tasks are organized, access to resources and benefits, promotion opportunities, authority structure, job ladders, and salary scales. Informally, they include the everyday comments, social arrangements, and interactions among employees. All of these may be gendered in ways that perpetuate inequality in jobs and occupations (Acker 2006).

Some factors do appear, however, to contribute to a decline in occupational gender segregation. Organizations that emphasize close camaraderie, a common identity, and limited choices among its members, such as the military

and military schools, reduce the probability of informal status systems arising and inequalities based on **ascriptive qualities** (Milner 2016). The development of new forms of work resulting from broad economic changes and white-collar service employment of an unspecialized nature also loosens the grip of gender segregation. Shakeups in the formal division of labor also appear to weaken traditional notions about appropriate roles for men and women. For example, reorganizing positions into work teams that cut across the usual job descriptions not only creates more public visibility for women and minorities, but undermines stereotyping of them, and opens up new work contacts. All of this can encourage the breakdown of gender segregation in occupations (Kalev 2009), though some argue that a greater reliance on teamwork encourages the development of homogenous work groups since both employees and managers tend to select people who are like one another to be group

Photo 6.3 An important source of power and mobility is the size and nature of a person's social network. Social capital can lead to job possibilities and promotions not only for oneself but for members of one's family as well. Being "in the know" has been a significant reason for the power and position of men in economic institutions, although women have increasingly strengthened their social networks in recent years.

© SpeedKingz/Shutterstock.

members (Williams, Muller, and Kilanski 2012). Greater formalization—that is, increased presence of written rules, tasks, procedures, and so on—has been linked to gender segregation, but also to the greater hiring of women. Research indicates that when organizations use formal, standardized procedures when recruiting rather than an informal network and word of mouth, they hire a greater proportion of women, including more for managerial positions (Szafran 1982; Reskin and McBrier 2000).

EARNINGS AND GENDER

As in occupational distribution, there are also significant earnings differences between men and women. In 1979, women earned only 63 percent as much as men. Despite a post-1970s decline in the wage gender gap, caused by a combination of reductions in men's wages and a slight rise in the median wages of women (Mishel, Bernstein, and Shierholz 2009), *weekly* earnings continue to differ between men and women, with median earnings for full-time working women in 2015 being about 81 percent those of men ($730 vs. $895). The differences exist across all major occupational groups (see Table 6.3), though the gap is greater among the higher paid occupations than among those that are lower paid (Davis 2015).

The gender differences in wages vary by race and ethnicity, with Black and Hispanic women who worked full-time earning 83 and 74 percent as much per week, respectively, as White women in 2014 (U.S. Bureau of Labor Statitics 2014). Increases in earnings among White women have been much higher in the last 20 years than those for minority women. Still the differences between men and women are greater among Whites than among either Blacks or Hispanics. In 2014, within the latter groups, women earned nearly 90 percent of what men earned, compared to 81 percent among Whites (U.S. Bureau of Labor Statistics 2014). Greater occupational specialization among Whites has been suggested as one possible reason for this difference (Greenman and Xie 2008).

The information given above is for *weekly* earnings. But we must keep in mind that weekly earnings are the result of *both* the number of hours worked and hourly wage rate. *Hourly* wage rate is often considered a more accurate gauge of earnings because it discounts the role played by hours worked, which is not the case when using weekly earnings as a measure. Just as in weekly earnings, however, women make lower hourly wages than men at every earnings and educational level. In 2013, median hourly wages for women were $12.20 versus $14 for men, with the greatest discrepancy found between White women and men

TABLE 6.3 Median Weekly Earnings of Full-Time Workers Age 16 and Older, by Occupational Category and Sex, Annual Averages: 2014

	Median Earnings		
Occupational Category	Men	Women	Ratio of Women's to Men's Earnings
Legal occupations	$1,765	$1,001	56.71%
Natural resources, construction, and maintenance	$764	$509	66.62%
Managerial and professional	$1,346	$981	72.88%
Production, transportation, moving	$689	$504	73.15%
Service occupations	$583	$461	79.07%
Sales and office	$766	$620	80.94%
Education	$1,141	$987	86.50%
Median earnings for all workers	$871	$719	82.55%

Source: U.S. Bureau of Labor statistics, 2015, Table 39, http://www.bls.gov/cps/cpsaat39.pdf.

($12.21 versus $14.24). Women do earn more than men in part-time work, earning in an average week $242 to men's $236 (U.S. Bureau of Labor Statistics 2014). Finally, the wage gap is greater for those in the 95th income percentile, 78.6 percent in 2014, than for those in the 10th percentile, 90.9 percent (McCann 2015).

How are differences in wages between men and women to be explained? Differences in human capital (experience, skills) may continue to account partly for the earnings gap. But differences in work effort or work interruptions, or attachment to labor force, which can take one away from the job, are not major variables in explaining gender earnings differences (Bielby and Bielby 1988). Research indicates that even when men and women work the same number of hours, and for the same tenure, pay gaps persist (Lips 2013). However, "interruptions" can be of many kinds. A study conducted recently in Indiana suggests that domestic work, especially child care, negatively affects women's earnings significantly more than men's. This is especially the case for women who are in non-working-class jobs. The gendered cultures of organizations that demand long hours and forbid family roles from intruding on work drive many women, particularly in the professions, out of their careers (Cahusac and Kanji 2014). Women appear to experience domestic and work pressures that men do not, and their earnings suffer as a result. Finally, women may downshift their career goals in anticipation of motherhood (Bass 2015).

One structural factor that is clearly important is the distribution among and concentration of men and women in occupational categories. Occupations that are culturally defined as appropriate for women and in which a high proportion of women work tend to have lower earnings attached to them regardless of who occupies them. Earnings for both men and women tend to be lower in those jobs that are dominated by women (Hegewisch and Liepmann 2013; Cohen and Huffman 2003; Cotter, Hermsen, and Vanneman 2003). For example, one of the fastest growing sectors of the economy is care work, or those jobs involving the care of others, such as child care,

home health care, or nursing. These jobs are overwhelmingly occupied by women, and are generally low wage (Dwyer 2013). These jobs frequently have shorter career ladders, which may further affect long-range earnings.

Within occupational categories, women are less likely to be in positions of authority and to be given distinct kinds of tasks—factors that also influence earnings (Blau and DeVaro 2007; Madden 2012). A recent study of U.S. companies suggested that most of the differences in compensation that existed between male and female executives were due not only to women being in smaller firms, but also to the fact that they were less likely than high-ranking male executives to be heads of their companies (Bertrand and Hallock 2001). In their study of variations in power at work, Elliott and Smith (2004) conclude that "there are strong findings to indicate that most superiors, regardless of their race and sex, tend to fill power positions they oversee with ascriptively similar others, . . . [and] because there are more white men at higher levels of workplace power than members of other groups, white men have greater opportunities to exercise this self-similar preference and, in the process reproduce their advantage over successive generations of employees" (p. 384). Until women reach higher-level positions in organizations, the inequalities are likely to continue.

Related to the occupational clustering of women and relegation to positions of lower authority are more subtle stereotypical beliefs about women that also lower their earnings. These include the perception that a woman's earnings are not as important to a family as those of a man, and that she is more committed to her family than to her job. Because salary and wage levels are based in part on subjective assessments of job performance, how bosses interpret worker behavior becomes an important factor in determining the earnings workers receive. The fact that salary and wage differentials between men and women persist even after differences in levels of education, college major, hours worked, family commitments, productivity, occupation, and related factors are taken into account, strongly suggests that subjective evaluations play a role in determining wage differentials (Dey and Hill 2007; Petersen, Snartland, and Milgrom 2007). The chances of a greater gender wage gap are higher when performance levels are either not clearly verifiable or open to interpretation, allowing biases to enter into the earnings equation (Gorman and Kmec 2009; Castilla and Benard 2010). This would suggest that having a greater proportion of women in high positions who evaluate work performance may result in a lower earnings gap between the genders. Indeed, this appears to be the case (Cohen and Huffman 2007).

Even women's perceptions of themselves may continue to affect the wage gap. Particularly when there are not clear rules on whether negotiation over salary is permitted or not, women are less likely then men to negotiate for a higher salary (Leibbrandt and List 2015). This behavior, in turn, may be related to their socialization into the traditional feminine gender role.

Finally, a slightly smaller percentage of employed women than employed men belong to unions, and union members consistently have had higher median earnings than nonunion workers. In 2014, 11.7 percent of men were unionized, compared to 10.5 percent of women. The median weekly earnings of full-time union workers were 21 percent higher than those of nonunion workers (U.S. Bureau of Labor Statistics 2014). Part of the reason for women's lower union membership rates relates to their lower percentage in occupations such as protective service and precision craft, where a significant proportion of employees are union members.

While the gender gap in pay remains, there has been a decline in its size in recent years. Two of the immediate factors that have increased annual earnings among women in working-class occupations are an increase in the number of married women who work and an increase in the number of hours worked by women. In contrast to women, however, the slower wage growth for men in working-class occupations since 2000 has been instigated in part by declines in the economic power of unions along with declines in and movement abroad of manufacturing and other jobs. Among women in higher positions, it has been a rise in their real hourly wages relative to men that explains most of their increases since 1979 (Mishel, Bernstein, and Allegretto 2007).

MICROINEQUITIES AND MICROAGGRESSIONS TOWARD WOMEN

Beyond the occupational and earnings differentials just discussed, there are other forms of inequalities experienced by women. Sexual harassment on the job is one of the areas that demonstrates this inequitable treatment. While forms of inequity relating to occupation and earnings have been in the public eye for years, microinequities between the genders permeate the everyday world that we take for granted. "**Microinequities** refer collectively to ways in which individuals are either *singled out*, or *overlooked, ignored,* or *otherwise discounted* on the basis of unchangeable characteristics such as sex, race, or age" (Sandler and Hall 1986, p. 3). These microinequities generally take the form of different kinds of language, treatment, or behavior exhibited toward women on a regular basis. A similar term used by many is **microaggressions**, or the "brief and commonplace daily verbal, behavioral, or environmental indignities, whether intentional or unintentional, which lie beneath visibility or consciousness and which communicate hostile, derogatory, or negative slights and insults toward targeted groups, persons, and/or systems" (Nadal et al. 2015, p. 147). Often microinequities and/or microaggressions are targeted at individuals based on the intersections of a number of identities, such as Muslim or African American women, or Latino men, or at individuals whose complex identities do not "fit" traditional gendered stereotypes. Thus Asian men are often targeted for being insufficiently masculine, Black women are seen as too assertive or angry and thus unfeminine, and Latina women are singled out in the workplace as not belonging (Nadal et al. 2014; Ridgeway and Kricheli-Katz 2013). In fact, a recent study demonstrated that minority women are far more likely to be harassed in the workplace than minority men or majority men or women, indicating a kind of "double jeopardy" of sexual and ethnic harassment (Berdahl and Moore 2006). This brief section merely points to some inequities and aggressions that appear in everyday language, communication, the media, and education.

As suggested, these inequities are often deeply rooted and seemingly unconscious. Growing up, we seldom sift through the reasons why we think the way we do. Even educated adults often find it difficult to identify these deep unseen inequities. All these experiences and events give evidence to our lack of conscious recognition of many everyday inequities.

Microinequities of a subtle sort permeate our culture. Sexism can sometimes be unnoticed and unintentional, as in instances when a person uses sexist language and does not know it. For example, the pronoun *she* is often used when speaking of occupations in which a majority of persons are women. Nurses, elementary school teachers, and the like are almost always referred to as *she*, whereas mechanics, doctors, and mathematicians are usually spoken of in terms of *he*. Choosing words that assume that only men and not women occupy a particular position (e.g., "chairman") is another example (Swim, Mallett, and Stangor 2004). While often unintentional, the use of such terms subtly reinforces gender stereotypes.

Even the styles of speaking and communication are often different between the genders, reflecting their social positions in society. For example, women's language tends to involve a greater use of fillers such as *um* or *you know*, conveying an image of uncertainty and insecurity (Laserna, Seih, and Pennebaker 2014). Women are also more likely to use "uptalk," or the practice of ending a sentence with an upward inflection or question, in their conversation. A recent study of contestants on the television show *Jeopardy* found young, White, female contestants were far more likely to use uptalk than men, and that those who did not engage in uptalk were more likely to win the game (Linneman 2013).

In a recent analysis of the representation of women in media, Collins (2011) also found gender stereotypes to be alive and well. Not only were women much less likely to be the leading characters in films, they were also more likely to be depicted in negative or sexualized manners, and to be shown in traditional feminine roles, such as homemakers. Images of women of color are frequently exoticized or hypersexualized (Nadal et al. 2015), such as representations of Black women in magazine ads wearing animal prints, or posing with large animals in a jungle motif. A study on microaggressions toward Muslim women (Nadal et al. 2012) recounts this scene from the *Office*, "in which Steve Carrell's character was traveling internationally for his business: He asked a female who walks into the office to say that she is from Abu Dhabi and he is like 'Pretend that you are from Abu Dhabi. I'm so ashamed of your naked face, I should cover you.' And he got his jacket and covered her face and said, 'Now you are sexy in your culture.'" In this instance, the sexuality of the Muslim women is seen as other and exotic. What is important about these media images of women's appropriate physical and psychological traits is that they help to lock women into traditional roles and reinforce their subservient position in society.

As in our earlier history, stereotypes and images have not kept pace with the reality of changes in women's social and economic lives. Though there has been great progress in access to a variety of roles and positions for women, toys remain more gendered than ever (see Nutshell 6.1). Toys for girls are in muted colors and focus on nurturing and involve less physicality, while toys for boys are presented in bolder colors and stress agency and physicality (Auster and Mansbach 2012; Sweet 2014).

Within schools, sex and gender biases remain significant. In primary and secondary schools, females are more likely than males to be ignored by their teachers and get less attention and encouragement in math and science. Though this has improved over the years, recent studies show that continued bias in assumptions about women's abilities in mathematics affect teachers' assessments of the abilities of female students (Riegle-Crumb and Humphries 2012). Textbooks continue to send hidden messages about women's

Photo 6.4   The toys children play with can reinforce limiting gender stereotypes.

© iStock.com/MattoMatteo.

NUTSHELL 6.1   Marketing Toys to Boys and Girls

The company Target made news in August of 2015 by announcing that they would no longer be separating toys and bedding into boys' and girls' sections. "We never want guests or their families to feel frustrated or limited by the way things are presented," Target's press release said. "Over the past year, guests have raised important questions about a handful of signs in our stores that offer product suggestions based on gender. In some cases, like apparel, where there are fit and sizing differences, it makes sense. In others, it may not" (Contrera 2015).

The marketing of toys based on gender is certainly not a new phenomenon, though given changes in gender roles, it is perhaps surprising that if anything the gender segregation of toys has increased (Sweet 2014). The gender-coding of toys was common from the 1920s through the 1960s, and began declining in the 1970s. Since the 1990s, however, gender-typing of toys has been on the increase (Sweet 2014; Auster and Mansbach 2012).

Marketers and toy producers signal to parents and children the appropriate toys for boys and girls in both direct and subtle ways. Not surprisingly, toys focused on war and physical action are marketed to boys, while toys centered on beauty and domesticity are marketed to girls. Even more subtle, the same toys are packaged differently

depending on whether the target is a boy or a girl. Girls' toys tend to be pastel-colored, whereas boys' toys use bolder colors such as reds or black. Based on research suggesting that girls are more likely to buy toys intended for boys than the other way around, toys that are purportedly "gender-neutral" are marketed in boys' colors, and more often with boys represented in the ads.

Why does it matter how toys are marketed? And in an age of increasing gender equity, other than the recent move by Target, why has gender-typing of toys persisted?

Sources: Contrera, Jessica. August 9, 2015. "Target Will Stop Separating Toys and Bedding into Girls' and Boys' Sections." *Washington Post.* Available at https://www.washingtonpost.com/news/arts-and-entertainment/wp/2015/08/09/target-will-stop-separating-toys-and-bedding-into-girls-and-boys-sections/; Sweet, Elizabeth. December 9, 2014. "Toys Are More Divided by Gender Now Than They Were 50 Years Ago." *Atlantic.* Available at http://www.theatlantic.com/business/archive/2014/12/toys-are-more-divided-by-gender-now-than-they-were-50-years-ago/383556/; Auster, Carol J., and Claire S. Mansbach. 2012. "The Gender Marketing of Toys: An Analysis of Color and Type of Toy on the Disney Store Website." *Sex Roles* 67 (7–8): 375–388. doi:10.1007/s11199-012-0177-8.

roles in society and their accomplishments. For example, Political Science textbooks tend to include very little discussion of women's political behavior, and relegate women to the chapters on civil rights (Cassese and Bos 2013). The contents of elementary school textbooks continue to portray men as competitive and aggressive while portraying women as characteristically warm, emotional, and nonconfrontational (Evans and Davies 2000). All of these treatments are part of the unofficial hidden curriculum of what schools teach their students.

Inequity problems can be found in colleges and universities. A glaring example of the sexual objectification of women among students took place in August 2015 at several universities as new students were welcomed to the community (New 2015). Students arriving at Old Dominion University were met with signs hanging from a fraternity university with phrases such as "Hope your baby girl is ready for a good time." A fraternity at Ohio State University placed a sign outside its door reading "Daughter Day Care." Such signs indicate to women that their role at college is to provide sex to men, and that they should be worried about their safety on campus.

Students also show bias against their instructors through the words they use in their course evaluations, the central mechanism for evaluating faculty for promotion and tenure. In this interactive display, a researcher demonstrates that students are more likely to use some words for women such as "bossy" or "disorganized," and men as "brilliant" or "knowledgeable" (http://benschmidt.org/profGender/). This assumption that men are more intelligent or knowledgeable is echoed in the distribution by gender in academic fields. While women have made great progress in achieving parity in most academic fields, women are less likely to be represented in fields seen as requiring greater innate ability, such as physics and math (Leslie et al. 2015).

A further indication that women's activities in education have not been taken as seriously as men's is evident in the history of women's athletics. Partly as a legislative reaction, Title IX was passed in 1972, which stated that no person can,

on the basis of sex, be denied access to, denied benefits of, or discriminated against in any education program that receives federal funding. While the law was not intended specifically for athletics, over the last three decades, a variety of lawsuits have been filed on behalf of female coaches alleging that they had been discriminated against because of their sex. These include complaints about unlawful termination, demotion in rank and pay, sexual orientation discrimination, punishment for whistle-blowing, and inequitable distribution of resources within athletic departments. Because of their predicament, female coaches often face a series of dilemmas out of which there is no satisfactory answer. For example, on the one hand, they are expected to produce winning seasons, but on the other, they are sometimes given inadequate resources to do so. In addition, female coaches may be taken advantage of if they exhibit behavior that is consistent with gender traditions, but also be punished if they act in a manner that is considered too masculine, that is, threatening to male colleagues or superiors (Buzuvis 2010).

These examples suggest the variety of problems that women face in U.S. society. Capodilupo et al. 2010 and Nadal et al. 2015 summarized the kinds of subtle gender discrimination that exist. Some are intentional and others are not, but generally they occur on an informal basis. Following are among the types they cited:

- Sexual objectification, including actions such as "cat-calls" or uninvited touching
- Treating women as second-class citizens by overlooking them for promotions or leadership, or treating them as invisible
- Assumptions of inferiority, where someone assumes that a woman cannot handle a task
- Denial of the reality of sexism, where a woman is accused of exaggerating claims of mistreatment
- Assumptions of traditional gender roles, such as when all women are assumed to be secretaries or assistants
- Use of sexist language

This list should serve as a reminder that sex discrimination can occur in several forms, not only in the formal institutional areas of occupation and earnings. The list also parallels the kinds of subtle discrimination that African Americans have experienced historically under paternalistic treatment of them as simpleminded children and tokens of their group.

GENERAL THEORIES OF SEX AND GENDER INEQUALITY

In addition to specific sources of gender inequality mentioned earlier, social scientists have proposed several general theories of gender inequality (i.e., inequality between males and females). Because of the broad range of theories available, our discussion will be limited to theories that are more sociological or anthropological in nature. Following a brief discussion of theories outlining the origins of gender inequality, we will divide the theories into three general categories: (1) cultural and interactional, (2) structural, and (3) intersectional. This set of categories does not, of course, exhaust all the types of theories of gender inequality that have been developed, nor are they mutually exclusive. The categories in the list overlap to some degree, but they also serve to separate theories whose foci and themes differ from each other.

Theories on the Origins of Gender Inequality

There have been many efforts to explain the origins of gender inequality and male dominance, many rooted in biology. Biological explanations of gender inequality suggest that basic genetic, hormonal, or physical differences determine gender inequality. These are, however, inadequate for several reasons. First, a close examination of the differences between males and females shows that on most measures the differences *within* categories is greater than the difference *between* categories (Epstein 1988). Thus, with many so-called **sex-typed** behaviors, there is a greater range of behaviors among men than is seen when comparing men and women. Second, although there are some

hormonal and physical differences between the sexes, these do not mandate that men will dominate women. These differences and any behaviors associated with them still have to be culturally and socially interpreted (i.e., gendered). Finally, much of what we know about the differences between the sexes is filtered through our existing cultural assumptions about sex as a binary, and the traits associated with that binary. "Our conceptions of the nature of gender difference shape, even as they reflect the ways we structure our social system and polity; they also shape and reflect our understandings of our physical body" (Fausto-Sterling 2000, p. 45).

The field of evolutionary psychology certainly provides some basis for understanding inequality (Crawford and Salmon 2004), but while there is some evidence for evolved sex differences, cross-cultural research suggests a complex picture that combines biological, ecological, and social influences (Wood and Eagly 2002). Therefore, we will focus here on research stemming mostly from sociology and anthropology, addressing two types of theories: 1) ecological models and 2) Marxian/socialist theories of gender inequality.

ECOLOGICAL MODELS Ecological models of gender inequality investigate how women and men interact and navigate their physical and spatial environments and how their adaptations affect the social order. For example, how societies gather or produce their food has a great impact on their social roles. Groups that were primarily foragers tended to be far more communal, and exhibited few divisions by age or gender (Lorber 1994). As technologies change, so do sex-typed behaviors. For example, as groups developed hunting technologies such as spears that required greater skill and organization, younger children could no longer participate in hunts, necessitating that someone stay home with the small children. "These gender roles emerge from the productive work of the sexes; the characteristics that are required to carry out sex-typical tasks become stereotypic of women and men" (Wood and Eagly 2002, p. 701). However, anthropologists demonstrate that there is a great diversity among humanoid and primate cultures in how sex-typed roles developed, making broad generalizations dangerous (Epstein 1988).

A classic work from an ecological approach is that of Peggy Sanday (1981). Her theory is based on her analysis of information from over 150 societies, most of them not known to the average reader and many of them extinct. But they provide clues to the origins of male dominance. Sanday defined male dominance in terms of the "exclusion of women from political and economic decision-making" and "male aggression against women" (p. 164). Her principal question addressed the origins of male dominance: Where does it come from? The basic generating cause for male dominance relates to the nature of the environment in which a society operates. If that environment is one in which risk is great, danger is present, or resources are uncertain or in scarce supply, then the society is more vulnerable to male dominance.

Different environments generate variable stresses for the people exposed to them, their relationships to the environment are defined differently, and the general cultural orientation and consequent sex-role plans they develop also differ as a result (Sanday 1981). In other words, a group develops its sense of peoplehood and cultural orientations as responses to its environmental circumstances. When those circumstances involve risk, uncertainty, and so forth, as in the case of societies that rely heavily on the hunting of large animals, then there is a greater reliance on the aggression of men. These societies, in which animals must be killed, in which death and destruction predominate, develop what Sanday calls an "**outer orientation**" in their worldview. "Men hunt animals, seek to kill other human beings, make weapons for these activities, and pursue power that is *out there*" (p. 5). On the other side are societies whose environments produce abundantly and with certainty, cultures that rely on the surrounding plants for sustenance. Nature is viewed in a friendly manner, as freely satisfying human needs. In many cases where this situation is present, a basic affinity is seen between women and nature. As women produce,

so does nature. Women are seen as being more in tune with nature, and men are largely extraneous to this relationship.

A strict sex-based division of labor is more likely when the society depends heavily on hunting as its means of subsistence, whereas a society that depends equally on hunting and gathering or inordinately on the latter for food is more likely to produce a division of labor that is sexually integrated. Cooperation rather than competition is likely to be emphasized. Females *achieve* power when a society has to depend on their economic activity for survival. This makes men more dependent on them. Women are *given* power when they are associated closely with nature and the society's continuity.

With Western colonialism, women lost much of the higher status they held in traditional societies. The infusion of new weapons and new technologies and the increased importance of aggression helped to redefine the roles of the sexes, with male activity becoming more highly valued. In many cases, the increased complexity of economic technology also led to the decline of women's status. In her survey of societies, Sanday concluded that "male dominance is associated with increasing technological complexity, an animal economy, sexual segregation in work, a symbolic orientation to the male creative principle, and stress" (1981, p. 171). Sex inequality is much more likely when the environment is unfavorable and unstable than when the opposite is the case.

To summarize Sanday's explanation, the nature of the surrounding environment gives shape to the economy and the stress in society and determines the relative worth of men's and women's behavior. Cultural orientations, myths, and sex-role plans develop that are consistent with these conditions. When environmental conditions create stress because they involve risk, danger, or uncertainty, greater reliance is placed on the economic efforts of men.

Sanday's theory has been criticized for overemphasizing the role of the environment in determining cultural beliefs and for ignoring the internal sources of stress in society. It also does not

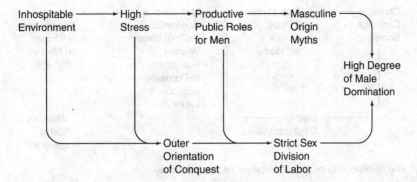

FIGURE 6.2 Sanday's Basic Model of the Genesis of Male Dominance

Source: Based on Sanday (1981), pp. 11–12, 64–75, 163–172ff.

take into account the fact that different cultures may react differently to similar environmental circumstances (Coontz and Henderson 1986). Additionally, her theory neglects the possibility that the difficulties men encounter in dealing with a harsh environment may strengthen them enough to dominate women directly.

Randall Collins has suggested, for example, that the form of the economic system and the habitability of the surrounding natural and political environments influence the extent to which warfare is an important element in the society. Men are generally larger and stronger than women and are therefore more likely to control the fighting that occurs. In such a potentially hostile environment, political alliances become important, and males use the exchange of females through marriage with surrounding groups as a means of establishing political, economic, and social ties. This control of females by males results in separate cultures and roles developing for each of the sexes (Collins 1971; 1988).

The causal nature of the relationships outlined by Sanday also needs to be more fully examined (England and Dunn 1985). One would suspect, for example, that cultural orientation and beliefs would have an impact on the degree to which the environment is interpreted as being hostile or friendly. In other words, not only can the environment affect the culture, but the culture may affect the definition of the environment as well.

MARXIAN THEORIES OF GENDER During the 1970s and 1980s, there were prominent efforts to integrate Marxian and feminist perspectives on gender inequality. Though this was never an easy alliance, as we will see below, they introduced to the literature important mechanisms underpinning the relationships between capitalism and **patriarchy** and the political economy of social reproduction (Brown 2012).

Vogel (1983) began the development of her theoretical framework by reviewing several Marxian concepts: production, reproduction, and labor power. **Labor power** refers to the capacities, mental and physical, individuals exercise whenever they produce something of use. *Production* is a result of labor power. But every act of production is also an act of *reproduction,* because whatever is produced lays the basis for its being reproduced later.

Specifically, a society needs a labor force to continue to produce products, and this labor force, in turn, needs food to maintain itself. In other words, part of the reproduction process involves reproducing the laborers who are involved in the labor process. Workers must be maintained and, when necessary, replaced. Sex becomes a significant factor in the generational replacement of bearers of labor power, because it is only women who can perform this function. But regeneration or replenishment of the labor force does not have to occur within the family. Other sources—such as migration, enslavement,

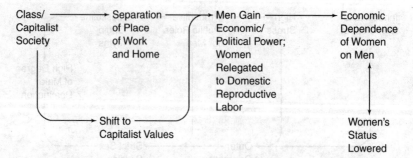

FIGURE 6.3 The Relationship of Class/Capitalism to Sex Inequality

and the enlistment of nonworkers within the family—also may serve as potential sources of labor power.

In order for the capitalist system of production to continue, labor power must produce the conditions necessary for the constant renewal of the labor process. The labor needed to reproduce workers and their replacements is **necessary labor**. For example, a certain minimum amount of labor is needed to provide basic subsistence to existing workers and to produce new workers. Part of this necessary labor is done at the workplace and is paid for by wages, with which the worker can buy those necessities needed to support himself or herself and other nonworkers in the working class. As it takes place in the social or public sphere it is the *social* aspect of necessary labor. But as mentioned, biological reproduction and the rearing of children are also needed, and as such constitute a second *domestic* component of necessary labor. In addition to necessary labor, there is **surplus labor**. This is the labor time that is left over after socially necessary labor has been subtracted from the total labor time spent on the job. It provides the profit to the employer.

It is the unavoidable performance of the domestic component of necessary labor by women that creates a basic sex division of labor. But their involvement in reproduction creates a dilemma for capitalists and constitutes an internal contradiction in the capitalist system. On the one hand, this domestic labor reduces any time women can spend in the labor force producing profit for employers.

So in the short run, capitalists suffer because of the smaller direct contribution of women to profit. On the other hand, if capitalism is to continue in the long run, replacement and reproduction are necessary. So in these terms, capitalism benefits.

In order to benefit both ways, capitalists try to minimize the amount of necessary domestic time needed for reproduction in order to maximize the surplus value of labor, thereby increasing their profit. Thus, employers may allow maternity leaves for female workers, but the leaves are kept short so as to maximize the work time of new mothers. At the same time, however, male workers try to get the best conditions and wages they can for themselves, their families, and their spouses. This may mean more and better-quality domestic time for their spouses. So while employers may be trying to enlist wives in the marketplace, husbands are trying to create conditions that will make it more possible for them to stay comfortably at home. This conflict is related to the gender issues involved in the balancing of home and work tasks discussed earlier. In trying to resolve this contradiction, according to Vogel, what almost invariably occurs is the involvement of men in the labor force and the production of surplus labor and profit on the one hand, and the involvement of women in the reproduction of the labor force at home on the other. Accompanying this resolution is a male supremacy based on males as the laborers who produce the means of subsistence and receive a wage.

It is in capitalism that a distinct and strong division is accentuated between the arena in which surplus labor is carried out and that in which domestic labor is performed. In order to increase profit, separate factories in which workers are concentrated that are socially and culturally isolated from the home are needed. "Capitalism's drive to increase surplus . . . forces a severe spatial, temporal, and institutional separation between domestic labor and the capitalist production process. . . . Wage labor comes to have a character that is wholly distinct from the laborer's life away from the job" (Vogel 1983, p. 153). Men are clearly associated with the social, working sphere, whereas women are associated with the domestic sphere. This is a carryover from earlier class societies.

As noted previously, according to Vogel, women's involvement in and relegation to domestic

labor is the basic source of their subordination. By working, receiving wages, and supporting women who are bearing and raising children, men gain economic power over women, and women remain in a subordinate position.

Since many of the immediate conflicts take place within the context of the family, it is easy to conclude that it is the sex division of labor within it that is at the source of the problems experienced by women. But Vogel reminds us again that it is the nature of the relationship of men and women to the capitalist system of production and women's role in reproducing it that is the basic cause. As long as capitalism remains unchanged, inequality between the sexes will continue. Figure 6.4 presents the core of Vogel's argument.

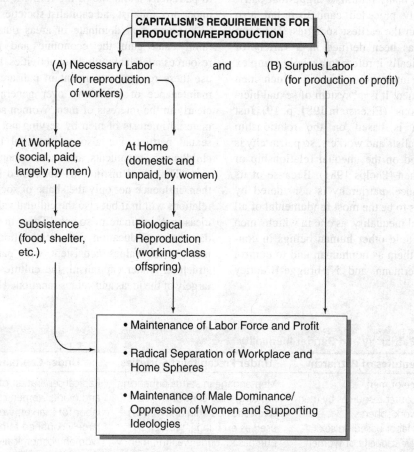

FIGURE 6.4 A Simplified Version of Vogel's Theory of Women's Oppression

One of the problems with Vogel's theory is that she dated the beginning of women's oppression with the advent of class societies. Many would argue that male domination predated class society (Nicholson 1984). Vogel's theory also heavily stressed economic factors to the exclusion of cultural, psychological, and other possible contributors to male domination.

THE ROLE OF PATRIARCHY Vogel acknowledged the division of labor and the inequality that exists between the sexes in capitalist society, but Sacks (1975) noted that in many nonclass societies the sexes were also unequal. This suggests strongly that sex inequality preceded capitalism and indeed is a form of domination distinct from class inequality.

In brief, many feminists argue that patriarchy not only preceded capitalism but also existed even in the earliest societies. The term **patriarchy** has been defined in a variety of ways, but basically it refers to a whole complex of structured interrelationships in which men dominate women. It is a "system of sexual hierarchical relations" (Eisenstein 1981, p. 19). Just as capitalism is based on the relationship between capitalists and workers, so patriarchy is a system based on the unequal relationship of men and women (Phelps 1981). Because of its early appearance, patriarchy is considered by most feminists to be the most fundamental of all forms of social inequality, as one in which "men learn how to hold other human beings in contempt, to see them as nonhuman and to control them" (Lengermann and Niebrugge-Brantley 1988, p. 306).

In other words, in this view, sexism and the domination of women did not appear with class societies as some Marxists would have it; rather, it existed long before capitalism came on the historical scene. The roots of patriarchy have been tied to the reproductive function of women in society (Eisenstein 1981; Phelps 1981; Chafetz 1988a). "On the basis of this capacity she has been excluded from other human activities and contained within a sphere defined as female" in Western society (Eisenstein 1981, p. 14). The division of labor between the sexes in this respect is ancient: "Where there is society, there is gender, and the gender division of labor is pervasive" (Smith 1987, p. 4). There was no primordial matriarchal society preceding class society. Table 6.4 suggests some of the basic elements tied to patriarchy and some of the forms it has taken under precapitalist and capitalist societies.

Once men dominate in areas outside the family and gain the economic and political resources attendant with those activities, they can use these resources to maintain patriarchy. The maintenance of patriarchy over generations is clearly in the interests of men. Women serve the material interests of men by serving not only as sexual partners but also as potential laborers, childbearers, ornaments, and status enhancers.

The social institutions dominated by men, then, influence not only the shape of society and relations within it but also the cultural values and ideas that dominate in society. Thus, in present-day society, education and socialization agents instill those values consistent with patriarchal structure. Under capitalism, the culture consists largely of the ideas and values sanctioned by those

TABLE 6.4 Patriarchy and Gender Inequality

General Features of Patriarchy	Under Precapitalist Societies	Under Capitalism
1. Power, force of men 2. Control of outer resources by men 3. Separate work spheres 4. Division of labor based on sex 5. Reproductive capacity of women critical	Men engage in status-enhancing hunting; men control domesticated animals; women used as exchange; women are purchased (bride wealth); men control military	Radical separation of home and work; women cheap labor for market; women largely confined to home; women economically dependent on men

in power—that is, men. This ruling ideology provides an official version of social reality, including beliefs about the real nature of men and women. Eventually, among women living under capitalism, a line of fault or disjuncture occurs between this official version of reality and how the system works and the concrete everyday experiences of women. But this experience is difficult to articulate because the symbols, language, and organization of thought in the society are those of men not women (Smith 1987).

The separation and inequality of men and women is reflected in dichotomies that go back to ancient times. The distinctions between rationality and passion, city and household, and public and private all derive from a belief in the basic differences and inequality between the sexes. In feudal and in capitalist societies, the public sphere is associated with the male, whereas the private sphere is the designated place for the female. In feudal society, females were considered private property of the male heads of families, and in capitalist society, women are largely relegated to the private sphere of the family. In other words, although the economic system may change, basic patriarchal relationships remain intact and only change form.

One of the difficulties with patriarchal theories is that the original source of patriarchy is not always clearly spelled out. Sometimes it is associated with the differences in the reproductive function between the sexes, sometimes with the physical force of men over women, and other times its source is left undescribed. Collins (1988) argued that the basic problem with theories that propose patriarchy as the fundamental, original cause of sex inequality is that they are merely restating the question using a different label. That is, if "patriarchy" *refers* to male domination of one sort or another, then how can it be used to *explain* male domination? This seems to be too severe a criticism, given that many of those proposing such theories do attempt to locate the sources of patriarchy itself. Since that source is often viewed as being tied to the elemental function of reproduction, the task remains to identify the exact conditions under which such distinctions

in the division of labor do *not* lead to patriarchy. For example, can socializing or spreading a large part of the child-rearing function free women to a degree from the destiny of remaining in the domestic sphere, thereby potentially raising their status in society?

SOCIALIST-FEMINIST THEORIES OF SEX INEQUALITY In contrast to those who would opt for viewing either capitalism *or* patriarchy as the principal cause of women's subordination, there are those who see the two as complementary causes. Women's oppression by men cannot be reduced to a matter of class exploitation, according to these scholars. *Exploitation* of women, Eisenstein (1999) argued, exists when men and women are wage laborers. But women are also in a lower sexual hierarchy in their roles as mothers and housewives. "The study of women's oppression, then, must deal with both sexual and economic material conditions if one is to understand oppression rather than merely understand economic exploitation" (Eisenstein 1999, p. 201). As we will see, those who use an internal-colonialism model in explaining Black–White inequality in the United States make a similar argument about understanding racial oppression.

Eisenstein and Hartmann both emphasized the mutual reinforcement between capitalism and patriarchy. Patriarchy supplies capitalism with generations of laborers it needs at minimal costs and with the techniques of control needed to keep oppressed women in their place. In turn, capitalism reinforces patriarchy by only hiring women for certain low-paying positions, thereby encouraging job segregation, women's relegation to the domestic sphere, and their continued economic dependence on males.

The domestic division of labor is the linchpin that connects capitalism and patriarchy (Philipson and Hansen 1990). Patriarchy defines the role of women as being in the home, whereas capitalism defines men's role as being in the wider economy and women's role as reproducer of workers in the economy. The division of labor, as it were, brings the private-domestic and public-economic spheres into contact. This has raised a number of questions about the nature of the relationship between the marketplace and the home.

One issue pits the obvious contributions of domestic work to the continuance of capitalism against the fact that domestic labor is basically unpaid low-status work outside the economy. If such work contributes to the economy by providing functioning laborers, why is it not paid labor? Because it is not paid, it has lower status in a society in which the amount of money labor brings in is a measure of its status (Benston 1969).

A second issue concerns the basic character of domestic labor. In contrast to work in the marketplace, which is seen by some as being alienating and rationalistic, work in the home is sometimes seen as much less alienating and more leisurely (Sontag 1973; Vogel 1983). The home and family life are viewed as the areas in which love, warmth, spontaneity, cooperation, and fun have a central place. In sharp contrast, the public sphere of paid labor is interpreted as one where work is forced, competitive, and rational. It is, of course, questionable whether those who feel trapped in the home would describe it in the glowing terms just used. But part of our socialization is aimed at fostering the belief that these terms accurately describe family life in modern society.

A third issue among scholars relates to the effects of involvement in the marketplace on women. Engels, Marx's collaborator, viewed industrialization as providing women with a means of escape from the drudgery of housework and the oppression of domestic life. Work outside the home was interpreted as a liberating experience. However, if capitalism creates work that is fundamentally alienating, a legitimate question can be raised about how liberating and beneficial such an escape would be for women. Are they not just escaping into work that is also alienating and compounding their alienation by doing not only paid labor but unpaid domestic labor as well?

A final area concerns the family's role in socializing new members of society into a dominant set of values and ideas that perpetuate patriarchy and capitalism (Hartmann 1979). The traits attributed to the ideal male—competitiveness, rationality, coolness—are those valued in the marketplace, whereas those attributed to the ideal female under capitalism—emotionality, sentimentality, and so on—are those valued in the family. These are values that keep patriarchy and capitalism intact.

The last point demonstrates that the concerns with profit in capitalism and with social control in patriarchy are "inextricably connected" and "cannot be reduced to each other." Capitalism and patriarchy, being mutually reinforcing, become an "integral process" (Eisenstein 1999, p. 208). The conditions in the marketplace affect what goes on in the family in terms of production, reproduction, and consumption; conversely, production, reproduction, and consumption in the family affect the production of commodities in the marketplace.

The centrality of the sexual division of labor in maintaining both patriarchy and capitalism has caused both Eisenstein and Hartmann to call for its elimination. Eisenstein argued forcefully that it is this division of labor that must be changed because it is the principal means by which men maintain control. It suggests that the roles and activities that divide men and women are rooted in nature (Eisenstein 1999). Eisenstein stated that for conditions to change, women must organize, and they can do so by becoming conscious of what they have in common with each other. They may differ in their ties to the marketplace, but their "commonality derives from the particular roles women share in patriarchy. From this commonality begins the feminist struggle" (p. 214). Similarly and even more pointedly, Hartmann (1976) believes that both men and women will be better off and more equal only when "we eradicate the socially imposed gender differences between us and, therefore, the very sexual division of labor itself" (p. 169).

One of the great values of seeing capitalism and patriarchy as dual systems is that doing so encourages us to examine the interlinkage between class and sex in trying to understand the relative roles of men and women in society. For example, Ruggles (2015) argues that changes in the structure of labor, particularly the decline in wage labor, combined with changes in family structure, indicate a waning of the patriarchal system. Clearly, an individual's position in the general system of inequality is an outcome of the confluence of economic, sexual, and racial/ethnic factors. Understanding the nature of this intersection and its paths will provide us with a more comprehensive and exact explanation of sex inequality.

Interactionist and Cultural Theories

Cultures expect different attitudes and behaviors from members of each sex, but those expectations vary among cultures. In some cultures, what we consider masculine behavior is expected of women, and in some cultures, men engage in what we would consider to be feminine behavior. "The content of gender categorizations may shift with society changes in the social roles of women and men" (Wood and Eagly 2015, p. 465). All this is to say that *sex* is a term used to describe a biological constant, and *gender* is a term used to describe socially and culturally approved expectations, and these vary among societies.

Thus, although women are members of the same sex category, their gender roles may be markedly different and differentially ranked among those same cultures. In the United States, as in other countries, sex is one of the fundamental ways by which we categorize individuals, and gender is a determinant of how we approach and interact with them. Consequently, our beliefs about the characteristics of each sex and appropriate gender roles help shape the positions individuals occupy in society. In this way, gender and the associated stereotypes serve as a basis for inequality between the sexes (Ridgeway 2011). These become embedded in labor market and organizational structures, and serve to maintain occupational, job, and status differences between men and women (Acker 2006). When women are viewed as too soft, less competent, less competitive, and generally lacking leadership qualities compared to men, it is no wonder that fewer women are found in high-paying, top-level positions. These gender categories are represented as a binary whose boundaries shift under different conditions. Men, for example, "distance feminine from masculine aspects of their ingroup identity more strenuously than women do and that they do so in part to protect and maintain a gender status that is 'hard won and easily lost'" (Bosson and Michniewicz 2013, p. 438). Thus during times of rapid change and threats to their status, those in power may hang on more tightly to traditional gender dichotomies.

One of the pitfalls of equating sex with gender has been to define the gender roles given to each sex as "natural," that by their nature men and women perform particular roles and have particular characteristics. The old phrase "men are men and women are women" captures this belief. The heterosexual matrix that holds cultural sway in our society posits direct, inviolate, and *normal* relationships between sex, gender, and sexuality. In this matrix, sex determines gender, and sexuality is a reflection of one's gender. Men are masculine, for example, and masculine men desire women. Violating this set of relationships in U.S. society creates problems. We discuss this at length in Chapter 7.

The cultural variability found in the relationships between gender and sex, sex and nature, and sex and sexuality have instigated questions about the stability of these concepts and their connections. The alleged binary nature of sex, gender, and similar dichotomies has come under attack in the last several decades. So have the beliefs that gender is a *consequent* and *cultural* creation whereas sex is a logically *prior* and *biological* fact, and that one's gender is determined by one's sex. If there is no fixed, necessary tie between gender and sex, then gender can be attached to anyone, male or female (Butler 1999). Gender itself is not an entity or property of the individual, says Judith Butler; rather it is "performative," a set of ritualistic, recurrent acts performed by individuals acting within a cultural and political system.

Borrowing from Foucault and French feminists, Butler argues that concepts such as "woman" and "female" are created within a cultural framework that is also a system of power. This framework is one that interprets heterosexuality as normal. Those who act in ways that are inconsistent with this framework are considered unintelligible or not normal (Butler 1999; Lloyd 2007).

Sex is just as culturally constructed as *gender*, contends Butler. Bodies have always been interpreted culturally and do not exist as social objects prior to their naming and interpretation. They appear to do so because culture is capable of producing "frames of reference which are so powerful that they congeal into the invariance and irreducibility of material reality" (Kirby 2006, p. 23). Even the expressions of women, as the traditional subject and object of liberation for feminist theory, sometimes indicate their unwitting adherence to frames of reference that are culturally dominant. In the 2010 congressional elections, for example, female candidates often challenged their opponents to "man up," to have the "cojones" to be tough and strong, thereby reinforcing the traditional sex-gender connection (Hennessy 2010, p. A3). The goal of a genealogy of the concept of gender is to uncover the acts that create and sustain it, and the social and political frameworks that underlie it and "police the social appearance of gender" (Butler 1999, p. 44).

Thus gender is not a static, inherent quality, but an accomplishment (Ritzer 2008). In their foundational 1987 article, Candace West and Don Zimmerman reconceptualize gender from a view that sees it as a set of traits residing within individuals to something that people *do* in their interactions. Gender involves a display of behaviors, the "activity of managing situated conduct in light of normative conceptions of attitudes and activities appropriate for one's sex category" (p. 127). In our everyday interactions each of us displays gender, including how we speak, dress, carry ourselves physically, or interact with others. We learn as young children how to display femininity or masculinity, though we certainly may not choose to at all times. By "doing gender," we reinforce the idea that there are essential differences between females and males. The act of accomplishing and displaying gender is a way of producing gender differences and reinforcing gender inequalities.

West and Zimmerman updated their theory in 1995 to encompass class and race as well,

arguing that class and race can also be seen as interactional "accomplishments," in the same way in which they describe gender. All three involve "doing difference," or enacting one's structural position in particular contexts, thereby reinforcing inequalities (West and Fenstermaker 1995). More recently Westbrook and Schilt (2014) expand on the concept by introducing the idea of "determining gender," an "umbrella term for the different subprocesses of attributing or, in some cases, officially deciding another person's gender" (p. 36). In their interactions, individuals engage in displays that indicate what gender they have determined someone to be, thereby announcing the appropriate expected behavior from that individual. All of the above theories highlight microinteractions (that is, interactions between individuals), but outline as well how these person-to-person interactions connect to the structure of society. The next set of theories, however, address explicitly how societies are structured to produce and maintain gender inequality.

Gender as Structure

Several of the most significant social-structural theories highlight the relationship between gender roles and social institutions such as work or family in generating inequality between the sexes (Risman and Davis 2013). Two particular theories illustrate a structural approach: Janet Chafetz's theory of sex stratification, and Barbara Risman's account of gender as structure.

CHAFETZ'S THEORY OF GENDER STRATIFICATION
Chafetz argued that there has never been a situation in which women dominated men on a systematic and long-term basis, so that societies vary "from near equality to radical inequality favoring males" (Chafetz 1988a, p. 51). She has tried to explain the degree of **gender stratification** in a given society—that is, "the extent to which societal members are unequal in their access to the scarce values of their society on the basis of their membership in a gender category" (Chafetz 1988b, p. 111) These values include material goods and services, prestigious roles,

political power, interpersonal decision making, freedom from unwanted constraints, and educational opportunities. In other words, Chafetz views stratification as multidimensional in nature. Moreover, some of these dimensions may vary independently of each other, causing women's positions to be high on some and lower on others.

Three of the factors most directly related to gender stratification, according to Chafetz, are (1) the nature of the work organization, (2) the type of kinship structure, and (3) the degrees of ideological and stereotyping support for sex inequality in the society. Of these, the most important is the work organization, which includes a number of specific elements. Gender inequality will be high in a society when the following circumstances exist: (1) women do not contribute significantly to highly valued tasks, (2) women are easily replaced, (3) occupational tasks are sex-typed, (4) attention span is an important variable in a valued task, and (5) women do not have ownership and control over the means and products of their production.

The work organization itself is affected by several other independent variables, most of which are directly related to the level and type of technology in the society. Specifically, the more time women have to spend on child-rearing activities, the greater the distance between workplace and home, the more the need for physical strength and/or mobility, and the less the emphasis that is placed on subsistence rather than surplus production for exchange, the less women can be meaningfully involved in valued work tasks and, consequently, the higher the degree of gender stratification will be.

In addition to work organization factors, kinship structure also has an impact. When (1) married women live with or in the same places as their husbands' families (patrilocal), (2) a society traces lineage through the male line (patrilineal), and (3) there is a domestic division of labor based on sex, then inequality between the sexes will be high.

Finally, Chafetz included both the degree of ideological/religious support for gender stratification and the degree of gender stereotyping as factors that affect the acceptance of inequality between the sexes. For example, some societies may support the notion that "women's place is in the home" or that a wife must be submissive to her husband, while other societies may emphasize above all the belief in the worth and equality of all individuals as human beings. In addition, cultures usually contain stereotypes of male and female characteristics and appropriate behavior for each gender. According to Chafetz, these factors are more important for sustaining and justifying inequality than they are for generating it.

There have been conflicting reactions to Chafetz's argument. In a discussion of his view of how sociological theory should be structured, Gerhard Lenski (1988) praised Chafetz's model for being presented in a diagrammatic and essentially propositional form. Lenski believed that this makes the theory clearer and more amenable to empirical testing. In sharp contrast to the praise of Lenski, Pierre van den Berghe (1985) was quite critical of Chafetz's formalistic approach to theory, which appears to be becoming more dominant in the field. In assessing her theory, he bluntly stated that "an exercise in loosely linking a grab bag of 'variables' does not constitute anything that a real scientist would recognize as a theory" (p. 1350). However, this is an extreme reaction to what is a useful predictive model. It brings together variables that have been cited as important by others into a somewhat coherent and testable package.

RISMAN'S GENDER AS SOCIAL STRUCTURE

Barbara Risman outlines a model for looking beyond individual-level theories to seeing gender as "structure" that argues that gender is "embedded in the individual, interactional, and institutional dimensions of our society" (2004, p. 429). When sociologists talk about structure, they are referring to patterned ways of organizing behavior "that exist outside individual desires or motives" (Risman and Davis 2013). Thus economics or politics are structures that affect how individuals interact at work, within families, and how they think about their relationship to the wider society. Structures also create stratification, including who benefits, who has access to resources, and who has political and ideological power. Risman endorses Giddens's (1984) structuration theory that argues that humans create structures and can act back on them and change them, thus though structures have great power over individuals and institutions, they do not fully determine either.

Risman argues that gender too is a structure, rather than solely being *created* by social structure. Based on the binary categorization of sex, the gender structure organizes and stratifies societies. In the example provided above regarding children's toys, the gender structure provides a framework for thinking about how toys should be displayed. Similarly, the gender structure differentially offers opportunities and constraints based on sex categorization. Risman offers this model to move beyond explanations for gender inequality rooted solely in socialization. Gender differences are "deceptive distinctions," in that men and women behave differently in part because they occupy different institutional positions. While socialization is important, merely changing how individuals are socialized will not address the economic and political structures supporting inequality. Similarly, however, it is not enough to understand structured inequalities without addressing interactional and cultural components.

Thus gender structure has implications at the individual, the interactional, and the institutional level. The individual level includes socialization, the development of gender identities, and the construction of selves. At the interactional level, gender structures cultural and status expectations, biases individuals may hold toward others, and promotes the "othering" of categories of individuals. Finally, at the institutional level, the gender structure contributes to organizational practices, laws, ideologies, and the distribution of resources (Risman 2004, p. 435).

Risman recognizes that gender structures are not homogeneous, and that they are constructed differently in various cultures, and at various times and places. "Even within contemporary American society, gender structures vary by community, social class, ethnicity and race" (Risman 2004, p. 442). However, though Risman acknowledges that individuals' experiences are affected by their position in various intersecting systems of stratification, she argues that there is value in analyzing gender as a structure separate from other forms of inequality.

Theories of Intersectionality

All the theories discussed above focus on the position of women in general. In recent years, however, numerous feminist and race theorists have stressed that we need to take into account that all women do not have the same experiences or live the same kinds of lives. We need to avoid what Adrienne Rich (1979) called "white solipsism"—the presumption that the experiences of Whites, in this case White women, represent the norm. While they may have some experiences in common because they are women, they vary along other dimensions, for example, with regard to race and social class. These dimensions intersect in different ways for different women and affect each other, the particular combination characterizing a given woman and having a unique effect on her life chances. As Browne and Misra (2003) put it in speaking about the relationship of gender and race, "[r]ace is 'gendered' and gender is 'racialized' so that race and gender fuse to create unique experiences and opportunities for all groups—not just women of color" (p. 488). We could add that race and gender are also "classed," and class has been "gendered" and "racialized" in our history. That is, the particular pattern *itself* has an impact independent of the separate effects that might flow from one's gender, race, or class. Each of these patterns has particular cultural images or stereotypes associated with it. For example, Black, lower-class men are often seen as dangerous, Black women as unusually sexually active, White women as dependent and feminine, and so on (Browne and Misra 2003).

This is what is meant by the importance of "intersectionality," or what Patricia Hill Collins (2002) calls "the matrix of domination." Collins continues in a later work by stating that "race, class, gender, sexuality, ethnicity, nation, ability, and age operate not as unitary, mutually exclusive entities, but as reciprocally constructing phenomena that in turn shape complex social inequalities" (Collins 2015b, p. 2). A woman's race, class, and gender may all affect her position in society. As we have seen in several instances, for example, the occupational and earnings positions of women vary with their race. The situation of women also depends on their class. In their study of power at work, Elliott and Smith (2004) found that "men and women of various races and ethnicities experience increasing inequality in workplace power, relative to white men, but they experience it to different degrees and via different mechanisms. . . . Evidence here suggests that a one-size-fits-all explanation hides more than it reveals" (pp. 384–385). Since each group faces problems that are in part unique, the solutions to their domination need to vary as well.

There have been many renditions of intersectional theory, but they have in common the "notion that gender is not an abstract and timeless essence, but an embodied and historical practice that is structured by other forms of inequality" (Williams 2013, p. 614). When first introduced, **intersectionality** focused primarily on the intersection between racism and sexism. More recently, researchers have turned to a much broader range of oppressions, such as disability, citizenship, age, and sexuality (McBride, Hebson, and Holgate 2015). Intersectional theory has been used in many ways, including to describe the variable experiences of individuals based on their social location and specific contexts, to develop theoretical and methodological approaches to understanding gender, and finally as a call for activism (Cho, Crenshaw, and McCall 2013). Given this multiplicity of approaches to the question of intersectionality, there has been much debate on issues such as how we define it, what metaphor should be used to describe it (i.e., is it a web, a matrix, a road intersection), how many categories we should include, and whether it is static or dynamic. Additionally, intersectional approaches might focus on groups, on systems, or on processes (Cho, Crenshaw, and McCall 2013).

In her foundational work, Leslie McCall (2005) suggests three possible approaches to intersectional research. The first is an *anti-categorical* approach. This approach emerged early in feminist discussion as a rejection of the viability of master, or overarching, categories. Examples include the works of writers such as Fausto-Sterling (2000), who critiqued the assumption that there are only two genders, and Omi and Winant (2005a), who argue that rather than being a stable category, race is an ongoing project involving power structures and cultural representations (see Collins 2015b). While addressing very different topics, these works challenge "the singularity, separateness, and wholeness of a wide range of social categories" (McCall 2005, p. 1778). Research from this approach questions our assumptions about categories, and studies individuals and social settings without any assumptions about what category someone might fit into.

The second approach, an *intracategorical* approach, looks at experiences within a category, and similar to the anti-categorical approach it highlights the complexity of categories and the diversity within categories. McCall states that this approach arose in part because of the recognition of the failures of earlier research to capture the realities of lived experiences. For example, research on Black women was flawed because previous studies combined research on women taken from the experiences of White women, and research on race stemming from understandings of Black men. Neither helped us understand the unique experiences of Black women (p. 1780). Therefore, by looking extensively into the varieties of experiences of Black women as a category that exists at the intersection of other categories, we can develop more complex theoretical models. Another compelling example of this approach is the recent work by anthropologist Lila Abu-Lughod (2013) that provides a rich detailing of the variety of experiences of Muslim women to demonstrate that the contemporary political assumption that Muslim women need to be "saved" by Westerners is problematic.

The final approach McCall discusses is an *intercategorical* approach, which compares experiences of individuals across categories. Often this approach looks at relationships between social groups to understand broader forms of inequality. Thus, for example, McDonald (2011) looks at how the intersection of race and class affect aspirations, and Gengler (2012) examines how race, class, and gender define power relations in battered women's shelters. An intercategorical approach focuses on the margins and on the intersections to understand further the structure of inequality.

Often intercategorical approaches help us understand how systems operate either within a society or globally. Thus Bose (2012) applies intersectional theory to understand how processes such as neoliberalism or globalization affect the experiences of women. She begins by recognizing that women's experiences vary greatly cross-culturally: "There is diversity across countries in their national-level gender inequalities based on intersecting axes of transnational, regional, cross-cutting, and unique national issues that structure gendered differences and concerns" (p. 70). But these variations help us understand cross-cutting themes, and the relationships between the various systems and power relations.

Globalization and the continual movement of people, jobs, and capital across national boundaries associated with it have had an impact on women's position in our own society and in others. Having examined a variety of general explanations of gender inequality, let us now examine the position of U.S. women in a global context and assess the specific roles played by globalization in determining the status of women around the world.

THE GLOBAL CONTEXT AND THE IMPACT OF GLOBALIZATION

The examination of gender inequality in the United States showed that women are generally below men in their earnings, income, and occupational statuses, and the families that they head are more likely to be poor. However, gender inequality and oppression encompass a broader range of life chances than just narrow economic opportunities. The life conditions for women in many parts of the world often entail subjection to extreme forms of discrimination.

There is great variation between countries in the quality of life experienced by women. In its analysis of international gender inequality, a recent United Nations study took into account women's (1) reproductive health, (2) empowerment, and (3) the labor market in its measure of gender-related-achievements inequality. Results in a 2015 ranking of 157 countries showed that, *compared to men*, women are worse off in Chad, Niger, Afghanistan, Mali, Yemen, and Côte d'Ivoire. Countries ranked best on the index were Slovenia, Switzerland, Germany, Austria, and Denmark. The United States ranked 55th, eight ranks lower than in 2014. If both men and women are not well off but are relatively equal in their status, a country will rank higher on the gender inequality index. In an assessment of their political decision-making power, women were most likely to be in high-level positions in Norway, Sweden, Finland, Denmark, Iceland, Andorra, Bolivia, and Cuba and least likely to have political power in Qatar, Kuwait, Lebanon, Iran, and Tonga (United Nations Development Programme 2015, pp. 224–227). Keep in mind that the "gender inequality index" used by the United Nations merely measures the *relative disparity* between men and women on the above three variables; it does not directly tap the level of quality of life in an *absolute* sense.

Save the Children is an independent, nonprofit organization that, for the last several years, has conducted an evaluation of conditions for women across the world. Its 2015 survey of conditions for mothers and children in 119 countries revealed results similar to those of the United Nations. Norway, Finland, Iceland, Denmark, Sweden, Netherlands, Spain, Germany, Australia, and Belgium ranked highest, respectively, in measures of mothers' well-being. The United States ranked 33rd, with maternal mortality having increased 136 percent since 1990 (S. Allen 2015). The nine countries with the lowest rankings, starting with the worst, were Somalia, Democratic Republic of the Congo, Central African Republic,

Mali, Niger, Gambia, Côte d'Ivoire, Chad, and Guinea-Bissau. In general, Scandinavian countries and industrial nations rank highest, while sub-Saharan African countries dominate the lowest rankings on this measure. The measure includes rates of maternal mortality, anemia, use of contraceptives, births by qualified professionals, female literacy, and participation of women in national government (Save the Children 2015). One of the problems with national-level data is that it obscures inequalities between subnational groups in a country. Ethnic cleansing, violence, and oppression often target some groups of women more than others.

Worldwide, there appears to be some evidence of a decline in gender inequality in a wide variety of areas (Dorius and Firebaugh 2010), but significant discrepancies still exist. As in the United States, the world's employed women are unevenly distributed across occupational categories. Women "are still rarely employed in jobs with status, power and authority or in traditionally male blue-collar occupations" such as craft, trade, and machine operator positions (United Nations 2010, p. ix). Over half of employed women are involved in various services (e.g., retail, restaurants, communications, insurance, personal services), and about one-quarter are involved in agricultural work. The rest participate in manufacturing (Current Population Survey 2015). Overall, women are heavily represented in professional, sales, clerical, and service positions. By and large, these patterns follow those found in the United States. In Europe, Latin America, and the Caribbean, women occupy about two-thirds of clerical and service jobs. Men are generally employed more equally across the three sectors (agriculture, industry, and services) than women are (United Nations 2010).

Among industrial countries, the gender gap in authority in the private economy appears to be lower in the United States than in many other countries. A study of employed individuals in Canada, the United Kingdom, Australia, Sweden, Norway, Japan, and the United States revealed that the gap was smallest in the United States and Australia, whereas Japan showed the widest difference in male and female authority. These differences persisted even after variations in characteristics in workplaces, jobs, and individuals were taken into account (Wright, Baxter, and Birkelund 1995).

Earnings constitute another area in which gender inequality is prominent. In none of the 50 countries in which men's and women's earnings have been analyzed are women's earnings equal to those of men. Unfortunately, these studies focus on earnings from just manufacturing and nonagricultural occupations. Since many women work in agricultural jobs, especially in developing nations, the picture given of wage discrepancies between the genders in these studies is, at best, incomplete. Those countries in which women receive earnings that are at least 85 percent of what men receive include Norway, Sweden, and Australia among industrial nations, and Tanzania, Vietnam, Sri Lanka, Colombia, Kenya, and Turkey among developing countries. In 2014, U.S. White non-Hispanic women earned about 78 percent of what White non-Hispanic men did, while Hispanic/Latina women earned 54 percent and African American women earned 63 percent of what a White non-Hispanic man earned (American Association of University Women 2015). This puts the United States near the middle in terms of earnings differences between men and women. Among industrial countries, the United States lags behind countries as disparate as Australia, Norway, Sweden, France, New Zealand, Germany, Belgium, Italy, Portugal, Greece, Austria, and Poland in gender earnings equality. Among the nations with the greatest earnings inequality are Suriname, Belize, Tunisia, Libya, Algeria, Jordan, Azerbaijan, and Mexico. In each of these countries, women's earnings equal no more than half those of men, even though they are ranked as having very high or high overall human development (United Nations Development Programme 2015, pp. 220–221). In sum, women's involvement in the economy, occupation segregation by sex, and lower authority for women are common around the world, but when compared to many other industrial countries, earnings differences between men and women have been higher in the United States.

In addition to their involvement in the formal economy, women throughout the world also spend significantly more time than men on unpaid housework. In industrial countries, women spend at least 30 hours per week on housework, compared to 10 to 15 hours for men. In developing countries, the figures are 31 to 42 hours and 5 to 15 hours, respectively. How equally housework is distributed between men and women is affected by *individual-level* variables such as belief in gender inequality and the time that women have for housework, and these factors in turn are affected by *national-level* factors that provide the context in which individual elements operate. Among the national-level variables that are important in this regard are level of economic development, gender ideology, and welfare policies (Fuwa 2004). This research supports several of the general theoretical arguments discussed earlier.

International differences in gender inequality as well as disparities within the United States are affected by globalization. Rather than being gender-neutral or impartial, globalization has profound and unique gender effects, effects that are generally more costly for women than for men (Chow 2003; Mills 2003; Gottfried 2004). This should not be surprising because globalization is simultaneously an economic, cultural, social, and political process; and in each of these spheres there are gender differences. Among the economic costs for women are "feminization of labor in segregated and low-paying work, wage dependency, labor exploitation, economic marginalization, poverty, sex tourism, and international human trafficking of women and young girls" (Chow 2003, p. 454). Economically, global capitalism can enlist sexist ideology to justify and perpetuate lower wages for women in a variety of cultural contexts. Women migrating from poorer to richer countries in search of better lives serve as domestic workers and nannies for two-career families in wealthy countries. As low as their wages may be by Western standards, the conditions and opportunities that immigrants experience in their new countries are often better than those they had in their countries of origin. We need to understand that a group's cultural and social experiences will affect its views of the costs and benefits of globalization. Whether globalization is seen as a largely positive or negative force depends in part on the vantage point from which it is viewed (Kabeer 2004).

The prevalence of women working in the United States along with continued gender inequities in housework and lack of child care support, for example, create a need and opportunity for domestic workers, many of whom are immigrants who expect better economic conditions than in their home countries (Kofman and Raghuram 2015). In other words, gender inequalities *within* a nation help spur the immigration of women *between* countries. The migration of women as workers is a widespread phenomenon. "In the United States, African-American women, who accounted for 60 percent of domestics in the 1940s, have been largely replaced by Latinas, many of them recent migrants from Mexico and Central America. In England, Asian migrant women have displaced the Irish and Portuguese domestics of the past. In French cities, North African women have replaced rural French girls. In western Germany, Turks and women from the former East Germany have replaced rural native-born women" (Ehrenreich and Hochschild 2005, p. 52). Lacking political, union, and economic power, these workers are open to exploitation by their employers.

Internationally, poverty and gender inequality are linked to the high prevalence of sex and slave trafficking of women and children. Estimates of trafficking range wildly; at least 700,000 victims and perhaps several million are trafficked every year (Troshynski and Blank 2008; Yen 2008). Some 100,000 to 150,000 individuals are believed to be in slavery in the United States. The United States ranks second in the world, behind Germany, as a destination or market for sex slavery. It is necessary to note, however, that prostitution is legal in Germany and illegal in the United States. That does not mean sex slavery and sex trafficking are legal in Germany, but it does mean that sex work and, consequently, sex trafficking look different in the two legal contexts. It must also be noted that human and sex trafficking statistics are difficult to obtain because tracking these illegal operations is extremely hard. Well over 90 percent of the sexually exploited are women (Schauer and Wheaton 2006).

In 2000, the United Nations estimated that sex trafficking yielded between five and seven billion dollars in profit (Shifman 2003; Meyer 2003). The technology of the Internet has made the buying and selling of women easier and increased its prevalence. In the demand for sex laborers, gender often intersects with racial, class, and age characteristics because men may have desires for particular kinds of women. Gendered values in a society may privilege certain qualities: "perhaps some of this demand grows out of the erotic lure of the 'exotic.' Immigrant women may seem desirable sexual partners for the same reason that First World employers believe them to be especially gifted as caregivers: they are thought to embody the traditional feminine qualities of nurturance, docility, and eagerness to please. . . . Some men seek in the 'exotic Orient' or 'hot-blooded' tropics a woman from the imagined past" (Ehrenreich and Hochschild 2005, pp. 53–54). In this way, globalization activates the use of gendered values in the perpetuation of gender inequality.

While domestic work and sexual labor offer two specific areas in which globalization has an impact, globalization has also had a broader effect on labor-force segregation. It has reinforced and reproduced traditional gender differences in the workplace, relegating women to positions of lower pay and authority than those of men. At the same time, globalization has created economic independence for some women and encouraged labor activism among them (Mills 2003). Some have even found that greater foreign investment by transnational corporations reduces occupational segregation (Meyer 2003).

How much globalization reproduces sex segregation in occupations within a nation depends in part on the relative position of the country in the world economic system as a whole. Globalization may exacerbate gender occupational inequality in some countries while lessening it in others. For example, Meyer (2003) found that high levels of trade and increased foreign investment have more

of a weakening effect on segregation and inequality in the occupational structure in less-developed countries than in more-developed countries. This results in part from the movement of women into traditional male occupations, such as manufacturing. But she cautions that this lessening of segregation does not reveal many of the qualitative properties of the jobs that women get, nor does it take into account the prevalence of women in the underground economy. She also observes that the segregation reductions may be temporary.

Occupational segregation and inequality in industrial countries appear to be much less affected by these globalization processes. From her study of 56 nations, Meyer (2003) contends that "[t]his is likely due to the fact that the economic structures in advanced industrialized nations counteract global forces and societal features . . . thereby promoting nominal segregation through the incorporation of women's traditional tasks into the formal economy" (pp. 370–372).

While occupational segregation may not be as affected by globalization in industrial countries like the United States as it is in less-industrialized nations, globalization does have other implications for gender inequality in the United States. For example, globalization has created more competition for major stockbroker firms on the international market and, consequently, greater pressure for increased effort and longer work hours for employees, most of whom are men. The result is the perpetuation and even intensification of gender inequity in housework. More time at work means less time for family, and higher pay means less need for spouses to work, thereby solidifying the traditional division of labor between husbands and wives (Blair-Loy and Jacobs 2003). More generally, globalization in the form of increased trade appears to be more likely to reduce gender wage inequality in concentrated than in competitive industries in the United States because it opens up these traditionally sheltered industries to international competition (Black and Brainerd 2004). Thus, as in other areas of inequality, conclusions about the effects of globalization need to take into account the economic and cultural contours of the units being examined.

Summary

This chapter has documented the historical socio-economic position of women in the United States. Despite having been consistently involved in the economy since colonial times, women have regularly faced sex segregation and relegation to lower statuses in their employment. Occupational conditions today still reveal distinct inequalities between men and women. Women (1) are involved in a smaller range of occupations, (2) are less likely to be in positions of authority, (3) are more likely to work in smaller organizations in the peripheral sector of the economy, (4) are more likely to occupy positions with short career ladders, and (5) make less money than men even when they work full-time, year-round, and have comparable educational levels. A variety of microinequities involving language, popular media and stereotypes, and education also pervade relationships between men and women.

Attempts to account for the inequalities between the sexes suggest that differences in human capital, commitment to the labor force, work effort, and interruptions due to childbearing and rearing do not account substantially for the differences in earnings and occupational placement. The differential arrangement of women and men along the occupational hierarchy is, however, directly related to the discrepancy in earnings between the sexes, especially when we consider the differences in the characteristics of the jobs most often held by men and women.

Broader theories of sex inequality have focused on (1) the cultural underpinnings of gender inequality, (2) the position of women in the work organization of society, (3) the hostile or friendly character of the natural environment, (4) capitalism's requirements and women's role in necessary labor, (5) early patriarchal structures, and (6) intersections with other statuses such as race and class. Women's roles in the domestic and economic public spheres appear to have direct consequences for their overall position in society.

Oppression against women varies widely around the world. Globalization has had an impact on the constraints and opportunities afforded women across the world. Its effects vary among nations depending on the position of the country in the world economic system. For example, the movement of women into careers in the industrial world has fostered a demand for more domestic workers, many of whom are immigrants from technologically less-advanced countries. This creates opportunities for some women but also the possibility for continued oppression.

Critical Thinking

1. Think about a specific occupation and its likely occupant (e.g., police officer, elementary school teacher, home builder). Does a specific gender come to mind? Why?
2. In your own life, how has gender limited you or allowed you to act a certain way or get involved in particular kinds of activities? What was it about your gender that created this effect?
3. In many parts of the world, women are pressed by customs to accept beatings by their male spouses for minor cultural infractions such as talking back and leaving the house without notifying the husband. How can this be changed without showing disrespect for the culture in those countries?
4. As technologies and the bases of the U.S. economy change, will men and women become more equal economically? Support your answer.

Web Connections

The Global Policy Forum is a nonprofit, tax-exempt organization that consults with the United Nations on issues of international law and equity among nations. In the section on global inequality, there are recommended articles on gender inequality and comparisons of countries on the gender gap. Visit www.globalpolicy.org/socecon/index.htm.

Film Suggestions

American Women of Achievement (1995). A 10-part series on important women in U.S. history.

Dreamworlds 3: Desire, Sex, and Power in Music Video (2007). Concerns sexual identity, masculinity, and femininity.

Miss Representation (2011). This is a documentary that discusses the stereotypes and double standards women face in media, and the expectations of appearance and persona women face in everyday life.

CHAPTER 7

Sexual Orientation, Gender Identity/ Expression, and Inequality

In itself, homosexuality is as limiting as heterosexuality: the ideal should be to be capable of loving a woman or a man; either, a human being, without feeling fear, restraint, or obligation.

SIMONE DE BEAUVOIR (1908–1986)

In the previous chapter, we focused on sex and gender and discussed a variety of inequalities that exist between males and females as the two traditionally recognized sexes. In this chapter, we will examine status inequality that results from sexual orientation, gender expression, and gender identity, although we principally focus on the inequities associated with being gay, lesbian, bisexual, and transgender.

One might wonder why we are combining sexual orientation and gender identity/expression in one chapter. Brynn Tannehill, an activist and director of advocacy for SPART*A, a group for LGBT veterans or current service members, gives several reasons why the combination makes sense (2013). First, gay people and transgender/genderqueer people violate gender norms—gay people because they love people of the "wrong" gender, and transgender/genderqueer people because they identify with and/or express themselves as the "wrong" gender. Second, gay, transgender, and genderqueer people all face discrimination, although, as we discuss later in the chapter, the discrimination against transgender people, particularly those who are people of color, is notably strong and dangerous. Third, it makes sense to talk about LGBTQ together because the groups are often conflated in the public mind, and various advocacy groups also combine them under one umbrella. While there are continuing tensions between the transgender and lesbian/gay communities, there is broader support for a political alliance than there was 20 years ago. Finally, social scientists have grouped LGBTQ people together in surveys, and, consequently, it is difficult to separate out the Q and T from the LGB in much of the data we have.

Unfortunately, sexual orientation and gender expression/identity have generally been ignored as bases for inequality. Speaking about gays and lesbians, Gamson and Moon (2004) comment, "With some noticeable exceptions ... sociologists of race, class, and gender nonetheless tended to treat sexuality as a weakly integrated addendum to the list of intersecting oppressions" (p. 52). While this invisibility is changing rapidly, scholars still need to do more work to understand how sexuality and gender identity intersect with other identities. Too often scholars and activists assume homogeneity in the LGBTQ population, ignoring how factors like class and race result in very different experiences and needs (Hutchinson 2001). Similarly, while statistics can be helpful in understanding averages, collecting data on LGBTQ people as a group obscures how being a lesbian is different from being a gay man or how transgender people face particularly high levels of poverty, incarceration, and violence.

Historically, mainstream Western society has viewed the either/or sets of male/female, masculine/feminine, and heterosexuality/homosexuality as exhausting sexual possibilities and as closely interlocked. We are told that men are meant to behave in a masculine manner while women are supposed to perform in a feminine manner, and heterosexuality is considered a part of their masculine and feminine performances. Heterosexuality has been viewed as natural and therefore normal, a view supported by dominant institutions, values, and behaviors. Some use the term **heteronormative** to describe our society because heterosexuality is taken for granted and is therefore rarely questioned. In fact, some scholars argue that heterosexuality is effectively compulsory—it is so entrenched in our society and deviations are punished so severely, it becomes too costly to explore alternatives (Rich 1980; McRuer 2006).

Societal sexual/gender dichotomies are legitimized by the existence of other typologies such as public/private, instrumental/expressive, and rational/emotional, and the continued emphasis on these dichotomies as "natural" lends them a seemingly timeless and universal quality. Theories of **biological determinism**, which see gender as inherent and natural, further support this view. Consequently, individuals who do not fit into neat categories or do not behave in the culturally prescribed manner have been thought of as deviant. Judeo-Christian dogma views normal, moral, and legitimate sex as having a reproductive function and as belonging in monogamous marriages between men and women, and views same-sex relations as sinful and abnormal (Herdt 1997).

But traditional binary categories of sex and related genders are neither timeless nor universal nor natural. They are social constructions found only in some societies during specific periods of time. Katz (2004) observes that, "'homosexual' and 'heterosexual,' the terms we moderns take for granted, are fairly recent creations. Although presented to us as words marking an eternal fact of nature, the terms 'heterosexual' and 'homosexual' constitute a normative sexual ethic, a sexual-political ideology, and one historically specific way of categorizing the relationships of the sexes" (p. 45). Categories such as these matter because they affect the lives, identity, and behaviors of both the people defined to be within the category as well as those defined as outsiders (Samuels 2014).

How one defines oneself sexually is not permanent but rather varies according to historical, situational, and cultural circumstances, and can be affected by one's race and class. Decena's work with Dominican men in New York (2008) illustrates how "coming out" as gay can incur a huge cost, especially for those who are poor or undocumented. Some of the men in his study strategically allowed their families to know that they loved other men without making an overt proclamation of being "gay." Coming out would not be liberating for them, but rather would violate their sense of privacy and would make it seem like they, rather than society, were the problem. This study is an example of how the meanings of sexuality intersect with cultural images of gender, race, and class. The meanings of masculinity, femininity, and sexuality in general also vary with one's race and class.

THE COMPLEXITY OF SEXUALITY AND GENDER

The fact that some individuals move between male and female, and engage in behaviors and demeanors that breach gender lines of masculinity and femininity, attests to the fluidity of gender. In some cases, gender can even be a temporary or situational experience, as when an individual routinely shifts behavior and physical presentation. "I'm not trying to be permanently that person [i.e., a man or a woman]. I just like [taking] the opportunity to be a man or a woman, if I want" (Irvine 2005, A5).

The simplistic, traditional, either/or categories of male/female, masculine/feminine, and heterosexuality/homosexuality miss much of the variety of actual human experiences (Lorber 1996). While the laws in most countries construct man and woman as mutually exclusive categories, a number of countries around the world recognize more than two sexes, sexualities, and/or genders. For example, in India, the *hijras,* while male at birth, define themselves as neither men nor women but as a third gender. They adopt many aspects of a feminine gender presentation. Yet they are not stigmatized, but are thought to exemplify the time-honored Hindu belief that each person possesses both masculine and feminine elements. *Hijras* challenge and question the masculine/feminine dualism and embrace ambiguity (Bakshi 2004). Another illustration of the complexity of sexuality concerns individuals who have intersexed anatomies. The term **intersex** refers to a set of conditions in which a person is born with reproductive or sexual characteristics that are not consistent with what we define as either the female or male category. A person may have some cells that have XX chromosomes while other cells have XY chromosomes. This variation in human anatomy covers a wide array of sex-anatomy combinations, and is thought to occur in about 1 out of 2000 children (Lahood 2012).

The traditional and allegedly universal pairs of male/masculine and female/feminine are also challenged by **transgender** individuals. Transgender people experience an incongruency between the gender they were assigned at birth and that with which they identify. For example, a person assigned male at birth may identify as a woman, or vice versa. Others may feel that they do not fit into the gender binary at all. Many transgender people choose to align their gender expression with their gender identity through a transition. This may involve changing names, dress, mannerisms, and, in some cases, pursuing hormonal or surgical prescriptions to create consistency between their physical bodies and psychological identities (Johnson, Mimiaga, and Bradford 2008).

One's gender identity is not necessarily tied to one's sexual orientation. Thus, individuals who are transgender may describe themselves as being heterosexual, bisexual, gay, lesbian, asexual, or pansexual (see Alternate Sexualities box). Most are attracted to the same gender(s) as they were before their transition. While gender and sexuality are not the same, gender transition can cause a redefinition of sexuality. For example, a transgender woman who identified as heterosexual prior to her transition will appear to be a lesbian after transition because she is still attracted to women. **Genderqueer** people bend the rules associated with masculinity and femininity, refusing to conform to the gender binary. They may identify as one gender but express another gender or they may be transgender. Being genderqueer is not necessarily linked to sexual orientation or gender identity.

Many transgender people do not challenge the idea that men should be masculine and women should be feminine. That is, they either accept the traditional gender categories, or they conform to them to decrease the chance of experiencing discrimination or violence. However, they define themselves as members of a gender they were not assigned at birth, and therefore adopt many of those roles and attitudes traditionally associated with that gender. Some argue that sexual and gender identity involve a variety of elements and thus their combinations can result in multiple possibilities. As described, these elements include one's biological sex assignment at birth, self-identity of gender, biological sex of partner, and the distribution of masculine and feminine traits in one's personality (Sedgwick 1998). The wide variety of self-identities, gender practices, and even biological differences found in contemporary society have led a growing number of scholars to urge replacement of the traditional dichotomies of male/female, masculine/feminine, and gay/straight with more complex classification systems of sexuality and gender (e.g., Lorber 1996; Herdt 1997; Fausto-Sterling 2000).

While there are political alliances between lesbian, gay, bisexual, and transgender people, the status of transgender people and bisexuals still remains somewhat ambiguous within the gay and lesbian community. For example, in a recent national poll, 28 percent of gays and lesbians said that they had "nothing at all" in common with transgender people. Only 13 percent said that they had "a lot in common" (Roper Center 2013). Some gays and lesbians worry about allying themselves with transgender people because it might weaken public support for anti-discrimination legislation (Weiss 2003). Bisexuals also hold an ambiguous place in the gay community. A study with college students found that 15 percent felt that bisexuality was not a legitimate orientation. While this was less true of gay and lesbian respondents than heterosexuals, the attitude was present in both groups (Friedman et al. 2014). Bisexuality challenges the idea that orientation is innate and immutable, an idea many straight and gay people believe. Additionally, when bisexual women partner with men or bisexual men partner with women, they may no longer feel welcome in the gay community. The final result is that transgender people and bisexuals are often relegated to a position of low status within a community that is itself stigmatized by the larger heterosexual society (Phelan 2001, pp. 115–117).

It appears that while knowledge of same-sex relations goes far back in history, the technical dichotomy of heterosexuality and homosexuality as we know it today is of nineteenth-century origin; it "is a product of the transition to modernity. . . . This sexual transformation involved such factors as the institutionalization of bourgeois middle-class values, the secularization of social medicine and state discourse on sexuality, the individualized concept of desire and identity, and the premium placed on reproduction within the

NUTSHELL 7.1 Alternate Sexualities

Heterosexuality, homosexuality, and bisexuality are often seen as the only possible sexual orientations. Other identifications, while still relatively rare, are receiving more attention. **Asexuality** as a named identity only traces back to the early 2000s (Cerankowski and Milks 2014). It is generally defined as a "lack of sexual desire or attraction" (S. Scott and Dawson 2015), but most writers on this topic note that asexuality does not necessarily mean a lack of intimacy or close emotional attachment. Asexuality is different from celibacy, in which people have sexual desire but choose not to act on it. The visibility of asexuality has been promoted by AVEN (Asexual Visibility and Education Network).

Little research has been done on inequality and asexuality, but one study (MacInnis and Hodson 2012) found that Americans see asexuals as "less human" than either heterosexuals or homosexuals. The study also found that respondents would be more willing to rent an apartment to a heterosexual person than either a homosexual or an asexual person.

Pansexuality is a term that refers to the potentiality of being attracted to all genders. It is closely related to bisexuality but is generally taken to be more inclusive because it includes attraction to transgender people and to people who identify outside the gender binary. Because this term is fairly new, we know little about whether there is a relationship between pansexuality and inequality.

nuclear family" (Herdt 1997, p. 39). At that time, homosexuality was considered abnormal and a disease, a kind of degeneracy from the healthy condition of heterosexuality. In fact, up until 1973, homosexuality was listed as a mental illness by the American Psychiatric Association (APA) in their *Diagnostic Statistical Manual* (DSM). Recent studies indicate that homosexuality *itself* is not a good predictor of mental illness, but the discrimination gay people face can contribute to illnesses like depression and anxiety (Bostwick et al. 2010).

Until recently, the DSM listed strong and consistent identification with the opposite gender as "gender identity disorder." The DSM V, published in 2013, however, clearly states that being transgender is not, in and of itself, pathological. This view is reflected in a new name: gender dysphoria. The description of gender dysphoria emphasizes the distress many transgender people feel as a result of societal prejudice and discrimination. In the run-up to the publication of the new DSM, some activists argued that there should be no category for transgender people at all, but others argued that without a diagnostic category, transgender people would not be eligible for hormones and other medical interventions under their health insurance policies.

PUBLIC OPINION

The last 15 years has seen remarkable change in public opinion toward gays and lesbians. Prior to that, the majority of Americans believed that homosexuality was unnatural and unhealthy, if not immoral. When one adds to this the belief by staunchly religious groups that homosexuality is also sinful, it is not surprising that, up until the early decades of the twentieth century in the United States, gay people tried to avoid harassment by keeping out of the public eye. In the mid-twentieth century, the anti-alien crusades of Senator Joseph McCarthy and FBI director J. Edgar Hoover as well as city police across the country continued to single out gays and lesbians as targets who were thought to undermine the heterosexual nuclear family as a cultural foundation. "Homosexual acts were illegal in most

states under existing anti-sodomy statutes. . . . Furthermore, gays and lesbians were specifically excluded from laws and policies regulating fair employment practices, housing discrimination, rights of child custody, immigration, inheritance, security clearances, public accommodations, and police protection" (Button, Rienzo, and Wald 1997, p. 24).

National survey data reveal a dramatic change in public opinion toward gays and lesbians over the last 15 years. Data from the General Social Survey, for example, showed that in 2002, 55 percent of American adults felt that homosexuality was "always wrong." In contrast, a 2008 Gallup poll found people split on the morality of homosexuality, and by 2015 a full 63 percent said that homosexuality was "morally acceptable" (Saad 2010; Jones 2015a). Consistent with these polls, a general review of surveys done between 1992 and 2015 revealed a consistent decrease in the percentage of those who believe homosexuality is morally wrong. The review also found that, by 2015, solid majorities supported the right of gay and lesbian people to adopt children, and believed that it was "okay to hire homosexuals as elementary or high school teachers" (Gallup 2015).

While public opinion toward homosexuality has undergone much change, there is still a significant minority who retain traditional views. When we look at these views, we see there is a contrast between Americans' reactions to homosexuals' *morality*, on the one hand, and their rights to *civil liberties*, on the other. This may in part be explained by how each of these is interpreted. While *morality* relates to *individual behavior* and activates traditional heterosexual and religious beliefs of Americans, *civil rights* relates to gays and lesbians as a *group*, does not refer to a specific behavior, and is not as easily linked to religious beliefs. Rather, the civil rights issue is more easily tied to ideas of equality and fairness (Loftus 2001). The difference in respondents' attitudes in these two areas exposes contradictions within the value systems of many Americans.

The framing of certain issues as involving civil rights increases support. For example, when asked whether homosexuals should have the "right" to adopt children, 63 percent of Americans say yes. About 68 percent also believe that homosexual relations between consenting adults should be legal (Gallup 2015). By and large, the belief that civil liberties ought to be curtailed among gays and lesbians has steadily declined since the early 1970s (Pew 2003). We see this support for civil liberties most dramatically in opinions about same-sex marriage. In 2001, 35 percent of Americans approved of legalizing same-sex marriage, while 57 percent opposed it. By 2008, 39 percent of Americans expressed approval and 51 percent disapproval (Pew 2010), and in 2015, a majority of Americans (55 percent) supported it with only 39 percent opposing (Pew 2015d).

However, Americans appear to disagree on whether the trend toward greater acceptance of lesbians and gays is a positive one. Republicans, White evangelical Protestants, less-educated, and older adults are more likely than other groups to see the trend in a negative light (Pew 2009b). Americans are also less accepting of homosexuality than citizens of other Western countries. For example, 60 percent of Americans said that homosexuality should be accepted by society. This compares with 88 percent in Spain, 80 percent in Canada, and 74 percent in Italy. Religion appears to account for some of the difference between countries; the more religious the country, the less accepting of homosexuality (Horowitz 2013).

There are a number of other predictors of support for gay and lesbian rights. For example, people's views on the origin of homosexuality help to determine their feelings about same-sex marriage. Specifically, those who think homosexuality is a choice are less supportive of marriage rights (Duncan and Kemmelmeier 2012; Haider-Markel and Joslyn 2008). Additionally, people who view marriage through a lens of **essentialism** (as an institution for one man/one woman that is natural and therefore invariant over time and place) are less likely to support same-sex marriage than those who see marriage as socially constructed (Duncan and Kemmelmeier 2012).

In general, men who identify as heterosexual appear to be more heterosexist than heterosexual women on a variety of dimensions. For example, they are more hostile toward homosexuals as *individuals*, especially when this involves gay men rather than lesbians. Researchers suggest that heterosexual male aversion to gay men may stem from a variety of factors including fear of sexual advances (and the threat to masculinity that they are perceived to represent) (Bortolin 2010). The eroticization of lesbians and bisexuals in popular culture may allay homophobia against them by heterosexual men (Kite and Whitley Jr. 1998). Men are also more opposed to civil rights, including same-sex marriage, than women (Pew 2015d).

In addition to gender, education is also related to homophobia, with more education being associated with lower degrees of prejudice. Among age groups, a greater proportion of those age 65 and older are prejudiced, compared to those under 30 years of age. This may be partially accounted for by the generally lower education and greater religious traditionalism among older adults. Table 7.1 lists the population categories

TABLE 7.1 Demographic Categories Most Negative on Morality and Civil Liberties of Homosexuals

Most likely to view homosexuality as immoral or to believe in restricting civil liberties of homosexuals are those who are:

- Older
- Less educated
- Male
- From the southern region of the United States
- Non-White
- Evangelical Protestant in religious affiliation

Source: Gallup, Saad 2012; Pew 2015d.

found by Gallup (Saad 2012) and Pew (2015d) to be most negative about the morality of homosexuality and most willing to restrict the civil liberties of homosexuals. Results from a sample of college students reveal similar results, with those who are male, non-White, conservative, and religious having more negative views of homosexuals. Additionally, college students who report having LGB friends and family members have more positive attitudes (Woodford et al. 2012).

Over the years, various polls have indicated that Blacks are more hostile to homosexuality than are Whites. For example, in one study, African American heterosexual undergraduate women had more negative attitudes toward gays and lesbians than their White counterparts. Religious views and perceived threats about AIDS and about the availability of acceptable men for marriage may have helped to account for these racial differences in attitudes (Vincent, Peterson, and Parrott 2009). Other research shows that an estimated 58 percent of Blacks and 59 percent of Hispanic voters (compared to 49 percent of Whites) in 2008 supported Proposition 8, which banned gay marriage in California. Ultimately, researchers found that the greater support of both Blacks and Hispanics was largely linked to their higher religiosity. Seventy percent of voters who attended religious services weekly, along with a greater percentage of politically conservative Republicans, voted for the ban (Egan and Sherrill 2009).

While Blacks are less supportive than Whites of gay marriage and are more likely to see homosexuality as immoral, they are also more likely to believe that wedding-related businesses should be required to serve same-sex couples (61 percent of Blacks compared to 45 percent of Whites), and they are more likely to say that gay people are discriminated against. It is likely that these views are a result of the empathy Blacks feel due to the historic, albeit quite different, discrimination they have faced themselves (Gecewicz and Lipka 2014). Blacks' views on homosexuality and gay marriage, like those of Whites, are becoming more positive. In fact, Black churches played a pivotal role in fighting for the passage of state-level gay marriage bills (Harris 2012).

There is ample polling data that can help us understand public opinion toward gays and lesbians, but much less data exists about attitudes toward transgender people. In fact, it was not until 2011 that the word "transgender" appeared in a poll (Roper Center 2013). This is largely because gender identity issues tended to be hidden or conflated—incorrectly—in the public mind with homosexuality. In recent years, however, well-known figures like Laverne Cox and Caitlyn Jenner have revealed that they are transgender, and television shows such as *Glee*, *Transparent*, the *Fosters*, and *Orange Is the New Black* feature transgender characters. As transgender people have become more present in the media, Americans also report higher levels of personal acquaintance. For example, in 2015, 22 percent of likely voters responding to a poll said that they knew or worked with a transgender person, up from 17 percent the year before (Halloran 2015). The increasing visibility of transgender people makes it likely that polling agencies will increasingly focus on this issue.

The data that has been collected suggests that a large majority of the public (71 percent) think that there is discrimination against transgender people. This is larger than the 68 percent who think there is discrimination against gays and lesbians (Roper Center 2013). In terms of the perceived morality of being transgender, in 2015, 33 percent of respondents to a national poll said that they believed it was immoral (14 percent said it was morally acceptable, and 39 percent said it was not a moral issue). The survey also asked whether people would be upset if their child were transgender. About 41 percent said they would be "very upset," while 39 percent said "not very upset" or "not upset at all" (YouGov 2015).

Stereotypes

The attitudes adults hold about gays, lesbians, and transgender people are at least moderately related to stereotypes held about them. These stereotypes include beliefs about gays' personality traits, behavior, and physical characteristics. Popular stereotypes of gays and lesbians suggest that negative reactions to them are due in part to the fact that they are seen as violating traditional gender rules about behavior and interests. The hostility toward men who violate masculine roles appears to be stronger than that toward women who violate feminine prescriptions (Kite and Whitley Jr. 1998; Herek 2002). Parents seem to be concerned that their sons, more so than their daughters, conform to the traditional gender role associated with their sex (Kane 2006). One particularly damaging and pervasive stereotype is that gay men are more likely than heterosexual men to sexually abuse children. As Herek (2013) points out, this stereotype should not be surprising given a history of discredited groups being blamed for hurting vulnerable members of the majority group (for example, Black men being portrayed as rapists of White women). The child predator stereotype began as early as 1977 in the U.S. and was fueled by the erroneous linkage of the two in the sex abuse scandals of the early 2000s. In fact, multiple studies show that gay men are no more likely to abuse children than straight men (Jenny, Roesler, and Poyer 1994; Holmes and Slap 1998). While the acceptance of this stereotype has decreased markedly among Americans, it has been hard to entirely erase (Herek 2013).

Stereotypes about gay men suggest that they are viewed as being feminine, emotional, neat, interested in fine arts, and creative. In a study at a private Midwestern university, Blashill and Powlishta (2009) found that students viewed gay men as less masculine than both heterosexual men and lesbians. They were seen as equally feminine as heterosexual women. The violation of traditional masculine roles is strongly held in popular stereotypes, and it is this dimension of the stereotype that may be most clearly linked to prejudice against gay men. Stereotypes about lesbians, like those of gay men, often contain violations of traditional gender roles in featuring many masculine traits. At the same time, stereotypes of lesbians appear to be somewhat less rigid; for example, an image of the highly feminine lesbian also exists in the public mind (Geiger, Harwood, and Hummert 2006).

Stereotypes can be harmful in a number of different ways. For example, when we assume that LGBTQ people have stereotypical traits—even if those traits are positive—it is harder to see them as full and complex human beings (Miller and Lewallen 2015). Conversely, labeling an individual as having the stereotypical traits of gay people, and therefore as being automatically lesbian or gay, can have significant consequences. For example, since as late as 1990, lesbian immigrants could be refused entry into the United States, and conscious attempts were made by border agents to identify lesbians. They looked for visible cues to the individual's sexual preference. Lesbian immigrants were often aware of this kind of screening, so they dressed and prepared themselves physically so that they would not appear to violate traditional images of what a woman *should* look like (sometimes called "straightening up") (Luibheid 1998, pp. 485–486).

Today there are no official immigration restrictions on gays and lesbians, and they may apply for amnesty in the United States if they are being persecuted for their sexual orientation in their home countries. Ironically, this leads to a situation where some gays and lesbians, in order to bolster their applications, are forced to do the opposite of straightening up by acting out gay stereotypes in front of the government agents deciding their cases. They fear that if they don't act "gay enough," their claim of being gay will be contested or they will not be seen as at risk for persecution back home (Bilefsky 2011).

Transgender people face particularly pernicious stereotyping. This may be because they throw into question both gender and sexuality dichotomies, showing the fluidity of both categories. In a content analysis of media images of transgender people between 2002 and 2012, for example, it was found that the most common images were of transgender people as victims, villains (often murderers), and sex workers (GLAAD 2012). Survey data suggest that another commonly held view of transgender people is that they are "confused" (Gazzola and Morrison 2014).

Since stereotyping often develops in the absence of regular contact between the groups involved, it would seem that increased contact and acquaintance with gay, lesbian, and transgender individuals might decrease prejudice against these groups, and, indeed, this appears to be the case, at least for gays and lesbians. An analysis of 41 studies revealed that contact reduces prejudice toward homosexuals, but contact is more effective in reducing negative attitudes about lesbians than it is in reducing prejudice by heterosexuals against gay men (Smith, Axelton, and Saucier 2009). The positive effect of contact on lowering prejudice has been found for other groups in many other studies as well (Pettigrew and Tropp 2006). This effect is especially likely if the contact is of an equal status type among individuals pursuing a common goal. It is possible that contact with transgender people will have the same effect, but this research has not yet been conducted.

LGBTQ PEOPLE AS STATUS GROUPS

As the surveys just discussed indicate, LGBTQ people form status categories with low prestige or social honor in the United States. As such, they possess all the core attributes of status groups. Most notably, they are viewed by others as sharing certain lifestyle characteristics and being qualitatively different from outsiders. Being gay or lesbian, for example, is associated with having certain kinds of occupations (e.g., hairdresser) and dress (high fashion, artsy) (Madon 1997). However, their differences are defined as even deeper. Recall that in his depiction of status groups, Max Weber argued that extreme status separation between groups is most likely if the differences that separate them are thought of as being "ethnic" in nature. Consistent with this conception, scholar Stephen Murray has referred to the homosexual community as a "quasi-ethnic group" (1996, p. 4). This suggests that the differences must be viewed as fundamental, almost biological in nature, for caste-like arrangements to develop between groups. As described above, about half of U.S. adults currently believe that homosexuality is biologically based (Jones 2015a). In their fight for political legitimacy and equal rights, the earliest gay-rights organizations in the United States (e.g., the Mattachine Society) characterized "homosexuals as a sexual minority,

similar to other ethnic and cultural minorities" (Button, Rienzo, and Wald 1997, p. 25).

In addition to being viewed as qualitatively different in lifestyle, being seen as a different "kind" of people, separated from the rest of society, and occupying a distinctive place on a hierarchy of social honor or prestige, a status group is also perceived as having an internal social cohesion that unites them. That is, they are seen as sticking together and being mutually supportive of each other. As with most status groups, outsiders lump them all together, even though there is a wide diversity of people and experiences within the group. For example, stereotypes often hide the fact that the experiences of gay/lesbian people of color are often quite different from those of White gays and lesbians. This is because race is generally less concealable than sexual orientation, and gay and lesbian people of color may be made more aware of it through the discrimination they experience. Because of their salience, race and class can cause divisions within the gay/lesbian community—especially when race is ignored or assumed to be a "completed project" (Eng 2010).

On the other hand, given that sexual orientation divides gays and lesbians from and is a primary basis for conflict with outsiders, it does help to unite them. This has resulted not only in the creation of informal friendship networks among gays and lesbians but also in the development of neighborhoods with high concentrations of lesbians and gays, separate institutions catering to a homosexual clientele, and political-rights organizations.

Finally, what further marks LGBTQ people as negatively defined status groups are fears of contamination and contact on the part of outsiders. Concerns about purity on the part of traditionalists and heterosexuals are indicative of concerted attempts to keep boundaries between heterosexuals and homosexuals intact. Publically known association by a heterosexual with homosexuals, especially of a personal kind, creates the risk that some of the ostracism held for lesbians and gays may "rub off" on the individual. In a few legal cases in the U.S. and elsewhere, defendants have used a "gay panic defense," alleging that a gay person propositioned them, causing them to panic and attack them. Other defendants have attempted a "trans panic" defense when they have become involved with transgender people who did not immediately reveal their status. In 2014, California banned both types of defenses, but other states have yet to follow suit. The fact that these panic defenses are considered legitimate enough to raise in court hints at a level of societal fear about personal contact between heterosexual and homosexual or transgender people.

In the 1960s, gay and lesbian parents who sought custody of their children were frequently denied it because court opinions were dominated by the beliefs that gay men and lesbian women were more likely than heterosexual parents to molest their children and pass on their sexual orientation to their children. These beliefs gradually eroded so that by the mid-1980s, court opinions were shifting (Rivers 2010). Recent research indicates that children who grow up with lesbian or gay parents are well-adjusted, more socially and academically competent, and less likely to engage in delinquent behavior than children of heterosexual parents (Gartrell and Bos 2010).

Still, negative beliefs persist in part because they are consistent with prevailing stereotypes and help justify hostile treatment of homosexuals.

Photo 7.1   This all-inclusive sign provides an option to traditional gender-binary bathrooms.

© iStock.com/Craig McCausland.

MINI-CASE 7.1

Bathroom Bills

The broad issue of transgender rights has sometimes been waylaid by debates over restrooms. Legislators in many states have proposed bills that would force people to use the restroom that matches the gender they were assigned at birth. Proponents of such bills say that they are concerned about protecting women and girls. They worry that a transgender person might sexually assault a child or that a man could enter a women's bathroom "in disguise" as a woman and assault someone. A content analysis of media reports about transgender inclusive legislation found that there is rarely any mention of concern about transgender men entering the men's bathroom in this debate (Schilt and Westbrook 2015). Instead, many of those who support bathroom bills assume that women need protection, that biological males are violence-prone, and that being transgender may be linked to sexual predation. Opponents of the laws point out that there have been no documented cases of assaults perpetrated by transgender people or people pretending to be transgender in bathrooms. They also point out that bathroom laws only recognize danger for **cisgender** women (those who were assigned female at birth and continue to identify as such). There is no consideration given to the much higher level of danger that faces a transgender person who must go into a bathroom that does not match their gender expression. What do you think? ■

Despite evidence to the contrary, opponents of gay rights often use "lurid stereotypes of gays as child molesters, sources of disease, and an abomination in the eyes of God" (Button, Rienzo, and Wald 1997, p. 195). It is feared that unless gays and lesbians are held in check, traditional morality and family structure as foundations of our society will become contaminated and seriously weakened. In the eyes of these opponents, social, cultural, and moral purity must be maintained, and contamination avoided at all costs.

THE LAW, SEXUAL ORIENTATION, AND GENDER IDENTITY

There are no federal laws that explicitly prohibit discrimination based on sexual orientation or gender identity. Title VII of the 1964 Civil Rights Act prohibits employment discrimination because of an individual's race, color, religion, national origin, or sex, but for many years was read to offer no such prohibition based on sexual orientation. Arguments in favor of protection for homosexuals, transgender, and other non-gender-conforming people under Title VII generally involved reference to the inclusion of "sex" in the law. Ironically, however, the word *sex* was added to Title VII at the last minute by a powerful anti–civil-rights representative who thought that, by adding it, Title VII would be voted down (Eskridge and Frickey 1995). It passed anyway. It is still difficult to know exactly what Congress had in mind, since *sex* was added to Title VII a day after it was presented. Consequently, there was little time for discussion of the meaning of this inclusion (Nathans 2001). Attempts to use other bases, such as the right to privacy, free speech, and equal protection to protect gays and lesbians, have not been particularly successful, and, consequently, the meaning given to the language in Title VII has become very important in efforts to legislate against employment discrimination (Zimmer et al. 2000).

Confusion and inconsistency in conceptualizing and defining "sex," "gender," and "sexual orientation" abound in legal venues and have affected the interpretation of Title VII. The manner in which these have been linked in legal cases reveals the biases in favor of traditional definitions and connections among these terms. Underlying these interpretations is the acceptance of heterosexuality as opposed to any other form. In this view, one's sex (defined biologically in terms of genitalia) is thought to automatically determine one's gender demeanor and role (social) as well as one's sexual orientation (sexual attractions and behavior). For example, males are expected to act in a masculine manner and to be attracted to females. They are not meant to be homosexual in their sexual orientation.

One consequence of these assumed associations is that courts have historically confused sex, gender, and sexual orientation, often in a way that results in denying the rights not only of gays and lesbians, but also of those who do not present themselves or act in a manner traditionally expected of their sex. A man, for example, who acts "effeminately" and who may or may not be gay might not be protected by a court because judges directly associate such behavior with being gay. As a consequence, while individuals who bring their complaints to court may argue that they are being discriminated against because they do not act in a "masculine" manner, courts often make decisions in these cases on the basis of sexual orientation, assuming that such behavior *means* that the persons are gay. In this way, gender expression and sexual orientation are conflated and incorrectly tied together (Valdes 1995; Nathans 2001). This results in plaintiffs losing because, as noted earlier, Title VII was not originally read to cover discrimination based on sexual orientation. An example of the narrow manner in which courts have often interpreted Title VII is revealed explicitly in a 1979 case involving three gay plaintiffs who lost their jobs. The Ninth Circuit Court judge argued that in including sex as a basis for discrimination in Title VII, "Congress had only the traditional notions of '*sex*' in mind," and that it "applies only to discrimination on the basis of *gender* and should not be judicially extended to include sexual preference such as homosexuality" (quoted in Zimmer et al. 2000, pp. 624–625; italics added).

The ruling discussed above shows how the court used the terms *sex* and *gender* interchangeably (see also Case 1995). The easy substitution of the terms *sex* and *gender* in legal arguments adds to the confusion concerning the terms' meanings. The case also reveals the narrow manner in which both sexuality and gender is framed by the court. The legal situation has been further complicated by the fact that some courts define *sex* according to the genitalia assigned to the person at birth, while others consider later operations that change an individual's biological makeup (Valdes 1995). Finally, the case shows how the legal system's actions have the effect of shoring up the gender binary.

Because of these areas of confusion in the law, the courts and the Equal Employment Opportunity Commission (EEOC), the federal agency charged with enforcing Title VII, have generally interpreted "sex" to refer only to biology and not to sexual orientation or gender identity. In a particularly notable case decided in 1978, *Smith v. Liberty Mutual Insurance Co.*, Smith was not hired as a mail clerk because he was seen as "effeminate" and, consequently, "not too suited for the job" (quoted in Valdes 1995, p. 138). The representative for the EEOC, which examined the case, reported that Smith liked "playing musical instruments, singing, dancing and sewing." These were viewed as "interests . . . not normally associated with males" (p. 138). Smith argued that he had been denied employment because he had hobbies that were not consistent with the masculine role and, therefore, was a victim of gender stereotyping. That is, his argument had to do with the traditional connection made between sex and gender behavior. In contrast, the employer argued that he had not been hired because Smith was "suspected" of being gay. In other words, the employer drew a conclusion about Smith's sexual orientation based simply on his gender behavior. The court ended up drawing the same connection, noting that Title VII did not cover an individual's sexual orientation. Thus, it ignored the argument of Smith and the fact that the evidence demonstrated that the discrimination had been based, as Smith proposed, upon his *gender behavior*

(effeminacy) and not his *sexual orientation*. This shows how the court used the plaintiff's behavior as a measure of his sexual orientation, and how stereotypical misinterpretations can result in legal defeats for lesbians, gays, and others.

It was not until 1989 that the courts began to recognize gender identity and expression as covered under Title VII. In the famous case of *Price Waterhouse v. Hopkins*, the U.S. Supreme Court found that Ann Hopkins had been discriminated against because partners refused to propose her as a partner in the firm on the basis of her gender behavior. To them, Ann displayed many of the characteristics traditionally associated with masculinity. She was described by some partners as "macho," as having "overcompensated for being a woman," and in need of "a course at charm school" (*Price Waterhouse v. Hopkins* 1989). In spite of her evidenced abilities and experience, Hopkins was passed over for partnership. In ruling against Price Waterhouse because of sex stereotyping, Justice Brennan stated that:

> [W]e are beyond the day when an employer could evaluate employees by assuming or insisting that they matched the stereotype associated with their group. . . . An employer who objects to aggressiveness in women but whose positions require this trait places women in an intolerable and impermissible catch 22: out of a job if they behave aggressively and out of a job if they do not. Title VII lifts women out of this bind.
> (*Price Waterhouse v. Hopkins*, p. 251)

The disposition in the Ann Hopkins case was the opposite found in the Smith case discussed earlier. It appears there was less tolerance for "sissies" than for "tomboys" (Valdes 1995, p. 179). "The man who exhibits feminine qualities is doubly despised" (Case 1995, p. 3). This is consistent with public opinion surveys, which find a greater contempt for men who violate their traditional roles than for women who act similarly.

Two important recent cases have established that both transgender and gay people are covered under the "sex" provision of Title VII.

Starting in 2004 with the *Smith v. the City of Salem* decision, federal courts began to rule that transgender people are protected from employment discrimination. Another important move forward happened in 2010 when Mia Macy, a transgender woman, was refused a job with the Bureau of Alcohol, Firearms, and Tobacco when she disclosed her transgender status. The EEOC initially refused to act in the case, as they did not define it as a case of sex discrimination. Macy appealed that decision to the courts, won the case in 2012, and today the EEOC protects transgender people under Title VII. Even more recently, in *Baldwin v. the Department of Transportation*, the EEOC changed its stance about whether gays and lesbians are also protected under the sex clause of Title VII. Decided in 2015, this case involved a gay man who was not hired for a permanent job because of his homosexuality. The EEOC decided that discrimination against gay people is, in effect, discrimination based on gender—the worker's gender and the gender of his or her partner.

The federal court precedents and EEOC decisions theoretically mean that most workers in the U.S. are protected from employment discrimination on the basis of sexual orientation and gender expression. Additionally, in 2014, President Obama issued an order prohibiting federal contractors from discriminating based on sexual orientation. There remains, however, a chance that the Supreme Court could rule against a gay or transgender person in a future case, setting a new precedent. It is also possible another president could overturn Obama's executive order or that the EEOC could reinterpret Title VII. To date, there are no federal laws that guarantee the protections that have been won.

While legal protection for those with nontraditional sexual orientations and gender identities has been weak at best at the federal level, a number of local and state governments have passed laws granting protection. Before 1985, only 2 states and 30 local governments provided protection for private and public employees, but by 1994, 9 states and 81 local governments had done so, and by 2015, 19 states provided protection for both gender identity and sexual orientation,

and an additional 3 offered protection for just sexual orientation. Additionally, over 200 cities and counties have passed laws against employment discrimination because of sexual orientation and, in some cases, gender identity (Phelps 2015; Klawitter and Flatt 1998). In 2015, 90 percent of Fortune 500 companies had protections based on sexual orientation. Even with these state, local, and company ordinances in place, however, a recent poll revealed that 47 percent of gays and lesbians have experienced employment discrimination (Human Rights Campaign 2015b). Additionally, there are states that have actively worked to limit or deny employment rights. For example, in 2015, Arkansas passed a bill preventing cities and localities from enacting anti-discrimination legislation that was stricter than any law at the state level. Since Arkansas has no anti-discrimination law protecting LGBTQ people, localities are now barred from doing so. Tennessee has a similar measure in place.

Estimates suggest that today half of all gays and lesbians are covered by legal employment discrimination protections granted by their states, localities, or through their employment with the federal government (Phelps 2015). The extension of Title VII means that most workers also now have federal protections. There are still limitations, however. For example, Title VII and many state and local laws do not protect workers in companies with fewer than 15 employees. In any company, if it can be proven that one's sexual preference is actually a "bona fide occupational qualification" for a position, then gays and lesbians may be excluded from that job (Zimmer et al. 2000, p. 634). Finally, most statutes exempt religious organizations from anti-discrimination laws. This is consistent with Title VII, which, in its original form, exempted religious institutions "to perform work connected with the carrying on by such corporation, association, or society of its religious activities." Congress amended this language in 1972, removing the word "religious" before activities. This allowed religious organizations involved in secular work (for example, a religious hospital) to discriminate if it was consistent with their religious principles (Thompson 2015).

Full legal protection for lesbians and gays has a long way to go. Most importantly, employment laws only cover discrimination at work. There is little protection against discrimination in other areas like housing. The Department of Housing and Urban Development tested whether there was discrimination in the online housing market. They sent out requests for information to people trying to rent out their apartments. Owners responded 15 percent less often to couples whose names suggested they were of the same gender (like John and Jacob) than to couples with traditionally opposite gender names (Jennifer and John) (Friedman et al. 2013). As of 2015, only 21 states had statutes prohibiting housing discrimination based on sexual orientation. Of those, 19 also had protections based on gender identity (Human Rights Campaign 2015b).

Because protections are scattered and are not enshrined in federal law, LGBT groups pushed for the passage of a federal law—the Employment Nondiscrimination Act (ENDA). This law would have added sexual orientation and gender identity to the list of protected classes in Title VII. It was

never successfully passed through both houses of Congress, at least in part over disagreements about the exemption religious organizations should be given. Now, the Equality Act has been up for consideration by Congress. This bill is much broader than ENDA—it would cover both sexual orientation and gender identity and would cover much more than just employment, with provisions for housing, credit, educational access, and public accommodations.

Same-Sex Marriage

Many see the legalization of same-sex marriage nationwide in 2015 as a victory for gay rights advocates. It was a victory for transgender people as well, some of whom were previously not allowed to marry. Prior to legalization of same-sex marriage, state law varied it how it handled marriage law and transgender people. In general, when a person transitioned prior to applying for a marriage license and legally established the new gender, they were allowed to marry—unless they wanted to marry someone of the same sex in a

Photo 7.2 The national legalization of same-sex marriage has enabled many couples, some of whom had been together for decades, to get married and receive the legal benefits associated with it.

© iStock.com/lisafx.

state that did not recognize such marriages. This was even more complicated in states, like Texas, that did not allow people to legally alter their gender. In those cases, a transgender man could only marry a legally male person (since the transgender person's birth certificate still listed him as female). When a transition occurred after marriage, the marriage was generally considered valid because it was valid at the time it was contracted. This led to the odd situation of legally wed same-sex couples in states that did not permit such marriages.

Marriage is important not only for its symbolism of inclusion; it also confers a wide variety of rights that have profound implications for inequality. Among others, these rights include hospital visitation if the partner is seriously injured, Social Security and pension benefits for a surviving partner, employer health insurance, and family leave if the partner is sick. The denial of these important benefits was one of the reasons same-sex couples began to fight for the right to marry.

The first same-sex couple to file for a marriage license did so in 1970 in Minnesota. They were denied the license and ultimately lost in court cases that came before the Minnesota Supreme Court and the U.S. Supreme Court. After 1970, multiple states passed bans preventing same-sex couples from marrying. The federal government became involved in the issue with the passage of the 1996 Defense of Marriage Act (DOMA). DOMA clearly illustrates how proposed legislation on sexual orientation is strongly tied to (1) the extent to which it is seen as supporting or undermining traditional values and social order and (2) how effectively and in what manner the issue is framed by proponents and opponents to the legislation. The subject of DOMA related directly to the moral dimension of public opinions on homosexuality. As we saw earlier, polls often uncover a schism in the public's view of the morality of homosexuality on the one hand, and the affording of civil rights to gays and lesbians on the other. A larger percentage of the public feel that the economic rights of lesbians and gays should be protected than say that homosexuality

is moral. On a broad level, this conflict is one that pits religious values against those of a secular democracy, and highlights the issue of separation of church and state.

Traditional U.S. values assign privilege to heterosexual over homosexual relationships, and assume a narrow and clear relationship between one's sex and gender role. Congressional sponsors proposed the DOMA bill "to define and protect the institution of marriage" and "to make explicit what has been understood under federal law for over 200 years; that a marriage is the legal union of a man and a woman as husband and wife, and a spouse is a husband or wife of the opposite sex" (Barr et al. 1996, p. 2). In arguing for its passage, the proponents of DOMA focused on the need to preserve traditional values of family and morality and on alleged attempts by the gay community to undermine "civilized" society. Traditional marriage was praised "as a 'corner-stone,' 'foundation,' 'bedrock,' and 'fundamental pillar' of any civilized society" (Lewis and Edelson 2000, p. 202). In these ways, proponents of DOMA sought to frame the legislation in *moral* rather than *civil rights* terms, knowing the public's perception of homosexuality as immoral.

Almost immediately after its passage, some states began to push back on the issue of gay rights. In 1999, California allowed for same-sex domestic partnerships, which conferred some, but not all, of the rights of marriage. Other states followed, either calling the new legal unions "domestic partnerships" or "civil unions." In 2013, the Supreme Court overturned DOMA, finding it unconstitutional. This federal-level victory came because the Court agreed that marriage is a civil right, not a moral issue. At the same time, they also declined to hear a California case brought by proponents of a state-level ban on gay marriage. In refusing to hear the case, the Supreme Court allowed a lower court ruling that overturned the ban to stand, but it did not prohibit states from having such bans. Between 2002 and 2015, 37 states legalized gay marriage, while bans were put into effect in 13 states. In 2015, the U.S. Supreme Court ruled that gay couples are protected under the Equal Protection clause of the U.S.

Constitution and that they cannot be banned from marriage.

Until DOMA was overturned, same-sex marriages were not recognized at the federal level, the result being that persons in long-term, same-sex relationships were not protected in the same ways that individuals in traditional marriages were. Today, however, gays and lesbians have the same federal and state rights granted to persons in traditional marriages. As a whole, the federal government offers 1,138 benefits based on marital status (Human Rights Campaign 2015a). Of these rights, Social Security survivor benefits are particularly important to families in terms of ensuring financial stability in case of a death of one partner. One analysis suggested that these benefits could be worth up to $343,000 for a family (Jurs 2015). While gay and lesbian married couples automatically became eligible for survivor benefits when the Court affirmed gay people's right to marry, it was not until August of 2015 that the Justice Department grandfathered in same-sex couples who had been married in a state where it was legal but lived in states that did not recognize their marriages. Couples who either chose not to marry or who were unable to afford to go to a state where gay marriage was legal, however, were unable to retroactively claim Social Security benefits.

SOCIOECONOMIC PROFILE OF GAY, LESBIAN, AND TRANSGENDER PEOPLE

Like data on the wealthy, we do not know very much about the actual socioeconomic position, or even the number, of gays, lesbians, and transgender people because many choose not to identify themselves for fear of their safety. This alone tells us a great deal about the stigma attached to being gay/lesbian or transgender.

Because transgender issues have only recently come to greater mainstream awareness, we have little data on how many transgender people there are. A 2011 survey conducted by the Williams Institute suggests that about 0.3 percent of Americans are transgender (Gates 2011). Another study (Harris 2015) used Social Security

records to count how many people changed either their gender or their name (from a name traditionally assigned to one gender to one of the other gender, for example Joseph to Josie). Harris found evidence of the existence of transgender people from 1936 when the Social Security Administration started keeping records. Numbers increased through time so that, by 2010, there were 90,000 living individuals who had changed their name and about 22,000 who had also changed their gender. Of course not all transgender people change their names with the Social Security Administration, and it is possible that some changed their names for reasons other than being transgender. At the same time, this study did give us a rough measure of prevalence. Pairing Social Security records with Census data also allowed the author to conclude that there are more transgender women than transgender men in the United States. Previous estimates of the population have found Whites to be overrepresented, and this data finds that to be the case as well, but not by a lot. Whites are overrepresented by about 4 percent, Blacks underrepresented by a little over 2 percent, and Hispanics underrepresented by about 4 percent.

There are disagreements about how to measure the gay/lesbian population. Measurement issues have revolved around how to define homosexuality and how to procure a representative sample so as to estimate the size of this population. Some estimates have put the figure as high as 10 percent, but that is considered by many to be too high. Generally, four national data sets are used to determine the gay/lesbian population in the United States. The General Social Survey (GSS), the National Survey of Family Growth (NSFG), Gallup, and the U.S. census provide the best estimates. At the same time, the data are still limited and may be inaccurate. For example, the Census does not ask about sexual orientation, only about whether a live-in partner of a respondent is of the same or opposite sex. Research suggests that the Census estimates may be incorrect because a surprising number of people in opposite-sex marriages mistakenly report having a "same sex husband/wife/spouse" (Lewis, Bates, and Streeter 2015). The GSS asks only about respondents' sexual practices—specifically, the number of female and male partners people have had during various time periods. It should be noted that historically and cross-culturally, determining a person's sexual identity on the basis of sexual behavior has been problematic. Just because a wife has sex with her husband for example, this does not necessarily mean that she identifies as heterosexual (Badgett 2001). The NSFG asks 18- to 44-year-olds about how they identify and the types of people to whom they are attracted. Gallup asks people about orientation but conflates sexual orientation and gender identity by asking, "Do you personally identify as gay, lesbian, bisexual or transgender?"

Not surprisingly, the estimates of the gay and lesbian population vary with the measure used. Recent Gallup data indicates that about 3.6 percent of the population identify as LGBT (Newport and Gates 2015). Pooling GSS data from 2008 and 2013, we see that while 4.6 percent of men have at least one homosexual experience after the age of 18, only 1.9 percent report exclusively homosexual encounters. For women, the equivalent percentages are 0.4 and 5.9 (GSS 2015).

Using data collected between 2011 and 2013, the NSFG finds that 92.1 percent of men say that they are only attracted to women, but 95.6 identify as heterosexual (1.8 say they are homosexual, and 1.2 say bisexual). The figures for women also vary with the measure. About 5.4 percent of women report a sexual experience with another woman since age 18, but only 0.4 percent report exclusively same-sex experiences. The NSFG reports that 81 percent of women say they are only attracted to men, and 92.3 report a heterosexual identity (with 1.3 percent saying they are homosexual and a notable 5.5 percent reporting a bisexual orientation) (CDC 2013).

Estimates from the census suggest that there were about 783,100 same-sex couples in the United States in 2014, with about 25,000 more female than male couples. About 8 out of 10 couples were White. The people designated as the "householders" averaged 48.4 years and their partners 46.5. In about three-quarters of the households at least one of the partners was employed, and in 60 percent both people were employed. Approximately 17.3 percent lived with children (10.4 percent of male couples and 23.7 percent of female couples) (U.S. Census Bureau 2015a).

California, New York, Texas, Florida, and Illinois have the largest number of same-sex couples, and Washington D.C. has the highest proportion (U.S. Census Bureau 2013b). San Francisco, Portland, and Austin have the highest percentages of gay people (6.2, 5.4, and 5.3 percent, respectively) (Newport and Gates 2015). Studies find that people are much more likely to identify themselves in surveys as gay in tolerant places, strongly suggesting that geographic comparisons are unreliable and that the overall gay population is undercounted (Coffman, Coffman, and Ericson 2013).

Stereotypes suggest that gays and lesbians tend to be highly educated and affluent. Recent data, however, suggests a much more complicated picture. It should first be noted that it is difficult to make comparisons about educational attainment between homosexuals and heterosexuals, largely because studies use different measures. For example, census data, which only identifies people as gay if they live with a same-sex partner, shows that a greater percentage of lesbians and gay men have higher degrees than other individuals. Specifically, about 46 percent of people in same-sex couples have college degrees compared to under one-third of those in heterosexual partnerships (U.S. Census Bureau 2015a). Gallup Poll data, however, which includes all people who identify as homosexual, bisexual, or transgender, indicates that this group, on average, reports lower levels of education than those who are heterosexual and gender conforming (Gates and Newport 2012). It is likely this discrepancy is due to the different populations studied.

Income data is similarly confusing to parse. Looking at census data, it appears that coupled lesbians are more likely to be in the low-income category than married straight couples. Coupled gay men, however, are less likely than individuals living with an opposite-sex partner to be in the low-income categories. An extensive analysis from the Williams Institute (Albelda et al. 2009) that controlled for important variables related to poverty, however, showed that poverty rates are higher among households with same-sex partners than those in heterosexual unions. This is particularly true for households with children, older lesbian couples, and couples living in rural areas. Notably, gay or lesbian households in which one or both of the partners are African American have poverty rates higher than other gay/lesbian households and higher than African Americans in opposite-sex partnerships.

The NSFG, drawing on data gathered from a national sample of 18–44-year-olds, shows an even more dramatic discrepancy between gay, straight, and bisexual people. While 15 percent of male heterosexual people and 21 percent of females are in poverty, the equivalent statistics for gay men were 20.5 percent and for lesbians 25.6 percent. Bisexuals fare the worst, with 25.9 percent of males and 29.4 percent of women in poverty

(Badgett, Durso, and Schneebaum 2013). Earlier studies that suggested that gay and lesbian couples had higher incomes than straight couples were based on small samples and tended to include disproportionate numbers of more affluent individuals, or only included gay people living with their partners, so their results did not accurately reflect the situation of the gay/lesbian population as a whole.

Stereotypes suggest that gay men and lesbians are clustered in gender atypical occupations. This appears to have only a small basis in truth, with gay people being slightly more likely to have gender atypical jobs—men more so than women. An extensive analysis of the data reveals that gender invariance in adolescence explains little of this difference (in other words, violating gender norms as a teenager does not predict later occupation). The difference is better explained by educational qualifications, parental status, and marital status (Ueno, Roach, and Peña-Talamantes 2013).

NUTSHELL 7.2   Official Gender Change

One important part of the transition from one gender to another is gaining legal recognition for the new status. As of 2010, the federal government allows for passports to be changed with documentation of "appropriate clinical treatment for gender transition to the new gender." This is a change from the past when surgical reassignment had to have taken place to get a passport issued in a different gender. Today, to get a regular 10-year passport, a doctor simply needs to certify that a person's transition is complete. This may or may not involve surgery (National Center for Transgender Equality 2015b).

There are two other important documents that establish legal gender: a birth certificate and a driver's license. Both of these are managed at the state level, and there is wide variation in laws regarding them. Currently, all states have a mechanism by which a driver's license can be changed. All but five states will either amend or issue a new birth certificate. While law is changing in this area, many states require proof of surgical change to change a birth certificate or driver's license. California, Washington, and Vermont do not require such

proof. Tennessee is the only state in which people are legally prohibited from changing their birth certificates, although other states (like Ohio and Idaho) make it impossible through policy and practice. Adding further confusion, it is possible to have been born in a state that does not allow for birth certificates to be changed, and then to be denied a driver's license change in one's current state because they require an amended birth certificate (Lambda Legal 2015).

There are important reasons for transgender people to change their gender legally. Inconsistent records can cause problems when multiple forms of identification are required. As is described later in this chapter, transgender people have faced harassment from police and other officials. Carrying an identification with a gender that does not match one's gender expression forces people to out themselves as transgender and can lead to harassment. Some states' requirement that surgery be completed to change identity papers is problematic because some people do not want surgery or cannot afford it (Lambda Legal 2015). Additionally, surgery can limit a person's ability to conceive or bear children later.

The U.S. military is among the most masculine of institutions, yet a significant number of gays and lesbians currently serve. In 2011, estimates suggested that over 47,000 lesbians, gay men, and bisexuals were on active duty with another 31,000 in the reserves. Gay men's representation in the military is slightly below their representation in the general population, while lesbian representation is somewhat higher (Rostker, Hosek, and Vaiana 2011). While it is likely there have been many gay men and lesbians in the military for a long time, numbers were hard to estimate prior to 2011 because gays were not allowed to enlist until 1994. From 1994 until 2011 they could serve but only if they did not reveal their homosexuality (under the "Don't Ask, Don't Tell" policy). Transgender people are still not allowed to serve in the military, but estimates suggest that there may be 149,000 current and former transgender soldiers (National Center for Transgender Equality 2015a).

In some situations, there is pressure for LGBTQ people to be dishonest or hide their sexual orientation or gender identity. In their social interactions with gender-conforming individuals, especially at work, they need to negotiate the relationships between their biological sex, gender identity, and gender performance. While moving between gendered behaviors, transgender individuals become highly sensitive to gender discrimination because they experience differences in their treatment as they change their gender performances (Connell 2010). Some give gender performances that are consistent with and expected of their biological sex; for example, a male exhibits masculine behavior. He will *do* the gender that is expected of him by gender-conforming colleagues, even though it is inconsistent with the gender with which he identifies. Others act with a mix of societally defined masculine and feminine behaviors or act openly in a manner consistent with their gender identity (Connell 2010).

NEGATIVE CONSEQUENCES OF STIGMATIZATION

As ostracized *status* groups, lesbians and gays have historically experienced a wide variety of recurrent stresses and obstacles in the United States, ranging from psychological difficulties, to personal physical attacks, to institutional and legal discrimination. Today, most gay men and lesbians report experiencing physical victimization at one time or another. Almost 40 percent of LGBT middle and high school students reported an incident of physical harassment in the most recent school year (GLSEN 2013). In this section, we will touch on some of the significant emotional and physical consequences of the stress placed upon gay and lesbian individuals. A brief discussion of hate crimes is included in Chapter 12.

Minority Stress

The stigma placed on homosexuality and alternative gender identities exposes people to a wide array of stresses. In Chapter 6 we discussed the microinequities and microaggressions women face. These types of incidents are frequent for LGBTQ people as well. Transgender people are called by disrespectful names ("trannies," for example), or people incessantly ask them about their genitalia. Gays and lesbians face slurs and often hear the expression "that's so gay" to refer to something negative. Other sources of stress for LGBTQ people can arise from a lack of acceptance by their families or discrimination in their churches or in the labor market. In turn, these stresses affect health and feelings of well-being, and have been related to recurrent headaches, depressive moods, and more serious psychological conditions. In the case of people of color who are homosexual or transgender, these stresses can be intensified because of their status as gender and ethnic/racial minorities (DiPlacido 1998). Indeed, gays and lesbians who experience discrimination because of their gender, race, or sexual orientation are almost four times as likely to have a substance abuse disorder as those who have not been victims of discrimination (McCabe et al. 2010). Minority stress is particularly notable in bisexuals, a group that receives relatively little attention. As described above, they have high rates of poverty, which may be a result of discrimination. They are also more likely to have a mood

Photo 7.3 Bullying is a major problem among youth, and it is more likely to occur in schools located in disadvantaged neighborhoods. Gay and lesbian youth are often easy targets. Research has suggested that boys are more likely to be victims of physical bullying, while girls are more likely to be victimized by indirect bullying such as teasing. Some data also indicate that victims are likely to be of lower social status in the school (C. Berger and Rodkin 2009; Carbone-Lopez, Esbensen, and Brick 2010).

© Mandy Godbehear/Shutterstock.

or anxiety disorder (Bostwick et al. 2010) and to smoke marijuana (Ford and Jasinski 2006). Bisexuals may feel isolated, as they lack clear acceptance in either the gay or heterosexual communities.

Family acceptance continues to be a problem for gay and transgender youth. A national survey of organizations providing services to homeless and near-homeless youth revealed that approximately 40 percent of all of their clients are LGBT. About half of these LGBT clients reported that the primary reason they needed housing assistance was family rejection. Over 70 percent said that they had experienced rejection from their families at one time or another (Durso and Gates 2012).

In schools, bullying and harassment is a serious problem for LGBT youth. They are often marginalized, stigmatized, and without support from fellow students (Craig, Tucker, and Wagner 2008). Results from a 2013 national survey indicated that harassment is common in schools: 55 percent

of LGBT students reported feeling unsafe at school, and 74 percent were verbally harassed about their sexual orientation in the year before the survey. Gender identity is strictly policed in schools as well; for example, 22 percent of LGBT youth reported being physically harassed for their gender expression (Kosciw et al. 2014). Harassment of LGBT students is more common in rural areas and in the Midwest and southern regions of the country (Palmer, Kosciw, and Bartkiewicz 2013). Online harassment of LGBT youth is also a serious issue: In survey data collected during the 2010–2011 school year, LGBT youth were three times more likely than gender-conforming heterosexuals to report that they had been bullied online (42 percent compared to 15 percent) (GLSEN 2013).

To avoid verbal and physical assaults in a normatively heterosexual culture, gay and lesbian people may try to pass as heterosexual by adopting gender-appropriate manners and behaviors. Transgender people may continue to live publically as the gender they were assigned at birth. It is a delicate matter for those who walk the tightrope of working to pass as heterosexual or gender-conforming in the public realm but to be accepted as themselves in their private lives. However, while passing may protect the individual, a continuous effort must be put forth to maintain it, and, when successful, it also perpetuates the heteronormative culture that demeans homosexuality (Rosenfeld 2009). These are the dilemmas of being a minority in a majority's society.

As this section shows, growing up gay, lesbian, bisexual, or transgender in a cultural and social setting in which there are strong expectations of heterosexuality and gender normativity can create deep stresses for an individual. At the same time, it is important to recognize that the situation has improved in some notable ways. While the Internet can be an avenue of bullying, it can also allow gay and transgender youth to feel less isolated. Such youths are able to gather information and connect with people like themselves who live far away. Adolescents' attitudes are shifting rapidly to become more accepting of both homosexuality and alternative gender expression. We see examples of inclusiveness, such as a lesbian student who was elected prom queen in Hesperia (a town located in a fairly conservative area of Southern California). She wore a suit to the dance. Many high schools across the country, even in rural areas, now allow same-gender couples to attend dances as well (Gray 2009).

Suicide

Heterosexism, social isolation, self-blame, and other stresses can have dire consequences for their victims. Reviews of research suggest that gay and lesbian youths are generally two to three times more likely to attempt suicide than their heterosexual counterparts (Suicide Prevention Resource Center 2008). In a recent study conducted with 237 LGBT youth, over 30 percent attempted suicide before the age of 21 (Mustanski and Liu 2013). Young transgender people have even higher rates, with a national study finding that 45 percent had attempted suicide in the year prior to the study (Grant et al. 2011). Adolescence

---

NUTSHELL 7.3   LGBT People, Prisons, and Immigrant Detention

As described, LGBT people face a host of stresses in daily life. These stresses are particularly acute, however, for those being held in immigration detention centers and prisons. Although policies are changing, transgender people are sometimes housed with people of the gender they were assigned at birth, rather than the gender they are living. Some are not able to access hormones that they may have been using for many years (Apuzzo 2015). Additionally, transgender people experience extremely high rates of sexual violence in prison. The Bureau of Justice Statistics reports that over a third experience sexual victimization in our nation's prisons (24 percent at the hands of other inmates and 17 percent at the hands of staff members). Twenty percent of substantiated sexual assaults in immigrant detention facilities were against transgender inmates. This is particularly notable given that only 1 percent of detainees are estimated to be transgender (GAO 2013b). In 2015, 35 members of Congress wrote to ICE (Immigration and Customs Enforcement) asking them to change their policies. ICE has vowed to collect better data and improve staff training.

Being in detention is dangerous for gay and lesbian inmates as well, with over 12 percent reporting sexual victimization at the hands of other inmates, and over 5 percent at the hands of guards. This compares to 2 percent of the total inmate population who reported being victimized by inmates, and another 2 percent who reported staff sexual misconduct toward them (Beck et al. 2013). Gay, lesbian, and transgender people who are harassed in either immigration or correctional custody are sometimes put in solitary confinement to protect them. Many negative psychological effects are associated with solitary confinement (Gruberg 2013).

has its own set of stressful events, and when homosexuality or being transgender is added to these, its problems are intensified.

- A 17-year-old transgender teenager from Cincinnati, Ohio, killed herself by running in front of a truck on the interstate. She faced rejection from her parents and was sent to Christian counseling in an attempt to force her to maintain a male gender identity (Kutner 2015).
- A 12-year-old California boy killed himself when he could not take the constant bullying and taunting he received at school as the only male member of the school's cheerleading squad (CBS 2014).
- A 13-year-old from Iowa killed himself as a result of persistent abuse from his classmates after he was outed as gay. He was mocked for his sexual orientation and the fact that he was half African American (Weber 2014).

However, suicide attempt rates are not spread evenly over this minority population. As in the general population, people with drug addiction or mental health issues are more likely to attempt suicide. Unlike the general population where women are more likely to attempt suicide, however, gay men have higher lifetime rates of suicide attempts than lesbians (King et al. 2008). This

may be because of the stronger stigma against male homosexuality. Among gays and lesbians, those who have been the victims of bullying, harassment, or violence at school have higher-than-average rates of suicide. Importantly, gays and lesbians who are rejected by their families are 8.4 times more likely to attempt suicide than those who are accepted by their families (Ryan et al. 2009). There is not a lot of data about the relationship between race/ethnicity and suicide risk among LGBT people, but in general, studies suggest that racial and ethnic minorities have higher rates of suicide (Haas et al. 2010). This is likely because of the problems they face as both racial/ethnic and sexual minorities (Meyer, Dietrich, and Schwartz 2008). Blacks and Latinos as opposed to Whites who are lesbian, gay, or bisexual experience greater continuing stress over their lifetimes and have fewer resources to help them cope (Meyer, Dietrich, and Schwartz 2008).

Despite the obvious need among these individuals for various kinds of social support, seeking out and obtaining such support is problematic because of the demeaned social status of LGBT people in U.S. society. Homosexual youths find themselves between a rock and a hard place. On the one hand, they may be willing to seek out individuals who might be able to help, but on the other hand, they may be unwilling to risk rejection or reveal their situation because of the stigma attached to the homosexual label. Finally, the

MINI-CASE 7.2

Religious Freedom and Gay Marriage

Since the Supreme Court decision legalizing same-sex marriage, a small number of officials have refused to perform the ceremonies or issue licenses. Some wedding service providers (like caterers and photographers) have also refused to participate in ceremonies. Those who have refused generally cite religious grounds: Their religious convictions forbid them from participating in a union they see as immoral. Two states have even passed laws allowing

these kinds of religious exemptions. Religious freedom is central to American philosophy and practice. At the same time, others argue that when one serves the public, one should not be allowed to discriminate. What if a religion, for example, encouraged its adherents to deny services to a racial or ethnic minority group? Is there a way to honor both religious freedom and equal rights for gays and lesbians? How would you resolve this issue? ■

invisibility of the homosexual group presents a further barrier for youths who are seeking a support network or role model to guide them through a difficult period.

SEXUALITY AND GENDER IDENTITY IN THE GLOBAL CONTEXT

Looking around the world, we see a wide variety of reactions to people who are homosexual or transgender. There are many examples of countries, where, like in the United States, discrimination against groups that do not fit traditional sex and gender categories is present. Homosexuals in Hong Kong, for example, often experience workplace discrimination that results in both psychological and financial costs (Lau and Stotzer 2011). In some Middle Eastern Muslim countries, homosexuality can be punished by death, and in many Asian countries it carries the threat of imprisonment. At the same time, there are examples of countries where there is far less discrimination than in the U.S. In 1989, Denmark became the first country in the world to legally recognize same-sex unions. The first law allowing same-sex marriage was passed in the Netherlands in 2000. Ireland, a majority-Catholic country, approved same-sex marriage in 2015. They were the first country to achieve this using a referendum.

Same-sex rights are not confined to Western nations. In fact, in June of 2011, the United Nations adopted a resolution saying that rights for homosexual and transgender people were a "priority issue." This resolution was introduced by South Africa and approved by 23 countries from every region of the world including Cuba, Poland, Slovakia, Mexico, and Guatemala. Nineteen countries voted against the resolution, including Angola, Russia, and Pakistan (Human Rights Watch 2011).

Not only do reactions to homosexuality vary internationally, but so do the very meanings of sex and gender. At the beginning of this chapter, we commented on the subjectivity and variety of sexual classifications across time and cultures. We also mentioned that members of different racial and class groups define and highlight masculinity and femininity in varying ways. In other words, there is no one way to classify sexualities, nor is there only one meaning for how one *does* sexuality. "Different cultures and different periods of history construct gender differently. Striking differences exist, for instance, in the relationship of homosexual practice to dominant forms of masculinity" (Connell 2015, p. 42). The complexity of classifications and sexual identities can only be expected to grow in the United States with globalization and the continued immigration of peoples of varying ethnicities and cultural backgrounds (Gamson and Moon 2004). The open borders that accompany these events will have an impact on our views of sexuality and the meanings that we give it. Individuals whose sexual identity is not honored in their own society can immigrate to another, more hospitable society and thereby affect and be affected by that society's cultural views.

Given that societies often differ in their sexual mores, meanings, and classifications, when different cultures meet it should not be surprising that clashes occur over these matters, as a host society seeks to impose its own hegemonic culture on those who immigrate into it. Movements by some rights groups to push for a more positive attitude toward homosexuality can inadvertently lead to backlashes by host governments, which establish policies that reinforce traditional meanings and definitions of sexuality (Massad 2002). A current example of this can be found in some countries in Africa where the U.S. government has actively promoted gay-rights policies. In fact, USAID has tied development money to gay rights, causing anger among some Africans who see it as a form of imperialism. As gays and lesbians have become more visible in those countries due to U.S. policies, discrimination and violence have increased. Making the situation even more complicated, Western religious groups have turned their attention to Africa in order to try and prevent the "mistakes" the U.S. has made in expanding gay rights (Onishi 2015).

Globalization can also result in situations where governments use progressive LGBTQ policies to help justify or cover for other oppressive practices. An example of this technique, called "pinkwashing," occurred in Israel when the government hired a public relations firm to highlight the gay-friendly nature of cities like Tel Aviv. Gays and lesbians were encouraged to support Israel and travel there even though the state's policies toward Palestinians are considered by many to be oppressive. A full-page ad ran in the *New York Times* saying, "Hamas, ISIS, and Iran kill gays like me – in Israel, I am free." Critics called these tactics propaganda because they distracted people from Israeli violence (Haaretz 2014).

The effects of globalization on definitions of sexuality and gendered behavior and their acceptance depend in part on the relative positions of countries in the world political-economic system. "The conditions of globalization, which involve the interaction of many local gender orders, certainly multiply the forms of masculinity in the global gender order. At the same time, the specific shape of globalization, concentrating economic and cultural power on an unprecedented scale, provides new resources for the dominance of particular groups of men" (Connell 2015, p. 46). Thus, as groups and individuals flow between countries, there are likely to be changes in and reactions to varying definitions of gender and sexuality. Which definitions and practices become dominant and accepted depends on relative power in the world order.

Altman (2005) contends that homosexual communities in other industrialized nations model themselves after such communities in the United States. The language used and histories evoked are those that originate not in their own countries, but in the United States. For example, the Stonewall riots that occurred in the United States as a result of police harassment are cited by European gays as giving birth to gay activism even though such activism occurred earlier in their own countries. This suggests the hegemonic position held by the United States in the world community.

Altman's argument that gay culture and identity are becoming homogenized across the world as a result of globalizing forces has been challenged by recent research, which describes a much more complicated picture of sexuality in varied settings. The "transmissions" relating to sexuality between globalizing forces and local cultures are complicated and result in sex and gender definitions that are neither fully global nor local (Berry, Martin, and Yue 2003; Boellstorff 2003). Adam, Duyvendak, and Krouwel (1999) argue that while there may be superficial similarities in tactics, terms, and symbols in gay movements across cultures, we must look to "local meanings of global tendencies" (p. 348). It is simply inaccurate to portray Western gay movements as the model to which others aspire (Jackson 2009).

Like variations in the legal and social treatment of gay people worldwide, we also see diversity in terms of transgender and genderqueer people. There are a number of countries where being transgender is illegal and can result in imprisonment or jail. In Malaysia, for example, it is illegal for a man to "pose" as a woman, and Human Rights Watch has documented multiple arbitrary arrests, torture, and sexual assaults of transgender people (Knight 2015). At the same time, we can also find many countries with more progressive policies than those in the U.S. For example, Argentina has now instituted the most open policies in the world, allowing transgender people to change their gender on official documents without the involvement of a judge or doctor. Government health care also covers all expenses related to transition.

Seven countries now include a third option on gender questions for people who do not identify on the gender binary. In Germany, parents of intersex babies can mark this third option on a birth certificate indicating that gender is indeterminate. Other countries (including Bangladesh, New Zealand, India, and Australia) allow adults to identify as a third gender on official documents. As described above, the United States sometimes serves as a model to other countries for new policies. At least in the area of transgender/genderqueer issues, it is clear that other countries are taking a strong lead. In the United States, activists have prepared a petition to the Obama administration asking that a third gender option be added to government forms. At the time of this writing, it has not yet gotten the required number of signatures to be considered.

Summary

This chapter has presented a brief overview of the inequities involved in being gay, lesbian, bisexual, transgender, or genderqueer. As a dishonored status group, LGBTQ people have been singled out and stigmatized as individuals who do not fit dominant cultural ideas about appropriate behavior and lifestyles. Although sympathy and opinions in specific areas of civil rights have improved in recent years, significant proportions and subgroups within the United States continue to be hostile to people who are not heterosexual or who do not conform to gender expectations. Stereotypes persist, and this group continues to be a minority with distinct status-group attributes, yet without many of the legal protections afforded other minority groups. At the same time that this group fits status-group definitions, there are also tensions within the group. For example, gays and lesbians sometimes resist being categorized with transgender people. When we focus on LGBTQ people as a group, it can hide important variations in experiences and discrimination by race and class.

Because of the difficulties that LGBTQ people face and the disregard in which they have been held, reliable and thorough statistics on this group are still lacking. Estimates about the size of the population and its characteristics vary from study to study. At the same time, our knowledge about gay people, lesbians, and transgender people is improving. Little continues to be known, however, about bisexuals, genderqueer people, asexual people, and pansexuals.

Discrimination against gays and lesbians is widespread globally. Globalization has had an impact on the sex categories used as well as the meanings ascribed to sexuality and masculinity and femininity. In the case of disagreements, which of these categories and meanings is privileged depends in part on the position of a society in the global context. Finally, while definitions, meanings, and experiences of being LGBTQ vary culturally, globalization has helped to link gay and lesbian groups across national boundaries.

Critical Thinking

1. What would be the social consequences if everyone accepted the belief that gender variation is a continuum rather than a dichotomy (i.e., if we believed that there are many more than two genders)?
2. In what ways do race and class intersect with sexual orientation and gender identity? What are some examples of how being gay, for example, might vary across classes and races?
3. Bullying appears to be a significant problem in many schools. What do you think can be done to curtail it?
4. What policies do you think colleges should employ in relation to transgender students? If you are in college, what policies does your school have?

Web Connections

For brief discussions of issues of concern to gay, lesbian, bisexual, and transgender groups, see the websites of the Human Rights Campaign (www.hrc.org) and the Williams Institute (http://williamsinstitute. law.ucla.edu). Visit also the National LGBTQ Task Force at www.thetaskforce.org/about/mission-history.html for reports on a wide range of issues related to LGBTQ rights.

Film Suggestions

Intersexion (2012). A documentary about the lives and experiences of intersexed people.

52 Tuesdays (2013). Follows a teenage girl named Billie as her mother transitions from female to male. Although fictional, the movie was filmed once a week for a year to mimic Billie's legal custody arrangement that only allowed her to be with her mother on Tuesday afternoons.

Tangerine (2015). Filmed with iPhones, this film is about a transgender woman who gets out of prison for prostitution only to discover that the pimp she loves has cheated on her.

The Case against 8 (2015). A documentary examining the efforts to overturn California's ban on same-sex marriage.

Out in the Night (2014). This documentary tells the story of a group of lesbians who were attacked by a man in New York City. Because he was wounded in the ensuing fight, the women were ultimately arrested, but four refused to plead guilty. The film explores the role of race, sexuality, and class in criminal justice.

CHAPTER 8

Racial and Ethnic Inequality

To be a poor man is hard, but to be a poor race in a land of dollars is the very bottom of hardship.

W. E. B. Du Bois (1868–1963)

The positions of women and minorities are often thought to have a lot in common. Moreover, as mentioned in Chapter 6, race and gender have both been associated with biological differences that have been given social and cultural meanings. While their specific histories and socioeconomic conditions are different, both women and members of minority groups tend to occupy lower positions than White males in our society. Each group has even been referred to as being in a lower caste when compared to White males. Finally, the terms *sex*, *gender*, and *race* each have specific meanings that vary with the cultural, historical, and social context in which they are used. Consequently, none of these concepts has a fixed, unvarying definition.

THE MEANING AND CREATION OF RACE

"What is a Black person?" This question, posed by a 7-year-old named Bridget, seems pretty straightforward. Bridget is a White U.S. citizen who lived abroad for many years; she has spent most of her life in England, not in the United States. Her mother responded to her question by saying that a Black person is a person who is "dark-skinned." Bridget responded: "You mean like Tarush [who is Indian]?" Her mother then went on to explain the traditional racial distinctions, but it was clear that Bridget thought her mother meant that a Black person is distinguished solely by the color of her or his skin. "Color" is an important social and cultural trait, and we know that within "races," individuals can vary in the color of their skin. In our society, individuals with lighter skin generally are accorded higher status than those with darker skin. We will discuss the issue of "colorism" more fully later in this chapter.

The exchange between Bridget and her mother hints at the complexity involved in defining race. *Race* is a slippery term. There have been past attempts to define it "scientifically" and to develop clear classifications of race, but these have always been found to be faulty for one reason or another, and virtually all have fallen by the wayside. Some of the earliest attempts classified individuals by their ancestry rather than physical features. These classifications tended to conflate ethnicity, nationality, and physical characteristics (e.g., Jewish or Irish "race"). Other classifications tended to identify and rank groups in an ethnocentric fashion, separating the socially dominant group from others and ranking it highest. The features chosen to distinguish the races were those that appeared to separate the dominant from lower-ranking groups, groups which could then be exploited for their alleged inferiority. The attempted annihilation of the "Jewish race" by the "Aryans" is an example of how racial categorizations can be based on and used for political rather than scientific reasons. As the social, economic, and cultural positions of groups changed, so did their race. While we usually think of a person's race as affecting his or her class position, in this case, *class* position helped to determine "*race*." For example, with assimilation, Jewish, Irish, and Italian immigrants, once defined as "non-White," became defined as "White."

The continual changing of racial categories in society and by governmental offices indicates that race is something that is created and anchored in the social, economic, and cultural conditions of the time. In the words of Omi and Winant (1994), it involves "racial formation," which is a "socio-historical process by which racial categories are created, inhabited, transformed, and destroyed" (p. 55). As historical conditions and contexts change, so do racial classifications. In a real sense, racial classifications reflect the structure of inequality in a society.

We need only to review changes that the U.S. Census Bureau has made since its first census in 1790. Native Americans and Blacks were separated out from others because of their political status, but it was not until 1820 that "race" or color was used in the census (Snipp 2003). Throughout the rest of the nineteenth century, the racial classifications used by the Census Bureau were rooted in cultural, social, and intellectual developments going on in the wider society. The addition of "Chinese" and "Japanese" to the 1890 census racial classifications reflected growing concern on the part of the dominant group about the increasing numbers and potential competition of these groups with native citizens on the West Coast. The added inclusion of "Octoroon" (one-eighth Black) and "Quadroon" (one-fourth Black) to the classifications symbolized the growing interest in and concern about racial purity at the end of the nineteenth century in the United States (Snipp 2003; Schaefer 2015).

The Census Bureau has not only changed the number of categories over time, but it has also restricted or expanded the definitions of some categories, changing the number of people in them. For example, states often defined a person as Black if they had only one drop of Black blood. They used this definition as a means to restrict "whiteness" and prevent and outlaw racial intermarriage (Brunsma and Rockquemore 2002). Historical records also show an example of a category being broadened when the number of Puerto Ricans classified as White dramatically increased in early twentieth-century censuses of Puerto Rico's population. In large part, this occurred because of "boundary shifting," that is, the definition of "White" was broadened to include more people (Loveman and Muniz 2007). These changes in turn reflect fluctuations in racial dynamics in the society at large.

When we examine historical fluctuations in the definition and meaning of race, it becomes apparent that racial definitions and classifications have served as indicators of which groups have political, economic, and social power and which ones do not. "Throughout the history of **racialization**, material (economic, social, and political resources) and ideological elements of race have been inextricably linked" (Lewis 2004, p. 625; emphasis added). At the same time, the dominant class is not always the force behind changing categorization. Political movements also sometimes fight for recategorization. This can be seen in recent attempts to create a new ethnic category, Middle Eastern and North African (MENA). Since the 1920s, people of Middle Eastern and

North African descent have been categorized as White. This decision was made, in part, due to lobbying on the part of the groups themselves in the early 1900s. They did not want to be categorized as Asian because that would have made them ineligible for U.S. citizenship under the Chinese Exclusion Act. Today, however, activists are calling for the establishment of the MENA category because they do not self-identify as White. They also argue that they experience discrimination like other minority groups. They point out that it makes little sense that today Pakistani-Americans can apply for minority small business loans because they are considered as "Asian," but Iranians do not qualify because they are counted as "White" (Aidi 2015).

The MENA categorization would allow for more accurate counts of the population, and it would also open the possibility of the group becoming eligible for federal, state, and local benefits as members of a minority ethnicity. The Census Bureau is currently testing the new category for possible inclusion in the 2020 census. One of the particularly effective social media campaigns that may have pushed the Census Bureau forward on this issue was "Check it Right, You Ain't White." This series of clever videos encouraged MENA respondents to write in their ethnic identification on the race question in the 2010 Census, rather than identifying as White (Wiltz 2014).

Another example of activists working to change ethnic categories involves the "Hispanic" ethnic identification. In today's census, Hispanic is not considered a racial category, but is listed as an ethnicity. This is because Hispanics can be of any race (for example, Hispanics from the Caribbean often look phenotypically Black, and there are Hispanics from Peru who look phenotypically Asian). The creation of the Hispanic category was result of work by state actors, ethnic leaders, and market groups (like the television network Univision) during the 1970s (Mora 2014). The new category was useful for counting purposes, and it allowed the government to extend benefits to Hispanics as a minority group (J. Lee and Bean 2004). While a Hispanic racial category was considered, the Census Bureau encountered resistance from a number of sources, including other minority groups who feared losing members (for example, there were concerns that Black Hispanics would check the "Hispanic" box rather than the "Black" box on the race question) (Mora 2014).

Today, the census is once again considering a combined race/origin question that would put Hispanic as a category alongside Black, White, and the other racial classifications. This is partly because in the last census a full 40 percent of Hispanic respondents checked "other" to the race question (Roth 2013). Additionally, two-thirds of Hispanics responding to a recent national survey report that they understand the category of "Hispanic" to better describe their race than their ethnicity (Pew 2015b).

In part because of problems encountered by census workers in accurately classifying a person's race, in 1960 the Census Bureau began to allow individuals to self-identify (Snipp 2003). In 2000, they made it possible for people to identify themselves as belonging to more than one race. The golfer Tiger Woods helped to call attention to this issue by calling himself a "Cabalinasian" (i.e., part Caucasian, Black, American Indian, Thai, and Chinese; White 1997). Currently, the Census finds that about 2.5 percent of individuals in the United States identify themselves as multiracial. Other surveys, however, suggest that some individuals with parents or grandparents of different races continue to identify as only one race, resulting in an undercount on the census (Pew 2015c). The move toward self-identification has further revealed the fluidity and complexity of race as a concept. In the future, high rates of immigration from Hispanic, Asian, and other countries will continue to accelerate the multiracial character of the United States and further complicate the racial/ethnic picture.

Interestingly, most Whites do not think of "White" as a race. Rather, when speaking of race, the tendency is to think of racial "minorities" as belonging to a race. Whiteness is invisible in this sense. "From an early age," observes Rothenberg (2008, p. 2), "race, for white people, is about everyone else." Whiteness is not racialized.

The invisibility of whiteness as a racial category fosters the illusion that being "white" is to be normal or the standard by which others are measured. Race is a term ordinarily used only in reference to other, non-White persons (Dye 2002). The claim that Whites are the regular, normal people and, therefore, representative of humanity allows whiteness to be a central basis for power and privilege in society. The racial categories with which people are identified have direct consequences for their lives because society's social structures and the opportunities and blockages they create are shaped in part by the dominant group.

It is clear that the term *white* has various meanings for different people. For some it has a distinct racial connotation, while for others it does not. The same is found for the term *black*. It has even been suggested that research in this area should focus not on "who is black" but "what does 'black' mean?" (Brunsma and Rockquemore 2002, p. 109). This is essentially what Bridget was asking earlier. How one defines oneself or others racially appears to depend on the geographical context, education, age, race of the identifier, and nativity (Farough 2004; Roth 2005). On nativity, for example, Pyke and Dang (2003) found that the adult children of Korean and Vietnamese immigrants thought of themselves as bicultural, but described others in their group as being either "fresh off the boat" or "whitewashed." In using these terms, these children were able to minimize or eliminate the stigma they faced by distancing themselves from their coethnic *others*. Doing this is a response to the racial hierarchy in U.S. society and the desire to maintain a respected position within it.

U.S. RACIAL AND ETHNIC RELATIONS: AN HISTORICAL SKETCH

Native Americans

The unequal treatment of racial minorities in the United States goes back to the early years of colonization. Anglo-Saxon colonists' earliest contact with a visibly different group were with American Indians. Ideas and stereotypes of the "savage" had developed in the sixteenth and seventeenth centuries and provided colonists with a framework within which to interpret American Indians. Rather than color or racial distinction, religious and ethnocentric criteria were used initially to separate groups into superior and inferior categories. Specifically, distinctions were made between "Christians" and "heathens" and between "civilized" and "savage" (Fredrickson 1981). Clearly, the American Indians were placed in the heathen and savage categories. Thus, distinct attitudes about this group were entrenched by the time the American Revolution occurred.

Despite these beliefs, early relations between colonists and American Indians were often cooperative since both groups were interested in trade and barter. In fact, American Indians frequently had quite a bit of power when it came to bargaining because of their prowess in the fur trade (Lurie 1982). But this cooperation was short-lived. Relationships with the British became increasingly belligerent, since the British were farmers and interested in obtaining American Indian land (Garbarino 1976). The American Indians whose economies emphasized agriculture and who were located near the East Coast were the first to be overwhelmed by the colonists (Lurie 1982).

In order for the colonists to spread their civilization, they had to obtain land held by American Indians. Many of the latter resided in villages and cultivated crops in a manner not very different from the traditional European way. But arguments about the savage and heathen way of life of American Indians were used as devices to justify taking over this land. Many of the arguments were similar to those used to justify slavery (Farley 1988). The belief was that such action would rescue the earth from these savages and speed progress and Christianity (Fredrickson 1981). This is an early instance of a group using an ideology to justify the taking of economic resources from another.

In the period roughly between 1880 and 1930, over 65 percent of the 138 million acres that had been held by American Indians moved to White ownership (Carlson and Colburn 1972).

By the last decade of the nineteenth century, most American Indians were on reservations where they were forbidden to practice their religions and their children were forced to attend boarding schools run by Whites where they had to speak English (Farley 1988). Much of the policy of this period was aimed at forcing American Indians to assimilate into the dominant White culture (Marden and Meyer 1973). Nevertheless, they were not allowed to vote since they were not considered citizens. The Constitution had never actively incorporated concerns for the rights of these groups, and it was not until the 1920s that American Indians were granted citizenship. Even as late as the 1920s and 1930s, there was a feeling among some influential individuals that American Indians were biologically inferior to White Anglo-Saxons (Carlson and Colburn 1972).

European Immigrants

Historically, the waves of immigrants who arrived in the United States from Europe during the nineteenth and early twentieth centuries were also victims of economic and social discrimination. Jews, Irish, and immigrants from southern and eastern Europe such as Italians, Poles, and Greeks were initially categorized as non-White and suffered the consequences. Widespread concerns about maintaining purity of the "White race," fascination with

eugenics and **Social Darwinism**, and the Red Scare early in the twentieth century, heightened fear of immigrants who were considered alien, and led to the restrictive immigration policies of the 1920s. Eventually, because of assimilation into American culture and economic mobility, many of these groups became classified as "White" (Brodkin 2008; Barrett and Roediger 2008). This shows again how racial classifications, rather than being scientifically based, were closely linked to the power and economic status of the groups involved.

African Americans

Land in early America was plentiful, but greater labor power was needed to take full advantage of its resources. The absence of large numbers of willing free laborers led to attempts to obtain forced labor that could be justified on ideological or philosophical grounds. American Indians were difficult to subdue and were a potential major threat because they were familiar with the countryside and could put up fierce resistance. On the other hand, large-scale, prolonged use of indentured White servants was unrealistic because they were freed after a period of servitude. This made the importation of non-White slave labor attractive. Slavery created a large labor pool of workers who did not know the land, and it helped to elevate all Whites to a higher status

---

NUTSHELL 8.1   Immigrants, African Americans, and West Virginia Coal Mines

During the 1800s, large numbers of European immigrants came to the United States. Life was extremely hard for many of these new arrivals. Atrocious working conditions, meager pay, and little power characterized their work-a-day existence. Discrimination in employment meant that many had to carve out niches in order to survive. For example, many Irish women became domestic servants, and many Eastern European Jews (both men and women) became peddlers (Hyman 2009; Library of Congress n.d.).

When coal began to be commercially mined in West Virginia in 1883, many immigrants and African Americans relocated there to find work. The mine

owners were willing to hire these groups largely because the local workforce was demanding unionization (Library of Congress n.d.). By hiring desperate immigrants and Blacks, the mining companies were able to pay extremely low wages, forcing the workers to shop at the overpriced company store, and charging them for the use of safety equipment (West Virginia State Archives 2015). This strategy of hiring powerless and desperate people also meant that the companies were able to prevent unionization. These events inflamed tensions between Whites, Blacks, and European immigrants. Whites felt that "their" jobs were being taken, resulting in heightened racism (Library of Congress n.d.).

(Fredrickson 1981). A major difference in the initial contacts, of course, was that whereas colonists conquered American Indians and annexed their land, in initial Black–White contact, it was a case of involuntary immigration (O'Sullivan and Wilson 1988).

Given English views of Blacks as evil, animalistic, uncivilized, and un-Christian, it is not surprising that the early colonies passed laws banning sexual mixing and intermarriage. Children of mixed parentage were considered Black (Fredrickson 1981). Enslavement was a thorny issue that troubled some of the Founding Fathers (e.g., Washington, Hamilton) more so than others (e.g., Jefferson). The result was that the problem of what to do with slavery after the Revolution was put off again and again. Several thousand African Americans had fought in the Continental Army, but nevertheless, at the Constitutional Convention it was decided that a Black man was only three-fifths of a man. Although Thomas Jefferson is associated with the belief that "all men are created equal," he owned 180 slaves when he died and thought of Blacks as inferior to Whites: "I advance it therefore as a suspicion only, that the Blacks, whether originally a distinct race, or made distinct by time and circumstances, are inferior to the Whites, in the endowments both of body and mind" (quoted in Feldstein 1972, pp. 52–53). Beliefs in the different endowments helped to justify slavery. After all, inhuman treatment could be tolerated if the members of a race were not considered fully human.

At the time of the first official census in 1790, the Black population was approximately 757,000, of whom almost 700,000 were slaves. The Black population grew to almost 4.5 million in 1860, of whom 89 percent were slaves. Between 1790 and 1860, about 90 percent of all Blacks in each census were slaves. Even though the slave trade was officially outlawed in 1808, it still flourished along the East Coast of the country (U.S. Census Bureau 1979). In 1790, 23 percent of all families had slaves, whereas in 1850, 10 percent of families owned them. Most of these families owned between seven and nine slaves (U.S. Census Bureau 1979).

The system of inequality that developed between the races during the heyday of slavery up to the Civil War was essentially a **caste system**. Laws forbade Blacks to (1) intermarry with Whites, (2) vote, (3) testify against Whites in legal cases, (4) own firearms, (5) use abusive language against Whites, (6) own property unless permitted by a master, (7) leave the plantation without permission or disobey a curfew, (8) make a will or inherit property, and (9) have anyone teach them to read or write, or give them books (Franklin 1980; Fredrickson 1981; Blackwell 1985).

The end of the Civil War, Emancipation, and Reconstruction did not end the misery for Blacks, and, in fact, appear to have done little to change their caste relationship with Whites (Turner, Singleton, and Musick 1984). Legal, intellectual, economic, and population changes were occurring that provided support for continued discrimination against Blacks. The Jim Crow laws in the South and beliefs about the inferior nature of Blacks, along with increased labor competition from a continuously rising number of White immigrants from all parts of Europe, conspired to keep Blacks in a lower socioeconomic position. Lynching of Blacks increased in the latter part of the nineteenth century. IQ tests, developed as early as the 1890s, were erroneously used to test intelligence, and then used to demonstrate the intellectual inferiority of Blacks. This occurred even though some of the early inventors of such measures cautioned against using them for this purpose (Weinberg 1989). Migration of Black southerners to the industrializing North during and after World War I resulted in severe clashes between Black and White workers, and in the years from 1917 to 1919, riots broke out in several cities (Brody 1980).

In the 1920s, anthropologist Franz Boas spoke out forcefully against the racially based theories being propagated at the time, and by the 1930s and 1940s, other important scientists joined him in attacking the idea that Blacks were inferior to Whites. Nazi racism also contributed to a reexamination of race domination in this country (Turner, Singleton, and Musick 1984). But discrimination continued, with Blacks still encountering problems within unions and industry.

Blacks also were segregated within the military. Riots occurred during World War II, which further demonstrated that the United States still had a long way to go to bring about equity between the races. Increasing organization and political power of African Americans during the late 1940s and 1950s helped to bring about some legislative changes and, eventually, the civil rights movement.

Wealth inequality between Blacks and Whites has been perpetuated since early in U.S. history, beginning with slavery, by governmental policies that prohibited Blacks from beginning certain kinds of businesses or entering particular markets. Agencies such as the Federal Housing Authority made loans and mortgages for Blacks more difficult to obtain, and there was a lack of opportunity to take advantage of the wealth-accumulation benefits of lower capital gains taxes, home mortgage deductions, and Social Security benefits. Joe Feagin (2006) calls this enshrine-ment of racism into the American system at its founding **systemic racism**. As we will see, the legacy of history continues in present-day struc-tures and outcomes.

Asian Americans

The preceding historical sketch reveals how extensive racial inequality has been in U.S. soci-ety. In addition to the groups already mentioned, Asian Americans have also suffered the effects of stereotyping and unfair treatment. Near the end of the nineteenth century, Japanese immigrants took laboring jobs but were disliked by unions and other employees. They were lumped in with the Chinese as part of the "yellow peril," the fear that yellow races would overtake the White race. The events at Pearl Harbor, initiating the entry of the United States into World War II, exacerbated negative feelings toward Japanese Americans. Under Executive Order 9066, people on the West Coast with virtually any Japanese ancestry at all were rounded up and moved into concentration camps. This was not done to either German or Italian Americans, even though the United States went to war against Germany and Italy as well as Japan. This strongly suggests a heavy influence of racism. The 113,000 Japanese sent to these camps without the benefit of trial could take only per-sonal items, leaving behind and often losing most of their property. After the war, terrorism and bigotry against Japanese Americans continued, although no instances of espionage by them were ever proved. Even while in the camps, they remained loyal to their adopted country.

Mexican Americans

Mexican Americans have been exploited for their land and labor since early in the history of the United States. In the last half of the nineteenth century, Mexican Americans frequently had their land taken away by European settlers. Over time, the use of Mexican workers has waxed and waned,

MINI-CASE 8.1

Multiculturalism versus Assimilation

In the United States and many European countries, economic problems have intensified nativist feelings and led to more limitations on and more careful screening of newly entering immigrants. One off-shoot of these developments is the issue of whether immigrants should be required to fully adopt their new country's cultural values and social rules or whether they should be allowed to keep their own language and cultural and social customs. The former solution suggests that a country should be a melting pot, while the latter preference promotes an image of nations as salad bowls, or patchworks of separate groups. What do you think? Can a nation still cohere if groups retain their separate identities? Can they identify with *both* their own groups and the nation at the same time? What requirements, if any, should be placed on immigrant groups in this regard? ■

depending on the demand for labor. They were used and then dispensed with when no longer needed. For example, early in the twentieth century, many Mexican immigrants came to the United States as agricultural laborers, only to be deported or repatriated after demand for their services declined. During World War II, Mexican workers were again imported, only to be sent back during the 1950s under "Operation Wetback" as expendable and undesirable. Illegal raids, threats, and expulsions have not been uncommon in our treatment of Mexicans (Farley 1988).

RACIAL AND ETHNIC INEQUALITY TODAY

Despite some advances, the different racial/ethnic groups in the U.S. continue to have significantly different incomes, occupations, and earnings. The tables and discussion to follow focus on data from Whites, Hispanics, and Blacks because these groups constitute roughly 95 percent of the U.S. population and thus provide a broad idea of the extent of inequality involving racial and ethnic groups. At the same time, it is important to point out that the economic status of American Indians is well below that of Whites in the United States. In the 2010 census, just under 1 percent of respondents (2.9 million people) identified themselves as American Indian or Alaska Native. An additional 2.3 million reported a mixed race identity that included American Indian or Alaska Native (U.S. Census Bureau 2012b). The West has the largest number of American Indians (41 percent), followed by the South, Midwest, and Northeast, respectively. New York and Los Angeles were the cities with the highest American Indian populations. About one out of five Native Americans live on reservations or other tribal lands.

In 2013, the median household income for American Indians and Alaska Natives was about $36,000 compared to just over $55,000 for non-Hispanic White households. About 29 percent had incomes that put them below the poverty line compared to 9.6 percent of non-Hispanic Whites (Economic Policy Institute 2014). Finally, American Indian unemployment rates are much higher and rates of health insurance coverage are lower than those found among non-Hispanic Whites. At the same time, in the last 25 years, there has been a dramatic increase in postsecondary education among American Indians, and in 2012, more than 270,000 businesses owned by American Indians and Alaska Natives brought in $38.8 billion. Members of tribes that have casinos tend to have higher incomes and better health care (U.S. Census Bureau 2012b; U.S. Census Bureau 2015c; Wolfe et al. 2012).

Asian Americans are also a relatively small proportion of the U.S. population (5.4 percent), but, on average, they have higher incomes and educational levels than other groups, including Whites (Pew 2013; U.S. Census Bureau 2015d). This has led to a "Model Minority" myth that attributes their success to a culture that places emphasis on hard work and education. This myth, however, masks tremendous disparities in outcomes between different groups of Asians. Hmong and Vietnamese people, for example, have much lower average educational and economic attainment than other Asian groups, but they receive little attention because they are lumped into the model minority category (Center for Immigration Studies 2012).

Discrimination against Asian Americans, prevalent historically, continues today. For example, in 2015 the government settled a suit with Honda that accused them of discriminatory lending practices against Asians as well as other minority groups (Myers 2015). In terms of public opinion about Asians, surveys reveal that while most White Americans see Asians as hardworking, they also tend to see them as outsiders, rating them low on measures like perceived patriotism (Xu and Lee 2013).

The tables and statistics in this chapter generally include a category labeled "Hispanics." This category, like the Asian category, hides a huge amount of diversity. Importantly, it includes both native and foreign-born people. Although other racial and ethnic groups contain immigrants, this is particularly true for Hispanics. Until recently, the largest share of immigrants to the U.S. have been Hispanic, and, as a result, they constitute the largest ethnic minority group in the country, accounting for over 17 percent of the population. By 2060, Hispanics are projected to make up 29 percent of the U.S. population (Colby and Ortman 2015). Of the roughly 53 million Hispanics in 2012, 35.5 percent were foreign-born, primarily from Mexico (Krogstad and Lopez 2014). There are important differences in inequality between the native and foreign-born. We discuss this at greater length in the immigration section below.

Wealth and Income

As we saw in Chapter 2, there are significant differences in the wealth of Whites, Blacks, and Hispanics, and while the gap between Black and Hispanic groups, on the one hand, and Whites, on the other, generally narrowed between 2001 and 2007, it began to increase after 2007. By 2013, the median net worth of non-Hispanic White households was 13 times as great as the net worth of Blacks and 10 times as great as Hispanics (Kochhar and Fry 2014). About one-third of Black and Hispanic households have zero or negative net worth, a rate that is about twice that of non-Hispanic Whites (Kochhar, Fry, and Taylor 2011). As mentioned earlier, wealth is much more unequally divided than income, and this is especially true among Blacks and Hispanics.

Historically, inheritance of family wealth, or lack of it, has been a significant factor in causing racial inequality. Data suggest that Whites are five times more likely to receive an inheritance or large financial gift than either Blacks or Hispanics (McKernan, Ratcliffe, Simms, and Zhang 2012). Among those who receive an inheritance, Whites receive 10 times more on average than Blacks (Shapiro, Meschede, and Osoro 2013). Looking at inheritance data in another way, Blacks receive about $5,000 less in gifts and inheritance every 2 years than Whites. This adds up considerably over a lifetime (McKernan et al. 2012).

The building of Black and Hispanic wealth for the next generation has been further hindered by discrimination in the mortgage industry. Regardless of credit history and income, Blacks

tend to be denied loans more often and be charged higher interest rates (Bayer, Ferreira, and Ross 2014; Zillow 2015). In the 4 years preceding the recession, Blacks were 7.7 percent more likely to get a high-cost loan than Whites, and Hispanics were 6.2 percent more likely. This was true even after researchers controlled for characteristics of both the lender and the borrower (Bayer, Ferreira, and Ross 2014). In 2012, Wells Fargo, the nation's largest mortgage lender, agreed to pay $175 million in damages to settle claims that they had discriminated against 30,000 Blacks and Hispanics between 2004 and 2009. The discrimination took the form of higher fees and rates. Wells Fargo was also accused of disproportionately steering minorities into subprime mortgages when they had enough income to qualify for regular loans (Savage 2012). These practices help to perpetuate wealth differentials and "sediment" Blacks into lower levels of wealth.

Income differences between groups are not as extensive as those in wealth. In 2013, the median incomes of Black households were about 60 percent that of non-Hispanic White households (DeSilver 2013). The later part of the 1990s witnessed the most equal income growth in two decades (Mishel, Bernstein, and Schmitt 2001). Starting in about 2000, however, things began to change. Incomes for White households and families stagnated between 2000 and 2007, but those for minorities declined. Minority groups were hit especially hard because of a softer labor market and industrial shifts, including losses in the manufacturing sector. The result is that the household income gap between groups that had been closing has grown since 2000.

Table 8.1 shows the trends in household incomes between 1980 and 2014 for different groups. The percentage of households with incomes below $25,000 went down for all groups between 1980 and 2000, and that for households with incomes of at least $75,000 went up for the same period. In the data from 2010, however, we see that there were increases for all groups in the percentages of those with incomes below $25,000, and decreases for all groups in the percentages with incomes of at least $75,000. This very likely

TABLE 8.1 Percentage of Households with Incomes under $25,000, $25,000–$74,999, and $75,000 or Higher, by Race and Hispanic Origin: 1980–2014 Incomes in 2013 Dollars

	Household Incomes Below $25,000				
	1980	1990	2000	2010	2014
Non-Hispanic White	22.60%	20.40%	18.40%	20.50%	20.40%
Black	44.90%	41.50%	32.40%	38.20%	36.80%
Hispanic	33.50%	33.30%	26.20%	30.10%	28.60%
	Household Incomes Between $25,000 and $74,999				
	1980	1990	2000	2010	2014
Non-Hispanic White	49.00%	45.50%	41.00%	40.20%	39.30%
Black	43.00%	42.10%	45.20%	41.40%	42.20%
Hispanic	50.30%	48.40%	48.90%	46.10%	45.90%
	Household Incomes $75,000 or Higher				
	1980	1990	2000	2010	2014
Non-Hispanic White	28.40%	34.20%	40.60%	39.00%	40.00%
Black	12.30%	16.50%	22.40%	20.00%	21.30%
Hispanic	12.90%	15.20%	24.80%	23.60%	25.40%

Source: Table H-17, http://www.census.gov/hhes/www/income/data/historical/household.

reflects the downturn in the economy from 2007 through 2010. The data from 2014 indicate that there has been an improvement in economic standing for all groups since the recession. It should be noted, however, that the proportion of White households with incomes of $75,000 or more remains significantly higher than those for Blacks and Hispanics. Conversely, the percentage of households with incomes below $25,000 remains noticeably higher for Blacks and Hispanics.

Concentrations in income distribution increased among Blacks, Whites, and Hispanics during the 1980–2014 period. Table 8.2 shows that for each of these groups, the proportion of income going to the top 20 percent increased. In 2014, the greatest concentration of income existed among Blacks. The increased polarization of income suggests a growth in class distinctions within these groups. Among Blacks especially, it complicates relative allegiances to class and race. The special vulnerability of Blacks to weak labor markets, reductions in manufacturing employment, the decline of union power, and the fact that the richest 25 percent of Blacks possess more than 90 percent of all Black wealth suggest that

economic discrepancies will continue to grow within this group.

Earnings and Occupations

Given the differences in household incomes, it should not be surprising that there are also inequalities in the earnings of these groups. The median *weekly* earnings of Blacks and Hispanics working full-time are lower than those of Whites, among both men and women (see Table 8.3). The earnings gap increased dramatically during the 1980s, and while it has slowed since then, significant disparities remain. The availability of manufacturing jobs, union membership, and public sector employment appear to be especially important for reducing Black–White wage inequality (Wilson, Roscigno, and Huffman 2013).

Part of the reason for the differences in earnings between racial and ethnic groups relates to differences in their occupational distributions. There seems to be at least a three-step process involved in producing the earnings discrepancy. First, Blacks are segregated into jobs that are dominated by other Blacks (Hamilton, Austin,

TABLE 8.2 Share of Aggregate Income Received by Bottom 20%, Middle 60%, and Top 20% Within Non-Hispanic White, Black, and Hispanic Populations: 1980–2014

Non-Hispanic Whites					
	1980	1990	2000	2010	2014
Bottom 20%	4.40%	4.30%	3.70%	4.50%	4.20%
Middle 60%	52.20%	50.00%	47.00%	49.10%	48.50%
Top 20%	43.40%	45.80%	49.30%	46.40%	47.40%
Gini Index	0.353	0.384	0.425	0.418	0.43

Blacks					
	1980	1990	2000	2010	2014
Bottom 20%	3.70%	3.10%	3.20%	2.60%	2.60%
Middle 60%	49.20%	48.00%	47.80%	45.60%	44.50%
Top 20%	47.10%	49.00%	49.00%	51.70%	52.90%
Gini Index	0.41	0.447	0.445	0.463	0.473

Hispanics					
	1980	1990	2000	2010	2014
Bottom 20%	4.30%	4.00%	4.00%	3.50%	3.60%
Middle 60%	51.10%	49.70%	47.40%	47.10%	47.30%
Top 20%	44.50%	46.30%	48.50%	49.40%	49.20%
Gini Index	0.386	0.416	0.444	0.456	0.452

Source: Tables H-2/F-4, http://www.census.gov/hhes/www/income/data/historical/inequality.

TABLE 8.3 Median Weekly Earnings of Full-Time Wage and Salary Workers 16 Years and Older, by Race, Hispanic Origin, and Sex: First Quarter 2015

Race	Male	Female
White	$918	$746
Black	$694	$614
Hispanic	$612	$547

Source: Table 3, http://www.bls.gov/news.release/pdf/wkyeng.pdf.

and Darity, Jr. 2011). A recent study in New York City found that Black and Latino applicants for low-level jobs were less likely than White applicants to receive second interviews or job offers even though their qualifications and experience were basically the same. Discrimination was not blatant, but took the subtle forms of seeing more potential in the resumes of White applicants, viewing minority Black candidates as a last resort, and shuttling minority candidates into positions with less customer contact and more physical work (Pager, Western, and Bonikowski 2009). Second, jobs in which there is a high concentration of minority employees have lower wages attached to them regardless of the qualifications of the workers or the characteristics of the place of employment. Evidence indicates a causal relationship between racial composition of jobs and their wages (Hamilton, Austin, and Darity, Jr. 2011). Third, minority workers tend to lose ground in wages to White workers as they get older and move through their careers (Willson 2003; Maume 2004). The initial lower levels of wages for these workers coupled with their cumulative disadvantage is another factor that makes it difficult to accumulate wealth or develop an inheritance for their children.

Examining broad occupational categories, we find that Blacks, Whites, and Hispanics are variously concentrated among them. There is, however, variation between men and women, and between regions of the country (Alonso-Villar, Gradin, and del Rio 2012). Blacks and Hispanics, especially women, are overrepresented in the service sector of the economy. Employed Black and Hispanic men are overrepresented in production, transportation, and material-moving occupations. A full quarter of Hispanic men work in natural resources, construction, and maintenance occupations (as compared to 18 percent for White men, 12 percent for Black men, and 7 percent for Asian men) (U.S. Bureau of Labor Statistics 2012).

An analysis of data from the Equal Employment Opportunity Commission indicates that racial integration among occupations increased in the 1960s and 1970s, but stopped after 1980. Interestingly, but perhaps not surprisingly, occupational integration is highest in low-wage industries, for example, retail trade (Tomaskovic-Devy et al. 2006). How smoothly Blacks and other minorities become harmoniously integrated into a business establishment depends in part on the latter's internal structure. Organizations that are larger and more formalized, and contain a smaller proportion of managers but higher percentages of minority managers, engender fewer complaints of racial discrimination (Hirsh and Kornrich 2008).

The evolving distribution of Blacks among occupations also reflects broader changes in the U.S. economy, culture, and polity. Among these have been the move toward a service-oriented economy, the decline in the centrality of unskilled work, and the decreasing power of unions. These types of macrolevel shifts are important for understanding the distribution of occupations among African Americans and Whites, but they are also directly tied to unemployment and poverty levels, the **hyperghettoization** of the inner city, and the size of the severely disadvantaged class. The decline in basic blue-collar jobs, especially those requiring little formal education, and the mismatch between the location of jobs and Blacks have intensified the unemployment problems of inner-city Blacks (Stoll and Covington 2012). These shifts in the economy, however, do not mean that race itself has become unimportant as a factor in accounting for occupational differences between Blacks and Whites. The relative significance of economic class and race will be discussed shortly.

Table 8.4 presents the current broad occupational distributions for Blacks, Hispanics, and Whites of each sex. The greatest concentration of White males is in the managerial/professional category, while Black males are most often found in production/transportation or managerial/professional occupations, and the highest percentage of Hispanic men occurs in the natural resources/construction group. Among women, the greatest concentration of White women is in managerial/professional occupations, while most Black women are in managerial, professional, or office

TABLE 8.4 Occupational Distribution of Employed Civilians Age 16 and Older, by Race, Hispanic Origin, and Sex: 2014 Annual Average

Occupation	White Male	White Female	Black Male	Black Female	Hispanic Male	Hispanic Female
Managerial/professional	35.50%	43.20%	23.60%	34.70%	17.00%	26.10%
Office/sales/adm. support	16.30%	30.60%	17.50%	29.50%	14.30%	30.90%
Service occupations	13.40%	20.10%	21.60%	27.90%	21.20%	32.00%
Natural resources/construction/maintenance	17.90%	0.90%	12.00%	0.60%	26.00%	1.80%
Production/transportation/moving	16.90%	5.10%	25.30%	7.20%	21.60%	9.10%

Source: http://www.bls.gov/cps/cpsaat10.pdf.

positions. Almost two-thirds of Hispanic women are in office or service positions.

But these general categories mask real discrepancies among more detailed classifications of occupations. As is evident in Table 8.5, Blacks are most underrepresented in certain high-level professional and upper-level skilled white-collar positions involving authority or decision making, and they are overrepresented in various private and governmental service and aide occupations. Those positions in which they are typically underrepresented require specialized training or high levels of education. Their overrepresentation lies in certain mid- to lower-level service jobs, such as security guards, barbers, and bus drivers. Some of these positions have direct or indirect ties to

government, suggesting to many that the government is a significant route to the middle class for Blacks. However, the economic benefits for Blacks of working for the government seem to have eroded since the 1970s (Hamilton, Austin, and Darity Jr. 2011).

One explanation for the paucity of Black men in leadership positions is their experience in occupational hierarchies. Even in some feminized occupations, it appears that while White men may be able to move up to supervisory and leadership positions, Black men are less likely to have access to such a "glass escalator." A study of nursing, for example, revealed that Black male nurses face hostility with White female colleagues, stereotyping from patients that damages caregiving, and

TABLE 8.5 Sample of Specific Occupations in Which Blacks and Hispanics Are Significantly Over- and Underrepresented: 2014

		Blacks	
Underrepresented	**%**	**Overrepresented**	**%**
Artists	2.1	Barbers	36.3
Environmental scientists	1.3	Nursing/home health aides	35.9
Farmers and ranchers	0.9	Security guards	30.3
Dentists	5.6	Baggage porters	17.2
News analysts/reporters	7.5	Postal service clerks	30.8
Millwrights	N.A.	Industrial truck and tractor operators	24.4
Carpet/tile installers	4.8	Taxi drivers	28.8
Aircraft pilots	1.9	Bus drivers	25.9
Veterinarians	3.1	Mail clerks	20.0
		Hispanics	
Underrepresented	**%**	**Overrepresented**	**%**
Editors	7.1	Agricultural graders/sorters	54.0
Environmental scientists	6.6	Cement masons/finishers	48.7
Farmers and ranchers	4.2	Drywall installers	61.5
Millwrights	N.A.	Construction laborers	42.1
Occupational therapists	5.2	Roofers	58.1
Lawyers	5.6	Packaging operators	36.0
Chemical engineers	3.6	Carpet/tile installers	44.2
Surveyors	N.A.	Sewing machine operators	34.6
Tax examiners	6.4	Maids and housekeeping cleaners	43.8
Public relations managers	12.9	Dishwashers	40.2

Source: http://www.bls.gov/cps/cpsaat11.pdf.

prejudice in promotion assessments (Wingfield 2009). Blacks in professional positions report that they are sometimes under pressure to "act white," which can exact a toll over time (Carbado and Gulati 2015). Moreover, even when Blacks do gain high-level positions in the public economy, their positions are tenuous because of the volatility of political conditions. This is particularly true in recent years with an increase in privatization and deregulation of government jobs (Wilson, Roscigno, and Huffman 2015).

Similar to Blacks, Hispanics are underrepresented in many professional, high-authority occupations and overrepresented in manual labor, agricultural, and personal-service positions. Interviews with agricultural employers suggested that they use monolithic cultural reasons to justify hiring Hispanics into low-level manual agricultural jobs. They view Hispanics as appropriate for these kinds of jobs because they are more willing to do hard physical labor than are White workers who, they say, seldom even apply for such jobs. Moreover, employers rationalize low pay and poor conditions by saying that the situation is better than workers would find in the countries their families are from. A steady flow of immigrants and use of race-neutral rhetoric on the part of employers ensures a low-wage ethnic working force, continued profit for White employers, and maintenance of a racialized division of labor (Maldonado 2009).

Blacks, Hispanics, and Whites differ, like males and females generally, with regard to (1) the authority they possess in their jobs, (2) the specific kinds of organizations in which they are employed, and (3) the economic sector in which they work. Similar to the situation for females, human-capital variables do not fully account for these discrepancies. Rather, structural factors, such as place of employment, along with discrimination, appear to be implicated in inequalities in the occupational structure. Evidence gleaned from 15 years of civil rights commission records suggests that Black women experience more job discrimination than White women and that it is most often race-based rather than sex-based (Ortiz and Roscigno 2009).

IMMIGRATION AND INEQUALITY

Since 1965, when changes took place in U.S. immigration laws that weakened the old quota system and opened the nation more fully to immigration of relatives, the proportion of immigrants coming from Asia and Latin America has grown significantly. In 1960, about 1 in 20 people in the United States were foreign-born, mostly from Europe. Today the number of foreign-born is 1 in 8, and most have come from Latin America and Asia (U.S. Census Bureau 2013a).

The manner and extent of adaptation of these U.S. immigrants have varied, and most of the recent Latino immigrants have not found assimilation to be a smooth or easy process. Nor has assimilation followed the same paths or resulted in the same experiences for different groups. Part of the reason for the lack of smooth assimilation of many immigrant groups is that Americans have decidedly mixed feelings about the effect of immigration on society and have varying attitudes about immigrants from different countries (*Newsweek* 2009). The variation between immigrant groups has resulted in "segmented assimilation," in which the quality of adaptation varies depending on the human capital of the immigrant group, the strength of its family structure, and the reception it receives in the host country (Portes and Rumbaut 2005). Some groups, such as Chinese immigrants, form economic enclaves that develop into a source of support and income for new immigrants. Other groups arrive in the U.S. with fewer community resources upon which to draw.

Generally, greater social and economic inequality in a country encourages emigration of poorer residents out of them and into less unequal countries. Thus, the movement is often from less- to more-developed countries such as the United States (Hao 2003). These new immigrants have less education and fewer high-level skills than native citizens. In 2011, for example, 29 percent of immigrants had not completed high school, compared to 7 percent of the native-born. At the same time, U.S. immigration policies also advantage highly educated and specially trained immigrants. About 29 percent of immigrants, compared to 33 percent of the native-born, had a bachelor's degree or higher (Center for Immigration Studies 2012). Physicians, for example, are disproportionately immigrants: About 26 percent of all U.S. physicians were foreign-born (McCabe 2012), and about one-quarter of all technology start-ups are founded by immigrants (Wadhwa, Saxenian, and Siciliano 2012). Immigrants from different countries tend to arrive with different levels of education. For example, while 57 percent of Mexican immigrants have less than a high school education, 80 percent of Indian immigrants have a bachelor's degree or higher (Center for Immigration Studies 2012).

In terms of average income, immigrants lag behind natives at every age, and they accumulate less in Social Security. This makes their retirement more financially precarious (Sevak and Schmidt 2014). They also have higher levels of poverty and lower levels of health insurance (Center for Immigration Studies 2012). Immigrant income does improve considerably with

length of residence in the U.S. For example, 28 percent of recent immigrants (in the country less than 5 years) are in poverty, while only 18 percent of those here 20 years or more are (Center for Immigration Studies 2012). As with education, Hispanic immigrants tend to lag somewhat behind other groups in terms of income. Their concentration in certain kinds of jobs such as textiles, cooking, tailoring, and other service positions helps account for their lower earnings (Camarota and Zeigler 2009).

While immigration can influence wealth inequality in the United States because of the diversity of newcomers, evidence indicates that immigration has little effect on the wages of native-born employees (Smith and Edmonston 1997; Hao 2003). In communities with large numbers of immigrants, native workers tend to shift away from manual labor jobs toward higher-paying positions that require strong communication skills. By working for low wages, immigrants allow some struggling businesses to survive, increasing the jobs available in the community

Photo 8.1 An Immigration and Naturalization Services truck patrols the U.S. border in Arizona. With increasing economic uncertainty, immigration issues have received more attention.

© iStock.com/Phototreat.

(Peri 2014; Waters, Kasinitz, and Asad 2014). Interestingly, Hispanic immigration has also helped to resurrect a number of dying Midwestern towns (Carr, Lichter, and Kefalas 2012). It also appears that when immigrants send money back home, it can have a positive impact on economic growth in their countries of origin. In fact, these remittances constitute about 8 percent of the GDP of low-income nations (Connor, Cohn, and Gonzalez-Barrera 2013).

Most immigrants in the U.S. are here legally, but there are also a substantial number of people who are here illegally. Mexicans make up the largest share of unauthorized immigrants in the country (5.2 million of the 11.3 million unauthorized immigrants) (Krogstad and Passel 2015). Central Americans, however, make up a growing share of illegal entries. What is particularly notable about the new Central American immigrants is the disproportionate representation of unaccompanied children. Most of these immigrants are fleeing violence and extreme poverty in their countries. Over 57,000 unaccompanied children were taken into custody illegally crossing the border between October of 2013 and June of 2014 alone (Krogstad and Gonzalez-Barrera 2014).

Negative attitudes about immigrants and immigration are fairly common across countries, with most natives preferring less immigration (Ceobanu and Escandell 2010). Concerns about increased Hispanic immigration in the U.S. often revolve around wage and job issues, welfare dependency, and ethnic allegiance. American public opinion about immigration is highly dependent on political and media attention to the topic at any particular time but generally appears to show a trend of increased concern about the issue. There also appears to be increasing support for immigration with about 55 percent of the public saying that the U.S. should increase or keep immigration at its current level (Gallup 2014). At the same time, there is wide variability in attitudes. Persons with higher educations and social networks that include immigrants are more likely to have positive attitudes about immigration than are those who are older, of lower socioeconomic status, and have social networks that contain no immigrants. The latter groups are more likely to feel threatened by a significant immigrant presence in their communities (Berg 2009; Ceobanu and Escandell 2010). There is even variability in attitudes about immigration among Hispanics. Those of Mexican heritage, the foreign-born, and those who identify less strongly with American culture express more favorable attitudes about immigration than other Hispanics (Rouse, Wilkinson, and Garand 2010).

The presence of "foreign" groups in U.S. cities has led to debates about what it means to be an American and about personal safety. These issues crystallized in the arguments for and against halting Muslim immigration in the 2016 presidential campaign. Perceived religious and cultural threats are not the only ones currently experienced by some White Americans who feel under assault. At a time when many people are struggling economically, it is not surprising that efforts would be made to identify and deal with perceived sources of their economic problems. One of these perceived sources is illegal immigrants, who many people view as both criminal and economic threats. Increased Hispanic immigration may, in fact, lead to interethnic competition for low-skill jobs in the agricultural, manufacturing, and construction sectors in some areas of the country (Shihadeh and Barranco 2010).

The recessionary climate, concerns about illegal immigration, and its extensive border with Mexico led Arizona to pass controversial immigration legislation in 2010. Principally, the "Support Our Law Enforcement and Safe Neighborhoods Act" required police to question an individual if they suspected that the person was in the United States illegally. Immigrants were expected to carry proper documentation at all times, and if they did not, they were charged with a misdemeanor. The law also penalized employers who hired or transported illegal immigrant workers. A number of states ended up passing their own versions of Arizona's law, with the most restrictive in Alabama. Today, the only provision of the acts that has survived court scrutiny involves the duty of the police to question citizenship status. The U.S. Supreme Court's decision reaffirmed that immigration is a federal matter; states have little power to make legislation. In response, the U.S. Congress considered but failed to pass a bill in its 2013–2015 session that would have allowed states much broader power to regulate immigration. The Strengthen and Fortify Enforcement (SAFE) bill would have allowed many of the earlier state bills, like Arizona's and Alabama's, to be reinstated.

Proponents of state-level legislation say the states should have the right to monitor their own borders, and that they need to act because the federal government has neglected its duty to protect citizens through its lax enforcement of current federal law. Opponents believe that the legislation unlawfully profiles certain kinds of people and thereby violates civil rights law. In addition, they contend that enforcement might undermine any trust minority groups have in the police. Since the 1980s, a number of cities have declared themselves "sanctuary cities" and refused to help federal efforts to deport immigrants. Because immigration has racial and ethnic undertones, the legal controversy over the control of immigration raises the issue of whether the law racializes immigration by profiling certain ethnic groups, reinforcing ethnic stereotypes, and providing another example of how some ethnic groups enjoy political power over others.

It should be noted that not all recent legislation affecting immigrants has been restrictive. In fact, some states have passed laws that aid illegal immigrants and may decrease inequality. For example, 10 states and the District of Columbia now allow a person to get a driver's license if they have proof of identity (which can include a foreign passport) or can prove residency in the state. Applicants do not need to prove citizenship. Twenty states allow unauthorized immigrants to attend public colleges at in-state tuition rates, and five allow them to receive state financial aid. Unauthorized immigrants, however, cannot receive federal financial aid (Park 2015). At the federal level, the Deferred Action for Childhood Arrivals (DACA) program has provided more than half a million young people (under the age of 31) who were brought illegally to the United States as children to receive two-year (renewable) temporary residency permits. This gives them certain limited rights including work authorization and eligibility for both federal and state financial aid to attend college.

An area that has not been well addressed in terms of immigration and inequality involves "mixed status" families. In these 2.3 million families, some of the children are citizens and others are not (this can happen when older children were born outside the U.S. and the younger children were U.S.-born). Mixed-status families can have some children with health insurance and some without, or some who can go to college and some who cannot afford to do so. This can cause painful inequalities within families (Castañeda and Melo 2014).

WHITE PRIVILEGE AND THE RELATIONAL NATURE OF RACIAL INEQUALITY

As suggested earlier, "race" has generally been thought to be a characteristic of non-White groups. Whiteness has been thought of as a noncolor and, therefore, invisible to most Whites. Critical-race theorists argue that (1) while whiteness is invisible to Whites, it is a position from which Whites view themselves as well as others; (2) it is a privilege of which Whites are unaware; and (3) society and cultural norms are organized in ways that privilege whiteness (Lucal 1996; Frankenberg 1997). That is, racism is rooted in the way institutions work, and laws are structured in society, rather than a psychological property of the individual (Feagin 2006). At the beginning of the chapter, we discussed historical examples of this kind of structural racism. An example today involves the effects of 30 years of zoning restrictions that have made it difficult for minorities and the poor to move to better neighborhoods (Massey, Rothwell, and Domina 2009). Another example involves criminal justice policy (which is discussed extensively in Chapter 12). Minority groups have also suffered structural disadvantages in the areas of education, employment, and health care.

From a **critical-race perspective**, viewing racism as an individual phenomenon masks its structural nature and prevents its eradication. Moreover, since Whites are generally unaware of how social arrangements benefit them above others, they do not see a reorganization of society as necessary. They assume its neutrality and argue for a color-blind perspective in which all are able to operate freely within the existing structure, thus leaving success solely up to the individual.

Defining racism in individualistic rather than structural terms allows one to ignore the institutional context within which individuals of different races are embedded, and to deflect attention from the issue of White privilege. Just as poverty is viewed by most as a problem of the poor, that is, *their* problem, the race problem is one focused on minorities as their problem. The result is that most studies of racism examine the oppression and discrimination minorities encounter and do not include the privileges that dominant groups enjoy and that foster racial inequality. Just as many view poverty as caused by individual deficiencies, traditional perspectives interpret racism as resulting from individual prejudice. The result is that remedies for racism emphasize enlightenment, education, and training to change the prejudiced individual rather than reorganizing the institutional structures that privilege the dominant group. In their study of how two school districts worked to address racial bias, for example, Vaught and Castagno noted that because school racial problems were interpreted "as the isolated struggles of individual teachers working with 'different' students," workshops focused on raising awareness and changing the perspective of individual administrators and teachers. "The racialized structural barriers that informed, maintained, and entrenched individual practice went unnoticed" (2008, p. 103).

Racism does indeed involve a set of relations between groups that is embedded in the structure of institutions. Just as the position and life conditions of a social class are determined by its structural relationship to other classes, so too the position and life conditions of a racial minority are determined by its structural relationship to the dominant racial group. Thinking about class or race as an individual's property blinds us from seeing how relational ties affect each group. The oppression of one group is related to the privileges of another, but, like being White, those privileges often go unnoticed. As Lucal (1996) has stressed, a relational model of race relations is needed to incorporate all sides of those relations. This means making visible the often unnoticed privileges enjoyed by Whites: "Because of the segregated structure of the material and discursive environments inhabited by most white people, racial privilege is lived but not seen; whites not uncommonly live much of their daily existence without coming into contact with people of color" (Lucal 1996, p. 247). The evidence that Whites are unaware of their race and its privileges, and that the societal structures are biased in their favor, is mixed. Results from one national survey, for example, indicate that while Whites are less likely than non-Whites to view their race as important to them or to interpret racial problems as caused by structural arrangements, these views are not held by all Whites (Hartmann, Gerteis, and Croll 2009).

MICROINEQUITIES AND MICROAGGRESSIONS AGAINST RACIAL MINORITIES

In the United States, it is clear that being White makes many of the daily aspects of life easier, while being a member of a minority group often makes everyday living more problematic. Like women, racial and ethnic minorities have been subjected to a host of everyday indignities. These indignities are independent of class position. Language, which reflects cultural values, helps to undergird the system of social inequality as it pertains to minorities, and yet because it is so much a part of our everyday lives, we seldom step back and look at it in any depth. The derogatory terms used to describe different ethnic and racial groups suggest the value placed on these groups and reinforce this negative imagery when terms referring to these groups are used to describe some disliked or despised behavior (e.g., "an Indian giver," to "Jew down," to "gyp"). Language is a powerful tool for shaping the attitudes toward and general beliefs about groups, and what makes it exceptionally influential is the fact that these terms are part of the matrix of everyday life and often used without intentional thought being given to their implications.

Embedded in this language are stereotypes of different racial and ethnic groups. Jokes and humor aimed at labeling and denigrating minorities have a long history in the United States, going back to the early seventeenth century when the first slaves arrived in the country. As new ethnic groups emigrated to the country, jokes that reinforced negative images of them increased. Such jokes helped to justify the stereotypes and poor treatment many immigrant groups received (Hughes 2003).

In the absence of real knowledge about specific groups, stereotypes provide a means by which individuals develop ideas about the characteristics of other groups. Most Americans, for example, have not had personal or extended contact with Native Americans. Yet many school and professional sports teams have adopted names and mascots that are supposed to represent Native American qualities. The Washington Redskins, the Atlanta Braves and the tomahawk chop of their fans, and the Chief Wahoo mascot of the Cleveland Indians are only a few examples of images that reinforce misperceptions about Native Americans. These terms and images are important because they shape our ideas about the supposed distinctiveness of Native Americans (King and Springwood 2001). They also damage the chances of accurately understanding the diversity and real qualities of Native Americans.

One reason for stereotypes is the lack of personal, concrete familiarity that individuals have with persons in other racial or ethnic groups. Lack of familiarity encourages the lumping together of unknown individuals. This happens even among social scientists. White interviewers have been found to view Black respondents as much darker

Photo 8.2 Stereotyping a group often results in all its members being thought of as the same and, therefore, deserving of the same treatment by dominant groups. The September 11, 2001, attacks on the Twin Towers of the World Trade Center in New York City provided an impetus to stereotyping and increased attacks on Muslims, as witnessed by this Minneapolis picketer on the 2010 anniversary of 9/11.

© Peter Marshall/Alamy Stock Photo.

than do Black interviewers, and, conversely, Black interviewers perceive White respondents as being much lighter than do White interviewers. In addition, each type of interviewer sees members of the opposite race as having little variation in color while seeing much more color variation among members of their own race. Familiarity encourages images of variation and individuality, while unfamiliarity fosters images of sameness (Hill 2002).

The media, especially movies and television, also have perpetuated stereotypes of African Americans learned in other contexts. Traditionally, African Americans and other non-White individuals have either been absent from the media or been portrayed in negative terms—for example, the African American as lazy, slow thinking, and subservient, and the American Indian as savage and hostile (Marger 1997). By ignoring heterogeneity among the more than 500 American Indian tribes through its presentation of the generic Indian and suggesting that American Indians are relics of the Old West, the media have contributed to the distortion in White Americans' image of American Indians.

The stereotype of the "drunken Indian" is also found among Whites. American Indians are viewed in the minds of many Whites as lacking a sense of control and responsibility. Such psychological factors are often used by Whites to explain alcoholism rates among American Indians, although the latter more often trace the problem to White invasions into Indian territory and culture. Allegations of psychological and cultural deficiencies are then used by Whites to explain the continued poverty and related problems among American Indians and to justify the paucity of attempts to alleviate these problems. In other words, such explanations continue to be used as part of an ideology to legitimate the inequalities that exist between Whites and American Indians (Holmes and Antell 2001).

The images of Asian Americans are also contradictory and problematic. As described above, they are often seen as the "model minority." This myth can cause pressure for individual Asian people when they are held to a higher standard than others. In fact, it appears that the stereotype of the model minority is so strong, Asians who are not highly successful experience negative outcomes. For example, while highly educated Asian Americans tend to earn more than similarly educated Whites, those Asians with low levels of education tend to earn less than similar Whites, suggesting that the incongruity between the model minority myth and reality results in those individuals being seen as defective (Kim and Sakamoto 2014). The model minority myth is also problematic as it implicitly denigrates other minorities by suggesting that their cultures are somehow inferior in relation to the "model." Focusing on cultural reasons for Asian success causes us to ignore the very different historical and structural contexts minority groups have faced upon arrival in the U.S.

There are many additional, subtle, taken-for-granted advantages that are attached to the status of being White. In their everyday experiences in school, Black undergraduates have typically been tokenized, stereotyped, and assumed to have gained college admission through affirmative action rather than through their own efforts. Hispanics often have their citizenship questioned and are treated coldly (Rivera, Forquer, and Rangel 2010; Watkins, LaBarrie, and Appio 2010). Asians report that they are often asked where they are from and that a truthful response like "Ohio" does not suffice. In many cases, the question is not about where the person is from but is rather about the ethnic origins of the person's family. Frequent repetition of the question suggests to the person that they are seen as a foreigner and outsider (see "26 Questions Asians Have for White People" (Buzzfeed 2015) for a humorous treatment of the topic).

Unfair treatment often sends coded messages about the perceptions of minorities by persons in the dominant group. For example, a White woman may unintentionally hold on to her purse extra tightly as a Black man passes by, suggesting she thinks that all Black men are criminals (Sue 2010). Indeed, as we will see in Chapter 12, the image of Black men as threatening, dangerous, and violent is a common one. This image often has more impact than the reality. Regardless of the actual incidence of violence and delinquent behavior, for example, public schools with larger percentages of Black students are more likely than others to use punishment in disciplining students, and more drastic forms of punishment as well, again implying that Blacks are seen as a threatening presence even if they follow the rules (ACLU 2015). Even President Barack Obama has been the victim of stereotyping because of his race and ancestry. Despite clear evidence to the contrary, some have made unfounded accusations that he is a Muslim rather than a Christian, and a Kenyan rather than a U.S. citizen.

One of the classic statements about every-day, taken-for-granted White privileges comes from Peggy McIntosh (1988). Among the 46 she lists are how being White allows her to:

- freely choose a place that she wants and can afford to live in;
- go shopping, feeling secure that she will not be harassed or followed;
- see others of her race prevalently displayed in the media;
- be fairly sure that her voice will be heard even in a non-White group;
- rely on her skin color to protect her from being seen as financially unreliable;
- feel that her children will receive an education that acknowledges the contributions of her race and in which teachers treat her children fairly;
- talk with her mouth full and not have people put this down to her color;
- not worry about acknowledging the views of non-White people;
- consider a wide variety of options in her life without worrying about whether her race would be a factor in limiting them;
- select a service or public accommodation without considering whether she will be treated poorly because of her race;
- not worry about her "shape, bearing, or body odor" being seen as a reflection of her race;
- use a "flesh-colored" bandage and have it blend with her skin.

Since its publication in the 1980s, McIntosh's list has proved extremely useful for uncovering the ways privilege invisibly manifests itself in the day-to-day experience of many Whites. Some academics and practitioners, however, argue that McIntosh's work should not be considered in isolation, as it insufficiently recognizes that whiteness is socially constructed. It also fails to acknowledge that different White people might have very different experiences (for example, a poor White man from a rural area may not experience privilege in the same way that a rich urban White woman might) (Lensmire et al. 2013). At the same time, the White privilege list can be an important step in interrogating the advantages that come with being categorized as White.

THE INTERSECTION OF CLASS, RACE, SEX, AND GENDER

In the preceding few chapters, we have examined the economic, racial, and gender dimensions of social inequality, and although they have been, to a large extent, treated separately, in the context of a *society* and in the lives of real *individuals*, these dimensions are interconnected. If we wish to understand how the dynamics and effects of each of these dimensions play out in actuality, we need to probe the nature of these interconnections at both the social/societal and individual levels. The significant meaning of these relationships can be uncovered by examining them at both levels.

When we speak of analyzing the interaction of class, race, and gender at the *social/societal level*, we are essentially considering each of these as separate variables that affect each other at the group or aggregate level. For example, consider the discussion of the relationship between the class measures of occupation and earnings on the one hand, and race on the other. Those relationships might be understood using references to racial compositions of occupations, group stereotypes, and interethnic relationships, without ever including the psychological effects or experiences of *individuals*.

The intersection of race and class can also be understood at the *level of individual experience*. Here, we are concerned with how race and class interact in the lives of individuals. How do people *experience* race and class in their lives? In their everyday lives, individuals accumulate *simultaneous* experiences as members of particular races, classes, *and* gender or sexuality groups. A person is all of these things at the same time. As described in Chapter 6, this is the meaning of *intersectionality*. The dimensions are not as readily separable but rather are nested into each other. How do these elements interact *within* the individual? Consider a person who is Black, upper-class, and male—a Black surgeon, for example. What is it like to be him? How do the effects of class and race and gender interact in his life? And, at the same time, what is it like to be poor, White, and female? To address these questions is to examine the intersection of race, class, and gender at the individual level.

The Relative Significance of Race and Class

One of the most controversial and prominent discussions on the intersection of race and class involves arguments about the relative effects of race and class on the life chances of individuals. Scholars differ on which they think is most important. Around the turn of the twentieth century, W. E. B. Du Bois suggested in his study of *The Philadelphia Negro* (1973) that not only racial discrimination but economic factors as well affected the everyday living conditions of Blacks. E. Franklin Frazier (1937) also suggested that both race and class play a role in determining what happens to Blacks, but finally felt that economics may be more important than race, an opinion later shared by Oliver Cox. Cox viewed race relations in the United States as stemming from and continuously being conditioned by economic-class relations. Racism exists as one of several devices used by capitalists to control, exploit, and keep workers down. As a result, it is rooted in economic conflict.

William Julius Wilson (1982) has argued that class has become more important than race in determining the life chances of Blacks today. This is because even though political and economic changes in society have opened up more potential opportunities for Blacks, these changes have also helped create urban joblessness. Blacks have been particularly affected, for example, by trends that continue today but began decades ago: the shift from a manufacturing to a service economy, a broadening split between low-wage and high-wage labor markets, and by the movement of industries out of the central cities (Bonacich 1980; W. J. Wilson 2012). "The net effect is a growing class division among Blacks, a situation, in other words, in which economic class has been elevated to a position of greater importance than race in determining individual Black opportunities for living conditions and personal life experiences" (Wilson 1982, pp. 399–400). Wilson has not argued that race is irrelevant today, but he has said that historically racism has had a major effect on the lives of Blacks that continues today. However, this *historical* discrimination has a more significant impact on Blacks' lives today than does *contemporary* discrimination. Still, it is broader economic and political forces that are most immediately important for understanding events and behaviors within the Black community.

In sharp contrast to those who stress the primacy of economic-class factors in explaining the socioeconomic condition of Blacks, others emphasize the greater and, in some cases, increasing significance of race in understanding the economic predicament of Blacks. They suggest that the gains that Blacks have made relative to Whites have been exaggerated or overestimated. For example, Black gains seem large when starting with a baseline of slavery, but appear much smaller when contemporary Blacks are compared to Whites (Feagin and Elias 2013; Shams 2015). On a day-to-day basis for adults, race often overrides class in its importance. For example, a longitudinal study of residential migration among Blacks and Whites suggests that racial factors are more important than wealth in explaining the slow rate of Black movement into heavily White neighborhoods (Crowder, South, and Chavez 2006). In other words, movement into White neighborhoods is slowed much more by racist practices than it is by a lack of ability to pay for homes.

Earlier in this chapter, we noted the high degree of wealth inequality within the Black population. There has been a long-standing suspicion between Blacks in different social classes. Since 1986, an increasing percentage of Blacks believe that the gap between the values of the middle and poor classes in the Black community has grown. By 2007 (the last time this question was asked in a national survey), more than 60 percent felt this way compared to less than half in 1986. Almost 40 percent felt that the diversity within the Black community was so great that they could no longer be considered a single race. But a majority still felt that both classes have at least some values in common (Pew 2007). These results suggest that class operates as a divisive force in the Black community, while race still has a cohesive effect. They pull in opposite directions.

Many examples presented in this chapter show that race has an effect on class standing. We saw, for example, that the class structure among Blacks is more compressed than that among Whites and that each class is different from its White counterpart. The position of the Black middle class, for example, is more precarious than that of the White middle class because of the generally lower stability of their jobs and the smaller "nest eggs" available for future expenses. "Wealthy" Blacks are not as rich as wealthy Whites; the white-collar positions held by members of the Black middle class tend to be of lower status than those occupied by middle-class Whites; and poor Blacks are generally poorer than poor Whites. Also, in contrast to the *invisibility* of whiteness as a color and of Whites as a race, consciousness of race is more prominent among Blacks, in part because of the continued segregation and other problems they face regardless of class.

In other areas, however, changes in class position seem to affect the salience of race. Among Blacks, an increase in class position in some situations can lead to greater racial allegiance. Evidence from voting studies in California suggests that as Blacks move into the middle class, a greater percentage vote in a pro-Black manner and more liberally than other classes on issues of central importance to Blacks. Among Blacks, "class gains appear to reinforce rather than erode race" (Hajnal 2007, p. 574). In contrast to effects in other ethnic groups, increases in class position appear to lead to more liberalism rather than more conservatism. There are other areas in which unity exists among Blacks in general. Regardless of class position, Blacks have a strong positive identity with their race and do not subscribe to negative images held of them by others (Hughes et al. 2015).

Despite these similarities among Blacks, class-related pressures still create fissures and disagreements within the Black community. Many of the issues between classes revolve around differences in lifestyles, attitudes, and child rearing. In her study of a Black middle-class neighborhood on the south side of Chicago, Mary Pattillo-McCoy (1999) found that residents often distinguish area individuals on the basis of whether they are "bourgie" (i.e., have a *bourgeois* lifestyle) or "uppity" (i.e., think they are better than everyone else). The economic middle class consists of both law-abiding and criminal elements. Perhaps most significantly, residents have to negotiate their daily lives using both "street" and "decent" lifestyles (see also Anderson 1999). While the decent lifestyle professes adherence to traditional, more mainstream middle-class values and behaviors, the street lifestyle requires values and behaviors that reflect the street smarts necessary for survival and respect in the neighborhood. The battle to balance these two lifestyles is constant, but especially intense during adolescence (Pattillo-McCoy 1999).

The conflict between traditional dominant lifestyle values and subgroup values also is found in school settings. In the hothouse environment of the elite prep school, all students, regardless of background, are expected to adhere to a given set of principles. But these principles often come into conflict with the values and attitudes that Black, working-class, and poor children have been taught at home. These children are marginalized in the school setting that is structured to prize and honor children from elite backgrounds. DeCuir-Gunby, Martin, and Cooper (2012), however, found that

Black students can learn to effectively combine the methods and lessons taught at home with those taught at school to navigate their way through the elite school. Parents were particularly helpful in supporting positive racial identity for the youth, enabling them to better weather racist incidents.

The interaction of race and class factors is certainly complex. We saw that, historically, economic and racial factors interacted in the treatment of American Indians and African Americans. Economic motives played a role in driving American Indians from their land and enslaving African Americans to create an extensive labor force. At the same time, we found that class distinctions existed among African Americans and women that were important for understanding the differences in life conditions. We also found that racism as a fully developed ideology was used to legitimate and sustain the economic systems that were being constructed. In the same way, ideologies about the sexes and their proper roles have helped to keep occupational sex segregation intact. Economic as well as other conditions helped bring about the migration of Blacks to the North and the consequent form of the class structure within the Black population. Evidence presented earlier shows that race affects one's occupation, and the racial composition of an occupation affects the earnings associated with it. Blacks receive less of a return on their educations than Whites, and race and class position both affect one's income (Kmec 2003; Pager, Western, and Bonikowski 2009).

Class, Color, and Race

Usually we think of race as a biologically fixed category that cannot therefore be affected by class. But as we saw earlier, races are socially constructed, and how one identifies with a given race and is placed in a racial category can depend on one's class position. Because of this, there is remarkable fluidity in racial identity. Saperstein and Penner (2012), for example, examined race and ethnicity data gathered between 1979 and 1998. Race was self-identified at two points in time and was also assigned by an interviewer at 19 points in time. Looking at the interviewer-assigned racial categories, it was found that over 20 percent of the sample changed races over the time period, some multiple times. While this fluidity was primarily between the White, Asian, and Hispanic categories, there was also movement into and out of the Black category. Similarly, self-identification (which was only measured in 1979 and 1998) also changed over time. Importantly, both self- and interviewer-assigned racial and ethnic categorizations were strongly correlated with class markers including unemployment, welfare use, poverty, and incarceration. In other words, unemployment or welfare use resulted in a higher likelihood that a person would be considered Black.

Race and class forces collide in the phenomenon of colorism. "'Colorism' is the discriminatory treatment of individuals falling within the same 'racial' group on the basis of skin color. It operates both intraracially and interracially" (Herring 2004, p. 3). Among Blacks, a greater proportion of those with darker skins have lower educations, incomes, and occupational statuses (Monk 2014). Colorism starts early; for example, African American adolescents with darker skin are more likely to be suspended than those who are lighter (Hannon, DeFina, and Bruch 2013). Similarly, skin tone predicts sentence length and time served among African American women (Viglione, Hannon, and DeFina 2011). Colorism also appears to be related to how individuals assess candidates for political office (Hochschild and Weaver 2007) and how intelligent Blacks and Hispanics are perceived to be by Whites (Hannon 2015).

Similar to racial and ethnic categorization, skin tone assessment appears to be affected by class and status markers. When respondents were prompted to believe that a Black person was well-educated, they later remembered the person as being lighter in skin tone than if they were prompted to think the person was not educated (Ben-Zeev et al. 2014). Similarly, in the 2008 election, some Blacks wondered whether the lighter-skinned Barack Obama was "Black enough" because his mother is White and he did not descend from a slave family or grow up in grinding poverty (Staples 2007). Being seen as authentically "Black" in this case means having a certain kind of socioeconomic background. Here again we see the complex effects when race, defined socially, and class mix.

The shading of one's skin is not only significant in the United States; throughout history, it has been socially important in countries around the globe. In her international analysis of what she calls a "yearning for lightness," Evelyn Nakano Glenn (2008) found rising demand for skin lighteners in all parts of the world, including Southeast and East Asia, India, and many countries in Latin America and Africa. In the United States, skin color made a difference early in its history. Slaves with lighter skins were treated better than those with darker skin or full African ancestry, later giving rise to groups such as "blue vein societies," associations of more prosperous freed Blacks whose blue veins could be seen because of their lighter skins. These organizations mirrored the "blue blood" societies among wealthy Whites.

The fact that skin color and social class interact may make growing class discrepancies within minority communities and between Whites and other groups even more significant. Saperstein and Penner (2012) point out that the "whitening" of successful or well-educated people of color can contribute to inequality because it widens the chasm between groups. In other words, if successful people of color become White, the people who remain in the minority category will appear to be very different from Whites, hardening racial categories. Colorism can operate within minority communities as well as outside them. In her study of women involved in high-society organizations, Diana Kendall (2002) found that within Black "high society," members used a **brown-bag test** to screen potential new members. Those whose skin was darker than a brown grocery bag were deemed ineligible (p. 129). This is significant because it denied people with darker skin access to social capital that could enhance their socioeconomic position.

Colorism is important because of its relationship to inequality. Bonilla-Silva (2004) also argues that it is a central marker in a new racial system emerging in the United States. He argues that increased multiethnicity, immigration, and globalization are among the forces leading the United States into a three-tiered racial system with "Whites," "Honorary Whites," and "Collective Blacks." The category of "White" is coming to include not only those groups we have traditionally categorized as White but also some light-skinned highly assimilated Latinos. "Honorary Whites" include a variety of ethnic groups that generally have been thought of as separate from "Whites" (e.g., Japanese Americans, Arab Americans, Asian Indians). The third category, labeled "Collective Black," includes not only African Americans, but newer, generally poorer East Asian immigrants, "dark-skinned and poor Latinos," and "reservation-bound Native Americans" (pp. 225–227). This suggested classification clearly shows the interaction of economic and racial/ethnic forces.

Gender, Race, and Class

As we discussed in Chapter 6, sex and gender discrimination plays an important role in shaping the class structure through mechanisms such as occupational segregation. In this chapter, we have discussed the important role racial discrimination plays. As Crenshaw (1989) points out, however, it is highly problematic to see gender and race as separate phenomena. When we do so, all "women" are too often assumed to be White and all people of color to be male. Sojourner Truth, in a famous speech at a Women's Convention in 1851 in Ohio, made exactly this point when she wanted to know why Black women's concerns were not being addressed. She asked, "Ain't I a woman?"

Census Bureau data on incomes of full-time workers make it evident that race *and* gender have an influence on income, earnings, and the distribution of occupations. Blacks and Whites differ on each of the latter, but within each race, males and females are differently situated with respect to income, earnings, and occupation. Census data clearly show that although Blacks and women, in general, have increased their representation in professional occupations, they continue to be severely underrepresented in professions dominated by males. Even though the proportion of male professionals declined, males continue to dominate certain high-ranking professions. In fact, their overrepresentation in these professions has increased. Black men are the next group most represented in these professions, followed by White women and Black women, respectively. These findings again suggest the complex interplay of race and gender that affects class position.

Attitudes toward the feminist movement both in the 1970s and today is another area that demonstrates the detailed interworking of race, gender, and class. In the 1970s, many African American women did not identify with the Women's Movement because they associated it with White, middle-class women, a group whose interests and needs differ in many ways from their own. They also experienced racism in some feminist groups (hooks 1981; Reid 1984; King 1988). Continuing into today, some Black women hesitate about identifying as feminists. They tend to take a more intersectional view of oppression instead, seeing race and gender as inextricably intertwined (Springer 2002). As is discussed in the Social Movements chapter, the Black Lives Matter movement is an interesting example of an intersectional approach with its clear welcome to women and to gender-nonconforming people.

The influences of race, class, and sex on the life chances of an individual are multiplicative because they interact in complex and different ways depending on the specific sociohistorical and cultural context and the area of life chances in question (King 1988). In this sense, African American women are often in a situation of "multiple jeopardy" because of their racial, sex, and class positions. It is inappropriate to lump Blacks and women into the same category because their current life experiences and past histories are unique. Whereas the races have been expected to restrict intimacy with each other, men and women have been expected to do the opposite. In this manner, Blacks have occupied a caste-like position, while women have not (Keller 1987). Even more specifically, Black women are often left to fall

between the cracks in discussions of Blacks (usually meaning Black men) and women (usually meaning White women). The lesson here is that even though the histories of the sexes and races have been unique in many ways, the influences of race, sex, and class interweave when affecting individual lives.

THEORIES OF RACIAL AND ETHNIC INEQUALITY

As is the case for sex and gender inequality, there have been a variety of attempts to explain racial inequality, ranging from biological to cultural and structural. Attempts to anchor an adequate explanation in biology have been widely criticized. The work of Herrnstein and Murray (1994) elicited an avalanche of commentary, most of it negative. Basically, these scholars argued first that an elite of highly intelligent people had developed that was increasingly separated from the rest of society, socially and economically. The high demands for intelligence and education in our sophisticated economy funneled these elite into the high-paying, high-prestige occupations and left the rest of the population behind, resulting in greater social inequality. The second part of their argument was that low intelligence was significantly linked to a wide array of social effects, including wages, poverty, crime, dropping out of school, and having an illegitimate child. A highly controversial position follows this discussion in which Herrnstein and Murray suggested that racial groups vary on intelligence, that a large portion of intelligence is very likely genetically based, and that most of those at the bottom of the socioeconomic ladder are also those who score low on intelligence.

Briefly, Herrnstein and Murray's work was criticized for, among other things, (1) its reliance on intelligence tests given later in life whose results might thus reflect both genetic and environmental influences, (2) the omission of other significant factors that can affect socioeconomic outcomes (e.g., labor-market experience), and (3) the belief in the fixity and rigidity of genetic mechanisms and related social problems (Haynes 1995; Massey 1995). Earlier research by the psychologist Arthur

Jensen, who argued that there are significant differences between Blacks and Whites in native intelligence, was also heavily criticized. But even if such differences could be demonstrated, their relevance for social and economic inequality between the races would still be problematic given the fact that numerous studies demonstrate that individual characteristics do not fully explain such inequality. Finally, the whole idea of racial differences in biology is based on the assumption that different races can be accurately, indisputably, and objectively identified. As we have seen, this is not the case.

Although biological explanations of racial and ethnic differences have largely been discredited, there is a current discussion about the link between genetics and race. Once the human genome was charted in 2000, it opened the door to research looking for a link between race and propensities for disease or criminality. While scientists claim their work to be race-neutral, social scientists have again pointed out that the empirical work that is being done relies on socially constructed categories of race. In other words, it assumes that "White" is a real category and attempts to find specific gene combinations linked to that category. This type of research also has the potential to mislead the public into false causational thinking. For example, it may appear that race causes a higher risk of cancer, but in reality, Blacks are simply more likely to live near toxic waste dumps that cause cancer (Duster 2015; Collins 2015a).

In the sections that follow, various interpretations of race relations and explanations for racial inequality will be presented. Most will focus on the United States even though they are frequently based on analyses developed for the characterization of intergroup relations in other countries such as India and developing countries in general.

Domination Theories of Race Relations

A variety of specific theories are included under this general category, but all of them incorporate the historically crucial role of power and/or domination in shaping racial inequality. They do not anticipate the eventual automatic assimilation of minorities, nor do they emphasize the stability of the system of inequality or the active complicity of the minority group. As was noted earlier, critical-race theory posits that the power of whiteness is woven into the structure and hegemonic culture of U.S. society. The effectiveness of dominant values as disseminated by political, economic, educational institutions, and the media helps to make White privilege invisible to most Whites, who are unaware of the everyday benefits that they enjoy because of their whiteness. In addition to critical-race theory, Noel's theory of ethnic stratification, imperialist/colonial models, and class-based theories also emphasize the centrality of power differentials in explaining racial inequality.

NOEL'S THEORY OF ETHNIC STRATIFICATION Noel (1968) generated a broad theory of the origins of ethnic stratification, which he then tested by applying it to the development of slavery in the United States. By ethnic stratification, he means "a system of stratification wherein some relatively fixed group membership (e.g., race, religion, or nationality) is utilized as a major criterion for assigning social positions with their attendant differential rewards" (p. 157). He begins with the assumption that before the possibility of such stratification even exists, there must be a period of prolonged contact between the groups involved. Whether contact results in stratification depends on the existence of (1) ethnocentrism, (2) competition, and (3) differential power. All three of these factors must be present for ethnic stratification to emerge.

Ethnocentrism, of course, refers to the belief that one's culture is the best, the center of the universe so to speak. All others are judged according to it. Cultures that are similar to one's own are ranked high, and those that are radically different are looked down on. Consequently, ethnocentrism fosters an in-group/out-group or us/them orientation toward others. Since people are so classified, double standards may be applied to the groups involved. What one expects of oneself may not be what is expected of others. It is important to note that each group is ethnocentric, thinking of the other in terms of mild or severe disdain. Each group measures the other in terms of its own values and beliefs, and of course, the other group is always found to be wanting to some degree. Each group also remains separate and autonomous from the other.

However, mere ethnocentrism is not enough to create ethnic stratification according to Noel. Groups can remain independent and relatively equal with a mutual and healthy respect for each other even though both are ethnocentric. Thus, it is also crucial that competition exists between the two or more groups in question. *Competition*, as defined by Noel, refers to the interaction between groups who are trying to attain "the same scarce goal." What is important about this interaction is that the goal is the same and that it is scarce. This could be competition over a prime neighborhood area or desirable jobs, for example. If the groups were after different goals, there would be no sense of competition and perhaps even lack of concern over the goals of the other group. If the goal is easily attainable and in abundant supply, there is no reason for one group to try to exploit or stratify the other. There is plenty for all.

If, on the other hand, the desired object or goal is actually or believed to be in scarce supply, then stratification may be seen as functional by each group. The intensity and terms of the competition along with the relative adaptive capacity of each group will affect the probability and form of ethnic stratification. Competition is more likely to be highly intense if there are many valuable, scarce goals that are shared by both groups, and will be less intense if those shared goals are few in number and relatively unimportant. The more intense the competition, the greater the likelihood of ethnic stratification, other factors being equal. The terms of the competition concern the values, rules, and structural opportunities present in the setting. If competition is regulated by agreed-upon rules and some basic human values are shared by the two groups, then ethnic stratification is far less likely to occur than if the competition is essentially a free-for-all and the groups have no values in common. Moreover, if there are few structural

outlets in the form of opportunities, then competition is more likely to lead to stratification.

Finally, the adaptive capacity of a group relative to its competitor also has an impact on ethnic stratification. Basically, the group that has more cultural and other internal resources to call on when problems of adaptation and adjustment arise will more likely be able to dominate the other group. The chances of stratification occurring are lower when both groups are equal in their adaptive capabilities.

According to Noel (1968), in addition to ethnocentrism and competition, a third variable, *differential power*, is also necessary for the emergence of ethnic stratification. "Highly ethnocentric groups involved in competition for vital objects will not generate ethnic stratification unless they are of such unequal power that one is able to impose its will upon the other" (p. 162). Ethnic stratification simply will not appear in the absence of differential power. Once the greater power of one group is established, the more powerful group develops measures to subordinate and regulate the other group and to stabilize the current distribution of differential rewards.

In sum, Noel argued for an interactive model in that all three variables—ethnocentrism, competition with particular characteristics, and differential power—are needed to produce ethnic stratification. In applying this theory to the development of slavery in the early English colonies of the United States, Noel concluded that it adequately explains ethnic stratification. "Given ethnocentrism, the Negroes' lack of power, and the dynamic arena of competition in which they were located, their ultimate enslavement was inevitable" (p. 172). Earlier, we saw how these factors also were implicated in the subjugation of American Indians.

The next two theories, which also focus on differential power, have a great deal in common. The colonial model of race relations owes a significant amount to the Marxian class framework, and early architects of that model generally acknowledge their debt to Marx (Fanon 1963; e.g., Memmi 1965). In recent years, there has been a lot of cross-fertilization of both the colonial and class perspectives, with each using concepts from the other. But since the primary impetus that gave rise to each was not the same, they will be presented as if they are distinct approaches. However, their overlap in general orientation will become clear as each is discussed.

INTERNAL COLONIALISM AND RACE INEQUALITY

Today, the terms "colonialism" and "postcolonialism" are used in a wide range of disciplines and theoretical perspectives. Mohanty (1988) explains that, "as an explanatory construct, colonization almost invariably implies a relation of structural domination, and a discursive or political suppression of the heterogeneity of the subject(s) in question" (p. 61).

"Internal colonialism" refers to one approach to understanding the structural domination of Whites over Blacks in the United States. It is based on discussions and analyses of relationships between colonizing countries and those who have been colonized. In this way, it bears a striking resemblance to world-system and dependency theories. The popularization of the internal-colonial perspective arose during the tumultuous 1960s when the War on Poverty, civil rights movement, and major urban racial confrontations were at their height. Militancy and discussions of "Black Power" and "Black nationalism" made the parallel between the Black predicament and that of other oppressed racial groups seem viable. In other words, the times were ripe for a colonial theory of U.S. race relations. Fanon (1963) and Memmi (1965), who wrote about colonial relationships in the developing world, had their writings adapted to the U.S. racial setting. Following them, a large number of scholars suggested and elaborated on what they felt was a basic parallelism between the dynamics in those relationships and those that occur in Black–White relations (cf. Carmichael and Hamilton 1967; Blauner 1972).

One of the noted differences between classic colonial relationships and the internal-colonial relationship said to exist between Blacks and Whites in the United States is that the former generally involves groups from one territory invading and dominating the territory of another group, whereas in the latter case, both groups are from and occupy the same country. What can be said in response to this difference is that it is the character of the relationship rather than the factor of geography that defines a relationship as colonial (Barrera 1979; Bonacich 1980).

Perhaps the most often-cited architect of the colonial model of race relations in the United States is the sociologist Robert Blauner. Blauner argued that although there are some important differences between classic colonialism and **internal colonialism**, they share several basic characteristics. First, the political domination and advanced technological level of the West was the basis for both slavery of African Americans and the colonization of many countries by Europe. Second, the economic and political superiority of the dominant group encourages a feeling of racial superiority used to justify the exploitation of the other group. In other words, since both types of colonialism have similar roots, Blauner (1972) said that they share "a common process of social oppression" (p. 84).

Blauner (1972) suggested that there are five basic characteristics in the colonization complex:

1. The dominant–subordinate relationship begins with forced, involuntary entry; that is, African Americans were brought here as slaves, and ghettos are controlled from the outside by the dominant group. White settlers also, of course, forcibly took over American Indian lands.

2. The indigenous culture and social organization of the dominated group is altered, manipulated, or destroyed; that is, African American culture and institutions are undermined. Native American culture also has been subjugated.

3. Representatives of the dominant group control the subordinate group through their legal and government institutions; that is, White institutions control much of the lives of African Americans. The placement of American Indians on reservations also serves as an example of control by the dominant group.

4. Racism as an ideology is used to justify the oppression of the subordinated group; that is, Blacks and other racially or ethnically distinguishable groups are seen as biologically or otherwise inferior to Whites.
5. The colonizers and colonized occupy different positions in the labor structure and perform different roles; that is, by and large, African Americans are relegated to menial, nonprestigious jobs while Whites dominate in higher-ranking positions. The dual-labor market characterizes the occupational positions of dominant and subordinate groups.

The listed characteristics suggest that Black neighborhoods, instead of being isolated from the rest of society in some kind of autonomous culture of poverty, are in fact tied to White society by bonds of exploitation and dependency. The educational, political, economic, and legal institutions of the dominant society infiltrate and permeate the dominated colony. Then racism is used to maintain and justify the lower status of Blacks.

In addition to these structural characteristics, there are also cultural and psychological ramifications to the colonial relationship. In the colony, individuals cannot break through the racial-ethnic barrier. Colonized individuals can move up in class but cannot change their position of being colonized except through successful revolutionary movements that transform the structure of society. They may try to gain entrance into the larger society, but "everything is mobilized so that the colonized cannot cross the doorstep, so that [they understand and admit] that this path is dead and assimilation is impossible" (Memmi 1965, p. 125). In attempting to assimilate, colonized persons may initially admire and even adopt aspects of their oppressors, but when it is realized that full structural assimilation is not possible, they begin to reassert themselves in part through resurrecting old traditions and through the advocacy of violence.

Most of these stages appear to apply to African Americans and their movements in the United States, although some of the protest behaviors of African Americans could be interpreted in ways

other than through the colonial mode (Omi and Winant 1994). Among the strengths of this model are its historical and comparative dimensions and the fact that it can account for a relatively large number of factors within a fairly straightforward theoretical framework (Barrera 1979). However, a weakness of simply transferring the colonial model intact to the American setting is that it omits consideration of the uniqueness of the American political and social context (Blauner 1972).

To effectively deal with this shortcoming, Blauner suggested that an adequate theory must incorporate elements dealing with characteristics of both colonialism and capitalism. Indeed, several of the attempts to develop a class-based theory of race inequality include references to both of these. Omi and Winant (1994) also pointed out that the internal-colonial model does not take into account class differences within the colonized (African American) group or relationships between minority groups. Despite these difficulties, the colonial model continues to provide a useful analysis of Black–White relations as well as White–Native American relations in the United States (Sabol 2012; Asadi 2011).

CLASS-BASED EXPLANATIONS OF RACE INEQUALITY Wilson (1970) has argued that economic and class dynamics are becoming more important for determining the life chances of Blacks. But well before Wilson developed his theory, others also argued that economic factors are behind the inequality between Blacks and Whites in the United States. One of the most sophisticated class-based theories of race relations in the United States was developed by Oliver C. Cox in the late 1940s.

Cox viewed race relations and inequality in the United States as a product of economic exploitation. Forcibly bringing slaves to the United States was essentially a way of getting labor to exploit the natural resources of the country. Racial exploitation is only one form of the proletarianization of labor according to Cox. Racism as an ideology was not the root of exploitation; rather, it followed from it and was used to justify economic exploitation of Blacks. Racism, therefore, is a relatively recent phenomenon. Given its character and economic basis, "racial antagonism is essentially political-class conflict." Racial antagonism is used by employers to divide Black and White workers, and racial ghettos are maintained because they facilitate control over Blacks and perpetuate a self-defeating lifestyle. Blacks may want to assimilate, but it is not in the interests of dominant Whites for them to do so (Cox 1948; Cox 1976).

What is attractive about Cox's arguments is that he intermingled elements of racism, colonialism, class inequality, and capitalism in a comparative framework. Racial inequality is bound up with the development and expansion of European empires and the rise of capitalism and its labor needs.

Trade is the lifeblood of international capitalism. The need to control potential markets and sources of raw materials strengthens the tendency of capitalism to colonize and exercise political control in the world economic system. Loans, raw materials, markets for manufactured goods, and imperialism each play a part in creating and fastening ties (chains) between dominant and subordinate nations in the worldwide capitalist system (Cox 1959; Cox 1964). Race prejudice is then used to justify imperialism. Much of Cox's later writing anticipated many of the ideas associated with world-system and dependency theory.

One of the thorny areas of disagreement among class-based theorists of race relations concerns who benefits from racism and the nature of the relationship between Blacks and the White working class. From one point of view, racism is used by employers to drive a wedge between Whites and Blacks in the working class, and nationalism is used to divide members of the working class from different ethnic/racial groups in different countries. White workers come to view foreign workers who labor for low wages as unfair competitors, and their racism, which is ultimately rooted in the worldwide development of capitalism, is an attempt to protect their own jobs (Bonacich 1980). Although White or dominant workers may benefit from this racism in the short run, in the long run, the inequality within the working class creates divisions that weaken its collective power against employers. Employers

exploit members of the minority for greater profits and money with which to pay the dominant working class. Accordingly, the principal beneficiaries of racism are employers rather than all Whites (Reich 1977).

In general, having an ethnic/racial working class provides capitalism with a surplus army from which to draw poorly paid workers to perform jobs that are necessary but that no one in the dominant group wants to perform. But as the capitalist economy advances and the revolutionary potential of minority groups grows, many large employers begin to feel that the long-term costs of race inequality may be too high and that it should be eliminated (Baran and Sweezy 1966). One obvious cost of racism to employers is the loss of bright minority members to employers who could use them to increase productivity.

Edna Bonacich (1980) attempted to integrate and synthesize many of the arguments in class-based theories of race inequality. She began by commenting on the motivations for imperialism abroad. One important source for this movement is the desire to find more malleable and cheaper labor because the cost of labor rises as capitalism develops within a country. Wages rise because (1) the absorption of the entire labor supply into the expanding economy creates labor scarcity, (2) workers have a need for higher wages to purchase the increasing number of commodities produced in the economy, (3) large factories create social conditions conducive to the political organization and greater union power among workers, and (4) increased state support of workers cushions them and enables them to hold out for higher wages (see also Piven and Cloward 1982).

Because of these pressures for higher wages by domestic workers, employers look outside national boundaries for new sources of cheap labor. Pick up a piece of clothing from a well-known and expensive brand (e.g., Tommy Hilfiger, Polo) and notice where the item has been sewn. The labels frequently cite places such as Honduras and the Dominican Republic. Wages are lower in less-developed countries because of the existence of additional sources of subsistence (production for use) and a traditionally lower standard of living. Members of the domestic working class then see themselves as competing with cheap laborers in Third World countries, and may (1) react with nationalist and racist fervor against such groups or (2) see both themselves and other working-class groups from around the world as victims of capitalist development. Which of the two reactions is pursued by the domestic working class depends in part on the extent to which capitalists can control the colonized working class and manipulate the domestic working class, on how imminent the experience of competition with outside cheap labor is in the domestic working class, and on how proletarianized this class is itself (Bonacich 1980).

It should be obvious by now that there are several similarities between the class and colony theories of race inequality. First, both have as a central theme the notion of the exploitation (especially economic) of a lower group—African Americans and/or the working class. Both perspectives view top and bottom positions in relational terms—that is, the position of one group is considered to be inextricably linked to that of the other group. Second, in both models, justifications (ideologies) are crucial for legitimating the power relationships that exist. But in both, the relationship is both "destructive and creative" (Memmi 1965). Third, both perspectives emphasize the polarization of society and the importance of rising consciousness among the exploited. In general theoretical terms, these basic congruencies between internal-colonial and class theories outweigh their differences (Wilson 1970; Blauner 1972; Barrera 1979).

THE GLOBAL CONTEXT AND GLOBALIZATION

Racial and ethnic inequality, a form of what Charles Tilly (1998) calls "categorical inequality," is found throughout the world. Historically, among the most well-known of these systems of inequality were those found in South Africa and India. We have chosen to highlight these two countries, in part, because their systems have been compared to the United States. In these societies, a significant axis of the system of inequality was centered around racial/ethnic differences, and cultural values and practices retained a grip even in the face of technological advances and globalizing forces. At the same time, we recognize the dangers in giving limited and non-contextualized cultural examples. We urge readers who are interested in this topic to study the cultures in more depth to understand the nuances of their systems.

Beginning in the late 1940s and lasting until the early 1990s, South Africa had in place a system of apartheid that enforced social, economic, and legal separation between Whites and Blacks. Even though they were heavily outnumbered by non-Whites, Whites dominated the country politically, socially, and economically. Blacks were required to live in certain areas, lacked political rights, had to use separate facilities, were limited in their job prospects, and were closely monitored by authorities. Under apartheid, the poorest 40 percent of the population, who were mostly Black, lived in conditions that were far worse than those of the richest 20 percent, who were mostly White. For example, in 1993, near the end of the apartheid era, among the crowded households of the poorest in South Africa, only about one-fifth had electricity, one-quarter had inside water, and less than one-fifth had toilets in their houses (United Nations 1998). A combination of growing Black organization and political power, economic requirements, and international sanctions and developments led to the decline of apartheid. In 1994, Nelson Mandela, a Black activist, was chosen as president in the country's first general election.

Since the formal breakdown of apartheid, significant racial differences exist about national priorities in South Africa. Blacks see unemployment and the need for widespread access to basic services like housing and water as critical issues, while Whites are more likely to be concerned with crime and political corruption. Despite these differences and more positively, however, there is a multiracial government and general agreement that democracy is the government of choice (Schaefer 2015).

Parallels have been drawn between apartheid and the Jim Crow system that flourished in the southern United States after the Civil War. As in South Africa, more powerful colonists and settlers pushed native peoples off the land and captured important resources. Also similarly, racist ideologies were used to justify the growing inequality between dominant and dominated groups. The elements of Noel's theory of racial inequality, including competition for resources, ethnocentrism, and unequal power—all operated in the U.S. and South African situations.

Similarities have also been suggested between India's traditional, now outlawed, caste system and Black–White relations in the United States. The caste system that was dominant in India provides an example of an extreme case of status stratification in Weber's sense. It was both a system of inequality and a means of integration for India, with each layer assigned specific and unique functions (Bidner and Eswaran 2015). The four major castes or **varnas**, beginning with the top, were the Brahmins, Kshatriyas, Vaishyas, and Shudras. Those at the top were assigned to perform the most honorific functions and were considered purer than those below. Legitimation for the caste system was rooted in early Hindu texts in which the four varnas are described and portrayed as metaphorically representing different parts of the Indian social body. A fifth stratum, the Untouchables (Harijans) were not part of the formal caste system itself; they were outside it. The real, everyday structure and operation of the caste system at the village level was much more complex than the four-varnas system would suggest. Although loosely associated by residents with the national caste system, castes or **jati** at the local level vary in number and character (Kolenda 1985).

While still influential in more rural areas, industrialization, trade, and globalization have helped to weaken the hold of the caste system and spurred a growing class system (Beckett 2007; Tiwari and Bandhu 2014). There is some evidence of avenues of social mobility, and some lower-caste persons have started their own religious movements, others have married upward, and the

relatively new Indian democracy and constitution have formally outlawed the caste system. At the same time, however, as in the United States, old traditions die hard. As Desai and Dubey (2011) note, "Access to productive resources, particularly education and skills remain closely associated with caste. Children from lower castes continue to be educationally disadvantaged compared to children from the upper caste. Once stripped of its religious and ideological trope, caste in modern India offers one of the most interesting examples of consolidation of material resources in hands of certain groups even as market mechanisms continue to take hold. The continued dominance of brahmins in Indian society and economy is perhaps the clearest example of this consolidation" (p. 47).

While change comes slowly to racial systems like those in India and the United States, immigrants bring in new ideas, cultural values, and practices that often clash with and foment change in the native culture. Recent economic crises and the increased popularity of more conservative political ideologies have led many countries to become more concerned and restrictive about their immigration policies. France, for example, has attempted to keep the influence of Muslims in check, pressed for removal of outward signs of their religious beliefs, and has expelled many Roma from the country. Even the traditionally more liberal Scandinavian countries have embraced more anti-immigration arguments. The influx of minorities, including Muslims, into these countries has strengthened the hand of conservative parties. In June of 2015, for example, the anti-immigrant Danish People's Party took 21 percent of the national vote.

As described earlier in the chapter, there are concerns about new immigrants as a social and economic threat in the United States as well. Yet attempts to screen and limit immigrants' entrance into a country fly in the face of the image of globalization as a process that opens the doors to technology, products, influences, and people from abroad. Concerns like this have led Ronen Shamir (2005) to argue that while theorists advocating globalization may see it as a liberalizing, open process, it is also a conservative, limiting, exclusionary process. This paradox arises from the desire for nations to control their borders and maintain their national identity even in the midst of globalization. Globalization produces "closure, entrapment, and containment" through the "prevention of movement and the blocking of access" since some immigrants are seen as potential threats, even terrorists. This produces a "paradigm of suspicion" in which profiling, quarantine, imprisonment, and other forms of containment are put in place to control the mobility of suspect immigrants (pp. 199, 206–206, 210). Most of these "suspects" are from poorer countries. These modes of control are "a structural response to the problem of maintaining high levels of inequality in a relatively normatively homogenized world" in which there is a "tension between universal rights and universal fears" (p. 214). In this manner, globalization helps to maintain racial hierarchies and status exclusion.

Summary

Historical and contemporary evidence documents the inequality that has existed between Whites and various minority groups, including African Americans, American Indians, Asian Americans, and Hispanic Americans. The exploitation of African Americans for their labor and American Indians and Mexican Americans for their land was justified by racist ideologies, stereotypes, and the force of law. Many minority groups have incomes, earnings, and occupational statuses that are lower than those of Whites, and their poverty rates are higher. Differences in family compositions, educational levels, and labor-force participation do not fully account for these economic discrepancies. African Americans and other minorities also experience day-to-day microinequities. Biases in language, education, and the media constitute many of these, but there are some, such as those noted by McIntosh (1988), that occur in a variety of settings.

A variety of theories have been developed to explain racial and ethnic inequality, ranging from conservative to more critical and radical explanations. In general, the latter are more sophisticated and focus on the centrality of differential power and economic domination in accounting for race inequality. As is the case with some gender inequality theories, several of these theories are couched in a comparative framework and intertwine class and economic processes in their explanation, which lends them some depth.

These theories and research evidence show how the variables discussed in the last several chapters—class, gender, and race—are intertwined and influence each other. Debates in recent years have centered on the relative importance of race, gender, and class in producing these inequalities between groups. Some have argued for the primacy of one of these over others, but it seems clear that all affect the life chances through complex routes. Early racial and ethnic antagonisms helped to justify the economic exploitation of American Indians, Mexican Americans, and African Americans, and gender stereotypes had the equivalent effect on women. At the same time, class differences within these groups created divisions that are sometimes hard to bridge. Gender and race also interact. For example, women of different races have different occupational and educational patterns. Race has been a source of division within the feminist movement as well.

Around the globe, most societies struggle with ethnic and racial divisions. Among the most notable of these are South Africa and India. Increased Latino and Asian immigration to the United States has reignited concerns about open immigration and its effects on economic inequality. Little support has been found for the argument that such immigration has a depressing effect on the earnings of native workers. Globalization encourages the free flow of material and human resources between countries, which suggests that every country might benefit from the process. But globalization has also renewed attempts by nations to monitor and maintain the security of their boundaries, the integrity of their cultures, and their position in the world economic order. Consequently, globalization also encourages tendencies toward closure and exclusivity at the same time that neoliberals publicize its open and fluid qualities.

In the last seven chapters, we have surveyed the extent of inequality along several axes: economic, status, power, gender, sexual orientation, and race/ethnicity. It is now time to examine in greater detail the most prominent explanations that have been given for social inequality in general. We begin in Chapter 9 with a discussion of classical explanations and then move on to an analysis of contemporary theories in Chapter 10.

Critical Thinking

1. How do historical events continue to play a role in racial and ethnic inequality today? Can the effects of these events ever be erased? How?
2. Does degree of darkness or shade of color play a role in the inequality between individuals that is independent of race? Explain and give examples.

3. Critical-race theory argues that racism is primarily structural in nature. What does this mean, and what kinds of examples can you provide to demonstrate this?
4. Why, and to whom, are Native American names and mascots for sports teams harmful? Who do they benefit? How?

Web Connections

Segregation is still widespread in the United States. To get an idea of how Blacks, Hispanics, and other ethnic groups are distributed within major U.S. cities, and how these distributions are related to the distribution of incomes in the cities, go to http://www.nytimes.com/interactive/2015/07/08/us/census-race-map.html?_r=0.

Film Suggestions

Race: The Power of an Illusion (2003). A three-part series that analyzes the meaning, nature, and creation of "race."

The State of Arizona (2014). A documentary about immigration into Arizona in the wake of strict new policies. It covers a wide range of immigration issues that are broadly applicable.

Irish in America (1997). Explores Irish immigration to America and the conditions these immigrants faced here.

What's Race Got to Do with It? (2006). Depicts the experiences of race relationships on a college campus.

PART 2

General Explanations of Inequality

CHAPTER 9

Classical Explanations of Inequality

Society as a whole is more and more splitting up into two great hostile camps, into two great classes directly facing each other.

KARL MARX (1818–1883)

The discussions throughout Part One make it clear that multidimensional inequality is extensive in the United States, and, in a number of ways, it is becoming even more pronounced and disconcerting for many Americans. The widespread nature of social inequality makes explaining it all the more important. Several previous chapters presented explanations of particular forms of inequality. This chapter examines the broad classical explanations of Marx, Weber, Durkheim, and Spencer, from which many modern thinkers have drawn. Karl Marx is discussed first because virtually all of his central ideas were formulated before any of the others and because subsequent theories are often viewed as reactions to Marx's own work.

KARL MARX (1818–1883)

Few social scientists have had as great a political and economic impact as Karl Marx. His perspectives on society have been used by social scientists and ideologues, and his influence on modern sociology, and even society, has been pervasive. The ideas of all scholars are in large part shaped by the historical events and life situations they experience. This appears clearly in the case of Marx. Karl Marx was born on May 5, 1818, in the city of Trier, Prussia (now part of Germany). His family was of Jewish background and provided a bourgeois setting for Marx in his youth. His father and a neighbor, Ludwig von Westphalen, introduced him to the thinkers of the Enlightenment. Ludwig von Westphalen in particular became an intellectual companion with whom Marx discussed philosophy and literature. Marx later married von Westphalen's daughter, Jenny.

While studying at the universities of Bonn and Berlin, Marx became a friend of a group known as the Young Hegelians. Although Hegel was dead, his ideas survived as an intellectual force at Berlin. The Young Hegelians helped to convert Marx from the study of law to the study of philosophy. The increasing radicalism of his ideas encouraged his departure for Paris in late 1843. It was in Paris, a center of invigorating intellectual activity, that Marx began his close association and collaboration with Frederick Engels, the son of a manufacturer who acquainted Marx more fully with the real conditions of the working class. Marx's writing caused his expulsion, and he moved from Paris to Brussels in 1845. By then, Marx already considered himself a socialist and revolutionary. He had aligned himself with several workers' organizations, and in 1848 he and Engels produced the *Manifesto of the Communist Party*.

After some moving around, in 1849 Marx left for London, where he stayed for most of the remainder of his life. It was there that he produced most of his major writing. During his stay, his life and that of his family were marked by poverty, which was relieved only by his occasional employment as a European correspondent for the *New York Daily Tribune* and periodic help from his friend Engels. He became a leader of the International, a radical movement made up of individuals from several European countries, and in 1867 published the first volume of his monumental *Capital*. In the last decade of his life, Marx was already an honored figure among socialists and was able to live somewhat more comfortably than he did during in his early London years. He died on March 14, 1883, only 1 year after the death of his elder daughter and 2 years after the death of his wife, Jenny (Coser 1971).

Despite the familiarity of Karl Marx's name to most, some analysts still do not have a proper understanding of many of his ideas. Two of these ideas are especially relevant to his statements concerning class relations. First, Marx did not believe that everything is determined by the economic structure, that all other institutions are merely reflections of the economic system and are without causal influence. Although Marx considered the economic aspect the "ultimately determining element in history" and the "main principle," he did not think it was the only determining one. In a personal letter, while admitting that he and Marx had probably contributed to the confusion on this point, Engels put the matter succinctly: "The

economic situation is the basis, but the various elements of the superstructure ... also exercise their influence upon the course of the historical struggles and in many cases preponderate in determining their *form*. There is an interaction of all these elements in which, amid all the endless host of accidents ... the economic movement finally asserts itself as necessary" (Marx and Engels 1970, vol. 2, p. 487, emphasis in original). Thus, political, religious, and cultural factors play a role, though the "ultimately decisive" one is economic. A second misconception is that Marx argued that only two classes exist in any society. On the contrary, Marx was aware of the diversity of classes that can exist at any one time, as well as the factions that can be present within a given class.

The Theoretical Context of Marx's Class Analysis

Marx subscribed to a materialist conception of social life. That is, he argued that activities are what characterize and propel human history. History consists of human beings going about producing and reproducing themselves in interaction with nature. Humans are a part of nature, and both nature and humans change as they interact, making both of them a part of human history. History is really a process of "active self-making" (Simon 1994, p. 98). It is *activity*, especially labor, that defines who we are. Consequently, a concentration on economic activity is fundamental for understanding history's process.

Labor is an expression of our nature. When freely engaged in, it allows us to realize our true human nature and satisfy our real basic needs (not manufactured ones). When freely done, labor is also an enjoyment because it is spontaneous. However, when forced or artificial, that is, alienated, it becomes more of a misery than an enjoyment. It twists our human nature. Alienated labor exists when private property and its owners hire or control others and define their labor for them. Instead of being for oneself, labor becomes a task that primarily benefits owners of property. One works to get food, shelter, and so on; that is, labor becomes a *means* to an end rather than an *end* in itself.

Under capitalism, as in other class societies, the laborer and her or his labor belong to the capitalist. As a commodity, laborers have been hired at a price to work for the capitalist; for this period, the capitalist owns the workers and exploits them. It is out of the exploitation of the laborer by the capitalist that new value or profit is created because what is needed to reproduce the laborer (i.e., wage) is less than the value of what the laborer produces. It is this difference in value that defines exploitation and generates surplus value or profit for the employer. It is also private property and its control that defines classes and their relationship.

Historically, there have been several types of societies with class systems. According to Marx, the earliest societies were classless, being based on a "common ownership of land" (Marx and Engels 1969, vol. 1, pp. 108–109). But all known subsequent societies have been class societies, and the engine of change in history has been class struggle. Private property spurs the development of classes. Although societies change and the specific names given to the various classes may change, the presence of dominant and subordinate classes remains. The particular form that relations take between the classes depends on the historical epoch and the existing economic mode of production. The **mode of production** refers to the particular type of economic system in operation, such as feudalism, capitalism, and so on. Within every mode of production are (1) means of production and (2) social relations of production. The **means of production** refer to the tools, machines, and other resources used in production, whereas the **social relations of production** refer to the property and power relationships among individuals in the economic system. Marx contended that up to his time there had been four major "epochs in the economic transformation of society" (p. 504). These were the Asiatic, ancient, feudal, and capitalist modes of production. Our primary focus here is on the last of these.

Generally, classes are defined by their relationship to the means of production. Hence, in the capitalist mode of production, "by bourgeoisie is meant the class of modern capitalists, owners of the means of social production and employers of wage-labour. By proletariat, the class of modern wage-labourers who, having no means of production of their own, are reduced to selling labour-power in order to live" (p. 108). But when viewed specifically, Marx's definition of *class* appears loose, and a variety of criteria are used differentially in different places. A full-fledged class that satisfied the criteria suggested by Marx would be one that possessed the following four features:

1. A distinct relationship to and role in the mode of production (in terms of ownership of the means of production, employment of wage labor, and economic interests).
2. A clear consciousness of its existence as a unified class with objective interests that are hostile to those of other classes.
3. An organization of the class into a political party aimed at representing and fighting for its interests.
4. A distinct set of cultural values and a separate style of life (Ollman 1968).

"The owners of mere labour-power, the owners of capital, and the landowners, whose respective sources of income are wages, profit, and rent of land ... form the three great classes of modern society based on the capitalist mode of production" (Bottomore and Rubel 1964, p. 178). Other transition classes exist, such as the petty bourgeoisie and small landowning peasants, but these would disappear as capitalism inexorably reached its peak as a mode of production. Marx believed that in his day of the "two great hostile camps," the "two great classes" that were being polarized were the bourgeoisie and the proletariat (Marx and Engels 1969, vol. 1, p. 109). However, his use of such terms as "strata," "gradation," "middle classes," and "dominated classes" makes it clear that Marx was aware of the complexity that can characterize a concrete system of inequality. What is also apparent is that mere occupation or source of income is not the criterion used by Marx to define a class. Each class has within it a hierarchy of strata. Thus, within the proletariat, for example, individuals vary according to their specific occupations and incomes.

Because of the classes' different relationships to private property (i.e., owners vs. nonowners), conflict is inherent in class society. Class antagonism is built into the very structure of society. Marx's theory is one of class struggle. The existence of a given class always assumes the existence of another hostile class. "'Who is the enemy?' is a question that can be asked whenever Marx uses 'class'" (Ollman 1968, p. 578). When the economic bases for classes are eliminated, classes themselves will disappear since the proletariat will be without the enemy, the capitalist.

Until then, in the process of class struggle, the proletariat develops from an incoherent mass (a class in itself) into a more organized and unified political force (a class for itself). The conditions that bring about this change are discussed in detail later.

Maintenance of Class Structure

The system of inequality—class positions, the given relations of production, and the profits of capitalists—is maintained and protected by a variety of mechanisms. The state, of course, is the ultimate arbitrator and represents "the form in which the individuals of a ruling class assert their common interests" (Bottomore and Rubel 1964, p. 223). "The executive of the modern State is but a committee for managing the common affairs of the whole bourgeoisie" (Marx and Engels 1969, vol. 1, pp. 110–111). The state has used its force and legislation to maintain capitalist class relations (Marx 1967, vol. 1, pp. 734–741). Struggles that do occur within the state are always class struggles.

A second mechanism used to maintain class relations is ideology, and the dominant ideology supports and legitimizes the position of the capitalist. "The ideas of the ruling class are in every epoch the ruling ideas: i.e., the class which is the ruling *material* force of society is at the same time its ruling *intellectual* force." Just as the ruling class has control over "material production," so too does it control "mental production," and the form these ideas take is clear: "The ruling ideas are nothing more than the ideal expression of the dominant material relationships" (Marx and Engels 1969, vol. 1, p. 47). Of course, the ideas generated have been mentally separated in their association with the dominant class and hence can appear as eternal laws (such as the "free market") or rules generated by all of the society. Members of the ruling class have themselves believed that. The ideas that support class relations are frequently promoted by bourgeois intellectuals who are often nothing more than "hired prize-fighters" for capitalism (Marx 1967, vol. 1, p. 15). Religion as an ideological institution similarly helps maintain the class system by preventing labor from seeing its real situation.

A third factor serving to bolster the set of economic relations is much less obvious than the two just mentioned. The capitalist structure itself strengthens its seeming inevitability by creating a working class that because of custom and training comes to view "the conditions of that mode of production as self-evident laws of Nature" (Marx 1967, vol. 1, p. 737). The condition of workers freely hiring themselves out to capitalists who freely employ them to work in factories run for maximum efficiency makes capitalism appear as an entirely natural process and creates a dependency of workers on the system that makes it difficult for them to resist or rebel. As Miliband (1977) wrote, "The capitalist mode of production . . . veils and mystifies the exploitative nature of its 'relations of production' by making them appear as a matter of free, unfettered, and equal exchange" (p. 45).

Stages of Capitalism

According to Marx (1967), capitalism as a mode of production has gone through three principal **stages**: (1) cooperation, (2) manufacture, and (3) modern (machine) industry.

COOPERATION Capitalism begins when a large number of laborers are employed in one place working together to produce a given product. "A greater number of laborers, working together, at the same time, in one place . . . in order to produce the same sort of commodity under the mastership of one capitalist, constitutes, both historically and logically, the starting point of capitalist production" (p. 322). It is when workers are thus brought together that "the collective power of the masses" for the individual capitalist can be realized. Workers become more productive and efficient under these conditions, resulting in greater profit for the capitalist. This and each successive change in the mode of production are motivated by the desire to increase the surplus value of labor power and, therefore, the level of profit.

MANUFACTURE "While simple cooperation leaves the mode of working by the individual for the most part unchanged, manufacture . . . converts the laborer into a crippled monstrosity, by forcing his detail dexterity at the expense of a world of productive capabilities and instincts" (p. 360). The period of manufacture begins in the sixteenth century and extends to the last part of the eighteenth century. Its characteristic is a strict and detailed division of labor among workers who have been brought together to cooperate in the production of the capitalists' products. Everyone has a specific function to perform; no one carries out all the tasks. Thus, with this change there no longer exists a group of independent artisans cooperating, but rather a group of individuals performing minute tasks dependent on each other. "Its final form is invariably the same—a productive mechanism whose parts are human beings" (p. 338).

Weber's later description of work under rationalized capitalism is strikingly similar, as we shall see. In manufacture, each person performs the same task over and over again until the job becomes routine and the laborer becomes a mere mechanism, but efficiency and perfection in production become reality. Skills that had been learned in apprenticeship become less necessary, and manufacture creates a set of unskilled laborers. The collective laborer, when organized in this fashion, increases production, and as a result, increases the surplus value of his labor power to the capitalist. The profit for the capitalist goes up, and conditions for him could not be better. For the laborers, however, conditions worsen. Under the capitalist mode, their labor is no longer their own,

because to increase capital, each worker must be "made poor in productive powers" (Marx 1967, p. 361). They become unfit to produce independently, and their labor power becomes productive only within the factory. They need the factory. Working on minute operations rather than whole products, they become "a never failing instrument," "a mere fragment of his own body . . . a mere appendage" (pp. 349, 360). And the constant regularity and monotony of the task "disturbs the intensity and flow of a man's animal spirits, which find recreation and delight in mere change of activity" (p. 341).

In essence, the workers become alienated from their own labor. The work being done (1) is not an end in itself but a *means* to an end, (2) is not voluntary but *forced*, (3) is not part of human nature (i.e., it is *external*), (4) is not work for the workers but for *someone else*, and (5) is *not spontaneous*. The object of their labor does not belong to the workers even though they have put a part of themselves into it. Rather, the product "becomes an object, takes on its own existence . . . exists outside [them], independently, and alien to [them], and . . . stands opposed to [them] as an autonomous power" (Bottomore and Rubel 1964, p. 170). As appendages, workers become alienated from themselves, each other, and nature.

Under manufacturing, therefore, capitalists prosper as workers' conditions deteriorate, and the real nature of capitalism as a mode of production becomes clear. Capitalists prosper *because* laborers suffer. The two classes are not merely different levels but are inextricably interlinked in the capitalist mode. People and their labor power become commodities, things of use value to the capitalist, who owns and controls the instruments of production, the raw materials—everything. The laborers, in turn, have nothing but their own labor power to sell, and even that becomes twisted into a form suitable for maximum production.

MODERN (MACHINE) INDUSTRY Like other forms of capitalist production, the development and use of machines are aimed at reducing the cost of commodity production for the capitalist by reducing the part of the day when the worker is working for themselves, and increasing that part when they are for the capitalist. That is, it is a way of increasing surplus value for labor. "The machine . . . supersedes the workman" (Marx 1967, p. 376). In modern industry, machines are organized into a division of labor similar to that which existed among laborers during the manufacture period. Since machines replace labor power, physical strength becomes less important, and capitalists seek to hire children and women. The result is a decrease in the value of the man's labor power, and a concomitant increase in the general exploitation of the family overall. When the value of the workman's labor power vanishes, laborers flood the market and reduce the price of labor power. Supply then outweighs demand for labor. In effect, machines are a means of controlling the collective laborer. "It is the most powerful weapon for repressing strikes, those periodic revolts of the working class against the autocracy of capital" (pp. 435–436).

With the advance of machines, production becomes more and more centralized, forcing many small bourgeoisie who cannot compete or find little use for their skills into the proletariat (Bottomore and Rubel 1964, p. 188).

Crises in Capitalism and Class Struggle

The increased competition for profit among capitalists generates crises at both the top and the bottom of the class structure, ultimately leading to the polarization of large capitalists and the massive class of the proletariat. The initial result of the introduction of machinery is to increase profit, but problems arise. Employees are thrown out of work, or work for low wages because they are not in demand. The proletariat increases in number and becomes more concentrated, and life conditions among members become equalized at a level of bare subsistence.

Competition among capitalists produces commercial crises, an "epidemic of over-production" which in turn leads to increased concentration of capital, since many go bankrupt (Marx and Engels 1969, vol. 1, p. 114). A **crisis of overproduction**

serves as an indication that the forces of production have become too strong for the property relations by which they are controlled ("fettered"). The capitalist responds by destroying productive forces and by trying to find new markets abroad, but these solutions are, at best, stopgap measures, and crises recur, each more serious than the previous. "Modern bourgeois society . . . is like the sorcerer, who is no longer able to control the powers of the nether world whom he has called up by his spells" (p. 113). The means of production that the bourgeoisie originally brought into existence to benefit their own position and that permitted them to supplant feudalism now become the means that destroy them.

Bourgeois society becomes the stage for the impending class struggle between the capitalists and the collective laborer, between the bourgeoisie and the proletariat. As capitalism improved from simple cooperation through modern industry, the bourgeoisie became more powerful and entrenched, their ideology and ideas became dominant, and the organization of the state more evidently reflected their power. But so, too, did the proletariat develop as a class with the progress of capitalism. Initially, struggle against the bourgeoisie takes the form of individual protests, then protests by larger groups—not against the relations of production, but against the forces of production: workers smash tools, machines, and so forth in order to maintain their status as workers. At this point, they are still just a mass rather than an organized whole. But as conditions for them worsen—that is, as they become increasingly massed together on an equal basis in a minute division of labor under conditions of extreme alienation and misery—and as their livelihood becomes more uncertain, their actions become more those of a united class and less those characteristic of individuals competing among themselves. The appalling work conditions experienced by the proletariat forge it into a social class.

During the struggle that has its roots in the domination of the means of production and appropriation of its products (i.e., in a peculiar set of property relations), the proletariat becomes honed as a class, and the struggle takes on a greater political character. Ironically, the bourgeoisie has created the conditions that develop the class that revolts against it. As the decisive hour approaches, and the class and crisis nature of the society becomes increasingly evident, those in the bourgeoisie who see what is happening on the historical level also join the working class (Bottomore and Rubel 1964, pp. 184–188).

Marx argued that a given social order is not replaced until all the forces of production that can be produced under it have been developed, and new relations of production (i.e., new social orders) do not appear until the material basis for their existence has been formed in the old society. This is essentially what happens, according to Marx, when revolution occurs. Revolutions do not take place until the material conditions for their appearance are present. The mode of production shapes all other aspects of social life, and "at a certain stage of their development, the material productive forces of society come in conflict with existing relations of production. . . . From forms of development of the productive forces these relations turn into their fetters" (Marx and Engels 1969, vol. 1, pp. 503–504).

With proletarian revolution, the bases for the class system are removed and the proletariat is emancipated. In the interim, between the capitalist and classless society, a "dictatorship of the proletariat" exists, paving the way for a communistic society and the beginning of truly human rather than class history. Figure 9.1 summarizes some of the key elements of Marx's model.

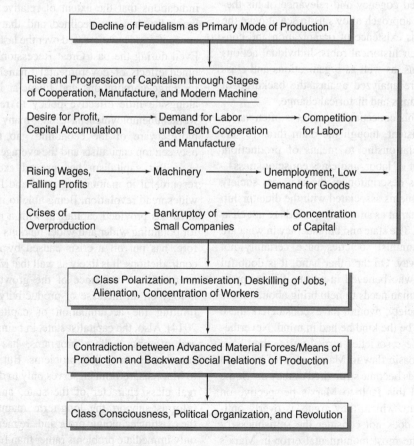

FIGURE 9.1 Core Elements in Marx's Theory of Class Struggle within Capitalism

Some Comments on Marx

There are few in the social sciences who have not had to confront the work of Marx. The sheer scope of analyses and critiques of Marx's theory of class struggle and capitalism is voluminous (e.g., Dahrendorf 1959; Mills 1962; Bottomore 1966; Giddens 1973; Miliband 1977). Consequently, only a few of the recurrent comments and criticisms about that theory are presented here.

Marx's theory has had a significant impact not only on the contemporary analysis of class structures but also on the study of society in general. His influence has radiated beyond social science to philosophy and the study of morals and to the political arena. That his work continues to generate discussion, as well as explanations and analyses built on his original ideas, is a tribute to the continued cogency and relevance of his theory. Marx's approach allows us to see at once the simultaneous existence of organization and conflict and their historical roots. Individual actions and emotions, as well as organizations and class structure, are analyzed against the backdrop of societal settings and historical change.

Still, his conception of class is often vague and inconsistent, though the main thrust of his criteria—relationship to means of production, employment of labor, and **class consciousness**—is clear. His description of the classless society and the problems associated with the dictatorship of the proletariat as an interim period are not clear and precise. The state and bureaucracy in what are called communist societies have certainly not withered away. On the other hand, it is doubtful that Marx, who believed in uniting theory, practice, and human needs to help bring about a more humane society, would have considered these societies to be the kind he had in mind. Nevertheless, that these societies turned out as they have suggests a basic flaw in Marx's view of how and why societies become structured as they do. Some have traced this fault to Marx's perspective on human nature which, they argue, is overly optimistic and does not consider the selfishness of people. "The most monumental error in Marx's thought," wrote Lopreato and Hazelrigg (1972),

"is his failure to accept the fact . . . that man is by nature a fallible and 'sinful' animal" (pp. 40–41). Moreover, Marx appears to have "seriously underrated" the ability of individuals to adjust to inequality (Duke 1976, p. 34).

It certainly seems true that Marx also underestimated the strength of nationalism as a force inhibiting the international union of classes. Miliband observed that "'nationalism' has proved a much more enduring and therefore a much more difficult problem to confront than early Marxists thought likely" (1977, p. 105).

Another criticism that has some validity is that the extent of pauperization and polarization of classes that Marx expected to occur in capitalism has not, as yet, occurred. How much one makes of this comment depends heavily on the time frame one selects, because certainly there are indications that the extent of relative economic inequality has not declined and that corporate concentration has increased over the last 100 years. Even during the past Great Recession, the combined effects of governmental financial support for large corporations and financial institutions alongside little effective policy to reduce high worker unemployment have made many Americans more aware of the economic gap that exists between top capitalists and the average worker.

But capitalism has proved exceptionally resourceful in maintaining itself and forestalling widespread revolution. Being able to internationalize has provided capitalism with a mechanism for obtaining wider and wider markets and, therefore, has put off a crisis caused by its internal contradictions. It is likely as well that Marx underestimated the influence of the growth in technology on an increase of productivity, therefore limiting the accumulation of capital (Piketty 2014). Also, the capitalist state, in being reformist and offering welfare programs, has alleviated some of its immediate problems. But, according to Marxists, reformism serves only to disguise the real class character of the state, and concrete reforms support the long-term maintenance of the existing economic order and are meant to solve only immediate problems rather than fundamental underlying ones (cf. Piven and Cloward 2012)

Moreover, Miliband contended that "capitalism, however many and varied the reforms it can assimilate, is unable to do without exploitation, oppression, and dehumanization" (1977, p. 39).

Marx thought that the members of the working class would be the "gravediggers of capitalism," but, to use Giddens's colorful phrasing (Giddens 1982, p. 63), "the grave remains undug, a century later; and its prospective incumbent, if no longer in the first flush of youth, does not seem seriously threatened by imminent demise." But the fact that the working class has not revolted is not conclusive proof of the inadequacy of Marx's theory or that capitalism is not a class society. This is because an effective class society, as Marx argued, can have a number of economic, political, and ideological characteristics that encourage false consciousness and minimize the chances for revolt by workers. Sooner or later, however (and Marx believed sooner), workers would become aware of their situation and act accordingly.

Although Marx's main predictions have not turned out exactly as he envisioned, many of the phenomena that he foresaw do exist to a degree. There has been a consistent trend toward more concentration of corporate power. There is also quite a bit of wealth inequality, and there are business ups and downs that capitalism follows. Moreover, every capitalist society has "class-based, working-class politics" to a certain degree (Collins 1988). U.S. government responses to the 2008–2010 economic crisis served to crystallize in the public's mind the differences in class interests of the capitalist and working classes. The effects of that crisis were felt worldwide. The international character of modern capitalism that Marx predicted means that the impact of its internal crises and contradictions reverberate throughout the world.

MAX WEBER (1864–1920)

Many of those who followed Marx, and especially the major social theorists of the period, were engaged in a "debate with Marx's ghost" (Zeitlin 1968). Among those most evidently aware of Marx's work and some of its shortcomings was Max Weber.

Weber is often considered to be the greatest sociologist in history. His "shadow falls long over the intellectual life of our era," wrote Mitzman (1970, p. 3). Much of what he contributed to social science still remains intact, and even those of his ideas that have proved weak or been discarded still provide a foundation from which further analysis can begin. Like Marx and other great theorists whose specific theories fit into a coherent whole, Weber's formulations regarding inequality must be considered in the context of his broader theory of the **rationalization** of the modern world. We will examine what Weber had to say about inequality, how U.S. sociologists have interpreted his work in this area, and if and how he added to Marx's own analysis of class structure.

Max Weber's life was quite different from Marx's, but like Marx's, his life experiences clearly affected the propositions about society that he developed. Weber was born in Erfurt, Germany, in 1864, 16 years after the publication of *Communist Manifesto* and 3 years before the publication of the first volume of *Capital*. His family was upper middle class. His father was a fun-loving conformist who disliked and feared upsetting existing political arrangements. In sharp contrast, Weber's mother was an extremely religious person of Calvinist persuasion, who often suffered the abuses of her much less moralistic husband, a fact that later became central in Max's repudiation of his father.

Despite its drawbacks for Weber, his parents' home was the site of frequent and diverse intellectual discussions featuring many of the well-known academicians of the day. So from the beginning, Max was exposed to a potpourri of ideas. Though he was a sickly child, he was very bright, becoming familiar with the writings of a variety of philosophers before setting off at the age of 18 for the University of Heidelberg, where he studied law, medieval history, economics, and philosophy. At age 19, Weber left for Strasbourg to put in his military service. It was there that he developed a lifelong and deep friendship with his uncle Hermann Baumgarten, an historian, and his aunt, a devout Protestant, who was effective in putting her religious fervor into action. Consequently, Weber developed a greater respect for the religious virtues of his own mother and less of a regard for the worldly and cowardly qualities of his father.

A year later, he returned to live with his parents and to study at the University of Berlin, where he wrote his dissertation on medieval business. Carrying on a strictly disciplined and rigid life, he served as a barrister in the Berlin court system and as an instructor at the university. He wrote several works on agrarian history and agricultural laborers. These investigations included discussions of the social and cultural effects of commercialization and the role of ideas in economic behavior.

After getting married and serving at the age of only 30 as a full professor of economics at the University of Freiburg, Weber and his wife, Marianne, left for Heidelberg, where he took a professorship, became more politically involved, and quickly developed a close circle of intellectual friends. During this period, Weber suffered a severe emotional breakdown and was able to do little of anything, even reading. He was only 33 years old at the time, and it was a number of years before his energy was restored. The breakdown may have been precipitated by a harsh confrontation with his father, very shortly after which his father died.

In the early 1900s, Weber's health was restored, and it was between this time and his death that Weber produced most of the works for which he is best known. He became enmeshed in German politics and volunteered for service during World War I, but later became disillusioned by the war and the German government's incompetence. Weber, unlike Marx, was accepted in polite society and was not a political radical, but he was generally a liberal and participated in the writing of the Weimar Constitution. There were many occasions when he fought bigotry and close-mindedness. Weber died of pneumonia on June 14, 1920, his broad knowledge leaving an unmistakable mark on social theory (Coser 1971; Mitzman 1970).

Rationalization of the World

Much of what Weber wrote had an undeniably unified theme. His discussions of bureaucracy, the Protestant ethic, authority, and even class, status, and party fit into his overall concern for social change and the direction in which he thought the Western world was moving. Thus, as is the case of Marx and many other nineteenth-century theorists, Weber's work on stratification must be understood within the context of his general perspective.

In contrast to Marx, who believed that capitalism and its accompanying denigration of the human spirit would eventually lead to a communistic and more humane society, Weber contended that alienation, impersonality, bureaucracy, and, in general, rationalization would be permanent societal features. Weber agreed with Marx that modern modes of technology have dehumanizing effects, yet he contended that bureaucracy and alienation are not temporary or peculiar to a passing period, but are instead at the core of an increasingly disenchanted world. What the future promised in Weber's view was not a wonderfully free society in which people are reunited to themselves and nature, but rather an "iron cage"; what we have to look forward to is not "summer's bloom," but rather a "polar night of icy darkness and hardness." Bureaucratization and technical rationality are not likely to decrease but rather to increase under socialism.

A bureaucracy is characterized by its impersonality, hierarchy of rational-legal authority, written system of rules, clear division of labor, and career system. According to Weber, bureaucracy is technically more perfect than other methods of organization and is the most efficient. "Precision, speed, unambiguity, knowledge of the files, continuity, discretion, unity, strict subordination, reduction of friction and of material and personal costs—these are raised to the optimum point in the strictly bureaucratic administration" (Gerth and Mills 1962, p. 214). Bureaucracy is the perfectly rational system. Business is carried out "without regard for persons," under "calculable rules." The lack of regard for persons is a central characteristic of all purely economic transactions. Since status honor and prestige are based on *who* a person is, the domination of the bureaucratic organization and a free market mean "the leveling of status 'honor'" and "the universal domination of the 'class situation'" (p. 215). The leveling of status strengthens the rule of bureaucracy by weakening status as a basis for position and encouraging the equal treatment of all regardless of background.

Capitalism and bureaucracy support each other; both are impersonal. Bureaucracy hastened the destruction of feudal, patrimonial organizations and local privileges. Whereas feudalism was characterized by ties of personal loyalty and was grounded in small local communities, bureaucracy denies or destroys personal loyalty and demands loyalty to position, thereby equalizing individuals. Capitalist production requires it. Conversely, capitalism can supply the money needed to develop bureaucracy in its most rational form (Roth and Wittich 1968, p. 224). Bureaucracy and capitalism are characteristics of the contemporary modern society.

Bureaucracy and capitalism increase the prevalence of authority based on rational-legal, as opposed to charismatic or traditional, grounds. In the rational-legal form, authority is based on the acceptance of rules regarding the right to issue commands as they apply to formal position in the organization. Authority is attached to the office, not the person; it is impersonal.

Putting all of this together, we see that capitalism and the secularized Protestant ethic, class, bureaucracy, and rational-legal authority are mutually supportive and are integral parts of the increasingly rationalized modern society that Weber saw emerging. They stand in stark contrast to feudalism, the personalism of status honor, tradition and charisma, and premodern forms of organization. An adequate understanding of Weber's perspective on class and status, their relationship, and their distinction can be obtained only if his broader theory of historical development and its associated concepts are incorporated in the analysis. Keeping Weber's broader theory in mind, we turn to discussion of his more specific ideas on inequality.

Tripartite Nature of Inequality

Weber argued that power can take a variety of forms. "Power," in general, refers to "the chance of a man or of a number of men to realize their own will in a communal action even against the resistance of others who are participating in the action" (Gerth and Mills 1962, p. 180). A person's power can be shown in the *social order* through his or her status, in the *economic order* through his or her class, and in the *political order* through his or her party. Thus, class, status, and party are each aspects of the distribution of power within a community. For example, if we think about an individual's chances of realizing his or her own will against someone else's, it is reasonable to believe that the person's social prestige, class position, and membership in a political group will have an effect on these chances.

Social order refers to the arrangement of social honor (prestige) within a society. Different status groups (e.g., professors, construction workers) occupy different places along the prestige continuum. Economic order, in turn, refers to the general distribution of economic goods and services (e.g., owners and nonowners)—that is, to the arrangement of classes within a society. Finally, political order relates to the distribution of power among groups (e.g., political action committees, parties) to influence communal decisions. Weber's general scheme for inequality is presented graphically in Figure 9.2.

Although these are presented as three distinct and separate orders, it is a mistake to see them strictly as such. All of them are manifestations of the distribution of power and can and usually do influence each other, often in a quite predictable manner. The inclusion of the social and political dimensions is ordinarily seen as a "rounding out" of the economic determinism of Marx (Gerth and Mills 1962, p. 47). But, as already pointed out, Marx was not a simple economic determinist; he viewed causal relationships in a more complex fashion. Moreover, Weber's own writing suggests that he did not view the three dimensions as being equally salient in capitalist society. Parkin (1971) persuasively argued that neo-Weberians have stressed the independence of these dimensions of stratification and thereby ignored, where Weber did not, the systematic relationship between the dimensions of

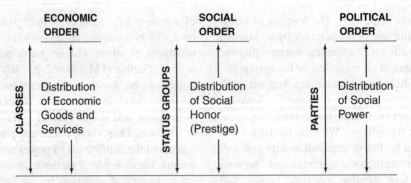

FIGURE 9.2 • Weber's View of the General Distribution of Power

inequality. Weber did not fully develop his political dimension, and the economic factor, as we shall see, outweighs the status element in the capitalist system of inequality. But at this point, it is necessary to examine each of Weber's three dimensions in greater detail.

CLASS   More so than Marx, Weber deliberately set out a number of formal definitions for his concepts (Roth and Wittich 1968). But Weber acknowledged his debt to Marx: "Whoever does not admit that he could not perform the most important parts of his own work without the work that those two [Marx and Nietzsche] have done swindles himself and others" (quoted in Mitzman 1970, p. 182). Weber's own conception of class parallels Marx's in several ways. Class, at its core, is an economic concept; it is the position of individuals in the market that determines their class position. And it is how one is situated in the marketplace that directly affects one's life chances, "a common condition for the individual's fate" (Miller 1963, pp. 44–45). Just as Marx indicated that capital begins when capitalist and laborer meet freely in the market, when the laborer is free to sell his or her labor and form a relationship with the capitalist, Weber pointed out that persons are members of a class only if they have "the chance of using goods or services *for themselves* on the market" (Miller 1963, p. 45; emphasis added). Consequently, slaves are not members of classes.

Weber distinguished three types of classes: property classes, commercial (acquisition) classes,

and social classes. Individuals belong to the same class if they are in the same "class situation," which refers to the probability of individuals obtaining goods, position, and satisfactions in life, "a probability which derives from the relative control over goods and skills and from their income-producing uses within a given economic order" (Roth and Wittich 1968, p. 302).

Property classes are "primarily determined by property differences." There are those who monopolize costly foods and status privileges, such as education, and those who control the bulk of wealth, capital, and sales in the society. Such classes usually are composed of "rentiers," who get income from a number of sources, including people, land, factories, and bank securities. Those who are not privileged are those who are unfree or are paupers. Weber stressed the distinction between the top and the bottom classes but did mention that in each set of classes there are "middle classes" (Roth and Wittich 1968, pp. 302–303).

Weber is not clear, but he does not appear to make a complete separation between property and commercial classes. Rather, he has a broad conception of property in terms of ownership, and it is "'property' and 'lack of property'" that are "the basic categories of *all* class situations" (Miller 1963, p. 44; emphasis added). These general categories in turn can be broken down "according to the kind of property that is *usable for returns*; and, on the other hand, according to the kind of *services* that can be offered in the market" (1963, p. 44; emphasis added). In a manner of speaking, one can own and dispose of property as well as skills and services.

Commercial-class position is determined by "the marketability of goods and services," in other words, by the opportunity to exploit the market (Roth and Wittich 1968, p. 302). Commercial classes, then, are determined by the skills and occupational characteristics members bring into the market. Hence, those who are privileged in this regard may monopolize management and exercise influence over government political policies that affect their interests. Merchants, industrial and agricultural employers, bankers, ship owners, professionals, and workers who have cornered certain skills are examples of the entrepreneurs who are members of privileged commercial classes. In contrast, those who are unprivileged are usually laborers (skilled, semiskilled, and unskilled) (Roth and Wittich 1968, p. 304). Again, there are middle classes, but these are treated more as residual categories when compared with the other classes.

Social classes make up all class situations "within which individual and generational mobility is easy and typical" (Roth and Wittich 1968, p. 302). That is, a social-class structure is one in which there is fluidity and movement of individuals between class situations. Upward mobility is most likely, however, between adjacent classes. Examples of such social classes are the "working class as a whole," "the petty bourgeoisie," "the propertyless intelligentsia and specialists," and "the class privileged through property and education" (p. 305).

Class Consciousness and Class Struggle According to Weber, classes of whatever kind need not be class conscious as Marx conceived them; they are not necessarily unified "communities." Class organization can occur in any one of the three types of classes, but class consciousness and class (communal) action are likely only under certain conditions. Weber argued that just because there are different property classes, for example, does not mean that they will necessarily engage in class struggle, although they may when circumstances are right. And when struggles do occur, they may not be over a basic change in the entire economy but may be more superficially over the distribution of wealth.

Class-conscious action is most likely if, first, "the connections between the causes and consequences of the 'class situation'" are transparent (Gerth and Mills 1962, p. 184). If individuals can plainly see that there is a connection between the structure of the economic system and what happens to them in terms of life chances, class action is more likely. Weber believed this had happened among the proletariat. A second condition for class unification exists if there is an immediate opponent on whom the class can focus. Hence, workers will react against their immediate employers rather than those who are most distantly and perhaps even more profitably involved (such as stockholders). Third, class organization is also more likely if large numbers of individuals are in the same class position. The increasing growth of the proletariat would increase the chances of class action by them. Fourth, if all of the individuals are in one place and therefore are easier to organize, class unity is more probable. Finally, if their goals are directed and interpreted by a group of intelligentsia who are actually outside their class, class organization is more likely (Weber 1947, pp. 427–428; Roth and Wittich 1968, p. 304). These conditions are not inconsistent with those that Marx thought would forge a mass of individuals in the same class situation into a "class for itself." However, Weber cautions us about the belief that fully developed classes are never wrong—that is, "falsely conscious"—about their own interests. They can be.

Class struggles have changed in content throughout history, according to Weber. The focus of conflict has evolved from struggles over debt and credit in antiquity, to struggles over the availability of consumer goods and their prices in the market during the Middle Ages, to struggles over the price of labor in the modern world. Historically, class struggles begin when a credit market exists in which debtors pay high and often increasing rates of interest to the wealthy, who monopolize the credits (Miller 1963, pp. 45, 48). But in each case, by definition, the struggle is of an economic character.

STATUS Standing in theoretical and practical opposition to the market principle of class, which "knows no personal distinctions" and "knows nothing of 'honor,'" is the principle of status. Traditionally, status groups are ranked in terms of the "*consumption* of goods as represented by special 'styles of life,'" whereas classes are determined by their relations to the production system and acquisition of goods" (Miller 1963, p. 56; emphasis in original).

In addition, then, to being ranked in terms of market situation, individuals can be ranked on the basis of honor or prestige. A person's "status situation" consists of all aspects of his or her "life fate" that are determined by a "social estimation of honor" (Miller 1963, pp. 49, 54). Status groups are based on a particular style of life, formal education, and/or inherited or occupational prestige. Certain groups may lay claim to (or, in other words, may usurp) a certain level of honor because of their hereditary background or family tree (such as the "First Families of Virginia"), because of their peculiar lifestyle or because of their power. The existence of status groups most often shows itself in the form of (1) endogamy or a restricted pattern of social intercourse, (2) sharing of food and other benefits within groups, (3) status conventions or traditions, and (4) monopolistic acquisition of certain economic opportunities or the avoidance of certain kinds of acquisitions. Thus, because of their formal education and occupational prestige, liberal arts professors might tend to socialize only among themselves and might have certain unwritten rules about how a member of the group should act or what kinds of goods and services are suitable for use in the status group and what kinds are not. The conventions associated with the status group control the kind of lifestyle allowable (Roth and Wittich 1968, pp. 305–306). It is clear that some of the bases of class and status may concern the same factor, such as occupation. However, their characteristics mean that status groups are usually cohesive communities. They tend toward closure, that is,

restriction of their memberships (Grabb 1984; Collins 1988).

The stability of status groups is linked to political and economic conditions in a society and is one way in which the latter two aspects of inequality are related to the social dimension. The likelihood of a conventionally recognized status group developing into a "*legal privilege*, positive or negative, is easily traveled as soon as a certain stratification of the *social order* has in fact been 'lived in' and has achieved stability *by virtue* of a stable distribution of *economic power*" (Miller 1963, p. 51; emphasis added). Weber is saying that status groups can be legalized and, therefore, become bases for political power differences when they have been around for some time and are buttressed by parallel differences in the distribution of economic resources. Where such stability exists, *caste groups* develop. Castes become supported by rituals (e.g., of purity), convention, and law. Separate castes may even develop their own religious beliefs. Usually, the status structure approaches this extreme form only when the fundamental differences between the groups are considered ethnic in nature (e.g., Jews). Caste is more than just simple ethnic segregation. The latter still permits each group in question to consider its own values (honor) to be high, but a caste system arranges these groups hierarchically, allotting one more honor than the rest. Any sense of dignity a lower-caste group might have would derive from its belief in a *future* beyond present conditions in which it would have an elevated status. In contrast, the privileged caste groups can and do derive their own sense of dignity from their *present and/or past* situation.

Weber stressed that class, status, and political power can be reciprocally related, with each affecting the others. Status can influence and even determine class (Roth and Wittich 1968, p. 306). However, his writing emphasized the effect of class on status in capitalist society. "Property as such is not always recognized as a status qualification, but in the long run it is, and with extraordinary regularity" (Miller 1963, p. 49). Frequently, the richest person has the greatest prestige, and those in similar economic situations normally socialize with each other rather than with persons from different classes. Equality of status among individuals in unequal classes can "in the long run become quite precarious" (Miller 1963, p. 49). Weber observed that although race, political power, and class have all been bases for status in the past, "today the class situation is by far the predominant factor, for of course the possibility of a style of life expected for members of a status group is usually conditioned economically" (Miller 1963, p. 53).

Despite the controlling importance of the class factor, Weber emphasized that status and class are not necessarily connected. Individuals who are low in class position can be high in prestige and vice versa. Analytically, status is opposed "to a distinction of power which is regulated exclusively through the market" (Miller 1963, p. 54). If individuals who were high in class automatically received high status, "the status order would be threatened at its very root" (Miller 1963, p. 55). Groups who base their high status on their lifestyle rather than crass property are likely to feel threatened when the basis for honor shifts to the economic order.

Weber said very little about the conditions under which stratification by class or status predominate. In fact, his whole definitional classification of class and status is too brief. Parkin (1971) argued that there was greater justification for seeing class and status as distinct and separate orders in the Middle Ages than is the case today, when status seems increasingly to be based on occupational and economic considerations. Weber maintained that, "when the bases of the acquisition and distribution of goods are relatively stable, stratification by status is favored" (Miller 1963, p. 56). If a status order is entrenched by virtue of a monopolization of certain goods by particular groups, then the free-market principle is hindered; it cannot operate. Under these conditions, "the power of naked property per se, which gives its stamp to 'class formation,' is pushed into the background." But "every technological repercussion and economic transformation threatens stratification by status and pushes class situation into the foreground" (Miller 1963, pp. 55–56). In contrast to commercial-class societies, which ordinarily operate in market-oriented economies, status societies are economically organized around religious, feudal, and patrimonial factors (Roth and Wittich 1968, p. 306). In capitalist societies, classes play a more important role than status (Giddens 1973).

PARTIES Political power generally is considered to be a third dimension of inequality included by Weber, though some interpret Weber to be saying that class, status, and party are each different forces around which the distribution of power can be organized (Giddens 1973). Although Weber's entire specific treatment of class and status is brief, vague, and sometimes even ambiguous and confusing, his treatment of parties is even briefer.

A **party** is an association that aims to secure "power within an organization [or the state] for its leaders in order to attain ideal or material advantages for its active members" (Roth and Wittich 1968, p. 284). Thus, Weber is not referring narrowly to what we think of as political parties (such as Democrats or Republicans) but to political groups more broadly conceived. Instead of parties being an outgrowth of class struggle, they can represent status groups, classes, or merely their own members and may use a variety of means to attain power. Well-organized interest groups would constitute parties in a Weberian sense.

Since parties aim for such goals as getting their programs developed or accepted and getting positions of influence within organizations, it is clear that they operate only within a rational order in which these goals are possible to attain and only when there is a struggle for power. Parties themselves, however, can be organized around a charismatic or traditional leader as well as being structured in a rational way with formal positions to which members are elected. Formally recognized political parties are not the only kind that exist; parties also can be organized around religious issues or those that concern the traditional rights of a leader in an organization (Roth and Wittich 1968, pp. 285–286).

Marx and Weber

Weber's theory of stratification has traditionally been hailed in U.S. sociology as a major improvement over the perceived narrowness of Marxian theory. Why is this so? To some extent, it reflects the nature of U.S. sociology and the interpretation of Weber by U.S. sociologists. The vagueness in parts of Weber's treatment has encouraged multiple interpretations of what he said on the subject of inequality and the unintentional shaping of what he said to fit the peculiar characteristics of one version of sociology. Weber's incorporation of noneconomic (status, party) and more general economic elements (such as market situation) is more appealing to a U.S. sociology rooted in a society that has been antiradical and staunch in the belief that individuals can distinguish themselves in a variety of ways other than economic. In some societies with long traditions of status ranking, such as Great Britain, the significance of the distinction between class and status in everyday life may be more obvious than in advanced open societies with shorter histories like the United States. Nevertheless, the separate operation of economic and social standings on individuals' situations is always a possibility. Consequently, the need to keep these concepts separate would seem to be important. Unfortunately, the conflation of the separate concepts of class and status into one measure, like socioeconomic status, blurs the real distinction between the concepts and their separate effects on individual lives. While economic class has effects in the areas of employment and income (life chances), the impact of social status is realized more in the area of "cultural consumption" (life choices) (Chan and Goldthorpe 2007).

Because they blend economic and social elements, not only do socioeconomic measures fail to separate out social status, they also fail to provide a purely Marxian economic measure of class. Despite superficial measures such as income and occupational status, until recently U.S. sociologists have generally neglected the development of Marxian measures of class and an adequate measure of Weber's market situation.

Part of the reason for this appears to lie in the fact that many sociologists have an ideological dislike of purely economic and especially Marxian theory, and that Weber's multidimensional theory offers a more complete portrait of social inequality than does Marx's.

However, it is very easy to exaggerate the differences between these two men. Lopreato and Hazelrigg (1972, p. 90), in fact, argued that Weber added little to what was at least already implicit in Marx's theory. For example, certainly the assignment of prestige (honor) to given positions can be viewed as one way in which the dominant ideology maintains the class system.

There are two basic similarities between Marx and Weber. First, both argued that capitalist society is a class society. Capitalism is characterized by laborers and capitalists meeting freely in the market; it creates a large pool of dehumanized workers of all types, and it broadens the market. Second, even though Weber talked about status and party as well as class, he argued that in a rationalized market society, such as capitalism, class becomes predominant, and there is a "leveling of status honor." The distinct separation of status honor from the market principle and property is most characteristic of traditional or premodern societies (Parkin 1971, p. 38). Thus, on the importance of class in capitalist society, Marx and Weber appear to agree.

In light of these core similarities, a good argument can be made that many U.S. sociologists have accepted Weber because they have trivialized his ideas by latching onto the multidimensional aspect of his theory and minimizing the systematic nature of the relationship between those dimensions. Their interpretation of Weber is that class, status, and party are separate and independent dimensions along which each individual can be ranked. By abstracting these concepts while ignoring their systematic interrelationship and the historical context in which they are embedded, Weber's theory becomes seriously distorted.

Of course, there are some basic differences between Marx and Weber. As mentioned earlier, Marx had a more optimistic view of the long-term future than Weber, who believed society would become increasingly rationalized and bureaucratized even under socialism, because bureaucracy once established was virtually "escape proof" (Grabb 1984). Socialism would only intensify the bureaucratic characteristics of the state. Thus, future society would not see the removal of alienation and impersonality but rather their enhancement. A second major difference between the theorists is that because Weber was concerned with status and party and defined class generally in terms of market situation, the system of inequality contained within it many more groups than are suggested by a class society in which only a few groups dominate. Market situation, for example, if defined broadly enough and in detail, could ultimately mean that each individual is in a distinct class position, meaning that there are as many classes as there are persons. Perhaps the greatest weakness in Weber's discussion is the brevity and ambiguity in his treatment of class, status, and party.

ÉMILE DURKHEIM (1858–1917)

In contrast to the theorists we have discussed, Émile Durkheim was not principally concerned with social inequality. Rather, he emphasized establishing sociology as a scientific discipline, uncovering the sources and forms of integration and moral authority, and tracking and understanding the place of individualism in modern industrial society (Giddens 1978). Most of his works revolve around issues of integration and cohesiveness—that is, the question of order in society. Although liberal and reformist in outlook, Durkheim was a central founder of the functionalist school of thought in sociology, which views society as a social system tending toward equilibrium. The organic analogy of society is evident in his writing. Despite his preoccupations with questions of order and the evolutionary growth of societies, however, Durkheim had something to say about social inequality, and so only a brief discussion is included here.

Émile Durkheim was born in 1858 in Alsace-Lorraine into a Jewish family, which expected him to become a rabbi. Later, as a young man, he turned away from religion and became an agnostic, even though his study of the "elementary forms of religious life" is one of his major works. Durkheim was a terrific student in his early youth, but was not entirely happy with the lack of scientific and moral emphases at the normal school he attended (Coser 1971). Later, he was to become a highly successful teacher at the high school and university levels.

Durkheim wanted to study a subject that would directly address issues of moral and practical guidance for society, and he wanted to use a scientific approach in the analysis of issues. He turned to sociology as his discipline of choice and, to the disdain of many colleagues, became an imperialistic advocate of sociology rather than the other social sciences (Giddens 1978). It is not surprising that topics related to order, development, and the relationship between the individual and the society would run as a common thread through Durkheim's body of work because of conditions in French society at the time. The early years of the Third Republic in France, when Durkheim was a young man, were marked by instability and conflicts between the political right and left.

Durkheim was actively involved in public affairs, including working toward restructuring the university system and helping early in the World War I effort by completing articles attacking Nationalist German writing (Coser 1971). Durkheim's major sociological works did not begin to appear until the end of the nineteenth century. *The Division of Labor*, the source we will be concerned with here, was completed in 1893, followed by *The Rules of Sociological Method* in 1895 and *Suicide* in 1897. Later, in 1912, he finished *The Elementary Forms of Religious Life*. Durkheim died in 1917 at the age of 59.

Durkheim and Inequality

In *The Division of Labor*, Durkheim developed his theory of the movement of society from "mechanical" to "organic" solidarity. A society organized on mechanical solidarity is homogeneous, with a simple division of labor, and based on the similarity of the individuals in it. There is a strong collective conscience that serves as a principal source of moral cohesion. The individual ego is not prominent in this kind of society. In sharp contrast, societies organized around the organic form of solidarity are characterized by differences and interdependence in their division of labor. Social uniqueness, along with the increased individualism, can threaten the cohesiveness and stability of society. Corporate groups and the division of labor serve as means for integrating individuals in this kind of society. They stand midway, as it were, between the state and individual.

In a fully developed organic society, characterized by individualism, equal opportunity, specialization, and interdependence, inequality is to be expected because at this point in evolution, Durkheim argued, it is based on differences in the *internal* abilities of individuals. A "normal" division of labor is based on internal differences between individuals, which include differences between men and women. Differences in the division of labor between men and women should persist, but other differences based on *external* qualities (e.g., race, inheritance), including classes, should decline and eventually disappear. As society evolves, differential rewards should, because of equal opportunity, directly reflect individual differences in abilities and differences in the social value of occupations. In short, Durkheim believed that as time moved on, modern society would be characterized by social inequalities between individuals based on their inner abilities rather than external characteristics. He believed that such internal differences existed between the sexes, and thus justified social inequalities between men and women, but he also argued that class and racial inequalities would diminish. Although there is some ambiguity in his treatment, this is Durkheim's primary position (Lehmann 1995).

Until this point in evolution is reached, however, the division of labor can take on "abnormal" forms that prevent its appropriate and efficient functioning. Durkheim argued that this occurs when individuals' positions in it are forced or determined without moral regulation. Individuals must recognize the rights of others in the division of labor and their duties to society as well as to themselves. Ideally, each person must have the opportunity to occupy the position that fits his or her abilities (Grabb 1984). When these conditions are not present, abnormal forms of the division of labor develop. Two of these are the **anomic** and **forced** forms of the division of labor.

In the first type, relations between people in the workplace are not governed by a generally agreed-on set of values and beliefs. Two of the developments that divided people were the split between "masters and workers" in which the organization is privately owned by the masters and the arrival of large-scale industry in which workers were each given very narrow and different functions to perform. Both of these factors served to drive a wedge between employers and workers. With large industries, "the worker is more completely separated from the employer." And "at the same time that specialization becomes greater, revolts become more frequent" (Durkheim 1933, p. 355). In smaller industries, in contrast, there is "a relative harmony between worker and employer. It is only in large-scale industry that these relations are in a sickly state" (p. 356). Large industry develops as markets grow and encompass groups not in immediate contact with each other. Producers and consumers become increasingly separated from each other. "The producer can no longer embrace the market in a glance, nor even in thought. He can no longer see its limits, since it is, so to speak, limitless. Accordingly, production becomes unbridled and unregulated" (p. 370); that is, a condition of anomie or normlessness exists. Economic crises develop, but industry grows as markets grow.

With the growth of industry and an increasingly minute division of labor, the individual worker becomes more "alienated," to use a Marxian term. Like Marx, Durkheim concluded that the worker becomes a "machine," performing mind-numbing, routine, repetitive labor without any sense of the significance of his or her role in the labor process. "Every day he repeats the same movements with monotonous regularity, but without being interested in them, and without understanding them" (p. 371). Although this description may sound intriguingly Marxist, Durkheim's view of the division of labor in modern society was quite different from that of Marx. Because of its nature, Durkheim viewed the division of labor as a central basis for integration in modern industrial society. It is only in certain abnormal forms that it becomes a problem. But basically, a complex division of labor is a necessity in *industrial* society. It is expected that as societies develop they become increasingly complex. In contrast, Marx viewed the division of labor as a source of basic problems in *capitalist* society. Class conflict was over fundamental issues in the property and social relationships involved in the division of labor. For Durkheim, class conflict was a surface symptom of an anomic state in which the employers and workers conflicted because of the absence of a common, agreed-on set of moral rules. The problems of the modern society are not due to contradictions within capitalism, "but derive from the strains inherent in the transition from mechanical to organic solidarity" (Giddens 1978, p. 36). Marx saw regulation in capitalist society as stifling human initiative, whereas Durkheim saw moral regulation as necessary for individual liberty and happiness.

However, the mere presence of rules is not enough to prevent problems in the division of labor because "sometimes the rules themselves are the cause of evil. This is what occurs in class-wars" (Durkheim 1933, p. 374). The problem here is that the rules governing the division of labor do not create a correspondence between individual talents or interests and work functions. The result is that the division of labor creates dissatisfaction and pain instead of integration and cohesiveness. "This is because the distribution of social functions on which [the class structure] rests does not respond, or rather no longer responds, to the distribution of natural talents" (p. 375). When the rules regulating the division of labor no longer correspond to the distribution of true talents among individuals, then the organization of labor becomes *forced* (the second type of division of labor referred to earlier.) Durkheim felt that inequalities that were not based on "internal" differences between individuals were unjust. "External" inequality, which is based on inheritance, nepotism, or simple membership in some biological group, must be eliminated, according to Durkheim, because it threatens the solidarity of society. Superiority that results from differences in the resources of individuals is unjust. "In other words, there cannot be rich and poor at birth without there being unjust contracts" (p. 384). The sense of injustice associated with the significance of external inequalities becomes greater as labor becomes more separated from employers and the collective conscience becomes weaker.

Despite his realization of the injustices suffered by workers in the division of labor, Durkheim was not an advocate of class revolution. As mentioned, he did not feel that there is anything inherently wrong with a complex division of labor and, consequently, believed that only reformist change was needed to eliminate the problems associated with it. Durkheim felt that complete revolution would destroy the delicate and complex membrane that made up society. "I am quite aware when people speak of destroying existing societies, they intend to reconstruct them. But these are the fantasies of children. One cannot in this way rebuild collective life: once our social organization is destroyed, centuries of history will be required to build another" (quoted in Fenton 1984, p. 31). Durkheim felt that deep, lasting change would take place gradually and through ameliorative reform rather than through drastic conflict. In this way also, he differed from Marx. Nor did he agree with Marx that the state was an instrument of oppression, but rather felt it could serve as an instrument of reform for a better society (Giddens 1978). However, like Marx and in contrast to Weber, he had an optimistic view of future society. Fundamental class conflicts would be minimized once problems in the division of labor could be ironed out with appropriate policies and moral regulations over time.

HERBERT SPENCER (1820–1903)

Herbert Spencer's star in social science fell as quickly as it rose. At the turn of the twentieth century, Spencer was highly regarded and popular in academic and public circles. But by the early 1930s, his fame and reputation had suffered greatly. Near the end of the 1930s, Talcott Parsons, who was to become the leading social theorist in the United States, indicated his belief in the irrelevance of Spencer by asking directly: "Who now reads Spencer?" By and large, attitudes have not changed. Spencer does not have the high standing in social theory today that is accorded to Marx, Weber, and Durkheim.

Despite the generally negative reaction to his work by social scientists, I include a brief discussion of Spencer here for three reasons: First, there are some today who argue that Spencer has been inappropriately neglected or ignored despite the value of some of his ideas (e.g., Turner 1985; Adams and Sydie 2002). Second, as we saw in Chapter 3, Spencer's arguments about inequality and its sources, as well as his beliefs about the proper role of the state in addressing poverty and related issues, are reflected in U.S. beliefs about poverty and welfare policies. Third, Spencer's individualistic orientation contrasts significantly and sharply with the more collectivistic views of Marx and Durkheim and, consequently, provides an alternative perspective on inequality. As in other instances, I will focus only on those ideas of greatest relevance to social inequality.

Herbert Spencer was born in 1820 in England to parents who were religious dissenters and who believed in religious freedom and social egalitarianism. Consequently, he grew to dislike the blind subjugation to authority demanded by traditional religion. His father was an independent, self-employed teacher who encouraged skepticism and freethinking. As a young boy, Spencer loathed formal education, and at 16 quit it for good. His greatest intellectual interests were in pragmatic and hard-scientific areas, such as mathematics and physics. Spencer's interest in concrete practical matters was evident in his inventions of a velocimeter, a fishing-rod joint, and other mechanical devices. He was not a romantic. He cared little for the softer fields of literature and poetry, and consequently, he was rather narrow in his reading. Because of his upbringing and the influence of the Enlightenment,

he believed in combining individual reason and the judicious use of scientific method as the means for uncovering social laws. As a young man, Spencer took a job as an engineer with a British railway firm, all the while continuing with his scientific reading.

Spencer was not fully healthy for much of his life, and in later years suffered from what may have been nervous breakdowns. His last years were marked by a bitterness resulting from the lesser publicity given to his later over his earlier works and his distaste for what he saw as England's aggressive militarism against other nations (Ashley and Orenstein 2005; Adams and Sydie 2002). Spencer died in 1903 and is buried in Highgate Cemetery, about 30 feet away and directly across from the tomb of Karl Marx. The worn state of his tombstone may be symbolic of the lack of attention and recognition his theories have received in recent years. In contrast, Marx's gravesite is quite grand and impressive.

Spencer's experiences as an engineer and his expertise in biological and physical/mechanical sciences informed his own interpretations of social evolution and equilibrium, and his work was quite influential in the latter half of the nineteenth century. Indeed, his texts on biology, sociology, and psychology were used at prestigious universities in England and the United States. This is despite the fact that Spencer held no higher degrees and never held an academic position. Part of the reason for his popularity was that his views on societal evolution, the state, and the sanctity of the free individual resonated with the ethos of the emerging U.S. capitalist industrial order of that time.

In Spencer's view, inequality originates in militancy, first involving men as a ruling class and women as a subject class. War then creates a slave class of the conquered. The slave class increases when slaves are bought or individuals are brought into slavery because of debt or crime. Serfdom also arises with military conquest and the annexing of land. Male descent rules and kinship with those in power increase men's wealth, as does the possession of slaves. Rank and wealth are tied together. Increases in inequality build on

themselves, as more wealth allows for greater accumulation and defense of it. Militancy and regulation in the larger society are reflected in the social structure of the family. Men are dominant in the domicile over women just as they are in the wider society.

The class structure is perpetuated by the abilities and habits developed over time by each respective class. Those on top become adept at control and domination, "an inherited fitness for command," while those below develop "an inherited fitness for obedience." These differences result in "strengthening the general contrast of nature." Eventually, these class relations are seen by all as "natural" (Spencer 1909, pp. 302, 309).

As a society becomes industrial, original class divisions based on rank, kinship, land, and/or locality break down. Classes and the distribution of rewards become based more "on differences of aptitude for the various functions which an industrial society needs," that is, on ability and performance in a competitive market (p. 310). Mental habits change as the increased economic exchange required in industrial society cultivates a "growing spirit of equality," that is, individuals become more "habituated to maintain their own claims while respecting the claims of others" (p. 307). Because human attitudes change, class and gender relations become more egalitarian.

Photo 9.1 and 9.2 Just as their views of inequality were opposite each other, so are their tombs. Karl Marx and Herbert Spencer are buried across from each other in Highgate Cemetery in Highgate, England. As the photos show, Marx's tomb is much grander and better kept than is Spencer's.

Photos by Charles E. Hurst.

Industrial societies mean more freedom and greater reverence for the individual.

Drawing on both biological and physical analogies, Spencer viewed society as naturally becoming larger, more complex, integrated, and adaptive. In its free and natural course, societies evolve in a manner that increases their adaptability. He argued that, left to its own devices and like any natural species, a society's best components survive, while its weakest die away. Evolution performs a cleansing function that makes society more adaptive to its environment. In the long run, this makes society stronger.

In the competitive battle of life, winners survive while losers die away. In this sense, inequality is to be expected in society. Spencer coined the phrase "survival of the fittest," which captures the spirit of this social competition. This is a natural process with which there should be no interference from any quarter. "Under the natural course of things each citizen tends towards his fittest function. Those who are competent to the kind of work they undertake succeed, and, in the average of cases, are advanced in proportion to their efficiency; while the incompetent, society soon finds out, ceases to employ, forces to try something easier, and eventually turns to use" (Spencer 1892, p. 138). As humanity evolves, Spencer believed, it develops traits that promote its survival. Unnecessary governmental legislation and other attempts to modify this process damage the natural evolutionary process. "Let the average vitality be diminished by more effectually guarding the weak against adverse conditions, and inevitably there come fresh diseases" (Spencer 1961, p. 310).

Freedom gives individuals the opportunity to develop their own adaptive traits. If individuals develop positive traits, they can be strengthened and passed on to future generations, making society as a whole much stronger and more adaptive. Even well-intentioned interference in this natural process only weakens the possibility of individuals developing these traits. Overall, it also weakens society's ability to survive since it encourages, or props up, its weakest members at the expense of everyone else. Because weak individuals do not have the properties necessary for survival, their dependence on state aid is "evil" because "all evil results from the non-adaptation of constitution to conditions," and it is in its advance to build its strength that society rids itself of "evil" (Spencer 1897, pp. 28–29).

In modern industrial nations, such as the United States, Spencer envisioned a free-market capitalist economy and a government that performed only basic defensive and protective functions for the nation's citizens. He argued that, by and large, the state should minimize its role in the individual's life. The free individual is a hallmark of an advanced society, and Spencer fiercely believed in the protection of individual rights.

MINI-CASE 9.1

Regulating Financial Institutions

Each of the theorists discussed in this chapter had distinct views about the role of government in society. Marx saw it as an instrument used by capitalists to maintain and enhance their economic interests. Weber believed government bureaucracy would become increasingly oppressive and intrusive, while Durkheim argued that government served as an effective and positive source of regulation and freedom for individuals. Finally, Spencer viewed the state and individual as being in an adversarial relationship; consequently, the state's functions and size should be kept to a minimum.

One of the alleged causes of the 2008–2010 economic crises in the United States was the failure of government to regulate the operations of financial institutions. The result was that many of these institutions bundled questionable mortgages into securities that were sold worldwide, causing many to lose large amounts of money. Considering the arguments of the classical theorists, should the government regulate financial institutions more rigorously or leave them alone to operate as they see fit? ■

As members of society, and at least before marriage, this applies to women as well as to men.

In contrast to Durkheim, Spencer (1897) believed that the state would become smaller and less intrusive and the individual freer as society evolved: "[T]he liberty which a citizen enjoys is to be measured ... by the relative paucity of the restraints [governmental machinery] imposes on him ... [especially] such restraints beyond those which are needful for preventing him from directly or indirectly aggressing on his fellows" (p. 19).

State size has implications for both the powerful and the powerless in society. What this means for the powerless and poor is that, in Spencer's view, governmental welfare programs should be eliminated for the good of society as a whole. Such programs actually weaken the poor and create bitterness among those who must be taxed to support them. In contrast to help given by volunteers to the needy, this aid is not freely given. No one benefits in the long run. It also weakens society because such suffering on the part of the weak must be endured if only to perfect society:

> Blind to the fact that under the natural order of things society is constantly excreting its unhealthy, imbecile, slow, vacillating, faithless members, these unthinking, though well-meaning, men advocate an interference which not only stops the purifying process, but even ... encourages the multiplication of the reckless and incompetent by offering them an unfailing provision, and discourages the multiplication of the competent and provident by heightening the difficulty of maintaining a family.... The process [of natural adaptation] must be undergone and the sufferings must be endured.
>
> (Spencer 1897, p. 151)

What smaller government means for the powerful is the creation of fewer opportunities for the rich and powerful to use it for selfish purposes: "It is a tolerably well-ascertained fact that men are still selfish ... and will employ the power placed in their hands for their own advantage ... directly or indirectly, either by hook or by crook, if not open then in secret, their private ends will be served" (Spencer 1897, p. 95). One need only think of recent governmental and corporate scandals to realize the applicability of this observation. In the long run, smaller government benefits all.

Spencer acknowledged the difficulties that the less fortunate face and the indignities and discrimination they suffer at the hands of the higher classes; he admitted that the distribution system gives too much to those on the top. But he contended that the problems that individuals face reflect the limitations of human nature at any given time. Unfortunately, governmental legislation and class organizations hinder this understanding. "[T]he welfare of a society and the justice of its arrangements are at bottom dependent on the character of its members. ... The defective natures of citizens will show themselves in the bad acting of *whatever* social structure they are arranged into. There is no political alchemy by which you can get golden conduct out of leaden instincts" (Spencer 1892, pp. 52–53; emphasis added).

In criticism, Spencer put too much faith in the natural process of evolution as the proper avenue through which inequality and its ills have to be solved. He appears to have been largely unaware of the negative consequences for many workers of the social-structural arrangements that evolve as a free-market economy "progresses." To wait for human nature to become less selfish seems like wishful thinking. Outside of voluntary charity and negative regulation that protected the rights of individuals, he left little room for using human activities of any kind as a means of alleviating poverty or inequality. This is because he viewed some inequality as a product of the survival of the fittest. On the positive side, Spencer's arguments call renewed attention to the selfish interests and biases of the powerful that are often present in governmental and other large organizations. As a champion of individual freedom, he also reminds us to be wary of constraints on both the rich and the poor, which may hinder their development as individuals. He reminds us that big government, regardless of its form, is no solution to the problem of social inequality.

MARX, WEBER, AND GLOBALIZATION

During the last three decades, "capitalism has intensified its grasp over the entire world, unleashing processes of economic change that intensify and render increasingly visible the links between the fate of people in the advanced capitalist countries and the rest of the world's population" (Gimenez 2005, p. 11). During this time, many corporations have established plants and markets in foreign countries and have outsourced thousands of jobs. New plants of foreign-owned companies have sprouted up in the United States, at the same time that older companies have left looking for more lucrative foreign markets. Marx's and Weber's analyses of capitalism and inequality provide a framework for understanding many of the processes associated with globalization. From a Marxian perspective, capitalism treats the world as a font of resources, a source of labor, and a large marketplace in which companies can sell their goods and services.

In its constant search for more profit through expanded markets and lower costs through cheaper labor and lower taxes, capitalism has expanded to the most remote parts of the globe. As Marx observed, capitalism is an international force that knows no national boundaries. In seeking economic efficiencies, it has left many unemployed and harnessed the cheap labor of workers in poor countries. Because it is able to cross national boundaries, capitalists extol the free market as a natural process because it leaves them unencumbered by governmental and other regulation. An unrestrained market allows capitalists to have free rein over its activities. Marx would view free-market arguments as an ideology that helps them maintain their powerful economic position. But what may be of short-term benefit to corporations can be harmful to others. When corporations modernize and introduce new efficiency measures, some workers are left without jobs, and small entrepreneurs who cannot compete are left to find more menial work to make ends meet (Chen et al. 2005).

While the "informal proletariat" composed of self-employed street workers and others like them is not the same group as Marx's factory proletariat, the growth in their numbers is still

Photo 9.3   A woman operates a sewing maching in Bangkok, Thailand. The increased demand for inexpensive goods in the West has lead to the growth of industrialization in less-developed countries.

© 1000 words/Shutterstock.

fostered by the movement of capitalist corporations into these economies (Choi 2006). When individuals are unemployed, their incomes fall, and they are left unable to spend on products being sold by multiple businesses. Their life

chances are diminished. The lower demand for goods (e.g., automobiles, televisions) creates more competition among sellers. In the battle for markets and profits, workers and consumers are viewed as commodities that can be manipulated

---

NUTSHELL 9.1   Republicans, Democrats, and Economic Crisis

The theorists discussed in this chapter are considered "classical" because many of their ideas live on in the thought processes and policies of contemporary leaders. As President Barack Obama noted, the basic philosophies of many Republicans and Democrats regarding the role of government and the workings of the economy differ, sometimes resulting in paralysis when policies need to be developed and legislation passed.

These philosophical differences were on ample display in recent Congressional discussions and wrangling over whether to increase the debt limit and how to alleviate the problems in the U.S. economy and restore its health. On the one hand, there are Republicans and conservatives who believe, like Spencer, that government should be small in a modern society and its functions minimal. For these groups, government, ideally, should not intrude in the free-market economy, but should let the market work out its own problems. There should be no "bailout." Like Spencer, they argue that market mechanisms will sort out the strong from the weak, and in the long term leave the economy in a healthier state. If some businesses go bankrupt, so be it. Most Democrats and liberals, on the other hand, believe that government has an important and large role to play in creating a just society and an economy that benefits everyone. Like Durkheim, they believe that government is a positive institution which often is needed to correct problems in the wider society. Consequently, they are less hesitant to suggest grand and sometimes expensive solutions to problems.

Many Democrats—as well as some Republicans—also argue that some financial and corporate capitalists have abused their power, and consequently, should be held accountable for many of the difficulties that individuals and institutions have experienced. "Greed" has often been mentioned as a principal cause of the crisis. As Marx observed, capitalists' primary motivation is to

increase profit, and leaders in financial markets tried to do so by creating new mechanisms, such as the bundling of faulty mortgages into securities for sale on the international market. Since individuals are viewed as being basically driven by egoistic motives, Democrats often contend, like Durkheim, that some regulation over individual behavior is advisable.

In dealing with economic crises, members of Congress often take sides when considering what group should be the primary focus in resolving problems. Should it be the banks since they are the source of needed funding and credit for businesses and individuals? Or should it be private businesses since they are the main source of employment in a capitalist economy? Or should it be average members of the public since they are often the first to experience unemployment and declines in their standard of living when crises occur? Like those for other questions, one's answers to these are conditioned by ideological and other beliefs.

Another point of disagreement is whether money should be put in the hands of citizens so they can spend it, or if it should be spent directly by the government to spur the economy. Generally, Republicans stress the conservative position of lowering taxes, providing more money for *individuals* to spend, while Democrats are more likely to value *government* spending as a means to create jobs and stimulate the economy. Ironically, like Marx, although not for the same reason, Republicans are more suspicious than Democrats of government.

Republicans and Democrats, conservatives and liberals, often differ on the thrust of their policy recommendations, but as Marx and Weber argued, the fact that capitalism is an interconnected system in which capitalists and workers, technology and bureaucracy, are all entangled, means that the unique problems of each constituency must be addressed and their real needs accommodated if economic crises are to be attacked effectively.

to increase revenue. In this battle, firms jockey for advantageous market position, often evolving through revolutionizing their technology and products. Some firms do not change and remain stagnant. As a result, some go bankrupt, leading to greater concentration in the market.

In the self-interested, rational drive for greater profit, the influence of tradition and social status is weakened. Weber observed that it is in periods of rapid change and tumult that staid beliefs and time-honored positions come under fire. Capitalism and the large state bureaucracy found in most advanced countries are antitraditional, in Weber's view. They operate "without regard for persons." In this climate, economic class position and money become more important as bases of power.

The inequalities created by these international economic processes engender some concerns and pockets of rebellion. But the alienation and false consciousness of many of those who suffer in this system, together with national ideologies that extol individualism and the free market, hold active resistance to a minimum. In Marx's view, conditions would need to get a lot worse before they get better for workers around the world.

Summary

It was mentioned at the outset of the chapter that a thorough understanding of what Marx, Weber, Durkheim, and Spencer had to say about inequality depends on seeing and analyzing that work in the context of their broader theories and perspectives on society and human beings. Too often, as a reflection of our specialization and departmentalization, we wrench out only those segments of an individual's theory in which we have an immediate interest. This is not the way in which these theories were developed, and so taking them out of context can lead to distortions and, at best, only superficial understanding. Consequently, the specific observations made by these individuals on inequality should be couched in the broader frameworks of their overall perspectives and life experiences. Hopefully, this leads to a fuller comprehension of what each of these theorists was trying to convey.

It is clear from the discussion in this chapter that these men differed significantly in their views on human nature, the forms that inequality could take, and the bases and future of inequality. Weber saw human beings as self-seeking, whereas Marx viewed them in more selfless terms. Durkheim felt that individuals required regulation and guidance. Spencer believed people were selfish but that their nature would be changed to become moral and respectful of others as industrialism took hold. Marx focused on economic classes, as did Durkheim in *The Division of Labor*, whereas Weber examined economic classes as well as status groups, and to some extent, parties. Spencer analyzed shifts in class, political, and gender inequality as societies moved from **militant** to industrial, and from simple to complex systems. Marx sought the source of inequality in an individual's relationship to the means of production, whereas Weber saw inequality arising from a number of sources, including market situation, lifestyle, and decision-making power. Durkheim argued that although inequality continued to be based on biological and inheritance factors, he assumed that eventually in organic society most social inequality would be founded solely on individual differences in abilities. Spencer placed the sources of the earliest and most rigid forms of inequality in militancy, conquest, and annexation of territory, while later, more fluid forms in industrial societies were based on one's function and performance in the economy. Weber, Durkheim, and Spencer did not see inequality as disappearing in the future, but Marx was more optimistic on this point.

Marx and Weber agreed that classes, class struggle, or both are significant elements in societies. Weber and Marx both felt that capitalism has dehumanizing effects and is class structured and that class is a predominant factor in modern society. Their conceptions of the effects of class anticipated many of the specific effects discussed in later chapters on life chances, crime, and protest. Similar conditions for class consciousness and protest were outlined by Marx and Weber. In contrast to Marx

TABLE 9.1 Summary of Basic Ideas on Inequality from Classical Theorists

Theorist	Major Concern	Forms	Causes	Inevitability	Future
			Theorists' Views on Inequality		
Marx	Classes in capitalist society	Historical class structures	Private property	No	Revolution and classless society
Weber	Dimensions of inequality and shifts in their prominence	Class, status, party	Market situation; granting of status honor; political power	Yes	Rationalization of society and growing salience of class
Durkheim	Abnormal forms of division of labor	Masters and workers	Anomic and forced divisions of labor	Mixed	Decline of class conflict in industrial society
Spencer	Evolutionary changes in bases and degree of inequality	Classes and gender relations	Form and evolutionary stage of society	Yes	Greater egalitarian ethos and inequality based on achievement

and Weber, Durkheim and Spencer argued that, because of its nature, industrial society contains less alienating and structured forms of inequality.

Table 9.1 highlights the central features of the main theorists covered in this chapter. The theories of Marx, Weber, Durkheim, and Spencer were presented because their perspectives have helped to shape modern social science. Their impact has not always been obvious, but it has been pervasive.

Critical Thinking

1. Is class or social status more important in understanding the everyday conditions and choices of individuals in the United States?
2. Is a classless society possible or even approachable? If so, what problems, if any, would arise from the classlessness? If not, why not?
3. In light of current trends in poverty, income, and wealth inequality in the United States, which of these theorists seem to make the most sense? Why?
4. Taking into account that the United States is a capitalist society, but also considering Spencer's arguments, do you think the federal government should or should not have a role in reducing inequality and poverty? Why?

Web Connections

Marx, Weber, and Durkheim were among the giants of sociology during its classical period. To find out more about them, and to read interviews that Marx and Engels had with various media representatives, go to the Marxist Archive, which also contains information on writers who followed in their footsteps. Comparisons of Marx with Weber and Durkheim can also be carried out by browsing and reading this website: www.marxists.org.

Film Suggestions

In Time (2011). A dystopian feature film that conveys Marx's social theory.

Up in the Air (2010). A feature film about a professional employment terminator (George Clooney) that illustrates many of Weber's ideas.

CHAPTER 10

Contemporary Explanations of Inequality

Fortunes . . . come tumbling into some men's laps.

FRANCIS BACON (1561–1626)

This chapter consists of a discussion of some of the more recent explanations of social inequality. Generally, theories of inequality tend to stress either the *structural* or *individual* causes of inequality (Gould 2002). Some explanations incorporate both elements and try to explain both the *structure of inequality* as well as *individuals' positions within it*. *Structural* explanations focus on the effects of the market's organization, occupational structure, institutional discrimination, and/or the social network of positions on social stratification in a society. Over time, as positions disappear and new ones appear, individuals' class positions also change. Position in the structure affects access, opportunities, and outcomes for individuals. The controversial **functionalist theory** of Davis and Moore (1945) and the dual labor market theory in this chapter stress the importance of structure and position within that structure for understanding inequality in rewards. In the last chapter, we saw that Marx's and Durkheim's theories are especially representative of this approach. *Individualist* explanations, on the other hand, emphasize the role of individual differences in qualities (traits, talents, education, etc.) in explaining the inequality among people. In other words, it is because of differences in effort, ability, training, experience, and the like that inequality in rewards emerges. In this chapter, neoclassical economic theories that focus on differences in human capital best exemplify this form of theory, while Herbert Spencer's explanation from the last chapter is also representative of the individualist type. Some explanations to be encountered shortly incorporate both structural and individualist, macro and micro elements. Included in these are certain forms of social constructionist and reproduction explanations. It can be inferred from some of these theories that even though it is helpful to make the analytical distinction between structural and individualist explanations, it is the case that structure and individual factors affect each other reciprocally in complex ways.

This chapter is not an exhaustive treatment of all contemporary theories of inequality. The work of Erik Wright, for example, a prominent American Marxist scholar, is not discussed in this chapter. Wright's principal publications have been concerned with the Marxian conceptualization and measurement of class and their application to understanding the shape of class structure in capitalist societies. As a result, his view of the class concept and class structure was reviewed in Chapter 2, along with other perspectives on class structure.

FUNCTIONALIST THEORY OF STRATIFICATION

Durkheim's belief that inequality in modern society is based primarily on differences in internal talents and the division of labor are echoed in the 1945 theory of Kingsley Davis and Wilbert Moore. Few theories of stratification called forth the attention and criticism that the Davis–Moore theory received. Though this theory is now quite dated, it provided a compelling framework that helped set the stage for a productive conversation across several decades among theorists of inequality.

Like Durkheim's theory, Davis and Moore's theory is based on a functionalist framework. The functionalist perspective views societies as social systems that have certain basic problems to solve or functions that have to be performed if the society is to survive. One of these problems concerns the motivation of society's members; if that motivation is absent, a society will not survive (Aberle et al. 1950, p. 103). If a society is to continue, important tasks must be specifically delineated and some means for their assignment and accomplishment created; for a society, "activities necessary to its survival must be worked out in predictable, determinate ways, or else apathy or the war of each against all must prevail" (p. 105). And since certain goods of value are scarce (property, wealth, etc.), "some system of differential allocation of the scarce values of a society is essential" (p. 106). The result of this differential allocation (stratification) must be viewed as being legitimate and "accepted by most of the members—at least by the important ones—of a society if stability is to be attained" (p. 106). Many functional prerequisites are assumed to be necessary for the survival of a society, but it is the assumption of the necessity of stratification that concerns us here.

The arguments in Davis and Moore's functionalist theory are quite easy to grasp and, on the surface, may appear to be commonsensical and even self-evident. One should keep in mind that the kind of thinking that is represented in their theory dominated sociology throughout the 1950s and much of the 1960s in the United States.

Davis and Moore (1945) indicated at the outset of their argument that they were trying to explain (1) the presence of stratification in all societies and (2) why *positions* are differentially ranked in the system of rewards in a society. Assuming that structure is at least minimally divided into different statuses and roles (i.e., a division of labor), Davis and Moore began by arguing that every society has to have some means to place its members in the social structure. A critical issue is the problem of motivating individuals to occupy certain statuses (full-time occupations) and to make sure that they are motivated to adequately perform the roles once they occupy those positions. Since some tasks are more onerous, more important for the society, and more difficult to perform, a system of rewards (inducements) is needed to ensure that these tasks are performed by the most capable individuals. "The rewards and their distribution become a part of the social order, and thus give rise to stratification" (p. 243). Like Durkheim's view of the ideal industrial society, Davis and Moore assumed that the society will run smoothly because the distribution of rewards to individuals will reflect the "internal inequalities" of their skills and capabilities.

Every society has a variety of rewards that it can use: (1) those "that contribute to sustenance and comfort" (money, goods of different kinds), (2) those related to "humor and diversion" (vacations, leisure plans), and (3) those that enhance "self-respect and ego expansion" (psychological rewards, promotion). Consequently, Davis and Moore are not simply talking about the distribution and system of economic rewards but all kinds of inducements that can promote motivation to perform tasks in the society. Not all positions have equal rewards attached to them, of course, and since that is the case, "the society must be stratified because that is precisely what stratification means. Social inequality is thus an unconsciously evolved device by which societies ensure that the most important positions are conscientiously filled by the most qualified persons" (p. 243). According to this approach, since every society has tasks that are differentially important to its survival, every society is stratified.

Davis and Moore specified two criteria that determine the amount of rewards that accrue to given positions: (1) functional importance of the task and (2) the "scarcity of personnel" capable of performing the task, or the amount of training required (pp. 243–244). Together these determine the rank of a given position in the system of rewards—that is, in the stratification system. Consequently, "a position does not bring power and privilege because it draws a high income. Rather it draws a high income because it is functionally important and the available personnel is for one reason or another scarce" (pp. 246–247). The exact contribution of each of these criteria, singly and in combination, to the level of rewards is not spelled out, so one can only guess as to how rewards would be affected if one of these criteria ranked high but the other low on a given position (Abrahamson 1973).

Davis and Moore (1945) implied that a third and more radical factor also is involved in determining an *individual's* (as opposed to a position's) rank and reward: economic power or control over resources. They recognized that having a great deal of money can give an individual an advantage in seeking a higher position. Power and prestige can be based on ownership, and "one kind of ownership of production goods consists in rights over the labor of others. . . . Naturally this kind of ownership has the greatest significance for stratification because it necessarily entails an unequal relationship" (p. 247). These comments are repeated in Davis's revised version of the theory (1948). Clearly, however, economic power takes a secondary place alongside functional importance and training or talent, especially since it is more clearly a determinant of why *individuals*, and not *positions*, are distributed as they are in a reward system.

Societies differ in their stratification systems because they contain different conditions that affect either one or both of the principal determinants of ranking—that is, either functional importance or scarcity. The stage of cultural development and their situation with respect to other societies vary between societies, causing certain tasks to be more important in one society than in another, and in personnel being more scarce for certain tasks than for others.

Figure 10.1 outlines the essential argument of the Davis–Moore thesis. Davis and Moore concluded their presentation by noting several dimensions along which stratification systems in different countries can vary. Among others, these include how fine the gradations are between ranks

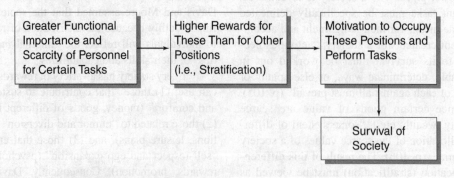

FIGURE 10.1   The Davis–Moore Theory of Stratification

specialization), the degree of social distance from the top to the bottom, the extent of mobility in the system, and the extent to which classes are clearly delineated in the society. What could be more logical? Certain tasks are more important than others, and some are more difficult to carry out. In order to make sure they are performed, more rewards are attached to them. Thus, people are motivated to perform them, and the society continues to function.

Critique of the Functionalist Theory of Stratification

For the first 40 years after its publication, Davis and Moore confronted a storm of criticism over their theory. The vehemence with which some of the arguments were made and the endurance of the debate suggest that a number of fundamental issues were involved. Three of these concerned (1) the issue of the differential functional importance of positions, (2) the question of whether the functionalists are addressing real societies, and (3) the neglect of the dysfunctions of stratification.

DIFFERENTIAL FUNCTIONAL IMPORTANCE A central problem of the Davis–Moore theory is how to establish the *functional necessity* of a task for a society. Davis and Moore acknowledged that it is difficult to define functional necessity, but they suggested two indicators of importance: (1) "the degree to which a position is functionally *unique*"— that is, there are no functional alternatives to the position; and (2) "the degree to which other positions are *dependent* on the one in question" (Davis and Moore 1945, p. 244; emphasis added).

It is not clear whether Davis and Moore are speaking of the *subjective evaluation* of positions as being differentially important or of positions being differentially important by some more *objective standard*. In the 1945 version, the indicators for measuring functional importance suggested that they were speaking of functional importance in an objective sense. But in a later statement, Davis (1948–1949) suggested that it is the *subjective evaluation* of a role's importance which is the significant determinant of

its functional importance. And, of course, if this is the case, about whose evaluation is he speaking— all of society or a select few? Moore (1970) also took a more subjective position later when he noted the importance of evaluating performance, qualities, and achievement in determining rewards. The bottom line is that Moore and Davis's criteria for defining *functional importance* are not clear, and studies attempting to measure the effect of functional importance on reward structures have yielded, at best, mixed results (Abrahamson 1973; Broom and Cushing 1977; Wallace 1997).

THE ISSUE OF DEALING WITH REAL SOCIETIES Another of the principal criticisms of the functional perspective is that it deals with highly abstract social systems (utopias) and has little to do with the operation of concrete societies (Dahrendorf 1958). As it applies here, the criticism means that if stratification of rewards is the means by which a society ensures that the most qualified people fill the most important positions, then it is crucial that there be a free flow of talent throughout the society. But, in fact, as Tumin (1953) made plain, this is not the case in real societies. People in the lower strata usually have restricted opportunities, societies are not freely competitive, and people probably are not taking full advantage of the talent they may have. The roles of conflict and lack of opportunity must be considered when trying to understand the socioeconomic arrangement of real societies (Dahrendorf 1958), and although Davis and Moore did mention the roles of power and wealth in determining and maintaining positions, they did not stress these as major determinants.

One way in which Davis and Moore tried to handle the criticism that some are hindered from attaining a high position was by reiterating that the theory is about *positions*, not the mobility of *people*. However, even given this insistence on their part, people do, in fact, become important in the theory because of Davis and Moore's belief that "it does make a great deal of difference who gets into which positions, not only because some positions are inherently more agreeable than others but also because some require special talents or training and some have more importance than others" (1945, p. 243). Moreover, differential power, as reflected in variations in resources and advertising, would certainly seem to play a role in determining which positions are defined as important in a society.

NEGLECT OF THE DYSFUNCTIONS OF STRATIFICATION Tumin (1953) was the first major critic to point out that stratification can have numerous dysfunctions for society and the individual, a point ignored in the original Davis–Moore argument. Among the dysfunctions he noted are that stratification (1) inhibits the discovery of talent, (2) limits the extent to which productive resources can be expanded, (3) provides those at the top with the power to rationalize and justify their high position, (4) weakens the self-images among those at the bottom and thereby hinders their psychological development, (5) can create hostility and disintegration if it is not fully accepted by all in society, and (6) may make some feel that they are not full participants and, therefore, make them feel less loyal to the society.

It is somewhat surprising that the original argument by Davis and Moore would neglect the question of dysfunctions, given their comments about power and wealth affecting the reward system. But, on the other hand, Tumin does not indicate that a condition of full equality may also generate problems of its own, such as lack of motivation and feelings of inequity. Wrong (1959), in fact, has indicated that many critics of the Davis–Moore theory point to the dysfunctions of stratification and the role of power and so forth in determining rank, but they neglect the dysfunctional effects of equality of opportunity. In a society where individuals can freely move up on the basis of their talent, would not the failures they suffer be felt even more acutely, knowing that they and not the system are to blame for their low position in the system of rewards?

THE SOCIAL CONSTRUCTION OF INEQUALITY

Traditionally, most dominant sociological theories have placed social structure, culture, and similar "social facts" at the center of their arguments. That is, they have tended to focus on the larger macro world around us as the principal source fo our individual fates and behaviors. Theorists have also been inclined to look at inequality on a broad social level rather than to focus on a more fine grained analysis of the changes occurring within occupational groups or classes. Reskin (2003) ha argued that we need to delineate the specific mechanisms that distribute resources and reward differently among different types of people. The focus should be on *how* rather than *why* inequality is produced. That is, through what process i inequality created in the first place? As Myle (2003) succinctly puts it: "The aim of the exercis is still to explain who gets what and why" (p. 556) A second related question concerns how individu als produce inequality by their everyday behavior

Identifying the mechanisms that explain inequality means providing details of the sequen tial causal process that brings it about (Sampso 2008; Gross 2009; Hedström and Ylikoski 2010) A **social constructionist** approach to understand ing inequality requires explanations to show hov individual actions and relationships in given situ ations actually generate inequality. That is, knowl edge of how and why individuals act (a micro-leve phenomenon) is needed to understand the macro level ranking of groups and the distribution o valued resources (Ridgeway 2013; Hedström and Ylikoski 2010).

Schwalbe (2008) suggests that, when w examine inequality over the long stretch of his tory, we find that unequal distributions of valuabl resources among racial and ethnic groups in th early United States were often the result of "thef extortion, and exploitation" (pp. 32–33). But it i the placement of groups of people into particula categories (e.g., less than human, biologicall distinct) that are different from "us" (human superior) that initiates and justifies the thef extortion, and exploitation. In this sense, rathe than being a natural inevitability, social inequalit is a humanly manufactured "accomplishment (Schwalbe 2008). Categorizations of individual such as male/female, gay/straight, citizen/noncitizen abled/disabled, and Black/White/Hispanic ar human creations, and the nominal characteristics of individuals that are developed into salient classifications which, in turn, become the bases of social distinctions, are results of the historical and cultural contexts (Ridgeway et al. 2009). As the shifting racial classifications of the U.S. Census Bureau demonstrate, changing historical and cultural situations produce changing classifications.

But what mechanisms spur the translation of simple nominal classifications such as race and gender into subjective rankings that evaluate a given race or gender as higher or lower in status than others? In a structural condition in which there is a perfect match between a socially recognized nominal characteristic such as race or gender and the distribution of jobs, creating economic and status inequalities among those jobs through exploitation and hoarding of opportunities by one group is easier (Tilly 1998; Tomaskovic-Devey et al. 2009). That is, when there is a clear and strong correlation between a recognized nominal trait like race or gender and possession of a valued resource (e.g., high salary), the nominal trait takes on a status value and becomes more salient in social situations (Ridgeway 2013). "It does so because it transforms the situational control over resources and power into a status difference between 'types' of people that are evaluatively ranked in terms of how diffusely 'better' they are" (Ridgeway 2013, p. 3).

The status value associated with one's race or gender is further reinforced and becomes broadly accepted when repeated interactions take place among individuals with similar perspectives (Ridgeway et al. 2009; see also Mark, Smith-Lovin, and Ridgeway 2009). Individual judgments made about the qualities possessed by others are shaped in interaction. This social influence, in turn, magnifies differences in the perceived qualities of individuals, with higher-status persons being "overvalued" and those of lower status "undervalued." Notable public persons receive high status from an individual simply because they get it from everybody else (Gould 2002). Individuals then carry these beliefs into other situations and actions. As a result, status beliefs get disseminated throughout the society (Ridgeway et al. 2009).

This legitimizes and helps to stabilize the different status evaluations individuals receive. At the same time, however, individuals will moderate the status they attribute to others depending on the extent to which they themselves receive attention or status from those others. If the demand for reciprocity in attention is pervasive, status inequality can be minimal.

The classifications that become important and broadly accepted bases for social status are generally invented by those who have economic, political, or social power (Rigney 2001). Consequently, the categories/classifications often reflect their interests and result in dividing up the social world in a manner that privileges them. For example, *intelligence* is generally defined by psychological experts or persons in authority using the "intelligence quotient" or IQ, even though in recent decades this measurement has come under attack from different, often less privileged groups. Using this definition, only certain persons are defined as "intelligent." Through classifications like this (intellectual, racial, status, etc.), we create "others" who simply do not measure up to the standards we have created. This process of "othering" creates and helps reproduce inequality (Schwalbe et al. 2000).

The concept of citizenship provides another example of how classifications are created. Classifying people on the basis of citizenship is a way of stating who belongs, who is recognized by the community, and who is deserving of the basic rights and resources provided to community members (Glenn 2011). The category of citizenship is a powerful one, as it interacts with and informs other key statuses such as gender, race, and ethnicity. For example, when the United States took over territories from Mexico in the Southwest in 1848, the government announced that all residents in the region would be declared U.S. citizens, unless they chose to return to Mexico. Thus, at a time when "full citizenship rested on white racial status, Mexicans, by implication, became 'white'" (Glenn 2011, p. 5). It was not until after 1930 that "Mexican" was a listed status in the U.S. census. Similarly, the term *illegal immigrant*, used almost exclusively when speaking about non-European origin immigrants, is a form of othering that justifies inequalities and the lack of access to resources such as education or work.

When their interests are at stake, groups will often compete for acceptance of their definitions or classifications. At different times, different groups may win, and some groups may win almost all of the time. Consequently, classifications may change or they may not. "When one group wins, its vocabulary may be adopted and institutionalized while the concepts of the opposing groups fall into obscurity. . . . The categories and meanings that they have created have direct consequences for the ways such phenomena are conceived, evaluated, and treated" (Spector and Kitsuse 1977, pp. 8, 15).

When one puts together all the accepted terms, definitions, classifications, and so forth that proliferate in society, it is easy to see why social constructionists view society as being made up of symbols and words, since it is these labels that constitute reality for us on a day-to-day basis. Different definitions and classifications suggest different realities. When sociologists, as "professional experts," create measures of social class and, using data on income, education, and so on, define given individuals as "working class" or "middle class" or "upper class," they are, in effect, inventing these classes or "doing class."

Individuals are "doing race" or "doing gender" when they engage in conversations or behaviors that create or reinforce differences between groups. In her engaging satirical novel about the experiences of a Nigerian immigrant, Adichie provides advice to other immigrants about what it means to learn to be Black in America (2014, p. 273): "Dear Non-American Black, when you make the choice to come to America, you become black. Stop arguing. Stop saying I'm Jamaican or I'm Ghanaian. America doesn't care." She goes on to explain why immigrants might distance themselves from the label "black": "You say 'I'm not black' only because you know black is at the bottom of America's race ladder. And you want none of that." Part of the non-American Black experience, then, is learning how to be a Black woman or a Black man, and learning what that

categorization implies about your actions and how others perceive you.

Similarly, we learn what gender means by how it is done, that is, by how different individuals are defined and treated. It is in this defining and treatment that different genders are created beginning early in life when boys and girls are treated differently. In this way, gender is socially constructed and is maintained through the recurrence of distinctions made in school, on the job, in the home, and in other institutions. We then define gender differences as inherent in each individual or as natural, and by treating individuals differently, we reproduce gender inequality (Lorber 2001). It is in our daily interactions with others that gender is invented. Women and men are viewed as being *meant* for different roles and positions. Once constructed, inequalities are then reproduced.

Part of the interest in examining the dynamics of inequality in everyday life is related to a larger concern for understanding the real, active processes by which inequality is generated. A few more recent attempts have tried to tease out more of the "nitty-gritty" processes involved in the development and maintenance of structures of inequality. They resonate with earlier and previously mentioned undertakings to *ground* theory, such as Omi and Winant's (2005) analysis of how racial categories are actually formed in historical context, for example, and West and Zimmerman's (1987) discussion of how individuals "do gender" in their everyday lives.

One of the most detailed and grounded explanations of inequality comes from Charles Tilly. Like Gould and others, he is interested in identifying the explicit mechanisms that generate and maintain structures of inequality. Tilly (1998; 2003) cites two mechanisms that produce "durable" inequality, *exploitation* and *opportunity hoarding.* Inequality becomes established when individuals use their resources to extract something of value (e.g., resources, labor) from others (i.e., exploitation), or when they deprive the access of other groups or categories of people to valued resources (i.e., opportunity hoarding). Among other things, "valued resources" include weapons, labor, land, machines, capital, knowledge, and media control, that is, those items that provide their owner with power over others.

In opportunity hoarding, the categories selected for exclusion may be determined in part by social categories already existing in the wider society, for example, those involving gender or race. These categories may be borrowed for use in specific situations or organizations, as when socially defined gender roles are extended to work positions in a corporation. Means that are effective in maintaining dominance over women at home, for example, may be used in the workplace as well. Or racial categories and meanings associated with them may be used to keep Blacks or other minorities out of certain establishments (e.g., Jim Crow laws). This process of borrowing categories from other spheres of life is what Tilly refers to as *emulation*.

Use of such preexisting categories can serve to clarify, justify, and maintain unequal arrangements in the work setting. As with other classifications, social categories of groups simplify relationships among individuals at the same time that they often function to rank them. "Categories matter. . . . [C]ategories facilitate unequal treatment by both members and outsiders. . . . The [c]ategories that matter most for durable inequality, however, involve both mutual awareness and connectedness; we know who they are, they know who we are, on each side of that line people interact with each other, and across the line we interact with them—but differently" (Tilly 2003, p. 33). Categories and the meanings attached to them come and go, as we saw with historical shifts in racial classifications. How they come about and change depends heavily on the nature of the contact and interactions between the groups involved.

Adaptation also aids in the maintenance of inequality (Tilly 2003). For example, in his study of total institutions, Goffman (1961) noted that one way inmates or residents adjusted to their

Photo 10.1 One of the reasons some low-income individuals remain poor is that the payday advance loans they take out to support themselves from week to week generally have exorbitant, even usurious, interest rates attached to them. Loans then have to be taken out to pay the interest on earlier loans, resulting in a vicious cycle that reproduces their low-income position.

Photo by Brendan R. Hurst.

controlled position was by becoming "model" inmates or residents, that is, by adjusting to and even accepting the role expected of them. Like emulation, such adaptation helps to sustain hierarchical arrangements. The four mechanisms of exploitation, opportunity hoarding, emulation, and adaptation along with the systematic use of social categories aid in the explanation of inequality structures and their durable nature. As a group, the ventures into identifying processes and mechanisms that create and maintain social inequality are all attempts to clarify the specific and concrete forces that underlie systems of inequality.

THEORIES OF SOCIAL REPRODUCTION

While social constructionist theories attempt to explain how social inequality *originates*, **social reproduction** theories examine how inequality is *reproduced* over and over again in our everyday behavior and situations. Social reproduction theories are generally built on a conflict model of society and are often aligned with Marxian views on inequality. Specifically, they are concerned with the question of how the class structure reproduces itself generation after generation. As MacLeod (2008) stated, "Social reproduction identifies the barriers to social mobility, barriers that constrain without completely blocking lower- and working-class individuals' efforts to break into the upper reaches of the class structure" (p. 8). Thus, even though they are concerned with the reproduction of inequality over time, these theories are in sharp contrast to those that emphasize a culture-of-poverty approach—that is, blaming the perpetuation of inequality on the values and other characteristics of poor individuals and their families.

Needless to say, there are a number of specific theories of reproduction. They variously focus on the role(s) of (1) institutions, (2) culture, and/or (3) the individual in the perpetuation of social inequality, or the intersection of all three. A social reproduction view of inequality recognizes that inequality is inextricably tied to the formation of our "self." "Social class experience

shapes the type of self that one is likely to become and defines the behaviors that are likely to be experienced as normative" (Stephens, Markus, and Phillips 2014, p. 612). Rather than being fixed or immutable, these selves are dynamic and related clearly to cultural context. As individuals engage in behaviors over time, given access to particular social and material resources, norms of behavior in these contexts emerge. For example, in the American context, an enduring cultural construct centers on the idea of independence and self-sufficiency. This ideal is expressed and experienced differently, however, within different economic classes, and is built into our institutions in different ways depending on resources. For middle-class individuals, independence is expressed in terms of self-expression, or "expressive independence." For working-class individuals, it is expressed as a "hard interdependence," or the recognition that "(i)n response to contexts that can be characterized as relatively chaotic, unpredictable, and risky, people have less freedom to chart their own course and to express themselves than in middle-class contexts" (p. 615). This sense of self develops in particular "gateway" contexts, or institutions, such as work, family, and school.

Institutions as social structures create avenues of and barriers to achievement. Societal and subcultural values encourage or discourage attitudes and behaviors that affect achievement. Finally, even though individuals may share values, they may enact them in different ways. Moreover, since each individual's situation is at least a little different, his or her immediate values that are grounded in this situation may also differ, and thus so may the individual's actions/reactions. Examples of arguments that stress each of these follow.

Institutions provide the normative framework that creates the accepted channels through which valuable resources can be obtained and accumulated. That is, they contain the legitimate rules, policies, and procedures that define acceptable (i.e., legal) and unacceptable behavior for individuals. This means that those who control institutions and shape their rules also shape the distribution of resources, and those with greater resources to begin with are in the most advantageous position to create and interpret the rules for a society (Schwalbe 2008). Critical among these institutions is the state, which develops the laws that regulate the economy. These laws concern business and economic behavior such as contracts and transactions, minimum wage rates, tax rates, loan and investment policies, and other regulations that define how wealth can be legitimately accumulated. Since these laws operate continuously and apply to the whole nation, they contribute to the reproduction of economic inequality's structure in a society.

The role of government has always been critical in shaping racial wealth inequality across generations (Oliver and Shapiro 2006). As reviewed in Chapter 8, through mortgage and other programs, governmental agencies have often created opportunities for wealth accumulation for some but not for others. Since degree of access to opportunities affects the growth of wealth for current and future generations, institutional conditions impact the economic gaps between racial groups. Historically, hoarding of opportunities and exploitation by the White majority were supported by U.S. laws during the period of slavery and Jim Crow, and during the government's treatment of Native Americans over the last two centuries (Massey 2007). In all cases, racist and other ideologies or official arguments were then used to justify the policies and perpetuate the inequality.

In addition to the state, the educational system is another institution that occupies a prominent place in some reproduction theories. Drawing on Marx's work, Bowles and Gintis's theory (1976) addresses how the educational system helps to reproduce class relationships in capitalist society. Rather than simply being an avenue to upward mobility and a means for developing the human personality, Bowles and Gintis view education as a vehicle to perpetuate the capitalist or class system in U.S. society. Even early in its development, education was a means "to help preserve and extend the capitalist

Photo 10.2   A central point of contention following the Great Recession was whether it is the responsibility of the government to rescue large banks that are in danger of failing due to risky lending practices.

© iStock.com/trekandshoot.

NUTSHELL 10.1   An Example of the Roles of Government and Financial Institutions in the Reproduction of Economic Inequality

During the summer and fall of 2008, the U.S. economy suffered a serious downturn. The stock market declined significantly, some high-powered financial institutions collapsed, unemployment rose, rates of home foreclosures skyrocketed, and the value of individuals' stockholdings and retirement savings eroded. This event provides some clues to the roles of government policy and the activities of financial institutions in the establishment of economic inequality in the United States.

One of the responsibilities of government is to provide conditions and a context in which markets can operate effectively and freely in our capitalist economy. In the United States, this has meant allowing economic activities to operate without heavy interference from the government. In the current political climate, for businesses this has meant deregulation and minimal monitoring of many financial activities, and favorable tax laws and allowances. For the consumer, this has meant easy access to credit and credit cards, and the freedom to select from a wide range of financial choices.

A central feature of capitalism is the privatization of profit. This provides a strong incentive for businesses and employers to seek out techniques and avenues that maximize their profits. In the absence of vigilant government oversight during 2007–2008, financial institutions were willing to take risks and try novel arrangements to maximize profits and increase the incomes of their top employees. Mortgage loans were given out to individuals who often could not afford them and for homes that were overpriced, because significant profits could be made on the interest being charged. These mortgages were then bundled into securities that were widely sold to other institutions. A relatively new financial device, the credit-default swap, served as a contract between institutions to insure against the possibility of losses on these securities. When the inflated value of these securities collapsed, the financial integrity of many financial institutions was endangered. Millions of consumers who had taken out loans found themselves unable to pay the mortgages on their price-inflated homes, the consequence being that many found themselves in foreclosure. Some

consumers went bankrupt. Others sought out payday lenders to get loans that had exorbitant interest rates attached to them. Lower-income individuals have often received "refund anticipation loans" from lenders in advance of their tax refunds. The interest rates generally range from 70 to 700 percent. Middle- and upper-income persons have access to loans at more competitive rates.

What all this means is that poorer individuals get caught up in seeking out credit and building up a pile of financial debt from which it is difficult to escape. They can do this because some financial institutions and lax government regulation create conditions in which institutions can profit while consumers can too easily lose. Americans in general have, in recent years, been encouraged to spend in order to possess the latest technologies, be competitive with their neighbors, and keep the economy going. One consequence has been that many in the middle class as well as those below them have saved little and accumulated high levels of debt, resulting in little financial security.

Of course, in the 2008 crisis, both financial institutions and ordinary citizens suffered because they were tied together in these economic arrangements. While profits were privatized, the costs of the crisis were socialized, that is, borne primarily by taxpayers. Taxpayer money was used to rescue failing financial institutions and to provide some relief to consumers whose homes were in foreclosure. The consequent unemployment in many industries also put downward pressure on the incomes of many middle- and working-class employees. Profits were made by a few, but many others shared in the cost of the crisis.

The encouragement to spend, to multiply the number of credit cards one has, and to buy on installment in a marketplace with little regulation is seductive, but it has led to a "debt culture" and a debt trap for many of the most vulnerable. For lenders and others, on the other hand, it has led to high incomes and short-term profits. This suggests that the manner in which government policies intersect with the economy shapes conditions that affect the distribution of economic resources, helping to reproduce inequality.

(continued)

NUTSHELL 10.1   *(continued)*

Sources: Steven Lohr, "Wall Street's Extreme Sport," *New York Times,* November 5, 2008, pp. B1 and B5; Children's Defense Fund, *The State of America's Children 2005* (Washington, DC: Children's Defense Fund); David Brooks, "Debt, the Great American Seduction," *Akron Beacon Journal,* June 11, 2008, p. A7; Institute for American Values, *For a New Thrift: Confronting the Debt Culture* (New York: Institute for American Values, 2008); James O'Connor, *The Fiscal Crisis of the State* (New York: St. Martin's, 1973).

order. The function of the school system was to accommodate workers to its most rapid possible development. . . . Since its inception in the United States, the public-school system has been seen as a method of disciplining children in the interest of producing a properly subordinate adult population" (Bowles and Gintis 1976, pp. 29, 37). A higher level of education for most people has not reduced economic inequality, nor has it developed their full creativity. Its structure rewards those who conform to its rules and obey authority.

As in the workplace, obedience to authority and rules is expected in school. There is a correspondence, Bowles and Gintis argue, between the structure of educational institutions and the workplace. Specifically, there is a similarity between the two spheres in (1) the nature of their authority structures, (2) students' lack of control over their classes and workers' lack of control over the work process, (3) the role of grades and other rewards (e.g., colored stars on papers) in schools and the role of wages in the workplace as extrinsic motivators, (4) ostensibly free competition among students and similar competition among workers, and (5) the specialization and tracking of courses in school and the narrow functional specialization and career paths in the workplace (Bowles and Gintis 1976; MacLeod 2008). These correspondences between the school and workplace reflect a parallelism between them.

In going through the educational process, individuals are prepared for their respective roles in the economy. In performing this function, "schools are constrained to justify and reproduce inequality rather than correct it" (Bowles and Gintis 1976, p. 102). By providing a setting in which success appears to depend solely on the individual and his or her talent and effort, schools give the appearance of rewarding those who are most meritorious. The school rewards certain attitudes and behaviors, and penalizes others. It rewards those who act and think in a manner that will serve them in the jobs they will perform in the division of labor. Not all who go to school will move on to higher white-collar professional jobs; many will perform the tasks of blue-collar work. As we noted in an earlier discussion of prep schools, education prepares each class differently, depending on the roles they will play when they collectively leave school. This means not only teaching the appropriate skills but also inculcating the appropriate values and demeanor for each class. Schools in different class neighborhoods differ in their organization and value structure.

Parents conspire with the school to sort students into their respective social classes. Parents from the middle class expect a more open school structure in which autonomy and creativity are valued. This reflects their image of what is needed in middle-class jobs. In contrast, working-class parents know from their job experiences that obedience and discipline are important. This is reflected in the organization and value structure of schools that are made up primarily of working-class students (Bowles and Gintis 1976, pp. 131–134). In her comparative study of preschools in upper-class and working-class neighborhoods in New York, Adrie Kusserow (2012) finds that children and parents are provided very different messages about what it means to be an individual. The upper-class preschool emphasized the cultivation of personal creativity and expression, individual feelings and preferences, while the working-class school emphasized "self-reliance, perseverance, determination, protectiveness, street smarts, stoicism, and toughness" (p. 195). When these perspectives clash, the student is left at a disadvantage. "In a New York upper-middle-class preschool, a child of Puerto Rican immigrants who is told at home not to talk back to adults, to be quiet, to speak only when spoken to, and to remember his or her place may be written up in an evaluation as anything ranging from naturally shy to sullen, rebellious, recalcitrant, suborn, lacking communication skills, or dull" (p. 207).

This form of education serves the interests of those in the dominant group. It is not liberating to those who receive it. Instead, it serves "to minimize or annul the students' creative power and to stimulate their credulity [which in turn] serves the interests of the oppressors, who care neither to have the world revealed nor to see it transformed" (Freire 1986). It launches a "cultural invasion" in which "those who are invaded come to see their reality with the outlook of the invaders rather than their own; for the more they mimic the invaders, the more stable the position of the latter becomes" (Freire 1986, p. 151). The educational experience, then, reproduces different workers for the economy and the social relationships on which the economy is based.

In sum, schools are not only interested in producing appropriate laborers for the economy but also serve the long-term goal of perpetuating the institutions and social relationships that will ensure the continued profitability of capitalism. An educational system accomplishes these goals in four ways:

1. It provides some of the skills needed to perform jobs for each class adequately. Curriculum tracking channels individuals from different classes into appropriate courses.
2. Through its structure and curriculum, the educational system helps to justify and legitimate the economic and occupational inequality present in society. It fosters a belief that individuals wind up in different positions solely because of differences in merit.

3. It encourages the development and internalization of attitudes and self-concepts appropriate to the economic roles individuals will perform. Those who conform to prized values (e.g., those of the upper or middle class) are rewarded, while those who do not are negatively labeled.
4. Through the creation of justified status distinctions within the school, education helps to reinforce a taken-for-granted acceptance of social stratification in the wider society (Bowles and Gintis 1976).

MacLeod (2008) has criticized the Bowles–Gintis theory as being too crude and mechanistic because it views individuals simply as outputs of capitalism and the educational system. It does not give adequate attention to the possible individual differences in reactions to structures that constrain a person. Nor does it take into account cultural or subcultural variations in values and lifestyles that may shape unique adaptations to structural barriers. Giroux (1983) has similarly criticized Bowles and Gintis for ignoring the active element in the individual within the structural framework of the school and economy. People *experience* the authority structure of the school and its teachers and react to them, sometimes through acceptance and sometimes through resistance. In Bowles and Gintis's theory, "the subject gets dissolved under the weight of structural constraints that appear to form both the personality and the workplace" (Giroux 1983, p. 85). In other words, attention to the micro processes of individuals' interpretations and interaction, like those specified in social constructionist arguments, are ignored. Structures may provide the broad parameters for behavior, but individuals interpret those structural constraints on their own.

A more culturally oriented theory of class reproduction is suggested by the work of Pierre Bourdieu. In this perspective, culture is a mediating element between class structure/interests and everyday life and behavior. By appearing to be objective and a source of knowledge, schools that produce both successful and failing students can justify the inequality that follows. Since schools represent the interests of the dominant culture, Bourdieu argued, they value the cultural capital of the dominant class more than that of the lower classes. **Cultural capital** refers to all the sets of beliefs, practices, ways of thinking, knowledge, and skills passed on from one class's generation to the next. Schools, especially those in higher education, espouse the cultural capital that is most characteristic of the privileged classes, thereby denigrating that which is characteristic of the working and lower classes (Bourdieu 1977a; 1977b). Since this occurs in the objective setting of the school, those in the latter classes who do not do well in classes develop an attitude in which they blame themselves and "actively participate in their own subjugation" (Giroux 1983, p. 89).

Generally, Bourdieu suggested that individuals compete within different "fields" in a struggle for economic, cultural, and social capital. These fields constitute networks of relationships among positions (Bourdieu and Wacquant 1992). As a result of these struggles, individuals come to occupy different classes that vary in the amounts and forms of their economic, social, and cultural capital. Research does indeed indicate that variations in capital are reflected in positional arrangements within fields (Anheier, Gerhards, and Romo 1995). Respectively, some possess great amounts of wealth, extensive social networks, and fancy tastes and lifestyles (whereas others do not) and can use these resources to justify their possession of capital. Individuals in higher occupational positions tend to have more diverse and extensive social networks that provide them with access to greater social resources. Moreover, since they tend to associate most often with similar kinds of individuals, most of the resources controlled by this group stay within it, helping to reproduce inequality (Erickson and Cote 2009). The presence or absence of these resources forms a large

part of the social context in which individuals live, and these objective conditions give rise to particular tastes, lifestyles, and ways of looking at the world. The upper class possesses a "taste of liberty and luxury," whereas the lower has "popular taste." "Distance from necessity" permeates the taste of the upper class, meaning that it is less directly functional and practical compared to the taste of the lower class.

An individual's **habitus**, or system of stable dispositions to view the world in a particular way, is a direct product of the person's structural situation; in fact, it is the psychological embodiment of the objective conditions in which one lives. Thus, different life conditions give rise to different forms of habitus, and those exposed to the same conditions will develop the same habitus (Bourdieu 1990). The habitus, in turn, has a direct, constraining effect on the social action of individuals, which, coming full circle, contributes to reproducing the social structure. Figure 10.2 gives a rough outline of Bourdieu's model. For example, an adolescent who lives within a structure with poor job opportunities as evidenced by the experiences of his or her parents will develop a view that chances of success are slight and that school makes no difference. This leads to behavior that accommodates him or her to a menial job, which in turn reinforces the existing job opportunity structure. Nothing changes.

A similar process involving the effect of social structure on outlook and decision-making appears to reinforce racial segregation in neighborhoods. Black neighborhoods in Chicago, for example, remain largely Black because Whites and Latino residents tend to move out when neighborhoods are or become disproportionately Black. Blacks, in turn, often remain in their own or similar neighborhoods, not because they prefer segregated neighborhoods, but because they find

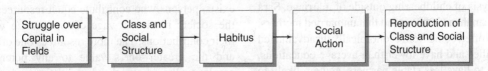

FIGURE 10.2 A General Model of Bourdieu's Explanation of Social Reproduction

their own neighborhoods more "hospitable" than richer White neighborhoods. Consequently, continued residential segregation and decisions to stay or move in part reflect the perceptions of different racial groups of each other (Sampson 2008; Sampson and Sharkey 2008).

Such an image of reproduction of social structure does not lend itself to reconstructing the social order, nor does it acknowledge the possibility of resistance or rebellion on the part of dominated groups (Giroux 1983). In Bourdieu's theory, the prospect of radically altering educational institutions or the system, in general, seems dim indeed (MacLeod 2008). MacLeod believes that while Bourdieu has incorporated an important cultural element into his theory of reproduction, a necessary corrective to the structural-correspondence theory of Bowles and Gintis, his theory is still too deterministic. MacLeod's case study of two groups of adolescent males in a public housing development reveals how social positions are reproduced, and how schools can work to foster within some students a sense of leveled aspirations and lower expectations. What ultimately leads some students to lower their aspirations is a combination of the devaluing of their cultural capital by school officials, lower teacher expectations, tracking, discrimination, and their own self-blame. Other groups, given their particular experiences and histories, maintain a faith in the achievement ideology, that is, the belief that opportunity exists for all and success is possible if one puts forth the proper amount of effort.

Too often, as well, class reproduction theories have ignored the separately lived and varied experiences of women and minority groups, an omission that can seriously limit the theories' ability to understand the habitus of these individuals and the reproduction of their economic situations. One of these lived variations concerns childbearing inside and outside marriage. In her analysis of childbearing outside of marriage, Sara McLanahan (2009) found that unmarried mothers, who often come from economically disadvantaged families and have lower-than-average educations, tend to have less stable partners, and are likely to have weaker social support, more mental stress,

and lower incomes than married mothers. The poorer resources and lower stability ultimately reduce their children's life chances and optimize the probability that their children will remain in a low economic position. Thus, low economic status is reproduced between generations.

LABOR MARKET THEORIES OF EARNINGS INEQUALITY

In contrast to the theories already discussed, labor market theories of inequality are derived principally from economics and focus narrowly on explanations for income and earnings differences. Some of these are based on rather old explanations of the working of the marketplace, while others are quite different. The treatment that follows is general and aimed at drawing out the core elements of the approaches. What is immediately appealing about these theories is that they make the detailed process of inequality more testable. Whereas it might be extremely difficult to satisfactorily test a theory of inequality based on the functional necessity of inequality, for example, it is possible to see what the effects of various kinds of human capital investment, such as education and training, are on an individual's earnings.

Neoclassical Labor Market Theory

This theory is based on the assumptions that: (1) a relatively free and open market exists in which individuals compete for positions; (2) position in that market depends heavily on the individual's efforts, abilities, experience, training, or human capital; and (3) there are automatic mechanisms that operate in the marketplace to ensure that imbalances between one's input (human capital) and one's rewards (wages) are corrected in a way that restores balance.

In a society in which free competition exists, persons who contribute equal resources in the society receive a wage commensurate with their contributions. The more resources one offers and the greater one's value to any potential employer, the greater the demand for one's services and the higher the wages (Thurow 1969;

Leftwich and Gordon 1977). Thus, factors such as one's education, training, skills, and intelligence are productivity components that are crucial in explaining an individual's wages. These are the elements that must be changed if one's wages are to change (Thurow 1969, p. 26). An extreme version of this argument would assume that individuals are free to choose the amounts of their human capital investments such as education, training, and so on, as well as their occupations. Thus, African Americans and women might be considered to have lower levels of income than White men because they have invested less in education and have less or interrupted work experience (Gordon 1972). The ultimate result is "that you take out what you put in" (Okun 1977, p. 41). Of course, as we have seen, it often does not work that way.

In addition to one's resources, the demand for one's skills is also important, and that demand depends on conditions in the marketplace. Demand for individuals, and therefore their wages, depends on the type of skills they possess and how talented they are at using them. In sum, it is the combination of supply and demand in the market and one's resources (human capital investments) that determines one's wages in the open marketplace (Cain 1976).

If an imbalance develops between what individuals contribute and the wages they receive, then supply and demand forces are set in motion to restore equilibrium in the market. For example, if wages for teachers are too low, the job will be viewed as undesirable and the supply of qualified teachers will go down. As the supply of teachers

shrinks, demand for teachers increases. If greater demand for quality teachers occurs, there should be an increase in the wages employers are willing to pay these workers. In this way, equilibrium is restored. If the opposite occurs—that is, individuals are paid too much for the resource(s) they offer—a large supply of potential workers will appear, too large for the demand for them in the market. In order to ensure getting jobs, they will lower the wages for which they are willing to work. With the lower wages, employment expands, thus leading to a clearing of the labor market and a balancing between supply and demand. Again, equilibrium is restored (Leftwich and Gordon 1977, p. 76). So, in addition to assuming a competitive market, this approach assumes that automatic mechanisms operate in the market to regulate it toward equilibrium. This tendency toward equilibrium, according to some critics, implies that there is a basic harmony between employers and employees (Gordon 1972, p. 33). Figure 10.3 summarizes the basic elements in the neoclassical explanation of earnings inequality.

If one accepts this argument, then what must be done to reduce earnings inequities is to attack the problems of human capital investment and the choices and returns associated with such investment. Thus, solutions might stress more education and training opportunities as well as accurate and appropriate assessment of individuals' skills and economic payoffs for those skills.

The pure neoclassical model has some distinct limitations, two of which are noted here. First, it is more concerned with wage differentials than with occupational differences and thus is less

Open Competitive Market

+

Differential Free Investment in Personal Human Capital

+

Differential Supply of and Demand for Positions

↓

Earnings Inequality

FIGURE 10.3   Basic Elements in the Generation of Earnings Inequality according to Neoclassical Theory

equipped to deal with sex segregation, for example (Mouw and Kalleberg 2010). Second, it presents an image of a U.S. economy that is freely competitive and tending toward equilibrium. Like the scarcity and functional-importance factors of the Davis–Moore theory of inequality, this model argues that the level of one's human capital (i.e., how scarce one's talents are) and the demand for them in the market (i.e., their functional necessity) largely determine differences in earnings. Like the kind of society conjured up in the functional approach, Dahrendorf would consider the open, largely conflict-free society of neoclassical theory to be a utopia. It should be mentioned that most economists are aware that the real marketplace does not operate without flaws and imperfections, and that discrimination does limit the opportunities of some in the market.

Segmented Labor Market Thesis

It has become increasingly obvious to some in recent years that explanations of income and earnings distribution, which rely on images of the free market and investments in human capital as the primary or sole factors in understanding economic inequalities, are inadequate. Critics of the orthodox view assert that the market simply does not work the way that pure traditionalists say it does. Rather, the major reasons for inequality lie deep within the workings and cleavages of the capitalist economy. A number of observations about continuing difficulties in the market have made many analysts skeptical about the orthodox approach and its potential effectiveness in reducing inequality. Issues that critics argue neoclassical labor theory does not explain include (1) the distribution of wages (who is paid what), (2) continued unemployment, and (3) discrimination in the labor market. A central concern is that individual workers do not have free choices in the labor market, and that the rewards they receive are often not commensurate to their human capital (Kwon 2014).

In the face of these alleged anomalies in the economy, some have tried to devise alternative explanations for continued poverty and income inequality. One of the more prominent of these is the segmented market approach. Briefly, this thesis consists of four basic assumptions: (1) the private economy is split into two major sectors; (2) the labor market is similarly divided into two parts; (3) mobility, earnings, and other outcomes for workers are contingent on place in the labor market; and (4) a systematic relationship exists between race/ethnicity, gender, and position in the labor market (Hodson and Kaufman 1982).

An early version of this theory was the **dual labor market** theory, which concludes that two markets exist which operate by different rules. In one market, the tasks seem to be menial, not intellectually demanding, and are associated with poor working conditions and low wages. The occupations are isolated and have no internal structures or career system. In other words, they appear to be qualitatively distinct from other kinds of jobs in the market.

Because of the poor nature of the work, workers in this **secondary labor market** often quit their jobs, which only encourages the belief that these jobs are unstable, and that performing these types of jobs to the exclusion of others encourages instability in the habits of the workers themselves. This secondary labor market is set off from the **primary labor market** in which jobs are characterized by stability, high wages, good working conditions, greater degree of internal job structure, and unionization (Gordon 1972, pp. 43–48). In the real economy, of course, the labor market is not neatly divided into only two parts. Many jobs possess a mixture of primary and secondary characteristics.

Dual labor market theorists contend that, to a large extent, the primary labor market is limited to a certain sector of the private economy, sometimes called the **core** or **monopoly sector**, whereas the secondary labor market exists primarily within the **peripheral** or **competitive sector** of the private economy. In the monopoly sector, firms tend to be large and capital intensive, with high productivity per worker, and operate in large, often national and international, markets. Examples of firms in this sector would be those in the automobile, railroad, steel, electric, and airlines industries. On the other hand, firms within the competitive sector are much smaller, more labor intensive, and more local in their markets, with low productivity per worker, and not in control of any stable product market (O'Connor 1973, pp. 13–16). Examples of firms in this sector would be local restaurants, gas stations, grocery stores, garages, and clothing stores.

Recent analysis of multiyear census data suggests that the degree of labor segmentation has increased, but largely due to an influx of immigrant labor, the decline in the influence of unions, and an increase in the size of the contingent labor force. These factors have become at least as important, if not more so, than race and sex as determinants of labor market placement. Nonunionized Hispanic immigrant labor and contingent workers have become significant sources of low-wage labor for employers (Hudson 2007).

Increasingly, some argue, the segmentation in the labor market is connected to a polarization of skills, wherein there are a few jobs requiring high technological skills that are highly paid, such as software development, and low-skill jobs characterized by low pay and job insecurity (Autor and Dorn 2013; Mouw and Kalleberg 2010). The role of technology plays out differently in these two sectors: In the highly paid sector, increases in technology result in rapid growth in employment and pay for those possessing the required skills. In the low-skill category, jobs are replaced by technology. A *caveat* to this model, proposed by Autor and Dorn (2013) and Dwyer (2013) is the rapid growth in jobs in the service sector, and particularly in the care-work industry. These jobs,

including child care work, health care, and retail work are not easily supplanted by technology. They remain, however, very low paid and are central contributors to inequality in wages.

The existence of segmentation in the U.S. economy, especially in the form of a dual labor market, helps to perpetuate income inequality and poverty. Changes in the occupational structure and a growing immigrant labor force have intensified the dual character of the labor market and the continued tendency for minorities to be overrepresented within the secondary market. Despite conclusions by early architects of dual labor market theory that there is little movement out of the secondary labor market once in it, national data show that between the 1970s and late 1990s, most workers who began their careers in the secondary market had left it by the time they were in their 30s. However, the rate of exodus was much lower for minorities and women than it was for White men. Greater concentration of minorities and women in the secondary job market is a significant source of earnings inequality (Wang 2008).

Figure 10.4 brings together several of the core elements of the dual labor market argument on the factors that produce earnings inequality. Notice that in sharp contrast to the neoclassical explanation, which stresses the characteristics of *persons*, the dual labor market theory focuses on the importance of *impersonal* labor markets and economic sectors in producing inequality. Being in either the secondary or primary labor market has an initial impact on an individual's wages. But once in either the secondary or primary market,

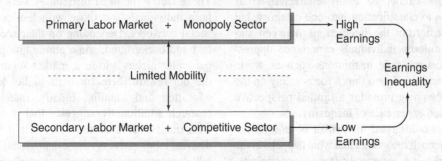

FIGURE 10.4   The Effect of the Dual Private Economy on Earnings

the determinants of earnings vary. In the primary market, earnings are affected by seniority and whether a person is in a career job hierarchy.

In applying the dual market theory to poverty, the central conclusion is that many individuals are poor not because they are unemployed or do not participate in the economy but because of the way in which they participate in the economy. Not only are they *excluded* from certain kinds of activities and organizations, they are *included* in the economic structure at particular places because "they have economic value where they are and hence . . . there are groups interested, not only in resisting the elimination of poverty, but in actively seeking its perpetuation" (Piori 1977, pp. 95–96).

Intersectionality and Labor Market Theory

In assessing these labor market theories, one of the weaknesses with both the orthodox explanation and the segmented labor market theories is that they both are unidimensional in many facets. Understandably, given their origin and focus, they are rooted in economics and center on the economic sphere. Additionally, much of the research relies on generalizations about types of work and types of workers within a section—thus there are often references to "women's work," or working-class jobs, with little attention to interactions between categories such as gender, race, or citizenship (Flippen 2014; McBride, Hebson, and Holgate 2015). An intersectional approach, however, recognizes that the experiences of workers in the labor market and thus explanations of inequalities cannot be easily characterized as being due to classification into one category, but rather stem from the interactions between statuses. Similarly, individuals experience oppression across multiple institutions such as work, family, and school, and thus a focus solely on the economic sphere provides a limited perspective on the lived experience of inequality.

As we discussed in Chapter 6, an intersectional approach recognizes that what happens in the labor market is experienced differently across categories. As Rashawn Ray (2014) states, "lumping Black men and Black women together, or White men and White women together, does not allow for the divergent patterns across racial and gender groups to be ascertained" (p. 484). Thus, in understanding the experiences of Latina women, it is not enough to explain their wages due to the sector of work they find themselves in, but whether or not they are considered to be "undocumented" must also be taken into account (Flippen 2014). Intersectionality forces researchers to recognize that there is diversity in any category of worker, and that individuals "within an intersectional space (i.e., of two overlapping categories) may be experiencing something completely different to those occupying one of the categories" (McBride, Hebson, and Holgate 2015, p. 335).

In discussing the limits of orthodox labor theory explanations for ethnic differences in occupation and wages, for example, Anthony Rafferty (2012) demonstrates the variability of success in the labor market by gender, ethnicity, and social class, after controlling for human capital. He finds a clear "ethnic penalty" in employment, meaning that members of some ethnic groups are more likely than native-born Whites to be overqualified for the jobs they occupy. Following the expected path of gaining more education and more training did not always result in higher-status jobs. "Ethnicity, gender and social class when taken together therefore provide a more nuanced picture of ethnic differences in labour market outcomes, interrelating in varying ways both between and within ethnic groups and shaped by the material and cultural contexts in which individuals exert agency toward socio-economic goals" (p. 992). Those facing the most difficulties were foreign-born individuals and those with less developed social networks. Depending on their social context and background, some ethnic groups found particular niches within a market segment that did not reward them for their higher levels of education and training. Finally, intersectional research additionally suggests that a difficulty with traditional labor theory is that it assumes discrete labor markets rather than global markets which interweave categories of work, workers, and global context.

THEORIES OF GLOBAL INEQUALITY

The major explanations that have been given for economic inequality between nations mirror those that have been offered to account for poverty and inequality in general. That is, inequality is said to exist because the parties (1) have simply not had enough time to catch up with each other; (2) differ in motivation and values related to economic success; and/or (3) differ in the chances they have for success, given their different circumstances or places in the social structure. The evolutionary/ stage, psychological/value, and dependency/ world system theories address each of these respective arguments.

Briefly, the older evolutionary perspective contends that economic progress for a nation requires that it pass through a set of stages brought about by processes at work within the society. In other words, progress is largely a matter of time. For example, Rostow (1960) suggested that societies go through five major stages in their movement toward development. In each stage, certain events must occur in order for a society to move on to the next phase. His fifth and final stage, "the age of mass consumption," is clearly modeled after the United States, which is viewed as the most fully developed nation. Cruder versions of this approach are found in earlier evolutionary theories that portray development as an almost automatic and universal process which comes with increasing population and progressive integration within the society. Leaving aside the ideological issues surrounding this perspective, Rostow's theory, like others in this school of thought, has been heavily criticized as being ahistorical, Western-biased, and weak in its consideration of how the ties between countries affect development and inequality.

A second set of theories, which developed during the 1950s to the early 1970s, stresses that a particular set of values has to be present in a significant proportion of the population for economic progress to occur. Countries differ in economic standing because their dominant values and traditions differ. Psychologist David McClelland (1961), for example, emphasized the importance of need-for-achievement as an individual value, and sociologists Inkeles and Smith (1974) argued that several values were important for a "modern man" personality to develop. Among the listed characteristics of a modern man are (1) a readiness for new experience, (2) a democratic orientation, (3) a belief in human efficacy, (4) faith in science and technology, and (5) a disposition to form and hold opinions. Traditional values such as superstition, ethnocentrism, fatalism, pride, dignity, and modesty are viewed as cultural barriers to development (Foster 1973). In these theories, the significance of structure and history for economic development pales next to the importance placed upon personality and values.

Both of the above **modernization theories** assume that there is a fundamental and irreconcilable conflict between tradition and modernity, and that the gap between them must be bridged if development is to occur. The idea that the two can coexist or aid each other is foreign to the logic of these explanations. By and large, these modernization theories also imply a narrow view of development and modernity, often implicitly offering the United States as the model of development. But it is possible that variations in development and national wealth may occur for reasons not suggested by these explanations. Dependency and world system perspectives offer such reasons, and were developed to counter the modernization arguments of evolutionary and psychological theories. Rather than emphasizing *internal* causes of economic development, these perspectives focus on *external* factors, the relative positions of nations in the world economy and polity (Sanderson 2005; Lee, Nielsen, and Alderson 2007; Kaya 2010).

The core arguments of **dependency** and **world system theories** share much in common, and, consequently, they will be treated together. Advocates posit that the capitalist world economy forms an expanding network of unequal relations between nations. The most economically advanced countries constitute a "core" that controls the world economy. The "periphery" nations are underdeveloped, and through exploited labor provide natural resources for the core. The third component of the world economy is the "semiperiphery" that structurally lies between the core and periphery and performs a stabilizing function in the world economy (Wallerstein 1974; 1979). These theories state that the principal reason some countries are underdeveloped and unequal to others is because they are linked to major nations through ties of exploitation.

The core dominates the periphery. Historically, core nations became dominant because of their protective trade policies, conquest, and economic support from the state. This allowed the core to siphon off natural and human resources from peripheral nations, many of which had been colonies of core nations. Dominance in the world economy is principally established through state control and legislation, trade policies, and economic penetration of poorer countries. While the periphery provides resources to the core, the core, in turn, uses peripheral nations as markets for its manufactured goods. In other words, each part of the world economy plays a particular role. Since a majority in the periphery nations are non-White while most in the core are White, the economic inequality that results takes on racial overtones.

The dependency and exploitation of peripheral nations goes through several phases during which dependency deepens and exploitative ties strengthen, resulting in a virtually permanent state of underdevelopment and subordinate position in the world economy (Frank 1969). In the first phase of dependency development, core nations return to sell finished products to peripheral nations, discouraging the development of local, indigenous manufacturers. In the second phase, peripheral nations borrow capital from foreign banks and transnational corporations to build capital-intensive factories that produce goods for the local market. To create these factories, heavy machinery must be purchased from core sources. This keeps dependency alive as more capital flows from the periphery to the core. In the third phase, the lower labor costs in peripheral countries attract transnational corporations that use the labor power in less developed nations to assemble products for export to developed nations. Lower labor costs, weaker unions, fewer environmental restrictions, and beneficial tax packages from host governments make movement into peripheral countries attractive to many corporations. Pharmaceuticals, electronic equipment, and clothing are among the products created (Ward 1993). These selective investments foster uneven development and greater income inequality within poorer nations. Because of these relationships, foreign investment is viewed as a drag on the economic growth of peripheral countries. According to this perspective, "these countries are trapped in relations of unequal world-economic exchange and world-political oppression" (Herkenrath et al. 2005, p. 371). The advance of one set of countries means the decline of others.

Since the 1970s, world system and dependency theorists have had a major impact in many social sciences because their arguments touch on economic, political, and social relationships in the world context (Sanderson 2005). Their roots in Marxian and radical theories made world system and dependency theories popular and compatible with the criticisms hurled at traditional modernization theories. But world system and dependency theories have also been criticized for, among other things, ignoring the role of women and gender inequality (Ward 1993) and assuming that core and peripheral positions are stable and permanent. Many countries that had been in the periphery have moved up into the semiperiphery (Sanderson 2005). This suggests that, in addition, world system theorists have paid too little attention to variations among peripheral nations themselves (Cardoso 1977; Herkenrath et al. 2005). Finally, they have not given full due to the role of internal factors, such as the state and past history, when explaining the degree of inequality and development in peripheral countries (Lee, Nielsen, and Alderson 2007; Kaya 2010).

The prominence of world system and dependency theories initiated a wave of studies attempting to test their central propositions. Among the most important of these propositions is that foreign investment and corporate penetration into peripheral nations increases their dependency and income inequality and slows their economic development. Trade flows and foreign investment are viewed by world system theorists as the most important causes of maintaining inequality in the world economic system (Kaya 2010). And yet, the research on this matter over the last several decades has yielded mixed results, suggesting that the relationships involved are not as simple as the theory argues. Some studies have found that foreign corporate penetration, foreign debt dependence, and export patterns of concentration are related to greater income inequality and slow development in the peripheral nation (e.g., Stack and Zimmerman 1982; Kentor 1998). Other studies have found that foreign penetration appears to have little, if any, effect on inequality and development, or that its effects depend on the reaction of the peripheral government to it and whether one is considering short-term or long-term effects (cf. Sanderson 2005; Lee, Nielsen, and Alderson 2007; Kaya 2010). These variations in findings also appear to be partially due to the kinds of "foreign-investment" measures used (Bornschier and Chase-Dunn 1985). For example, Jaumotte et al. (2013) suggest that trade and export growth are associated with lower income inequality, but that global processes that increase openness in financial markets has led to high inequality. Finally, they find that the growth of technology has a greater net effect than globalization itself. Needless to say, the argument over the effects of inter-nation economic relationships on income inequality and development needs more careful specification and is far from settled.

Summary

The focus in this and the previous chapter has been on general explanations of inequality. Each of the theories covered views the concept of inequality in a different way and is suggestive of different measures of it. Nevertheless, all of them are concerned with the distribution of scarce resources in society, principally political power, economic power, or both. One of the primary values in looking at the classic theorists is that each of them suggests different ways of viewing inequality and makes us sensitive to different aspects of it.

Several of the theories covered in this and the previous chapter have basic elements in common. Most generally, one can see the influence of Marxian thought in social reproduction theory and dual labor market theory. The role of the social construction of categories in producing inequality resonates with Weber's discussion of status and subjective side of social inequality. On the more conservative side, Durkheim's functionalist tradition has been carried through most fully in neoclassical economic theory and the Davis–Moore theory.

All of these theories organize the phenomenon in diverse ways and evoke different images of how to view society. Some of these, such as the functionalist and labor market theories, assume a society that is largely free, competitive, and lacking in organized constraints and conflict, while others, most notably social reproduction and dual labor market theories, view society as consisting of constraining structures and systemic conflict between groups. Because this is so, each of the theories provides us with alternative tools and concepts with which to approach the study of inequality; together, they anticipate the kinds of questions and issues that significantly can be raised about inequality.

While each of the explanations discussed in this chapter is distinct in many ways, this does not mean that they cannot complement or build on each other. For example, social constructionists suggest how minority and majority groups come to be labeled and evaluated in society. The labels given to groups, in turn, affect their treatment by educational, political, and other institutions. This treatment, as explained by reproduction theories, helps to account for patterns of social and economic capital within groups. Finally, it also serves to solidify inequalities such as those found in neighborhoods, occupations, and labor markets.

Critical Thinking

1. What is wrong, if anything, with an argument that says that rewards are simply a reflection of one's skills and credentials as well as the importance of one's job?
2. Is it possible to categorize people without ranking them? If so, how? If not, why not?
3. What role do you think parent–child relationships play in the reproduction of social and economic inequality?

4. It has been argued that networks of interactions between countries and individuals have become faster, more complex, and widespread (Herkenrath et al. 2005). Will this lead to more or less inequality, or will it have no effect on it?

Web Connections

As suggested in this chapter, Pierre Bourdieu was one of the most influential social reproduction theorists. A summary of his ideas can be found at http://routledgesoc.com/profile/pierre-bourdieu.

Immanuel Wallerstein is a principal architect of world systems theory. Read how his ideas developed at http://iwallerstein.com/intellectual-itinerary.

Film Suggestions

Inside Job (2010). A documentary on the mechanisms in economic, financial, and political policies that led to the 2008–2009 economic crisis.

Waiting for Superman (2010). A documentary that follows students through their education and demonstrates failures within the public school system.

The Corporation (2004). A documentary that investigates and reports on "the corporation" as the dominant institution of today, much like the Catholic Church and the Communist Party of the past. It also discusses how corporations are viewed as individuals under the U.S. Constitution, and what that means for their "character" and responsibilities.

PART 3

Consequences of Social Inequality

CHAPTER 11

The Impact of Inequality on Personal Life Chances

A large income is the best recipe for happiness I ever heard of.

JANE AUSTEN (1775–1817)

There would not be much point in studying inequality if it did not affect individuals and society. Inequality is an important subject because, ultimately, its existence affects the day-to-day lives of people. The social positions that individuals occupy help to determine who they are, what they think and do, where they are going, and what happens to them. Close your eyes for a moment and imagine yourself as a very poor or extremely wealthy person. What do you see? As a person in either position, how do you feel about life in general and yourself in particular? How do you view the future and your prospects?

Most basically, social inequality affects the life chances of individuals. But as Figure 11.1 suggests, its effects are far-reaching, reverberating outward from individuals themselves to their immediate families and the wider society. Chapters 12 and 13 will address some aspects of the *social* effects of inequality, beginning with a discussion of its relationship to the broader issues of crime, and proceeding to examinations of environmental justice, social trust, and social movements. The present chapter will focus on the relationship of inequality to *individuals'* chances for physical and mental health, adequate food, and shelter. More specifically, we will see how socioeconomic status, gender, and/or minority status affect personal lives at the most basic level.

BASIC LIFE CHANCES: PHYSICAL HEALTH

There is nothing more basic to life than physical health, and it is evident that individuals rate their own health status differently, depending on their race and income. Generally, Blacks, Hispanics,

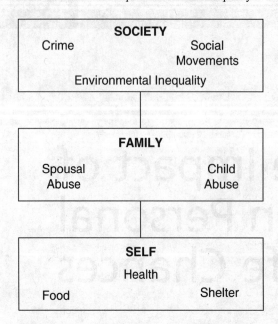

FIGURE 11.1 A Sampling of the Range of Effects of Social Inequality

and American Indians are more likely than Whites to rate their own health as only fair or poor, and individuals who are poor are more than twice as likely as nonpoor persons to consider their health this way. Similarly, a slightly greater percentage of women than men classify their health as below average (see Figure 11.2).

Interestingly, this self-assessment is a good predictor of a person's actual health, and, indeed, minorities and poor individuals are worse off on a wide variety of health measures (CDC 2014). The life expectancies at birth of Blacks and Whites, males and females, have varied historically, and these differences are expected to continue in the twenty-first century. In 2013, average life expectancy for all Americans was 79 years, lower than that of most other industrial countries, including Japan, Australia, Canada, and most western European countries (World Bank 2015b). The life expectancy of Whites at birth was 3.8 years longer than that of Blacks, largely due to the lower life expectancy of black men. Within each racial group, those with lower incomes were expected to live a shorter time (CDC 2014).

The divergence in life expectancy is partly a result of poverty. A report from the National Academies of Science, Engineering, and Medicine (2015) looked at the difference in life expectancy between people born in 1930 and those born in 1960. Those in the highest of five income brackets made substantial gains (about 7 years) across cohorts, but the lowest income bracket actually lost a year. This was true for both men and women. Generally, women live longer than men, but the life expectancy of Black women is closer to that of White men than to

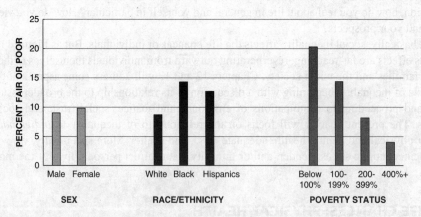

FIGURE 11.2 Percent of Respondents Assessing Health Status as Fair or Poor, by Sex, Race/Ethnicity, and Poverty Status: 2013

Source: Centers for Disease Control, http://www.cdc.gov/nchs/data/hus/2014/050.pdf.

White women (CDC 2014). Research shows that gains in life expectancy have been greater in urban than rural areas (Center for Advancing Health 2014). This is largely because of higher rates of smoking, less access to high-quality health care, higher rates of suicide and accidents, more poverty, and more chronic conditions like hypertension in rural areas (National Rural Health Association 2015).

Differences in mortality rates parallel the discrepancies in life expectancies with higher rates among those in the lower socioeconomic classes (Elo 2009). Mortality rates also vary by status. For example, as Table 11.1 indicates, death rates in 2013 for major diseases varied by race and ethnicity. With the exception of suicide and respiratory disease, death rates were higher for Blacks than for other groups. Homicide and HIV rates were especially high among Blacks compared to other groups. Interestingly, the death rates for heart disease, cancer, respiratory disease, and stroke were lowest among Hispanics.

The years of life lost to these long-term or **chronic illnesses** are also greater for Blacks. Five-year survival rates for cancer in general are higher for Whites than Blacks. Death rates from all causes for those with less than a high school education are about three times higher than those found among higher-educated individuals. This

holds for both men and women, although men in general tend to have higher mortality rates regardless of the cause (CDC 2014). The gap in mortality rates between educational groups increased at the end of the twentieth century, in part because of greater use of new heart disease treatments and declines in smoking among more highly educated individuals (Elo 2009).

While it is true that lower-status individuals have higher mortality rates, a much-publicized recent study revealed that there have been surprising increases in mortality for White middle-class people. Case and Deaton (2015) traced this increase to a rise in opioid use, alcohol abuse, and suicide. The researchers also noted an increase in chronic pain in this population. A later reanalysis of the data (Aron et al. 2015) found, however, that it was not White middle-class people generally, but rather White middle-class women specifically, who were driving the increase. They call for a deeper look into the conditions of women's lives to understand the gender disparity.

Status differences in mortality rates extend to children as well. The infant mortality rate among children of Black mothers, for example, is more than twice that of White children. The rate for Hispanic children is lower than it is for either of these groups, and the rate for Asians is even lower. For all groups, children of mothers with

TABLE 11.1 Age-Adjusted Death Rates for Selected Causes of Death by Sex, Race, Hispanic Origin: 2013

	Rate Per 100,000 Population*		
	Non-Hispanic Whites	Blacks	Hispanics
Heart disease	171.8	210.4	121.2
Cancer	167.7	189.2	114.5
Alzheimer's	24.8	20.1	17.7
Respiratory disease	47	29.5	18.7
Unintentional injuries	44.2	32.6	26.9
Diabetes	18.6	38.4	26.3
HIV disease	0.9	8.9	2.1
Suicide	15.9	5.4	5.7
Homicide	2.5	17.8	4.5

Except for *respiratory disease for Whites* and *respiratory disease for Blacks*, all rates have decreased from 2007.
Source: http://www.cdc.gov/nchs/data/hus/2014/018.pdf.

lower educations have higher infant mortality rates (Mathews and MacDorman 2013).

Health and Status

The social and economic *context* in which lower socioeconomic individuals live has a causal effect on their rates of mortality and morbidity that is independent of the effects of the *personal* status of the individuals. This can cause confusion, even for scientific researchers. When researchers examine whether there are racial/ethnic differences in various health markers, they will often find them. They may then see race as "causing" the disparity, although it is usually the different social and economic conditions under which the groups live that actually explain the difference (Collins 2015a; Fujimura 2015).

When people of different races and ethnicities live in the same circumstances, there tends to be little difference in their health. For example, neighborhoods with high unemployment and poverty have higher rates of suicide among both Blacks and Whites than more affluent neighborhoods (Kubrin and Wadsworth 2009; Denney et al. 2009). Although Blacks have higher rates of hypertension and diabetes than Whites, a recent study of Black and White men living in the same neighborhood in Baltimore found that their rates were the same (Thorpe et al. 2015).

Individual-level factors do play a role in health outcomes as well. Research shows that low socioeconomic status contributes to earlier mortality and probability of sickness. This is partly because poor people tend to have lower rates of preventive care. They also possess less knowledge of and access to newer treatments for HIV/AIDS, helping to account for the higher rates of HIV mortality among Blacks (Rubin, Colen, and Link 2010). The link between status and morbidity is causal; lower status is more likely to lead to sickness than sickness is to lead to a lower status (Warren 2009; National Center for Health Statistics 2010).

Key to understanding this relationship is identifying the significant mechanisms among lower-status groups that lead to illness. Health-related factors such as smoking, poor diets, lack of exercise,

and obesity are more prevalent among lower socioeconomic groups (Pampel, Krueger, and Denney 2010). Obesity rates are especially high among minority women, and the rate of smoking is highest among Black men. Health outcomes for Hispanics are different from either Blacks or Whites. Foreign-born Hispanics tend to have better health and live longer than either Blacks or non-Hispanic Whites. Those Hispanics who were born in the U.S., however, have illness and death rates between those of Blacks and Whites. Part, but not all, of the gap between foreign- and native-born Hispanics is due to the fact that immigrants smoke at lower rates (Cantu et al. 2013).

A variety of explanations, all of which derive from low status position, have been given for the higher rates of unhealthy behaviors among lower socioeconomic groups: (1) higher stress leading to smoking, etc., as a means of coping; (2) greater fatalism about their longevity; (3) life-style differences between status groups; (4) less knowledge about the health effects of some behaviors; (5) weaker sense of efficacy and self-control; (6) lower incomes creating fewer opportunities for exercise, etc.; (7) poor neighborhood influences; and (8) weaker social networks and support (Elo 2009; Pampel, Krueger, and Denney 2010). Finally, compared to Whites or the nonpoor, minority and lower-status individuals generally experience more traumatic events in their lives that affect their health, and are more likely to be limited in their daily activities because of chronic health problems (Hatch and Dohrenwend 2007).

The poor health disproportionately experienced by Blacks is a continuation of racial differences in health that exist all through the life cycle. Moreover, it appears that it is largely these racial groups' differing socioeconomic positions that account for their differences in health (Lin and Harris 2009). Both current low socioeconomic status and poor childhood socioeconomic condition have a negative effect on being able to physically function as an adult (Haas 2008; Huguet, Kaplan and Feeny 2008). Continuous **economic hardship** throughout one's life cycle appears to increase the chances for being functionally disabled, having a chronic condition, and experiencing recurrent physical symptoms (Kahn and Pearlin 2006). Largely because of these poverty-linked conditions, Blacks lose about twice as many years of life before age 65 as Whites. Of Black males born in 1946, only about 76 percent were still alive in 2006, compared to 86 percent of White males. Similar discrepancies existed among females as well (Arias 2010).

All these findings make it clear that health is related to *individual* socioeconomic status. But as noted earlier, the health of individuals is also related to the socioeconomic status of the *community* as a whole and to the degree of income inequality in a *society*, independent of the effects of one's individual status. A 2011 study randomly selected people in public housing to receive a voucher allowing them to move to a wealthier neighborhood. Ten years later the researchers found that the group who moved had lower rates of obesity and diabetes than the group who remained in their original location (Ludwig et al. 2011). The physical deterioration, environmental problems, lack of access to medical care, and social disorder found in poorer neighborhoods, along with the fear that they create, play significant roles in the poorer mental and physical health statuses found among their residents (Galster 2012). Similarly, Lovasi et al. (2009) found that disadvantaged communities had fewer places to work out and fewer stores with healthy food, impacting everyone's health.

In sum, there have been and continue to be distinct gaps in the health statuses of different racial and socioeconomic groups, and in some areas the gap appears to have widened in recent years. Gender is also related to differences in health. In general, women live longer than men but suffer from more illnesses, some of which, such as arthritis, are related to their longer lifetimes (Read and Gorman 2010). Women have higher rates of disability; of acute conditions such as respiratory, infective, and digestive problems; and of most chronic conditions. Women over the age of 65 are more likely than older men to report difficulty in their daily activities. Among chronic conditions, the rates for *nonfatal* varieties are

especially higher for women. These include various digestive problems, anemias, osteoporosis, arthritis, migraine headaches, urinary infections, and varicose veins. The rates for fatal chronic conditions, such as heart disease, are higher for men (Federal Interagency Forum on Aging-Related Statistics 2012; AARP 2009).

Read and Gorman (2010) suggest that while biology plays some role in explaining gender discrepancies in health, we must also look to differences in work and leisure risks, consistent health care, lifestyles and role behaviors of the sexes, and proactive health care. Riskier behaviors and greater exposure to serious violence contribute to men's lower life expectancy. On the positive side, women tend to engage in healthier lifestyles and seek more preventive care than men. Women also tend to be more attentive to their bodies and therefore more sensitive to symptoms. They take more continuous care of their health problems than men do. Finally, women are better at reporting minor health problems, which might help minimize the seriousness of those problems later in life and help account for their higher life expectancy.

On the other hand, the lower occupational and earnings status of women raises their vulnerability to illness, as do the greater family stresses and intimate violence they face (Read and Gorman 2010). However, even when their initial health is the same, women become healthier and have fewer physical limitations the longer and more continuously they are employed than women who are either intermittently employed or not in the labor force. Those who are recently unemployed or who are intermittently employed are the least healthy (Hergenrather et al. 2015). In addition to employment itself, the number of work hours also affects health among men. Working more than 40 hours per week has a positive impact on their health, but when their wives work longer than 40 hours per week, husbands' health suffers. In contrast, long work hours by their husbands do not harm wives' health, nor does the number of their own work hours affect their health (Kleiner and Pavalko 2014).

Finally, increases in one's own earnings are positively related to health, but the effects of increases in *spousal* earnings appear to be more complicated. For example, research finds that among heterosexual married couples, an increase in wives' earnings has a positive impact on their health but raises the chances of husbands dying, whereas the reverse is true for wives when husbands' earnings increase (McDonough et al. 1999; Schnittker 2007). These results on the effects of work hours and earnings on health suggest that men are most likely to suffer when their wives become more involved and successful in the world of work, a sphere which, traditionally, has been more of a man's province. Providing support for this hypothesis, a recent study found that unequal incomes had different effects in same-sex and heterosexual couples. Earning about the same amount of money appeared to protect same-sex couples from breaking up, while equal-earning heterosexual couples were more likely to break up. This suggests that gendered expectations about work and who should be the breadwinner are the issue: Even today, violation of traditional gender norms in a heterosexual relationship can be difficult for couples to navigate (Weisshaar 2014).

Use of Health Services and Access to Health Insurance

Given the differences in health conditions between groups, one would expect to find parallel differences in the preventive use of physicians and other health care providers. There is little disagreement that there are significant differences in the quality of care received by nonpoor Whites on the one hand, and the poor and minorities on the other (Nelson, Smedley, and Stith 2002; Schnittker, Pescosolido, and Croghan 2005). Indeed, Black and Hispanic mothers are less likely to have had a Pap smear in the last year, and less likely to have had prenatal care when pregnant. They are more likely to die during pregnancy or while giving birth. Minorities, the poor, and the uninsured are less likely to have a family physician whom they see on a regular basis, and are less likely to have visited a physician's office in the last year. Poor children are also less likely to have received a full set of vaccinations. Unmet dental needs are more

likely among the poor and minorities (National Center for Health Statistics 2010). Among the consequences of lower rates of preventive care among the poor and minorities are greater numbers of emergency-room visits and higher rates of hospitalizations that might have been avoided had preventive care been taken.

There is no widespread agreement on a single reason as to why the poor and minorities receive less than adequate health care. Perhaps it is simply that those in lower socioeconomic positions choose not to seek care for their health problems. This does not appear to be the case, however. A national study found that, regardless of income or education, Blacks are no less likely to seek care than Whites, and may be even more inclined to do so. Nor do they expect less benefit from modern medicine. Instead, disparities in care may result from a confluence of patient and physician expectations, beliefs, and behaviors (Schnittker, Pescosolido, and Croghan 2005). In their 2002 review of more than 100 studies, researchers at the Institute of Medicine concluded that while patient attitudes do not appear to be a major factor, "research suggests that healthcare providers' diagnostic and treatment decisions, as well as their feelings about patients, are influenced by patients' race or ethnicity" (Nelson, Smedley, and Stith 2002, pp. 10–11). A recent Pew Research poll (Patten 2013) supported this position, finding that a full 47 percent of Blacks felt that they were treated less fairly than Whites when getting health care.

The argument that differences in care may be linked to beliefs and expectations held by health care professionals suggests a need for more research on the "culture of medicine." Most of the attention has been on patients' attitudes rather than on professionals' culture. But service involves both patient and physician. Stereotypes and general beliefs about racial and ethnic minorities and the poor held by physicians can affect diagnosis and treatment of patients. These orientations, in turn, have their source in racist ideologies that are widely dispersed in the larger society (Nelson, Smedley, and Stith 2002; Green et al. 2007). Researchers have also found that physicians believe—incorrectly—that poor patients are more likely to sue them. This can cause doctors to treat poor patients differently or refuse to accept Medicaid patients (McClellan et al. 2012). Despite the potential importance of cultural factors, however, it is most likely that a full explanation of disparities in health care service involves multiple causes.

Other explanations offered for disparities in health care treatment include lack of access and affordability. Kirby and Kaneda (2005) found that access to health care was negatively affected by living in a neighborhood where a disproportionate number of residents were poor, unemployed, and poorly educated. They speculate that such neighborhoods may create fear in residents, receive worse city services than others, and not be attractive to health care providers. Additionally, as mentioned above, not all health care providers accept Medicaid. One study (Decker 2012) found that a full third of doctors refused to take new Medicaid patients (as opposed to the 18 percent who refused new private patients). Another study found that lists of Medicaid providers had a large number of errors including disconnected phone numbers and physicians listed who were no longer practicing (O'Brien 2015).

In some cases, access to effective care may be compromised by language barriers. Although many clinics and hospitals have translation services available, they are insufficient to meet the needs of a large and diverse group of immigrants. Consequently, children sometimes "broker" care for their parents—translating both language and culture during appointments. This is a difficult job, as medical terminology is complex and the child may not know the highly specialized words in either language. Brokering can also be difficult when parents feel embarrassed by the health issue, when the prognosis is extremely upsetting, or when directions for care are very detailed (Katz 2014).

Medical costs are an important cause of economic and health inequality. In the United States, per capita spending on health care increased from between 3 percent and 7 percent per year from 1980 through 2013, with the most recent years seeing lower increases (World Bank 2015a). At the same time, insurance coverage by private employers declined, affecting both white-collar and blue-collar workers and employees from all educational levels. For example, between 2000 and 2006, 6.4 million employees lost their employer-sponsored insurance (Bernstein and Shierholz 2008). The percentage of individuals without insurance peaked in 2013 when a full 18 percent had no coverage at all (Levy 2015). Not unexpectedly, minority persons and those lower in socioeconomic status were more likely to be uninsured. Even those with insurance, however, saw premiums rise and co-payments, especially for prescription drugs, increase. This meant that a greater proportion of health care costs had to be borne by private individuals.

Because of increasing costs and reduced insurance coverage, many Americans struggled to pay their medical bills. In fact, in 2013, three in five bankruptcies were primarily due to medical bills (LaMontagne 2014). About 34 percent of all Americans said that they did not get needed medical care or prescription drugs during the previous year because of the cost involved. This was a particularly acute problem for poor people, even those with insurance. Those without insurance, however, were at the highest risk of forgoing care, with 59 percent reporting skipping care in the last year (Collins et al. 2014).

The Affordable Care Act (ACA) was passed into law in 2010 with most of its major provisions taking effect in 2014. The goal of the ACA was to increase the number of people with health insurance and to improve the quality of care while also decreasing costs. The law has many different provisions. For example, it requires more private companies to provide insurance to their employees. It also prohibits health insurers from removing sick people from coverage or rejecting people with preexisting conditions. At the same time, the ACA requires that individuals obtain health insurance or they face fines. To help them obtain affordable insurance, all but 19 of the states have expanded their Medicaid programs, and individuals can also buy subsidized coverage on state and federal exchanges. In the first year of the individual mandate (2014), the uninsured rate dropped 4.2 percentage points, from 17.1 percent to 12.9 (Levy 2015). The largest drops during this period were among Blacks (7 points) and among those earning less than $36,000 a year (6.9 points). By August of 2015, only 10.8 percent of Americans were uninsured. Rates of insurance were much higher in states that opted into expanded Medicaid coverage. States who did not opt in were primarily located in the Southeast and Midwestern regions of the country.

While the ACA has been successful at increasing the rates of coverage, it has not yet solved all the problems with the health care system. In particular, poor and minority people are still less likely to be insured. In 2015, for example, over 30 percent of those who earned less than $36,000 a year were still uninsured (see Figure 11.3). The rate decreased to 11.7 in the middle-income bracket and to 5.8 percent among those who earned $90,000 or more. Hispanics had the lowest rate of insurance (30 percent), compared to Blacks at 13.9 percent and Whites at 8.9 percent (Levy 2015). The ACA also does not address the problem of rising premiums or deductibles. In a recent national survey, the *New York Times* found that 46 percent of respondents said that paying for basic medical care was a hardship. About 33 percent reported that their health care costs had "gone up a lot" in the last few years (Rosenthal 2014). It is clear that this is a problem that will need to be addressed. Medical bills can create economic hardship for upper income Americans but can be absolutely devastating for those in the middle or lower classes.

BASIC LIFE CHANCES: PSYCHOLOGICAL HEALTH

Consider for a moment how important physical health is in anyone's life. It affects one's chances in employment, social activities, travel, and relationships with others. Psychological health is also a basic element of a meaningful life, but are the chances for such health evenly distributed among groups in U.S. society? In 2013, over 45 million adults in the United States had some diagnosable mental illness. This represented 18.5 percent of the population. Of those, 10 million had serious mental illnesses, defined as disorders that substantially reduced their ability to carry out major activities (National Institute of Mental Health 2015). Native Americans, those between the ages of 26 and 49, and women had the highest rates of mental illness in general and serious mental illness in

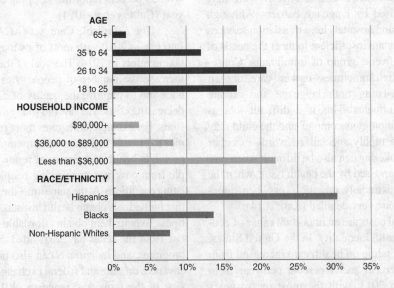

FIGURE 11.3 Percent of Persons without Health Insurance, by Race/Ethnicity, Income, and Work Experience: 2015 (Q1)

Source: http://www.gallup.com/poll/182348/uninsured-rate-dips-first-quarter.aspx.

particular. Interestingly the rate of mental illness among Whites was higher than those for Blacks and Hispanics. Historically, the vast majority of those admitted to inpatient mental health facilities have been White and disproportionately poor. Men and members of minority groups, especially Blacks, have been more likely than White women to be placed in state and county psychiatric facilities than in private or general hospitals.

Class, Race, Gender, and Distress

As we describe below, many studies have found a link between lower socioeconomic status and poor mental health. But the nature of the relationship is complex, and the direction of causality is a source of controversy. One argument is that individuals who become mentally ill lose their jobs and incomes, and are socially selected or "**drift**" into a lower class as a result. The alternative view is that the characteristics of a class position create conditions that foster mental health or illness. This is the **social causation** position. Both positions may apply in different circumstances, and the nature of the relationship may vary depending on the specific illness in question. It is difficult to unravel these complexities especially because evidence suggests that the diagnoses psychiatrists give patients vary by both the patient's socioeconomic status and their race (Read 2010).

But, as with physical health, there appears to be little question that economic conditions affect the degree of an individual's psychological distress and whether they receive treatment for it. To have "serious psychological distress" a person must have had feelings of worthlessness, sadness, nervousness, or hopelessness in the last year (Ward et al. 2015). A 2009–2013 national survey of adults confirmed higher rates of "serious psychological distress" among minorities, women, and the poor. Individuals with incomes below the poverty line had rates that were over three times those of persons with incomes that were at least 200 percent above the poverty level (Weissman et al. 2015). Not surprisingly, low income creates multiple hardships, such as the inability to pay monthly bills, which, in turn, foster depression

and other psychological issues. Low income also prevents people from seeking treatment. In 2014, 45 percent of adults who needed mental health care said they did not seek it because they could not afford it (SAMHSA 2015, table 1.42A).

Unemployment, like poverty, is linked to higher rates of mental illness. In a study of people who were unemployed, Young (2012) found that it was not so much the loss of the job that lead to worsening mental health, but the subsequent period of unemployment. This effect was not purely financial, as receiving unemployment insurance did not mitigate the negative psychological effects of unemployment. Classen and Dunn (2012) also linked the duration of unemployment to an increased probability of suicide; as the period of unemployment increased so too did the chances of suicide. Rosenthal et al. (2012) also found that unemployment led to unhealthy behaviors (like alcohol use and poor nutrition) that, in turn, led to poor physical health outcomes.

Besides its economic impact on probability of treatment, how does living in poverty contribute to mental distress? We know that lower socioeconomic status contributes to an accumulation of physical health problems in later life, which is linked to depression (Danese et al. 2009). At the individual level, family poverty directly influences childhood mental health (Reiss 2013), and it has a long-term impact on children's later feelings of well-being as adults because it strains relationships within the family and depresses children's later educational and economic attainment (Sobolewski and Amato 2005). Living in a poor neighborhood also takes its toll on health. Latkin and Curry's study (2003) of over 800 respondents in disadvantaged neighborhoods in Baltimore uncovered a strong correlation between perceptions that a neighborhood had serious trash, theft, and vacancy problems and the degree of depression felt by respondents. They linked this effect to the high levels of stress and powerlessness along with weak networks of social support produced by living in such neighborhoods.

Recent research suggests that impoverished people have an elevated risk for developing post-traumatic stress disorder (PTSD), particularly if they live in disordered or high crime areas

(Gapen et al. 2011). PTSD is an anxiety disorder precipitated by one or more traumatic incidents. People with PTSD can have a range of symptoms including flashbacks and hypersensitivity to stimuli. An Attorney General's National Task Force on Children Exposed to Violence (2012) found that children who are exposed to multiple kinds of trauma have a greatly elevated risk for PTSD and other mental disorders.

Evidence indicates that life stresses are implicated in the higher rates of general anxiety disorders experienced by Black youth and the higher rates of depression among Hispanic youths. Black and Hispanic youths are less likely than other groups to attend high-performing schools with many extracurricular activities. They are more likely to be targeted for disciplinary action like suspension or expulsion and are more likely to experience other negative events in and out of school. In turn, these conditions contribute to stronger feelings of anxiety and depression (Gore and Aseltine 2003; Merikangas et al. 2010; Lewis, Byrd, and Ollendick 2012). Moving into a middle-class occupation does not necessarily alleviate distress either, since their placement in racially segmented positions creates another source of stress because these individuals compare themselves to others around them who are primarily Whites (Hudson et al. 2012). As Black adults age, they also experience more traumatic losses than Whites, which further enhances the probability of depression (George and Lynch 2003). One of the factors that appears to serve as a buffer against psychological distress for young Black adults is the extent to which they identify with their race. Strong racial identity appears to reduce the distress effects that arise from racial discrimination young Black adults might experience (Sellers et al. 2003).

As described above, women tend to experience greater psychological distress when compared to men and are more likely to have experienced feelings of "serious psychological distress" during the previous month (Ward et al. 2015). It appears, however, that a greater breadth of roles for women may produce healthy results. In 2012, Gallup found that stay-at-home moms suffered higher rates of depression, sadness, and anger than working moms

(Mendes, Saad, and McGeeney 2012). While this can be partly explained by lower household income, there is also evidence that individuals with multiple roles display a greater sense of psychological well-being, and that loss of roles is related to increased feelings of distress. People with multiple roles—for example, employee, spouse, and parent—tend to have better health than those with none of these roles (Ruderman et al. 2002). Sociologically, it makes sense that multiple roles lead to higher well-being since roles provide people with their identities. "The greater the number of identities held, the stronger one's sense of meaningful, guided existence. The more identities, the more 'existential security,' so to speak. A sense of meaningful existence and purposeful, ordered behavior are crucial to psychological health" (Thoits 1983, p. 175). On the other hand, involvement and responsibility in *too many* areas can increase a person's feeling of loss of personal control and thereby increase stress and depression symptoms (Mirowsky and Ross 2003).

Obviously, some conditions and life events may help prepare and strengthen individuals for stressful conditions. For example, in the early 1980s, Elder and Liker analyzed data from middle-class women who were young adults during the Great Depression. They found that those women who had suffered serious economic loss during the Depression felt less helpless and more assertive and in control of their lives 50 years later than those middle-class women who did not experience such losses. Working-class women, on the other hand, who entered the Depression with fewer resources to begin with and experienced serious reductions in economic resources, felt less assertive and had a greater sense of being victimized (Elder Jr and Liker 1982). What this suggests is that life's obstacles are more easily overcome and can even have long-term beneficial effects when those experiencing them have had, at the outset, ample resources on which to build a strong life.

Labeling, Diagnosis, and Inequality

General cultural images and expectations pertaining to different categories of people appear to be important for how mental illness symptoms are interpreted. Blacks are diagnosed most frequently with schizophrenia and at a much higher rate than Whites, whereas Whites are more likely to be labeled as having a bipolar disorder (for a review of the literature, see Schwartz and Blankenship 2014). Some research suggests that cultural differences in language and symptom interpretation as well as physician biases enter into diagnoses of illness (Feisthamel and Schwartz 2009). Clearly, interpretations of mental illness interact with racial, gender, and class characteristics of patients. The same symptoms in a White patient tend to be interpreted more negatively when found in a Black patient. Part of the stereotype of Black men is that they are dangerous and potentially violent; this is related to the diagnosis of schizophrenia more often given to them (Nelson, Smedley, and Stith 2002).

Stereotypes and gender role expectations may also affect how mental illness in men and women in general is handled. "[I]t is possible that our American culture addresses mental illness differently for women than men, with women seeking treatment when distressed whereas men may be more predisposed to break laws when distressed. There are significantly more men than women incarcerated in the United States . . . many of whom have a mental illness" (Bye and Partridge 2003, p. 44). Stereotyping and labeling the mentally ill according to traditional gender and racial roles is nothing new, however. In the seventeenth and early eighteenth centuries, the artistic and scientific images of "the mad" were decidedly male in nature, depicting someone who was "aggressive," "muscular," "seminude," and "raving," with "uncivilized animality." By the first half of the nineteenth century, the image of madness had changed to a feminine one: "antisocial, violent, unruly, and oversexed. . . . The figure of the sexually aggressive madwoman effectively displaced the previously more common figure of the raving male lunatic" (Kromm 1994, pp. 507–508, 530–531). In part, this shift reflected concerns about the increasing political involvement of women in Europe after the French Revolution. This imagery served to control women's power (Kromm 1994).

Sense of Control, Choice, and Inequality

Mental illness and distress indicate the presence of serious psychological difficulties. But there are other psychological feelings that, while not requiring institutionalization, are indicators of one's general sense of well-being and life satisfaction. Central among these are feelings of control over one's life and that one's actions make a difference. In fact, feelings of control and

PL. VII.

Gravé par Ambroise Tardieu.

Photo 11.1 Early in the nineteenth century, the image of the insane person as female and feminine became established, reflecting concerns about the rising political power of women after the French Revolution.

From Etienne Esquirol's Des Maladies Mentales, 1838, courtesy of the National Library of Medicine.

mastery have been linked to making better health choices (Cobb-Clark, Kassenboehmer, and Schurer 2014). Those in high-ranking or professional positions are more likely to have such feelings, because those who spend much of their lives in occupations that are characterized by autonomy and decision-making ability are also likely to feel that they are responsible for and can take control of their lives. Moreover, this effect of work on feelings of self-direction is long lasting (Schooler, Mulatu, and Oates 2004).

In contrast, the greater feelings of distress found in the lower socioeconomic groups have been linked to greater feelings of vulnerability, powerlessness, and alienation, while those in higher positions have a greater feeling of mastery and control (Brender-Ilan 2012; Mirowsky and Ross 1983). Women (particularly older women), people in lower-status jobs, those with less education, and those who are unemployed have less of a sense of control over their lives (Ross and Mirowsky 2002). Individuals with a sense of powerlessness have feelings of little control over their lives, believing that they cannot master or determine the paths that life will take. Rather, they believe that factors outside the individual—fate or "society," for example—determine what happens to them and that there is little they can do to change that. Feelings of self-mastery and control over one's life appear to be an important set of mediating influences on mental health. Those in low socioeconomic positions generally have a greater sense than those in higher statuses that their lives are determined by factors beyond their immediate control. These feelings, in turn, are related to higher levels of chronic depression (Wiersma et al. 2011). The importance of mastery over one's life for mental health is further implied by findings that show that job insecurity, over which individuals have little control, increases depressive feelings (Meltzer et al. 2010). Of course, those with few resources lack the choices available to others. In a critical sense, lacking a sense of power and control is about lacking choices. The luxury of considering choices is not available to someone who is scrambling to merely stay alive or to have a little bit of comfort.

It should not be surprising that the self-image of individuals with this perspective would differ from those who feel they can and do control their lives. Consistent with this view are the findings of a 2003 Gallup survey that revealed that groups with more resources were more likely than others to have excellent self-images. Interestingly, both this Gallup poll and other recent surveys find that a higher percentage of non-Whites than Whites have a positive self-image or higher levels of self-esteem (see Table 11.2). This suggests that strong racial identities and unusual adversity may toughen individuals psychologically, helping to create stronger feelings of mastery and purpose in their lives (Erol and Orth 2011; Ryff, Keyes, and Hughes 2003). Whites, in contrast, are not as likely to think of their whiteness as a race and are in a weaker position to justify their difficulties using external adversities such as discrimination. As Table 11.2 indicates, men of both races report higher self-esteem than women.

Sharply contrasting with the belief that one has little control is traditional American individualism, the belief that individuals are responsible for their own fates. Imagine how you would feel if, on the one hand, you believed in individualism and, on the other hand, had little opportunity to improve your situation. The presence of different opportunities for classes combined with an ingrained belief in individual responsibility can produce self-damaging feelings and doubts among those who are not economically successful, and feelings of self-confidence and entitlement among those in successful families.

Individualism encourages the desire to excel, and some do excel while others do not. Those who *do* excel develop feelings of competence and freedom, while those who *do not* develop feelings of guilt and suspicions of their own inadequacy. For those at the top, individualism reinforces their belief in the deservedness of their position and abilities and reaffirms their high self-worth, while for those at the bottom, especially Whites, individualism has the doubly damaging effect of confirming the deservedness of their lowly position and reinforcing in their minds that they do not have what it takes. Analyses of survey data from multiple countries (including the U.S.) across time show that greater percentages of those with high incomes say that they are satisfied with where they are in life. However, *increases* in income result in similar increases in life satisfaction for individuals in all income categories (Stevenson and Wolfers 2013). Figure 11.4 summarizes this process.

Education is often seen as a way to gain control over one's life, to gain autonomy and choices, and to increase life satisfaction. Indeed, those with lower levels of education are more likely to feel vulnerable and less in control of their lives (Mirowsky and Ross 2007). The working-class respondents in Sennett and Cobb's (1973) study realized the potential of education to give

TABLE 11.2 Percentage of Survey Respondents Saying They Have "High Self-Esteem" by Race and Gender

	Agree			Disagree		
	Strongly	**Somewhat**	*Neither*	**Somewhat**	**Strongly**	*No Opinion*
All	55	34	3	5	3	1
White women	43	45	3	7	2	*
Black men	72	22	2	3	1	*
White men	59	32	2	5	1	–
Black women	67	22	2	6	2	*

Source: Washington Post/Kaiser Family Foundation Poll (November 2, 2011), http://www.washingtonpost.com/wp-srv/politics/polls/postkaiserpoll_110211.html.

Note: The question was, "Please tell me whether you agree or disagree with the following statement: I see myself as someone who has high self-esteem. Do you agree strongly, agree somewhat, disagree somewhat, disagree strongly or neither agree or disagree?"

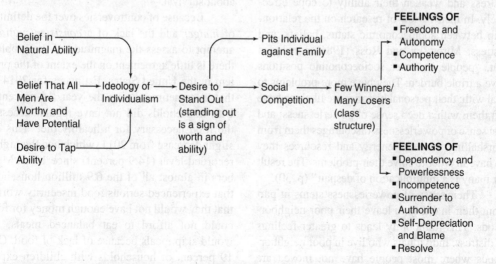

FIGURE 11.4 Ideology, Class Inequality, and Their Effects on Self-Perceptions among Men of Different Classes

Source: Based on Sennett and Cobb (1973).

their children independence in their lives, but they also suspected that educated people can get away with things that the average person cannot, and that education drives a wedge between less-educated parents and their children. More recent research bears this out. In a study of first generation students at a small college, Banks-Santilli (2014) found that over a third felt a sense of emotional separation from their families. Jade was one of the young women in the study. She and her brother were raised by a single mother who had finished high school but did not attend college. Banks-Santilli comments, "Although Jade has always looked up to her mother and sought her help with homework and assignments over the years, she discovered that while in college, she can no longer rely on her the way she used to. 'I don't talk about [name of college] at home. I keep it to myself'" (p. 17). Like many of the other youth in the study, Jade's growing independence and high level of education were hard on the relationship between her and her family members.

To summarize, the conditions and resources with which people live affect their beliefs and outlook. The feelings of lack of control, vulnerability, and powerlessness held by many in lower socioeconomic groups generate higher levels of distress and weaken their ability to cope effectively. In their review of research on the relationship between socioeconomic status, beliefs, and distress, Mirowsky and Ross (1986) concluded that, "people in lower socioeconomic positions have a triple burden: They have more problems to deal with; their personal histories are likely to have left them with a deep sense of powerlessness; and that sense of powerlessness discourages them from marshalling whatever energy and resources they do have in order to solve their problems. The result for many is a multiplication of despair" (p. 30).

Their sense of powerlessness stems in part from their inability to leave their poor neighborhoods. This immobility leads to greater feelings of distress. Individuals who live in poor neighborhoods where most people have not moved are more likely than residents of stable nonpoor neighborhoods to experience depression and anxiety; living in a neighborhood where everyone is poor reduces feelings of happiness, regardless of one's personal income (Firebaugh and Schroeder 2009). This is due in part to perceptions that their neighborhood is physically broken down and dangerous: "The stress of living in a place where the streets are dirty, noisy, and dangerous takes its toll in feelings of depression and anxiety" (Ross, Reynolds, and Geis 2000, p. 594).

BASIC LIFE CHANCES: FOOD AND SHELTER

The research on physical and psychological health clearly shows that economic, racial, and gender inequality are deeply implicated in the chances of individuals for a healthy life. It does not warrant belaboring that food and shelter, like health, are basic to a decent life, and it is the poor who are disproportionately found among the hungry and homeless.

According to some, the kind of food one eats has become a status marker for the middle and upper classes in the United States, and as a result, the more nutritious, freshest foods have increased in price at a greater rate than other foods (Miller 2010). But those who are hungry are very likely less concerned about status than they are about survival.

Because of controversies over the definition of *hunger* and the lack of a *consistent national* attempt to assess the magnitude of the problem, there is little agreement on the extent of the problem in the United States. Estimates for 2014 are that at sometime during the year, 14 percent of U.S. households did not have regular access to the food necessary for a healthy diet. This is a slight decrease from 2011, which had the highest recorded level (14.9 percent) since 1995. Members in almost all of the 6.9 million households that experienced serious food insecurity worried that they would not have enough money for food, could not afford to eat balanced meals, and would skip meals because of lack of food. Over 19 percent of households with children experienced food insecurity. The rate was much higher in single-parent homes, however (Coleman-Jensen et al. 2015).

Black and Hispanic households had rates of food insecurity that were over twice as high as those of White households, and, not surprisingly, poor households had rates that were five times higher than those with incomes at least twice that of the poverty level. Low-income, minority, and children-present households also spend much less on food than higher socioeconomic and childless households. When surveyed, over 60 percent of food-insecure households in 2014 indicated that they had participated in a major federal food program during the previous month (Coleman-Jensen et al. 2015).

Photo 11.2 Over the last decade and a half, the proportion of people who are hungry has increased, and many of these individuals are also homeless. While single men are still the modal group, children, women, and minorities are composing a higher percentage of the homeless. Violent crimes against the homeless have also been on the increase.

© Xavier Marchant/Fotolia LLC.

Major cities have food programs that serve the hungry, but they are not always adequate. In a 2012–2013 survey of 25 cities, need for food increased over the previous year, the result being that three-quarters of the cities had to reduce the number of times individuals and families were allowed to come to the food bank. Additionally, over 20 percent of residents who needed food had to be turned away (U.S. Conference of Mayors 2013). Estimates are that 5.7 million are served each week in Feeding America's food pantries, shelters, and kitchens. This represents an increase of 46 percent over 2006 levels. More than one-quarter of these clients do not have high school degrees, over three-fourths are unemployed or out of the workforce, and 80 percent live in households with incomes low enough to meet the government standard for welfare eligibility (130 percent of the poverty line) (Weinfield et al. 2014).

The problem of hunger, of course, is linked to the issue of good health. The Physician Task Force on Hunger in America reports that inadequate diet has an impact on the health of pregnant women and on the children to whom they give birth. Higher infant mortality rates, low birth weight, slower or deficient brain growth, poorer resistance to infection, and general stunting and anemia are among the conditions related to poor nutrition among children. Independent of other factors, children who experience severe hunger also report more stress and anxiety than children who are not hungry (Frongillo et al. 2013). Thus, the consequences of chronic hunger can be life-long. Other negative effects are found among older persons who are chronically hungry. Many of the health problems among older people—for example, hypertension and weakening of the bone mass (osteoporosis)—require careful attention to quality and quantity of diet, and hunger worsens these maladies (Seligman, Laraia, and Kushel 2010).

Many of those who are hungry are also homeless, although it is primarily those homeless who have personal health problems and those who have been consistently homeless who are most likely to experience hunger (Lee and Greif 2008). Determining the extent of homelessness, however, is another difficult matter. Because of methodological differences, national surveys yield wildly different appraisals on the extent of homelessness in the United States, with estimates ranging from several hundred thousand to several million. Indications are that homelessness increased for over two decades but, starting in 2007, has declined by about 10 percent. Estimates based on single counts at a given time ("point-in-time counts") tend to be lower than estimates based on counts of those who are homeless sometime during a period of time ("period prevalence counts"). One point-in-time study estimated that there were 591,000 homeless during the month of January 2013. A period estimate, on the other hand, showed that almost 1.42 million used a shelter or transitional housing during the calendar year 2013 (Solari et al. 2014).

The homeless population has become much more heterogeneous since the 1980s. Of the approximately 114,785 people reportedly living on the streets, in shelters, or transitional housing on any given night in 25 major cities in 2012–2013, 47 percent of the adults were either mentally ill or physically disabled, 81 percent were unemployed, 16 percent were victims of domestic violence, and 13 percent were veterans (U.S. Conference of Mayors 2013). Not surprisingly, a higher degree of homelessness is found in urban than in rural areas. While single men are still the modal group, children, women, female-headed families, and minorities (especially Blacks) make up an increasing proportion of the homeless. Generally, the composition of the homeless population in a given area reflects the composition of the local population (Lee, Tyler, and Wright 2010).

What is it like to be homeless? In Washington D.C., David feared going to the shelter because it is dangerous and some of the bedding had lice. Instead, he slept on the streets, worrying that he might freeze to death in the winter. In Pittsburgh, Marlene did everything she could to avoid sleeping outside at night to avoid being raped. Two homeless teenage brothers in Pennsylvania were kicked out of their school because they had been forced to take up residence in a camping trailer outside their original school district (NPR 2012; Uchegbu 2015; Klein 2013).

These vignettes suggest the unique set of stresses faced by the homeless. Homeless persons suffer greater emotional pressures than those encountered by the housed poor. They have higher levels of physical and mental illness, particularly depression (APA 2015). Again, the relationship between health and socioeconomic status appears reciprocal. Mental disorder may precipitate homelessness, and homelessness generally intensifies psychological distress. Adding to this distress is the distinct stigma placed on the homeless by the public. National research indicates that the stigma of being homeless adds to the stigma of just being poor. One supported explanation for the stigma is that the homeless "are viewed as dirty, smelly, lice-ridden, or diseased," resulting in a desire on the part of the public to keep from being contaminated by them (Phelan et al. 1997, p. 333). A survey in Los Angeles County found that housed respondents vastly overestimated the number of homeless people with drug, alcohol, and mental illness issues (Agans et al. 2011). Although the public does not fully blame homeless individuals for their plight, these perceptions of the homeless mark them as a negatively evaluated status group, as defined in Chapter 4.

Violent crimes against the homeless have increased in the last decade. Between 1999 and 2013, a total of 1,437 violent crimes were reported in the media or by homeless services organizations. This is probably an undercount of actual violence committed against homeless people. In 2013 alone, there were at least 109 attacks, resulting in the deaths of 19 of the victims. In some cases the perpetrators were police officers. Most of the victims and perpetrators were men, and most of the perpetrators were youths under 30 years of age (Stoops 2014). The stigma and low social status attached to homelessness encourages attacks against them: "Young men see the way we treat homeless people – criminalizing them, shoving them out of sight, and they get a message: These people are less than human and it is OK to attack them" (quoted in Chancellor 2008, p. A4).

A number of factors have been linked to the rise in homelessness. Primary among these is the lack of affordable housing. The higher cost of housing is due in large part to declines in the building of affordable private homes and in public housing. In addition, stagnation in wages and the decline in the value of the minimum wage has made decent housing difficult to obtain for low-wage workers. This has left a larger poor population competing for smaller numbers of affordable residences. The increased demand has pushed rents up (National Low Income Housing Coalition 2015). The destruction or conversion of housing units for other purposes, along with gentrification, has worsened the problem. Most of the homeless also list unemployment, evictions, and poverty as major causes of their homelessness (U.S. Conference of Mayors 2013).

Health difficulties and the associated lack of services available to the homeless have helped maintain homelessness. The declining value of public assistance benefits, a lack of low-cost treatment options for mental illness and drug addiction, and high numbers of people reentering society from prison contribute as well. During the Great Recession, homelessness among families increased as the number of foreclosures rose. Thus, many of the elements that affect the extent of homelessness are "macroprocesses" related to the government and

NUTSHELL 11.1 The Stresses of Too Much Versus Too Little

Throughout the text, there are numerous discussions of the negative effects of being on the bottom of the socioeconomic ladder. The poor are worse off when it comes to basic life chances such as health, hunger, and homelessness. They also have less social status and political power than others. Does this mean that the very wealthy are without significant problems? After all, they can afford the homes, vacations, and lifestyles they want. Money can provide the physical comforts and much of the security that everyone desires.

But what are the stresses, if any, associated with being wealthy? Many religious groups consider too much wealth to be dangerous because it can potentially weaken a sense of community and increase egoism. One of the authors of this text found this to be the case among the Amish (Hurst and McConnell 2010). Wealth is seductive, but it holds hidden dangers: "It's just like eating," one Amish businessman told me, "we have to eat but if we don't discipline ourselves we become gluttons."

In their interviews with 130 millionaires, some of whom had inherited their wealth while others were self-made millionaires, Schervish and his colleagues found that most felt that a lot of money does not guarantee happiness or that one will be taken seriously (Schervish, Coutsoukis, and Lewis 1994). One millionaire entrepreneur, for example, admitted that while she has been very successful, she also believes that she is often not taken seriously because she is a woman. In effect, her wealth does not save her from being a victim of

prejudice. Some of the interviewed wealthy wish they had spent more time with their children. Guilt about having inherited wealth is also a recurrent theme in the self-told stories of many of these millionaires. It is a feeling that makes many want to prove their worth by their own achievements and contributions. Wealth also draws the jealousy and envy of others, and the sense that one was just lucky or more ruthless than others.

Recent research suggests that the wealthy may differ from those in the lower class in other ways as well. For example, it appears that wealthy people score lower on tests of empathy, generosity, helpfulness, and compassion (Kraus, Côté, and Keltner 2010; Piff et al. 2010; Stellar et al. 2012). One hypothesis that explains this finding is that poorer people are forced to rely more on personal connections for survival and thus they need to be very aware of the emotions of others. A related hypothesis is that poor people are more aware of their environments because they have less control and more often have to respond to threats (like foreclosure or crime). When you think you might have to respond quickly to a threat, it pays to be very aware of your surroundings and the feelings of the people in those surroundings.

The lesson here is that while wealth may allow one to have more possessions, better health care, and a fancier lifestyle, it has its own attendant pressures and stresses. A question for you to consider is how much wealth is enough to live a happy, meaningful life. What do you think?

market economy (National Alliance to End Homelessness 2015). And it is the poor who are especially vulnerable to shifts in these processes. "As long as the distribution of shelter security remains tied to income and social class the poor will bear the burden of going homeless" (Hoch 1987, p. 29).

LIFE CHANCES IN A GLOBAL CONTEXT

So far our discussion has focused on relationships between inequality and life chances in the United States. But connections between economic inequality, on the one hand, and health and sustenance, on the other, exist in the international setting as well. The United States spends a much higher percentage of its gross domestic product on health care compared to other industrial nations. In comparison to the United States spending 17.1 percent of its gross domestic product on health care, for example, Canada, United Kingdom, and Sweden, which have national health plans, spend 9–11 percent (World Bank 2015a). In 2013, U.S. health care spending at $9,146 per capita was the highest in the world except for Switzerland and Norway (World Bank 2015a).

When compared to other wealthy nations, however, the United States does not fare very well on some morbidity rates and life expectancy and infant mortality measures. Mortality rates for circulatory, respiratory, and nervous system disorders in the U.S. are higher than the average for industrialized countries (Kaiser Family Foundation 2015a). Although life expectancy in the United States is longer than in many countries around the world, it is shorter than in most other industrialized countries. The list of countries with longer life expectancies numbers more than 15 and includes Australia, Costa Rica, France, Greece, Slovenia, and South Korea (World Bank 2015b). In data aggregated from 2011 to 2015, the United States also ranked relatively high on infant mortality rates with a rate of 6 infant deaths per 1,000 live births. In contrast, Cuba had a rate of 4 and Denmark a rate of 3 (World Bank 2015c).

Of course, when compared to individuals in low-income countries, persons in wealthier nations can expect to live much longer. In 2012, the average life expectancy for low-income nations was only 60, compared to 76 for high-income countries. Between 1990 and 2012, however, life expectancies rose in parts of Asia, the Middle East, and North Africa. For example, Liberia increased its life expectancy by 20 years over the period and Ethiopia by 19 years (World Health Organization 2014). At the same time, upcoming life expectancy figures in Liberia, Sierra Leone, and Guinea will be depressed by the Ebola outbreak of 2014 (Helleringer and Noymer 2015).

High-income countries also have 10 times the number of physicians per capita than low-income countries. The distribution of dentists and mental health professionals is even more unequal. High-income countries have a median 9.1 dentists per 10,000 persons, while the median for low-income countries is close to zero (0.3). The disparity in the number of psychiatrists is even greater, with low-income countries only having .05 psychiatrists per 100,000 people. This compares to 7.47 in high-income countries (World Health Organization 2011). The lack of access to mental health professionals and other widespread deprivations in poor countries coincides with higher rates of major depression found in countries that rank low on the UN's Human Development Index (HDI). Among high-HDI countries, a higher degree of income inequality is associated with higher rates of depression episodes (Cifuentes et al. 2008).

A lack of adequate food also haunts poorer countries. Estimates are that 98 percent of the 795 million who are undernourished live in developing countries. Many hungry people live in rural areas or shantytowns on the periphery of large cities. About half of the undernourished are farmers living in small communities around the globe. Malnutrition has been linked to a wide range of poor health outcomes. For example, half of women in developing countries are iron deficient, leading to 315,000 deaths of pregnant women from hemorrhaging at birth (U.N. World Food Programme 2015).

Summary

This chapter has focused on a variety of areas concerning personal life chances in different racial, gender, and socioeconomic status (SES) groups. It appears clear that the latter factors are related to physical and mental health in several ways. Moreover, these groups also tend to use health services in different ways, to contact doctors and dentists at different rates, and to differ in the likelihood of possessing health insurance and taking preventive health measures. Inequality also is related to the problems of hunger and homelessness.

Two points should be made about the research conducted on these relationships. First, frequently different measures of SES have been used in studies on the same issue, and, for the sake of convenience, the term *social class* has been used in this chapter as if it were synonymous with SES measures. Second, although significant relationships have been found between race, gender, and SES, on the one hand, and health, on the other hand, we do not want to suggest that these are the only variables or always the most important variables in explaining variations. Rather, the question of interest has been whether inequality in its various forms plays any role in producing various personal life chances. It seems apparent that it does. Indirectly, the organization of a competitive capitalist society and, more directly, the system of inequality that it creates, results in individuals and families being placed in different positions regarding access to and possibilities of gaining the "good things" in life. The role of poverty and inequality in affecting life chances extends beyond U.S. borders into the world as a whole. Income inequality and poverty are implicated in physical and mental health and food inequalities between nations. In many ways, then, the effects of inequality reach inside the intimate lives of individuals in the United States and elsewhere. In Chapter 12, we turn from these personal effects of inequality to more society-wide effects—crime, environmental justice, and social trust.

Critical Thinking

1. Imagine your starting point in life as a young child and the path you are likely to follow to adulthood. If you were born into a poor family in the United States, what barriers and detours would you be likely to encounter while traveling on this path? Would your race or gender or sexual orientation/gender identity make a difference? Compare those to the obstacles likely to be encountered by a person born into a wealthy family.

2. To what extent should individuals be held responsible for their health and actions if these are shaped by their opportunities and circumstances?

3. Why do research results regularly show that women have higher rates of mental illness and distress than men in the United States?

4. What effect do you think the requirement for everyone to have health insurance will have on the health of the U.S. population? Will it reduce, increase, or simply maintain the overall level of health in the country? Why?

Web Connections

Health, United States, a volume published yearly by the National Center for Health Statistics, contains a wealth of longitudinal and cross-sectional information on the life expectancy, mortality, and health conditions of the U.S. population, including information on all the states. Check it to see how your income, age, and educational group compare on health measures, as well as how your state compares to others. Go to http://www.cdc.gov/nchs/hus.htm.

Film Suggestions

African-American Women: Where They Stand: Health-care (2007). Part of a five-part series on the status of African American women produced by NBC News.

Google Baby (2009). A documentary exploring the global "baby production" trade. Rich clients can purchase eggs from one place (like Appalachia) and hire women in India to carry the children.

Deadly Deception (1993). The story of the infamous Tuskegee experiment.

Unnatural Causes: Is Inequality Making Us Sick (2008). A seven-part series on socioeconomi status, race, and health.

Lost in America (2015). Focuses on the lives of home less youth in the United States. This documen tary explores a wide range of issues includin sex trafficking, foster care, and the overrepreses tation of LGBTQ kids living on the streets.

CHAPTER 12

Social Consequences of Inequality

*History teaches that grave threats to liberty often come in times of urgency,
when constitutional rights seem too extravagant to endure.*

THURGOOD MARSHALL (1908–1993)

he previous chapter focused on how position in the system of social inequality affects an individual's *personal* life, that is, its impact on physical and mental health, access to food, and chances f homelessness. In addition to affecting the personal life chances of individuals, social inequality as broader effects on the quality of life and stability of society as a whole. Through its impact n different forms of crime, environmental degradation, and general trust, inequality creates a roblematic context in which we must all live. In the long run, inequality affects all of us.

NEQUALITY AND THE MEASUREMENT OF CRIME

he quality of life in any society is affected by the amount of crime within it, and many aspects f crime and its consequences appear to be closely related to social inequality. Inequality has een connected to the nature and collection of crime statistics, the likelihood of arrest, the social roduction of crime, and sentencing. In other words, its effect appears to permeate most phases f the criminal justice process. Unfortunately, discussions about the relationship between inequaly and crime are mired in disagreements about the definition of *crime* and the varying statistics bout it.

Clearly, labels applied to persons and actions have an impact on what behaviors are defined s criminal, how much laws are enforced, and how the behavior of individuals is interpreted. ecause of this, the definition of the "crime problem" is a social construction, and the definitions ven by some groups may be favored over those of others. Perhaps you consider the crime probm to consist mainly of street crimes such as rape, robbery, murder, and the like, but others may el that the real crime problem is found in white-collar crime that costs billions of dollars every ear and yet receives less attention in the popular press. In the small city in which we live, it is illegal to "cruise" the downtown in the evenings. What defines *cruising* is rather arbitrary, however. *Loitering* is another rather vaguely defined illegal act. The more one examines various "crimes," the more it becomes evident that they are defined into existence. Similarly, once laws and crimes are defined, their enforcement may also be uneven. In sum, these and similar observations should make us wary in drawing conclusions about crime because statistics about it have several shortcomings.

Because (1) "crimes" are the result of only certain behaviors being defined as illegal, and because (2) police actions appear to be affected by the socioeconomic and racial characteristics of citizens, many have questioned the fairness of the criminal justice system. A 2015 national survey found that only 30 percent of Blacks and 46 percent of those with incomes below $30,000 had "a great deal" or "quite a lot" of confidence in the criminal justice system (Jones 2015b). An examination of men whose guilty verdicts were later thrown out as a result of DNA tests seems to give credence to these feelings. Most were either working class or poor, and 70 percent were either Hispanic or Black (Grimsley 2012). The discussion that follows of the relationship between inequality and crime covers street, white-collar, corporate, and hate crimes. Included are discussions of phases of the criminal justice process, starting with arrests and the commission of crime and ending with sentencing.

STREET CRIME AND INEQUALITY

Crime rates are ordinarily determined by using the FBI's Crime Index, which includes both property crimes (burglary, larceny-theft, motor vehicle theft, arson) and violent crimes (murder, forcible rape, robbery, and aggravated assault). One of the problems with this list of **street crimes** is that it does not include any serious, very costly white-collar, corporate, or "suite" crimes, as they are sometimes called. Since the latter are largely crimes perpetrated by middle- or upper-class individuals, it would be a mistake to look only at the index crimes to reach a conclusion about the relationship between race, sex, socioeconomic status, and crime. To do so would

bias the conclusion against individuals in lower social and economic rankings.

Another point to keep in mind is how perceptions about racial groups affect individuals' fears and views of crime rates. Racial stereotypes and fears may be reinforced by crime reporting by the media that, evidence shows, overrepresents Blacks in stories of criminal perpetrators and that minimize their portrayal as victims of crime. If Whites rather than Blacks are continuously portrayed as the victims, Whites may begin to be more fearful of crime than warranted by the facts, and the lack of attention paid to groups that are the most victimized may result in less public support for policies that would lessen their rate of victimization (Bjornstrom et al. 2010).

Evidence from several cities also indicates that respondents' perceptions of the extent of the crime rate in a neighborhood is affected by the percentage of residents who are Black. The greater the percentage of Blacks in an area, the more likely is the perception of a high crime rate. In fact, the racial makeup of a neighborhood actually has stronger impact on perceptions of high crime rate *than does the actual crime rate*. This provides ample evidence that racial stereotypes are at work in labeling neighborhoods (Schulz et al. 2008). Feelings that one might be a victim of crime are also affected by neighborhood racial composition (Pickett et al. 2012).

This stereotyping of neighborhoods as dangerous according to their racial composition appears evident also in research on police interpretation and actions. A study in Chicago found that Blacks who live in a poor neighborhood are more likely to feel they are treated unfairly compared to those who live in White and higher socioeconomic neighborhoods. Interestingly, the relationship goes the other way for Hispanics, with those in more wealthy neighborhoods more likely to perceive police injustice. The authors speculate that this might be because there is more gentrification in Hispanic neighborhoods, encouraging police to monitor the behavior of the remaining poor people more closely (Schuck and Martin 2013). While these findings are different, they both show the importance that differences in class have for perceptions of police.

Photo 12.1 Thousands of people protest against the police in New York City in 2014. Minorities who live in poor neighborhoods are more likely than others to view police and other governmental authorities with suspicion and to feel they are treated unfairly in the justice system.

©iStock.com/Leonardo Patrizi.

Most Whites believe that police treat people impartially. Minorities, however, tend to see law enforcement as another institution that maintains their subordination (Weitzer and Tuch 2005). There is evidence to support this view. Research finds that racial minorities are more likely to be arrested than Whites in similar circumstances. In a meta-analysis of 27 different datasets, Kochel, Wilson, and Mastrofski (2011) found that Blacks are about 30 percent more likely to be arrested than Whites in comparable situations. The racial characteristics of the victim also seem to make a difference in arrest rates. A South Carolina study showed that when the rate of Black crimes against *Whites* increased, the rate at which Blacks were arrested also increased. When the rate at which Blacks committing crimes against other *Blacks* went up, however, the arrest rate did not increase. This may mean that when Blacks are perceived as a criminal threat against the White majority by authorities, arrest activity intensifies (Eitle, D'Alessio, and Stolzenberg 2002).

Research in Seattle, using multiple data sources, supports the conclusion that racial differences in drug arrest rates are not primarily caused by actual differences in drug usage or the violence associated with it. Rather, arrest rates are strongly tied to police perceptions of the "drug problem" as a "Black" problem, and to "crack" rather than "powder" cocaine as the more dangerous drug (Fellner 2009). Historically, sentencing for crack cocaine crimes was significantly more severe than that for powder cocaine convictions. This had racial effects, as Whites were more likely to be in court for powder cocaine use and Blacks for crack cocaine. In the last 6 years, however, the states and federal government have moved to reduce, but not eliminate, that discrepancy (Steiker 2013).

Whether or not youth have actual encounters with police or are arrested also appears to be related to the socioeconomic status of the persons involved. Police generally have particular images of delinquents, stereotypes that result in lower-class persons being arrested more often (Tapia 2010). In essence, police have certain expectations of the criminal behavior of youths, and these images lead them to more frequently monitor and arrest youths in the lower class, regardless of the frequency of their actual criminal behavior.

Socioeconomic status can have an effect on an individual level, but it can also impact communities. Specifically, the general socioeconomic status of a neighborhood can influence the attention paid to it and its inhabitants by authorities. For example, during the 1990s and early 2000s, a number of cities, led by New York, began to engage in "aggressive order policing." This type of policing requires officers to intervene in situations of minor disorder in communities (for example, loitering or public drinking) on the theory that this will prevent a slide into more serious types of crime. The idea for aggressive order policing was taken from Broken Windows Theory (Kelling and Wilson 1982). Kelling and Wilson found that when police clamped down on small infractions in a neighborhood, residents began to feel less fearful of crime. They extrapolated this finding to argue that aggressive order policing would also ultimately reduce not just fear but crime as well. Aggressive order policing has been highly criticized because it focused police attention on poor neighborhoods and led to "stop and frisk" policies that resulted in poor and minority youth having a disproportionate number of contacts with the police (Howell 2009).

Policies such as aggressive order policing affect the relationship between official rates of crime/delinquency, race, and social class, complicating efforts to draw conclusions about the relationships between them. This should be kept in mind when viewing the information in Table 12.1, which presents the arrest distributions for FBI Crime Index offenses by race and sex of those arrested. In 2013, almost three-fourths of those arrested were men. The highest arrest rate for women was for larceny-theft (43.1 percent). In recent years, the arrest rates for women have increased. While most of those arrested in 2013 were Whites, Blacks were disproportionately represented in the arrest rates for all index crimes. In total, 38.7 percent of all those arrested for violent crimes and 29 percent of those arrested for property crimes were Black. A small percentage of arrests, generally 2–3 percent, involved American Indians, Alaska Natives, Asians, or Pacific Islanders.

TABLE 12.1 Arrests by FBI Crime Index Offense Charged, Estimated Distributions by Sex and Race: 2013

Offense Charged	% Male	% Female	% White	% Black	% Other[a]
Murder and non-negligent manslaughter	88.3	11.7	45.3	52.2	1.3
Forcible rape	98.1	1.9	66.2	31.3	1.3
Robbery	88.6	13.4	41.9	56.4	0.8
Aggravated assault	77.0	23.0	62.9	33.9	1.6
Burglary	83.0	17.0	67.5	30.4	1.1
Larceny-theft	56.9	43.1	68.3	28.7	1.7
Motor vehicle theft	80.1	19.9	66.7	30.5	1.4
Violent crime[b]	79.9	20.1	58.4	38.7	1.4
Property crime[c]	62.2	37.8	68.2	29.0	1.6

Source: http://www.fbi.gov/about-us/cjis/ucr/crime-in-the-u.s/2013/crime-in-the-u.s.-2013/tables/table-43, arrests by race; http://www.fbi.gov/about-us/cjis/ucr/crime-in-the-u.s/2013/crime-in-the-u.s.-2013/tables/table-42

[a]American Indian, Alaska Native, Asian, or Pacific Islander.
[b]Violent crimes are murder and non-negligent manslaughter, forcible rape, robbery, and aggravated assault.
[c]Property crimes are burglary, larceny-theft, motor vehicle theft, and arson.

Social Class, Inequality, and the Commission of Crime

The relationship between social class and actual *commission* of crime/delinquency has been a source of great controversy. While we do not have strong evidence that poverty, in and of itself, leads to delinquency, it is linked to certain circumstances that may increase delinquency. For example, we know that poor children are more likely to end up in foster care, and foster care is linked to increased delinquency (Birckhead 2012). As described in the end of this chapter, poverty is also linked with exposure to lead-based paint, another predictor of delinquency (World Health Organization 2015). On the other hand, there are arguments that suggest that it is the definition of crime, the enforcement of laws, and the judicial and sentencing procedures that work against the lower classes, resulting in higher crime rates and more severe sentencing for those groups. For example, a survey of 187 cities found that, since 2011, there has been a dramatic increase in laws that criminalize behaviors the homeless are more likely to engage in like camping in public (city-wide bans up 60 percent) and begging (up 25 percent) (National Law Center on Homelessness and Poverty 2014).

Past overviews of studies done on the relationship between social class/socioeconomic status and crime/delinquency have yielded inconsistent conclusions (Ellis and McDonald 2001). Part of the explanation for discrepancies in findings on this relationship appears to relate to the measures used for social class and crime. Many of the studies have used occupational prestige, income, or educational hierarchies as measures of class, rather than Marxian measures (e.g., ownership, control over labor). Hagan and his colleagues (1985; 1987), for example, suggested that differences in power ought to be more fully incorporated into studies of class and crime. When one considers that power differences exist between races, classes, and frequently between men and women in families, and may be directly linked to the probability of white-collar crime, the request for other measures of class seems more than reasonable.

The data on the relationship between most measures of class and crime is less clear than that on employment. It appears that employment has a deterrent effect. Research does suggest, however, that the deterrent effect of employment is much stronger for high-quality stable jobs than menial, low-paying, unstable work. For example, Uggen (1999) found that when prisoners return home and obtain a high-quality job, they are less likely to return to prison than if they are employed but at a less desirable job. Among teenagers, we see that employment and criminal behavior also appear to be used as substitutes, at least to a point. Teenagers who work fewer than 20 hours a week are less likely to engage in delinquency, but after 20 hours, work appears to be associated with higher delinquency (Bachman et al. 2011; Staff and Uggen 2003). It is not clear why this is the case.

When it comes to the commission of crime, an analysis of its relationship to inequality involves more than just examining the connection between the statuses of individuals and criminal acts. At the social-structural level, or macro level, the system of inequality itself may be related to crime rates. Unemployment, employment in unstable jobs, gender and racial inequality, poverty rates, and economic deprivation have all been found to be positively related to crime rates (e.g. Chiricos 1987; Devine, Sheley, and Smith 1988; Kposowa, Breault, and Harrison 1995; Phillips and Land 2012).

In a longitudinal study, Phillips and Land (2012) examined data from 1978 to 2005 on the commission of seven index crimes at the county, state, and national levels. Their results are valuable because they indicate that unemployment can have both positive and negative effects on crime, depending on the type of crime. Specifically, unemployment can have a dampening effect on the crime rate because it means that the opportunity to be a victim of a property or violent crime is lower. When people are unemployed, they are at home, among friends and relatives, "guarding" property more often. This means that they are less likely to be victims of crimes by a stranger. On the other hand, unemployment has a positive effect on criminal motivation, thereby increasing the probability of crime, especially property crime. Consistent with these arguments, Fallahi, Pourtaghi, and Rodríguez (2012) analyzed national employment data and found that, in the short term, unemployment increases motor vehicle theft but decreases burglary.

In addition to property crime, violent crime is also related to inequality of different types. In a review of literature from around the world, Nivette (2011) found that countries that have a higher level of income inequality tend to have higher violent crime rates. Hunnicutt and LaFree (2008) analyzed data from 27 countries and found that income inequality was linked to higher rates of infanticide, particularly of female infants. Fajnzylber, Lederman, and Loayza's research (2002) looked at 37 countries and compared income inequality and violent crime (homicide and robbery). They found the two were related both within countries and across countries, suggesting a strong causal relationship. The employment rate also appears to be linked to violent crime. An analysis of 2,462 U.S. counties suggests that high levels of employment (even if it is less than full-time) can lower violent crime rates (Lee and Slack 2008).

The Blau and Blau study (1982) of inequality and violent crime rates in metropolitan areas used official crime statistics from 125 of the largest metropolitan areas in the United States to find out if the crime rates varied with the extent of socioeconomic inequality in the area. Theoretically, they reasoned that in a democracy, inequalities based on skill or other achieved qualities are perceived as justifiable, while those based on ascribed characteristics such as race or sex are not. When a nominal or horizontal trait like race is closely connected to the vertical structure of economic inequality, racial and class differences become consolidated, and conflict between groups occurs. One result of this situation is higher violent crime rates. Their findings bear out this theory. Economic inequality generally, and socioeconomic inequality *within* racial groups in particular, is related to the production of violent crimes (Hipp 2007).

Indeed, homicide rates in democratic societies, including the United States, are related to the degree of economic inequality and the relative deprivation that accompanies moderate levels of inequality. When inequality is moderate so that individuals in the lower ranks can see and compare their own circumstances with others who are better off, feelings of relative deprivation are more frequent and result in higher rates of violence. As the Blau theory suggests, the most volatile combination is when the existing inequality is highly related to ascriptive qualities such as race, and when, at the same time, the society is based on meritocratic principles (Messner 1989). In these societies, where economic differences are closely tied to race, the inequality is seen as illegitimate and more likely to result in violence. Crime rates are positively related to income inequality, especially in situations where individuals in different classes interact and where the inequality is not seen as based on merit. Such inequality fosters a sense of injustice that can instigate criminal behavior among some individuals (McVeigh 2006).

However, high homicide rates are less likely in polar situations where there is either little inequality or extreme inequality. In the latter instance, comparisons that generate feelings of relative deprivation are less probable because of the presence of segregation that eliminates most contact and visibility between higher- and lower-status groups. "Resentment is more likely among the relatively deprived in an affluent society than it is among the absolutely deprived in an impoverished society" (Jacobs and Richardson 2008, p. 31). Given that economic inequality is higher in the United States than in other democratic, industrial nations, it should not be surprising that its homicide rates are noticeably higher as well (Jacobs and Richardson 2008; Pryor 2010).

A reanalysis of the Blau data by Williams (1984) suggested that the level of poverty may also be related to homicide rates, especially in areas outside the South. This supports the findings of other studies (e.g., Danziger and Wheeler 1975; Williams and Flewelling 1988). Resource deprivation is related to higher rates of violent crime (Lee and Slack 2008). As Williams and Flewelling (1988) stated, "It is reasonable to assume that when people live under conditions of extreme scarcity, the struggle for survival is intensified. Such conditions are often accompanied by a host of agitating psychological manifestations, ranging from a deep sense of powerlessness and brutalization to anger, anxiety, and alienation. Such manifestations can provoke physical aggression in conflict situations" (p. 423).

Race, Inequality, and the Social Production of Crime

The statistics presented in Table 12.1 suggest strongly that Blacks are more likely to commit crimes than their counterparts in other groups. This difference in rates, however, is not due primarily to cultural differences, but to differences in the structural contexts in which the groups live. That is to say the causes of Black crime are similar to the causes of crime by any group, but Blacks are exposed more forcefully and thoroughly to social contexts that encourage criminal behavior (this argument about race and social context is sometimes called the "**racial invariance hypothesis**"). Much of this context involves elements related to inequality such as poverty, economic discrepancies, social isolation, poor jobs, and unemployment. For example, one of the arguments used to explain the economic stress faced by minorities has emphasized the role played by the decline of manufacturing and the deindustrialization of cities, leaving only low-wage employment or high rates of unemployment in their wake.

Let us consider the relationship between Black residential segregation and crime more closely. This segregation has been highly intransigent but has declined since 1970. It continues to be extensive, however, especially in the East and Midwest (Iceland, Sharp, and Timberlake 2013). Many cities remain "hypersegregated." Farrell 2008) comments, "The divide between the urban core and suburban ring remains a substantial if not defining component of segregation and racial distinctions between suburban communities are increasing" (p. 467). Segregation of Asian and Hispanic immigrants is present but less extreme than that of Blacks (Parisi, Lichter, and Taquino 2011). Such residential segregation itself is largely a result of inequality processes. Early in the twentieth century, Blacks moved in large numbers from the South to the North, frequently recruited by employers who were fighting unions and who wished to use Blacks as strikebreakers. This only intensified racist feelings among Whites. Fear by Whites led to "restrictive covenants" in neighborhoods and **blockbusting** by real estate dealers who hoped to profit from the Black migration. Later, movement of industry out of cities and increasingly poor opportunities for stable employment impoverished these areas. These developments led to the consequent concentration of Blacks into isolated, overcrowded, poor neighborhoods.

The current extreme segregation experienced by Blacks is not one of choice; in contrast to Whites, most prefer a decidedly mixed neighborhood. Rather, it has been the actions of government, real estate agencies, banks, and the construction industry that have shaped and maintained segregation through their loan and mortgage policies, gatekeeping of neighborhoods, and construction requirements. Sometimes the stereotypes are evident but the style of discrimination is soft and nuanced, as found in these comments by real estate agents who guide Whites away from certain areas:

> Black people do live around here, but it has not gotten bad yet; [or] "That area is full of Hispanics and blacks that don't know how to keep clean"; or (This area) is very mixed. You probably wouldn't like it because of the income you and your husband make. I don't want to sound prejudiced.
> (Farley and Squires 2005, p. 36)

What is important about such segregation is that it means that the tools and avenues needed to succeed are largely out of reach for isolated Blacks; access to decent education, health care, and employment is severely limited. The possibility of investing in a desirable home that would increase in value over time, laying a foundation for future wealth, is also almost nonexistent. These conditions perpetuate the low socioeconomic position of residents and freeze the positions of those middle-class persons who live there. As a structural fact, these conditions are beyond the power of any person to change them (Massey and Denton 1993; Farley and Squires 2005).

The concentration of poverty and unemployment in these isolated and highly dense areas of cities has led to a stable disadvantaged class, the collapse of effective institutions (leading to family disorganization, poor housing, poor employment opportunities), and the development of cultural adaptations that are sometimes different from the mainstream. There is little to bind individuals to the community. Consequently, social controls to minimize crime are not in place; neither institutions nor cultural values are effective in controlling crime in this context. Segregation and Black isolation are highly and directly related to worse neighborhood conditions and thus higher rates of violence and other negative outcomes for youth (Galster and Santiago 2015). This setting results in fewer opportunities and less attachment of Blacks to the wider society. Higher crime rates follow, as do victimization rates, and since it is Blacks who are concentrated in these areas, it is their rates that spiral upward. In 2013, for example, 44 percent of murder victims were Black, even though they compose only about 13 percent of the population (FBI 2013, Table 6). The victimization rates of Blacks and low-income individuals for other kinds of violent crimes are also disproportionately higher than those of Whites and higher-income persons (see Table 12.2). They are higher, too, for urban dwellers.

What is clear from research is that there is strong evidence for the racial invariance thesis—that the causes of crime and victimization among Blacks are not unique. Any individual exposed to an isolated and impoverished environment over time is vulnerable to criminal behavior and victimization (Kposowa, Breault, and Harrison 1995; Sampson and Wilson 1995). At the same time, however, new research suggests that we should be open to the idea that the unique history and cultures of different racial/ethnic groups might strengthen or weaken the relationship between environment and crime (Unnever 2016). For example, poverty may have a stronger impact on Blacks than on other groups because of the history of discrimination against them (Steffensmeier et al. 2010). Future research will allow us to better understand how structural conditions interact with history and culture to produce variations in crime.

It will also be important to further study how community conditions play a role in crime. Living in a poor family that is located in a community that is also suffering economically intensifies the effects of family and neighborhood disadvantage on crime. Thus, it is not just one's immediate poverty but the surrounding context that contribute to violent and other crime rates (Hay et al. 2007; Peterson and Krivo 2009). Thus, to understand differences in crime and victimization rates between rich and poor, Blacks and Whites, we need to appreciate the social context and history that generate such differences.

Gender, Inequality, and the Social Production of Crime

There are a number of theories about why males commit more crime than females. For example, it is possible that crime is a way of expressing masculinity, especially when other routes are blocked (Messerschmidt 1993). Other research finds that males tend to have more delinquent peers, encouraging criminality. This appears to be particularly true in higher-income neighborhoods where the gap in delinquency between males and females is consequently larger (Zimmerman and Messner 2010). While these are important theories, here we focus most on the power control theory of Hagan and his colleagues (1985; 1987) because of its relevance to inequality.

Hagan and his associates collected data from students in Toronto and used a measure of authority and ownership to determine the position of men and women in the households. The authors hypothesized that in families in which wives and daughters have little power, there is less freedom and risk taking on the part of women. Hence, they will be significantly less likely than the sons to commit delinquent acts. It is in these types of families that gender differences in delinquency will be most pronounced. On the other hand, in those families in which females have some freedom and can take risks, there will be little difference between the sexes in their delinquency rates.

The data the researchers collected supported their hypotheses and also revealed that the gender differences in delinquency declined as one went down the class hierarchy. Gender differences were largest in the employer class. A large part of the reason for this gender difference seems to be that sons in this class have greater power relative to their mothers and are not taking as great a risk in being punished as are daughters. In other words, the authors pointed out again that gender differences in delinquency are linked to power differences in the family, which in turn are a reflection of power differences in the workplace. In more recent updates to their theory, Hagan and his colleagues (Hadjar et al. 2007) expand the explanation of gender difference in delinquency to include gender dominance ideology. They posit that families who subscribe to traditional gender roles in the home are more likely to closely monitor daughters. Thus there will be higher rates of delinquency among sons.

Inequality and Criminal Sentencing

The criminal justice system has a number of stages, beginning with the definition of crime, and continuing with labeling of individuals as potential criminals, arrest procedures, court procedures, and sentencing. Because there are so many stages of the criminal justice process, so many different jurisdictions, and because of the complexity of factors that determine outcomes, it can be hard to isolate the impact of race and ethnicity at any specific place or at any given historical moment. At the same time, there is strong and consistent evidence of racial and ethnic disparities at all points in the process (Kalogeras and Mauer 2003). More importantly, however, bias appears to accrue over the criminal justice stages so even if there is not a large disparity at any one point in time, the cumulative effect on a given individual is large (Stolzenberg, D'Alessio, and Eitle 2013).

One of the points at which bias can occur involves release decisions. A recent study of bail decisions in New Jersey found evidence of racial and ethnic bias in the requirement to pay bail, how high the bail was set, and how able the defendant was to meet the bail. Specifically, Blacks and Hispanics were more likely than Whites to be required to pay bail to get a pretrial release, Blacks were assigned somewhat higher bail, and both Blacks and Hispanics were less able than Whites to pay it (Sacks, Sainato, and Ackerman 2015). In another study using analysis of data from 5,000 felony defendants in Ohio, the researchers found that race was generally not a determinant of whether people were released on their own recognizance (without bail). One group was an exception, however; young Black men were less likely to be released on their own recognizance than equivalent young White men (Wooldredge 2012). It is possible that this is because "judges and other court actors develop 'patterned responses' that express both gender and race-ethnicity assessments relative to blameworthiness, dangerousness, risk of recidivism or flight" (Demuth and Steffensmeier 2004).

TABLE 12.2 Estimated Rates of Violent Victimization, by Race/Ethnicity, Sex, and Residence: 2014

Victim/Household Characteristics	Violent Crime Victimization Rate*
Race	
White	20.3
Black	22.5
Hispanic	16.2
Other	23.0
Sex	
Male	21.1
Female	19.1
Residence	
Urban	22.2
Suburban	19.3
Rural	18.3

* Rates for violent crime are per 1,000 persons age 12 and older and do not include murder or manslaughter; rates for property crime are per 1,000 households. All rates rounded.

Source: http://www.bjs.gov/content/pub/pdf/cv14.pdf, Tables 9 and 10.

If a person is convicted of a crime, sentencing is the next stage. Sentencing goes to the heart of questions about the fairness of the criminal justice system. As is the case with likelihood of arrest and conviction, those who are lower in status do worse than others when it comes to sentencing. Even when the type of offense and previous criminal record are taken into account, lower-income individuals have been found to receive longer sentences. After examining results from many studies, Jeffrey Reiman and Paul Leighton (2012) concluded that, generally, "*for the same crime*, the system is more likely to investigate and detect, arrest and charge, convict and sentence, sentence to prison and for a longer time, a lower-class individual than a middle- or upper-class individual" (p. 162). We see this phenomenon play out in the percentage of state prison inmates who reported being in poverty prior to their most recent arrest. In 2004 this figure topped 60 percent, while the percentage of Americans who were in poverty stood at 15 percent (Wheelock et al. 2008).

Black or Hispanic men are especially likely to receive lengthy sentences compared to their White counterparts. Often, although not always, this relationship is found even when other relevant factors such as previous records are taken into account. Harsher penalties are also meted out if the victim of the crime is White and the perpetrator is Black. In cases of murder, the death penalty is more likely to be given to Blacks who have been convicted of killing Whites (Kansal and Mauer 2005). In an analysis of death-penalty eligible cases from 1999 through 2015 in Colorado, researchers found that prosecutors were about five times more likely to pursue the death penalty when the defendant was Black than when he or she was White, even when they controlled for the seriousness of the crime and other variables (Beardsley et al. 2015). In his analysis of 7 years of data from Harris County, Texas, Scott Phillips (2009) found that the probability of receiving the death penalty was 20 times greater for a poor Black person who murdered a respected, culturally and socially involved, high-status person than if a White high-status person killed a low-status, unsophisticated, marginal individual. Moreover, some research suggests that darker-skinned Blacks are more likely than lighter-skinned Blacks to receive the death penalty (Trei 2006).

In January 2014, 42 percent of the 2,979 prisoners under a death sentence were Black, 56 percent were White, and 14 percent reported being of Hispanic ethnicity (they could be of any race). Just under half of death-row prisoners possessed less than a high school education; only 9 percent had any college education at all. Almost all (98 percent) were male (Snell 2014).

MINI-CASE 12.1

Parking Tickets and Jail Time

Should individuals be put in jail or prison if they cannot afford to pay a monetary penalty? In many jurisdictions in the United States, people can be jailed for failing to pay parking tickets or other court-related costs (for example, some defendants are charged for public defenders, and some inmates are charged for room or board or medical care) (Eisen 2015). Recently, a suit about this was lodged against the towns of Ferguson and Jennings in Missouri. In 2013, Ferguson issued 33,000 arrest warrants in these kinds of failure-to-pay cases. One of the people suing Ferguson, Tonya DeBerry, is a 52-year-old grandmother who lives on disability and food stamps. Because she was unable to pay the fines for old traffic tickets, the city issued a warrant for her arrest. In 2014, she was pulled over while giving her 4-year-old grandson a ride in a car with expired license plates. The officer discovered the warrant, and she was handcuffed and taken to jail where she stayed for 2 days (Shapiro 2015). Critics of the jailing for nonpayment of fines policy note that it effectively criminalizes poverty. Others say that people need to find a way to pay fines. What do you think about this question? Should people be sent to jail or not? ■

Most of those people who are given a death sentence are not actually executed (their sentences are overturned or their sentence is commuted or they die a natural death or commit suicide) (Baumgartner and Dietrich 2015). The probability of being executed, however, is higher for Black inmates convicted of killing Whites than it is for other death-row inmates (Jacobs et al. 2007). Not surprisingly, a significantly larger percentage of Blacks than Whites are against the death penalty, in part because they believe the criminal justice system is biased against them. Rather than attributing Black incarceration to bias, Whites, on the other hand, are more likely to believe that Blacks are more prone to violence (Unnever and Cullen 2012).

In addition to the death penalty, length of prison sentences are also related to race. Burch (2015) found that Blacks in Georgia receive sentences that are, on average, 4.25 times higher than similar Whites. Notably, she also found that light-skinned Blacks are given lower average sentences than Blacks with darker skin. Another study found that Blacks were more likely than Whites or Hispanics to be sentenced to prison (Bales and Piquero 2012). At the same time, there is evidence that racial and ethnic disparities vary by crime type, with especially long sentences meted out to Blacks for drug crimes (Warren, Chiricos, and Bales 2012). This may be because drug offenses are considered minority crimes, and consequently result in stiffer punishment for Blacks and Hispanics (Steffensmeier and Demuth 2000). Steen, Engen, and Gainey's (2005) work suggests that sentencing varies across crime types because of racial stereotyping about "normal" crime and dangerousness. Black males fare worse in drug-crime sentencing because it is perceived to be a Black crime and because Blacks are seen as more dangerous.

In contrast to the correlations of race with sentencing, the relationship between gender and sentencing is a little more complicated. In general, however, recent studies suggest that women receive more lenient sentences than men. For example, both Jill Doerner (2015) and Sonja Starr (2012) found that women in federal court are sentenced to less time than are men. There are a number of reasons this may be the case. First, it is possible that judges look paternalistically on women, seeing them as weak and in need of protection (Franklin and Fearn 2008). It may also have to do with the fact that women are more often caretakers of children or elderly adults. A study by Freiburger (2009) found that judges tend to be more lenient toward caretakers. It should be noted that while the research supports the idea that women receive more leniency in court, it also suggests that there is variation based on the type of crime, the circumstances, and the race of the defendant. Crimes in which women act in stereotypically masculine ways, for example, may result in higher sentences. This hypothesis is supported by the fact that women are less likely to be sentenced to prison than men for property or drug crimes, but not for violent crimes (Rodriguez, Curry, and Lee 2006). Women accused of violent crimes are also more likely to be referred for psychiatric evaluations (Thompson 2010).

Photo 12.2 The negative effects of imprisonment go far beyond the isolation, monotony, and regimentation experienced by inmates. They also include strained family relationships, disenfranchisement, and dampening of future economic prospects.

© Dan Bannister/Shutterstock.

Whether a judge is male or female also affects the probability of incarceration and length of sentence, although there is some contradictory evidence as to the direction of the effect. Most research prior to 2005 showed that, in contrast to the image of women as more lenient, female judges tended to be harsher in their sentencing. For example, in a study of the sentencing of white-collar offenders, researchers found that between 1994 and 2004, female defendants received more lenient sentences than men, especially if they appeared before a male judge (Van Slyke and Bales 2013). In an older study, researchers found that female judges were more likely than males to incarcerate an offender and to sentence them for a longer period of time. Judges of both genders were less likely to incarcerate White, older, and female offenders, but this was especially the case for female judges. Female judges were significantly more likely than their male counterparts to give longer sentences to Black repeat offenders. In other words, offender characteristics affect the decisions of women on the bench more so than those of male judges (Steffensmeier and Hebert 1999).

Today new evidence suggests that female judges, at least in the federal system, may actually be more lenient than male judges. In 2005, the Supreme Court case *U.S. vs. Booker* forbade judges to enhance sentences using evidence that was not reviewed by a jury. At the same time, however, it made sentencing guidelines advisory, not mandatory, increasing the potential role of judge discretion. A study of sentencing decisions since 2005 showed that female judges are actually more lenient in terms of sentencing, assigning prison times that were, on average, 1.4 months less than male judges (Yang 2014). Importantly, the study found that the Booker ruling is linked to an increase in sentencing disparities by judge demographics. This does not just include gender, but also includes political affiliation. Further research needs to be conducted in this area.

Prison and Inequality

Incarceration in the United States has grown enormously over the last 30 years. Since 1985,

the number of individuals in federal and state prisons in the United States has increased more than 500 percent to reach almost 2.2 million persons in 2015, giving this nation the largest rate of incarceration in the world (Sentencing Project 2015a). *Jail* inmates totaled more than 744,000 in 2014. Table 12.3 profiles the populations for jails and state prisons. Compared to the outside population, inmates have lower levels of education. Jail inmates are also 8 to 11 times and prison inmates 4 to 6 times more likely than individuals in the general population to have been homeless at least sometime during the year before their incarceration (Greenberg and Rosenheck 2008a; 2008b).

Much has been written about the reasons for mass incarceration and its effects. Several important scholars have linked it to the maintenance of inequality in society. In a widely read book, Michelle Alexander (2012) argued that incarceration is the "New Jim Crow." This new system, like slavery and Jim Crow before it, ensures that Blacks remain economically and socially subservient. Unlike the prior systems, however, the New Jim Crow appears, on its face, to be racially neutral. Loïc Wacquant (2009) makes a similar argument, tracing what he calls "hyper-incarceration" to slavery and Jim Crow. He sees the reduction of the welfare state and the loss of jobs in urban centers as leading to hyper-incarceration becoming the new system to control the poor.

Incarceration has a deep impact on inequality through its effects on individual people. For example, a criminal record makes it very difficult to get a job, particularly for Blacks. Research in Milwaukee found that even with identical résumés, not only were job applicants with criminal records less likely than noncriminals to be called back for interviews, but Black *noncriminals* even got fewer callbacks than Whites with *criminal* records. Whether Black or White, having a criminal record decreases the chances for employment, but this is especially true for Blacks (Pager 2003).

Imprisonment also erodes the employment skills and related human capital of inmates, making them less likely and less eager to seek employment after being in prison (Apel and Sweeten 2010). It should not be surprising, therefore, to find that criminal conviction also reduces one's future income. A spell of incarceration, on average, reduces White men's wages through the age of 48 by 52 percent. The equivalent percentage for Black men is 44 percent and for Hispanic men 41 percent (Western and Pettit 2010). The loss of an inmate's income while in prison, the lower earnings after release, the cost of visiting inmates, and the high probability that the conviction carried monetary fines which need to be paid, all exacerbate the already low incomes of most inmates and their families (Harris, Evans, and Beckett 2010; Wakefield and Uggen 2010; Wildeman and Western 2010). These effects further reduce the chances of building up wealth for the next generation and help reproduce inequality.

TABLE 12.3 Percent Distribution of Jail Inmates and State Prison Inmates

	Jail Inmates (2013)	State Prison Inmates (2014)*
Sex		
Male	86	93
Female	14	7
Race, Hispanic Origin		
White, non-Hispanic	47	35
Black, non-Hispanic	34	38
Hispanic	16	21
Other	3	6

* Includes only those sentenced for 1 year or more in state prisons. "Other" includes persons of two or more races in addition to Asians, Native Americans, and Pacific Islanders.

Source: Minton et al., Census of Jail Populations Changes 2009–2013, U.S. Department of Justice, Bureau of Justice Statistics, December 2015, Table 7 and page 2. Online at http://www.bjs.gov/content/pub/pdf/cjpc9913.pdf. Carson, E.A., Prisoners in 2014. U.S. Department of Justice, Bureau of Justice Statistics, December 2015. Appendix Table 4.

Incarceration also reduces a person's political power because 48 out of 50 states in the United States do not allow prison inmates to vote. Many of these states also severely limit the ability of individuals with felonies voting even after they have served their sentences. As a result, in the 2014 midterm election about 5.85 million citizens, only one-quarter of whom were incarcerated, were not allowed to vote due to having felonies on their records. As described in Chapter 5, this included 1 in every 13 Black men (Sentencing Project 2015b). Many of the disenfranchisement rules were passed after the Civil War during Reconstruction, when Blacks were a potential political force. States in which non-Whites make up a large percentage of the prison population are those most likely to have the most restrictive disenfranchisement laws (Behrens, Uggen, and Manza 2003). Beyond simply forbidding prisoners to vote, strict disenfranchisement rules may also have a dampening effect on voting rates of Blacks and lower socioeconomic groups in general, further weakening the impact of these groups on political outcomes and policies (Bowers and Preuhs 2009). Such laws can affect who gets elected to the U.S. Congress and the presidency (Sentencing Project 2014). Whether intentional or not, both imprisonment and disenfranchisement serve as means of controlling and disempowering Black men.

While we generally think about individual level effects of incarceration, there are also community and macro-level effects. The prison system tends to draw from particular impoverished urban neighborhoods, resulting in what Laura Kurgan and Eric Cadora (2006) called "million dollar blocks." This name reflects the fact that the state is paying at least a million dollar a year to imprison people from these blocks. These neighborhoods suffer as their residents bounce in and out of the prison system. Sociologist Todd Clear says, "Concentrated incarceration in those impoverished communities has broken families, weakened the social-control capacity of parents, eroded economic strength, soured attitudes toward society, and distorted politics; even, after reaching a certain level, it has increased rather than decreased crime" (2009, p. 5).

WHITE-COLLAR CRIME, CORPORATE CRIME, AND PUNISHMENT

All the adult crimes discussed thus far involve those listed on the FBI's Crime Index. **White-collar** or **suite crimes** are not part of the FBI's Crime Index, which raises further questions about equity in the treatment of types of crime generally associated with different segments of the population. Generally, though not always, white-collar crime refers to crimes committed by white-collar persons in the course of their occupations. It is the latter part of the definition that is critical; thus, blue-collar workers who steal or defraud in the course of their jobs might be considered guilty of similar crimes, but ordinarily the focus has been on those in the higher-status occupations.

Since the crime occurs in the context of a job, white-collar crime usually involves a violation of trust. Thus, such acts as misadvertising, price fixing, identity theft, computer scams, insurance fraud, and other kinds of duplicities and misrepresentations are a part of white-collar crime. Losses to the victims of white-collar crime are estimated to be over $250 billion annually, compared to estimates of $18 billion for ordinary street crimes, which receive more publicity (Holtfreter et al. 2008).

More recently, larger-scale corporate scandals have involved alleged insider trading, and accounting irregularities and misrepresentation of company assets that have bilked stockholders and drained the retirement packages of thousands of average employees. Because corporate fraud takes many years to investigate, some of the biggest cases in 2014 were a result of actions taken preceding the recession of 2008. For example, multi-billion dollar settlements were reached with JP Morgan Chase and Bank of America for mortgage fraud that occurred 6 years prior (Henning 2014). Of course, **corporate crime** has not ceased since the recession. For example, there are many recent cases of Medicare fraud by health care professionals including instances of fake clinics that falsify billings in order to get large sums of money from the government. In many cases, the alleged procedures were never performed. In 2013, it was estimated that Medicare fraud cost taxpayers about $36 billion (Center for Medicare and Medicaid Services 2014).

Corporate crime appears to be extensive, and it is expensive. As only one example, an analysis of 959 cases of occupational fraud committed between 2006 and 2008 estimated that organizations lose over $900 billion each year to crimes involving bribery, kickbacks, extortion, deceitful billing, and related offenses. Owners, executives, or managers are the offenders in more than half of the cases, with other employees accounting for the remainder (Association of Certified Fraud Examiners 2008).

Generally, individual white-collar crimes involve many more than one victim. When safety-code violations or price fixing occur, for example, many are harmed or seriously injured. In fact, although one ordinarily does not think of white-collar crime as violent, "there is considerable evidence that so-called 'nonviolent' white-collar criminals kill and maim more people each year in the United States than do violent street criminals" (Messner and Rosenfeld 2012, p. 31). In 2014, over 4,600 workers died from occupational injuries, with 20 percent of the deaths occurring in the construction industry (OSHA 2015). Many non-lethal occupational injuries involve the back. A 2015 investigation, for example, found that 35,000 nursing employees suffer back injuries each year from lifting patients. Many of these painful and debilitating injuries could be prevented if hospitals implemented the correct technology and training (Zwerdling 2015). Health is affected by other types of corporate crime as well. For example, in 2015, an egg company in Iowa bribed an official from the USDA to release eggs that had been held back because of concerns about their quality. Over 2,000 people were sickened with salmonella as a result (FBI 2015).

During the 1970s and 1980s, researchers were interested in understanding the sentencing of white-collar offenses (Simpson 2013). The results from these studies were somewhat contradictory. Some studies found that those in the occupational hierarchy with higher prestige were sentenced more harshly, while others found less harsh punishments (see, for example, Wheeler, Weisburd, and Bode 1982; Benson and Walker 1988).

More recent research on sentencing of white-collar crime is scarce and tends to address disparate sets of questions (Simpson 2013). For example, Bussman and Werle (2006) looked at 5,500 companies around the world. They found high rates of fraud, but low rates of prosecution by companies, largely because the companies did not want to suffer harm to their reputations. This finding is further bolstered by Karpoff, Lee, and Martin's (2008) work looking at the costs to firms who are caught committing fraud. While fines were relatively small, firms incurred huge losses on the market as a result of their damaged reputations. Looking at a different question, Eitle (2000) argued that the people in firms with the most power and authority were less likely to be sanctioned than those who were at lower levels. In contrast, Brickey (2006) found that top management was not more likely to escape prosecution. It is clear that more work needs to be done to understand the dynamics of the prosecution of white-collar crime.

The studies just described investigate interesting and important questions, but they do not address the issues of what percentage of alleged white-collar crimes are actually brought to court, or the length of sentences perpetrators receive. In these areas, there appears to be a greater discrepancy between white-collar and street crimes. This is especially the case for high-level crimes: "The U.S. regulatory and judiciary systems . . . do little if anything to deter the most damaging Wall Street crimes" (Leaf 2002, p. 64). White-collar criminals convicted of massive fraud in the 1980s savings-and-loan crisis served an average of just over 3 years in prison, while common burglars (usually stealing $300 or less) received sentences of 4.5 years, and first-time drug criminals got about 5.4 years (Leaf 2002).

In the fiscal year ending in September of 2014, 8,459 individuals were charged with white-collar crimes and 8,039 (95 percent) were convicted (U.S. Attorneys 2014). On closer examination, however, we find that all kinds of crimes, including welfare fraud, are included in the "white-collar" category, and that only 139 of these cases were for securities or commodities fraud—a common kind of white-collar crime more likely to be perpetrated by well-off individuals. In fact, the number of federal prosecutions of white-collar crime was at a 20-year low in the first three quarters of 2015 (Syracuse University 2015). This may be in part because the Department of Justice increasingly uses "deferred prosecution agreements" and "non-prosecution agreements" in corporate cases. These agreements allow an accused person or corporation to avoid prosecution by agreeing to sanctions (such as fines or changes in policies) (Alexander and Cohen 2015).

Although there is a trend of decreasing prosecution, since 2002 there have also been a number of high-profile convictions of corporate executives for fraud, grand larceny, conspiracy, obstruction of justice, and/or money laundering. These include CEOs at WorldCom, Tyco International, and Adelphia Communications. Former CEOs of Enron and WorldCom were sentenced to 24 to 25 years, for example; a former stock analyst at Goldman Sachs & Co. was sentenced to almost 5 years for his role in a $6.7 million fraud; and British Petroleum (BP) was fined $20 million for its oil spill in Prudhoe Bay, which was a violation of the Clean Water Act (Podgor 2007; "BP Pleads Guilty, Will Pay $20 Million Penalty for Oil Spill" 2008; United States Attorney Southern District of New York 2008). In 2009, a sentence of 150 years was given to stockbroker and investment advisor Bernie Madoff for a **Ponzi scheme** that defrauded thousands of investors of $50–$65 billion.

In 2015, the U.S. Sentencing Commission proposed a number of changes for the handling of white-collar crime. Prior to that, these types of crimes were sentenced based primarily on the total economic gain the defendant received from the crime, with some consideration given to the total number of victims. This led to a situation where a person could get a very high sentence by defrauding a lot of people of very little money, causing little harm. A person who defrauded a few people of a lot of money, however, would receive a lower sentence. Today the Sentencing Commission has proposed that harm and intent be taken into account. They have also lowered the dollar amounts at each sentencing level to account for inflation (United States Sentencing Commission 2015).

At the beginning of this chapter, we noted how crime is often "defined" into existence. The terms used to describe street crime—robbery, theft, murder, and so on—leave little doubt of the nature of the behavior involved. In contrast, white-collar crimes are often described in more ambiguous and softer terms like financial "malfeasance," bookkeeping "irregularities," and "misconduct." "Misconduct" does not seem quite as criminal as "theft," even though *stealing* may be what is involved in both cases. This terminology and the complicated nature of these cases, along with the physical appearance and self-definition of white-collar defendants as upstanding citizens, encourages a different treatment of white-collar defendants. Some argue that the terminology has to become more straightforward: "you've got to boil it down to lying, cheating, and stealing," says a securities board commissioner (Leaf 2002, p. 76).

The special manner in which white-collar crime is treated—including special names for the crimes, special kind of legislation that regulates it, the special kind of enforcement groups used, and the generally minimal types of punishment meted out—indicates that white-collar crime is treated differently than street crime in the U.S. justice system, even though its cost to victims is much greater. Importantly, an additional heavy cost of white-collar crime is the erosion of faith in social institutions that occurs when such crime takes place. Trust is a basis of solidarity, and when it is damaged, society as a whole suffers. Thus, the damage resulting from white-collar crime radiates from the immediate victims to include many more.

The Roots of White-Collar and Corporate Crime

The lower probability that white-collar or corporate crimes will result in convictions and incarceration reflects difficulties and deficiencies in the system of justice: case overloads, ambiguous and vague regulatory laws, powerful law teams at the disposal of some but not others, and the complexity of the cases themselves. These deficiencies help to account for the commission of these types of crime.

But there are other proposed explanations. One argument focuses on the greed and immorality of individual perpetrators. In this view, white-collar crime is the result of a few "bad apples" with character flaws. Cullen, Hartman, and Johnson (2009) argue that the "bad apple" argument is popular in America but that it is dangerous because it diverts attention from the structural conditions that promote white-collar crime. A second—more structural— view emphasizes the role that U.S. and corporate cultures play in encouraging this type of crime. U.S. culture encourages free enterprise and open competition, honors economic winners rather than losers, and winks at those clever people who are able to "pull the wool" over others' eyes. Similarly, and over other values, corporate culture sometimes encourages success and profit making and taking full advantage of opportunities to maximize the bottom line. This may even involve intentionally protecting valuable executives from accusations of criminality (Lyons 2002). Corporations have also begun to publicize their philanthropic acts as a way to seem ethical and above-board, making it even easier for Americans to accept the individualistic bad-apple explanation (Laufer 2014).

A third, and potentially more perceptive, view involves the political structure and economic context within which corporations operate. This is especially relevant for corporate rather than simple white-collar crime. A significant part of the structure that affects corporations is the federal regulation to which they are subject. In this case, regulations are often vague and ambiguous, leaving room for multiple interpretations. They are also complex: "[J]uries have a hard time grasping abstract financial concepts, and well-counseled executives have plenty of tricks for distancing themselves from responsibility" (France and Carney 2002, p. 35). The broadness of the regulations means that while a given activity might be considered immoral, it is not necessarily illegal.

Sometimes changes in rules create opportunities for crime. Banking deregulation in the 1980s, for example, made it possible for savings and loans associations to engage in fraudulent actions because deregulation removed many of the controls that held these institutions in check. Repeal of earlier laws such as the Glass-Steagall Act removed central limitations that had been placed on banks. Deregulation created an economic climate in which greed, risk taking, and corporate crime were encouraged. In addition to lack of effective regulations and lax monitoring of financial trans-actions, resource inadequacies and case overloads in enforcement agencies encourage illicit and unethical activity by lessening the chances of get-ting caught or being indicted. As described, finan-cial fraud cases are extremely complicated, and sometimes juries cannot understand them well enough to render a verdict. The complexity also means that such cases are extremely expensive to try (Kolhatkar 2015).

Finally, corporate lobbying for favorable legislation facilitates regulations that are pro-business. The result is that, while the average person may consider certain legal behaviors to be unethi-cal and even "criminal," they may be allowable under law. For example, the "business-judgment rule" permits business executives to carry out almost any transaction as long as it could be inter-preted as economically sound, committed in good faith, and is not clearly illegal. The broadness of this rule has resulted in executives being protected from many legal actions against them. Rules allowing corporations to export earnings to avoid taxation, allowing stock options to be left unde-fined as company costs, and allowing executives but not other employees to sell company stock during certain times reveal the corporate bias in many regulatory laws. In Charles Derber's opin-ion (2000, p. 148), "[T]he business-judgment rule and the growing set of constitutional rights vested in the corporation have created an unaccountable entity with sovereign powers far greater than nat-ural entity theorists of the Gilded Age could ever have imagined."

Favorable rules and laws, when combined with the lobbying power of corporations, optimize the opportunity to *define* what is legal and what is not. In a broad sense, these conditions demonstrate the role of economic power in directing operations within the criminal justice system. At the same time, there has been change in recent years. For example, the Sarbanes–Oxley Act of 2002 created the Public Company Accounting Oversight Board,

which oversees the mandatory auditing of public companies. It investigates and enforces compliance with financial regulations (Simon 2009). In the wake of the recession, additional regulations have also been put in place. For example, the Dodd-Frank bill went into effect in 2010. It increases the number of crimi-nal offenses that can be invoked in cases of financial wrongdoing. It also expands the number of actors to whom the regulations apply. In an effort to ensure compliance, new regulatory agencies have been cre-ated and others have been combined. At the same time, a number of high-profile corporate crime cases have come to light since the passage of these new regulations, suggesting they are far from perfect (Pontell and Geis 2014).

With respect to corporate crime, a capitalist society in which corporations must successfully compete to survive creates pressures to violate the law. The uncertainties in the social, political, and economic environments in which corporate prof-its must be obtained make success problematic. Additionally, if some firms are engaging in illegal activities, it puts pressure on other companies to do the same so that they can compete (Pontell and Geis 2014). Corporations, like other large organi-zations, try to control their environments in order to create a level of certainty in their operations, and they are powerful actors in their own right. One of the means to create predictability in the resource and consumer markets is to behave in an illegal manner. When legitimate means to obtain-ing organizational goals are either difficult to use or unavailable, pressure exists to obtain legitimate goals such as profit by illegitimate means. This suggests that capitalism itself helps to generate corporate and white-collar crimes.

HATE CRIMES AND INEQUALITY

Social conditions affect the number of crimes committed against members of demeaned status groups. **Hate crimes** are violent or property crimes against someone or some group primarily because of the victim's race, religion, disability [mental or physical], gender, sexual orientation, gender identity, or ethnicity/national origin. One characteristic that distinguishes them from other crimes is the nature of the motivation. Hate crimes have a symbolic function in that they are directed as a *warning* against groups of low status. Consequently, who the specific victims are may be irrelevant to the perpetrator(s) since they serve only as a representative of the group. As warnings, hate crimes are aimed at reinforcing the existing social hierarchies and keeping groups in their place. Thus, their effects of intimidation and fear reach into the entire group, not just the individual victim. Expectations are that hate crimes will not only continue but also increase in the future as the United States becomes more diversified and as pressures mount for dominant groups to share scarce economic, political, and other resources (Perry 2001; Craig 2002).

Knowledge about the extent, causes, and consequences of hate crimes is incomplete for several reasons. First, there has been little systematic research on hate crimes. Second, states vary in the groups that they include as potential victims, making rate comparisons difficult and conclusions about total numbers suspect. Third, hate crimes are underreported and enforcement of hate crime laws is particularly lax in states with a history of lynching and large Black populations (King, Messner, and Baller 2009).

Despite deficiencies, the FBI data are generally used to reach conclusions about hate crimes in the United States as a whole. The gathering of these data began as a result of the Hate Crimes Statistics Act in 1990. In 2013, according to FBI statistics, 5,928 hate crime incidents were reported, involving 7,242 victims. Just under half were racially motivated, with about two-thirds of those crimes directed against African Americans. Race crimes were followed by biases based on sexual orientation, religion, ethnicity/nationality, and disability, respectively (see Table 12.4). About 52 percent of the perpetrators were White, and just under a quarter were Black. Extreme concerns about racial and ethnic purity, continued immigration, job competition, residential infiltration, and the sanctity of marriage and Christianity most often lie behind these biases. Target groups are viewed as threats to the living standards of perpetrators, who see their own way of life as under siege from contaminating elements.

Biases against particular groups are long-standing. As we saw in Chapter 8, abusive acts against Blacks were permitted during slavery, and the creation of the Ku Klux Klan (KKK) after the Civil War helped keep racist fires burning. Current White separatist groups in the United States include the various segments of the KKK, neo-Nazi and skinhead groups, and some extreme Christian groups such as Christian Identity and the Christian Defense League. Today estimates suggest there are about 900 such groups operating in the United States, up from about 600 in 2000 (Berman 2014). Prejudice against gays and lesbians also has deep historical roots, principally highlighted by laws against sodomy, which were in place as early as the 1600s in the United States, and which required the death penalty or severe mutilation as punishment. Such laws continued in many states until 2003, when the U.S. Supreme Court declared them unconstitutional. Among other elements, feelings of superiority and concerns about competition over resources demonstrate the role of status inequality in the production of hate crimes.

One of the more publicized instances of a hate crime was committed in the fall of 1998. Matthew Shepard, a 21-year-old gay college student, was kidnapped, robbed, beaten, and tied to a fence in Laramie, Wyoming. Shepard died from his ordeal less than a week later (Brooke 1998). More recently, Dylann Roof was charged with 33 federal hate crimes and firearms violations when he shot and killed nine Black churchgoers at Charleston's Emanuel African Methodist Episcopal Church (Reuters 2015). In November of 2015, Frazier Glenn Miller Jr. was sentenced to death for the shooting of three people in Kansas. Although all of the victims were Christian, they were shot outside of Jewish institutions. Miller was known to have said that he wanted to kill Jewish people (Associated Press 2015).

Hate crimes legislation is not without its critics, on both the left and the right of the political spectrum. One critique says that crimes such as assault are already illegal, making enhancements to the law unnecessary. Others argue that it is too difficult to figure out intent in a criminal situation. How can you tell if someone committed a crime because of hate or

TABLE 12.4 Number of Incidents and Victims of Hate Crimes by Bias Motivation: 2013

Motivation	No. of Incidents	No. of Victims
Race		
Anti-White	653	754
Anti-Black	1,856	2,371
Anti-Asian	135	164
Religion		
Anti-Jewish	625	737
Anti-Islamic (Muslim)	135	167
Anti-Other Religion	117	137
Sexual Orientation		
Anti-Male Homosexual	750	890
Anti-Female Homosexual	160	191
Anti-Lesbian, Gay, Bisexual, or Transgender (Mixed Group)	277	329
Ethnicity		
Anti-Hispanic	331	432
Other	324	389
Disability		
Anti-Physical	22	24
Anti-Mental	61	75
Multiple-Bias Incidents	6	12
Total	5,928	7,242

Source: http://www.fbi.gov/about-us/cjis/ucr/hate-crime/2013/tables/1tabledatadecpdf/table_1_incidents_offenses_victims_and_known_offenders_by_bias_motivation_2013.xls.

if it was for some other reason? Sometimes a free speech argument is made: that while assault should not be condoned, expressing hate should be considered protected under the first amendment. Some progressive activists also oppose hate crime laws because they believe they do little to deter crime. Others see the laws as a way to placate oppressed people without addressing the systemic roots of inequality. Finally, an argument has been made that we should be working to dismantle the massive prison-industrial complex rather than consigning people to more time in prisons that do little to rehabilitate them (Reddy 2011; Black and Pink 2009).

SOCIAL INEQUALITY AND ENVIRONMENTAL EQUITY

Criminal justice is an issue closely linked to conditions of social inequality, and it affects the community at large. **Environmental equity** is another social problem that has been tied to social, especially racial, inequality. This problem principally concerns the unequal access to land resources and variations in proximity to dangerous environmental hazards. Generally, environmental equity has not been considered a part of the area of social inequality, and consequently, few social-inequality researchers have addressed this issue. Indeed, the first serious studies of environmental equity go back only to the early 1980s.

Since it is reasonable to hypothesize that in the competition for a decent and healthy life, those with fewer resources and less power will lose out to those with more, and since the accessibility of attractive land and geographic location of potentially dangerous wastes likely affect the chances citizens have for a healthy life, the study of environmental equity legitimately belongs in the field of social inequality. Whatever the effects of accessibility and location are, "those impacts will fall unevenly, along existing divisions of wealth/poverty, power/powerlessness; the transformations of nature will tend to occur in a way that reproduces and exacerbates existing social inequalities. In effect, environmental inequality is one facet or moment of social inequality. . . . [It is] a necessary and inevitable facet of social inequalities, embedded in the very fabric of modern societies" (Szasz and Meuser 1997, pp. 116–117).

Awareness of the link between inequality and the environment is not new. One clear example is the 1960s activism of farmworkers, led by Cesar Chavez, to reduce exposure to toxic pesticides and to improve working conditions in the fields. In the 1980s, two major events occurred that led to a wider coalition. The first was the well-publicized success of a group of poor citizens who organized to prevent the construction of an industrial-waste landfill in their North Carolina county. The second involved the publication of three studies, providing evidence that hazardous waste facilities were disproportionately located in areas with large Black populations (Bullard 1983; U.S. General Accounting Office 1983; United Church of Christ 1987). The term "environmental racism" became a popular descriptor for this problem.

In the 1990s, more researchers began to study the locations of treatment, storage, and disposal of hazardous waste facilities (TSDFs). They also examined the degree of exposure to toxic chemical releases as measured by the U.S. Environmental Protection Agency's (EPA) Toxic Release Inventory (TRI). In general, reviews of these TSDF and TRI studies concluded that race was a significant predictor of TSDF location, even though some of the studies had methodological limitations (Ringquist 2000; Lester, Allen, and Hill 2001). Research also found that poor, working class, and Black individuals are more likely than other groups to live near environmental hazards or facilities that emit polluting chemicals (Mohai et al. 2008; Scanlan 2009). Daniels and Friedman (1999) examined aerial release of more than 300 toxic chemicals over all U.S. counties, as recorded by the TRI. The results showed a positive relationship between the proportion of the population that was Black and the emission of toxic chemicals, even when controls such as urbanization and presence of manufacturing were considered. Researchers found that income was curvilinearly related to the amount of chemical releases. Poor and wealthy areas had lower emissions than moderate-income or working-class counties.

Similar findings were uncovered by Ringquist (1997) in his study of the location of TRI facilities across the country. Briefly, he found that zip codes that had disproportionate numbers of Blacks and Hispanics were also more likely to have TRI facilities. This was also the case for working-class, older, urban, industrial areas. However, somewhat paradoxically, Ringquist also found that even though wealthy areas are less likely to contain any TRI facility at all, those that do are more likely to have multiple facilities. That is, income is positively related to the *density* of TRI facilities.

The fairly consistent research finding that minority populations are more likely to live near TSDFs or be exposed to toxic chemical releases from manufacturing plants raises the question of causality. How do minority populations come to be at higher environmental risk? Is it pure racism? What were these areas like when plants first decided to move into them? Were they disproportionately composed of minorities? Do such plants intentionally locate in these areas because of the high minority population or for other reasons? Or do minority populations move into these areas because of the greater affordability of homes and availability of industrial jobs? And if they do move into these areas, is it by choice or because they are constrained to do so? The process by which race, class, and environmental risks become linked needs to be more clearly identified to reach a fully satisfactory conclusion about the existence and nature of environmental racism.

Some of the described research does suggest that racism is involved because housing segregation may indirectly contribute to the disproportionate exposure that Blacks receive. That is, because Blacks are more limited than Whites in where they can live, they are more often funneled into living in urban industrial areas where manufacturers emit toxic chemicals (Boer et al. 1997; Daniels and Friedman 1999). Another potential reason for the relationship is that some areas may have been zoned or targeted for industrial development by local officials, and TSDF plants, for example, may locate in a particular area because of these regulations (Boone and Modarres 1999). On this level, if racism is present, it may have resulted from the actual zoning or local planning process rather than from policies of company plants. Local residents sometimes have little power or awareness in these types of decisions. While the EPA does allow communities to file civil rights complaints, 9 out of 10 are rejected or dismissed (Lombardi 2015).

Environmental inequities can take forms other than hazardous waste or airborne chemicals. Lead poisoning is a problem that many people associate with the 1970s and 1980s, but, in fact, it continues to be a problem today, particularly for the poor. In 2014, there were a half million children diagnosed with dangerously high lead levels (CDC 2015). In the past, both paint and gasoline were made with lead. Most houses before the 1950s were painted with this lead-based paint. The lead was added to make the paint more water resistant, durable, and vivid. Lead was also added to automotive gasoline starting in the 1920s to decrease wear and tear on the engine, to increase the octane rating, and to reduce engine knocking.

While lead certainly has useful properties, it is also toxic, especially to children. Lead exposure can lead to a large range of negative health outcomes in children, including lowered IQ, behavioral problems (like decreased attention span), and reduced educational attainment (WHO 2015). There are also a wide range of physical symptoms from lead exposure, up to and including death. While controversial, some scientists have linked increases in the crime rate during the 1960s and 1970s with high levels of lead exposure in children who came of age during those years (Drum 2015). Regardless of whether this association is true or not, we know that when children are lead poisoned, the inequalities can last a lifetime. Children generally get lead poisoning from eating chipped paint or inhaling dust in old houses. While people of all backgrounds are susceptible, the problem has hit poor communities disproportionately hard because the houses in these neighborhoods are older and more run-down. The poor are also less likely to have their children tested for lead exposure and/or to have access to information about lead poisoning.

While its use decreased from the 1950s to the 1970s, lead paint was not outlawed for houses until 1978, although the government ordered a phase-out starting earlier in the decade. Sales of leaded gas for on-road vehicles became illegal in the U.S. in 1996. Even with these restrictions, about 34 percent of houses with children under the age of six still contain lead-based paint. The percentage is considerably higher among low-income households (HUD 2011). Other cases of lead poisoning have been tied to toys and jewelry imported from China. An example of a recent spike in lead poisoning occurred in New Orleans after Hurricane Katrina (Rabito et al. 2012). As people returned to their badly damaged homes, they were forced to renovate, uncovering lead paint.

Another tragic example of lead poisoning and environmental injustice plagues the former manufacturing boomtown of Flint, Michigan. In the 1950s, Flint was the second largest General Motors (GM) auto manufacturer in the United States. As the deindustrialization of America began in the 1980s and continued through the 1990s, GM closed and relocated some of its manufacturing plants. This left many rust belt cities, including Flint, reeling. The 2014 American Community Survey found that even 20 years after the GM plant closings, Flint had not recovered. Today 41.6 percent of the city lives below the poverty level (U.S. Census Bureau 2014a; 2014b). Though poverty is a problem for all demographic groups, the rate for Blacks is particularly high, hovering just under 50 percent (U.S. Census Bureau 2014a; 2014b).

Because of these high poverty rates, there is a low tax base to support city services. This has caused budget problems for many years, and ultimately the state took over the management of the city, giving a great deal of power to a governor-appointed city manager. In April 2014, the manager (in consultation with state-level workers and agencies) approved a switch in the city's water source from the more expensive Lake Huron, which is Detroit's water source, to the local Flint River (Graham 2016). Although river water is more corrosive than lake water, the switch was done without using any type of corrosion inhibitor, causing the pipes to begin to leach lead into the water (Roy 2016a). Marc Edwards, a professor and water engineer began an independent study of the water quality in the summer of 2014 (Graham 2016). His team found blood-lead-level spikes as early as that summer, just months after the switch (Bliss 2016).

Through the Freedom of Information Act, Edwards was able to obtain a July 2015 internal report from the Michigan Department of Health and Human Services that alerted officials that lead poisoning rates "were higher than usual for children under age 16 living in the City of Flint during the months of July, August, and September, 2014" (Bliss 2016). Edwards continued on with his study and in the fall of 2015 found that the water in Flint had many times the recommended EPA [Environmental Protection Agency] limit for lead particles (Graham 2016).

After the EPA warned Michigan officials in February 2015, Governor Snyder and the emergency manager commissioned two state agencies to conduct further studies (Maddow 2015). However, there were methodological problems in how the tests were conducted, and the details of the results were withheld from Flint citizens. By the fall of 2015, however, reports from pediatricians of high lead levels in children could no longer be ignored (Bliss 2016; Roy 2015). It was clear that although Flint residents were paying some of the highest water bills in the United States, they were slowly being poisoned (Roy 2016b). The governor authorized the switch back to Detroit water in October 2015, but lead poisoning cases continued to emerge. It was not until January 2016, however, that the governor finally took action to address the effects of the lead poisoning. This was 20 months after the water switch and at least several months after he knew about the toxic lead levels (Bliss 2016; Graham 2016).

At the time of this writing, there is no law on the Michigan books "to punish state employees who intentionally distort data to change the outcome of an official report," though one state representative

had planned to introduce such a law (Carmody 2016). In the meantime, the United States Department of Justice and the United States Attorney's Office are looking into the water contamination and the subsequent handling of the situation (Bliss 2016). This leaves Flint residents to await their fate and attempt to plan for their own medical futures. Though the water has been switched back to the safe Lake Huron source, it still remains dangerous to drink, and officials are not sure how long it will remain dangerous (Ingraham 2016). It is likely that an entire generation of poor Flint city children—many of whom were already struggling with poverty—will grow up with the consequences of lead poisoning.

A final example of how environmental issues and inequality are related involves natural disasters. Obviously, events like hurricanes and tornados do not discriminate, but inequality can shape both preparedness for disasters and what happens in their wake. For example, in August of 2005, Hurricane Katrina struck the southern coast of the United States. It caused extensive damage and was the costliest storm on record in United States history; Katrina displaced more than a million people, killed over 1,800, and caused $151 billion of regional damage (Dart 2015). Preparedness plans were put into action as government officials and citizens from Texas to Florida watched the massive hurricane approach. After the storm hit, however, it became obvious that the preparedness plans had left some communities more vulnerable than others.

Poor and majority Black communities, especially in metropolitan New Orleans, were inadequately unaccounted for in the evacuation plan and recovery process. For example, the New Orleans evacuation plan assumed people would use their own cars to flee the city. The 100,000 people who did not own cars were supposed to find someone, a "good Samaritan," to help transport them to safety (Strolovitch, Warren, and Frymer 2006). Because New Orleans was and remains divided along class and race lines, poor Blacks were left stranded when they could not escape the storm.

One of the poorest areas in New Orleans, the Lower Ninth Ward, is geographically isolated from

Photo 12.3 Toxic waste sites, which can be significant health hazards, are more likely to be located in areas populated by minorities and those of lower socioeconomic status. Home property values near these sites suffer, making it more likely for those with little capital to be able to afford homes there, but also making it less likely for residents to move from there.

© deserttrends/Fotolia LLC.

rest of the city by a shipping channel. New leans is already below sea level, but this portion the city was directly surrounded by floodwalls lding the water back. When the storm surge broke levees, the entire city was flooded, and the wer Ninth Ward experienced the worst of it with ter up to 12 feet deep (Neuman 2015; G. Allen 15a). The people and families that remained in w Orleans throughout Hurricane Katrina found ir way to the city's last-resort shelter: the Louisi-a Superdome. The Superdome ended up serving a shelter for between 9,000 and 20,000 people day during and after Katrina. The National ard only had enough water to give two bottles a y to each adult, there was no electricity, the toilets rflowed for days, and many waited in line for rs to get meals only to be told there was no food (Gerhart 2005). One National Guard militiaman nmented that there was no plan in place to help vide these basic necessities (Gerhart 2005).

A week after the storm, the Pew Research nter conducted a poll to see how Whites and Blacks viewed the recovery effort. Fifty-five percent of Whites and 77 percent of Blacks thought that the federal government was only doing a fair or poor job in responding to Hurricane Katrina. Seventeen percent of Whites and 66 percent of Blacks believed that the response would have been faster if most of the victims had been White (Ross 2015). This poll showed two distinct views about how the federal government treated their citizens in crisis: "Race so clearly shapes American life that black and white Americans do not view even cataclysmic events in anything approaching the same way" (Ross 2015).

This disparity in how Whites and Blacks felt during the storm and the recovery was furthered when wealthier areas of New Orleans were cleaned up first and the Lower Ninth Ward was last to get its power and water back (G. Allen 2015a). Many had hoped that Hurricane Katrina would provide an opportunity for the city to start over without duplicating the racial and class inequities that existed before the storm. However, today the poverty rate for the metropolitan area is 27 percent, the same as pre-Katrina levels, but the median household income of Whites continues to be considerably higher than that of Blacks. For example, within the city, the 2013 median household income for Blacks was 54 percent lower than it was for metro-area Whites. Nearly half of Black households made less than $20,900 a year, and the bottom 20 percent made less than $12,301 a year (Data Center et al. 2015). Even more telling, today average incomes for White residents of New Orleans are on par with national income averages for Whites, but Black median household incomes are 20 percent lower than the national Black median household income level (Dart 2015). These racial disparities make residents believe that recovery efforts have helped Whites and the wealthy more than minorities and the poor (Hamel, Firth, and Brodie 2015).

The city's business district has made a significant economic recovery, but the wealth has not been distributed to the poorer areas that are still in need of rebuilding. Several uptown neighborhoods surrounding the business district are quickly gentrifying—the character of the neighborhood is changing and the majority of the original residents can no longer afford to live there (G. Allen 2015b). With gentrification pushing out original residents, the city continues to segregate itself along Black and White race lines. The index of dissimilarity is used to measure segregation between two racial groups. New Orleans has a dissimilarity index of 68; this means that 68 percent of the population would have to move to a different area in order for Blacks and Whites in the city to be equally distributed. In the city, segregation has increased since Hurricane Katrina (Brown University 2010).

Post-Katrina New Orleans was not seen as welcoming by many of the Black and poor prior residents. In fact, about 100,000 never returned to the city (G. Allen 2015b). Their homes were too destroyed to rebuild, and they were forced to seek opportunity elsewhere. The limited resources distributed to poor Black citizens of the city after Katrina serve as a reminder that "while a hurricane is natural, the shape and extent of its damage is largely determined by man-made factors" (Snyder 2005).

INEQUALITY, TRUST, AND SOCIETAL WELL-BEING

Like the effects of a stone thrown on the water, the effects of inequality ripple outward from the individual, to groups and neighborhoods, and ultimately to the society as a whole. Moreover, its negative effects do not simply impact the unfortunate and minorities. *Everyone's* quality of life is damaged by high levels of inequality. In their review of evidence from dozens of studies, Wilkinson and Pickett (2009) found that greater income inequality was related to higher rates of violent crime, including homicide, obesity, poor educational achievement, mental illness, racism, hostility, morbidity, teenage births, imprisonment, and drug overdose. Inequality also helps generate governmental corruption, a greater sense of injustice among citizens, more political activism outside the voting booth, and less participation and charity-giving in the community. In a broad sense, it creates what Rory McVeigh (2006) refers to as a "social structure of discontent." Times of economic difficulty further weaken civic participation because people in tough financial straits "lose some of their trust in society" (McManus 2010, p. A11).

Within the structure of inequality in which we all live out our lives, social relationships are more tenuous and more restrictive. At the same time, in a democracy like the United States, increased contact between individuals from different income classes can intensify feelings of relative deprivation among those in the lower ranks, and magnify perceptions of the degree of economic difference between themselves and others. Inequality weakens the belief that we are all in this together; rather, it "draws attention to conflicting interests between the haves and the have-nots" (McVeigh 2006, p. 521). Social solidarity is especially weakened when inequality is tightly linked to religious and racial heterogeneity in society. This is because social ties *within* each racial, religious, and economic group will be stronger than those *between* different groups. The implication here is that societies which have less inequality will create stronger feelings of trust among its citizens as well as a sense of a common fate (Jordahl 2007).

Indeed, in cross-cultural studies and in research in the United States, the degree of economic inequality is inversely related to the degree of trust among populations. Greater inequality means less trust (Rothstein and Uslaner 2005; Jordahl 2007; Wilkinson and Pickett 2009). Multiyear data from the General Social Survey indicate that states with less inequality and more racial/ethnic homogeneity have higher levels of trust. States in the North and Northwest (North Dakota, Montana, Minnesota, South Dakota, and Wyoming) are relatively more homogeneous, have more income equality than other states, and are highest in trust. In contrast, states in the South and Southeast (Mississippi, Alabama, Arkansas, and North Carolina), which have more racially mixed citizenries and significantly more income inequality, exhibit less trust within their populations (Alesina and La Ferrara 2002).

If one thinks of a civil society as one in which most individuals are fully and cooperatively joined with others in a common enterprise that benefits all of society, that is, one in which social capital is widely and deeply spread, and one in which civility, diversity, and justice are respected (Persell 1997), then it is clear that economic inequalities weaken our civic life as a society. One of the central casualties of income inequality and inequality of opportunity is a decline in social trust within the population. This decline is significant because increases in distrust weaken faith in governmental institutions, involvement in civic activities, tolerance toward those who are different, personal happiness, and feelings of control over one's life. Trust in others implies that there is some underlying agreed-upon morality which knits different groups of society together in basic ways (Rothstein and Uslaner 2005; Zmerli and Newton 2008). The absence of such a common moral standard makes it less likely that all groups can work together effectively in the common cause that is the whole society.

Trust is especially critical in large, complex, increasingly heterogeneous societies like the United States in which virtual strangers with frequently conflicting interests must interact with each other. The instability, unpredictability, and openness of social relationships make trust a valuable commodity in part because it lowers the psychological, social, and economic prices we pay for monitoring others' behavior and enforcing rules (Jordahl 2007). "Generalized trust links us to people who are different from ourselves . . . [and it] depends upon a foundation of economic and social equality" (Rothstein and Uslaner 2005, p. 45). When inequality is high, trust is low, and in this context, the probability is low that the government will successfully enact social programs in which all groups are seen to benefit. Ultimately, inequality makes it difficult to find widespread acceptance for broad public policies that would address inequality. Thus, inequality is related to trust both as a cause and as a consequence, the result being that some countries find themselves in a repeating cycle of inequality and distrust (Rothstein and Uslaner 2005).

The fact that inequality increases distrust suggests that groups having varying positions of advantage in the income and status hierarchies will display different levels of trust—and they do. Compared to other groups, greater percentages of Blacks and those with lower incomes and educations have little trust in others (Alesina and La Ferrara 2002; Smith 2010). The reasons for these relationships appear to be relatively straightforward. Individuals from these groups are more likely to have experienced some recent traumatic event in their lives (e.g., unemployment, hunger, prejudice), and to have experienced discrimination or mistreatment historically. They are also less likely to have been materially successful. Blacks and other minorities, for example, distrust more often because they believe that they have been treated unfairly, compared to other groups. Living in neighborhoods that suffer from high rates of unemployment, poverty, and violent crime exacerbate feelings of fear and distrust, feelings that can be passed on to the next generation (Alesina and La Ferrara 2002; Smith 2010).

SOCIAL CONSEQUENCES ON A GLOBAL SCALE

In this chapter we focused on how inequality is linked to crime within the United States. Pratt and Godsey's study (2003) reveals that the crime/inequality relationship exists globally as well. They analyzed data from 47 countries and found that income inequality was positively related to a country's homicide rate. Its effect was especially noticeable when the amount of social support provided for the population by the government was low. The percentage of a country's gross domestic product used in public spending on health care was how the authors measured the degree of "social support." This suggests that the civic and political framework within which citizens live has an impact on the role that inequality plays in generating violent crime. If not paid by the government, health care costs can place an economic strain on individuals, a strain that may, together with other economic needs, instigate crime.

This chapter also described how inequality is linked to environmental risk in the United States. Poor and minority people are more often exposed to lead and other contaminants and, in the wake of environmental disasters, are less likely to get help. Looking globally, we find this relationship on a macro scale. For example, poor countries are more likely to have environmental problems than rich countries, and, in many cases, these problems can be traced back to actions taken by the richer countries. This is true in the case of the disposal of electronic waste like old computers and phones. More than 20 percent of the waste that OECD countries (which includes the U.S. and many other developed countries) dispose of are shipped to developing countries such as China, India, Nigeria, and Ghana. Workers in these countries sometimes burn the devices, releasing dangerous toxins into the air and potentially harming their own health. The soil at the disposal sites ends up with hazardous levels of heavy metals (Bradley 2014).

The state of Brazil's Amazon rainforest is another example of the ecological damage developed countries cause at the expense of less-developed countries. Brazil has destroyed large swaths of its rainforest in order to use the land for other purposes. For example, they will soon become the second largest producer and exporter of soybeans in the world, growing them on land that was once rainforest (Garcia-Navarro et al. 2015). Brazil also makes money from the rainforest through its export of Amazonian wood. The United States is the biggest importer of this wood, with a full third coming from Brazil. Even though the U.S. has regulations about the sources of the imports, it is difficult to track wood's origin and illegal imports can easily enter the country (Garcia-Navarro et al. 2015).

At the same time that developed countries benefit from products that destroy the rainforest, they also pressure Brazil's government to engage in conservation efforts. Brazil has, overall, decreased the rate of deforestation, but the cumulative rainforest loss is still growing. In 2014, the amount of the Amazon rainforest that was destroyed was equal to the entire Olympic National Park in Washington State. One of Brazil's wealthiest senators, who has been called "the founding father of deforestation," has criticized the U.S. for pressuring Brazil to conserve the rainforest (Garcia-Navarro et al. 2015). He says that because the U.S. "made the mess to begin with," and continues to benefit from the Amazon's deforestation, the nation should not be forcing Brazil to carry out costly conservation efforts. There is compelling evidence to suggest, however, that the continued destruction of the Amazon may result in increasingly intense droughts and severe heat waves that will have worldwide effects (Garcia-Navarro et al. 2015). These potential environmental disasters will be difficult for poorer nations to escape, as they will not have the resources to take care of their people or safeguard their economies like wealthier nations can.

In the first major global study to estimate the costs of rich countries' ecological impact, researchers examined human activities during the period 1961–2000, and estimated that the cost of the damage brought about by practices in wealthy countries totals well over $2 trillion. "The imbalance of activity and harm is most pronounced for low-income countries. Our analysis highlights the ecological harm poor countries bear to indirectly enable the living standards of wealthier countries" (Srinivasan et al. 2008, p. 1771). The authors suggest that continued globalization and economic development may even widen the gap in ecological harm borne by poor and rich countries. Global climate change—which is predominately caused by developed countries—is likely to have a disproportionate impact on poor countries and on poor individuals within countries. For example, India is dependent on the monsoon for drinking water and for water for agriculture. The Intergovernmental Panel on Climate Change believes that climate change is already resulting in a more erratic monsoon season. Too little rain can result in famine, and too much rain too quickly can cause flooding and crop damage. If India sees a number of erratic seasons in a row, it is likely to force impoverished rural people into the cities, causing chaos and even deeper poverty (*Economist* 2015).

Given the worldwide movement of capital, finances, and resources, it should not be surprising that the ill effects of inequality spread beyond national boundaries. Many of the same processes evident in the United States are manifested on the global stage. Importantly, economic or environmental actions taken in one country can have a severe impact on others.

Summary

Inequality can affect behavior and social events in several ways. At the outset it was stated that not only individual position in the system of inequality but also the system as a whole can have such effects, and in this chapter concern was expressed for both aspects. We looked at the relationship between class, race, sex, and crime rates, as well as the relationship between capitalism/inequality and crime rates in general, and found that in each case inequality is implicated in the incidence of crime. Official statistics reveal a relationship between being Black and of low income and the probability of being arrested. The bulk of the studies on sentencing suggests a bias against groups of lower socioeconomic standing. A variety of data, then, raise questions about the fairness of the criminal justice system. The definition of the crime problem in terms of FBI Crime Index offenses, the special treatment given to white-collar crime, the frequent discovery that SES is related to likelihood of arrests, official reporting of crimes, and type of punishment strongly suggest that justice is not evenly meted out in U.S. society. Moreover, the findings of a relationship between income inequality and property crime rates further suggest that inequality helps produce crime and that reductions in inequality may produce reductions in property crime. Hate crimes, motivated by biases against particular demeaned status groups, also reflect the social inequalities perceived by different clusters of people.

Recent evidence has also raised the possibility of environmental racism. There appears to be a relationship between the presence of minority and working-class populations and environmental pollutants. The social consequence of this inequity is that these populations are disproportionately exposed to potential health hazards. Issues of environmental equity and competition over land will become only more prominent as the U.S. population grows and diversifies.

Finally, it was stressed that inequality has negative implications for the whole society because it creates an environment that lowers the quality of life for everyone. In fomenting distrust between individuals and groups, inequality stalls the development of a vibrant civic culture in which community interest takes precedence over self-interest. In an increasingly heterogeneous society, social and economic inequality becomes an even stronger predictor of division and separation.

Critical Thinking

1. What must be done to change the living conditions in inner-city and low-income neighborhoods that help generate street crime?

2. Historically, why has ordinary street crime received more attention from authorities than white-collar and corporate crimes when evidence suggests they

result in greater costs for individual victims and society than street crime?

3. How can trust between individuals be increased, given that the United States is a religiously, ethnically, and racially heterogeneous society? Is complete equality necessary for this to happen?

4. As competition for them increases, how can access to desirable spaces and land be made equitable? What role, if any, should the government play in this process?

Web Connections

The Sentencing Project regularly collects and reviews information on prison populations, state laws, sentencing issues, and criminal justice in general. It is a good place to find data summaries on a variety of law enforcement topics. Go to www.sentencingproject.org.

Film Suggestions

Broken on All Sides (2012). A documentary about mass incarceration in the United States with a focus on race and inequality.

The Great Invisible (2014). Examines the Deepwater Horizon oil spill—both its causes and its consequences. Corporate negligence and health impacts are both covered.

Prison Kids (2015). Provides a view into the juvenile justice system through the stories of four different young people.

Chasing Ice (2012). Breathtaking images of the Arctic glaciers taken over 3 years with time-lapse photography. Provides evidence for and discussion of climate change.

CHAPTER 13

Social Inequality and Social Movements

If I can't dance, I don't want to be a part of your revolution.

EMMA GOLDMAN (1869–1940)

In societies where extensive social inequality not only exists but is also perceived as being unjust, it is not unusual for people to demonstrate their feelings against it. The large-scale Black Lives Matter protests in 2015 across the country are a good example. Systems of inequality instigate social movements aimed at altering them, and conversely, the degree of ultimate success of social movements is measured in terms of their impacts on those systems. The extent to which either of these relationships is actualized, as you will see, depends on structural, cultural, and historical conditions in the society at the time. Economic shifts, prevalent ideologies, political policies, and unique historical events all impress themselves on the shapes of inequality and social movements.

Consistent with the multidimensional focus of treatment, this chapter will explore three social movements related to class, race, and gender that were explicitly aimed at reducing inequality and improving the life chances of the groups in question or individuals at the intersections of these groups. The early labor movement of the latter part of the nineteenth century and the first decades of the twentieth century in the United States, the civil rights movement of the 1950s and 1960s, the current Black Lives Matter movement, and the women's movement of recent decades are examples of concerted efforts to change social and economic conditions for their constituencies. The purpose here is not to provide an exhaustive history of these movements, but rather to demonstrate systematically how each of them grew out of conditions relating to the structure of social inequality at the time, and how that structure affected the ebb and flow, goals, and tactics of those movements.

THE LABOR MOVEMENT

One of the first things to understand when examining any social movement is that the wider social, historical, and cultural context in which it takes place has an impact on the development, shape, and ultimate fate of the movement. Raymond Hogler and colleagues contend that the viability of a continuously strong labor movement has been made problematic in the United States by cultural values associated with the founding of the country. Beliefs in individualism, small government, a Protestant ethic, the sanctity of private property, free markets and free labor, have made it difficult for the labor movement to prosper on a consistent basis (Hogler, Hunt, and Weiler 2015).

Obviously, the poor conditions and deprivations experienced by industrial workers in the latter part of the nineteenth and early part of the twentieth centuries created dissatisfaction and feelings of hostility. Even though there was some improvement in wages after 1880, hours were long, wages remained low, and working conditions were dangerous. There were few, if any, protections against the hazards of chemicals, machinery, and inhalants from work in the mines and mills. Laborers on the railroads and in construction and logging industries also were exposed to extreme dangers. There was little concern for safety, and many of the wildcat strikes of this time were related to safety issues.

Writing of the period between 1865 and 1917, Asher (1986) observed that "industrial workers have been victimized by low wages, company stores, blacklisting, arbitrary dismissals, forced overtime, sexual exploitation, company spies, police brutality, and a host of other ills" (p. 115). Some of the dangers were inherent to the nature of the work and the technology used, and the fear of competition and concern for profit kept employers preoccupied with matters other than safety (Asher 1986). The early scientific-management movement among employers sought to organize, systematize, and thoroughly gain control of the workplace for management. In order to keep production and efficiency up in the early twentieth century, the pace of work in many plants was accelerated, stopwatches were used, and work was constantly checked by inspectors. This created further alienation among workers.

Living conditions in most instances also left much to be desired. Dubofsky (1975) described a typical immigrant residential area in Pittsburgh: "Situated in what is known as the Dump of Schoenville runs a narrow dirt road. Frequently strewn with tin cans and debris, it is bereft of trees and the glaring sun shines pitilessly down on hundreds of ragged, unkempt, and poorly fed children" (p. 23). The company towns and cramped urban ghettos made for dreary living conditions. In his study of "How the Other Half Lives," Riis (1890) described the conditions in which New York City workers lived. He found "an urban jungle of exploitation, family disintegration, crime, and human degradation" (quoted in Green 1980, p. 20). Even as late as the 1920s, living conditions for most workers were still poor. During these years, although some improvements were made, work was hard, hours were long, and the level of wages left little money for leisure and recreational activities. In 1929, 42 percent of families had incomes below $1,500, which was barely enough to keep a four-person family going (Zieger 1986). In sharp contrast, the richest 1 percent held almost one-third of all the nation's private wealth. Economic inequality was obvious and extensive.

The awful circumstances of the lives of most industrial workers alone do not explain the development and continuation of the labor movement over time. The growth of the labor movement was affected by a combination of external and internal factors. Externally, the strength of workers tended to be greater when there was a tight labor market; this gave them greater bargaining power. Strength also grew when economic opportunities were plentiful. The chances of a labor movement being successful also were enhanced when society allowed a variety of political and legal expressions and permitted greater access to resources (Hogler 2015). This occurred, for example, during the 1930s after Franklin Roosevelt's election and passage of the Wagner Act, which legalized the right to unionize. These events created alternate sources of power, and when the potential for political and economic power of labor was high, so was the solidarity of workers. The belief by workers that they would be spending a large part of their lives in their jobs and that they could make a political difference in society also increased their solidarity and the probability of a labor movement.

Sources of Control over Workers

Not surprisingly, employers were interested in keeping the power of labor to a minimum, and used a variety of techniques to divide and control workers (Griffin, Wallace, and Rubin 1986). With their superior political resources and generally better organization, employers fought workers in bloody battles in the latter part of the nineteenth century and well into the twentieth century. To weaken worker solidarity, employers replaced native workers with unskilled immigrants and used them and Blacks as strikebreakers. This created animosity and weakened the cohesiveness of labor in general.

A second technique that created divisions within the ranks of labor involved reorganizing the division of labor. For much of the nineteenth century, craftsworkers had exercised a great deal of control over their work and occupied indispensable positions in the iron, steel, and machinery industries (Dubofsky 1975). Nevertheless, employers and their foremen controlled the workers through direct personal control, "intervening in the labor process often to exhort workers, bully and threaten them, reward good performance, hire and fire on the spot, favor loyal workers, and generally act as despots, benevolent or otherwise" (Edwards 1979, p. 19).

The scientific-management movement further strengthened the power of supervisors over workers by taking away control of the work process from the worker. **Scientific management** divided the work process into its smallest components in order to increase efficiency and output. But in so doing, it also introduced extreme specialization and monotonous work on the shop floor. Tasks were divided into such small parts that even completely unskilled individuals could perform them. Numerous early confrontations occurred over the question of who should direct the pace of work tasks (Dubofsky 1975; Piven and Cloward 2012; Edwards 1979; Stephenson and Asher 1986).

The use of foreign and African American labor along with changes in the mechanisms of control were only two of the techniques used to weaken labor. Industrial management also used **welfare capitalism** to minimize solidarity among workers. Briefly, welfare capitalism included special savings plans and bonuses, homeownership aid programs, stock-purchasing options, and group insurance plans. Most significant among the programs offered were employee representation plans or work councils and company unions. The latter plans presumably gave workers a meaningful voice in the operation of the organization. Around the time of World War I, the concept of "industrial democracy" had become quite popular. Clearly, these employee representation plans, while suggesting a democratic and more equal relationship between employer and employee, were aimed at reducing worker allegiance to outside unions and slowing their attempts to organize themselves (Brody 1980; Griffin, Wallace, and Rubin 1986). The motivation for these programs was very likely a combination of paternalistic concern for workers, the belief that a more satisfied workforce would increase productivity and efficiency, and a desire on the part of employers to control labor. The latter function, however, appears to have been the most important (Brody 1980; Griffin, Wallace, and Rubin 1986).

Employers also opposed the organized labor movement by fighting against closed or union shops, advocating open shops in their place. In the latter, employees need not be members of unions to remain employed. This push for open shops under the "American Plan" label was especially dominant during the first decade of the twentieth century. The National Association of Manufacturers launched a campaign for open shops across industries, while other business-oriented groups (e.g., National Civic Foundation) argued that if unions were to exist and be acceptable, they had to be "responsible" in nature. In response to business attacks on union shops, some trade unions began to take in more unskilled workers as members (Green 1980). The conservative trade unionism of the American Federation of Labor (AFL) was preferred by business over the more militant and revolutionary approach of the International Workers of the World (Griffin, Wallace, and Rubin 1986). The espousal of welfare capitalism and a conservative brand of labor organization helped employers appear as being reasonable and fair. But neither of these enhanced the ability of labor to organize effectively in its own interests.

Employers had, of course, other resources by which to resist encroachment by labor. Spies were employed to monitor labor activities; legal actions were encouraged against militant workers and organizations; and the power of police, state militia, and federal troops also were used to quell labor unrest. Some states had laws specifically outlawing unions that were considered to be revolutionary or that openly advocated the taking over of industries by workers (syndicalism). Leaders of such unions could be and were put in prison or deported (Perlman and Taft 1935; Griffin, Wallace, and Rubin 1986). The informal political alliance between business and government was reflected in the frequent use of police or military might in putting down worker protests.

In the late nineteenth century, workers often had the support of local officials, so industries had to get help from state and federal sources (Dubofsky 1975; Green 1980). In numerous strike actions between 1890 and 1920, state militia and federal troops were used against workers. The 1892 steel plant conflict at Homestead, Pennsylvania, and the Pullman railroad boycott of 1894 are only two instances in which soldiers were used against strikers. In Lawrence, Massachusetts, in 1912, the American Woolen mill employed roughly 40,000 individuals, about half the city's population. About half of the employees were young women and most were foreign-born. But when a group of young Polish women were given reduced wages for no explicit reason, a strike was organized and spread to other mills. In this case, too, police and militia were used against strikers, but after a couple of months, the workers in the "Bread and Roses" strike, as it was called, won wage gains (Green 1980). Many other labor–employer confrontations occurred during this period. But in most cases, employers emerged as the victors (Piven and Cloward 1979; Brody 1980).

In the last years of the nineteenth century and the early years of the twentieth century, workers simply did not have the political or organizational power to be consistently successful against industrial owners. The only effective legal control on the contract imposed by the employer at the turn of the century was the condition of the labor market. As long as employers had government, the press, and the market behind them and a large number of immigrant workers available, there was little that could get employers to voluntarily improve their contracts with workers (Ginzberg and Berman 1967).

Internal Divisions in the Labor Movement

The particular directions taken by the labor movement have been explained in a variety of ways, but not altogether successfully (Laslett 1987). The varying images of the roles of unions, industrial changes, and social and cultural heterogeneity within the working class and disagreements on the goals of unions all helped to shape the differentiation within the movement. At various times, unions were seen as having educational functions, playing a key role in the class struggle over the means of production, and as tools for increasing the economic benefits of workers.

There is no question that some of these frequently conflicting emphases were reflected in the internal structure of the organized labor movement of the early twentieth century. The forms the labor movement took in the United States were also conditioned by industrial changes. In the waning decades of the nineteenth century, the social organization of the economy was undergoing rapid change, and these changes had implications for both employers and employees. For example, the period beginning with the late 1880s was one in which economic enterprises dramatically increased in size and frequently merged with each other. In other words, it was a period in which economic power became more consolidated and concentrated (Edwards 1979). Industrialization brought in its wake a more simplified, detailed division of labor, increasing the need for less-skilled laborers.

Machines often fomented dissatisfaction among skilled craftsworkers and encouraged antagonism between the unskilled industrial workers who could do simple work and operate basic machines, and those who were skilled craftsworkers before machines became dominant (Stephenson and Asher 1986). Machines rapidly took the place of workers, and control over the workplace more frequently fell into the hands of owners and their foremen. These shifts in technology helped to drive wedges between unskilled and skilled workers, thereby stimulating the different directions in which the organized labor movement would go.

Along with technological changes, productivity rose rapidly, but so did the demand for labor. Immigrants flooded into the United States from a variety of countries. Consequently, the late nineteenth century was also a period in which the size of company workforces increased. The industrial working class grew significantly, but it was composed of individuals from sharply contrasting social and cultural backgrounds. The industrial working class for much of the latter half of the nineteenth century was a conglomeration of native-born craftsworkers, farmers who had left the land to come to the cities of New York and New England, skilled immigrants from Britain and western Europe, Irish who came to the United States after the potato famine in their native land, and Chinese who became employed primarily in the railroad industry.

After 1880, immigrants from eastern and southern Europe joined the ranks of the less skilled in industry and became an increasingly large part of the industrial working class (Aronowitz 1973). As the demand for labor grew and these immigrants flooded into the country to take lower positions in the mines, mills, and factories, the labor force in the North was almost as segregated by nationality in 1900 as the southern market was by race (Green 1980). Moreover, as the century came to an end, the proportion of women and African Americans involved in industry also increased. In 1900, almost a quarter of all women were in the labor force. The point of all this is that the heterogeneous nature of the working class at this time created divisions that often hindered the solidarity of workers when conflict arose with their employers. As noted earlier, this heterogeneity was exploited by employers to minimize worker cohesion.

The racial and ethnic differences within the working class meant language, skill, and religious differences as well, making control of working-class militancy easier. So these internal divisions had direct implications for both the working class and its employers. Some labor leaders had no wish at all to bring non-Whites into the organized labor movement, but rather were primarily interested in advancing the interests of White, skilled craftsworkers. Exclusionary practices, including explicit policies prohibiting admission of non-Whites, were not uncommon among many AFL unions (Green 1980). This was to be a bitter source of antagonism within the labor movement. Samuel Gompers, who founded the American Federation of Labor in 1881, was against the inclusion of non-White, nonskilled workers. In 1905, Gompers proclaimed to a group of union members in Minneapolis that "caucasians" were "not going to let their standard of living be destroyed by Negroes, Chinamen, Japs, or any others" (quoted in Green 1980, p. 46). The miscellaneous category of "others" referred to people from what were considered at that time the less desirable regions of Europe, such as the Slavic countries and Italy. Keep in mind that ideas about the biological inferiority of different groups were still circulating at this time (see Chapter 8).

In contrast to the American Federation of Labor, which sought to unionize skilled White craftsworkers, other organizers felt that it was crucial to organize all industrial workers. Among those groups that supported the organization of all workers, some had socialist or communist leanings. The Knights of Labor, briefly popular in the 1880s, was among those groups that argued that all workers should be included in the organized labor movement. Rather than advocating the homogeneous composition found in the trade and crafts unions of the AFL, the Knights preferred mixed groupings of workers. The Socialist Party of America, founded in 1901 and under the leadership of the charismatic Eugene Debs, also favored an organizational umbrella that would cover the mass of workers in industry. A few years later, the Industrial Workers of the World, and several decades later, the CIO also actively sought the membership of Blacks and all industrial workers.

As their views about the compositions of labor organizations varied, so did labor leaders' views on the appropriate goals for the labor movement. The goals of the Knights of Labor were broad and involved the reorganization of the industrial order to create a more just society. These utopian goals were eschewed by the newer AFL trade unions that sought more immediate narrow rewards for their members, such as higher wages and better working conditions. This "pure-and-simple" or "business" unionism was more consistent with native American values according to some interpreters. A large part of the reason for this orientation, argued Lipset (1971), is related to the openness of the class structure, and the values of materialism, egalitarianism, and individual opportunity. Individuals in this context see themselves more as individuals than as members of a class, and see social change as resulting more from individual efforts than from mass organization or social structure. The American values of work, social and geographic mobility, comfort, and common sense also lie behind the belief that individuals do and should determine their own economic fates (Dunlop 1987).

The AFL's trade unionism has aimed at working within the present economic system rather than trying to change it. The emphasis on increasing labor's power has been for the purpose of more effective collective bargaining than for political reasons. Early AFL leaders felt that government should not interfere in labor matters. It should be up to labor to chart its own course and make its own gains (Brody 1971). Gompers's "voluntarism" perspective underscored the belief that labor should not solicit aid from the government for those goals it can accomplish by itself (Green 1980). Paradoxically, this stance helped to create a bond between the AFL and establishment forces, fostering increased cooperation between the union, management, and the government (Rogin 1971; Brody 1980).

In this interpretation, U.S. workers were not as interested as their European counterparts in a basic change *of* the economic system as much as they were in changing their individual positions *within* the system. Brody (1980) concluded that in the waning years of the nineteenth century, the labor movement was (1) practical rather than utopian or theoretical, (2) nonrevolutionary with narrow material interests, and (3) impatient with

intellectuals and academicians who had theories about the direction the labor movement should pursue.

Despite the narrow orientation of many workers, however, one should not conclude that there has been no revolutionary fervor or concerns within labor. "Such an approach has always been unfair, especially during the heyday of the IWW between 1905 and 1917, and in the early years of the history of the CIO. It was especially untrue during the period of the Knights of Labor . . . which . . . upheld producer's and consumer's cooperation, equal pay for women, and a 'proper share of the wealth that they (the workers) create'" (Laslett 1987). Organized labor has not been a uniform homogeneous mass.

Just prior to World War I, then, organized labor contained several different types of organizations and orientations. The trade-union wing, exemplified by the AFL, was solidly on its way but did not incorporate most unskilled and semi-skilled industrial workers. The Socialists had political influence on many workers even though the latter's trade-union orientation remained intact. The IWW organized those left out by the more conservative AFL affiliates, was active and militant, and was led by the imposing Big Bill Haywood (Brody 1980).

The Russian Revolution, America's involvement in World War I, and the accompanying patriotic fervor that swept the nation legitimated political and coercive attacks on Socialist organizations and the IWW. As a result, the power of the left in organized labor declined. "The labor hopes of the American left, hitherto bright, died in World War I and its aftermath" (Brody 1980, p. 41). In the patriotic context of the postwar period, organized labor, in general, was a victim of attacks from industry. The "American Plan" of business proclaimed the consistency of the open shop with U.S. values. In this hostile atmosphere, the AFL became more cooperative with industry and government. With the restrictive immigration laws of the 1920s reducing the inflow of unskilled labor from culturally undesirable countries, industry's source of fresh workers was weakened. By the late 1920s, labor unrest had calmed down even though the cost of living was increasing, erasing many of the gains that had been made by some workers (Zieger 1986).

From the Depression to the Present

On the whole, the 1920s and the early 1930s were not kind to U.S. workers. "The symbol of the twenties is gold . . . the twenties were, indeed, golden, but only for a privileged segment of the American population. For the great mass of people—workers and their families—the appropriate symbol may be nickel or copper or perhaps even tin, but certainly not gold" (Bernstein 1960, p. 47). Bernstein labeled the 1920 to 1933 period as "the lean years" for the worker (p. 47). A litany of the problems for workers would include the stagnation of the union movement during the period (union membership fell from 5 million in 1920 to 3.5 million in 1929) and the absence of any effective industry-wide collective-bargaining tools. Employers could hire whom they wanted, and workers had little recourse in the matter. Older workers found it more and more difficult to hold on to their jobs, as farm migrants and women increasingly entered the urban labor force. Mechanization displaced workers. Between 1920 and 1929, it is estimated that about one-third of those displaced by machines in the manufacturing, coal mining, and railways industries remained unemployed (Bernstein 1960). Moreover, the shift to more mechanized professional positions did not help many workers, who did not have the qualifications for such positions. Income inequality was also extensive in the society. The combined incomes of the top 0.1 percent of families were as great as those of the bottom 42 percent of the population. Within the working class there were also divisions in wages based on regional, ethnic, racial, skill, union membership, sex, and residential differences. Irish, Italian, Jewish, African American, and Mexican workers were generally worse off than native White workers (Bernstein 1960).

The effects of the Great Depression on employment were disastrous. In the middle of 1930, almost 4.5 million were without jobs. Shanty areas cropped up in and around cities, places of makeshift residences sometimes called "Hoovervilles." Hunger also rose dramatically. By early 1931, an estimated 8.3 million were unemployed, but the number was to rise even further to 13.6 million by the end of that year, and to 15 million by early 1933. At that time, about one-third of all wage/salary workers were completely out of work. Many others were only working on a part-time basis (Bernstein 1960).

Needless to say, the Depression in the early 1930s changed political dynamics inside and outside the labor movement. The AFL had successfully cultivated close relationships with industrial management and government forces. It stressed union–management harmony and fought against leftist elements in the labor movement. The Depression made many workers and unions recognize the need for state help and intervention. It spurred questions among the unemployed about the ability of the present economic and political systems to deal with catastrophic problems, especially as it became clear over the bitter years of the 1930s that it was not the lack of individual efforts but rather broader social forces that were behind much of the misery being experienced (Piven and Cloward 1979). At the same time, however, the vast majority of citizens still had faith in the U.S. system and did not see socialism or communism as a viable alternative. Nor did they think of themselves as a cohesive working class fighting capitalism (Aronowitz 1973; Zieger 1986).

In the early part of the twentieth century, labor had received little help from the federal government, especially during the Republican administrations of the 1920s. Several critical events strengthened labor's hand during the 1930s, in addition to the political-administration changes that had occurred. One was the rising prospect of war in Europe. U.S. companies that had armament contracts with European countries could not afford major labor unrest to disrupt production. A second event was the passage of the Wagner Act in 1935, which legalized the right of workers to organize and bargain collectively under the protection of the National Labor Relations Board, which could monitor business compliance with the law. This law, bitterly fought by business, resulted in a rapid upsurge in union membership. In the mid- and late 1930s, union membership tripled, reaching about 9 million in 1939 (Zieger 1986). A third event that increased the power of labor was the creation of the CIO in 1935. The CIO unionized many of the previously unorganized mass-production industrial workers. Unlike the AFL, it aimed at being a union for all workers. Its leader, John L. Lewis, also realized that the CIO had to recruit skeptical Blacks to prevent their being used as strikebreakers. In 1937, the CIO had about 4 million members. The New Deal and events during the 1930s left in their wake a triumvirate of power: big government, big business, and

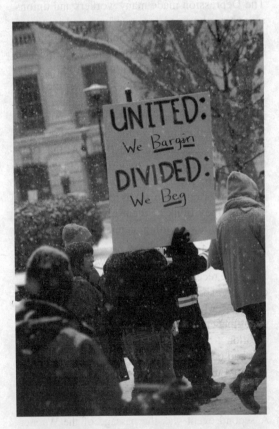

Photo 13.1 Historically, unions have been a major source of organized strength for workers, helping to improve wages, benefits, and working conditions.

Photo by Brendan R. Hurst.

big labor. During and after World War II, union membership was still high and growing, and unions were an effective force for improving working conditions for their members.

Despite this growth in union power, the ideological tide had already begun to shift against organized labor by the end of the 1930s. The recession of 1938–1939, which led to a weakening of federal recovery programs, factionalism within the CIO (which many suspected had communist leanings), the growing patriotism during the early years of World War II, and the impatience of many with the increased militancy of workers immediately after the war strengthened conservative forces against unions (Zieger 1986). The increased bureaucratization and job consciousness of unions over the years and the routinization of formal contracts and the "rule of law" in industry also helped to institutionalize labor–industry conflict. Employers were more willing to buy off workers with higher wages than to relinquish control of the production process (Brody 1980; Zieger 1986). The Taft–Hartley Act of 1947 renewed many of the powers that had been lost to business by the Wagner Act. It also curbed the power of unions to strike, required an anti-Communist pledge from workers, and redefined labor's rights in much narrower terms (Piven and Cloward 1979; Zieger 1986).

The increased conservatism and narrowness of unions meant that workers often fought against the wishes of union leadership. The interests of workers and those of the union leadership did not always coincide. This internal division within the labor movement has continued. Although union membership generally grew during the 1950s and 1960s, and more public employees initiated unionization drives, differences of opinion within the labor community surfaced over Vietnam and the civil rights and women's movements of the 1960s. During the conservative 1980s and early 1990s, unions were again under attack, membership declined, and union leadership appeared weaker than in the earlier heyday of organized labor. More specifically, the breach of traditional understandings between unions and management coupled with vigorous business attacks on union since the 1970s, helped to weaken unions. In addition, globalization, and the rapid employment growth in new areas coupled with higher unemployment in traditional occupations, the lack of national unity among unions, and a hostile political climate have certainly contributed to the decline of union power (Western 1993; Clawson and Clawson 1999). Elements internal to labor unions themselves have also contributed to their decline. Publicized corruption, ethnic and gender biases within unions, and a lack of union democracy for rank-and-file workers have weakened their moral authority (Kallick 1994). In 2014, only 11.1 percent of wage and salary workers in the United States were union members. The rate among public employees was much higher than that found among workers in the private sector (35.7 versus 6.6 percent), and it is much higher in traditionally more liberal regions like the Northeast, Midwest, and Pacific West, than in more conservative areas like the South and Mountain West (U.S. Bureau of Labor Statistics 2015b).

It must be recognized that labor is not a monolithic force. Different unions continue to react differently to the challenges their workers face, with some more willing than others to adopt nontraditional tactics to increase their influence (Martin 2008; Martin and Dixon 2010). The current splintering and weakness of unions is reminiscent of the labor movement of the 1920s, and these developments come in a -decade period marked by relatively stagnant wages and significant economic uncertainty for many in the middle and working classes. Nonunion employees are suffering disproportionately. Workers who are not union members have pensions and insurance benefits valued at less than half those of union workers. Retirement and health insurance benefits have been significantly curtailed by many corporations. In fact, in 2014, 2 million Americans were still without health insurance, although this represented a decrease of 9 million from 2013, likely due to the implementation of the Affordable Care Act (Kaiser Family Foundation 2015b). Historically, union membership has meant significantly higher wages and better benefits.

Importantly but not surprisingly, the decline of union membership is occurring at a time of conservatism, increasing globalization, and open markets, when transnational corporations have gained more economic and political leverage (Faux 2003). The weakness of labor against business does not bode well for a decline in economic inequality. Indeed, a study by Western and Rosenfeld (2011) finds that the decline in unions accounts for between a fifth and a third of the growth in inequality from 1973 to 2007. "The decline of American labor and the associated increase in wage inequality signaled the deterioration of the labor market as a political institution" (Western and Rosenfeld 2011, p. 533).

Perhaps the labor movement has come full circle and will again mobilize its constituencies to restore labor's power, but to do this in an international marketplace, it may have to embrace not only differences in class, race, and gender, but those of nationality as well. The difficulty of this task is perhaps exemplified in the failure of the Occupy Wall Street movement of the past few years to mobilize toward cohesive action, in part due to the fragmentation across interests and demographics (Calhoun 2013). There is some evidence that unions realize this need and are actively trying to organize the growing number of immigrant workers. Union influence in the Democratic Party has remained strong (Francia 2007). Most of the public are also sympathetic. Perhaps because of high corporate bonuses and the infamous financial scandals of the 1990s and 2000s, a variety of recent polls show that a majority of the public view unions in a positive light and as helpful to workers. The public is also much more likely to see big business and big government as threats to the nation than they are to see big labor as a threat (Panagopoulos and Francia 2008). At the same time, most do not feel that union members who work in the public sphere such as teachers, police officers, and firefighters, should be allowed to strike. Indeed, in light of local and state budgetary problems, unionization and collective bargaining by public employees has become a hot issue (see Nutshell 13.1).

NUTSHELL 13.1 Collective Bargaining: A Dying Species?

The power of labor unions in the private sector has been in steady decline since the passage of the Taft-Hartley Act in 1947 that weakened worker rights. The trend to weaken unions has coexisted with a corresponding rise in political conservatism and the increased lobbying and economic power of business. In 2015, 25 states, mostly in the South and Midwest, had right-to-work laws prohibiting closed-shop employment. In early 2011 and again in 2015, a proposal for a "National Right to Work Act" was submitted in Congress to eliminate the right of unions to collect dues and fees from nonunion workers. With economic deficits and the 2010 election of more conservative state governors, labor unions in the public sector have also come under attack.

Ohio and Indiana are two states engaged in the contest over worker rights between public employees and state government. But Wisconsin has been the lightning rod for the recent debate about collective bargaining by public employees. Battles between legislators, union members, and sympathizers on both sides in Wisconsin provide a vivid example of the attempts to balance state budgets by stripping union members of some of their historically hard-won rights to strike and collectively bargain for better wages and benefits. In March 2011, the Wisconsin governor signed a bill increasing the amount of health care and pension contributions by state employees, and eliminated virtually all of their collective bargaining rights. Because of a political maneuver, Republican senators were able to pass the bill without the presence of 14 Democratic senators who had left the state because of disagreement over the proposed bill. Mass protests by public employees and members of other unions did not sway the governor, who argued that the bill not only would help balance Wisconsin's budget but also attract business to the state and create 250,000 jobs. Senate

Democrats viewed the bill as an assault on workers, with one senator saying that, "in 30 minutes, 18 state senators undid 50 years of civil rights in Wisconsin" (Davey 2011, p. A3).

The bill has deepened splits among workers at a time when unity would strengthen the working class. A 2015 Gallup poll revealed that 58 percent of Americans approved of labor unions, representing a 9 percent increase from 2009 (Saad 2015). Many workers in the private sector who have lost wages and benefits, however, feel that public sector workers should also have to share the burden of the recent economic downturn. "Everyone else needs to pinch pennies and give more money to health insurance companies and pay for their own retirement," claimed one private sector worker. "I don't get to bargain in my job, either," argued another (Sulzberger and Davey 2011, p. A17). At the same time, the leader of the Wisconsin State Employees Union believes that "public employees did not create the recession and the deficit here in Wisconsin. It was Wall Street" (Greenhouse 2011, p. A12).

At a time when income and wealth differences are higher than they have been in decades, a reasonable question to ask is how these legislative acts will affect economic inequality. Will these laws actually result in more employment and higher incomes for some or just exacerbate the growing divide between top and bottom?

Sources: Monica Davey, "Wisconsin G.O.P. Ends Stalemate with Maneuver," *New York Times*, March 10, 2011, pp. A1 and A3; "Americans' Support for Labor Unions Continues to Recover," Lydia Saad, Gallup Institute, August 17, 2015; Steven Greenhouse, "Wisconsin Union Leader Minces No Words When Labor Issues Are at Stake," *New York Times*, February 23, 2011, p. A12; A. G. Sulzberger and Monica Davey, "Union Bonds in Wisconsin Begin to Fray," *New York Times*, February 22, 2011, pp. A1 and A17.

THE CIVIL RIGHTS MOVEMENT

Although it often discriminated against both Blacks and women, the labor movement was driven by concerns over inequities in political and economic power, and historical, cultural, and social conditions shaped its development and form. In

general terms, the same can be said of the civil rights movement of the mid-1950s and 1960. Although an indisputable specific date for its beginning cannot be given, there is general agreement that it began in the period between 1953 and 1955 during which the Supreme Court's histori

Brown v. Board of Education decision was made, and systematic bus boycotts had occurred in Baton Rouge, Louisiana, and Montgomery, Alabama. The nonviolent movement extended into the mid-1960s up to the point when other, more radical, Black Power elements were becoming increasingly important.

As was the case in the labor movement, there had been many instances of protest by African Americans against Whites before the civil rights movement. Revolts by slaves against their masters, the Underground Railroad, the massive growth of the National Association for the Advancement of Colored People (NAACP) membership to almost half a million during World War II, the demands that led Roosevelt to establish a Fair Employment

Practices Committee, and A. Philip Randolph's political activity in Washington and before Congress in the 1940s all provide evidence of racial protest and a push for racial equality before the civil rights movement (Morris 1986). Thus, the movements of the 1950s and 1960s did not suddenly appear out of nowhere. Consequently, what may appear to be the beginning of a social movement may only be a resurgence of activism that had been kept in abeyance because of lack of opportunity structures in the social context (Taylor 1989). As was evident in the labor movement's history, particular historical, political, economic, and social conditions created a context in which effective mass protest could be initiated, and the civil rights movement could be nurtured.

MINI-CASE 13.1

Affirmative Action: Yes or No?

As we have seen, significant racial inequality continues to exist in the United States, and the question continually arises about what to do about it, if anything. Two approaches to affirmative action have been implemented, one stressing the need for "equal opportunity" for all (e.g., as in the Equal Employment Opportunity Commission), and the other, assuming that there is racial bias built into our institutions, emphasizing "equal representation" of racial and ethnic groups (e.g., as in the Office of

Federal Contract Compliance). The arguments in favor of affirmative action cite past wrongs and continued discrimination as well as success in reducing racial discrepancies and increasing diversity, while those who oppose it argue that it constitutes reverse discrimination, lowers the self-esteem of minorities, and reinforces stereotypes of minorities. What do you think? Should some form of affirmative action be continued, or should it be eliminated entirely? ∎

In the late nineteenth and early twentieth centuries, African Americans had few resources with which to launch a massive civil rights campaign. First of all, racist ideologies discouraged support from Whites. Second, most African Americans were fully but exploitatively integrated into the Southern economic and political structure. There were few economic opportunities open to them, and Jim Crow laws kept them in their assigned place. In other words, the social context offered few political and economic opportunities or alternatives. Third, the federal government did little to alleviate the oppressive conditions under

which Blacks lived. Earlier, national leaders had written into the Constitution that Black men, who were unfree, were to be considered only three-fifths persons. Now Congress stood by as Blacks were disenfranchised and treated violently in the South.

The North and the federal government did little while Black subjugation and White supremacy were being systematically institutionalized in the South. This structured inequality was especially evident in the political realm. Blacks were effectively prevented from voting through the use of various devices, including poll taxes, tests of literacy and "good character," grandfather requirements, and primaries limited to Whites. Laws in the South prohibited the integration of Blacks and Whites in schools, hospitals, motels, places of recreation, and even funeral homes and cemeteries. These Jim Crow laws made it legal to spend less public money on Black than on White institutions (Sitkoff 1981).

The Changing Context of Racial Inequality

After World War I, it was clear that changing economic and political conditions would strengthen the power position of African Americans in the United States. Among these economic changes was a decline in the centrality of agriculture in the Southern economy coupled with increasing industrialization of the urban South. This agrarian decline was fostered, in part, by declines in immigration and agricultural exports during the war. Accompanying the decline in immigration was an increase in the demand by northern industry for laborers from the South. Both "King Cotton" and industry needed workers, but changing circumstances created a shift in demand from agriculture to industry. Before and after World War I, there was massive African American migration to the North and to cities to seek employment in industries (Piven and Cloward 1979; Sitkoff 1981; McAdam 2010). Southern agriculture suffered again during the Great Depression of the early 1930s. An overproduction of cotton due to decreased demand led to a drastic decline in its price, which spelled disaster for many Southern farmers. In Mississippi, at that time perhaps the greatest stronghold of White supremacy, farmers lost their land at about twice the national rate (Bloom 1987). Later, during the 1940s, as mechanization also became more and more essential in agriculture, some farmers left agriculture behind, and the average size of landholdings increased. This meant that more Black as well as White farmworkers were economically displaced and needed to seek employment in the industries of northern and southern cities (Piven and Cloward 1979). Southern agriculture also had to diversify its products to feed the soldiers in

military camps during World War II (Bloom 1987). All of these circumstances served to shake up the foundations of the traditional economy in the South.

The changed geographic and economic base of Blacks helped to develop their voting power and the indigenous institutional bases needed for the civil rights movement (McAdam 2010). Cities provided greater opportunities for Blacks to get organized, to receive more education, and to lay the basis for an expanded Black middle class. The growth of these basic strengths within the Black community was important in the genesis of the civil rights movement. There is good evidence that, despite the importance of external resources to the movement, its origins and development can be traced to reliance on institutions indigenous to the Black community (Oberschall 1973; McAdam 2010; Morris 1986; Jenkins and Eckert 1986).

African American colleges, churches, and civic and fraternal institutions provided not only economic resources but also the communication network and most of the leaders needed to organize the movement. Martin Luther King Jr., for example, was influential as a movement leader not only because of his charisma but also, crucially, because of the personal and organizational backing he received. The influence of the Southern Christian Leadership Conference during most of the movement's career suggests the relevance of religious institutions. Local colleges also provided most of the students who, early in the 1960s, were involved in the civil disobedience actions that helped bring about legislative changes.

External support of protests generally comes after the protests themselves. These additional resources are a *product* rather than a *cause* of protest (McAdam 2010). The patronage that did come later from outsiders appears to have been given less out of feelings of conscience and injustice than out of concern to keep the movement moderate, weaken the radical element, and exercise some control over the direction of the movement (Jenkins and Eckert 1986). The nonviolent sit-ins of college students and others in the South in the early 1960s, for example, brought much financial and other support from outside, northern groups

The violent protests later in the 1960s in northern and western cities, on the other hand, produced a White backlash, partly because of the violence, but also because of the switch in focus of problems from the rural South to the urban ghettos of the North.

The economic and attending geographic shifts that were occurring in the South, then, provided African Americans with the opportunity to "construct the occupational and institutional foundation from which to mount resistance to White oppression" (Piven and Cloward 1979, p. 205). On the other side, changing economic and social conditions also created a split in the "Solid South" between the interests of business and agriculture.

Establishment forces were further weakened by the increased stridence and militancy of the reaction against African American protests for equality, which helped to isolate the South, especially the Deep South, from the rest of the nation. The traditional social and political structure had been grounded in a particular kind of economy. A weakening in the basis of that agricultural economy threatened the survival of sociopolitical arrangements that primarily benefited the rich landowner and discriminated against African Americans. "Racial patterns and racial consciousness have as their foundation particular class structures, and they develop and change as these structures themselves change" (Bloom 1987, p. 3).

This last point is very important. Class and economic factors were implicated in the shifting allegiances to racial inequality. However, *racist ideology* was still an underlying element in accounting for not only social and economic inequality in the South but also reactions to Black attempts to eliminate it. Recall that in the latter part of the nineteenth and well into the twentieth centuries, there were a variety of established racial ideologies justifying unequal treatment of Blacks. Beliefs about the inferiority of Blacks go back even further than that to the early founding of the United States (see Chapter 8). The continued significance of racism itself was manifested in the support given by lower-class as well as upper-class White Southerners to the discriminatory treatment of Blacks. Upper-class White Southerners who had vested local economic interests fought the hardest against voting rights for Blacks because to afford this right would have been tantamount to surrendering power to them.

Although the voting regulations effectively prohibited many lower-class Whites as well as Blacks from voting, the former went along with their upper-class brethren in supporting the laws. The Southern aristocracy played on racist images of Blacks and used the image of competition between Blacks and Whites as a means to obtain the support of lower-class Whites (Piven and Cloward 1979). In addition, not only Southern agricultural aristocrats but also local town and city business people fought against those who pushed for integration into local restaurants, motels, and so on. In essence, both economic factors and racism played roles in the dynamics of racial inequality and reactions to it.

Other cultural events and employment issues also gave strength to the Black effort to confront both racial and economic inequality. During the 1920s, the Harlem Renaissance encouraged Blacks to take pride in themselves and their cultural and literary heritage. Most Blacks who had jobs in northern industrial cities during the 1930s and 1940s were working class, and consequently, fought not only against racism, but also for better working conditions and economic fairness (Isaac 2008). The civil rights activists of the late 1920s and 1930s often fought alongside White radical unionists who were pushing the New Deal policies (Sitkoff 1981). Radical union leaders, it will be recalled, wanted to include not only Whites and skilled workers but also Blacks and unskilled industrial workers as well. Both radical unions and Black organizations, however, were often labeled as communist. This would become a familiar theme again after World War II, especially with the rise of McCarthyism.

In addition to the changes in the U.S. economy and social-cultural factors that strengthened Black unity, other historical events and conditions also helped to lay the groundwork for the civil rights movement that was to come in the 1950s. Migration to the North not only meant a greater probability of voting but also led to Blacks holding political office in several major cities (Sitkoff 1981; Bloom 1987). Politicians with presidential aspirations became increasingly concerned about potential Black political defections and, as a result, often courted the Black vote.

Despite this courtship, governmental policies continued to underrepresent the interests of Blacks. But they also, perhaps inadvertently, strengthened the position of Blacks. As we saw in the history of the labor struggles, the New Deal's policies had an impact on the fate of the labor movement. Similarly, the public works programs of the New Deal provided Blacks with an alternate source of income outside the relatively narrow range of private positions open to them. Having another source of income, which meant less dependence, created a source of power with which to fight oppression (Piven and Cloward 2012; Bloom 1987). This federal source of work and the increased demand for labor in industry helped to drive wages up—wages that dominant agricultural groups were increasingly hesitant to pay (Bloom 1987). Federal loans also became available as a substitute for local ones, again making Blacks less dependent on local White funding institutions.

World War II brought further changes to the situation of Blacks. Unionization of Blacks was less difficult than had been the case only a decade earlier. Employment conditions had improved, especially with the wartime economy. But national unity was the preferred emphasis, and most Blacks did not favor protest in these circumstances (Sitkoff 1981). Despite continued demands by Black groups, any serious attempts to deal with racial problems took a backseat to dealing with the Axis powers. Although the war brought some positive changes, Blacks were still much worse off than Whites politically and economically, and discrimination was still prevalent.

After the war, several political events occurred that affected efforts for racial equality. The liberation struggles abroad against colonialism heartened many Black leaders who became convinced that change was possible (Rollins 1986). These events, coupled with the racist overtones of Nazism, against which the United States had fought, meant that continued racial inequality

at home could prove to be an embarrassment. Harry Truman, in running for the presidency in 1948, had to present a platform that showed a strong desire for civil rights if he was to defeat opponents who also were courting the vote of those Blacks who had migrated to the cities of the North. He also ordered the desegregation of the military. The economic and political context had shifted to the extent that Truman was advised to court Blacks even at the risk of turning away Southern Democrats (Piven and Cloward 1979).

A final political element in the late 1940s that affected civil rights efforts came out of the developing "cold war" with the former Soviet Union. "Red-baiting" was fashionable, and civil rights groups and leaders were not immune to accusations of being communist. White supremacists argued that communists were behind the movement for Black equality. It will be recalled that similar accusations had been made about unions and their leadership when they also pushed for greater economic and political power. McCarthyism frightened Blacks, and the majority of Black leaders took a gradual and calm approach. "The NAACP became less a protest organization and more an agency of litigation and lobbying after World War II" (Sitkoff 1981, p. 18). All of the conditions discussed thus far comprise the context in which the Supreme Court made its momentous *Brown v. Board of Education* decision in 1954.

A Brief History

The *Brown v. Board of Education* decision was a true watershed in the effort for civil rights. It declared segregation in education to be unconstitutional. In concluding his argument, Chief Justice Earl Warren stated simply, "We conclude that in the field of public education the doctrine of 'separate but equal' has no place. Separate educational facilities are inherently unequal" (quoted in Sitkoff 1981, p. 22). This decision had a powerful effect on both Blacks and Southern Whites. The Black movement for equality was given a boost, but at the same time, a White countermovement was established to fight these advances. While Blacks were jubilant about the decision, the South's White lite were not about to accept it without a fight. Many said unequivocally that they would not comply with the law in this case. "The prospect of desegregating public schools was fundamentally appalling to the average White Southerner" (Morris 1986, p. 27). Even though the decision by the Court to desegregate had been unanimous, it had not come to this decision easily. In order to get the unanimous ruling, Warren had to agree on a policy of gradual implementation of the desegregation policy. The qualification of gradualism left room for Southern dissenters to fight enforcement, and it led to frustration on the part of Blacks who wished speedy implementation of the law.

There was no strong push on the part of the government for swift implementation of the law; the dominance by conservative elements of the major political parties in Congress meant no rapid enforcement would be forthcoming. The FBI's J. Edgar Hoover still saw racial unrest as being communist inspired (Bloom 1987). In the South, White churches and the press generally opposed the ruling, and local White Citizens' Councils were set up to fight desegregation (Sitkoff 1981). In 1956, the membership in these councils approached 250,000 (Piven and Cloward 1979).

In the mid-1950s, notable bus boycotts by Blacks occurred in Baton Rouge, Montgomery, and Tallahassee. Perhaps the most famous of these was initiated by Rosa Parks in Montgomery in December of 1955. Parks, who was an active NAACP participant and had been put off a bus previously for refusing to move to the back, had gotten on a crowded bus and refused to surrender her seat to a White man. At the next bus stop, Parks was taken off the bus and arrested for violating the local bus ordinance (Sitkoff 1981). News of her arrest spread, and a bus boycott was organized by a group of local Black leaders. Assuming that it would be best to appoint an outsider as its leader, they appointed a hesitant, young, middle-class, nonviolent, and intellectually sophisticated Black minister to lead the boycott.

The Reverend Martin Luther King Jr. was well educated, a newcomer to the area, and had attended theological school in the North. He was stunned by the blatant racism that seemed to be so out of place in a period when Blacks had become more educated and urbanized (Sitkoff 1981). Given his background and training, King assumed initially that Whites would respect logic and listen to reason, but he was wrong. "He now realized that the matter was one of power, not reason, that 'no one gives up his privileges without strong resistance'" (Sitkoff 1981, p. 51). Under his new organization, dubbed the Montgomery Improvement Association, King led a nonviolent boycott of the bus system. Local Black churches provided sites for meetings and arranged for alternative modes of transportation. The boycott went on for over a year, and during that time, White resistance tried a range of tactics to bring it to an end. Legal tactics such as arrests and jailings for minor or fictitious infractions of local laws were used. Economic sanctions also were tried; some deeply involved in the boycott lost their jobs. Finally, violent tactics were used: Many beatings occurred, and four Black churches and the homes of King, his associate Ralph Abernathy, and another supporter were bombed. In the last analysis, however, the nonviolent boycott prevailed, and the U.S. Supreme Court declared Alabama's bus segregation laws unconstitutional.

The nonviolent, long-suffering, patient approach of the boycott contrasted in the national media with the harsh White reaction. Many outside the South were appalled at the tactics used by the White resistance. In contrast, King's "neo-Gandhian persuasion" seemed reasonable and acceptable as a means for obtaining equal rights. Above all, it was nonviolent and embraced the Christian beliefs of turning the other cheek and not condemning individual racists. It blamed the system of segregation rather than the individuals who enforced it (King 1958; Sitkoff 1981). As a result of the boycott, King and his approach to injustice gained worldwide attention. Out of the boycott, other civil rights groups were organized, most notably the Southern Christian Leadership Conference (SCLC) under King's leadership.

A familiar pattern of Black–White confrontation began to develop as a result of the early boycotts. Basically, the sequence would begin with nonviolent Black protests, followed by a militant

White response, which in turn often led to federal intervention. It did not take long for Black leaders to figure out how to get the attention of federal officials who had been unreliable and largely unresponsive in the past in enforcing rights that were theirs under the Constitution.

The violent repressive tactics of Whites against nonviolent protestors angered many in the Black community, and some of them were not altogether happy with King's patient, nonmilitant approach. This was especially the case as hostile White resistance intensified during the late 1950s and early 1960s. However, many young college-educated Blacks had had their resolve stiffened by the growing number of successes from King's approach. Beside boycotts and marches, additional nonviolent tactics were used. Among these was the sit-in, which also had been used effectively in the past in union strikes.

In the early 1960s, sit-ins were held throughout the South as a way of protesting segregation of public facilities. Similar protests were held in northern cities to demonstrate sympathetic support of the civil rights protestors. These protests involved thousands of individuals, many of them college students. One of the most famous of the sit-ins occurred in early February 1960 in Greensboro, North Carolina. Four Black students sat down at a Woolworth's lunch counter and asked for coffee and donuts. When refused, they kept their seats until the store closed. The next day, more students did the same thing, but White officials remained implacable, and it was only after repeated sit-ins that Greensboro allowed such service 6 months later. This sit-in inspired similar protests throughout the South and afforded a means by which college students could become meaningfully involved in the civil rights movement. Adults also joined in these protests. Within a year and a half of the Greensboro sit-in, demonstrations had been carried out in over 100 cities and towns in all the Southern states (Blumberg 1991). Not only sit-ins at lunch counters, but sleep-ins in the lobbies of motels, swim-ins at pools, play-ins at recreational areas, kneel-ins at churches, and read-ins at libraries followed. Boycotts also were carried out against merchants who refused desegregation (Sitkoff 1981).

Local White reactions were often swift and violent Floggings, kickings, pistol whippings, dog attacks, jailings, and even acid throwings were among the repressive means used against the protestors. But still the sit-ins continued.

One result of these demonstrations was that they showed Southerners the depth of Black feelings about these matters. They were also powerful in bringing to the attention of the nation the injustice of widespread legal segregation practices Largely as a result of the active concern of Black college youths, their impatience with years of waiting, and the seemingly futile legal maneuverings of the more conservative approaches in the civil rights movement as typified by the NAACP, other, more militant types of organizations (such as the Student Nonviolent Coordinating Committee [SNCC] began appearing in the early 1960s (Sitkoff 1981 Blumberg 1991).

In 1961, the Congress of Racial Equality (CORE), which had been founded in 1942 and had advocated direct nonviolent means of protest, organized a "freedom ride" from Washington, D.C., to New Orleans to see if states and municipalities were complying with the federal law against discrimination in interstate bus terminals. These rides went into the Deep South where White resistance was strongest. As with other peaceful protests these rides too evoked violent White resistance Beatings and deaths of protestors, for example took place in several Alabama cities, including Birmingham and Montgomery. Again, much of the violence was broadcast through the media.

It was only when waves of public sympathy came that the federal government acted to protec the protestors and enforce the law. When there was no publicity, little was done; violations of the law were left unpunished. It became clear to protestor that they apparently had to elicit a violent response to receive public attention and sympathy, and to prod the government to act. When the White resistance reacted with legal nonviolent measures, such publicity and sympathy were not as likely, nor, as a result, was governmental intervention. Barkar (1984) suggested that had Whites used these mean more often, the results may have been different Examining the confrontations in Montgomery

Selma, Birmingham, Albany (Georgia), and Danville (Virginia), he concluded that in those cities where legal means such as arrests, high bails, court proceedings, and injunctions had been used, protestors were less successful (see also Sitkoff 1981).

One of the most brutal reactions to the nonviolent demonstrations of King and the SCLC occurred in Birmingham in the spring of 1963. Sit-ins, marches, and similar techniques had been used to protest local segregation. After these had been going on for a time, the local police commissioner, Eugene "Bull" Connor, came down violently on the protestors. His violent response was seen by millions on television. Officials used dogs, high-pressure hoses, cattle prods, clubs, and even a police tank to beat down the protestors. President Kennedy and his brother Robert, who had wanted "cooling-down" periods by Blacks and a more gradual approach to desegregation, sent federal representatives to help reach a compromise between King and local officials. But the protestors would not back down. Finally, the SCLC obtained desegregation of some public facilities, a promise of nondiscriminatory hiring, and the formation of a biracial committee in Birmingham (Sitkoff 1981).

As successful protests became more frequent, more working-class Blacks were drawn into the movement. Greater competition among the major Black organizations (SCLC, SNCC, CORE, NAACP) occurred with each group vying for the dominant position. They sponsored massive demonstrations throughout the country. A national March on Washington occurred in August 1963, sponsored by numerous civil rights, union, and church organizations and involving well over 200,000 individuals. During the summer of 1964, hundreds of individuals worked in Mississippi to increase voter registration, and three workers were brutally murdered. The government asked workers to remain calm, but this request only deepened their distrust of administration policies and motives. Riots broke out in several cities. President Kennedy began to press for a civil rights law in 1963, and shortly thereafter the Civil Rights and Voting Rights Acts were passed under President Johnson. This national legislative response to the basic problems of Blacks, particularly in the South, helped to delegitimize the need for protest, especially in the eyes of northern Whites.

Despite the passage of these laws, several other changes had occurred that helped alter the nature of the Black movement from the nonviolent protest tactics of King to cries for "Black Power" and Black "liberation." First, the slow, compromising approach of the federal government to the problems experienced by Blacks on a day-to-day basis, coupled with the patient nonviolent method of King, convinced some in the civil rights movement of the need for more drastic action on their own behalf. The consistently violent reactions by Whites to the nonviolent protests of Blacks over the years widened the gap between factions within the civil rights movement in the early 1960s.

Second, the focus of the civil rights movement had been on the South, but the migration of many Blacks into the cities of the North and West led to a shift in goal emphasis within the movement. The problems of Black city dwellers became the focus: poverty, employment, housing, poor schools, and so on. The civil rights movement has been interpreted by some as largely a movement by and for middle-class individuals, while the focus of the Black movement on problems of city residents appeared to demonstrate a greater concern for the Black working and lower classes (Oberschall 1973; Blumberg 1991; Bloom 1987). In total, the shift in the movement was from an emphasis on integration, political and social rights, and nonviolence to one on Black separatism, economic needs, and more militant tactics (Blumberg 1991; Bloom 1987). Different segments stressed the importance of cultural and Black nationalism, while others spoke of Black Power. Despite their dissimilarities, all of these more militant perspectives betrayed a basic distrust of White institutions, the need for Blacks to develop their own institutions or identities, and the need for stronger reactions to discrimination against Blacks. Stokely Carmichael's statement about the need for Black Power suggests the feelings that some were having: "Power is the only thing respected in this world, and we must get it at any cost" (quoted in Sitkoff 1981, p. 214).

Violent riots occurred during the "long hot summers" of the 1960s in many major cities, including Chicago, Cleveland, Milwaukee, Dayton, San Francisco, Detroit, Newark, New Haven, Boston, Buffalo, and others. During 1967 alone, there were 150 such outbreaks (Sitkoff 1981). Certainly with this turn of events, it was clear that by the mid-1960s, while the Black push for equality was continuing, the nonviolent civil rights movement phase had passed.

There is evidence that the shift in focus from the South to the North during the 1960s weakened support for the movement and encouraged its decline. The strength of the civil rights movement was also sapped by declines in other movements, such as the antiwar movement against the Vietnam War. The vitality of the civil rights movement appears to have been tied to the vigor of other protest movements (Martin et al. 2009). In addition, shifts in the economy, greater political conservatism and complacency, the rise of Hispanics and concerns about new immigrants, and growing economic inequality outside and inside the Black community over the last couple of decades have softened the national focus on Blacks' living conditions and created divisions among Blacks themselves. There have even been attempts to eliminate affirmative action policies originally aimed at equalizing opportunities for all groups; in fact, at the time of writing, the Supreme Court is deliberating a case challenging affirmative action policies in higher-education admission.

The civil rights movement has left its imprint on a variety of social and cultural changes in U.S. society. It helped to break down Jim Crow and segregation laws, sparked programs to help the disadvantaged, and inspired hope for social progress. It certainly stimulated and provided major parts of the strategic and tactical frameworks for other rights movements such as those on behalf of women and LGBT individuals. Perhaps most significantly, the battles for civil rights in the 1950s and 1960s changed American culture by fostering more liberal and fair-minded attitudes among those who have clear memories of those days. In this way, the civil rights movement has continued to influence most Americans as we move further into the twenty-first century (Griffin and Bollen 2009; Isaac 2008; Martin et al. 2009). The legacy of the past civil rights movement is most keenly seen in the current efforts to address issues of racial injustice, the Black Lives Matter movement.

THE WOMEN'S MOVEMENT

In both the civil rights and early labor movements, women experienced discrimination and inequality, and their interests were rarely central to the movements. Women needed their own movement to advance their interests. Like the civil rights movement, the women's movement has had an uneven history. Its unevenness is reflected in the fact that some scholars suggest that there were two or three separate such movements in history, yet others suggest that a single women's movement went through several phases. Freeman (1975a), for example, stated that "sometime during the 1920s, feminism died in the United States" (p. 448). But as is the case in the other movements, the push for political, economic, and other rights for women never completely "died." Rather, during the natural history of the women's movement, there were times when the movement was widely and publicly active, and other times when those in the movement were retrenching and the movement was, so to speak, being held in suspension or in abeyance (Taylor 1989). As was the case with the other movements we have surveyed, internal conditions interacted with external circumstances to determine the nature of the movement. Many of those conditions were related to structures of economic, racial, and sexual inequality in the society.

The women's movement in the United States began in the late 1700s and early 1800s and has continued, although not always actively and publicly, to this day (Hole and Levine 1975; Chafe 1977; Snyder 1979). Throughout its history, feminism has incorporated two seemingly paradoxical general goals. One is the belief that since women are, in most respects, the *same* as men in their potential and abilities, they are deserving of the *same* rights as men. The other is the belief that since women are *different* from men and encounter different life experiences, they deserve special protections. At different times and by different groups, each of these positions has been emphasized. Women's rights, then, are defined according to which of these two sets of beliefs and goals is stressed (Cott 1986).

The earliest organized efforts by women involved attempts to increase their educational rights and to fight for the abolition of slavery, and it was during involvement in the abolitionist movement of the 1830s that some women began expressing an acute awareness of their own low political status. As proved to be the case with their involvement in other historical movements, women were not given significant status or voice in the abolitionist movement. Indeed, while this movement was fighting for an end to slavery, women were being prevented from joining some abolitionist organizations and were being muzzled in their attempt to speak in public on the issues. Women had to create their own antislavery organizations because they were being excluded from many of the men's organizations (Hole and Levine 1975). Women had experienced similar issues in the early labor union movement. While demanding rights and social justice for workers, many unions were at the same time barring women from membership. In those cases where women were members, few held leadership positions.

In 1840, a world antislavery meeting was held in London. Men at the meeting, including so-called radicals, were shocked to see women present, and so had them put in galleries where they could not participate effectively in the meeting. Later, in 1867, Sojourner Truth, a crusader for both women's and African Americans' rights, wrote of the neglect of women's rights among those who advocated such fights for African Americans: "There is a great stir about colored men getting their rights, but not a word about colored women; and if colored men get their rights and not colored women theirs, you see the colored men will be masters over the women, and it will be just as bad as it was before" (Hess and Ferree 1985, p. 32). Time and again, it became clear to many women that they would have to have their own organizations and movement if equal rights

were ever to be achieved (Hole and Levine 1975; Snyder 1979).

Two of the women who had attended the antislavery convention in London were Elizabeth Cady Stanton and Lucretia Mott. Convinced of the need for an organization exclusively for women's rights, these women organized a meeting that was held in Seneca Falls, New York, in July of 1848. About 300 men and women attended, including Frederick Douglass and Susan B. Anthony. The attendees approved a "Declaration of Sentiments" based loosely on the wording of the Declaration of Independence. Among other things, this document argued for the basic equality of men and women and stressed that historically men had dominated over women in religious institutions, employment opportunities, and family and political life. Included among the declarations made was a demand for the right to vote. Although this latter demand has been said to signal the beginning of the suffrage movement, most of the women at the Seneca Falls meeting were more concerned with issues in their immediate experience: control of property and earnings, rights over children, rights to divorce, and so forth. From 1848 to the Civil War, women's conventions were held almost every year in different cities of the East and Midwest (Hole and Levine 1975).

The Early Social Context and Directions

The social environment within which women were advocating greater freedoms and rights was not hospitable. This was reflected not only in women's imposed marginal status in male abolitionist and labor organizations but also in the reactions within other dominant institutions. Religious institutions and the media railed against the embryonic women's movement. It was as if natural and supernatural orders were being violated by the attempts to gain women rights equal to those of men. In order to spread the word, women had to rely on some abolitionist papers and their own journals. Late in the nineteenth century, Stanton and others produced *The Woman's Bible*, a systematic critique to demonstrate that the traditional Bible was a major source of the subjugation of women.

The early formation of the movement also was affected by the forces of early industrialization. Not being allowed to learn skills, women who needed to work were relegated to either household or low-paying work (Huber 1982). Women who were from the middle or upper class, on the other hand, were not expected to work but rather to appear and act as "ladies," or the "angel in the house" (Collins 1998). "The nineteenth-century concept of a lady was that of a fragile, idle, pure creature, submissive and subservient to her husband and to domestic needs. Her worth was based on her decorative value, a quality that embraced her beauty, her character, and her temperament. She was certainly not a paid employee" (Fox and Hesse-Biber 1984, p. 19). Not only working-class women but also Black women especially were not in a social and economic position to live up to the ideals of this image. They had to work, and in places and ways that did not foster an image of them as "ladies." If a woman was lacking in the qualities expected of a "lady," it "meant a woman was unnatural, unfeminine, and thus a species of a different—if not lower—female order. . . . Women who worked outside the home, or whose race had a history of sexual exploitation, were outside the realm of 'womanhood' and its prerogatives" (Giddings 1984, pp. 48–49). Thus, race as well as class circumstances divided women.

This class division among women had an impact on the membership and goals of the early women's organizations. It was largely middle- and upper-class women who initiated the early movement and who fashioned its goals to fit their problems and desires, such as the desire for education in the professions and civil service, and property and voting rights. At the same time, they pushed for lower numbers of hours for female factory workers (Huber 1982). Although the latter appeared as a form of protection for women, it also was seen by many men as a way to minimize work competition from women. This suggests, as discussed earlier, the varying emphases on women as being different as well as the same as men. A desire for protection implies that women are different and

more vulnerable than men, whereas the desire on the part of some women for equal employment opportunities implies that they are the equals of men. In sum, the religious and cultural milieu along with the conditions of industrialization and slavery, helped to shape the form of the early women's movement as well as reactions to it.

After the Civil War, when the Fourteenth and Fifteenth Amendments on Black rights were being debated, women were told that attempts to include women in these amendments would only diffuse the focus that was being placed on rights for Blacks alone. The incorporation of women as well as men into the amendments, they were told would hinder their passage (Hole and Levine 1975; Snyder 1979). The thrust for a separate women's movement accelerated, and basically two strands developed. One, under Elizabeth Cady Stanton and Susan B. Anthony, formed the National Woman Suffrage Association. It emphasized a variety of rights for women and viewed the vote as a means to obtaining them. The other, exemplified by the American Woman Suffrage Association under Lucy Stone and others, focused only on the vote. Eventually, the emphasis on the vote won out in the movement and the two organizations merged into the National American Woman Suffrage Association (Hole and Levine 1975). It is during this period that the term *feminism* came on to the public scene. It would have been unthinkable to use such a term during the "woman movement" of the nineteenth century. Feminism suggested a radical change in all relations with men and also attracted smaller numbers of followers than the earlier "woman movement" (Cott 1987).

In this *first wave* of the feminist movement two of the most militantly active groups pushing for the enfranchisement of women were the Congressional Union and the group derived from it the National Woman's Party (NWP). Both were at the forefront of the movement between 1916 and 1920.

The NWP was viewed as having a single objective, and any diversion from its pursuit was considered harmful. The rigid adherence to this philosophy resulted in insensitivity to the unique goals and problems of subgroups within the female population. "Only women holding cultur-ally hegemonic values and positions—that is, in the United States, women who are White, hetero-sexual, middle class, politically midstream—have the privilege (or deception) of seeing their condi-tion as that of 'woman,' glossing over their other characteristics," observed Cott perceptively (1986, p. 58). For example, some Blacks felt that the NWP was basically racist and did not care about the rights of Blacks. Most suffragist groups of the time were imbued with the racism of the broader culture and did little to combat it. Black women's concerns were considered to be racial rather than feminist problems (Cott 1987). This initial wave of the movement has been criticized for its narrow focus on the vote and absence of a broader con-sciousness of women's issues (Nachescu 2008).

In 1919, shortly before the passage of the Nineteenth Amendment enfranchising women, Walter White, leader of the NAACP, remarked about the NWP and its leadership: "If they could get the Suffrage Amendment through without enfranchising colored women, they would do it in a moment" (quoted in Cott 1987, p. 69). Just as women had been marginalized in the abolitionist movement by those fighting for Black rights, the specific problems of Blacks were now being put aside to focus on those of women only. In the same vein, some educated women were fighting for the same right to vote that "drunken male immigrant layabouts" possessed. This implied a kind of elitism among some segments of the suf-frage movement (Hess and Ferree 1985). But it also reflected a class and race elitism present in the wider society in the early 1900s, a division whose implications for the suffrage movement were not fully understood by its leaders. Those in the movement "profoundly misread the degree to which ethnic, class, and family allegiances under-mined the prospect of sex-based political behavior" (Chafe 1977, p. 118).

After the enfranchisement of women was accomplished in 1920, the movement for women's rights changed drastically. Rather than completely dying, the movement fractured internally, in large part because the attainment of the franchise had meant different things to different organizations and individuals. In essence, some women saw enfranchisement as an end in itself, while others viewed it as a means to reach more important goals, such as an equal rights amendment (ERA) for women.

The latter was now the goal of the National Woman's Party, while the more conservative National American Woman Suffrage Association fought against the ERA, formed the League of Women Voters, and worked for the active citizen-ship of women. The idea of universalistic legisla-tion covering women's rights also was opposed by the Women's Bureau of the Department of Labor and a number of voluntary women's organizations. They feared that the legalization of equality with men would remove the shelters women received under the protectionist legislation of the 1920s, which limited women's involvement in the labor force. Some of the motivation on the part of the government for passing protective legislation was concern over the declining fertility rate early in the twentieth century. Officials feared that too drastic a decline would have harmful effects on the size of the defense forces and on the growth of the econ-omy. It was believed that encouraging women to remain at home might stem the tide toward a lower birthrate.

At the bottom of everything, what divided women was the question of the priority of wom-en's maternal roles compared to their employment opportunities. Protectionist legislation was inter-preted by its adherents as conserving the maternal role of women (Huber 1982). Those pressing for an ERA, on the other hand, expressed an interest in the full potentiality of women, not merely their roles in the family. In a real sense, this difference of opinion on ERA resurrected the old question about the natures of men and women. Those who were in favor of the ERA were saying that women and men were basically the same, whereas those opposed to it and in support of protective legisla-tion were saying that the two groups were basi-cally different. Although both groups believed that sex inequality existed, the first group saw it as unnecessary and undesirable, whereas the second saw it as a given and, therefore, women needed protection (Cott 1986).

The movement also was splintered by the multiple ties of many women to other social movements. Once the Nineteenth Amendment had passed, many women moved on to other causes, such as temperance, birth control, union organizing, and poverty (Hess and Ferree 1985). Black women and working women had concerns other than those held by educated middle- or upper-class women, and some eventually formed their own organizations. Black women, for example, did not put the passage of the ERA and goals of the birth control movement anywhere near the top of their agenda: "For them, racial concerns overwhelmed those of sex" (Giddings 1984, p. 183). Lynching was a problem that hit much closer to home for them.

From Limbo to Resurgence

From 1945 to the 1960s, the women's movement was in limbo. In the years immediately after World War II, the social and cultural environment was not hospitable to protest from any minority group. The "feminine mystique" perception of the perfect woman was dominant. This woman was expected to be married, have children, be a helpmate to her husband and his career, and be happy in her domestic life. In other words, it was a conservative cultural period—one that sanctified the traditional male and female roles. Women who protested or sought "masculine" roles were considered not only unstable and possibly neurotic but also deviant (Rupp 1985; Taylor 1989). Thus, even if some women wanted to protest, there were few effective avenues through which to do so, and their protests would not have had the support of the federal government. The media ridiculed feminism and reinforced traditional husband and wife roles (Taylor 1989). It will be recalled that during this postwar expansion period, social inequality, in general, was an issue that was minimized.

Adding to the inhospitality of the social and cultural context, support for feminism also dwindled, and extant women's groups had little mass power. The Women's Bureau of the Department of Labor had little influence and was anti-ERA anyway, and the National Woman's Party had been reduced to a relatively small number of faithful followers. Most of the women still present in this organization after World War II were White, middle or upper class, employed, well educated, unmarried, and older than 50 years of age (Rupp 1985; Taylor 1989). The Alva Belmont House, which served as the national headquarters of the NWP in Washington, D.C., had its own set of hired cooks and servants, suggesting the privilege of class. None of these groups made much progress during this period, although they kept the movement for women's rights alive.

In light of its persistence through the difficult climate of the postwar period, the National Woman's Party served as the organization of abeyance for the women's movement. It provided tactics, social networks, and an identity to spur the resurgence of the activist phase of the *second wave* of feminism in the 1960s and 1970s. The National Organization for Women (NOW), which was founded in 1966, used many of the tactics of the NWP, such as political pressure and lobbying. NWP activists kept pressure on the government, thereby encouraging President Kennedy's decision to form a Presidential Commission on the Status of Women, and to include "sex" in Title VII of the 1964 Civil Rights Act.

Although the 1945–1960 period was not marked by significant advances in the women's movement, several other social, cultural, and economic changes were occurring that created the structure necessary for a resurgence of the movement in the 1960s. In the period after World War II, an increasing number of women were obtaining educational degrees and participating in the labor force. Opportunities to work, coupled with a trend toward smaller families and a desire for more consumer goods on the part of families who could get on the installment plan, encouraged more women to enter the market. More children were moving out to attend college, which further increased the need in most families for added income. The contour of the female labor force changed from one that had been primarily composed of single women in 1940 to one that consisted mainly of married women and mothers in 1950. But women also experienced significant job segregation following their removal from jobs after the war and the return of more men to the labor force (Freeman 1975b; Huber 1982). Nevertheless, successful participation in traditionally male positions during the war convinced many women that they could do the same jobs as men in most cases. Moreover, their increasing participation in the labor market was at odds with the vision of the perfect family in which the wife/mother stays at home to perform domestic and wifely chores.

In other words, by the time the 1960s arrived, women were more educated, had more earnings, and many had significant experience in the labor force. This experience brought women face-to-face with their limited occupational opportunities. Added to this was the fact that the civil rights movement was peaking in the early 1960s and ideas about equality and personal intimacy were becoming more popular. The "sexual revolution" of the mid-1960s, which encouraged control of one's own body and tolerance of different sexual practices, also was consistent with feminist goals (Chafe 1977). All these events and conditions made the context ripe for a resurgence of the women's movement.

It should be kept in mind that this resurgence took place at a time and at the partial expense of the civil rights movement. Despite the occurrence of all the racial incidents in the South during this time, sudden concern was deflected from racial issues and focused on the problems of women, especially, it appeared, those of White middle-class women. The concerns that Betty Friedan expressed in *The Feminine Mystique*, those of the alienated suburban housewife, seemed far removed from the real everyday problems of Black women. The issues posed clearly described a kind of woman unfamiliar to the average Black woman. Many Black women considered White women to be simply another part of the White enemy, and considered their own problems to be both more serious and qualitatively different from those of White women. They resented White feminists' equating sexism with racism, and promoting the idea that Blacks and women experience a "common oppression" (Nachescu 2008, p. 47). Consequently, during this period most activist

Black women did not identify with the priorities of the White women's movement, and did not join it (Breines 2007). Further souring feelings between Black and White women was the fact that the women's movement was seen as having benefited from the earlier and costly efforts of the civil rights movement (Giddings 1984).

In June 1966 a meeting of state commissions on the status of women convened in Washington, D.C. (Freeman 1975b; Hess and Ferree 1985). It was here that the National Organization for Women was created, largely because of the belief that the Equal Employment Opportunity Commission, which had developed out of the Civil Rights Act of 1964 and was supposed to deal with sex discrimination, was doing little about the problems of women in the labor market. Race and sex again appeared to be working at cross purposes. NOW's early emphasis on equal rights, which was attractive to many middle- and upper-class women, turned off Black women, lesbians, and those who were members of unions (Giddings 1984). Conversely, when NOW leaders desired membership in the Leadership Conference on Civil Rights, they were denied with the argument that women's problems did not constitute a civil rights issue (Hess and Ferree 1985).

The civil rights movement and the newly resurgent women's movement of the 1960s intertwined race and sex issues in other ways as well. Experience in civil rights activities provided many women with knowledge about tactics and organizing problems and gave them a sense of their own capabilities. At the same time, however, their participation made it clear, as it had been made clear to women involved in the abolitionist movement, that they needed to develop their own organizations and movement. Women, Black and White, were not accorded high status in the civil rights movement, especially in the later Black Power stage. This is despite the fact that, though largely unrecognized, Black women had performed many varied leadership roles in the civil rights movement (Barnett 1993).

Young women's experiences in the student New Left movement also left much to be desired. While the movement preached fewer restrictions on sexuality, the men generally treated the women who were members as objects available for the taking. Women did not have positions of power in the New Left. The experiences of many younger women in both the Black Power and New Left movements helped motivate them to create a network of feminists committed to their own unique cause. Thus, another less formal branch of the women's network developed alongside the more centralized and national-level organizations of the women's movement. In contrast to the older, more bureaucratic sector of the feminist movement that sought equality through formal institutional channels, this strand of the second wave of the movement consisted of more informal, locally based groupings composed primarily of younger women. While the formal national organizations stressed legislation and lobbying as routes to women's rights, the younger, less formal, and more radical strand emphasized the importance of education and consciousness-raising to personal power and women's liberation. These groups arose all over: in Chicago, Toronto, Detroit, Seattle, Gainesville, and many other places.

The diversity hinted at should suggest the level of richness and depth of the current women's movement. But its complexity, broadness of constituency, and decentralized organization is only one of the ways in which it differs from the earlier suffrage phase of the women's movement. A second difference lies in the fact that its development during the 1960s was more in tune with broader changes in the society at large, as well as more in touch with the real experiences of many women. The cultural contexts during the suffrage and abolitionist movements, it will be recalled, were much more hostile to a woman's movement for equal rights or liberation. Third, in contrast to the earlier active phases of the movement, the goals became much more diverse during the second wave. The suffrage movement concentrated on a single issue—the vote (Chafe 1977). Similarly, the abolitionist movement concentrated on a single problem—slavery.

Despite its successes, the women's movement has continued to encounter an array of fearsome obstacles. The political, economic, and social conditions of the 1980s generated a strong antifeminist countermovement. By the end of the 1970s, many average citizens had been told by the media that women had reached their goals. Added to this message was another that portrayed "feminists as anti-male, lesbian, humorless, and politically correct ideologues" (Anderson 1997, p. 313). In 1980, Republicans dropped advocacy of the ERA from their platform after 40 years of supporting it. The New Right began to flower in the late 1970s and has consistently attacked the feminist agenda. This movement is composed of professionals, ministers, and politicians who subscribe to a combination of fundamentalist religious dogma and conservative politics antagonistic to feminism. Since 2000, an increasing number of women have been drawn into right-wing movements.

Nevertheless, a *third wave* of feminism, dominated by younger women, continued into the 1980s and 1990s, and emphasized intersectionality, particularly the influence of queer studies; an emphasis on a variety of perspectives and theoretical approaches rather than grand narratives; and an inclusivity in definitions of feminisms (Snyder 2008; Evans and Chamberlain 2015). Instead of pursuing equality through political action, third-wave feminists often focus on personal empowerment in the cultural sphere, through music, fashion, transgender behaviors, and other multiple identities (Aronson 2003; Diamond 2008; Wrye 2009). Some suggest that in the early years of the twenty-first century, a *fourth wave* of feminism is emerging that reaches outward to others, stressing the importance of an "internal sense of gender inequality," a spirituality that views all humans as part of one community, and actions that aid the whole world and its downtrodden populations (Diamond 2009, p. 218; Wrye 2009). Additionally, some cite the increasing use of social media and technology as a hallmark of a fourth wave (Evans and Chamberlain 2015).

Since the 1970s, support for the women's movement and feminism has increased, though public opinion is contradictory (Huddy, Neely, and Lafay 2000). The vast majority of Americans appear to support many of the specific ideas associated with the equality of men and women. At least

55 percent of Americans believe in equality for women, and over 75 percent of women believe that the women's movement has made life better for them (Kliff 2015; Rhode 2014). "And when polls give the dictionary definition of feminism as someone who supports political, economic and social equality for women, most polls find 65–77 percent of women and 58–70 percent of men consider themselves feminist; in one 2013 survey, 82 percent of Americans agreed with the statement" (Rhode 2014, p. 10).

However, most Americans do not identify themselves as "feminist," in great part due to its association with activism and with negative stereotypes related to feminism (Rhode 2014; Leaper and Arias 2011). Only 18–25 percent of Americans currently embrace the label "feminist" (Kliff 2015; Frankovic 2014), though younger women are more likely to do so than older women (Fitzpatrick Bettencourt, Vacha-Haase, and Byrne 2011).

The ambivalence and divisions in perceptions of feminism are reflected in a recent survey of young women who differ in the ways they define "feminism" and vary in their identification with feminism. The priorities given to life's issues depend heavily on the everyday experiences and the racial and class backgrounds of these women. Most of the women interviewed were ambivalent, supporting some feminist ideals but not others, and were hesitant to define themselves as feminists (Aronson 2003). In light of the historical divisions within the women's movement and the conflicting social and cultural forces currently at work in society that were noted earlier, it is perhaps not surprising to find that many young women have ambiguous and ambivalent feelings about feminism.

It has been argued that using the imagery of "waves" of feminism makes the diversity within the various women's movements less visible, and makes it appear that the movement has been monolithic (Springer 2002). Since the so-called first wave, there have been movements focused on the concerns of a diversity of women, addressing issues of race, class, ethnicity, and sexuality. However, the women's movement has traditionally been seen as a White middle-class one that does not address the needs of all women (Rosen 2006). One veteran feminist observes that most of the achievements of the women's movement have not really affected poor women: "I think living in poverty is an unresolved problem of the women's movement" (Bolgar 2009, p. 198). The diversity within the movement with respect to race, sexuality, gender expression, class-specific goals, and assumptions about the nature of men and women has provided a source of strength. But under the pressures of a countermovement against feminism, these divisions could widen and splinter the movement. What can be a source of strength can also be a source of damaging division. Like the labor movement, the women's movement has yet to bring everyone under its umbrella.

THE BLACK LIVES MATTER MOVEMENT AND THE REEMERGENCE OF STUDENT ACTIVISM

Having been in a fairly quiescent phase until recently, in the past several years, civil rights movements have enjoyed a substantial upsurge, exemplified by movements such as Occupy Wall Street and the fight for marriage equality. Most recently we have seen the emergence of Black Lives Matter as well as a range of campus-based activism by college students. These movements all build on past efforts and continue the often invisible work of organizing that continues in the background: "Movements often proceed in alternating phases of intense public action and seeming dormancy, and much of the work that shapes the long term is in fact done during what appear superficially to be mere spaces between waves of activism. The waves, moreover, are often conjunctures among multiple movements" (Calhoun 2013, p. 26). As such, the Black Lives Matter movement represents both a continuation of past racial justice movements and the confluence of several other social justice movements.

In 2012, Trayvon Martin, an unarmed 17-year-old Black boy, was shot and killed by George Zimmerman while walking in a Florida neighborhood. Prosecutors in the case argued that Zimmerman was suspicious of Martin because he was "an unfamiliar tall black teenager in a hoodie walking around Mr. Zimmerman's gated community" (Alvarez 2015). Zimmerman ignored a police dispatcher's advice to not engage with the teenager and forced a confrontation with Martin. Martin defended himself against Zimmerman, who responded by shooting and killing Martin. Zimmerman was acquitted of second-degree murder, successfully pleading self-defense (Alvarez 2015). This event sparked national outrage centering on issues of racial profiling and racial injustice.

The viral #BlackLivesMatter movement was created in response to the death of Trayvon Martin and the subsequent acquittal of Zimmerman. The term was coined when queer Black activist Alicia Garza wrote on social media that "the anger people felt was justified and that 'black lives matter'" (Craven 2015). Patrisse Cullors assigned the hashtag to the phrase and began posting it on social media, leading to the rise of the movement (Craven 2015). Black Lives Matter strives to bring social media to the streets to celebrate the value of Black lives in the face of systemic racism. The movement maintains a continuity to previous efforts, most particularly the Black Liberation movement, but in many respects differs in strategy and approach from earlier movements.

The strategies and goals of the Black Lives Matter movement are greatly informed by an intersectional approach to understanding oppression and injustice (Shor 2015; Garza 2015). Specifically, the organizers take an *intracategorical* approach to their work (see Chapter 6), in that through underscoring and understanding the diversity of experiences of Black individuals based on statuses such as gender, class, sexuality, gender expression, citizenship, and ability, they can better move toward achieving racial justice. In her explanation of the goals of the movement, Garza states, "Progressive movements in the United States have made some unfortunate errors when they push for unity at the expense of really understanding the concrete differences in context, experience and oppression. In other words, some want unity without struggle. As people who have our minds stayed on freedom, we can learn to fight anti-Black racism by examining the ways in which we participate in it, even unintentionally, instead of the wor-

Photo 13.2 The past few years have seen a resurgence of activism centered on issues of police shootings and persistent racism.

© Rena Schild/shutterstock.

out and sloppy practice of drawing lazy parallels of unity between peoples with vastly different experiences and histories" (Garza 2015).

The approach of the movement borrows directly from the Black Liberation movement, and more specifically from the efforts of the Student Nonviolent Coordinating Committee (SNCC) from the 1960s (Shor 2015). The model they employ is a decentralized, community-based structure that brings together loosely organized chapters across the country. As did SNCC organizer Ella Baker, Garza and her colleagues very much wanted to break away from the more traditional, male-dominated civil rights organizational structure in which the work of women and LGBTQ individuals in the movement was greatly marginalized and made invisible. Garza explains that "(t)he narrative of this movement's beginnings counter the typical origins of black leadership, which are often personified via cisgender, heterosexual black men. If people were looking for a remake of Martin Luther King Jr., Jesse Jackson or Al Sharpton, they'd be disappointed, and rightfully so" (Garza 2015). At times the movement has come into conflict with older generations of organizers, as was seen in December of 2014 when Black Lives Matter members stormed the stage after the Reverend Al Sharpton refused to allow any younger speakers during a rally protesting the killings of young black men (Shor 2015).

The movement has garnered a fierce social media following, at least in part because of its dedication to inclusion. The movement has become even more relevant as police shootings and violence against Blacks gain media attention. The deaths of Tamir Rice, Freddie Gray, Eric Garner, Michael Brown, and Sandra Bland have been highlighted as Blacks who were killed at the hands of the police under questionable circumstances. The attention to these cases is partly a result of the work of the Black Lives Matter movement.

The #BlackLivesMatter movement has seen significant backlash from people who argue that it ignores the value of White people who are also victims of violence. The #AllLivesMatter platform was created to represent this view. Similarly, the #BlueLivesMatter platform was focused on valuing and remembering the lives of police officers lost in the course of their work. Critics of All Lives Matter, however, argue that Black Lives Matter is intended to highlight the systematic disparity in the way Blacks and Whites are treated under the law. This inequality, further detailed in Chapter 12, is entrenched in the law as well as in its enforcement. Critics also point out that All Lives Matter fails to recognize that the Black Lives Matter movement is not suggesting that White lives do not matter, but rather that Black lives have been limited by institutionalized inequalities that do not face Whites in the same ways (Garza 2015).

The success of the Black Lives Matter movement has encouraged the formation of other "hashtag" movements. Most of these support and act as subgroups to the original #BlackLivesMatter movement. For example, #SayHerName and #(insert name of slain Black individual) have received attention. The Say Her Name platform was created to bring Black women's lives to the public's attention and ". . . offer a more complete—not competing—narrative about policing and race" (Workneh 2015). #(Insert name of slain Black individual) has been posted along with the Black Lives Matter hashtag in order to make the name of the victim of police violence known to the public. It humanizes the victim and allows for each victim's narrative to stand on its own while acknowledging its position in the greater problem of systemic racism in American society.

In conjunction with the Black Lives Matter movement and the various hashtag movements, student activism has been proliferating in the United States and globally for the past several years (Wong 2015; Wong and Green 2016). Blogger and historian Alan Johnston (Johnston 2016) has mapped and analyzed 160 separate student protests focused on issues of racial justice both globally and within institutions of higher education, but including as well the cost of higher education, sexual assault, and gender expression in the classroom. Most recently, students at many institutions have presented lists of demands to their administrators on issues of campus climate and racial inclusion (see www.thedemands.org for a partial listing of institutions and student demands).

These demands range widely, but common to many are the hiring of more faculty and administrators of color and the creation of mandatory cultural competency training courses for students, faculty, and staff (Wong and Green 2016). As Johnston states, "One of the things that ties (the campus movements) all together is a sense that the future doesn't look as rosy as it might have a few years ago" (quoted in Wong 2015).

The Black Lives Matter movement and the wave of student activism represent an important new wave of civil rights activism. The Black Lives Matter movement played a crucial role in debates about the 2016 presidential candidates. Although there has been significant backlash to the movement, it has placed racial inequality and violence squarely into the public consciousness.

Summary

All of the social movements discussed were focused on reducing social inequalities of one sort or another. But as has been noted before, such grievances are not sufficient for either the development or continuance of a social movement. The surrounding social structure must generate openings and opportunities for movements to develop and prosper. Conditions such as social unrest and economic upheaval create potential economic and political opportunities that lead to the appearance of social movements.

The cultural context also affects the life and structure of a social movement. You have seen how a variety of societal values and ideologies have been reflected in the character of labor, women's, and civil rights movements. Racist, sexist, and class values and their intersection deeply influenced the shape of and membership in each movement, creating internal divisions and pressures toward homogeneous organizations.

In addition to structural opportunities and cultural milieu, the resources available to a group affect the development of a movement. Of course, whether an aggrieved group can obtain such resources also depends on the structure of opportunities and the cultural milieu.

Finally, the presence of opportunities, resources, and a favorable cultural milieu fosters the development of power and a sense of a *cognitive liberation* in which groups of aggrieved individuals redefine their situation and their potential for successful solutions (McAdam 2010). On the other hand, when groups have few opportunities and no resources, and the culture is adverse, the chances of a new revolutionary consciousness and a successful social movement are slim indeed. Until equity is achieved, however, movements for class, racial, and gender equality are likely to continue in the United States, if only sporadically.

Critical Thinking

1. Given current economic difficulties in the United States at large, what do you think the prospects are for a resurgence of a vibrant labor movement? Explain your answer.
2. What effect, if any, do you think the conservative movements that have arisen in the United States since the early 1980s will have on inequality in the country?
3. What kinds of new inequalities are emerging from which movements might develop? What conditions might maximize or minimize the chances for these movements?
4. Why has it been difficult for those in the labor, civil rights, and women's movements to join forces?
5. To what extent would you describe the Black Lives Matters movement as an intersectional movement?

Web Connections

Visit the AFL-CIO's website at www.aflcio.org to learn about issues of importance to unions. To read about the goals of the feminist movement in the 1960s and 1970s, go to http://womenshistory. about.com/od/feminism. The story of the civil rights movement as told by its veterans can be read at www.crmvet.org.

The Black Lives Matter website (http://blacklives matter.com) provides a detailed history of the movement and its political underpinnings, as well as a dynamic representation of current activities and changes in the movement. Compare the tactics in this movement to that represented in the AFL-CIO website above.

Film Suggestions

Democracy in America: #05 Civil Rights: Demanding Equality (2003). This film examines guarantees of equality and the roles played by government and individuals in ensuring these guarantees for vulnerable groups in society.

American Women of Achievement (1995). This series looks at the lives of 10 notable American women from Abigail Adams to Wilma Rudolph to Sandra Day O'Connor.

Selma (2014). This film depicts a 3-month period in 1965 in which Dr. Martin Luther King Jr. led a march from Selma to Montgomery, Alabama. Though they faced violent opposition, the march ultimately ended in the signing of the Voting Rights Act of 1965.

PART 4

Stability and Change in the System of Social Inequality

CHAPTER 14

Social Mobility and Status Attainment

It's all right to tell a man to lift himself by his own bootstraps, but it is cruel jest to say to a bootless man that he ought to lift himself by his own bootstraps.

MARTIN LUTHER KING JR. (1929–1968)

The United States as a storied land of opportunity and freedom is chronicled in many myths and fables about how the individual, no matter how humble and lowly, can succeed. Children in U.S. society often are told that if they work hard enough and want something badly enough, they will obtain it. They are taught that opportunities are there to be grasped, if a person just has the aspirations and perseverance required to take advantage of them.

Americans tend to have a rosy view of the opportunities and prospects attainable in their country. A 2014 Pew survey found that about 65 percent of Americans think that people can get ahead if they just work hard (Pew 2014b). Just about the same percentage expect their personal financial situation to improve over the next year. Interestingly, a full 57 percent of Americans disagreed with the statement, "Success in life is pretty much determined by forces outside our control" (Gao 2015). In other words, most Americans believe it is the attributes of the person rather than outside forces that are most important for advancement. Having little education, too much debt, and making poor choices are the factors most often mentioned for why some persons are downwardly mobile (Economic Mobility Project 2009).

In light of these values about the individual and achievement, it is not surprising that a central question raised in the study of inequality has concerned the extent to which the United States is an open society. The issue of openness raises a number of questions:

- In terms of sheer amount, how much mobility has there been and is there now in the United States? How does the United States compare with other countries on mobility?
- What is the nature of the mobility that has occurred? Is it more often long-distance or short-range mobility?

- What have been the trends in intergenerational inheritance? Are individuals more or less likely to have the same socioeconomic status as their parents?
- What roles do socioeconomic background and individual qualities play in determining an individual's present status? To what extent is social mobility determined by forces beyond individuals' control rather than by their own actions?
- What conditions in the economic, social, and cultural structures affect the chances for and levels of attainment by individuals?

Each of these questions concerns a separate issue, but all of them are relevant to the general question of how open U.S. society is, and each of them has been addressed in research. The first three questions have been the concern of traditional mobility studies, whereas the last two have been a main focus of status attainment research.

U.S. MOBILITY OVER TIME

Serious mobility research began in the 1940s, and even then there was concern about what the future held. Changes in mobility studies since the 1940s have been driven by changes in the databases used and increases in the sophistication of techniques for analyzing them.

Estimates of Mobility Trends from World War II through the 1990s

One of the first attempts to arrive at some conclusions regarding post–World War II mobility trends using national sample data was carried out by Jackson and Crockett (1964). The authors compared data for **intergenerational mobility** between father and son collected in 1957 by the Survey Research Center at the University of Michigan with national data collected in 1945, 1947, and 1952 to determine trends in mobility from 1945 to 1957. The results suggested that greater mobility occurred in 1952 and 1957 than in 1947. Some mobility would have occurred simply because of changes in the occupational structure between

generations. The amount and type of social mobility that occurs in a society is in part affected by the opportunities that are created, changed, or eliminated by the structure within which individuals operate. For example, World War II veterans often received occupational training while in the military; they were also able to take advantage of the educational opportunities afforded by the GI bill. Taking advantage of these opportunities allowed veterans to strengthen their human capital and later attain higher wages and more prestigious occupations (Teachman and Tedrow 2004). The structure of opportunities had broadened because new avenues for social mobility had opened up. Indeed, many veterans were able to go to college using the GI bill.

The character and composition of the occupational structure at any given point in time make up part—a very important part—of the **opportunity structure** within which individuals may be able to move. The structure places limits on the possibility and degree of occupational mobility in a society. Increases in the white-collar governmental sector after World War II, for example, even encouraged working-class and middle-class youths to leave high school or college to get jobs in the expanding economy (Shanahan, Miech, and Elder 1998).

In other words, between any two periods of time, some mobility is bound to occur if the occupational distributions in the two generations in question are different. The difference between that minimum amount of *expected* mobility and what *actually* occurs is often referred to as the amount of social fluidity or **circulation mobility**. Most consider this to be a better measure of the openness of a system than the total amount of mobility because it allegedly has already taken into account changes caused by alterations in the occupational structure. Circulation mobility is also a more direct measure of the impact of family background on an individual's mobility. Greater openness suggests a weaker tie between background and mobility. A greater proportion of the total mobility in 1947 appears to have been due to circulation than to structural conditions or **structural mobility**, whereas in 1952 and 1957, the reverse is the case.

Blau and Duncan (1967) added 1962 national data to that used by Jackson and Crockett. Blau and Duncan's data suggested that circulation increased between 1957 and 1962 and that the son's occupation was less dependent on that of the father. In other words, the system of inequality appears to have been more open in 1962 than in the earlier years.

Some of the principal findings from Blau and Duncan (1967) revealed clear patterns:

1. Despite a good deal of mobility, especially of the short-range variety, occupational inheritance was higher than would be expected if no relationship existed between the father's status and the son's 1962 occupational status.

2. Upward mobility was much more prevalent than downward mobility, most of it being structurally induced.

3. The highest rates of *inflow* into an occupational category from other categories occurred among the lower white-collar and lower blue-collar occupations. That is, they recruited individuals from a wide variety of occupational backgrounds.

4. The highest rates of *outflow* from an occupational category occurred among the two lowest white-collar groups and the blue-collar and farm groupings. That is, a greater proportion of these sons went to other occupations, suggesting that they had greater chances for mobility. In the salaried professions, on the other hand, just the opposite situation occurred. The sons were much less likely to outflow to other occupations, suggesting a high degree of inheritance.

5. An increasing proportion of men with non-farm/manual origins moved up into the white-collar occupations. But men who started their own careers in a blue-collar occupation were less likely to be mobile than those who began their careers as white-collar workers or farmers (pp. 28–41).

In the 1970s, Featherman and Hauser (1978) replicated Blau and Duncan's study and found some similar results. There was a great deal of intra- and intergenerational mobility, most of it short-distance, and there was more upward than downward mobility. More mobility took place than would be expected looking only at changes in the occupational structure. Most of the mobility took place in the middle of the occupational hierarchy, for example, in upper blue-collar positions. The top and bottom were fairly closed, suggesting "barriers to movement across class boundaries" (p. 180). Still there was a decline in the relationship between occupational origins and destinations and between fathers' and sons' occupations. Featherman and Hauser concluded that, "among American men a reduction of obstacles to occupational change appears to be a long-term and continuing tendency" (p. 136). At least for men, background seemed to have become less important in determining occupational position. This has been substantiated for the period from 1972 to 1985 as well. The decline in the association between an individual's social background and where they end up occupationally appears to be linked to the rise in the proportion of workers who have higher education. This is the case for both men and women (Hout 1988).

Race, farm background, and paternal occupation were still important predictors of occupational status and mobility, but contemporary changes moderated their impact. On the one hand, the educational level of Blacks increased. Black fathers were more able to pass on their status to sons, and the growing "rationality" of the economy created pressures to reduce discrimination. But discrimination did not appear to be any less significant than in the 1960s, racial differences in returns to human-capital investments still remained, and the likelihood of young Blacks being in the labor force was smaller in the 1970s than in the 1960s. Stratification within the Black community became more visible and clear. Blacks became more differentiated with respect to socioeconomic status, creating more distinct classes and greater inequalities among them.

With respect to the last point, results from the analysis of several national surveys conducted between 1972 and 1985 indicate that the openness of the U.S. occupational structure may have increased, whereas changes in the composition of the occupational structure may have slowed. This means that, overall, the extent of observed mobility remains unchanged because the increase in openness has been offset by a reduction in mobility resulting from changes in the occupational structure. In the 1980s, both men and women were more likely to have had parents with similar occupational status than was the case even in 1970. For example, the share of men and women whose origins are upper middle class had grown, whereas the proportion with farm backgrounds had declined. For most of the twentieth century, the extent of mobility in the United States was due primarily to changes in the occupational structure between generations. From the late 1960s into the 1980s, however, mobility shifts may have been due especially to increases in openness and related factors.

In contrast to the Blau and Duncan (1967) and Featherman and Hauser (1978) studies, which projected a society with increased openness and decreasing inheritance of occupation, evidence suggests that occupational mobility and intergenerational mobility slowed and perhaps even declined in the last decade of the twentieth century. The amount of social fluidity or openness for men born since the mid-1960s appeared to be lower than that for children born earlier in the twentieth century (Aaronson and Mazumder 2008). Interestingly, this was partly because the link between mothers' class and sons' occupational status became stronger over time (Beller 2009). Earlier analyses, which did not include measures of mother's social class or employment status, were unable to assess this link.

During the 1990s, intergenerational mobility at the top and bottom of the economic hierarchy remained fairly restricted. There was a distinct tendency for individuals born into a high- or low-status family to remain in that position (Hertz 2005; Mazumder 2005). For example, in the 1990s, it was estimated that a son born into the top 10 percent of the income hierarchy had at least a 1 in 5 chance of attaining the same position, but that one born into the bottom 10 percent had only a 1 in 100 chance of moving up into the top income decile. The chances were much greater

that the latter would remain at the bottom (Bowles and Gintis 2002). Nam's (2004) study of sons from low-income and high-income backgrounds confirmed this conclusion, finding that intergenerational transmission for those in the high-income group increased over time, but that the chances of low-income persons moving up from their poorer position did not change significantly. "These findings imply that America is not becoming more equal for its children" (p. 202).

Rytina's longitudinal study of occupational mobility (2000) revealed that the relationship between fathers' and sons' specific occupations may be strengthening. Using data from a national sample of families that have been tracked for 36 years since the late 1960s, a study compared parents' 1968 family incomes with those of their children in the late 1990s and early 2000s. While most children had incomes higher than that of their parents, children's income was strongly influenced by those of their parents. Parental influence on children's *wealth* was also present, although it was not as strong as the impact on *income* (Isaacs, Sawhill, and Haskins 2008).

Current U.S. Mobility Patterns

The most recent studies of intergenerational mobility show mixed results. Some scholars predicted that there would be drops in social mobility since 2000 because of documented increases in income inequality. The link between income inequality and social mobility has been well established. For example, looking at the country level we see that high income inequality is strongly associated with low social mobility (Corak 2013). Given this, we would expect that the recent increases in U.S. income inequality would lead to mobility decreases. While some studies have found this to be the case (Aaronson and Mazumder 2008), others have found less evidence for the link. Chetty, Hendren, Kline, Saez, and Turner (2014), for example, analyzed tax returns from all U.S. citizens born between 1980 and 1993 and found that intergenerational mobility has not changed significantly from the 1970s. They speculate that income inequality has not had the predicted effect because much of the change is in the upper end of the income distribution (the top 1 percent increasing its share of income) and has not had a lot of impact on the middle class. Chetty et al. point out, however, that while mobility has not significantly decreased, this should not be taken to mean that increasing income equality has no effect on people's lives. In fact, inequality has a profound impact on other domains like health and education.

One important recent finding about social mobility is that there are strong variations by region of the country. For example, there is comparatively low mobility in the Southeast region and high mobility in the Mountain West and the rural Midwest. The researchers use two cities to illustrate this regional difference. In Charlotte, North Carolina, the chances of a child from the lowest quintile of the income distribution making it to the top quintile is 4.4 percent. The equivalent number in San Jose, California, is 12.9 percent. The researchers find five features that distinguish high from low mobility areas. High mobility areas tend to have less income inequality, less residential

segregation, more stable families, better schools, and stronger social capital (Chetty, Hendren, Kline, and Saez 2014).

As described at the beginning of this chapter, Americans tend to be optimistic about their chances of becoming rich even though rags-to-riches mobility is very unusual in the United States (DiPrete 2007; Kotkin 2010). The chances of becoming wealthy by being a Horatio Alger–type entrepreneur are much less for those from poor backgrounds than they are for individuals who come from middle- or upper-class families. In fact, recent data show that only 4 percent of adults who were raised in the lowest income quintile make it to the top quintile (Pew Charitable Trusts 2012). It is paradoxical that, on the one hand, most citizens believe in the openness of U.S. society, while on the other hand, the family one is born into has a significant effect on one's **status attainment**. This reflects a conflict between a value that extols openness for all, and one that exhorts parents and families to do the best they can for their children. These values clash in struggles over issues of

Photo 14.1 This mural in a poor urban neighborhood shows the importance of "choosing the right path" to leave behind the darkness of poverty and crime and to move toward a brighter future.

Photo by Brendan R. Hurst.

equal opportunity and inheritance (McNamee and Miller Jr. 2013; Bowles, Gintis, and Groves 2009).

Mobility toward and at the Bottom

Evidence of growing numbers of poor people, rising income/earnings inequality, and speculation about a declining middle class have spurred questions about whether downward mobility has increased in the United States in recent years. Research suggests that in some respects it has, but that the answer depends somewhat on whether such mobility is measured in absolute or relative terms. **Absolute downward mobility** refers to a downward shift in economic resources without a simultaneous change in an individual's position relative to others. For example, one's income may decline, but because the income of others is also declining or because those below are much poorer, one may still remain in the same place on the income ladder. **Relative downward mobility**, on the other hand, refers to an actual shift in position on the ladder, a switching of position with others. So, for example, one may start out in the third quintile in the income distribution, but then fall into the fourth because of declines in income.

Evidence from large nationally representative samples suggests that 84 percent of Americans earn more than their parents did at their age (absolute upward mobility). It should be noted, however, that the gains are much higher at the upper end of the income spectrum than the lower. In terms of relative mobility, we see that the upper and lower ends of the spectrum are particularly "sticky" (meaning that poor people tend to stay poor and rich people tend to stay rich). Moreover, larger amounts of relative downward mobility came from the middle and lower quintiles than from the upper quintiles. The chances of falling into poverty are much greater for Blacks and those who are **near poor** (Pew Charitable Trusts 2012); they are also greater for women than for men. Together with evidence cited earlier about growing economic inequality, these trends fit the saying that the "rich get richer and the poor get poorer."

Regardless of similarity in experience, credentials, and human capital, Blacks in high-status occupations early in their careers are more likely than Whites to face downward mobility during their first four years in their occupations. This is especially the case in the private sector. This downward movement has negative repercussions for occupational experiences later in their careers. Human capital and other predictors of occupational status appear to be more predictive and protective of high-status White than Black employees. Decisions for Black displacement are "broadly based" and less affected by standard, expected factors like education and background (Wilson and Roscigno 2010, p. 69). Blacks in lower middle-class positions are also more apt than Whites to suffer downward mobility. Blacks who are relatively new to a middle-class status are more vulnerable than their White counterparts to falling in class position because they often lag behind Whites in education and wealth (Hardaway and McLoyd 2009).

Mobility at the bottom of the economic ladder has become a growing concern as questions about the severely disadvantaged class and possible intergenerational transmission of poverty have arisen. National data suggest that the chances of upward mobility of both White and Black children are reduced when raised in a poor family. Being from a Black family increases the negative effects of poverty. Generally, about half of all Blacks who were raised in poor families stay poor in early adulthood, compared to about a third of Whites who were raised poor (Pew Charitable Trusts 2012). Almost two-thirds of Black children grow up in the bottom 20 percent of families in the nation, compared to only 11 percent of White children, and when they become adults, Black children, especially those in the middle class, are much less likely than White children to have incomes that exceed those of their parents. About 56 percent of Black children compared to only 32 percent of White children with middle-class parents wind up falling into the bottom income quintile when they are adults (Pew Charitable Trusts 2012).

Children who are raised poor are significantly more likely to be poor when they are adults than children brought up in nonpoor families. Compared to poor children, those brought up in wealthy families are more likely to inherit large amounts of wealth, obtain it earlier, attain high levels of education, and develop patterns of consumption and methods of asset allocation that will maintain and even enhance their wealth (Isaacs, Sawhill, and Haskins 2008). In contrast, even if poor children move out of poverty as adults, having come from a poor family negatively and significantly affects children's future education, working hours, earnings, and incomes. The effects of poverty are particularly severe when experienced in early childhood (Duncan and Magnuson 2011). *Why* these effects occur has been a subject of debate.

The mechanisms linking background to future poverty are multiple. Lack of economic resources may affect the ability of parents to provide enriching educational experiences such as high-quality day care or summer camp. Poor parents may also be hindered from providing enriching experiences in their homes because they work long hours or struggle with anxiety and depression. In turn, these factors affect the economic futures of their children (Duncan and Magnuson 2011). Children raised in lower-income families are less likely to complete their schooling and more likely to have children outside of a marriage—two conditions that seem to increase the chances of poverty (Shattuck and Kreider 2013). The effects of early poverty are cumulative and stretch across the life course. For example, a study of persons 55 and older found that those who had less than a high school education and were engaged in low-wage work for most of their lives were much more likely to fall into poverty in old age than people who had more education and had been employed in higher-wage stable work (O'Brien, Wu, and Baer 2010).

Evidence also strongly suggests that employment opportunities and neighborhood conditions are important. The number and nature of economic opportunities in an area also affect poverty risks (Chetty, Hendren, and Katz 2015). Poor neighborhoods become socially isolated from nonpoor areas as economic and employment flight from them occurs (W. J. Wilson 2012). It should not be surprising, then, that elderly *urban* residents are also less likely than elderly *rural* residents to become poor since the presence of economic opportunities are greater in metropolitan areas than in rural places.

STATUS ATTAINMENT: WHAT DETERMINES HOW FAR ONE GOES?

Most mobility studies have not provided us with a systematic picture of the *process* through which mobility occurs. That is, they do not lay out the mechanisms and pathways that explain the connection between the positions of parents and their adult children. Status attainment studies attempt to identify the factors that are primarily responsible for this connection by focusing on *how* individual parental status affects the status of offspring. These studies provide us with another way to measure a society's openness. A society is considered open to the extent that the economic statuses of children are not dependent on those of their parents. It is the extent of this dependence and how it is maintained that has been the focus of status attainment research.

The first large-scale set of national data specifically collected for the study of intergenerational mobility in the United States became available with the study of Occupational Changes in a Generation (OCG), later published by Blau and Duncan under the title *The American Occupational Structure*. The data were obtained as part of the Current Population Survey (CPS) of the Bureau of the Census in March 1962. Over 20,000 men formed the basic sample for the OCG study by Blau and Duncan. This sample represents about 45 million men between 20 and 64 years of age who were in the civilian, noninstitutionalized population in March 1962 (Blau and Duncan 1967, pp. 10–19). Thus, this study said nothing about changing economic conditions among women, youths, or the elderly. Nevertheless, the data were considered to be of unusual reliability and completeness because they were collected by trained individuals using established techniques and working for an institution that had been carrying out such surveys for decades.

Blau and Duncan's basic attainment model is presented in Figure 14.1. They were concerned

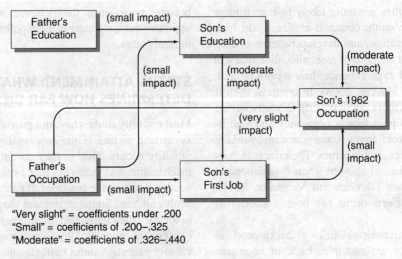

"Very slight" = coefficients under .200
"Small" = coefficients of .200–.325
"Moderate" = coefficients of .326–.440

FIGURE 14.1 Effects of Father's Status on Occupational Status of Son

Source: Based on Blau and Duncan (1967).

with the relative role of socioeconomic origins in the determination of the son's occupational status. From the diagram, it can be observed that the greatest direct effects on the occupational status of the son in 1962 came from education. A father's education had an indirect effect on 1962 status through its effect on education, whereas a father's occupation had a direct as well as an indirect effect through its connections with the son's first job and education.

In summarizing the findings of Blau and Duncan, social origin, education, and first job accounted for less than 50 percent of the variation that occurred in 1962 occupational attainments. The lower the position from which a person begins, argued Blau and Duncan, the greater the probability that he or she will be upwardly mobile, if only because there are more occupational categories above the individual than below. But as men get older and move through their careers, their social origins appear to have less effect on their attainment than past experience and career accomplishments.

The Blau–Duncan findings also suggest that having a stable family life, having fewer siblings, and being the youngest or oldest male are positively related to occupational success. But those who come from large families *and* overcome

obstacles are also likely to move up occupationally more readily than others who have not had such challenges. Moreover, evidence suggested that the role of education, which Blau and Duncan viewed as an achievement variable, had become increasingly important to occupational attainment. They suggested that this indicated an increase in the importance of universalistic factors in attainment.

While it only focused on men and did not include housework as a form of occupation, *The American Occupational Structure* opened the door to a whole new way of examining the problem of the openness of the system of inequality, gave impetus to scores of studies, and made some valuable contributions to our understanding of movement in the occupational hierarchy.

Explanations of Status Attainment

Basically, the Blau–Duncan model relies on *structural* factors as explanatory variables. It is clear that this model does not consider social-psychological factors, such as aspirations and the influences of parents and peers, that may have a significant effect on attainment.

To deal with the issue of the effect of varied social-psychological factors on educational and occupational attainment, Sewell and others developed what is known as the **Wisconsin model** of socioeconomic attainment (e.g., Sewell and Shah 1967; Sewell, Haller, and Ohlendorf 1970). The large volume of studies of this model grew out of an initial survey in 1957 of over 10,000 high school seniors in Wisconsin. Most of the early research was devoted to studying the influence of socioeconomic background and social-psychological factors on aspirations. Follow-up surveys were done in 1964 and later decades.

WISCONSIN MODEL A basic version of the Wisconsin model of early occupational achievement is presented in Figure 14.2. Essentially, it shows that socioeconomic background (father's and mother's education, father's occupational status, and parental income) does not affect grades and is independent of academic ability. However, it does have a sizable ultimate effect on educational and occupational attainment through its influence on the mediating variables of significant others' influences and educational and occupational aspirations. Overall, the model explains about 57 percent of the variation in educational attainment and about 40 percent of the variation in early occupational attainment for the men in the sample. The percentages are somewhat smaller for women (Sewell and Hauser 1976). The model has been applied to individuals from both rural and urban backgrounds, although it was first applied to a sample of farm residents and then later applied to groups from a variety of residential backgrounds.

The Wisconsin model is more effective in explaining the variation in educational and occupational attainment than the basic Blau–Duncan model. The earlier structural model accounts for 26 percent and 33 percent in educational and occupational attainment, respectively. It seems clear from the Wisconsin model that a variety of social-psychological factors play mediating roles linking socioeconomic background and ability to attainment (Haller and Portes 1973, p. 68).

Studies conducted after the development of the Wisconsin model and using national longitudinal samples tended to support the general arguments of the model. What is revealing in the other findings, however, is that none of these models explains a great deal of the variation that exists among individuals in earnings and income, and what small proportion they do explain (under 20 percent) is due primarily to the effect of objective factors, such as SES, rather than to social-psychological variables.

The Role of Education in Attainment

The discovery that neither the Blau–Duncan nor the Wisconsin model of attainment accounts for

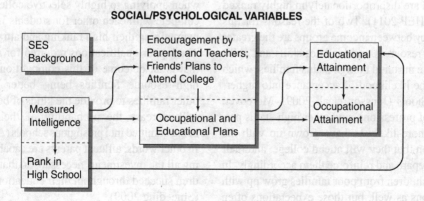

SOCIAL/PSYCHOLOGICAL VARIABLES

IGURE 14.2 A Simplified Version of the Wisconsin Model Showing the Mediating Role of Social-Psychological actors in Individual Attainment

ource: Adapted from Sewell, Haller, and Ohlendorf (1970), p. 1023.

very much of the variation in earnings and income has given rise to a variety of speculations about what the really significant factors might be. The connection between education and economic achievement, while not always strong, has been among the most important predictors included in past achievement models. In considering the role that education plays in future occupational and earnings attainment, it must be kept in mind that the timing of education during one's life cycle has an impact on future earnings. Generally, those who go smoothly through high school, college, and professional training early in their careers do better than those who stop going to school and then either resume their educations later in life or do not return at all. Needless to say, those who come from higher-status backgrounds, especially White males, are more equipped with advantages that allow them to attain their highest level of education early, creating a further advantage over others that increases with time. "The enduring effects of social origins and ascribed statuses on educational transitions into adulthood are starkly evident. Childhood socioeconomic status has long-term effects that are not completely reduced by adult strategies to improve human capital" (Elman and O'Rand 2004, p. 154).

Background clearly has an impact on the probability of attending college. As we will see below, a much greater percentage of students in the top income quartile attend higher-education programs and are disproportionately in highly ranked schools (IHEP 2011). Two of the reasons for this discrepancy between income groups are the greater economic resources and kinds of skills and abilities that are nurtured in high-status families, which increase the likelihood of acceptance into higher-ranked schools (Jonsson et al. 2009). Moreover, children of professional and other high-status parents are more likely to have grown up with the expectation that they will attend college, and their parents prepare and reinforce them accordingly. In contrast, children from poor families grow up with expectations as well, but those expectations often do not include college educations (Bozick et al. 2010). Highly educated mothers, for example, are more likely than others to have their children placed in early child care programs that lay a foundation for later school success (Augustine, Cavanagh and Crosnoe 2009). When they are 3–5 years old a greater percentage of children of highly educated parents recognize all the letters of the alphabet, can write their first names, can count to 20, and are read to every day (College Board 2010).

Statistics support these arguments. In 2012, 84 percent of high school graduates from families in the highest income quartile enrolled in college compared to 45 percent from the lowest quartile. A much greater percentage of those in the top quartile (77 percent) than those in the bottom (9 percent) graduate within 6 years of having entered. This means that high-income youths are 8 times more likely to graduate from college than low-income youths, a gap that has increased from 1970 (Cahalan and Pema 2015). This gap cannot be explained by ability. A recent study found that among students who scored between 1200 and 1600 on the SAT and went on to enroll in college, 78 percent of those from high-income families graduated compared to only 44 percent from poor families (Carnevale and Strohl 2010).

In addition to family background characteristics, another factor affecting the chances of children going on to college concerns the increasing competition among schools for students. Students from lower socioeconomic groups not only are less likely to be accepted at colleges and universities, but they also are at a distinct disadvantage when applying to highly selective colleges which compete with each other for students in hopes of maintaining their high ranking and attractiveness. The higher qualifications required for attendance that is an outcome of this competition results in high-resource families being better able than other families to provide the kinds of benefits that will increase the probability of their children being admitted into prestigious schools (Alon 2009). In other words, affluent parents are capable of making all the investments necessary so that their children succeed throughout their educational careers (Smeeding 2009).

The cumulative advantages or disadvantages that accrue to different individuals over time are matched by the inequalities found within the different educational systems attended by individuals. Moving from the state level to the classroom level, inequalities abound. Within the public school system, states vary in their economic support of education and students, and within states, school districts vary in quality. Schools within districts are often unequal, as are classes within schools, and students within classes. Generally, schools in poor areas do not have the resources available to schools in more advantaged neighborhoods and, consequently, are not as able to prepare their students for successful college entrance (Smeeding 2009). Not surprisingly, across the world, students tend to do better if they are from higher-status families and attend schools in which there are high amounts of varied resources (Chiu 2010). Schools that are predominately White are more likely than predominately Black and Latino schools to have multiple resources. Consequently, regardless of socioeconomic background, students who attend predominately White high schools are more likely to graduate and to get a college degree (Goldsmith 2009). At the same time, however, minorities and students from low socioeconomic backgrounds who attend high schools dominated by higher-income students face problems because of their disadvantages relative to White and

better-off students. Crosnoe (2009) found that the greater the proportion of high-income students in the school, the lower the scores in math and science were for disadvantaged students, even though they might have been higher than those they would have received at schools that had predominately minority or low-status student bodies. These students also experienced higher levels of psychosocial problems.

This set of telescoping, **nested inequalities** creates different levels of opportunities and cumulative advantages or disadvantages for students in different educational systems (Hochschild 2003). Being a student in a low-level track, in a poor school, in a weak school district, and in a state that provides minimal support for education has long-term effects for that student. The generally greater deficiencies of poor children in terms of preschool attendance, high school preparation, and college education lower their incomes as adults and reduce the chances of escaping the poverty of the family in which they were raised (Isaacs, Sawhill, and Haskins 2008).

Table 14.1 makes it clear that having a higher education is associated with economic and personal benefits. In addition to the educational advantages listed there, research also indicates that

TABLE 14.1 Education and Its Economic and Personal Benefits: 2007–2012

Benefits	Less than High School	High School Graduate	Bachelor's Degree or Higher
After tax earnings (2011)	$21,000	$29,000	$45,000–$78,000
Lifetime earnings ratio (2011)	0.72	1.00	1.65–2.92
Very satisfied with job (1972–2012)	42%	47%	48–51%
Sense of learning new things on the job (Strongly agree, 2010)	35%	32%	44–56%
% of indiv. 25 and older living in poverty (2011)	28%	14%	5%
Obesity rates for boys age 2–19 (2007–2010)*	24%	19%	11%
Obesity rates for girls age 2–19 (2007–2010)*	22%	21%	7%
Vigorous exercise for those 55–64 (2012)	18%	25%	53%

Source: The College Board, Education Pays, 2013, https://trends.collegeboard.org/sites/default/files/education-pays-2013-full-report.pdf.

*Levels of education on statistics related to children refer to the highest level attained in the household.

higher-educated persons have a greater sense of personal control in their lives. This follows from their jobs, which are generally more challenging, interesting, enriching, economically rewarding, and controlled more fully by them than is the case with lower-status occupations (Schieman and Plickert 2008).

Even though education is a predictor of first occupation, earnings, and other benefits, the explanation for its importance has been a source of controversy. The traditional argument has been that advances in technology and upgrading of the occupational structure have created a need for the greater skills and training that education is supposed to supply. Others have argued that the importance of education for attainment does not lie primarily in the cognitive skills it imparts to students. Cobb-Clark and Tan (2011), for example, found that other skills—such as communication ability, attitude, work habits, and other personal characteristics that may be influenced by the education experience—affect occupational success independently of any cognitive skills a person may possess. College major, which may serve as a proxy for some of these skills, does have an impact on occupational status and economic mobility (Wolniak et al. 2008).

Collins (1971) and more recent scholarship (see Brown 2001 for a review of the literature) also challenged the technical skill argument, saying there is evidence that what is important about education is not the training it provides but the fact that it represents an introduction into a particular "status culture." Many individuals, argued Collins, are overeducated for their jobs, and those who are better educated do not necessarily perform better than the less educated. In fact, Collins stated, U.S. schools generally are not very good at providing students with the vocational skills they need to be successful in the performance of their jobs. What is important about schools for early occupational achievement is that they teach students a particular set of values and ways of acting and defining things. Employers then select those who will fit into the status culture of the elite and those who might be willing to serve under them because of their adherence to the prescriptions of a particular status culture. In this manner, schools can be used to control membership in economic institutions.

While education has an impact on economic status for a variety of reasons, it does not explain all of the variations in individuals' earnings and income. Gender, race, labor market, industry, parenthood status, economic conditions, and economic sector of employment are all involved. For example, because of pressures in male-dominated fields, mothers disproportionately enter lower paid female-dominated occupations, or they enter a male-dominated field but leave due to pressure to work longer hours than a standard work week (Cha 2013). Recent research also suggests that some male-dominated professions are "task segregated," meaning that women are given the more repetitive, less desirable tasks leading to exhaustion, frustration, and ultimately to less income mobility (Chan and Anteby 2015).

Another suggestion is that factors associated with an individual's current experiences may be better predictors of earnings than traditional education. In a meta-analysis, Haelermans and Borghans (2012) found that on-the-job training increases earnings. The amount of time spent in the labor force also affects an individual's earnings (Friedberg and Owyang 2004). But as already noted, the length of time spent in a high-paying position depends in part on the pressures to which one is subjected. Perhaps not surprisingly, job satisfaction is positively related to tenure on the job and income (Supeli and Creed 2015).

In addition to these factors, networking and connections may play important roles in the explanation of earnings and income. Research suggests that individuals who get jobs through personal contacts are more likely to get wage increases and promotion opportunities than those who secure jobs without such contacts. By providing positive information and optimizing the chances of good matches between individuals and jobs, contacts can help create work environments for their acquaintances that are favorable for promotion and pay raises (Loury 2006). These networks appear to be especially important for women (Aguilera 2008).

NUTSHELL 14.1 Being a First-Generation College Student

In the early 1990s, Charles Hurst, the original author of this text, researched faculty at eight selective liberal arts colleges, aiming to explore the relationships between their socioeconomic backgrounds and the degree of comfort they felt on their campuses and among their colleagues. He wondered if those from working-class families would feel comfortable or out of place in their elite, high-priced colleges where many of the faculty have upper-middle-class origins. He found that some of the working-class faculty sensed a lack of fit between themselves and the college setting in which they worked, while others had accommodated themselves easily to their surroundings.

Like some working-class faculty, first-generation college students also face challenges when entering the alien environment of higher education, although some experience a sense of alienation more strongly than others. Some schools have offices and programs to assist first-generation students, while others do not. It is often hard for a well-educated faculty member from an upper-middle-class family to fully understand the unique personal issues that first-generation students face, and the feelings they experience as they move through the alien environment of the college campus (Merullo 2002).

What *are* these feelings? Bobby Allyn, a first-generation university student from a working-class family, engages in a kind of impostor behavior, not wanting his fellow students to know that he is from a lower class than they are. While he has a sense of satisfaction because he is effective in masking his class identity, he knows inside that he is still an outsider (Allyn 2009). Another person who was attending a prestigious prep school sensed that he was "trying to find a way to weld two very different worlds," but it is often difficult to articulate what the problem is (Merullo 2002). For many students from impoverished backgrounds, there is "a shadow" over the achievement of getting into college because they feel they are on their own without the benefit or support of friends who had been to college who can guide them (Merullo 2002).

Because many of these students are White, they are invisible on campus, and must deal with their unique problems on their own. Bobby Allyn laments the absence of a meeting ground for students in a similar situation (Allyn 2009). But he does not know if such students are present because they are invisible. Most colleges and universities have offices to assist minorities and women, but have not created support programs for students from poor or working-class backgrounds. What, if anything, do you think should be done to support these students?

Finally, some people just happen to be in the right spot at the appropriate time. For example, a person might happen to be in a community that has a greater range of jobs than others, or the weather might suddenly destroy jobs in construction, or a person might run into someone who unexpectedly gives them a job lead. Some of these kinds of events may be appropriately labeled as luck, but others are factors that are systematically related to earnings and background but have not yet been incorporated into attainment models (McDonald 2009).

Structures in the Process of Attainment

The notion that luck or being in the right place at the right time may play a role in attainment suggests that one's position in a broader social structure is significant for mobility. Most of the early research on the process of occupational and income attainment focused on characteristics of the individuals involved (i.e., their educations, parents, attitudes). In questioning what determines how far people get, especially when compared to their parents, U.S. sociology trained its eye almost solely on human capital factors and the peculiarities of people's backgrounds. This was one of the primary limitations of early research.

Especially since the mid-1980s, however, there has been an emphasis on structural factors in status attainment. When one looks outside the individual for reasons for success or failure, one finds that structures in society and in organizations play a significant role in the chances for upward or downward movement. Moreover, while earlier research was concerned primarily with accounting for socioeconomic attainment *in general*, many post-1990 investigations examined the attainment process as it is played out within the structural context of a given economic sector or organization. Attainment always takes place within a concrete organizational or economic context, and variations in the structural networks, hierarchies, and career pathways between organizations can help account for differences in attainment processes and outcomes. This latter realization has led to a focus on **intragenerational mobility** rather than on differences between parents and children.

How, specifically, is structure involved in the attainment process? At a broad level, shifts in the national occupational structure obviously create openings and closures in positions. They create new occupations and eliminate others. For example, there has been a lot of discussion of the United States moving rapidly from a manufacturing to a service-based economy, causing layoffs in one area and creating new openings in the expanding service sector. Over the long run, occupations rise and fall in their dominance of a nation's employment structure. These national economic changes are in turn rooted in technology changes, international competition, and the movement of capital between and within nations. Attendant streamlining, downsizing, and actual closures also affect the alternatives available for attainment.

So-called **vacancy-driven mobility** models stress the fact "that mobility depends on the availability of empty positions and that the filling of jobs is interdependent. One person's move to a new job or out of a job system creates an opening to be filled" (Rosenfeld 1992, p. 41). For example, historically, many immigrants have dominated certain types of lower-status positions as natives have moved on to the greener pastures of more prestigious jobs. At the national level, attainment is also affected by legislative changes. Affirmative action and equal employment opportunity policies are aimed at broadening the opportunity structures of women and racial/ethnic minorities (Rosenfeld 1992).

Below the national level, attainment is also tied to the structure of opportunities within different economic sectors and organizations. Within large formal organizations of the core economic sector, for example, jobs are more likely than in the peripheral sector to be part of a career ladder (i.e., an internal occupational hierarchy along which an individual can move). Frequently, the ladder may be multifaceted or have multiple branches, or an organization may have several job ladders of varying heights, widths, and connections. The relative location of a person in that structure affects the criteria needed and the chances for advancement. Upward mobility is generally slower if one is in a job that is close to the top of a ladder. The pathways to advancement also can vary within the same structure (DiPrete and Krecker 1991; Rosenfeld 1992). The presence of this treelike structure creates opportunities for differential attainment that are independent of the characteristics of individuals.

Some mobility is not vacancy driven, however. For example, in some unionized plants, one's time-in-grade or seniority affects economic advancement, and in colleges and universities, time-in-rank affects promotion up the professorial hierarchy. Knowledge about and access to information about the various avenues to advancement within an organization also are important, and may vary with one's position in the organization and the internal network of which one is a part. Being an insider, having connections, and being "in the know" affect one's chances for attainment, especially within an organization whose opportunity ladder is open solely or primarily to current employees (DiPrete and Krecker 1991).

Research suggests that, in addition to connections, social skills and personality characteristics determine both hiring and promotion. Robert Jackall's intensive study of corporations (1988) was important in showing how these factors are often more important than hard work, education, and other achievement-based factors in moving up the corporate ladder. More recent research has come to the same conclusion. For example, Rode et al. (2008) found that personality characteristics like extroversion and agreeableness had a strong effect on the salary of recent graduates. Measures of ability showed no significant correlation with either salary or perceived job success. Having the ppropriate mentor and sponsor also helps one's hances for upward mobility (Lim et al. 2015).

MOBILITY AMONG AFRICAN AMERICANS AND HISPANICS

The experience of mobility and the process of attainment vary between races. In their landmark study of U.S. men in the early 1960s, Blau and Duncan (1967) argued that Blacks generally start out from a lower position, but instead of moving up in a manner commensurate with their education and other human capital, they become involved in a vicious circle in which they are hindered at each step along the way in the attainment process. That is, their disadvantages are *cumulative*. They have a hard time getting a higher education, and when they do, the occupational returns for that education are less than those received by Whites. For example, Blacks with a bachelor's degree earn 20 percent less than Whites with the same degree (Carnevale, Rose, and Cheah 2011). Knowledge of this fact may lower the incentive of Blacks to obtain such education, and thereby reinforce the negative stereotype of Blacks as unwilling to be educated.

Blau and Duncan did not include an analysis of Hispanics, but we can use more recent work to understand their mobility patterns as well as those of Whites and Blacks. While smaller percentages of Blacks and Hispanics than Whites graduate from high school and obtain bachelor's degrees, their rate of increase in college enrollment has been much higher. This is particularly notable among Hispanics, with enrollment jumping 240 percent since 1996. Black enrollment also increased a significant 72 percent during the same time period. The equivalent percentage for Whites was 12 (Krogstad and Fry 2014). Because more Blacks and Hispanics are enrolled in college, they receive more bachelor's degrees than in the past. At the same time, the graduation rate has not risen by the same amount as the enrollment rate. Today only about 18 percent of bachelor's degree holders between the ages of 25 and 29 are either Black or Hispanic.

Why is increasing enrollment not directly translating to an equivalent level of graduation? This can be explained by the fact that Blacks and Hispanics are more likely to drop out due to financial and other concerns and a higher percentage attend schools that do not award bachelor's degrees (Krogstad and Fry 2014). Additionally, schools that have low enrollment of Blacks or which are located in predominantly White rural areas have lower graduation rates for Black students (*Journal of Blacks in Higher Education* 2006).

While Blacks are still not proportionately represented in the middle class, their representation has grown in recent decades. Data from 1983 to 2010 indicates that the proportion of Blacks in the middle class increased by about 10 percent (Landry and Marsh 2011). One new feature of middle-class growth has been the increase in young Black single people who live alone. They are estimated to make up one-quarter of all middle-class Black households in which the householder is under the age of 34 (Marsh et al. 2007). The number of middle-class Hispanics has also increased. By 2012, over 29 percent of Hispanic adults earned more than $50,000 a year. Projections suggest that these figures may increase dramatically by 2050. Not surprisingly, middle- and upper-class Hispanics have become the intense focus of marketing efforts from a range of companies (Nielsen 2013).

As we discussed in Chapter 2, both the Black and Hispanic middle classes were hit particularly hard by the recession. This was because they had a greater percentage of their wealth tied up in the housing market. In recent years, middle-class Blacks have also been severely affected by cuts in public sector jobs. Blacks are 30 percent more likely than Whites and twice as likely as Hispanics to hold a public sector job (Cohen 2015). Additionally, both Hispanics and African Americans who are in the middle or upper class are more likely than Whites to be in managerial rather than professional positions. Managerial positions may be more precarious, particularly in tough economic times (Alba and Barbosa 2015). Mobility into the higher-paying core sector or into a higher-status occupation may be hindered by residential segregation which limits access and opportunities to move up (Hout 1986; Andersson et al. 2014). As we have seen, Blacks and Hispanics both experience high levels of residential segregation, but this is particularly the case for Blacks.

Researchers have identified a set of processes in organizations that limit the mobility of Blacks and Hispanics (and other minorities). **Tokenism**, for example, is when a White-dominated company or institution admits a very limited number of people of color in an effort to prove that they are inclusive. Research finds that these "tokens" become highly visible and their performance is scrutinized more than that of the majority group. This leads to considerable stress (Kanter 1977b). In a study of Black and Latino police officers, Stroshine and Brandl (2011) found that both men and women experience the negative effects of tokenism. **Pigeonholing** (Cose 1993) is another phenomenon that affects mobility for minorities. It is when people of color are steered into positions within organizations that are defined as appropriate for them. In the professional realm, these are often the "diversity management" jobs or jobs that serve high numbers of minority clients. These jobs tend to have limited power and mobility associated with them (Hall and Stevenson 2007).

A phenomenon related to pigeonholing is "cultural taxation" or "identity taxation." These terms are normally used in reference to faculty jobs in higher education but can easily be applied more broadly. Cultural taxation (Padilla 1994) is when people of color are asked to take on extra work to add diversity on committees or when they are asked to provide extra support services for students of color. Hirshfield and Joseph (2012) coined the term "identity taxation," which is broader than cultural taxation. They defined identity taxation as when, "faculty members shoulder any labour—physical, mental, or emotional—due to their membership in a historically marginalised group within their department or university, beyond that which is expected of other faculty members in the same setting" (p. 214). Both cultural and identity taxation result in a situation where minorities (including gay, lesbian, and gender-nonconforming people) do not have time or energy left to do the work they need to do to be promoted.

Race and the Status Attainment Process

Research has been done to determine if the models that have been developed to explain educational and occupational attainment apply to Blacks as well as they do to Whites. Work still needs to be done to compare these findings to the experiences of Hispanics and other groups. Since race has an effect on a variety of areas in U.S. life, we might suspect that what applies to Whites does not apply to Blacks. Since race is an ascribed characteristic, a model based on achievement norms may not fit Blacks as well as Whites. Also, race affects mobility, and the relationship between many of the variables that are included in these standard models differ from one race to another.

An early study by Portes and Wilson (1976) suggested that the process of educational attainment does differ among Blacks. Analyzing a nationwide sample of boys surveyed over a period of several years, and using a variant of the Wisconsin model of status attainment (described earlier), they found several differences between Blacks and Whites:

1. The variables in the model are better at explaining attainment among Whites than among Blacks, which suggests that factors not traditionally considered are more important for Blacks.
2. The more objective factors of socioeconomic background, mental ability, and academic performance are more important for White attainment, whereas among Blacks, the later and more subjective variables of self-esteem and educational aspirations are the significant ones.
  a. There is a much stronger connection between mental ability and academic performance and between academic performance and educational attainment among Whites than among Blacks. Among Blacks, there is no significant direct connection between academic performance and attainment.
  b. Conversely, the ties of mental ability to self-esteem and the ties of self-esteem to attainment are much stronger among Blacks than Whites.

In summarizing their findings, Portes and Wilson suggested that the results imply a distinction among Whites and Blacks as insiders and outsiders in the U.S. achievement system. In an open society, one would expect that performance and ability would be quite important, and they are for Whites. But for Blacks, educational attainment is more dependent on self-reliance and ambition. In a manner of speaking, then, while Blacks have had to rely on these qualities, Whites "have at their disposal an additional set of institutional 'machinery' which can, in effect, carry them along to higher levels of attainment" (p. 430).

Porter (1974) examined early occupational as well as educational achievement among Blacks and Whites and also found significant racial differences in the processes involved. His study of a large sample of males suggests that among Blacks, grades are largely a function of personality factors, such as conformity and ambition, whereas among Whites, both personality and intelligence play roles. As in the Portes and Wilson (1976) findings, subjective rather than objective conditions appear to play a greater part in the attainment process for Blacks. "It would appear that the official sanctions of the school system operate primarily with reference to the visible being of the pupil, and only secondarily, and on the condition that he is White, with reference to academic ability" (Porter 1974, p. 311). Another interesting finding of this study is that in contrast to the results among Whites, grades have no direct effect on either educational or occupational attainment. This seems to reinforce Wilson and Roscigno's (2010) finding that factors other than expected predictors such as education and experience are more significant predictors of downward mobility among Blacks.

Confirming the significance of nonrational, subjective factors in the attainment process of Blacks is the fact that "color" also has an impact on the socioeconomic attainment of African Americans. Simply put, Blacks whose physical appearance more closely approximates the European/U.S. ideal of beauty do better socioeconomically than others (Hill 2000).

Blacks themselves feel that their path to occupational attainment is made more difficult by the lack of decent available jobs for which they are qualified, the concentrated poverty of their neighborhoods, and their lack of social contacts in the inner city. They believe that luck, connections, education, help from those who have made it, and being from the right neighborhood make all the difference (Venkatesh 1994).

These beliefs suggest the importance of the context in which people live as an explanation for why some get ahead while others remain stuck. In her longitudinal study of women's changing economic fortunes over a 30-year period, Andrea Willson (2003) found that Black women were much more likely than White women to be at financial risk in their old age. White women who were married benefited financially from their marriages; this was not the case for Black women. Poor health, especially that on the part of the husband, significantly reduced household income among married couples. Continuous employment benefited both Black and White women, although unmarried Black women did not get the same income returns from their employment as White women in part because of their generally lower levels of education and lower-status occupations. The higher economic benefit of marriage and continuous employment for White women meant that they lost more than Black women in old age due to widowhood and loss of employment. On the whole, Black women had flatter and lower earnings trajectories over their lifetimes than White women. Consequently, they did not have as far to fall, experiencing smaller declines. This study demonstrated not only the relevance of marital status for some women but also the significance of the availability and quality of jobs, and indirectly the importance of education for women's long-term income. The labor market and education are parts of the varying contexts within which women of different races must navigate their careers.

PATTERNS OF MOBILITY AND ATTAINMENT AMONG WOMEN

The major national studies done on intergenerational mobility during the 1960s and 1970s concentrated on the occupational statuses of *men*.

MINI-CASE 14.1

Educational Choice versus the Law

In January 2011, a woman in Akron, Ohio, was arrested and convicted of falsifying records about her residency. She lived in Akron with her two school-age daughters. Her grandfather lived in a smaller suburb known for its better schools. The woman's Akron home had recently been burglarized, and because she worked as a teaching assistant and was pursuing a teaching degree, she was not always at home. Consequently, she worried about the safety of her daughters. Residency laws require that students attend the school district in which they are living. The mother recorded her grandfather's home as her daughters' residence so they could attend schools in that district even though, the court says, her legal residence was still in Akron. She says her reason for putting the girls in the suburban school was safety, but the school also has a fine reputation and is funded heavily by property taxes paid by local residents. So some felt that the mother had also defrauded the school system by sending her children to a school for which she had not contributed taxes. Others sympathized, arguing that the mother's desire to send her children to a safer and better school was praiseworthy since it demonstrated that she only had her daughters' future in mind. Who would you side with in this case and why? ■

Part of the reason for the omission of women in these studies is that they were based on the assumption that women's positions, especially those among women who are married, are dependent on those of their husbands or fathers, and that to know the mobility patterns of men is, therefore, to know the patterns for the entire society. The central problem with all this is that women are not considered as independent persons, even though many married and unmarried women have their own occupational, educational, and income resources. From discussions earlier in this book, you know that sex and gender inequality exists along a variety of dimensions, and yet people's concepts (like class position) reflect a concern primarily for the attributes of males.

Recently, the Brookings Institution published "Women and Mobility: Six Key Facts" (Reeves and Venator 2014). It summarizes the most current research, and we excerpt (and adapt slightly) the six main points here:

1. Today's working women (henceforth described as "daughters") have higher wages than their mothers—but do not have higher wages than their fathers. Men have higher wages than both their fathers and their mothers.
2. The poorest women are doing best. Eighty percent of daughters raised in the bottom quintile have higher wages than did their fathers.

3. When looking at married couples, men's wages are more important than women's in increasing family income.
4. Women who grew up in households where their mother did not work actually have the highest family incomes today—but not because they themselves earn more. Daughters' individual incomes do not vary significantly by mother's work status, but family income does—suggesting that daughters whose mothers didn't work have higher-earning husbands. Perhaps those raised in more traditional settings are more likely to replicate a traditional division of labor?
5. There's a lot of stickiness at the top and bottom of income distribution—*but women suffer more than men at both ends*. Women born at the bottom are more likely to remain in the bottom two quintiles than men, but men born at the top are more likely to stay at the top than woman born at the top.
6. More work for women has been good for mobility, particularly for those at the bottom. Pew looked as what would happen to mobility if women's wages increased as they have over the past 40 years, but women's labor force participation (i.e., hours worked) were the same as in their mothers' generation. They found that increased work hours resulted in an 11 percentage point increase in upward mobility for women born at the bottom.

These facts indicate that women have made important mobility gains but still lag behind men on key indicators. Notably, a greater percentage of women than men who were born into families in the bottom income quintile are likely to remain at the bottom, and women in all but the highest income quintile are more likely than men to experience downward mobility in income (Reeves and Venator 2014).

While women may have less mobility than men, they are excelling in educational attainment. Overall in 2009–2010, women earned 57.4 percent of bachelor's degrees, 62.5 percent of master's degrees, and 53.3 percent of doctoral degrees. When the data are broken down by race, we see that all groups follow the same pattern of women having higher graduation rates than men, but the disparity is particularly pronounced among Blacks (National Center for Education Statistics 2012). There are a variety of possible explanations for the gender disparity (see Bailey and Dynarski 2011 for a summary of the literature). For example, it is possible that men sense that they are less likely to need a degree for their future jobs. There is also evidence to suggest that the predominance of female teachers influences young people's educational aspirations, encouraging young women more than men.

Certainly, along the road to adulthood, whether people receive encouragement, help, and access to opportunities plays a role in their status attainment. The importance of encouragement and help is perhaps most critical for those at the bottom of the socioeconomic hierarchy. Monthly interviews with low-income minority women in 2000 and 2001 demonstrated the role of social capital in affecting upward mobility for these women (Dominguez and Watkins 2003). Strong kin groups can either aid or hinder mobility through their expectations and demands. Sometimes "[s]upport networks can exert a pull away from social mobility ties that is difficult to resist. They enforce kinscripts that levy time-consuming and professionally limiting expectations on women" (p. 131). On the other hand, an employment situation can create access to social networks of different people who may have resources or information that open up new possibilities for mobility. "Heterogeneous networks may encourage low-income women to look beyond their present circumstances and learn from those who are more upwardly mobile" (p. 131).

The occupational attainment of women who are employed is affected by a pattern of factors that is different from the pattern that affects the attainment path of men. Thus, the attainment process of employed women is quite different from that of married, unemployed women, whose attainment path is directly tied to that of their husbands. The differences are largely due to the features of the opportunity structure that women encounter when they move into the labor force—features that frequently involve curves, bumps, and walls not often encountered by men. Think of the road to attainment as akin to a maze, and some mazes are more complex and difficult than others. How successful one is in getting through it may depend partially on individual attributes, but it also depends heavily on the structure of the maze itself.

Obstacles and Pathways in Status Attainment for Women

To fully understand the process of status attainment, it is important to remember that such mobility always takes place within a given social and cultural context. This context helps define the ease with which attainment can occur. Some pathways make attainment much easier than others. Generally the opportunity structure for men makes attainment a less troublesome process than is the case for women.

By and large, status attainment in the United States occurs within a culture in which there are different beliefs about and expectations for men and women that affect their role prospects. It should not be surprising, then, that women are more affected by household-related variables than are men. For example, Michelle Budig (2014) uncovered a "motherhood penalty" and "fatherhood bump" in her analysis of income data. This means that fatherhood is associated with higher wages, but motherhood is linked to lower wages. The fatherhood bump is particularly pronounced at higher levels of the income scale. Budig argues that this may be because fathers are seen as more responsible and warm (and therefore desirable as workers) but mothers are seen as less committed to their careers.

In the United States, strong attachment to work is expected and valued, and so the price paid by a new mother for taking even a short time-out can be significant. Many American women are aware of this and, thus, are more attached to the marketplace, taking as little time off as possible (Aisenbrey, Evertsson, and Grunow 2009; Gangl and Ziefle 2009). But when mothers are successful in higher managerial positions, they are often criticized as not being "feminine" by being less warm and interpersonal, and this affects how they are evaluated. Since most high-level executive positions are assumed to require "masculine" qualities, men are not as subjected to these criticisms (Benard and Correll 2010).

Gender segregation and the level of earnings associated with it are affected by what Petersen and Saporta (2004) called "the opportunity structure for discrimination" (p. 852). This refers to the variety of opportunities available to employers to discriminate against given categories of individuals. Using data collected over a nine-year period, Petersen and Saporta's research on a large service-producing organization revealed that employers were most likely to discriminate against women at the point of hiring, rather than during their job tenure, because discrimination is less detectable and less costly at this juncture. Once hired, women were more often placed in lower-level jobs and received lower wages than men even though their educational levels were roughly similar. Thus, women went through a gatekeeping or filtering process that resulted in their being relegated to specific kinds of positions. This was a feature of the opportunity structure within which women had to operate. Interestingly, the authors found that women were more likely to be promoted and received higher salary raises than men. Possible reasons for this included the company's desire to change its sexist image and concerns about lawsuits alleging discrimination, which is more detectable and measurable at this point of employment.

But while women were more likely to be promoted once in a job, women were not likely to occupy the highest positions because (1) they were unlikely to be placed in these positions when hired and (2) there was only a small pool of women with seniority who were eligible to be promoted into the top echelons of the organization.

In her study of an industrial corporation, Kanter (1977a) found that at the top is an inner circle of individuals who have to be counted on to share a similar view of the organization and to behave in a manner consistent with that view. There are distinct pressures for homogeneity and conformity at the managerial level. A large part of the reason for this pressure to conform arises from the open nature of organizations and the managerial positions within them. Since position tasks are not well defined at that level and the organization operates in a "turbulent" environment with other organizations, the conclusion is that executives have to be able to trust one another and see one another's behavior as predictable. "Women were decidedly placed in the category of the incomprehensible and unpredictable" (p. 58).

More recent research in corporate law firms by Gorman and Kmec (2009) confirms Kanter's arguments. Their findings showed that women face a disadvantage when promotions near the top are being considered, and similar to Kanter, they attribute this disadvantage to an interaction of gender stereotyping and job characteristics. Specifically, they argue that assumptions about women's competence and appropriateness for particular tasks, together with the uncertainty and variety of the job itself and male dominance at the top, lead to lower chances for upward mobility for female members of law firms. This experience can further dampen the ambition and skills of women colleagues, further reinforcing low mobility rates.

One of the difficult dilemmas for women's mobility concerns the fact that the hiring and promoting of women at given managerial levels may depend on the proportion of women already present in an organization at or below those levels. A study of top executive positions in Fortune 1000 companies (Helfat, Harris, and Wolfson 2006) found that when there is very low to no women in high ranks of a company, executives generally decide to hire a few token women. It appears, however, that women have to be present in relatively high percentages before women are hired or promoted in good numbers. This creates a circular trap, as women need to be hired before women are hired.

Women, of course, have traditionally been socialized into the same general beliefs about the sexes as men, and their beliefs can have an impact on the probability of their being upwardly mobile. This is Sheryl Sandberg's argument (2013) in her bestselling book *Lean In*. Sandburg argues that women internalize the idea that they will not be able to combine work and family so they fail to strive for high positions, even early on in their careers. She argues that in order for women to achieve greater social mobility, they need to believe in their own abilities and shoot high. While criticisms have been raised that she fails to properly acknowledge structural barriers to women's success, Sandberg's argument does fit with other literature indicating that women can internalize negative stereotypes that affect their chances of mobility (Gneezy, Niederle, and Rustichini 2001; Bonnot and Croizet 2007). Similarly, researchers have identified **stereotype threat** as a problem for many marginalized groups. This means that people perform poorly because they fear confirming a negative stereotype (for example, if a girl is aware of the stereotype that females are worse at math, she will become anxious and score lower on a math test than she would if she were unaware of the stereotype). Stereotype threat could influence women's performance and thus chance for mobility in some high-level or stereotypically male professions (Bergeron, Block, and Echtenkamp 2006).

Self-definitions and expectations combine with race, class, occupational segregation, and the internal market structure of organizations to limit mobility by women. For example, in a study of Hispanic schoolteachers in California, Flores and Hondagneu-Sotelo (2014) documented how social forces colluded to steer second-generation Hispanic American women into teaching, rather than the higher-status occupations to which they had originally aspired. Limited funds made most graduate programs out of reach, and most of the women could not afford to do the unpaid internships required by some professions. Importantly, many needed to help support their families as quickly as possible. Teaching jobs were plentiful for college-educated bilingual people and seemed to promise a measure of financial security. While teaching is certainly an important profession, it has limited mobility and income attached to it.

GLOBALIZATION AND COMPARATIVE STUDIES OF MOBILITY

How does the rate of social mobility in the United States compare to rates in other industrial countries? One argument is that all rates are similar. The **industrialism thesis** contends that "industrialization, directly or indirectly, demolishes old barriers, opens new avenues for ascendance, and shifts the basis of status attainment from ascription to achievement. It therefore loosens the dependence of destinations on origins and generates a gradual openness in the mobility structure, in addition to transforming the occupational structure and promoting structural mobility" (Wong 1994, p. 122). According to this argument, industrialism has an "inner logic" that, when introduced into countries, overshadows the distinctive cultural and social characteristics of industrial nations.

The argument that industrialization inevitably increases upward social mobility in a similar manner in all industrial countries has come under severe attack, however (Van Leeuwen and Maas 2010). In the United States, for instance, income inequality has increased, as has the proportion who are poor or near poor. Concerns about increased downward mobility have also intensified in this highly advanced nation. Moreover, as education becomes more important, lack of it gives those at the bottom a smaller chance of moving up.

Many recent studies also indicate that industrial countries vary in their *rates* and *patterns* of mobility. Comparative studies suggest that *overall* observed mobility rates in Western industrial nations are not that similar (e.g., Esping-Andersen 2014; Van Leeuwen and Maas 2010). Roughly, the same can be said for upward social mobility rates in industrialized nations (Wong 1994).

What this suggests is that the industrialism thesis is flawed because it ignores the central role of the often unique historical, cultural, and institutional context of countries in which mobility does or does not occur. The patterns of mobility vary between countries because of differences in their contexts. First of all, the process of industrialization does not follow the same route in all countries. Historical and political conditions help shape the occupational structure and mobility within the country (Webb 2009). Second, varying characteristics of educational institutions affect access to quality education and the connection between education and employment. Thus, the pathways to mobility vary between countries (Esping-Andersen 2014). Think about this: Every society provides institutional pathways through which a citizen needs to move if he or she is to be mobile. These pathways differ not only in their structure but also, because of the culture, in terms of who is eligible to use them and when they can use them. Between one's origin and one's destination lies a patterned structure through which one must pass to be socially mobile. What did your parents have to go through to get where they are? How about your grandparents? The pathways to mobility for different generations vary to the extent that economic, social, political, and cultural structures also change

between generations, creating new opportunities while eliminating or altering old ones.

In comparisons with other industrial countries, the association between sons' and fathers' earnings is stronger in the United States and the United Kingdom than in Canada and some European countries, suggesting less *intergenerational* mobility in those countries. For example, it is estimated that about half of the economic advantage or disadvantage of a father is passed on to his son in the U.S., Italy, and the UK. In contrast, the corresponding figure for Denmark, Finland, and Norway is one-fifth (Corak 2013). This means that earnings mobility is lower in the first set of countries. Similarly, we see that in Denmark, Finland, Canada, Norway, and the United Kingdom, a higher percentage of poor children have incomes greater than their parents. In Denmark, the correlation between parental and child income is three times less than it is in the U.S. (Esping-Andersen 2014).

The United States ranks in the middle of the industrialized countries in most measures of mobility, for example, when we look at the rate of mobility during individuals' own lifetimes (i.e., *intra-generational* mobility). At the same time, we see lower rates of mobility in many developing countries like Ecuador, Peru, and Brazil. In these countries, the relationship between fathers' and sons' income appears even stronger (Isaacs, Sawhill, and Haskins 2008).

Summary

This chapter surveyed some of the research that has dealt with trends in the openness of industrial societies, especially the United States. Generally, study findings suggest that the trend in mobility has not been altogether uniform in U.S. society. Most of the mobility that occurred in the twentieth century appears to have been brought about by changes in the occupational structure over time rather than through greater democracy and freedom in the society. The United States has more upward than downward mobility, but most of the upward mobility is of short distance. There does not appear to have been much significant change

through most of the twentieth century in the extent to which the occupational status of the son is dependent on that of the father, and in general, the last couple of decades have witnessed at least a stabilization, if not a decline, in overall occupational mobility in the United States. Some broad socioeconomic advances have occurred for Blacks and women in recent years, but they still lag significantly behind White males.

Status attainment research reshaped the study of mobility. Two basic models of status attainment surfaced early: the Blau–Duncan model which emphasizes the importance of structural factors for attainment, and the Wisconsin model, which incorporates social-psychological elements. Both models explain occupational and educational attainment better than they account for differences in earnings and income. In addition to education and family background, other factors in attainment include economic and organizational opportunity structures and one's place in them. The process of attainment among African Americans and females varies from that found among White males. Both experience nonrational barriers not faced by White males. Traditional status attainment studies often neglected discrimination as a significant factor in mobility, instead focusing on individuals' personal characteristics and backgrounds as predictors. This made attainment models less effective in explaining the attainment processes of minorities and women. Discrimination, along with the varying opportunity structures available to different groups, can help us understand why some are rich and others poor, or why some occupy positions of high status or power while others are stuck farther down the social ladder. The continued presence of these inequalities raises the possibility that many may consider them unjust.

Critical Thinking

1. The United States is often thought of as a land of opportunity, one in which there are few obstacles in the path of anyone who wants to move up. What do you think most accounts for this image?
2. Trace your own social mobility or that of your parents. What best explains the degree of attainment and its route?
3. Mobility of children is affected by the socioeconomic status of their parents, putting poorer children at a disadvantage. Does this mean that to eliminate this disadvantage we need to eliminate wealth inheritance between children and parents?
4. Do you think objective criteria to evaluate individuals can be established and agreed upon so that evaluations of the educational and job performances of minorities and women, especially mothers, can be fairer and not reflect prejudices about these groups? Explain your answer.

Web Connections

Change in the occupational structure was the primary factor behind social mobility for most of the twentieth century. What occupations are growing the fastest? Which are declining in employment? What trends exist in wages for specific occupations? How do these vary by state? Visit www.bls.gov/oes/current/oessrcst.htm to search your state for trends in occupations and wages.

Film Suggestions

First Generation (2011). Shot over 3 years, this documentary follows the challenges four high school students face as they strive to be the first people in their families to attend college.

Shooting Women (2008). Features 50 camerawomen from all over the world talking about their profession and the barriers to entry and mobility for women within it.

Country Boys (2006). A three-part PBS series about two Appalachian youths trying to move up in the face of great odds.

CHAPTER 15

Justice and Legitimacy

Assessments of the Structure of Inequality

Slaves are generally expected to sing as well as to work.

FREDERICK DOUGLASS (1818–1895)

Think about situations when you were rewarded differently from someone else. If the situations were important to you, undoubtedly you had feelings about whether such treatment was or was not justified. These feelings become issues and problems when you feel that your treatment was unjustified. What made the difference in whether you felt you were treated fairly or unfairly, and why are some unequal distributions of rewards considered just while others are thought of as unjust?

Virtually every chapter in this book so far has provided evidence of extensive economic, political, gender, and racial inequality in U.S. society. There is no denying that this inequality is present, but is it unfair? It is difficult, if not impossible, to avoid the question of fairness in the presence of such pervasive inequality. Increases in income and wealth inequality since 1980 and recent revelations about excessive executive compensation, golden parachutes, and corporate bailouts while employees are downsized or asked to work for lower wages have helped to stimulate questions about fairness and inequities in earnings and wealth. As Thomas Piketty (2014) observes, "The history of inequality is shaped by the way economic, social, and political actors view what is just and what is not, as well as by the relative power of those actors and the collective choices that result" (p. 20).

Is it fair that between 1978 and 2014, the average chief executive officer's compensation (CEO) at a major corporation increased 997 percent and the average worker's compensation only increased 10.9 percent? Or that in 2013 the richest 1 percent in the United States holds over one-third of all wealth while what the bottom 40 percent owns fluctuates between 1.5 and –0.9 percent (DeSilver 2015)? Recent surveys suggest that about half of Americans feel they are underpaid for the work they do and that the rich should be taxed more heavily to redistribute wealth (Newport 2015b).

What is fair? Who considers it fair? What determines whether individuals think the present distribution of resources is just or not? What criteria do people use before reaching a conclusion about the fairness of inequality? These are the empirical questions to be addressed in this brief chapter.

How people evaluate the inequality around them depends on what they think is primarily responsible for it, on the criteria they use when making their evaluative assessment about the extent of inequality, and on the effectiveness of national ideologies and institutions in justifying extensive inequality. When individuals come to the conclusion that a given distribution of rewards is fair, they also tend to believe that it is legitimate. Beliefs in the fairness and legitimacy of the structure of inequality in a society are two elements that contribute to its stability and continuity over time. Thus, when trying to account for its perpetuation, it is important to know how people feel about inequality and what factors underlie its legitimacy.

U.S. ATTITUDES ABOUT THE DISTRIBUTION OF INCOME AND WEALTH

Americans often have ambivalent attitudes about social and economic inequality because the issues surrounding it touch on different, often conflicting, values held dear by most Americans.

While the recognition of inequality has increased in recent years, Americans' views about inequality are complex. Most Americans appear to believe there should be a limit on the amount of inequality. About two-thirds think that the current amount of income inequality is too large, and 63 percent believe wealth and income should be more equally distributed (Newport 2015b). These numbers have remained unchanged for the past 30 years. However, Americans are more concerned with people at the top getting too much than people at the bottom not getting enough (Osberg and Smeeding 2006). At the same time, however, they

are split on whether the government should do more, and more than 8 out of 10 believe that the government should focus on improving the economy in general rather than trying to redistribute wealth (Newport 2007). Thus, while Americans are concerned about inequality, they are wary of redistributive systems aimed at ameliorating inequality (McCall 2014).

How much credence we should put into individuals' judgments about whether an economic distribution is fair, however, depends on whether those people have an accurate grasp of the *actual* extent of economic inequality upon which they base their judgments. Compared to those found in most other industrial countries, individuals' *perceptions* of inequality in the United States tend to understate the *actual* discrepancies in earnings that exist. How people feel about existing inequalities also depends on what they think created them. Inequalities are viewed as justified or unjustified, depending on their perceived sources.

An international survey of nine countries, including the United States, confirmed that citizens feel that those in the highest-ranking occupations should be paid, on average, three to five times the salary of those in the lowest-ranking positions (Kelley and Evans 1993). More so than their citizen counterparts, older persons with higher education, incomes, and self-identified social classes favor greater pay for individuals in high-ranking occupations. For example, a conservative, high-income, 60-year-old man with a college education who identifies with the upper class, and who is also a supervising manager of his own company, feels that those in high-prestige positions should be paid seven times the minimum wage. In contrast, an individual with the opposite characteristics believes that a person in that kind of occupation should receive a salary of only three times the minimum wage. These preferences certainly understate the pay discrepancy noted earlier between CEOs and average workers. When it comes to the lowest-status jobs, however, the results are distinctly different. There is general consensus across groups about the appropriate wages for unskilled workers. Surprisingly, the single difference shows those with higher incomes favoring higher pay for those at the bottom. In essence, then, the only major disagreement among individuals revolves around the size and legitimacy of the salaries accorded high-prestige occupations. At the same time, however, virtually no one in these countries is in favor of a completely egalitarian distribution of income. Nor, argues Adam Swift, would completely open mobility be a sufficient criterion for defining fairness since it alone ignores the rights and duties of parents to help their children, ignores issues related to different rewards for positions, and sidesteps the role of luck in attainment (Swift 2004).

Almost two-thirds of Americans believe that inequality continues because it helps the rich and powerful (Davis and Smith 1996). Perhaps the cynical attitude expressed by a majority of adults about why inequality continues is related to their belief in a link between wealth and corruption.

Jong-Sung and Khagram's study (2005) of the relationship between inequality and beliefs about corruption in 129 countries revealed that higher degrees of inequality are associated with stronger beliefs in the presence of corruption. "Inequality increases corruption, especially in democracies, and corruption produces policy outcomes closer to those preferred by the rich than those favored by the median voter" (p. 154). Compared to the United States, however, much higher percentages of individuals in postcommunist societies like Russia, Hungary, and the Czech Republic believe wealth is obtained by dishonest means or because of problems in the economic system. U.S. respondents are more likely to stress hard work as a source of wealth (Kreidl 2000). Recent disclosures of high-level fraud on the part of some extremely wealthy individuals like Bernard Madoff, however, may cause a shift in these attitudes. Remember as

NUTSHELL 15.1 Our Values and Fairness in Policy

Sharon Hays spent 3 years talking to welfare recipients and visiting two welfare offices in different-sized cities. Her study, *Flat Broke with Children*, examined the cultural values underlying welfare reform and the effects of reform policy on the poor. Oftentimes, controversies involving fairness or justice are based in allegiances to different and seemingly contradictory values. Current welfare policies reflect these contradictions, which are in turn visited upon the poor who must adhere to the policies. Hays says that while support for dependent women and adequate wages for men who are supporting families were expected under the New Deal established under President Franklin Roosevelt in 1935, neither the government nor free-market processes have resulted in such support.

To back up historical principles of support realistically, Hays argues that we need to provide more economic aid for caregivers through tax credits and supplemental income so that dependents like children and stay-at-home mothers can be effectively supported. National standards also need to be set for caregivers so that the quality of care is uniform and high. Conditions at work should also be tailored to demonstrate that employers value the work of caregivers. This can take the form of good family-leave policies and availability of flexible work hours. Such support would create the opportunity for employees with families to act effectively and consistently on their responsibilities at home.

To further ensure economic independence for all adults, Hays feels that minimum wages need to be raised to help keep families together and keep individuals off welfare rolls who would prefer not to be there. Governmentally supported job training programs and even public employment opportunities would further promote financial independence for those in the working and lower classes. Finally, Hays notes that many of the economic problems faced by the disadvantaged are mirrored in the high degree of income inequality between those on the top and those on the bottom. To address this issue, Hays suggests a more progressive tax policy and a reduction in the various subsidies that favor the well-to-do.

Do any or all of Hays' ideas seem fair or just to you?

Source: Sharon Hays, *Flat Broke with Children* (New York: Oxford, 2003), pp. 235–236.

well the study by Hahl and Zuckerman (2014) mentioned in Chapter 4 indicating that high-status people are perceived as cold and calculating, and that people believe that they have received their wealth through questionable means.

In sum, a majority of Americans appear to support the *principle* of income inequality as being fair, but they do not see the present system as necessarily equitable. They also underestimate the extent of economic inequality in the country, and they are decidedly split on whether the government should do something about income inequality. In sum, Americans' attitudes about inequality are complex and often contradictory.

WHAT IS A JUST DISTRIBUTION?

The question of what constitutes a just distribution of scarce and desired goods is an issue that people have wrestled with for centuries. There seem to be two broad principles used to define a just distribution, but each of these is more complex than it first appears. One principle argues that a just or equitable distribution exists when equal people are treated equally and unequal people are treated unequally. It assumes that people (1) start out with different abilities and traits, (2) are free to realize their potentials, and (3) are therefore entitled to make different claims on scarce resources and rewards. This is what Hochschild (1981) called the "**principle of differentiation**," and it approximates what Ryan (1981) called the principle of "fair play." Given that individuals vary in their talents, abilities, and interests, it is predictable that they also will and should vary in their socioeconomic success, and that those with high levels of appropriate talents will assume higher positions in the hierarchy of inequality (Ryan 1981). If persons of *unequal* talent and ability are given *equal* rewards, then this must be justified (Hochschild 1981). While this position is consistent with a belief in meritocracy, one complication is that one's competencies and motivations may be due to luck related to biology or environment, factors over which one may have little control. So if people are not fully responsible for their competencies or motivations, a question

can be raised as to whether they really *merit* what they get (Marshall, Swift, and Roberts 1997). Generally speaking, this position is consistent with conservative theories such as functionalism and human-capital theory, both of which imply that one should get out of a system what one puts into it. Findings from the international study cited earlier are broadly consistent with this view.

A second broad principle, the "**principle of equality**," argues that people are of "equal value and can make equal claims on society. Differences in treatment must be justified" (Hochschild 1981, p. 51). This conception approximates Ryan's notion (1981) of "fair shares" as a basis for a just

Photo 15.1 Distributive justice is often seen as giving people what they deserve, for example, blaming those who are viewed as causing a problem and not blaming those who view themselves as the victims of the problem.

Photo by Brendan R. Hurst.

distribution. People ought to have equal rights and equal access to society's resources in order to live decent lives. This principle is consistent with more radical, Marxian views of inequality and its roots, such as those that consider private property to be a major source of explanation. Although there are a number of variations on these two principles, none of which are agreed on by all, we cannot pursue them here. While the principle of differentiation and the principle of equality appear to be incompatible, there is some evidence that people's perceptions of the fairness of inequality are affected by the arguments of both these criteria, that is, on their personal assessment of both the distributive *outcome* of rewards as well as the *process* that led to it. Moreover, how people feel about the process is related to their feelings about the outcome, and vice versa (Törnblom and Vermunt 1999).

Causal Attributions for Inequality

How do Americans define a just distribution of economic rewards in society? This partly depends on their characteristics and history, the criteria suggested by the society's dominant ideology, and their beliefs about the causes of economic inequality (Shepelak and Alwin 1986; Stolte 1987). With respect to the latter, Americans appear to give mixed messages when asked what they believe determines an individual's economic position.

Generally, most people attribute poverty and wealth to either *individualistic* or *structural* factors. "Individual" arguments include beliefs that poverty and wealth are due to personal qualities such as effort, ability, and ambition, while those who take a "structural" position argue that one's economic status is due to factors beyond the individual's control, such as inheritance, government policy, wage rates, discrimination, and availability of work. Historically, Americans have more often aligned themselves with the individualistic position, believing that hard work, ambition, personal investment in education, and natural ability are critical for economic success (Hanson and Zogby 2010). The widespread endorsement of this position is consistent with the belief that the United States

is a free and open society in which anyone can succeed. Most Americans subscribe to the dominant ideology that (1) opportunity for economic mobility is prevalent; (2) each individual is personally responsible for the extent of his or her own economic success; and (3) in general, therefore, the system of inequality is fair (Kluegel and Smith 1986). "In . . . the United States, principles of justice are based on the assumption that the playing field is level and that opportunities to succeed are the same for everyone" (Flanagan et al. 2003, p. 717). However, a review of recent surveys suggests that an increasing percentage of Americans are not satisfied with the degree of opportunity available for working-class people to succeed even if they work hard, and believe that the American Dream will be harder for the next generation to obtain (Hanson and Zogby 2010).

Not everyone, of course, is equally likely to subscribe to the belief that individuals are primarily responsible for where they wind up. Social class affects one's perceptions. Generally, greater proportions of individuals in high-status positions subscribe to individualistic rather than structural explanations of inequality. The possible exception is individuals with high education, who are less likely to attribute poverty to lack of effort or low morality (Kreidl 2000; see also Hunt 2007). In Bullock and Limbert's study (2003), for example, when low-income women were asked what they believed were the principal causes of poverty, structural explanations were favored over individualistic ones (see also Hunt 2004). Inheritance and being able to go the best schools, that is, being privileged, were the most frequently given explanations for why some people are wealthy (Bullock and Limbert 2003).

Another indication that the disadvantaged often see success as out of their personal control is the finding that Blacks and Latinos consider genetics more important for success in life than do more advantaged groups, though they do not believe that genetics explains differences in intelligence (Shostak et al. 2009). The belief in genetics may be strong because, in addition to the fact that genes are something we cannot control, genetic differences may be believed to explain health differences which then limit success. Additionally, among Blacks and Hispanics, working-class persons are also more likely than middle-class persons to argue that discrimination is an important cause of racial inequality. Paradoxically, higher-educated Blacks are more likely than their less-educated counterparts to believe that discrimination is a significant reason for inequality between the races (Hunt 2007; see also Pew 2007). In another study of teens' attitudes about social justice and equality of opportunity, researchers found that 90 percent of teens believe that equal opportunity to attain a good education exists in the United States. Surprisingly, students from private schools were more likely than those from public schools to identify inequalities in the educational system (p. 439). However, overall, Black students were more likely than Whites to report higher levels of inequality. Males, especially White males, are more likely than females to believe in individualistic causes. White women are more likely than men to take a structural position and to believe that the government should help care for the poor. Among Blacks and Hispanics, gender has less of a differentiating role (Hunt 2007).

Race and ethnicity are also significant predictors of beliefs about the sources of poverty and wealth. Interviews in 2000 with over 1,000 White and minority individuals in Los Angeles revealed that, as a group, respondents were more likely to attribute wealth to individualistic causes such as ambition, effort, and talent, but attribute poverty to structural causes such as inheritance, connections, dishonesty, or the economy. In other words, most believe that the "sky is the limit" for most people, but that those at the bottom are held down by factors beyond their control (Hunt 2004). Hunt found that Whites, Blacks, and Latinos were equally likely to attribute wealth to individualistic causes, but Blacks and Latinos were more likely than Whites to also attribute wealth to structural sources. Interestingly, Blacks and Latinos are more structuralist but *also* more individualist than Whites in their beliefs about what causes poverty. This "dual consciousness" is more prevalent among minorities (Hunt 2004, p. 845). In recent years, while race differences still exist, an increasing percentage of Blacks and Hispanics are attributing racial inequality to differences in motivation

and willpower, and are less willing to cite discrimination as the principal explanation. This "conservative" trend has reduced the racial gap in explanations for inequality (Hunt 2007).

What Americans believe the determinants of income *are*, of course, may be different from what they believe the determinants *should* be. Thinking of a system of inequality as legitimate helps to reduce uncertainty and makes persons feel better and more relaxed. Justification is easier in the United States than in some other countries because in this country there is a strong association between what people believe the determinants of wealth/income distribution actually *are* and what they think they *should* be. As a society with a capitalist, competitive, market-driven economy, personal attributes like ambition, hard work, and ability *should* and *do* operate as the primary bases for success according to most Americans. Individuals who exhibit these qualities to a higher degree merit higher rewards than others (van der Toorn, Berkics, and Jost 2010).

Performance and effort are widely believed to be appropriate bases for rewarding employees. Data from 31 countries indicate that an average of almost three-fourths of the persons in each of the countries considered performance and effort as legitimate determinants of pay. There is much more disagreement about need and education as bases for wages and salaries, however. Women, churchgoers, and individuals in lower socioeconomic positions are more likely to subscribe to "welfare/needs" as an acceptable basis for pay (Evans, Kelley, and Peoples 2010).

Perceptions of economic inequality are generally viewed differently and separately from views of racial and gender inequality. With racial and gender inequality, inequalities of *outcome* are seen as evidence of inequalities of *opportunity*. That is, if we find that there are differences in outcome by race, it is a fair assumption that there are unfair obstacles in the way of some, and thus the inequality is seen as unjust. With economic inequality, however, inequality of outcome coexists with inequality of opportunity—inequality of outcome may be due to differences in efforts or skills. Thus, as McCall suggests, an intersectional model of

Equality and Equity

Findings from a number of studies cited in previous chapters indicate that socioeconomic background has an impact on one's life chances. This suggests that the socioeconomic condition of a person's family can affect how far he or she can get in life. At the same time, numerous surveys have shown that Americans' idea of fairness is defined not in terms of equal family conditions, but primarily in terms of equal opportunity. That is, a system of inequality can be seen as fair if it is one in which everyone has an equal opportunity to succeed. Americans are much less inclined to believe in equality of condition, that is, an equal distribution of income, and so on. The question is, Can equality of opportunity exist without equality in socioeconomic conditions of families? Are equal starting conditions needed to achieve equality of opportunity? How would you reconcile these two principles to achieve a fair and equitable society? ▪

income inequality should ask: "How are perceptions of rising class inequality affected: by perceptions of trends in racial and gender inequality? by racial and gender differences in education, wealth, poverty, employment, and residential segregation? by racial and gender identities? and by intersections of these with social class identities and social movements" (2014, p. 30).

BASES FOR THE LEGITIMATION OF STRUCTURED INEQUALITY

The preceding studies indicate that most people in the United States believe that it is the individual more than anything else that determines upward mobility in the socioeconomic hierarchy. In other words, most people use the "principle of differentiation" in defining a just distribution. It is the *process* that must be seen as being just. The evidence also suggests that criteria over which the individual presumably has great control, such as effort and skills, *should be* used more than other kinds of factors to determine income. These beliefs obviously fit into the dominant American ideology that if people invest in themselves, they can improve their economic fate in life. Yet, as mentioned earlier, the evidence suggests that there are obstacles to equal opportunity for certain categories of individuals, and that not everyone with the same kind of job and education earns the same amount of income.

The question, then, is how do individuals come to accept a belief system even though there is evidence that it is not completely fair? How is an ideology internalized so that Americans come to believe that inequality is legitimate and justified? Mechanisms to assist internalization exist on the micro level of *individuals* in their everyday experiences as well as on the *institutional* macro level, working through the family, the education system, and other institutions.

Legitimation at the Level of the Individual

How do ideologies become internalized by people? This is a question addressed by Della Fave (1980), who tried to describe how individuals develop self-evaluations and judgments about the fairness of inequality. Interaction seems to be critical. To begin with, individuals are social beings, meaning that they develop only in relationship with each other. As individuals grow and develop, they come into contact with greater numbers of people who react to them in a variety of ways. Individuals learn the expectations others have of them by noticing how others behave toward them. This combination of the expectations and reactions of others toward us makes up what Mead called the "generalized other" (Della Fave 1980). It is through relationships with the generalized other that individuals develop a definition and image of themselves. Seeing how others react to us leads to the development of a particular self-image. By viewing ourselves as others see us, we come to a conclusion about our own worth and our contributions to society. A consistent self-image over time requires the social support of others. "A person who maintains a self-definition with no social support is mad; with minimum support, a pioneer; and with broad support, a lemming. Most of us are lemmings" (Huber 1988, p. 92).

The generalized other helps us understand why we evaluate *ourselves* as we do. How we evaluate the quality of *others* also depends on interaction. When individuals with different *amounts* of money or other resources *and* different *kinds* of noticeable nominal characteristics (e.g., race, sex, age) interact, each person draws associations between those characteristics, competence, and the differential amount of resources. Eventually, there develops a belief in the greater competence of those with more resources. One result is that better-off individuals can and are expected to present their opinions more forcefully and effectively, resulting in higher esteem for them and lower esteem for the less well-off. To the extent that the better-off tend to be male or White, beliefs in the greater quality of these types of people develop and are accepted by both parties in these interactions. "In effect, double dissimilar encounters [i.e., those in which individuals differ in resources and nominal characteristics] become beacons that continually broadcast support for status beliefs about the nominal distinction, encouraging and under pinning their diffusion and eventually their consensuality as well" (Ridgeway et al. 1998, p. 334).

Further strengthening of beliefs in the legitimacy of "who has how much" occurs because people believe that hard work and ambition are critical and justifiable reasons for wealth. Thus, the wealthy are viewed as deserving of their high positions. This positive assessment of the wealthy influences not only individual images of them but people's own self-images.

But how does the individual reach the conclusion that those who are wealthy work harder, contribute more to society, and therefore deserve more than others? Briefly, Della Fave (1980) argued that individuals reach conclusions about the reasonableness of their beliefs from what they consider to be an "objective outside observer."

In other words, it is from this observer that individuals develop ideas about what reality is and how it operates, and it is this observer whose judgments are internalized. It is the generalized other who fulfills the role of this observer, and it is the reactions of the generalized other to others that individuals internalize. Since a wide variety of people subscribe to a dominant ideology that emphasizes hard work and talent as the main reasons for success, they react to the wealthy as being deserving. The old saying "If you're so smart, why aren't you rich" captures this belief that wealth is a product of one's intelligence and talent. This appears to be an objective evaluation, and so they come to interpret others, and themselves, accordingly. Those who are reacted to favorably or treated as if they were important by almost everyone, including other important people, develop a very positive self-image, whereas others develop self-evaluations that are not quite as positive. "It is from the generalized other that individuals form an evaluation of self and, thus, of the worth of their 'contributions.' It is upon these evaluations, in turn, that judgments of equity are made in accordance with the principle of distributive justice" (Della Fave 1980, p. 961).

Those who are successful also develop feelings of self-efficacy; that is, they believe that their own actions can bring about successful rewards. This is largely because of positive reactions to their success by others, which then encourage them to do more and reinforce their high self-efficacy. Viewing their own success as being a result of their own actions, they come to define it as legitimate and deserving (Stolte 1983).

Individuals who possess very positive self-evaluations, in turn, come to view their own high level of rewards as being deserved relative to others, whereas those with more negative self-images see themselves as being worthy of fewer rewards. In a large complex society, individuals generally have to piece together broad images of what others are like and what their contributions are on the basis of the limited information to which they have access. Thus, individuals make conclusions about the contributions of others based on the information that shows on the surface—namely, their wealth and income. Those with high incomes, in turn, can use their resources to manage the impressions that others have of them—that is, manipulate the interpretations of others in such a way that the latter develop a positive image of them (Goffman 1959). Moreover, their ability to maintain high positions in educational, economic, and other institutions reinforces the image of their greater contributions and worthiness for higher rewards. Those with greater amounts are viewed as making greater contributions, and, therefore, as deserving of their economic resources. Essentially, the process of legitimation in this case is circular: Those with greater rewards elicit greater respect and the feeling from others that they deserve what they have, which in turn reinforces the inequality found in the hierarchy of rewards (Della Fave 1980). A skeletal interpretation of this process is presented in Figure 15.1.

According to Della Fave (1980), the entire internalization and social process—the **legitimation process**— just described bears directly on the extent to which the system of inequality is legitimated. The greater the degree to which the distribution of self-evaluations in society matches the distribution of rewards, the more legitimate the system of inequality will be considered and the more stable the society's structure of inequality will be. Conversely, if the two sets of distributions are not matched, then the stratification system is less likely to be defined as legitimate. This is consistent with Durkheim's views on the importance of the match between internal differences and rewards. More exposure and media coverage of corruption among individuals of high status and wealth, however, may increasingly counteract the power of personal resources to justify the level of rewards upper-class individuals receive.

Several of the relationships suggested have been tested recently. Following Della Fave's theory, Shepelak (1987) tested relationships among income, self-evaluations, and the belief in individual responsibility for a person's position. Her interviews with over 300 Indianapolis residents revealed that those with higher incomes did indeed have more favorable self-evaluations than those

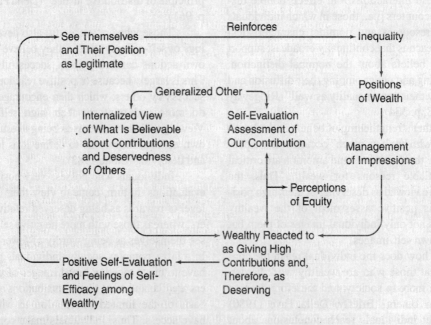

FIGURE 15.1 The Internalized Process of the Legitimation of Inequality

Source: Based on Della Fave (1980), pp. 955–958.

with low incomes, and that those with better self-evaluations were more likely than others to attribute their incomes to their own effort. However, the latter explanations were not related either to family income or estimates of equity/fairness. Family income and self-appraisals were both found to be positively related to the feeling that an individual's income was fair. Conversely, those with low incomes were more likely to say that they were being underrewarded. In other words, contrary to Della Fave's self-evaluation theory, those with lower incomes do not feel that they deserve less than those above them. In fact, family income is more strongly linked to beliefs in the fairness of one's family income than are either self-evaluations or explanations of income level. "These findings fail to substantiate the view that disadvantaged persons believe they deserve less" (Shepelak 1987, p. 501). Rather, they provide support for those who found that income is inversely related to the belief that the system of inequality is legitimate (e.g., Robinson and Bell 1978). On the other hand, support was found for the conclusions that a person's income standing and explanation of present position do affect feelings of self-worth. Figure 15.2 shows the interrelationships found

among self-evaluations, income, perceptions of fairness, and perceived causes of income.

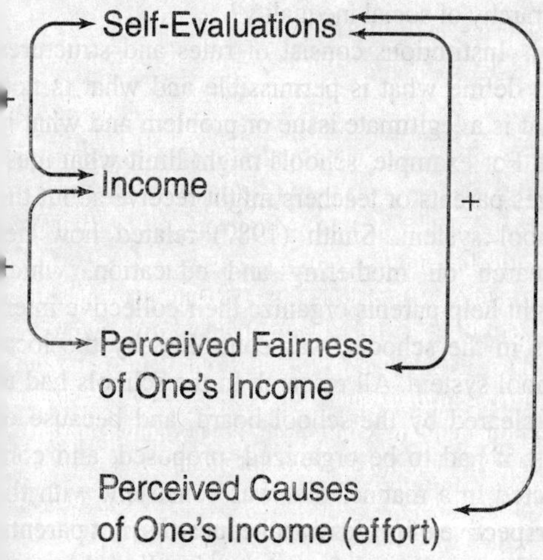

As a further test, experiments on university students examined the relationships among position, rewards, self-evaluation, and views of the fairness and structure of rewards. Sutphin and Simpson (2009) found that higher-positioned individuals who earned higher rewards also developed more positive self-evaluations, and also viewed the system of unequal rewards as legitimate and their own rewards as fair. Individuals in less-advantaged positions, however, varied in their conclusions about the fairness of the system. Those who had high evaluations of themselves were more likely than those with low self-evaluations to see their rewards as unfair.

In addition to the self-evaluation process just discussed, there are other elements in the everyday lives of individuals that promote feelings of system legitimacy. Most people, perhaps especially those who have to scramble to eke out a living, are too wrapped up in their daily lives and personal troubles to give much thought to the broad public issues of legitimacy and stability. Some research studies show that the social activities of those in the working and lower classes are usually limited to those involving friends and relatives; exposure to a wide range of types of people and geographic areas is restricted. The value and belief system that develops out of involvement in this immediate environment is basically accommodative in nature, helping individuals to make sense out of their everyday situation. Thus, it also tends to be parochial—tailored to explain or deal with the specific and immediate context in which these individuals live (Parkin 1971). As it concerns social inequality, part of the accommodation in this value system is to accept inequality but also to try to improve one's position within it. Thus, the value system generated in the local neighborhood does not ordinarily lead to a basic questioning of the system of inequality and its bases or to development of a radical ideology. Rather, people accept it in the abstract and then try to concretely adjust to it. So, "dominant values are not so much rejected or opposed as modified by the subordinate class as a result of their social

FIGURE 15.2 Relationships between Self-Evaluations, Income, and Fairness

Source: Based on Shepelak (1987), pp. 500–501.

circumstances and restricted opportunities" (Parkin 1971, p. 92).

Legitimation at the Cultural/Institutional Level

Although it is clear that self-evaluation and similar social-psychological processes are involved in legitimating social inequality, a society's culture and its social institutions are also directly implicated in the legitimation process. After all, during most of their routine activities, individuals are embedded in institutions. As in the case of self-evaluation's role, the basic question is how institutions and cultural values operate in ways that justify and maintain the hierarchy of social inequality.

It has been noted that Americans have ambivalent feelings about inequality. A large part of the reason for this ambivalence lies in the frequently inconsistent values that make up U.S. culture. At the abstract level, a core value in the culture is the belief in equal opportunity or fair play. But, in addition, Americans also tend to believe in competition, achievement, success, work or activity, efficiency, individual personality, freedom, nationalism, humanitarianism, and morality (Williams 1970). We have seen that differential rewards are more often believed to be the result of variations in effort or work by individuals striving to achieve success in a context of free, open competition with others. To attack capitalism or the structure of inequality that has existed for generations would be, for many, not only unfair but also unpatriotic. So these values, by and large, push people in the direction of supporting the existing system, while other values such as humanitarianism and moralism may suggest that inequality is inequitable.

The impact of values is often reflected in stereotypes that are held about different groups, and these stereotypes, in turn, often help to justify and sustain social inequalities. For example, images of ability and competence have limited the success and mobility of disabled workers. Research suggests that stereotype threat, or individuals' worry that they will be judged negatively based on stereotypes, can lead to underperformance in work and school environments, thus increasing inequalities.

In an experimental study of blind subjects, Silverman and Cohen (2014) found that those blind individuals with higher levels of stereotype threat were more likely to avoid challenges, had a lower sense of well-being, and were less likely to be employed. "Stereotype threat experiences threaten self-integrity, and people may defend their self-integrity by avoiding future situations that could arouse stereotype threat" (p. 1337).

In sum, images and stereotypes function to justify and maintain occupational inequality based on disability. Obviously, negative stereotypes of racial or ethnic minority groups perform a similar function. Perceiving Blacks, for example, as being less intelligent, less interested in education, and having less work incentive than Whites also serves to legitimize the economic and political inequalities that exist between the races. The power of these beliefs persists even when the evidence in each of these cases does not warrant such beliefs.

The beliefs and values that individuals endorse derive, in large part, from the broader institutional and cultural framework in which they operate. The task now is to describe how the system of inequality and the supporting values infiltrate the social institutions so that institutions foster activities and reinforce beliefs that legitimate inequality. How do institutions help to maintain the hierarchy of social inequality?

Institutions consist of rules and structures that define what is permissible and what is not, what is a legitimate issue or problem and what is not. For example, schools might limit what messages parents or teachers might receive about the school system. Smith (1987) related how her research on mothering and education, which might help parents organize their collective interests in the schools, was controlled by the local school system. All research in the schools had to be cleared by the school board, and because of this, it had to be organized, proposed, and conducted in a manner that was consistent with the perspective of professional educators, not parents. *Professionalism* defines what is allowable, and professionalism is defined by those most esteemed and dominant in the profession (generally White, higher-status males). This creates limits on what information can be collected and what can be done with it.

The preceding example suggests that one of the tools used by institutions to legitimate the social structure, including the system of inequality, is to frame the image of that structure and the processes associated with it in a particular way with the use of certain kinds of concepts and terms. Language can greatly influence the interpretations placed on issues such as poverty, welfare, and political participation. The terms used to describe what is defined as a social problem also can influence how people react to it. There is no more apt example than the government's recent intervention into the shaky economic market through its subsidization of private corporations. The program was initially termed a "bailout," with some calling it "corporate welfare." Given the high value that a "free" market has in our society, the negative reaction to the government "bailout" was understandable. So the terminology was changed to describe it as a "rescue plan" rather than a "bailout" in an attempt to legitimize the plan and make it more palatable to the public. Governments can affect the extent to which citizens interpret "poverty" as legitimate by using particular symbols to describe it. To most Americans, to indicate that some people are "on welfare" suggests something about the character of these individuals and their responsibility for their own fates. Someone who is considered a "welfare case" by an outsider is usually thought to be a person who does not work and probably does not want to work, one who is "living off" the rest of society. The term *welfare* itself evokes an image quite different from the term *poor*.

Similarly, referring to income as "rewards" or "earnings" plants the belief that the money is earned and thus deserved. Attributing the high rewards of a position to its "functional importance" to society helps to legitimize differential rewards. People have been socialized to react positively to the needs of society, the national interest, and earnings. Terms such as these encourage the acceptance and legitimation of "material sacrifices, constricted roles, political weakness, existing power hierarchies, and unfulfilled lives" (Edelman 2013, p. 153–154).

Institutions of all types use language and symbols to create an image that legitimates the existing social reality. The use of certain terms to evoke specific images, and thus to encourage the acceptance of inequalities between individuals, applies to economic differences not only between rich and poor but also between men and women and Blacks and Whites. Because of the symbolic power of the concepts used by institutions and because of the intrusion of major institutions into most corners of their lives, people develop certain interpretations about society and other people, including those who are meritorious and deserving and those who are not. The institutions of family, education, and religion all contain elements that encourage acceptance of inequality.

FAMILY Because they differ in resources and structure, it is clear that families contribute to the reproduction of economic, racial, and gender inequalities. Poor parents do not have the material resources to support and pass on to their children that wealthier parents possess. Fewer resources also means that poorer parents are less able to provide their children with safe environments or with access to enrichment activities such as music lessons or participation on sports teams (Pew 2015f).

Economic differences also affect the structure of families. The propensity for people to marry people like them, known as "assortative mating," means that we increasingly have "power couples" that magnify levels in inequality across generations (Cowen 2015). Wage inequalities between races create an incentive for minority women to postpone or eliminate marriage as an attractive option because the low wages paid to male minority members reduces the availability of appealing marriage partners. For poor women, this increases the likelihood that they will have children before marrying, since there are few opportunity costs for them and welfare is available. Moreover, in the absence of alternative sources of fulfillment available to higher-status women, motherhood is a principle source of identity for less-advantaged women. This is especially true for single-parent families, which are found in greater proportions among minority and poor populations. Single mothers bear a wage penalty that single fathers do not, and carry out most of the child rearing, further exacerbating economic and status inequalities between the sexes (McLanahan and Percheski 2008; Swartz 2009).

The differences in structures and resources between families means that the benefits and experiences of children in families also differ. This has implications for the kind of socialization that occurs between parents and children. The family has always been considered a major instrument of socialization. It is within the domestic sphere that men and women learn much about how they should define themselves, their proper roles, and what they can expect from each other and society. For example, individuals develop within families' understandings about sexuality, including whom they should love and how they should express their sexuality. For some families, this means socialization into a model of **heteronormativity**; for others, sexuality, and therefore the meaning of family, is defined more fluidly. Socialization within families into gendered or sexualized roles can therefore serve the function of perpetuating traditional roles, or in some cases disrupting these roles, leading to social change.

EDUCATION Schools perpetuate and legitimize inequality between the sexes, races, and classes through a variety of mechanisms. In education, individuals with varying abilities and levels of effort are channeled into appropriate levels of the occupational structure. The school appears as a forum in which students openly compete with each other and then are objectively evaluated by the experts. Skills and abilities are often measured through the use of standardized tests; differences in scores are seen as differences in abilities. Of course, performance on such tests depends in part on the learning opportunities that have been afforded students, and these vary by socioeconomic status. The expectation is that students who have had more of these opportunities will do better on tests than other students (Grodsky, Warren, and Felts 2008). Still, different scores are seen as objective measures of the different levels of ability existing between students. "The educational system fosters and reinforces the belief that economic success depends essentially on the possession of technical and cognitive skills—skills which it is organized to provide in an efficient, equitable, and unbiased manner on the basis of meritocratic principle" (Bowles and Gintis 1976, p. 103). Consequently, schools are in the business of preparing students to be funneled into work roles at appropriate status levels.

At another level, various aspects of teacher–student relations encourage acceptance of an individual's traditional place in the structure of inequality. By teaching students about the nature of social reality, such as the values of the free market, intellectuals help to support the status quo. In Gramsci's phrase (1971), intellectuals often have been "managers of legitimation." This includes members of the helping professions, such as social workers, psychiatrists, and teachers. Although educators often have encouraged happiness through adjustment to the status quo, those involved in these professions "have reinforced inequality by equating adjustment to existing social, economic, and political institutions with psychological health" (Edelman 2013, p. 152). People who deviate from their expected roles or who criticize the social structure are defined as "deviant" and are dealt with accordingly (Mills 1959).

Some of the teacher behaviors that encourage adjustment also reinforce traditional gender roles in U.S. society. Teachers in middle and high schools hold the expectation that boys will be stronger in math than girls. These expectations influence the attitudes and expectations of their students, resulting in traditional gender stereotyping of ability in mathematics (Gunderson et al 2012). These expectations are intertwined as well with race and ethnicity, as teachers are more likely to hold the belief that White males are stronger in math than Black or Hispanic males, and stronger than White females (Riegle-Crumb and Humphries 2012).

Schools also provide an environment where children are often sorted or segregated by sex leading to a perpetuation of gender stereotypes. Children are asked to "line up" or separate by sex at playtime, and are often encouraged to find playmates of the same sex. Children who mor frequently choose playmates of the same sex are also more likely to engage in traditional gender-typed play (Martin et al. 2013). The assumption by teachers that boys and girls are different helps to reinforce a socialization into gendered behaviors.

Along with gender roles, traditional images of minorities are also reinforced. By and large, the information presented in classrooms and textbooks usually offers a favorable interpretation of the United States and its history. Children have seldom been told in detail about unethical acts by national leaders or of the brutalization of such groups as American Indians. Recently, an Oklahoma legislative committee voted to ban the teaching of Advanced Placement History courses becomes they emphasize "'what is bad about America' and characterizes the United States as a 'nation of oppressors and exploiters'" (Rampell 2015). "None of this is very surprising. . . . Throughout history all children have been socialized to accept the dominant values and institutions of their society" (Kerbo 1983, p. 388).

Teacher expectations of Blacks and Whites and students from higher and lower classes also have been shown to be different (Ferguson 2003). The images teachers have of lower-status groups influence their expectations of them. Less is expected from them, which ultimately affects how well they do in school. Their lower performance only reinforces the initial negative image held by teachers, resulting in a self-fulfilling prophecy. Their lower performance also appears to justify their lower attainment, further strengthening the belief that attainment is linked to merit. The lower expectations by teachers of lower-status individuals influence the teachers to place these students in lower non-college-oriented tracks. Their placement in these tracks helps to ensure their lower educational attainment.

What is important about all these mechanisms is that their effects are largely unrecognized. The overriding belief is that in schools teachers are the objective experts, and that students study and take valid tests, are judged on the basis of their performance, and end up at a place in the attainment hierarchy that reflects their performance. What level they attain appears to be solely up to

them. This reinforces and legitimates the belief that inequality in society is largely the result of differences in individual efforts and abilities.

RELIGION French sociologist Émile Durkheim argued that religion is integrative for society because its beliefs and rituals take individuals out of their secular private lives and bring them together to form a community. It is out of the social gathering of individuals in a religious setting that feelings of a superior force or power outside individuals first arise. Thus, Durkheim argued that the worship of supernatural forces in religious rituals is really an adoration of the powers in society. "In the divine, men realize to themselves the moral authority of society, the discipline beyond themselves to which they submit, which constrains their behavior even in spite of themselves, contradicts their impulses, rewards their compliance, and so renders them dependent and grateful for it" (Sahlins 1968, pp. 96–97).

Given this description, it should come as no surprise that images of the supernatural world often mirror the social structure of society. Swanson (1964) showed concretely in his study of non-Western societies that a social hierarchy on earth is reflected in a social hierarchy in the supernatural realm. In societies in which older people occupied positions of importance, ancestors were a subject of worship, and in societies in which there was a great deal of social inequality, religion helped to legitimate the differences between the top and the bottom. A good example of this legitimation occurs in Hinduism in which the concepts of karma, dharma, and samsara combine to explain and justify the continuous inequality generation after generation. *Karma* indicates the belief that a person's present situation is the result of his or her actions in a previous life, and *dharma* refers to the duties and norms attached to each caste. Finally, *samsara* refers to the continual birth and rebirth of life. In other words, central beliefs in Hinduism absolve society or others from responsibility for social inequality. It is the result of individual actions (Turner 1986).

Particular branches of Christianity have also legitimated people's beliefs about inequality, for example, in their dictum that self-denial, continuous effort, and hard work result in success. This kind of spirit is what is embodied in Weber's concept of the "Protestant ethic." Hard work and religious beliefs were intermingled by many famous preachers early in U.S. history. Cotton Mather, a charismatic Puritan preacher of the late seventeenth century, lectured that business and people's occupations were "callings" and not to be ignored. If individuals do not engage in their occupations, but rather remain idle (slothful), poverty will befall them. Riches are the result of industry, and poverty is the result of individual laziness. Those who are poor should expect no help from others since it is their own behavior that has resulted in their dismal situation. By engaging in business, people are doing what God intended: "Yea a *calling* is not only our *Duty*, but also our *Safety*. Men will ordinarily fall into horrible *Snares*, and infinite *Sins*, if they have not a *Calling*, to be their preservative. . . . If the Lord Jesus Christ might find thee, in thy *Store House*, in thy *Shop*, or in thy *Ship*, or in thy *Field*, or where thy *Business* lies, who knows, what *Blessings* He might bestow upon thee?" (cited in Rischin 1965, pp. 24, 26). It is only a short jump from this statement to the belief that those who are successful are so because of their own efforts and are among the favored of God, while those on the bottom do not work and are sinful.

Advocates of Dutch Calvinism justified slavery by viewing Blacks as sinners and slavery as a just condition for their sins and inferiority in the eyes of God. The legacy of these beliefs can be found in the contemporary dilemmas of inequality in South Africa (Turner 1986). In the United States, a slave catechism was used in many churches during the period of slavery to justify domination by masters, to encourage work, and to attribute lack of work to personal laziness. White pastors told Blacks that God created the masters over them and that the Bible tells them that they must obey their White masters (Fishel and Quarles 1967). There are additional elements in Christianity that have been used to support continual subordination of women to men, including the biblical argument about the origins of woman out of man and the injunctions to obey one's husband in marriage.

The impact of religion on beliefs about inequality has continued. Members of dominant religions, especially Whites who espouse Protestantism and Catholicism (though Catholics to a lesser extent), are more likely than members of minority religions such as Judaism to support the inequality status quo, believing that poverty is a result of individuals' flaws rather than a consequence of luck or structural defects (Hunt 2002).

Civil religion is used to justify the "American way of life." It is a mixture of religious and political ideology in which the U.S. social structure and culture are seen as favored by God. God and Americanism go hand in hand in this ideology. This is a nation "under God," and its institutions are sanctified by the Almighty. At civil ceremonies and during certain public occasions, such as the opening of Congress, presidential inaugurations, and the Pledge of Allegiance, it is suggested that God is the benefactor of the United States. The "American way" that is so blessed incorporates the values of individualism, freedom, capitalism, and equality of opportunity, which make up a core part of the ideology supporting inequality. Some televangelists conjoin Christianity and Americanism in a manner that makes them not only mutually supportive but almost indistinguishable. In this ideology, to attack Americanism becomes tantamount to committing a serious sin. Americanism is supposed to be accepted, not criticized or undermined.

More recently, the "prosperity gospel," arising within American Evangelical and Pentecostal denominations post-1940 emphasizes a belief consonant with key American principles, including a personally engaged God who demonstrates individuals' salvation by conferring wealth and health. Consistent with capitalist views of consumerism and materialism, individual effort and hard work are rewarded with prosperity and ultimately salvation. A belief in the prosperity gospel is negatively associated with socioeconomic status, perhaps because wealthier individuals do not believe that divine intervention is necessary to achieve success (Schieman and Jung 2012).

Karl Marx viewed religion under capitalism as having many of the effects on inequality just discussed. People are expected to put up with inequality; religion lulls them into a false sense of complacency. That is, it makes them *falsely conscious* of their real situation. It blinds them to the real causes of their predicament (i.e., class exploitation, not personal sin). In this way, socioeconomic inequality is seen as legitimate by those who blame only themselves or look forward to another life when conditions will be better for them.

Of course, Marx realized that historically, before capitalism, religion had been used to support the oppressed; even in our own time, religions have not always supported the status quo. Martin Luther King Jr. and the Southern Christian Leadership Conference used religious ideas to try to improve conditions of Blacks in the United States, and Catholic bishops have fought on the side of the poor against many Latin American dictatorships (Hehir 1981; Light, Keller, and Calhoun 1989).

More recently, Pope Francis has been very vocal in speaking against inequality, tweeting on April 28, 2014, that "(I)nequality is the root of social evil," and in a speech in Bolivia in 2015, he stated that "Working for a just distribution of the fruits of the earth and human labor is not mere philanthropy. It is a moral obligation. For Christians, the responsibility is even greater: it is a commandment" (Huddleston 2015).

Despite these instances in which religion has opposed inequality, historically it has been more closely associated with its legitimation and maintenance. This has been the case with each of the social institutions we have discussed. By and large, each has served to support the dominant value system as it pertains to inequality, and it is through each of them that individuals come to believe that the social inequality around them is legitimate.

Summary

The principal focus of this chapter has been on examining the assessments of the fairness of social and economic inequality and the criteria that define such fairness, and exploring the factors that contribute to the legitimation and, therefore, the stability of inequality in the United States. Americans are clearly torn on the fairness issue. On the one hand, they believe that hard work, education, and similar personal investments are important for economic achievement and believe that they should be important. On the other hand, most feel that the extent of inequality is too great; on the other hand, they do not think that full equality of income or wealth would be fair either. Moreover, when asked what they think determines success, they tend to overestimate the significance of some factors and underestimate the impact of others, most notably race and sex. Attributing poverty and wealth to individualistic and/or structuralist causes varies with one's class, gender, and minority status. In their assessments of the criteria to be used in determining a fair income, Americans tend to use a mixture of achievement and other factors (e.g., education, marital status, sex, occupational status).

The system of inequality itself is legitimated at the individual and institutional levels. Individuals develop interpretations of their own and others' rewards and contributions from the reactions of others to inequality. Their position in the rewards hierarchy affects their own self-evaluations and their appraisal of the fairness of their own incomes. At the same time, those with positive self-evaluations interpret their own incomes as being the result of their own efforts.

Through its culture and institutions, society helps to encourage traditional beliefs about the causes of inequality, thereby maintaining the structure of inequality. Generally, the values impressed on members and clients of those institutions are those of individualism and capitalism. Through the language and symbols used and their rules of knowledge, institutions define what is real and proper. In the case of the family and education, institutions shape beliefs and roles for those in different positions of the system of inequality and encourage a belief in the legitimacy of their positions. Religion also has used its resources on many occasions to legitimate the socioeconomic inequality that surrounds individuals.

Critical Thinking

1. If wealthy individuals are more likely than others to consider the system of inequality fair, what are the chances that the system will ever change?
2. Is it possible to develop a formula for the fair distribution of resources that is objective and generally agreed on by most in society? Explain your answer. If you agree that it could be developed, what might go into such a formula?
3. Is there such a thing as *too much* inequality if that inequality is the result of free-market forces and individual differences in effort and talent? How could one determine if there is *too much* inequality?
4. The family, educational institutions, and religion have often perpetuated and justified inequality. Are there any aspects of these institutions that undermine inequality or encourage its decrease?

Web Connections

In considering how wealth might be distributed and whether we should help the poor of the world, consider the arguments at www.sevenoaksphilosophy.org/ethics/distribution-of-wealth.html.

Film Suggestions

Income Inequality (2007). In this episode of the PBS program *NOW*, two authors discuss inequality in the United States and who it is helping and who it is hurting.

Bread and Roses (2000). Janitorial workers fight for better working conditions and unionization.

Inequality for All (2013). Former labor secretary Robert Reich explores the widening wealth inequality in America post-recession and what it means for overall economic health in this documentary.

GLOSSARY OF BASIC TERMS

absolute downward mobility a downward shift in economic resources without a simultaneous change in an individual's position relative to others.

anomic division of labor an abnormal condition in which the rules of relationships among those in the production process and limits in the marketplace are unclear.

ascriptive inequality or ascriptive qualities qualities conferring status that are mostly inherited or beyond an individual's control, such as race, ethnicity, or class at birth.

asexuality a sexual orientation defined by the absence of sexual desire.

biological determinism theories that view human behavior as innate rather than influenced by culture or societal structures.

blockbusting when real estate agents convince Whites that minorities are moving into the neighborhood, the Whites then sell their houses for low prices, and the real estate agents resell the houses at higher prices to minority families.

brown-bag test criterion used to screen individuals from membership in a group or organization if their skin color is darker than a brown grocery bag.

capitalism an economic system based on private ownership, competition, and open markets.

caste system a closed social ranking system dividing categories of individuals in which position is ascribed and which is legitimated by cultural and/or religious institutions.

chronic illness health problems that continue over a long period of time.

circulation mobility mobility that reflects the cultural and social openness of a society.

cisgender an adjective describing people whose gender identity matches the sex they were assigned at birth.

class defined variously as individuals or groups who (1) occupy the same position on hierarchies of occupational prestige, income, and education; (2) are in the same relation to the system of production;

or (3) are in the same relation to the system of production and are also class conscious.

class consciousness the full awareness within a group of its class position and relationship with other classes, along with action based on this awareness.

contingent workforce includes people who work on a non-permanent basis as contractors, freelancers, or consultants.

core economic sector the section of the private economy occupied by large, capital-intensive, highly productive firms with large, sometimes international, markets (also called **monopoly sector**).

corporate crime crime generally committed by corporate officials for the immediate benefit of their corporation rather than themselves.

crises of overproduction the inability of capitalism to sell all that it produces, largely because of the inconsistency between low, impoverished wages and advanced technology.

critical-race perspective views racism and race relations as rooted and hidden in the structure and historical social arrangements of society rather than as issues of individual prejudice.

cultural capital a group's cultural values, experiences, knowledge, and skills passed on from one generation to the next.

dependency theory argues that international inequality is due to relationships of dependency and exploitation between strong and weaker nations.

digital divide inequality between social classes in technology ownership and use.

drift hypothesis in the study of the relationship between mental illness and social class, the argument that illness causes one's downward mobility through the class system.

dual labor market the view of the market as being split between a primary market with better jobs and a secondary market characterized by lower-paying and less stable jobs.

economic hardship spending more than 40 percent of one's income on debt payment.

embourgeoisement the taking on by the working class of middle-class cultural and social characteristics.

environmental equity/justice concerns the extent to which groups have equal access to public land resources and equal exposure to environmental hazards.

essentialism the idea that people are born with a certain unchanging, underlying "essence" that can include sexual orientation or gender identity.

ethnic group a group distinguished on the basis of its native cultural and linguistic characteristics.

ethnocentrism belief that one's culture is the best and should be used as a standard to rate other cultures.

financial wealth those forms of wealth that can be easily and quickly converted to cash.

forced division of labor an abnormal condition in which the distribution of accorded positions and occupations is inconsistent with the distribution of talents and skills among individuals.

functionalist theory of stratification the argument that stratification is a necessary device for motivating talented people to perform society's most difficult and important tasks, and that it arises from scarcity of talent and the differential social necessity of tasks.

gender a set of attitudinal, role, and behavior expectations, which are socially and culturally defined, associated with each sex.

gender stratification the degree to which access to valued resources is restricted because of gender.

genderqueer people whose feelings and behaviors are not confined by the gender binary.

glass escalator the presumption that men in traditionally female occupations rise more quickly then women.

globalization *economically*, the acceleration of international trade and flow of financial capital; *politically*, the opening of national borders to foreign goods and services; and *socially*, the free flow and exchange of cultural ideas and structural arrangements among nations.

habitus Bourdieu's term for a system of stable dispositions to view the world in a particular way.

hate crime a violent or property crime that is motivated at least in part by a bias against the victim's race, religion, disability, sexual orientation, ethnicity, or national origin.

heteronormative a worldview that assumes heterosexuality is the normal and natural state.

human capital the investments one makes in oneself (i.e., education, acquisition of skills, and experience).

hyperghettoization the extreme concentration of underprivileged groups in the inner city.

income deficit how far below the poverty level one's income falls.

industrialism thesis the argument that, regardless of the country, industrialization breaks down barriers to social mobility and results in an emphasis on achievement rather than ascription as a basis for vertical mobility.

in-kind benefits noncash outlays given to recipients of government programs, such as food stamps, medical assistance, and job training.

inner circle a network of leaders from large corporations who serve as top officers at more than one firm, who are politically active, and who serve the interests of the capitalist class as a whole.

inner/outer orientation a view of the environment as hospitable, fruitful, and freely giving (inner) or as one in which the environment is alien and hostile, and must be conquered (outer).

institutional view of social welfare belief that since poverty is often beyond the control of individuals, and one of government's legitimate roles is to help those in need, welfare should be available to help people out of poverty.

intergenerational mobility a change in economic or social hierarchical position between generations.

internal colonialism a situation in which minority group is culturally, socially, and politically dominated as if it were a colony of the majority group.

intersectionality the idea that one's race, sex, ethnicity, and social class, when combined, create distinctive social positions that have effects that are independent of the separate effects of each component taken separately.

intersex term used to describe a variety of conditions in which a person is born with a reproductive or sexual anatomy that does not seem to fit the typical definitions of female or male.

intragenerational mobility vertical economic or social movement within one's own lifetime.

jati the complex system of local castes found in Indian villages.

labor power the mental and physical capacities exercised by individuals when they produce something of use.

legacy college and university preferences given to the children of alumni.

legitimation process the means and manner by which social inequality is explained and justified.

mass society a society in which the vast majority of the population is unorganized, largely powerless, and manipulated by those at the distant top.

means of production the material (e.g., machines) and nonmaterial (e.g., lectures) techniques used to produce goods and services in an economy.

microaggressions or microinequities everyday ways in which, because of their social ranking, individuals are ignored, put down, highlighted, or demeaned.

militant societies societies in which there is heavy regulation of individuals and groups; the regulatory system is the dominant institution in the society; contrasted with industrial societies and associated with Spencer.

mode of production the particular type of economic system in a society, including its means of production (e.g., technology) and social/authority relations among workers and between workers and owners. Capitalism and feudalism are two modes of production.

modernization theory assumes that there is a fundamental and irreconcilable conflict between tradition and modernity in "underdeveloped" countries, and that the gap must be eliminated for development to occur.

near poor those whose total incomes fall between 100 percent and 125 percent of their poverty thresholds.

necessary labor the labor needed to reproduce workers and their replacements.

neoliberalism a theory that views globalization as an opening up of opportunities and boundaries that results in greater benefits for all countries.

nested inequalities inequalities existing at various levels within a given institutional sphere that have a cumulative or layered effect.

net worth one's wealth minus one's debts.

opportunity structure characteristics of the cultural, social, political, legal, occupational, economic, and other institutions that affect chances of social mobility either positively or negatively.

pansexuality a sexual orientation denoting the possibility of attraction to people of all gender identities.

party an association aimed at or specifically organized for gaining political power in an organization or society (Weber).

patriarchy a complex of structured interrelationships in which men dominate women.

peripheral economic sector part of the private economy occupied by small, local, labor-intensive, less productive, and less stable economic organizations (also called **competitive sector**).

phantom welfare government cash, tax, and in-kind programs and policies that largely benefit the nonpoor.

pigeonholing steering members of a particular category (for example, racial or gender) into positions deemed appropriate for them.

pluralism the view stressing that power is distributed throughout society among various groups rather than concentrated.

political action committee (PAC) a group that organizes around a broad or narrow common interest to influence political policy in its favor.

Ponzi scheme economic fraud in which investment money is manipulated to make illegal profit.

power elite a small group or set of groups that dominate the political process and masses in a society.

prestige the social ranking accorded a position or occupation; a synonym for status honor.

primary labor market the labor market associated with jobs that are stable, good paying, and unionized; have good working conditions; and in which there is an internal job structure through which one can move.

principle of differentiation the belief that it is fair that those with unequal talents should receive unequal rewards.

principle of equality the belief that since all people are ultimately of equal value, they should therefore receive equal consideration or treatment.

proletarianization the conversion of white-collar and middle-class occupations into occupations with traditional working-class characteristics (e.g., boring, routine).

public assistance programs cash and in-kind government programs for the poor that are means tested (i.e., require that individuals prove their eligibility) and to which there is a social stigma attached.

racial invariance hypothesis the idea that causes of crime are the same for all racial groups but that the groups are differentially exposed to those causes.

racialization social and psychological process by which poverty and welfare are defined as Black issues.

rationalization the increasing bureaucratic, technological, and impersonal character of the modern world (Weber).

relative downward mobility a shift in one's position on the economic ladder to a lower position and involving a switch in place with another person or group.

residual view of social welfare the belief that since poverty is caused by personal flaws, welfare programs should be minimal, with low benefits and strict eligibility requirements to discourage their use.

ruling class the broad Marxian view that the upper class, or an active arm of it, generally dominates the political process in society to protect its interests.

scientific management a system of control used by management in which labor tasks are simplified and standardized by being broken down into their smallest elements.

secondary labor market the labor market associated with poor, unstable, low-paying, and often dead-end jobs.

sedimentation the reproduction and perpetuation of lower levels of wealth over generations for given groups.

sex-typed activities, qualities, roles, or behaviors presumed to be appropriate for one sex.

social capital the size and nature of networks of social relationships possessed by a person or group.

social causation thesis in the study of the relationship between mental illness and social class, the argument that social class position is causally related to the probability of mental illness.

social constructionism a perspective that explains how social phenomena are socially created through definitions, classifications, and categorizations used by individuals.

Social Darwinism a social philosophy stressing perfection of society through a natural, unfettered process of survival of the fittest.

social insurance governmenvt programs, such as Social Security, for which individuals who have worked for a certain period of time are automatically eligible and seen as deserving of aid.

social relations of production the nature of property and power relationships among workers, between workers and managers/supervisors, and between owners and nonowners in an economic system.

social reproduction the process by which structural conditions reproduce themselves.

social stratification a condition in which the ranking system among groups or categories of individuals is firmly established, resulting in a set of social layers separated by impermeable boundaries.

socioeconomic status a person's position on several continuous social and economic hierarchies such as education, income, occupation, and wealth.

soft power national power that is based on a country's values, cultural traditions, ideals, and foreign policy rather than on its physical might.

stages of capitalism capitalism's movement through phases of cooperation, manufacture, and modern industry (Marx).

status the ranking of individuals and groups on the basis of *social* and evaluated characteristics; contrasts with **class**, which is largely an *economic* ranking.

status attainment the study of the factors and processes that account for the educational, occupational, and economic attainment of individuals.

stereotype threat individuals' worry that they will be judged negatively based on stereotypes, leading to underperformance in work and school environments.

street crimes crimes listed by the FBI's Crime Index, including burglary, larceny-theft, motor vehicle theft, arson, murder, forcible rape, robbery, and aggravated assault.

structural mobility mobility that is due to shifts in the occupational distribution or changes in technology.

suite crime a synonym for **white-collar crime**.

surplus labor labor time that is left over after socially necessary labor has been subtracted from the total labor time spent on the job. It produces profit for the employer.

systemic racism discriminatory practices and ideologies that were built into social institutions (like the economy and the educational system) from early in a country's history.

tokenism recruiting one or a small number of minorities as a symbolic gesture of inclusion.

tokens individuals who are the only persons seen as representing a distinct minority within a group.

transgender referring to individuals who do not self-identify with the gender they were assigned at birth.

underclass a small, urban, largely unemployed, chronically poor, welfare-dependent group of individuals living in impoverished neighborhoods, whose children often wind up in the same position.

vacancy-driven mobility mobility that depends on the availability and distribution of open positions.

varna a major ritual caste in India, such as the Brahmins.

welfare capitalism special benefits used by management to minimize solidarity among workers.

white-collar crime crimes committed by individuals of high status or corporations using their powerful positions for personal gain.

Wisconsin model a model of status attainment that stresses the impact of social-psychological as well as structural factors on attainment.

world inequality the total amount of inequality between nations and the average amount of inequality within nations combined.

world system theory posits that the world economy is composed of core, semiperipheral, and peripheral nations, which determines each nation's function and place in the world system.

REFERENCES

Aaronson, Daniel, and Bhashkar Mazumder. 2008. "Intergenerational Economic Mobility in the United States, 1940 to 2000." *Journal of Human Resources* 43 (1): 139–172.

Aaronson, Daniel, and Daniel G. Sullivan. 1998. "The Decline of Job Security in the 1990s: Displacement, Anxiety, and Their Effect on Wage Growth." *Economic Perspectives—Federal Reserve Bank of Chicago* 22: 17–43.

AARP. 2009. "Chronic Condition Prevalence in the 50+ US Population." Washington, D.C.: American Association of Retired Persons Public Policy Institute.

Aberle, D. F., A. D. Cohen, M. J. Davis, and F. X. Sutton. 1950. "The Functional Prerequisites of a Society." *Ethics* 60: 100–111.

Abrahamson, Mark. 1973. "Functionalism and the Functional Theory of Stratification: An Empirical Assessment." *American Journal of Sociology* 78: 1236–1246.

Abramovitz, Mimi. 2000. *Under Attack, Fighting Back: Women and Welfare in the United States*. New York: Monthly Review Press.

Abramovitz, Mimi. 2001. "Everyone Is Still on Welfare: The Role of Redistribution in Social Policy." *Social Work* 46 (4): 297–308.

Abu-Lughod, Lila. 2013. *Do Muslim Women Need Saving?* Cambridge, MA: Harvard University Press.

Acker, Joan. 2006. "Inequality Regimes: Gender, Class, and Race in Organizations." *Gender & Society* 20 (4): 441–464.

Ackerman, Bruce A., and Anne Alstott. 1999. *The Stakeholder Society*. New Haven, CT: Yale University Press.

ACLU. 2015. "The School to Prison Pipeline in Black and White." Providence, RI: American Civil Liberties Union of Rhode Island. Available at http://riaclu.org/images/uploads/School_to_Prison_Pipeline_in_Black_and_White_2015.pdf.

Adam, Barry D., Jan Willem Duyvendak, and Andre Krouwel. 1999. "Gay and Lesbian Movements beyond Borders? National Imprints of a Worldwide Movement." In *The Global Emergence of Gay and Lesbian Politics: National Imprints of a Worldwide Movement*, edited by Barry D. Adam, Jan Willem Duyvendak, and Andre Krouwel, 344–372. Philadelphia, PA: Temple University Press.

Adams, Bert N., and Rosalind Ann Sydie. 2002. *Classical Sociological Theory*. Thousand Oaks, CA: Pine Forge Press.

Adams, Charles Francis. 1969. *The Works of John Adams*. Vol. IX. Freeport, NY: Books for Libraries.

Adamy, Janet. 2015. "America's Middle Class Is No Longer the Majority." *Wall Street Journal Blogs—Real Time Economics*. December 9. Available at http://blogs.wsj.com/economics/2015/12/09/americas-middle-class-is-no-longer-the-majority.

Addo, Fenaba R., and Daniel T. Lichter. 2013. "Marriage, Marital History, and Black–White Wealth Differentials Among Older Women." *Journal of Marriage and Family* 75 (2): 342–362.

Adichie, Chimamanda Ngozi. 2014. *Americanah*. New York: Anchor Books.

Adler, Patricia A., and Peter Adler. 1998. *Peer Power: Preadolescent Culture and Identity*. New Brunswick, NJ: Rutgers University Press.

African Development Bank Group. 2012. "Briefing Notes for AfDB's Long-Term Strategy." Briefing Note 5. Available at http://www.afdb.org/fileadmin/uploads/afdb/Documents/Policy-Documents/FINAL%20Briefing%20Note%205%20Income%20Inequality%20in%20Africa.pdf.

Agans, Robert P., Guangya Liu, Mary Jones, Clementina Verjan, Mark Silverbush, and William D. Kalsbeek. 2011. Public Attitudes Toward the Homeless. AAPOR. Available at http://www.amstat.org/Sections/Srms/Proceedings/y2011/Files/400188.pdf.

Aguilera, Michael Bernabe. 2008. "Personal Networks and the Incomes of Men and Women in the United States: Do Personal Networks Provide Higher Returns for Men or Women?" *Research in Social Stratification and Mobility* 26: 221–233.

Aidi, Hisham. 2015. "Middle Eastern Americans Push Census Change." Al Jazeera America. February 2. Available at http://america.aljazeera.com/opinions/2015/2/middle-eastern-americans-push-census-change.html.

Ainsworth, Claire. 2015. *Sex Redefined*. London: MacMillan.

Aisenbrey, Silke, Marie Evertsson, and Daniela Grunow. 2009. "Is There a Career Penalty for Mothers' Time out? A Comparison of Germany, Sweden and the United States." *Social Forces* 88 (2): 573–605.

Alba, Richard D., and Guillermo Yrizar Barbosa. 2015. "Room at the Top? Minority Mobility and the Transition to Demographic Diversity in the USA." *Ethnic and Racial Studies* 39 (6): 917–938.

Albelda, Randy, M. V. Badgett, Alyssa Schneebaum, and Gary Gates. 2009. "Poverty in the Lesbian, Gay, and Bisexual Community." Los Angeles, CA: The Williams Institute. Available at http://escholarship.org/uc/item/2509p8r5.pdf.

Alderson, Arthur S., and Francois Nielsen. 2002. "Globalization and the Great U-Turn: Income Inequality Trends in 16 OECD Countries." *American Journal of Sociology* 107 (5): 1244–1299.

Alesina, Alberto, and Eliana La Ferrara. 2002. "Who Trusts Others?" *Journal of Public Economics* 85 (2): 207–234.

Alexander, Cindy R., and Mark A. Cohen. 2015. "The Evolution of Corporate Criminal Settlements: An Empirical Perspective on Non-Prosecution, Deferred Prosecution, and Plea Agreements." *American Criminal Law Review* 52: 537–703.

Alexander, Herbert E. 1992. "The PAC Phenomenon." In *Almanac of Federal PACs: 1992*, edited by Ed Zuckerman, ix–xv. Washington, D.C.: Amward.

Alexander, Michelle. 2012. *The New Jim Crow: Mass Incarceration in the Age of Colorblindness*. Revised edition. New York: New Press.

Allard, Scott W. 2009. *Out of Reach*. New Haven, CT: Yale University Press.

Allen, Greg. 2015a. "Ghosts of Katrina Still Haunt New Orleans' Shattered Lower Ninth Ward." Morning Edition – Hurricane Katrina: 10 Years of Recovery and Reflection. National Public Radio. Available at http://www.npr.org/2015/08/03/427844717/ghosts-of-katrina-still-haunt-new-orleans-shattered-lower-ninth-ward.

Allen, Greg. 2015b. "Some Moved On, Some Moved In and Made a New New Orleans." Special Series—Hurricane Katrina: 10 Years of Recovery and Reflection. National Public Radio. Available at http://www.npr.org/2015/08/26/434288564/some-moved-on-some-moved-in-and-made-a-new-new-orleans.

Allen, Michael Patrick. 1987. *The Founding Fortunes: A New Anatomy of the Corporate-Rich Families in America*. New York: Truman Talley Books.

Allen, Samantha. 2015. "United Nations: U.S. Is Failing Women." *Daily Beast*, December 15. Available at http://www.thedailybeast.com/articles/2015/12/15/united-nations-u-s-is-failing-women.html.

Allyn, Bobby. 2009. "Among Privileged Classmates, I'm an Outsider." *Chronicle of Higher Education*, October 11. Available at http://chronicle.com/article/Among-Privileged-Classmates/48730/?key=-Sm0mJ1lmMyhPbXVjLnNKLiNWO3spcxgpbHYTayUaZlFd.

Almond, Gabriel A. 1991. "Capitalism and Democracy." *PS: Political Science & Politics* 24 (3): 467–474.

Alon, Sigal. 2009. "The Evolution of Class Inequality in Higher Education Competition, Exclusion, and Adaptation." *American Sociological Review* 74 (5): 731–755.

Alonso-Villar, Olga, Carlos Gradin, and Coral del Rio. 2012. "Occupational Segregation of Hispanics in U.S. Metropolitan Areas." Working Paper ECINEQ 2012–242. Verona, Italy: Society for the Study of Economic Inequality.

Altman, Dennis. 2005. "The Globalization of Sexual Identities." In *Gender Through the Prism of Difference*, edited by M. B. Zinn, P. Hondagneu-Sotelo, and M. A. Messner, 216–226. New York: Oxford.

Alvarez, Lizette. 2015. "U.S. Won't File Charges in Trayvon Martin Killing." *New York Times*, February 24. Available at http://www.nytimes.com/2015/02/25/us/justice-dept-wont-charge-george-zimmerman-in-trayvon-martin-killing.html.

American Association of University Women. 2015. "The Simple Truth about the Gender Pay Gap." Washington, D.C.: American Association of University Women.

American Express. 2014. "The 2014 State of Women-Owned Businesses Report." Available at http://www.womenable.com/content/userfiles/2014_State_of_Women-owned_Businesses_public.pdf.

American Society of Plastic Surgeons. 2014. "2014 Plastic Surgery Statistics Report." Arlington Heights, IL: American Society of Plastic Surgeons. Available at http://www.plasticsurgery.org/Documents/news-resources/statistics/2014-statistics/plastic-surgery-statsitics-full-report.pdf.

Anderson, Elijah. 1999. *Code of the Street*. New York: Norton.

Anderson, Margaret L. 1997. *Thinking about Women*. Boston: Allyn & Bacon.

Anderson, Monica, and Andrew Perrin. 2015. "15% of Americans Don't Use the Internet. Who Are They?" Pew Research Center. July 28. Available at http://www.pewresearch.org/fact-tank/2015/07/28/15-of-americans-dont-use-the-internet-who-are-they.

Andersson, Fredrik, John C. Haltiwanger, Mark J. Kutzbach, Henry O. Pollakowski, and Daniel H. Weinberg. 2014. "Job Displacement and the Duration of Joblessness: The Role of Spatial Mismatch." Cambridge, MA: National Bureau of Economic Research. Available at http://www.nber.org/papers/w20066.

Anheier, Helmut K., Jurgen Gerhards, and Frank P. Romo. 1995. "Forms of Capital and Social Structure in Cultural Fields: Examining Bourdieu's Social Topography." *American Journal of Sociology* 100 (4): 859–903.

APA. 2015. "Health & Homelessness." American Psychological Association. Available at http://www.apa.org/pi/ses/resources/publications/homelessness-health.aspx.

APA. 2016. "Disability & Socioeconomic Status." American Psychological Association. Available at http://www.apa.org/pi/ses/resources/publications/factsheet-disability.aspx.

Apel, Robert, and Gary Sweeten. 2010. "The Impact of Incarceration on Employment during the Transition to Adulthood." *Social Problems* 57 (3): 448–479.

Appalachian Regional Commission. 2011. "Appalachian Region Income Report 2011." Washington, D.C.: Appalachian Regional Commission. Available at http://www.arc.gov/images/appregion/Sept2011/IncomeReportSept2011.pdf.

Apuzzo, Matt. 2015. "Transgender Inmate's Hormone Treatment Lawsuit Gets Justice Dept. Backing." *New York Times*, April 3. Available at http://www.nytimes.com/2015/04/04/us/ashley-diamond-transgender-hormone-lawsuit.html.

Arias, Elizabeth. 2010. "United States Life Tables, 2006." *National Vital Statistics Reports* 58 (21): 1–38.

Aron, Laudan, Lisa Dubay, Elaine Waxman, and Steven Martin. 2015. "To Understand Climbing Death Rates among Whites, Look to Women of Childbearing Age." Health Affairs. November 10. Available at http://healthaffairs.org/blog/2015/11/10/to-understand-climbing-death-rates-among-whites-look-to-women-of-childbearing-age.

Aronowitz, Stanley. 1973. *False Promises: The Shaping of American Working Class Consciousness*. New York: McGraw-Hill.

Aronson, Pamela. 2003. "Feminists or 'Postfeminists'? Young Women's Attitudes toward Feminism and Gender Relations." *Gender & Society* 17 (6): 903–922.

Asadi, Muhammed. 2011. "Internal Colonization and the International System: Gender Stratification in the US and Its Global Implications." *Societies Without Borders* 6 (1): 1–32.

Asher, Robert. 1986. "Industrial Safety and Labor Relations in the United States, 1865–1917." In *Life and Labor: Dimensions of American Working-Class History*, edited by Charles Stephenson and Robert Asher, 115–130. Albany, NY: SUNY Press.

Ashley, David, and David Michael Orenstein. 2005. *Sociological Theory: Classical Statements*. Needham Heights, MA: Allyn & Bacon.

Associated Press. 2015. "Kansas: Death Sentence Imposed on Man Who Sought to Kill Jews." *New York Times*, November 10. Available at http://www.nytimes.com/2015/11/11/us/kansas-death-sentence-imposed-on-man-who-sought-to-kill-jews.html.

Association of Certified Fraud Examiners. 2008. "2008 Report to the Nation on Occupational Fraud & Abuse." Austin, TX: Association of Certified Tax Investigators.

Asteriou, Dimitrios, Sophia Dimelis, and Argiro Moudatsou. 2014. "Globalization and Income Inequality: A Panel Data Econometric Approach for the EU27 Countries." *Economic Modelling* 36 (January): 592–599.

Atkinson, Rowland, and Oliver Smith. 2012. "An Economy of False Securities? An Analysis of Murders inside Gated Residential Developments in the United States." *Crime, Media, Culture* 8 (2): 161–172.

Attorney General's National Task Force. 2012. "Defending Childhood: Protect, Heal, Thrive." Washington, D.C.: Attorney General's National Task Force on Children Exposed to Violence. Available at https://www.hopeforchildrenfoundation.org/children-exposed-to-violence.

Augustine, Jennifer March, Shannon E. Cavanagh, and Robert Crosnoe. 2009. "Maternal Education,

Early Child Care and the Reproduction of Advantage." *Social Forces* 88 (1): 1–29.

Auster, Carol J., and Claire S. Mansbach. 2012. "The Gender Marketing of Toys: An Analysis of Color and Type of Toy on the Disney Store Website." *Sex Roles* 67 (7–8): 375–388.

Autor, David H. 2010. "The Polarization of Job Opportunities in the US Labor Market: Implications for Employment and Earnings." Center for American Progress and The Hamilton Project. Available at http://www.researchgate.net/profile/David_Autor/publication/227437438_The_polarization_of_job_opportunities_in_the_U.S._labor_market_implications_for_employment_and_earnings/links/00b7d520285b657fd8000000.pdf.

Autor, David H., and David Dorn. 2013. "The Growth of Low-Skill Service Jobs and the Polarization of the US Labor Market." *American Economic Review* 103 (5): 1553–1597.

Autor, David H., Lawrence F. Katz, and Melissa S. Kearney. 2008. "Trends in US Wage Inequality: Revising the Revisionists." *The Review of Economics and Statistics* 90 (2): 300–323.

Bachman, Jerald G., Jeremy Staff, Patrick M. O'Malley, John E. Schulenberg, and Peter Freedman-Doan. 2011. "Twelfth-Grade Student Work Intensity Linked to Later Educational Attainment and Substance Use: New Longitudinal Evidence." *Developmental Psychology* 47 (2): 344–363.

Badgett, M. V. Lee. 2001. *Money, Myths, and Change: The Economic Lives of Lesbians and Gay Men*. Chicago: University of Chicago Press.

Badgett, M. V. Lee, Laura E. Durso, and Alyssa Schneebaum. 2013. "New Patterns of Poverty in the Lesbian, Gay, and Bisexual Community." Los Angeles: The Williams Institute. Available at http://escholarship.org/uc/item/8dq9d947.pdf.

Bailey, Martha J., and Susan M. Dynarski. 2011. "Gains and Gaps: Changing Inequality in U.S. College Entry and Completion." Cambridge, MA: National Bureau of Economic Research. Available at http://www.nber.org/papers/w17633.

Baker-Sperry, Lori, and Liz Grauerholz. 2003. "The Pervasiveness and Persistence of the Feminine Beauty Ideal in Children's Fairy Tales." *Gender & Society* 17 (5): 711–726.

Bakshi, Sandeep. 2004. "A Comparative Analysis of Hijras and Drag Queens: The Subversive Possibilities and Limits of Parading Effeminacy and Negotiating Masculinity." *Journal of Homosexuality* 46 (3–4): 211–223.

Bales, William D., and Alex R. Piquero. 2012. "Racial/Ethnic Differentials in Sentencing to Incarceration." *Justice Quarterly* 29 (5): 742–773.

Banks-Santilli, Linda. 2014. "First-Generation College Students and Their Pursuit of the American Dream." *Journal of Case Studies in Education* 6: 1–32.

Baran, Paul, and Paul Sweezy. 1966. *Monopoly Capital*. New York: Monthly Review Press.

Barkan, Steven E. 1984. "Legal Control of the Southern Civil Rights Movement." *American Sociological Review* 49: 552–565.

Barnett, Bernice McNair. 1993. "Invisible Southern Black Women Leaders in the Civil Rights Movement: The Triple Constraints of Gender, Race, and Class." *Gender & Society* 7 (2): 162–182.

Barr, Bob, Steve Largent, Jim Sensenbrenner, Sue Myrick, Ed Bryant, Bill Emerson, Harold Volkmer, and Ike Skelton. 1996. "'Defense of Marriage Act' 5/96 H.R. 3396 Summary/Analysis." The 'Lectric Law Library. Available at http://www.lectlaw.com/files/leg23.htm.

Barrera, Mario. 1979. *Race and Class in the Southwest: A Theory of Racial Inequality*. Notre Dame, IN: University of Notre Dame Press.

Barrett, James E., and David Roediger. 2008. "How White People Became White." In *White Privilege*, edited by Paula S. Rothenberg, 35–40. New York: Worth.

Bartels, Larry M. 2004. "Partisan Politics and the U.S. Income Distribution." Department of Politics and Woodrow Wilson School of Public and International Affairs, Princeton University.

Bartels, Larry M. 2008. *Unequal Democracy: The Political Economy of the New Gilded Age*. New York: Princeton University Press.

Bass, Brooke Conroy. 2015. "Preparing for Parenthood? Gender, Aspirations, and the Reproduction of Labor Market Inequality." *Gender & Society* 29 (3): 362–385.

Batteau, Allen. 1984. "The Sacrifice of Nature: A Study in the Social Production of Consciousness." In *Cultural Adaptation to Mountain Environments*, edited by Patricia Beaver and

Burton Purrington, 94–106. Athens: University of Georgia Press.

Baumann, Robert. 2006. "Changes in the Appalachian Wage Gap, 1970 to 2000." *Growth and Change* 37 (3): 416–443.

Baumgartner, Frank R., and Anna W. Dietrich. 2015. "Most Death Penalty Sentences Are Overturned. Here's Why That Matters." *Washington Post*, March 17. Available at https://www.washingtonpost.com/blogs/monkey-cage/wp/2015/03/17/most-death-penalty-sentences-are-overturned-heres-why-that-matters.

Baxter, Janeen, and Erik Olin Wright. 2000. "The Glass Ceiling Hypothesis: A Comparative Study of the United States, Sweden, and Australia." *Gender & Society* 14 (2): 275–294.

Bayer, Patrick, Fernando Ferreira, and Stephen L. Ross. 2014. "Race, Ethnicity and High Cost Mortgage Lending." Working Paper 2014-023. Chicago: Human Capital and Economic Opportunity Global Working Group. Available at http://real.wharton.upenn.edu/~fferreir/documents/BFR_Rate_Spread%20final.pdf.

Beardsley, Meg, Sam Kamin, Justin F. Marceau, and Scott Phillips. 2015. "Disquieting Discretion: Race, Geography & the Colorado Death Penalty in the First Decade of the Twenty-First Century." *Denver University Law Review* 92 (August): 431–452.

Beck, Allen, Marcus Berzofsky, Rachel Caspar, and Christopher Krebs. 2013. "Sexual Victimization in Prisons and Jails Reported by Inmates, 2011–12." NCJ 241399. Washington, D.C.: U.S. Department of Justice, Bureau of Justice Statistics. Available at http://www.prearesourcecenter.org/taxonomy/term/57/0.

Beckett, Paul. 2007. "Caste Away." *Wall Street Journal*, June 24, sec. News. Available at http://www.wsj.com/articles/SB118256120981545474.

Beckfield, Jason. 2003. "Inequality in the World Polity: The Structure of International Organization." *American Sociological Review* 68 (3): 401–424.

Behrens, Angela, Christopher Uggen, and Jeff Manza. 2003. "Ballot Manipulation and the 'Menace of Negro Domination': Racial Threat and Felon Disenfranchisement in the United States, 1850–2002." *American Journal of Sociology* 109 (3): 559–605.

Béland, Daniel. 2007. *States of Global Insecurity: Policy, Politics, and Society*. New York: Macmillan.

Bell, Winifred. 1987. *Contemporary Social Welfare*. New York: MacMillan Publishing Company.

Beller, Emily. 2009. "Bringing Intergenerational Social Mobility Research into the Twenty-First Century: Why Mothers Matter." *American Sociological Review* 74 (4): 507–528.

Benard, Stephen, and Shelley J. Correll. 2010. "Normative Discrimination and the Motherhood Penalty." *Gender & Society* 24 (5): 616–646.

Bensman, Joseph. 1972. "Status Communities in an Urban Society: The Musical Community." In *Status Communities in Modern Society*, edited by H. R. Stub, 113–130. Hinsdale, IL: Dryden.

Benson, Michael L., and Esteban Walker. 1988. "Sentencing the White-Collar Offender." *American Sociological Review* 53: 294–302.

Benston, Margaret. 1969. "The Political Economy of Women's Liberation." *Monthly Review* 21: 15–16.

Ben-Zeev, Avi, Tara C. Dennehy, Robin I. Goodrich, Branden S. Kolarik, and Mark W. Geisler. 2014. "When an 'Educated' Black Man Becomes Lighter in the Mind's Eye." *SAGE Open* 4 (1): 1–9.

Berdahl, Jennifer L., and Celia Moore. 2006. "Workplace Harassment: Double Jeopardy for Minority Women." *Journal of Applied Psychology* 91 (2): 426–436.

Berg, Justin Allen. 2009. "Core Networks and Whites' Attitudes toward Immigrants and Immigration Policy." *Public Opinion Quarterly* 73 (1): 7–31.

Berger, Christian, and Philip C. Rodkin. 2009. "Male and Female Victims of Male Bullies: Social Status Differences by Gender and Informant Source." *Sex Roles* 61 (1–2): 72–84.

Berger, Jonah, and Morgan Ward. 2010. "Subtle Signals of Inconspicuous Consumption." *Journal of Consumer Research* 37 (4): 555–569.

Berger, Joseph, and M. Hamit Fişek. 2006. "Diffuse Status Characteristics and the Spread of Status Value: A Formal Theory." *American Journal of Sociology* 111 (4): 1038–1079.

Bergeron, Diane M., Caryn J. Block, and Alan Echtenkamp. 2006. "Disabling the Able: Stereotype Threat and Women's Work Performance." *Human Performance* 19 (2): 133–158.

Bergmann, Barbara R. 2006. "Reducing Inequality: Merit Goods vs. Income Grants." *Dissent* 53 (1): 67–72.

Berman, Mark. 2014. "The Current State of White Supremacist Groups in the U.S." *Washington*

Post, December 30. Available at https://www.washingtonpost.com/news/post-nation/wp/2014/12/30/the-current-state-of-white-supremacist-groups-in-the-u-s.

Bernstein, Aaron. 1996. "Is America Becoming More of a Class Society?" *Business Week* 26: 86–91.

Bernstein, Irving. 1960. *The Lean Years: A History of the American Worker, 1920–1933*. Boston: Houghton Mifflin.

Bernstein, Jared, and Heidi Shierholz. 2008. "A Decade of Decline: The Erosion of Employer-Provided Health Care in the United States and California, 1995–2006." EPI Briefing Paper 209. Washington, D.C.: Economic Policy Institute.

Berry, Chris, Fran Martin, and Audrey Yue. 2003. "Introduction: Beep-Click-Link." In *Mobile Cultures: New Media in Queer Asia*, edited by Chris Berry, Fran Martin, and Audrey Yue, 1–18. Durham, NC: Duke University Press.

Bertrand, Marianne, Claudia Goldin, and Lawrence Katz. 2010. "Dynamics of the Gender Gap for Young Professionals in the Financial and Corporate Sectors." *American Economic Journal: Applied Economics* 2 (3): 228–255.

Bertrand, Marianne, and Kevin F. Hallock. 2001. "The Gender Gap in Top Corporate Jobs." *Industrial & Labor Relations Review* 55 (1): 3–21.

Berube, Michael. 2006. "Foreword: Another Word Is Possible." In *Crip Theory: Cultural Signs of Queerness and Disability*, edited by Robert McRuer, vii–xi. New York: New York University Press.

Besley, Timothy, Stephen Coate, and Timothy Guinnane. 2004. *Incentives, Information, and Welfare: England's New Poor Law and the Workhouse Test*. Stanford, CA: Stanford University Press.

Bianchi, Suzanne M., Liana C. Sayer, Melissa A. Milkie, and John P. Robinson. 2012. "Housework: Who Did, Does or Will Do It, and How Much Does It Matter?" *Social Forces* 91 (1): 55–63.

Bidner, Chris, and Mukesh Eswaran. 2015. "A Gender-Based Theory of the Origin of the Caste System of India." *Journal of Development Economics* 114 (May): 142–158.

Bielby, Denise D., and William T. Bielby. 1988. "She Works Hard for the Money: Household Responsibilities and the Allocation of Work

Effort." *American Journal of Sociology* 93: 1031–1059.

Bilbao-Osorio, Beñat, Soumitra Dutta, and Bruno Lanvin. 2014. "The Global Information Technology Report 2014." Geneva, Switzerland: World Economic Forum.

Bilefsky, Dan. 2011. "For Gays Seeking Asylum in U.S., a New Hurdle." *New York Times*, January 28. Available at http://www.nytimes.com/2011/01/29/nyregion/29asylum.html.

Birchfield, Vicki L. 2012. *Income Inequality in Capitalist Democracies: The Interplay of Values and Institutions*. Philadelphia: Penn State Press.

Birckhead, Tamar R. 2012. "Delinquent by Reason of Poverty." *Washington University Journal of Law and Policy* 38: 53–107.

Bishaw, Alemayehu, and Kayla Fontenot. 2014. "Poverty: 2012 and 2013." American Community Survey. Available at: https://www.census.gov/content/dam/Census/library/publications/2014/acs/acsbr13-01.pdf.

Bishop, Bill. 2009. *The Big Sort: Why the Clustering of Like-Minded America Is Tearing Us Apart*. Boston: Houghton Mifflin Harcourt.

Bittman, Michael, Paula England, Liana Sayer, Nancy Folbre, and George Matheson. 2003. "When Does Gender Trump Money? Bargaining and Time in Household Work." *American Journal of Sociology* 109 (1): 186–214.

Bjornstrom, Eileen E. S., Robert L. Kaufman, Ruth D. Peterson, and Michael D. Slater. 2010. "Race and Ethnic Representations of Lawbreakers and Victims in Crime News: A National Study of Television Coverage." *Social Problems* 57 (2): 269–293.

Black and Pink. 2009. "A Compilation of Critiques on Hate Crimes Legislation." Dorchester, MA: Black and Pink. Available at http://www.againstequality.org/wp-content/uploads/2009/10/critiques-on-hate-crimes.pdf.

Black, Sandra E., and Elizabeth Brainerd. 2004. "Importing Equality? The Impact of Globalization on Gender Discrimination." *Industrial & Labor Relations Review* 57 (4): 540–559.

Blackwell, James E. 1985. *The Black Community: Diversity and Unity*. New York: Harper & Row.

Blair-Loy, Mary, and Jerry A. Jacobs. 2003. "Globalization, Work Hours, and the Care Deficit among Stockbrokers." *Gender & Society* 17 (2): 230–249.

Blashill, Aaron J., and Kimberly K. Powlishta. 2009. "Gay Stereotypes: The Use of Sexual

Orientation as a Cue for Gender-Related Attributes." *Sex Roles* 61 (December): 783–793.

Blau, Francine D. 1978. "The Data on Women Workers, Past, Present, and Future." In *Women Working: Theories and Facts in Perspective*, edited by Ann H. Stromberg and Shirley Harkess, 29–62. Palo Alto, CA: Mayfield.

Blau, Francine D. 1984. "Occupational Segregation and Labor Market Discrimination." In *Sex Segregation in the Workplace*, edited by B. F. Reskin, 117–143. Washington, D.C.: National Academy Press.

Blau, Francine D., Peter Brummund, and Albert Yung-Hsu Liu. 2013. "Trends in Occupational Segregation by Gender, 1970–2009: Adjusting for the Impact of Changes in the Occupational Coding System." *Demography* 50 (2): 471–492.

Blau, Francine D., and Jed DeVaro. 2007. "New Evidence on Gender Differences in Promotion Rates: An Empirical Analysis of a Sample of New Hires." *Industrial Relations: A Journal of Economy and Society* 46 (3): 511–550.

Blau, Francine D., and Lawrence M. Kahn. 2013. "Female Labor Supply: Why Is the US Falling Behind?" Boston: National Bureau of Economic Research. Available at http://www.nber.org/papers/w18702.

Blau, Judith R., and Peter M. Blau. 1982. "The Cost of Inequality: Metropolitan Structure and Violent Crime." *American Sociological Review* 47: 114–129.

Blau, Peter M., and Otis Dudley Duncan. 1967. *The American Occupational Structure*. New York: Wiley.

Blauner, Bob. 1972. *Racial Oppression in America*. New York: Harper & Row.

Bliss, Laura. 2016. "Government Response to Flint's Water Crisis Comes Far Too Late." CityLab. January 13. Available at http://www.citylab.com/cityfixer/2016/01/flint-lead-water-national-guard-too-late/423822/.

Bloom, Jack M. 1987. *Class, Race, and the Civil Rights Movement*. Bloomington: Indiana University Press.

Blumberg, Rhoda Lois. 1991. *Civil Rights, the 1960s Freedom Struggle*. Boston: Twayne.

Bocian, Debbie Gruenstein, Wei Li, and Keith S. Ernst. 2010. "Foreclosures by Race and Ethnicity." Durham, NC: Center for Responsible Lending. Available at http://www.nwfairhouse.org/images/1277759877.pdf.

Boellstorff, Tom. 2003. "I Knew It Was Me: Mass Media, 'Globalization,' and Lesbian and Gay Indonesia." In *Mobile Cultures: New Media in Queer Asia*, edited by Chris Berry, Fran Martin, and Audrey Yue, 19–51. Durham, NC: Duke University Press.

Boer, J. Tom, Manuel Pastor, Jr., James L. Sadd, and Lori D. Snyder. 1997. "Is There Environmental Racism? The Demographics of Hazardous Waste in Los Angeles County." *Social Science Quarterly* 78: 793–810.

Bolgar, Hedda. 2009. "A Century of Essential Feminism." *Studies in Gender and Sexuality* 10 (4): 195–199.

Bolzendahl, Catherine, and Clem Brooks. 2007. "Women's Political Representation and Welfare State Spending in 12 Capitalist Democracies." *Social Forces* 85 (4): 1509–1534.

Bonacich, Edna. 1980. "Class Approaches to Ethnicity and Race." *Insurgent Sociologist* 10 (2): 9–23.

Bonica, Adam, Nolan McCarty, Keith T. Poole, and Howard Rosenthal. 2013. "Why Hasn't Democracy Slowed Rising Inequality?" *Journal of Economic Perspectives* 27 (3): 103–124.

Bonilla-Silva, Eduardo. 2004. "From Bi-Racial to Tri-Racial: The Emergence of a New Racial Stratification System in the United States." In *Skin Deep: How Race and Complexion Matter in the "Color-Blind" Era*, edited by C. Herring, V. Keith, and H. D. Horton, 224–239. Chicago: University of Illinois.

Bonnot, Virginie, and Jean-Claude Croizet. 2007. "Stereotype Internalization and Women's Math Performance: The Role of Interference in Working Memory." *Journal of Experimental Social Psychology* 43 (6): 857–866.

Boone, Christopher G., and Ali Modarres. 1999. "Creating a Toxic Neighborhood in Los Angeles County." *Urban Affairs Review* 35: 163–187.

Boris, Eileen, and Jennifer N. Fish. 2014. "'Slave No More': Making Global Labor Standards for Domestic Workers." *Feminist Studies* 40 (2): 411–443.

Bornschier, Volker, and Christopher Chase-Dunn. 1985. *Transnational Corporations and Underdevelopment*. New York: Praeger.

Bortolin, Sandra. 2010. "'I Don't Want Him Hitting On Me': The Role of Masculinities in Creating a Chilly High School Climate." *Journal of LGBT Youth* 7 (3): 200–223.

Bose, Christine E. 2012. "Intersectionality and Global Gender Inequality." *Gender & Society* 26 (1): 67–72.

Bositis, David A. 2007. "Black Political Power in the New Century." In *The Black Metropolis in the Twenty-First Century*, edited by Robert D. Bullard, 221–242. Lanham, MD: Rowman & Littlefield.

Bosson, Jennifer K., and Kenneth S. Michniewicz. 2013. "Gender Dichotomization at the Level of Ingroup Identity: What It Is, and Why Men Use It More than Women." *Journal of Personality and Social Psychology* 105 (3): 425–442.

Bostwick, Wendy B., Carol J. Boyd, Tonda L. Hughes, and Sean Esteban McCabe. 2010. "Dimensions of Sexual Orientation and the Prevalence of Mood and Anxiety Disorders in the United States." *American Journal of Public Health* 100 (3): 468–475.

Bottomore, Thomas Burton. 1966. *Classes in Modern Society*. New York: Pantheon.

Bottomore, Thomas Burton. 2006. *Elites and Society*. New York: Routledge.

Bottomore, Thomas Burton, and Maximilien Rubel. 1964. *Karl Marx: Selected Writings in Sociology and Social Philosophy*. New York: McGraw-Hill.

Bourdieu, Pierre. 1977a. "Cultural Reproduction and Social Reproduction." In *Power and Ideology in Education*, edited by Jerome Karabel and Albert Henry Halsey, 487–510. New York: Oxford University Press.

Bourdieu, Pierre. 1977b. *Outline of a Theory of Practice*. Vol. 16. Cambridge, MA: Cambridge University Press.

Bourdieu, Pierre. 1990. *The Logic of Practice*. Stanford, CA: Stanford University Press.

Bourdieu, Pierre, and Loïc J. D. Wacquant. 1992. *An Invitation to Reflexive Sociology*. Cambridge, MA: Polity Press.

Bowers, Melanie, and Robert R. Preuhs. 2009. "Collateral Consequences of a Collateral Penalty: The Negative Effect of Felon Disenfranchisement Laws on the Political Participation of Nonfelons." *Social Science Quarterly* 90 (3): 722–743.

Bowles, Samuel, and Herbert Gintis. 1976. *Schooling in Capitalist America: Educational Reform and the Contradictions of American Life*. New York: Basic Books.

Bowles, Samuel, and Herbert Gintis. 2002. "*Schooling in Capitalist America* Revisited." *Sociology of Education* 75: 1–18.

Bowles, Samuel, Herbert Gintis, and Melissa Osborne Groves. 2009. *Unequal Chances: Family Background and Economic Success*. Princeton, NJ: Princeton University Press.

Bozick, Robert, Karl Alexander, Doris Entwisle, Susan Dauber, and Kerri Kerr. 2010. "Framing the Future: Revisiting the Place of Educational Expectations in Status Attainment." *Social Forces* 88 (5): 2027–2052.

"BP Pleads Guilty, Will Pay $20 Million Penalty for Oil Spill." 2008. *Andrews Environmental Litigation Reporter* 28 (12): 11–14.

Bradley, Laura. 2014. "E-Waste in Developing Countries Endangers Environment, Locals." *U.S. News & World Report*. August 1. Available at http://www.usnews.com/news/articles/2014/08/01/e-waste-in-developing-countries-endangers-environment-locals.

Brady, David. 2009. *Rich Democracies, Poor People: How Politics Explain Poverty*. New York: Oxford University Press.

Brady, David, Andrew S. Fullerton, and Jennifer Moren Cross. 2009. "Putting Poverty in Political Context: A Multi-Level Analysis of Adult Poverty across 18 Affluent Democracies." *Social Forces* 88 (1): 271–299.

Brady, David, and Kevin T. Leicht. 2008. "Party to Inequality: Right Party Power and Income Inequality in Affluent Western Democracies." *Research in Social Stratification and Mobility* 26 (1): 77–106.

Brady, Henry E., Kay L. Schlozman, and Sidney Verba. 2015. "Political Mobility and Political Reproduction from Generation to Generation." *The Annals of the American Academy of Political and Social Science* 657 (1): 149–173.

Breines, Winifred. 2007. "Struggling to Connect: White and Black Feminism in the Movement Years." *Contexts* 6 (1): 18–24.

Brender-Ilan, Yael. 2012. "How Do Income and Its Components and Perception Relate to Alienation?" *Journal of Applied Social Psychology* 42 (2): 440–470.

Bricker, Jesse, Lisa J. Dettling, Alice Henriques, Joanne W. Hsu, Kevin B. Moore, John Sabelhaus, Jeffrey Thompson, and Richard A. Windle. 2014. "Changes in U.S. Family Finances from 2010 to 2013: Evidence from the Survey of Consumer

Finances." 100 (4). Federal Reserve Bulletin. Washington, D.C.: Board of Governors of the Federal Reserve System. Available at http://www.federalreserve.gov/pubs/bulletin/2014/pdf/scf14.pdf.

Brickey, Kathleen F. 2006. "In Enron's Wake: Corporate Executives on Trial." *The Journal of Criminal Law and Criminology* 96 (2): 397–433.

Brimeyer, Ted M. 2008. "Research Note: Religious Affiliation and Poverty Explanations: Individual, Structural, and Divine Causes." *Sociological Focus* 41 (3): 226–237.

Brodkin, Karen. 2008. "How Jews Became White." In *White Privilege*, edited by Paula S. Rothenberg, 41–53. New York: Worth.

Brody, David. 1971. *The American Labor Movement*. New York: Harper & Row.

Brody, David. 1980. *Workers in Industrial America: Essays on the Twentieth Century Struggle*. New York: Oxford University Press.

Brooke, James. 1998. "Gay Man Dies from Attack, Fanning Outrage and Debate." *New York Times*, October 13, pp. A1, A17.

Brooks, John. 1979. *Showing Off in America*. Boston: Little, Brown.

Broom, Leonard, and Robert G. Cushing. 1977. "A Modest Test of an Immodest Theory." *American Sociological Review* 42: 157–169.

Brown, Abram. 2013. "Where the Rich Live in America: Connecticut, California and Virginia Top the List." *Forbes*. February 12. Available at http://www.forbes.com/sites/abrambrown/2013/02/12/where-the-rich-live-in-america-conneticut-california-and-virginia-top-the-list.

Brown, B. Bradford. 2011. "Popularity in Peer Group Perspective: The Role of Status in Adolescent Peer Systems." In *Popularity in the Peer System*, edited by Antonius H. N. Cillessen, David Schwartz, and Lara Mayeux, 165–190. New York: Guilford Press.

Brown, B. Bradford, and Mary J. Lohr. 1987. "Peer-Group Affiliation and Adolescent Self-Esteem: An Integration of Ego-Identity and Symbolic-Interaction Theories." *Journal of Personality and Social Psychology* 52 (1): 47.

Brown, David K. 2001. "The Social Sources of Educational Credentialism: Status Cultures, Labor Markets, and Organizations." *Sociology of Education* 74: 19–34.

Brown, Heather. 2012. *Historical Materialism Book Series, Volume 39 : Marx on Gender and the Family: A Critical Study*. Leiden, NLD: BRILL.

Brown, Roy. 1996. "Partnership and Marriage in Down Syndrome." *Down Syndrome Research and Practice* 4 (3): 96–99.

Brown University. 2010. "New Orleans City." Database. US2010: Discover American in a New Century. Available at http://www.s4.brown.edu/us2010/segregation2010/city.aspx?cityid=2255000.

Browne, Irene, and Joya Misra. 2003. "The Intersection of Gender and Race in the Labor Market." *Annual Review of Sociology* 29: 487–513.

Bruins, Jan. 1999. "Social Power and Influence Tactics: A Theoretical Introduction." *Journal of Social Issues* 55 (1): 7–14.

Brunsma, David L., and Kerry Ann Rockquemore. 2002. "What Does 'Black' Mean? Exploring the Epistemological Stranglehold of Racial Categorization." *Critical Sociology* 28 (1–2): 101–121.

Bucks, Brian K., Arthur B. Kennickell, and Kevin B. Moore. 2006. "Recent Changes in U.S. Family Finances: Evidence from the 2001 and 2004 Survey of Consumer Finances." Federal Reserve Bulletin, March, A1–38.

Budig, Michelle J. 2014. "The Fatherhood Bonus and the Motherhood Penalty: Parenthood and the Gender Gap in Pay." Washington, D.C.: Third Way and Next. Available at http://www.thirdway.org/search?q=budig.

Bullard, Robert D. 1983. "Solid Waste Sites and the Black Houston Community." *Sociological Inquiry* 53: 273–288.

Bullock, Heather E., and Wendy M. Limbert. 2003. "Scaling the Socioeconomic Ladder: Low-Income Women's Perceptions of Class Status and Opportunity." *Journal of Social Issues* 59 (4): 693–709.

Burch, Traci. 2015. "Skin Color and the Criminal Justice System: Beyond Black–White Disparities in Sentencing." *Journal of Empirical Legal Studies* 12 (3): 395–420.

Bussmann, K.-D., and Markus M. Werle. 2006. "Addressing Crime in Companies: First Findings from a Global Survey of Economic Crime." *British Journal of Criminology* 46 (6): 1128–1144.

Butler, Judith. 1999. *Gender Trouble*. New York: Routledge.

Butler, Sandra S., Janine Corbett, Crystal Bond, and Chris Hastedt. 2008. "Long-Term TAN

Participants and Barriers to Employment: A Qualitative Study in Maine." *Journal of Sociology and Social Welfare* 35: 49–69.

Button, James W., Barbara Ann Rienzo, and Kenneth D. Wald. 1997. *Private Lives, Public Conflicts: Battles over Gay Rights in American Communities*. Washington, D.C.: CQ Press.

Buzuvis, Erin. 2010. "Sidelined: Title IX Retaliation Cases and Women's Leadership in College Athletics." *Duke Journal of Gender Law & Policy* 17: 1–45.

BuzzFeed. 2015. "26 Questions Asians Have For White People." BuzzFeed. September 27. Available at http://www.buzzfeed.com/dayshavedewi/26-questions-asians-have-for-white-people.

Bye, Lynn, and Jamie Partridge. 2003. "Factors Affecting Mental Illness Hospitalization Rates: Analysis of State-Level Panel Data." *The Social Science Journal* 40 (1): 33–47.

Cahalan, Margaret, and Laura Pema. 2015. "Indicators of Higher Education Equity in the United States." Washington, D.C.: The Pell Institute and PennAhead. Available at http://www.pellinstitute.org/downloads/publications-Indicators_of_Higher_Education_Equity_in_the_US_45_Year_Trend_Report.pdf.

Cahusac, Emma, and Shireen Kanji. 2014. "Giving Up: How Gendered Organizational Cultures Push Mothers Out." *Gender, Work & Organization* 21 (1): 57–70.

Cain, Glen G. 1976. "The Challenge of Segmented Labor Market Theories to Orthodox Theory: A Survey." *Journal of Economic Literature* 14: 1215–1257.

Cairns, Robert B., and Beverly D. Cairns. 1994. *Lifelines and Risks: Pathways of Youth in Our Time*. Cambridge, MA: Cambridge University Press.

Calhoun, Craig. 2013. "Occupy Wall Street in Perspective." *The British Journal of Sociology* 64 (1): 26–38.

Camarota, Steven A., and Karen Zeigler. 2009. "Jobs Americans Won't Do? A Detailed Look at Immigrant Employment by Occupation." Center for Immigration Studies. August. Available at http://cis.org/illegalImmigration-employment.

Campbell, Andrea Louise. 2007. "Parties, Electoral Participation, and Shifting Voting Blocs." In *The Transformation of American Politics*, edited by Theda Skocpol and Paul Pierson, 68–102. Princeton, NJ: Princeton University Press.

Campo-Flores, Arian, and Howard Fineman. May 30, 2005. "A Latin Power Surge." *Newsweek*, p. 7.

Cancian, Maria. 2001. "Rhetoric and Reality of Work-Based Welfare Reform." *Social Work* 46 (4): 309–314.

Cancian, Maria, and Daniel R. Meyer. 2004. "Alternative Measures of Economic Success among TANF Participants: Avoiding Poverty, Hardship, and Dependence on Public Assistance." *Journal of Policy Analysis and Management* 23 (3): 531–548.

Cantu, Phillip A., Mark D. Hayward, Robert A. Hummer, and Chi-Tsun Chiu. 2013. "New Estimates of Racial/Ethnic Differences in Life Expectancy with Chronic Morbidity and Functional Loss: Evidence from the National Health Interview Survey." *Journal of Cross-Cultural Gerontology* 28 (3): 283–297.

Caplan, Patricia. 1987. *The Cultural Construction of Sexuality*. London; New York: Tavistock.

Capodilupo, Christina M., Kevin L. Nadal, Lindsay Corman, Sahran Hamit, Oliver B. Lyons, and Alexa Weinberg. 2010. "The Manifestation of Gender Microaggressions." In *Microaggressions and Marginality: Manifestation, Dynamics, and Impact*, edited by Derald W. Sue, 193–215. Hoboken, NJ: John Wiley & Sons.

Carbado, Devon W., and Mitu Gulati. 2015. *Acting White? Rethinking Race in "Post-Racial" America*. Reprint Edition. New York: Oxford University Press.

Carbone-Lopez, Kristin, Finn-Aage Esbensen, and Bradley T. Brick. 2010. "Correlates and Consequences of Peer Victimization: Gender Differences in Direct and Indirect Forms of Bullying." *Youth Violence and Juvenile Justice* 8 (4): 332–350.

Cardiff, Patrick. 1999. "Profiles of Poor Counties: Some Empirical Evidence." HHES/SAIPE FB3-1065. Washington, D.C.: U.S. Bureau of the Census.

Cardoso, Fernando Henrique. 1977. "The Consumption of Dependency Theory in the United States." *Latin American Research Review* 12: 7–24.

Carli, Linda L. 1999. "Gender, Interpersonal Power, and Social Influence." *Journal of Social Issues* 55 (1): 81–99.

Carli, Linda L., and Alice H. Eagly. 2007. "Overcoming Resistance to Women Leaders." In *Women and Leadership: The State of Play and Strategies for Change*, edited by Barbara Kellerman, Deborah L. Rhode, and Sandra Day O'Connor, 127–148. San Francisco: Wiley.

Carlson, Lewis H., and George A. Colburn. 1972. *In Their Place: White America Defines Her Minorities, 1850–1950*. New York: Wiley.

Carlyle, Erin. 2013. "How Self-Made Forbes 400 Billionaires Earned Their Money." *Forbes*, September 18. Available at http://www.forbes.com/sites/erincarlyle/2013/09/18/how-self-made-forbes-400-billionaires-earned-their-money/.

Carmichael, Stokely, and Charles V. Hamilton. 1967. *Black Power: The Politics of Liberation*. New York: Vintage.

Carmody, Steve. 2016. "State Employees Who Intentionally Distort Data Could Face Jail Time under a Proposed Law." Michigan Radio: News for Michigan. January 4. Available at http://michiganradio.org/post/state-employees-who-intentionally-distort-data-could-face-jail-time-under-proposed-law.

Carnevale, Anthony P., Stephen J. Rose, and Ban Cheah. 2011. "The College Payoff: Education, Occupations, Lifetime Earnings." Available at https://repository.library.georgetown.edu/handle/10822/559300.

Carnevale, Anthony P., and Jeff Strohl. 2010. "How Increasing College Access Is Increasing Inequality, and What to Do about It." New York: The Century Foundation. Available at http://tcf.ejaeworks.com/assets/downloads/tcf-CarnevaleStrivers.pdf.

Carr, Deborah. 2005. "Political Polls." *Contexts* 4 (1): 31–32.

Carr, Patrick J., Daniel T. Lichter, and Maria J. Kefalas. 2012. "Can Immigration Save Small-Town America? Hispanic Boomtowns and the Uneasy Path to Renewal." *The Annals of the American Academy of Political and Social Science* 641 (1): 38–57.

Carrier, James G., and Don Kalb, eds. 2015. *Anthropologies of Class: Power, Practice and Inequality*. Cambridge, United Kingdom: Cambridge University Press.

Cartwright, Bliss, Patrick Ronald Edwards, and Qi Wang. 2011. "Job and Industry Gender Segregation: NAICS Categories and EEO–1 Job Groups." *Monthly Labor Review* 134 (11): 37–50.

Case, Anne, and Angus Deaton. 2015. "Rising Morbidity and Mortality in Midlife among White Non-Hispanic Americans in the 21st Century." *Proceedings of the National Academy of Sciences* 112 (49): 15078–15083.

Case, Mary Anne. 1995. "Disaggregating Gender from Sex and Sexual Orientation: The Effeminate Man in the Law and Feminist Jurisprudence." *Yale Law Journal* 105: 2–3.

Cassell, Dana K., Robert C. Salinas, and Peter S. Winn. 2005. *The Encyclopedia of Death and Dying*. New York: Facts On File.

Cassese, Erin C., and Angela L. Bos. 2013. "A Hidden Curriculum? Examining the Gender Content in Introductory-Level Political Science Textbooks." *Politics & Gender* 9 (2): 214–223.

Castañeda, Heide, and Milena Andrea Melo. 2014. "Health Care Access for Latino Mixed-Status Families: Barriers, Strategies, and Implications for Reform." *American Behavioral Scientist* 58 (14): 1891–1909.

Castilla, Emilio J., and Stephen Benard. 2010. "The Paradox of Meritocracy in Organizations." *Administrative Science Quarterly* 55 (4): 543–676.

Catalyst. 2007. *The Double-Bind Dilemma for Women in Leadership: Damned If You Do, Doomed If You Don't*. New York: Catalyst.

Catalyst. 2015. "Catalyst. Pyramid: Women in S&P 500 Companies." New York: Catalyst. Available at http://www.catalyst.org/knowledge/women-sp-500-companies.

Cauthen, Kenneth. 1987. *The Passion for Equality*. New York: Rowman & Littlefield.

CBS. 2014. "Family, Friends Remember 12-Year-Old Boy Who Committed Suicide." CBS Sacramento. December 4. Available at http://sacramento.cbslocal.com/2014/12/04/family-friends-remember-12-year-old-boy-who-committed-suicide/.

CDC. 2013. "Key Statistics from the National Survey of Family Growth." Centers for Disease Control and Prevention. Available at http://www.cdc.gov/nchs/nsfg/key_statistics.htm#sexualorientation.

CDC. 2014. "Health, United States, 2013: With Special Feature on Prescription Drugs." Washington, D.C.: U.S. Department of Health and Human Services. Available at http://www.ncbi.nlm.nih.gov/pubmed/23885363.

CDC. 2015. "CDC – Lead – Home Page." Centers for Disease Control and Prevention. Available at http://www.cdc.gov/nceh/lead.

Cech, Erin A. 2013. "The Self-Expressive Edge of Occupational Sex Segregation." *American Journal of Sociology* 119 (3): 747–789.

Center for Advancing Health. 2014. "Gap in Life Expectancy Between Rural and Urban Residents Is Growing." CFAH: Health Behavior News Service. January 23. Available at http://www.cfah.org/hbns/2014/gap-in-life-expectancy-between-rural-and-urban-residents-is-growing.

Center for Immigration Studies. 2012. "Immigrants in the United States: A Profile of America's Foreign-Born Population." Center for Immigration Studies, July 21. Available at http://cis.org/node/3876.

Center for Medicare and Medicaid Services. 2014. "Medicare Fee-For-Service 2013 Improper Payments Report." Washington, D.C.: Center for Medicare and Medicaid Services. Available at https://www.cms.gov/Research-Statistics-Data-and-Systems/Monitoring-Programs/Medicare-FFS-Compliance-Programs/CERT/CERT-Reports-Items/Downloads/MedicareFee-for-Service2013ImproperPaymentsReport.pdf.

Center for Responsive Politics. 2010. "Super PACs." OpenSecrets.org, Center for Responsive Politics. Available at http://www.opensecrets.org/pacs/superpacs.php?cycle=2016.

Center for Responsive Politics. 2015. "Top 20 PAC Contributors to Candidates, 2013–2014." March 9. Available at https://www.opensecrets.org/pacs/toppacs.php?Type=C&cycle=2014.

Center on Budget and Policy Priorities. 2015a. "Policy Basics: Introduction to SNAP." Center on Budget and Policy Priorities, January 8. Available at http://www.cbpp.org/sites/default/files/atoms/files/policybasics-foodstamps.pdf.

Center on Budget and Policy Priorities. 2015b. "Policy Basics: Where Do Federal Tax Revenues Come From?" Center on Budget and Policy Priorities, March 11. Available at http://www.cbpp.org/research/policy-basics-where-do-federal-tax-revenues-come-from.

Center on Budget and Policy Priorities. 2015c. "Chart Book: TANF at 19." Center on Budget and Policy Priorities, August 20. Available at http://www.cbpp.org/research/family-income-support/chart-book-tanf-at-19.

Ceobanu, Alin M., and Xavier Escandell. 2010. "Comparative Analyses of Public Attitudes toward Immigrants and Immigration Using Multinational Survey Data: A Review of Theories and Research." *Annual Review of Sociology* 36: 309–328.

Cerankowski, Karli June, and Megan Milks, eds. 2014. *Asexualities: Feminist and Queer Perspectives*. Routledge Research in Gender and Society. New York: Routledge.

Cha, Youngjoo. 2010. "Reinforcing Separate Spheres: The Effect of Spousal Overwork on Men's and Women's Employment in Dual-Earner Households." *American Sociological Review* 75 (2): 303–329.

Cha, Youngjoo. 2013. "Overwork and the Persistence of Gender Segregation in Occupations." *Gender & Society* 27 (2): 158–184.

Cha, Youngjoo, and Kim A. Weeden. 2014. "Overwork and the Slow Convergence in the Gender Gap in Wages." *American Sociological Review*, 79 (3): 457–484.

Chafe, William H. 1977. *Women and Equality: Changing Patterns in American Culture*. New York: Oxford University Press.

Chafetz, Janet S. 1988a. *Feminist Sociology: An Overview of Contemporary Theories*. Itasca, IL: FE Peacock.

Chafetz, Janet S. 1988b. "The Gender Division of Labor and the Reproduction of Female Disadvantage: Toward an Integrated Theory." *Journal of Family Issues* 9 (1): 108–131.

Chan, Curtis K., and Michel Anteby. 2015. "Task Segregation as a Mechanism for Within-Job Inequality: Women and Men of the Transportation Security Administration." *Administrative Science Quarterly*, October.

Chan, Tak Wing, and John H. Goldthorpe. 2004. "Is There a Status Order in Contemporary British Society? Evidence from the Occupational Structure of Friendship." *European Sociological Review* 20 (5): 383–401.

Chan, Tak Wing, and John H. Goldthorpe. 2007. "Class and Status: The Conceptual Distinction and Its Empirical Relevance." *American Sociological Review* 72 (4): 512–532.

Chancellor, Carl. 2008. "Violent Attacks Plague the Homeless." *Akron Beacon Journal*, May 10, p. A4.

Chen, Martha, James Heintz, Renana Jhabvala, Francie Lund, and Joann Vanek. 2005. *Women, Work & Poverty*. New York: UNIFEM.

Chen, Stefanos. August 15, 2013. "Million-Dollar Mausoleums." *Wall Street Journal*. Available at http://www.wsj.com/articles/SB1000142412788 73234776045786540840036648860.

Chertoff, Emily. 2012. "The Racial Divide on . . . Sneakers." *The Atlantic*. August 20. Available at http://www.theatlantic.com/national/archive/2012/08/the-racial-divide-on-sneakers/261256.

Chetty, Raj, Nathaniel Hendren, and Lawrence Katz. 2015. "The Effects of Exposure to Better Neighborhoods on Children: New Evidence from the Moving to Opportunity Experiment." Cambridge, MA: Harvard University and National Bureau of Economic Research. Available at http://www.nber.org/mtopublic/final/MTO_IRS_2015.pdf.

Chetty, Raj, Nathaniel Hendren, Patrick Kline, and Emmanuel Saez. 2014. "Where Is the Land of Opportunity? The Geography of Intergenerational Mobility in the United States." Cambridge, MA: National Bureau of Economic Research. Available at http://www.nber.org/papers/w19843.

Chetty, Raj, Nathaniel Hendren, Patrick Kline, Emmanuel Saez, and Nicholas Turner. 2014. "Is the United States Still a Land of Opportunity? Recent Trends in Intergenerational Mobility." Cambridge, MA: National Bureau of Economic Research. Available at http://www.nber.org/papers/w19844.

Chiricos, Theodore G. 1987. "Rates of Crime and Unemployment: An Analysis of Aggregate Research Evidence." *Social Problems* 34 (2): 187–212.

Chiu, Ming Ming. 2010. "Effects of Inequality, Family and School on Mathematics Achievement: Country and Student Differences." *Social Forces* 88 (4): 1645–1676.

Cho, Sumi, Kimberle Williams Crenshaw, and Leslie McCall. 2013. "Toward a Field of Intersectionality Studies: Theory, Applications, and Praxis." *Signs* 38 (4): 785–810.

Choi, Wai Kit. 2006. "Proletarianization, the Informal Proletariat, and 'Marx' in the Era of Globalization." Paper presented at Annual Meeting of American Sociological Association, August 10, Montreal.

Chow, Esther Ngan-ling. 2003. "Gender Matters Studying Globalization and Social Change in the 21st Century." *International Sociology* 18 (3): 443–460.

Chu, Johan S. G., and Gerald F. Davis. 2015. "Who Killed the Inner Circle? The Decline of the American Corporate Interlock Network." SSRN Scholarly Paper ID 2061113. Rochester, NY: Social Science Research Network. Available at http://papers.ssrn.com/abstract=2061113.

Cifuentes, Manuel, Grace Sembajwe, SangWoo Tak, Rebecca Gore, David Kriebel, and Laura Punnett. 2008. "The Association of Major Depressive Episodes with Income Inequality and the Human Development Index." *Social Science & Medicine* 67 (4): 529–539.

Cigler, Allen J., and Burdett A. Loomis, eds. 2015. *Interest Group Politics*. 9th ed. Washington, D.C.: Congressional Quarterly.

Classen, Timothy J., and Richard A. Dunn. 2012. "The Effect of Job Loss and Unemployment Duration on Suicide Risk in the United States: A New Look Using Mass-Layoffs and Unemployment Duration." *Health Economics* 21 (3): 338–350.

Clawson, Dan, and Mary Ann Clawson. 1999. "What Has Happened to the US Labor Movement? Union Decline and Renewal." *Annual Review of Sociology* 25: 95–119.

Clear, Todd R. 2009. *Imprisoning Communities: How Mass Incarceration Makes Disadvantaged Neighborhoods Worse*. New York: Oxford University Press.

Cleaveland, Carol. 2008. "'A Black Benefit': Racial Prejudice among White Welfare Recipients in a Low-Income Neighborhood." *Journal of Progressive Human Services* 19 (2): 71–91.

Cobb-Clark, Deborah A., Sonja C. Kassenboehmer and Stefanie Schurer. 2014. "Healthy Habits The Connection between Diet, Exercise, and Locus of Control." *Journal of Economic Behavior & Organization* 98: 1–28.

Cobb-Clark, Deborah A., and Michelle Tan. 2011 "Noncognitive Skills, Occupational Attainment and Relative Wages." *Labour Economics* 18 (1) 1–13.

Coffman, Katherine B., Lucas C. Coffman, and Keith M. Marzilli Ericson. 2013. "The Size of the LGBT Population and the Magnitude of Anti-Gay Sentiment Are Substantially Underestimated." Cambridge, MA: National Bureau of Economic Research. Available at http://www.nber.org/papers/w19508.

Cohen, Patricia. 2015. "Public-Sector Jobs Vanish Hitting Blacks Hard." *New York Times*, Ma

24. Available at http://www.nytimes.com/2015/05/25/business/public-sector-jobs-vanish-and-blacks-take-blow.html.

Cohen, Philip N., and Matt L. Huffman. 2003. "Occupational Segregation and the Devaluation of Women's Work across US Labor Markets." *Social Forces* 81 (3): 881–908.

Cohen, Philip N., and Matt L. Huffman. 2007. "Working for the Woman? Female Managers and the Gender Wage Gap." *American Sociological Review* 72 (5): 681–704.

Colby, Sandra L., and Jennifer M. Ortman. 2015. "Projections of the Size and Composition of the US Population: 2014 to 2060." Current Population Reports. Washington, D.C.: U.S. Census Bureau. Available at http://www.census.gov/content/dam/Census/library/publications/2015/demo/p25-1143.pdf.

Coleman-Jensen, Alisha, Matthew P. Rabbitt, Christian Gregory, and Anita Singh. 2015. "Household Food Security in the United States in 2014." Washington, D.C.: United States Department of Agriculture.

College Board. 2010. *Education Pays*. New York: College Board.

Collins, Patricia Hill. 1998. "It's All in the Family: Intersections of Gender, Race, and Nation." *Hypatia* 13 (3): 62–82.

Collins, Patricia Hill. 2002. *Black Feminist Thought: Knowledge, Consciousness, and the Politics of Empowerment*. New York: Routledge.

Collins, Patricia Hill. 2015a. "Science, Critical Race Theory and Colour-Blindness." *The British Journal of Sociology* 66 (1): 46–52.

Collins, Patricia Hill. 2015b. "Intersectionality's Definitional Dilemmas." *Annual Review of Sociology* 41 (1): 1–20.

Collins, Randall. 1971. "Functional and Conflict Theories of Educational Stratification." *American Sociological Review* 36: 1002–1019.

Collins, Randall. 1988. *Theoretical Sociology*. New York: Harcourt College.

Collins, Rebecca L. 2011. "Content Analysis of Gender Roles in Media: Where Are We Now and Where Should We Go?" *Sex Roles* 64 (3–4): 290–298.

Collins, Sara R., Petra W. Rasmussen, Michelle M. Doty, and Sophie Beutel. 2014. "The Rise in Health Care Coverage and Affordability Since Health Reform Took Effect." Issue Brief 1800, volume 2. New York: Commonwealth Fund.

Connell, Catherine. 2010. "Doing, Undoing, or Redoing Gender? Learning from the Workplace Experiences of Transpeople." *Gender & Society* 24 (1): 31–55.

Connell, R. W. 2015. "Masculinities and Globalization." In *Gender through the Prism of Difference*, edited by Maxine Baca Zinn, Pierrette Hondagneu-Sotelo, and Michael A. Messner, 5th ed., 41–52. New York: Oxford University Press.

Connolly, William E. 1969. *The Challenge to Pluralist Theory*. New York: Lieber-Atherton.

Connor, Phillip, D'Vera Cohn, and Ana Gonzalez-Barrera. 2013. "Changing Patterns of Global Migration and Remittances." Pew Research Center's Social & Demographic Trends Project. December 17. Available at http://www.pewsocialtrends.org/2013/12/17/changing-patterns-of-global-migration-and-remittances/.

Contrera, Jessica. August 9, 2015. "Target Will Stop Separating Toys and Bedding into Girls' and Boys' Sections." *Washington Post*. Available at https://www.washingtonpost.com/news/arts-and-entertainment/wp/2015/08/09/target-will-stop-separating-toys-and-bedding-into-girls-and-boys-sections.

Cookson, Peter W., and Carolyn Hodges Persell. 2010. "Preparing for Power: Twenty-Five Years Later." In *Educating Elites: Class Privilege and Educational Advantage*, edited by Adam Howard and Ruben Gaztambide-Fernandez, 13–30. Lanham, MD: Rowman & Littlefield.

Coontz, Stephanie, and Peta Henderson, eds. 1986. *Women's Work, Men's Property: The Origins of Gender and Class*. London: Verso.

Corak, Miles. 2013. "Income Inequality, Equality of Opportunity, and Intergenerational Mobility." *Journal of Economic Perspectives* 27 (3): 79–102.

Correll, Shelley J., Erin L. Kelly, Lindsey T. O'Connor, and Joan C. Williams. 2014. "Redesigning, Redefining Work." *Work and Occupations* 41 (1): 3–17.

Cose, Ellis. 1993. *Rage of a Privileged Class*. New York: HarperCollins.

Coser, Lewis A. 1971. *Masters of Sociological Thought: Ideas in Historical and Social Context*. New York: Harcourt Brace Jovanovich.

Cott, Nancy F. 1986. "Feminist Theory and Feminist Movements: The Past Before Us." In *What Is Feminism?* edited by J. Mitchell and A. Oakley, 49–62. New York: Pantheon.

Cott, Nancy F. 1987. *The Grounding of Modern Feminism*. New Haven, CT: Yale University Press.

Cotter, David A., Joan M. Hermsen, and Reeve Vanneman. 2003. "The Effects of Occupational Gender Segregation across Race." *The Sociological Quarterly* 44 (1): 17–36.

Cowen, Tyler. 2015. "The Marriages of Power Couples Reinforce Income Inequality." *New York Times*, December 24. Available at http://www.nytimes.com/2015/12/27/upshot/marriages-of-power-couples-reinforce-income-inequality.html?_r=0.

Cox, Oliver Cromwell. 1948. *Caste, Class and Race: A Study in Social Dynamics*. New York: Monthly Review Press.

Cox, Oliver Cromwell. 1959. *The Foundations of Capitalism*. New York: Philosophical Library.

Cox, Oliver Cromwell. 1964. *Capitalism as a System*. New York: Monthly Review Press.

Cox, Oliver Cromwell. 1976. *Race Relations: Elements and Social Dynamics*. Detroit, MI: Wayne State University Press.

Craig, Kellina M. 2002. "Examining Hate-Motivated Aggression: A Review of the Social Psychological Literature on Hate Crimes as a Distinct Form of Aggression." *Aggression and Violent Behavior* 7 (1): 85–101.

Craig, Shelley L., Edmon W. Tucker, and Eric F. Wagner. 2008. "Empowering Lesbian, Gay, Bisexual, and Transgender Youth: Lessons Learned from a Safe Schools Summit." *Journal of Gay & Lesbian Social Services* 20 (3): 237–252.

Crandall, N. Fredric, and Marc J. Wallace. 1998. *Work and Rewards in the Virtual Workplace: A New Deal for Employers and Employees*. New York: American Management Association.

Craven, Julia. 2015. "Black Lives Matter Co-Founder Reflects on the Origins of the Movement." *Huffington Post*, September 30. Available at http://www.huffingtonpost.com/entry/black-lives-matter-opal-tometi_560c-1c59e4b0768127003227.

Crawford, Charles, and Catherine Salmon. 2004. *Evolutionary Psychology, Public Policy and Personal Decisions*. Mahwah, NJ: Lawrence Erlbaum.

Credit Suisse. 2013. "Global Wealth Report 2013." Zurich: Credit Suisse Research Institute.

Crenshaw, Kimberle. 1989. "Demarginalizing the Intersection of Race and Sex: A Black Feminist Critique of Antidiscrimination Doctrine, Feminist Theory and Antiracist Politics." *University of Chicago Legal Forum* 1989 (1): 139–167.

Critelli, Filomena, and Marsha Schwam-Harris. 2010. "'In a Bind': Foster Mothers' Experiences with Welfare Reform." *Journal of Children and Poverty* 16 (2): 123–143.

Crosnoe, Robert. 2009. "Low-Income Students and the Socioeconomic Composition of Public High Schools." *American Sociological Review* 74 (5): 709–730.

Crosnoe, Robert, Kenneth Frank, and Anna Strassmann Mueller. 2008. "Gender, Body Size and Social Relations in American High Schools." *Social Forces* 86 (3): 1189–1216.

Crowder, Kyle, Scott J. South, and Erick Chavez. 2006. "Wealth, Race, and Inter-Neighborhood Migration." *American Sociological Review* 71 (1): 72–94.

Crutchfield, Robert D., and David Pettinicchio. 2009. "'Cultures of Inequality': Ethnicity, Immigration, Social Welfare, and Imprisonment." *The Annals of the American Academy of Political and Social Science* 623 (1): 134–147.

Cullen, Francis T., Jennifer L. Hartman, and Cheryl Lero Jonson. 2009. "Bad Guys: Why the Public Supports Punishing White-Collar Offenders." *Crime, Law and Social Change* 51 (1): 31–44.

Current Population Survey. 2015. "Employed Persons by Detailed Industry, Sex, Race, and Hispanic or Latino Ethnicity." Household data annual averages. Bureau of Labor Statistics Available at http://www.bls.gov/cps/cpsaat18 htm.

Current Population Survey. 2016. "2014 Family Income." Bureau of Labor Statistics. Available a https://www.census.gov/hhes/www. cpstables/032015/faminc/finc01_000.htm.

Dahrendorf, Ralf. 1958. "Out of Utopia: Toward Reorientation of Sociological Analysis." *American Journal of Sociology* 64: 115–127.

Dahrendorf, Ralf. 1959. *Class and Class Conflict in Industrial Society*. Stanford, CA: Stanford University Press.

Dahrendorf, Ralf. 1970. "On the Origin of Inequality among Men." In *The Logic of Social Hierarchies*, edited by Edward Otto Laumann, Paul M. Siegel, and Robert William Hodge, 3–30. Chicago: Markham.

Danese, A., T. E. Moffitt, H. Harrington, B. J. Milne, G. Polanczyk, C. M. Pariante, R. Poulton, and A. Caspi. 2009. "Adverse Childhood Experiences and Adult Risk Factors for Age-Related Disease: Depression, Inflammation, and Clustering of Metabolic Risk Markers." *Archives of Pediatrics & Adolescent Medicine* 163 (12): 1135–1143.

Daniels, Glynis, and Samantha Friedman. 1999. "Spatial Inequality and the Distribution of Industrial Toxic Releases: Evidence from the 1990 TRI." *Social Science Quarterly* 80: 244–262.

Danziger, Sandra K. 2010. "The Decline of Cash Welfare and Implications for Social Policy and Poverty." *Annual Review of Sociology* 36: 523–545.

Danziger, Sheldon H., and Sandra K. Danziger. 2006. "Poverty, Race, and Antipoverty Policy before and after Hurricane Katrina." *Du Bois Review* 3 (1): 23–36.

Danziger, Sheldon H., Robert Haveman, and Robert D. Plotnick. 1986. "Antipoverty Policy: Effects on the Poor and the Nonpoor." In *Fighting Poverty: What Works and What Doesn't*, edited by Sheldon H. Danziger and Daniel H. Weinberg, 50–77. Cambridge, MA: Harvard University Press.

Danziger, Sheldon, and David Wheeler. 1975. "The Economics of Crime: Punishment or Income Redistribution." *Review of Social Economy* 33 (2): 113–131.

Dart, Tom. 2015. "What Katrina Left behind: New Orleans' Uneven Recovery and Unending Divisions." *Guardian*, August 22. Available at http://www.theguardian.com/us-news/2015/aug/22/hurricane-katrina-recovery-lower-ninth-ward.

Data Center, Allison Plyer, Nihal Shrinath, and Vicki Mack. 2015. "The New Orleans Index at Ten: Measuring Greater New Orleans' Progress toward Prosperity." The New Orleans Index. The Data Center. Available at https://s3.amazonaws.com/gnocdc/reports/TheData-Center_TheNewOrleansIndexatTen.pdf.

Datta Gupta, Nabanita, Nancy L. Etcoff, and Mads M. Jaeger. 2015. "Beauty in Mind: The Effects of Physical Attractiveness on Psychological Well-Being and Distress." *Journal of Happiness Studies*, June: 1–13.

Davis, Alyssa. April 7, 2015. "Women Still Earn Less than Men Across the Board." Economic Policy Institute. Available at http://www.epi.org/publication/women-still-earn-less-than-men-across-the-board.

Davis, Georgiann, and Rachel Allison. 2013. "Increasing Representation, Maintaining Hierarchy: An Assessment of Gender and Medical Specialization." *Social Thought and Research* 32: 17–45.

Davis, James Allan, and Tom W. Smith. 1996. "General Social Surveys, 1972–1996." Chicago: National Opinion Research Center, producer; Storrs, CT: Roper Center for Public Opinion Research, University of Connecticut, distributor.

Davis, Kingsley. 1948. *Human Society*. New York: MacMillan.

Davis, Kingsley, and Wilbert E. Moore. 1945. "Some Principles of Stratification." *American Sociological Review* 10: 242–249.

Decena, Carlos U. 2008. "Tacit Subjects." *GLQ: A Journal of Lesbian and Gay Studies* 14 (2–3): 339–359.

Decker, Sandra L. 2012. "In 2011 Nearly One-Third Of Physicians Said They Would Not Accept New Medicaid Patients, But Rising Fees May Help." *Health Affairs* 31 (8): 1673–1679.

DeCuir-Gunby, Jessica T., Pamela P. Martin, and Shauna M. Cooper. 2012. "African American Students in Private, Independent Schools: Parents and School Influences on Racial Identity Development." *The Urban Review* 44 (1): 113–132.

De Jong, Gordon F., Deborah Roempke Graefe, and Tanja St. Pierre. 2005. "Welfare Reform and Interstate Migration of Poor Families." *Demography* 42 (3): 469–496.

Della Fave, L. Richard. 1980. "The Meek Shall Not Inherit the Earth: Self-Evaluation and the Legitimacy of Stratification." *American Sociological Review* 45: 955–971.

Demuth, Stephen, and Darrell Steffensmeier. 2004. "The Impact of Gender and Race-Ethnicity in the Pretrial Release Process." *Social Problems* 51: 222–242.

DeNavas-Walt, Carmen, and Bernadette D. Proctor. 2015. "Income and Poverty in the United States: 2014." Current Population Reports. U.S. Census Bureau. Available at https://www.census.gov/content/dam/Census/library/publications/2015/demo/p60-252.pdf.

DeNavas-Walt, Carmen, Bernadette D. Proctor, and Jessica C. Smith. 2010. "Income, Poverty, and

Health Insurance Coverage in the United States: 2009." U.S. Census Bureau, pp. 60–238.

Dencker, John C. 2008. "Corporate Restructuring and Sex Differences in Managerial Promotion." *American Sociological Review* 73 (3): 455–476.

Denney, Justin T., Richard G. Rogers, Patrick M. Krueger, and Tim Wadsworth. 2009. "Adult Suicide Mortality in the United States: Marital Status, Family Size, Socioeconomic Status, and Differences by Sex." *Social Science Quarterly* 90 (5): 1167–1185.

Derber, Charles. 2000. *Corporation Nation: How Corporations Are Taking Over Our Lives–and What We Can Do About It.* New York: Macmillan.

Desai, Sonalde, and Amaresh Dubey. 2011. "Caste in 21st Century India: Competing Narratives." *Economic and Political Weekly* 46 (11): 40–49.

DeSilver, Drew. 2013. "Black Incomes Are Up, but Wealth Isn't." Pew Research Center. August 30. Available at http://www.pewresearch.org/fact-tank/2013/08/30/black-incomes-are-up-but-wealth-isnt.

DeSilver, Drew. 2015. "The Many Ways to Measure Economic Inequality." Pew Research Center. September 22. Available at http://www.pewresearch.org/fact-tank/2015/09/22/the-many-ways-to-measure-economic-inequality.

Devine, Joel A., Joseph F. Sheley, and M. Dwayne Smith. 1988. "Macroeconomic and Social-Control Policy Influences on Crime Rate Changes, 1948–1985." *American Sociological Review* 53: 407–420.

Dewan, Shaila, and Robert Gebeloff. 2012. "The 1 Percent Paint a More Nuanced Portrait of the Rich." *New York Times*, January 14. Available at http://www.nytimes.com/2012/01/15/business/the-1-percent-paint-a-more-nuanced-portrait-of-the-rich.html.

Dey, Judy Goldberg, and Catherine Hill. 2007. *Behind the Pay Gap.* Washington, D.C.: American Association of University Women Educational Foundation.

Diamond, Diana. 2009. "The Fourth Wave of Feminism: Psychoanalytic Perspectives." *Studies in Gender and Sexuality* 10: 213–223.

Diamond, Lisa M. 2008. "Female Bisexuality from Adolescence to Adulthood: Results from a 10-Year Longitudinal Study." *Developmental Psychology* 44 (1): 5–14.

DiMaggio, Paul, and Bart Bonikowski. 2008. "Make Money Surfing the Web? The Impact of Internet Use on the Earnings of US Workers." *American Sociological Review* 73 (2): 227–250.

Dinovitzer, R., and J. Hagan. 2014. "Hierarchical Structure and Gender Dissimilarity in American Legal Labor Markets." *Social Forces* 92 (3): 929–955.

Dionne, Eugene Joseph. June 13, 2004. "'E Pluribus Unum'?" *Akron Beacon Journal*, B2.

DiPlacido, Joanne. 1998. "Minority Stress among Lesbians, Gay Men, and Bisexuals: A Consequence of Heterosexism, Homophobia, and Stigmatization." In *Stigma and Sexual Orientation: Understanding Prejudice against Lesbians, Gay Men and Bisexuals*, edited by Gregory M. Herek, 138–149. Thousand Oaks, CA: Sage.

DiPrete, Thomas A. 2007. "Is This a Great Country? Upward Mobility and the Chance for Riches in Contemporary America." *Research in Social Stratification and Mobility* 25 (1): 89–95.

DiPrete, Thomas A., and Margaret L. Krecker. 1991. "Occupational Linkages and Job Mobility within and across Organizations." *Research in Social Stratification and Mobility* 10: 91–131.

DiTomaso, Nancy, Corinne Post, and Rochelle Parks-Yancy. 2007. "Workforce Diversity and Inequality: Power, Status, and Numbers." *Annual Review of Sociology* 33: 473–501.

Dobson, M. C. 2011. "Insecurity, Professional Sociability, and Alcohol: Young Freelance Musicians' Perspectives on Work and Life in the Music Profession." *Psychology of Music* 39 (2): 240–260.

Docquier, Frédéric, and Hillel Rapoport. 2012. "Globalization, Brain Drain, and Development." *Journal of Economic Literature* 50 (3): 681–730.

Doerner, Jill K. 2015. "The Joint Effects of Gender and Race/Ethnicity on Sentencing Outcomes in Federal Courts." *Women & Criminal Justice* 25 (5): 313–338.

Dolan, Kathleen. 2005. "How the Public Views Women Candidates." In *Women and Elective Office: Past, Present, and Future*, edited by Sue Thomas and Clyde Wilcox, 41–59. New York: Oxford University Press.

Dolgoff, Ralph, and Donald Feldstein. 2012. *Understanding Social Welfare: A Search for Social Justice*. 9th ed. New York: Pearson Higher Ed.

Dollar, David, and Aart Kraay. 2004. "Trade, Growth, and Poverty." *The Economic Journal* 114 (493): F22–49.

Domhoff, G. William. 1971. *The Higher Circles.* New York: Vintage.

Domhoff, G. William. 1998. *Who Rules America? Power and Politics in the Year 2000.* Mountain View, CA: Mayfield.

Domhoff, G. William. 2006. "Mills's 'The Power Elite' 50 Years Later." *Contemporary Sociology* 35: 547–550.

Dominguez, Silvia, and Celeste Watkins. 2003. "Creating Networks for Survival and Mobility: Social Capital among African-American and Latin-American Low-Income Mothers." *Social Problems* 50 (1): 111–135.

Dorius, Shawn F., and Glenn Firebaugh. 2010. "Trends in Global Gender Inequality." *Social Forces* 88 (5): 1941–1968.

Doucouliagos, Hristos, and Mehmet Ali Ulubaşoğlu. 2008. "Democracy and Economic Growth: A Meta-Analysis." *American Journal of Political Science* 52 (1): 61–83.

Dowd, Maureen. May 5, 2005. "Ugly Duckling Has No Chance." *Akron Beacon Journal*, B2.

Drori, Gili S. 2006. *Global E-Litism.* New York: Worth.

Drum, Kevin. 2015. "Lead and Crime: The Brennan Center Weighs In." *Mother Jones.* February 12. Available at http://www.motherjones.com/kevin-drum/2015/02/lead-and-crime-brennan-center-weighs.

Dublin, Thomas. 1979. *Women at Work.* New York: Columbia University Press.

Dubofsky, Melvin. 1975. *Industrialism and the American Workers, 1865–1920.* Arlington Heights, IL: AHM.

Du Bois, W. E. B. 1973. *The Philadelphia Negro.* White Plains, NY: Kraus-Thomson.

Duke, James T. 1976. *Conflict and Power in Social Life.* Provo, UT: Brigham Young University Press.

Duncan, Greg J., and Katherine Magnuson. 2011. "The Long Reach of Early Childhood Poverty." *Pathways* Winter: 23–27.

Duncan, Melanie L., and Markus Kemmelmeier. 2012. "Attitudes toward Same-Sex Marriage: An Essentialist Approach." *Analyses of Social Issues and Public Policy* 12 (1): 377–399.

Dungan, Adrian. 2015. "Individual Income Tax Shares, 2012." *Statistics of Income Bulletin.* Washington, D.C.: Internal Revenue Service.

Dunlop, John T. 1987. "The Development of Labor Organization: A Theoretical Framework." In *Theories of the Labor Movement*, edited by Simeon Larson and Bruce Nissen, 12–22. Detroit, MI: Wayne State University Press.

Durkheim, Émile. 1933. *The Division of Labour in Society.* New York: Free Press.

Durr, Marlese, and Adia M. Harvey Wingfield. 2011. "Keep Your 'N' in Check: African American Women and the Interactive Effects of Etiquette and Emotional Labor." *Critical Sociology* 37 (5): 557–571.

Durso, Laura E., and Gary J. Gates. 2012. "Serving Our Youth: Findings from a National Survey of Services Providers Working with Lesbian, Gay, Bisexual and Transgender Youth Who Are Homeless or at Risk of Becoming Homeless." Los Angeles, CA: The Williams Institute with the Palette Fund and the True Colors Fund. Available at http://escholarship.org/uc/item/80x75033.pdf.

Duster, Troy. 2015. "A Post-Genomic Surprise. The Molecular Reinscription of Race in Science, Law and Medicine: A Post-Genomic Surprise." *The British Journal of Sociology* 66 (1): 1–27.

Dwyer, Rachel E. 2013. "The Care Economy? Gender, Economic Restructuring, and Job Polarization in the U.S. Labor Market." *American Sociological Review* 78 (3): 390–416.

Dyck, Joshua J., and Laura S. Hussey. 2008. "The End of Welfare as We Know It? Durable Attitudes in a Changing Information Environment." *Public Opinion Quarterly* 72 (4): 589–618.

Dye, Thomas R. 2002. *Who's Running America? The Bush Restoration.* Upper Saddle River, NJ: Prentice Hall.

Economic Mobility Project. 2009. "Findings from a National Survey and Focus Groups on Economic Mobility." Philadelphia: Economic Mobility Project of The Pew Charitable Trusts, Greenbergy Quinlan Rosner Research and Public Opinion Strategies.

Economic Policy Institute. 2014. "2013 ACS Shows Depth of Native American Poverty and Different Degrees of Economic Well-Being for Asian Ethnic Groups." Economic Policy Institute, September 18. Available at http://www.epi.org/blog/2013-acs-shows-depth-native-american-poverty.

Edelman, Murray. 2013. *Political Language: Words That Succeed and Policies That Fail.* New York: Elsevier.

Economist. 2015. "If India's Monsoon Fails: A Billion-Person Question." The World. July 30. Available at http://worldif.economist.com/article/13/what-if-india%E2%80%99s-monsoon-fails-a-billion-person-question.

Eder, Donna. 1995. *School Talk: Gender and Adolescent Culture.* New Brunswick, NJ: Rutgers University Press.

Edin, Kathryn, and Maria Kefalas. 2011. *Promises I Can Keep: Why Poor Women Put Motherhood Before Marriage.* Revised. Berkeley, CA: University of California Press.

Edin, Kathryn, and H. Luke Shaefer. 2015. *$2.00 a Day: Living on Almost Nothing in America.* New York: Houghton Mifflin Harcourt.

Edwards, Richard C. 1979. *Contested Terrain: The Transformation of the Workplace in the Twentieth Century.* New York: Basic Books.

Egan, Patrick J., and Kenneth S. Sherrill. 2009. *California's Proposition 8: What Happened, and What Does the Future Hold?* Washington, D.C.: National Gay and Lesbian Task Force Policy Institute.

Ehrenreich, Barbara, and Arlie Russell Hochschild. 2005. "Global Woman." In *Gender Through the Prism of Difference*, edited by Maxine Baca Zinn, Pierrette Hondagneu-Sotelo, and Michael A. Messner, 49–55. New York: Oxford University Press.

Eichner, Alana, and Katherine Gallagher Robbins. 2015. "National Snapshot: Poverty Among Women & Families, 2014." Poverty Data Fact Sheet. Poverty and Family Supports. National Women's Law Center. Available at http://www.nwlc.org/sites/default/files/pdfs/povertysnapshot2014.pdf.

Eisen, Lauren-Brooke. 2015. "Charging Inmates Perpetuates Mass Incarceration." New York: Brennan Center for Justice. Available at https://www.brennancenter.org/sites/default/files/publications/Charging_Inmates_Mass_Incarceration.pdf.

Eisenstein, Zillah R. 1981. *The Radical Future of Liberal Feminism.* New York: Longman.

Eisenstein, Zillah R. 1999. "Constructing a Theory of Capitalist Patriarchy and Socialist Feminism." *Critical Sociology* 25 (2/3): 196–220.

Eisler, Benita. 1977. *The Lowell Offering: Writings by New England Mill Women (1840–1845).* Philadelphia: J.B. Lippincott.

Eitle, David J. 2000. "Regulatory Justice: A Re-Examination of the Influence of Class Position on the Punishment of White-Collar Crime." *Justice Quarterly* 17 (4): 809–839.

Eitle, David J., Stewart J. D'Alessio, and Lisa Stolzenberg. 2002. "Racial Threat and Social Control: A Test of the Political, Economic, and Threat of Black Crime Hypotheses." *Social Forces* 81 (2): 557–576.

Elder Jr, Glen H., and Jeffrey K. Liker. 1982. "Hard Times in Women's Lives: Historical Influences across Forty Years." *American Journal of Sociology* 88 (2): 241–269.

Eller, Ronald D. 1982. *Miners, Millhands, and Mountaineers: Industrialization of the Appalachian South, 1880–1930.* Knoxville, TN: University of Tennessee Press.

Elliott, James R., and Ryan A. Smith. 2004. "Race, Gender, and Workplace Power." *American Sociological Review* 69 (3): 365–386.

Ellis, Lee, and James N. McDonald. 2001. "Crime, Delinquency, and Social Status: A Reconsideration." *Journal of Offender Rehabilitation* 32 (3): 23–52.

Ellwood, David T., and Mary Jo Bane. 1984. "Family Structure and Living Arrangements Research: Summary of Findings." Working Paper 92A-82. U.S. Department of Health and Human Services.

Ellwood, David T., and Lawrence H. Summers. 1986. "Poverty in America: Is Welfare the Answer or the Problem?" In *Fighting Poverty: What Works and What Doesn't*, edited by S. H. Danziger and D. H. Weinberg, 78–105. Cambridge, MA: Harvard University Press.

Elman, Cheryl, and Angela M. O'Rand. 2004. "The Race Is to the Swift: Socioeconomic Origins, Adult Education, and Wage Attainment." *American Journal of Sociology* 110 (1): 123–160.

Elo, Irma T. 2009. "Social Class Differentials in Health cand Mortality: Patterns and Explanations in Comparative Perspective." *Annual Review of Sociology* 35 (1): 553–572.

Elwell, Craig K. 2014. "The Distribution of Household Income and the Middle Class." RS20811 Washington, D.C.: Congressional Research Service. Available at http://digitalcommons.ilr.cornell.edu/key_workplace/1263/.

Embrick, David G., and Kasey Henricks. 2013. "Discursive Colorlines at Work: How Epithets and Stereotypes Are Racially Unequal." *Symbolic Interaction* 36 (2): 197–215.

Eng, David L. 2010. *The Feeling of Kinship: Queer Liberalism and the Racialization of Intimacy.* Durham, NC: Duke University Press.

England, Paula. 2010. "The Gender Revolution: Uneven and Stalled." *Gender & Society* 24 (2): 149–166.

England, Paula, and Dana Dunn. 1985. "Why Men Dominate." *The Women's Review of Books* 2: 14–15.

Epstein, Cynthia Fuchs. 1988. *Deceptive Distinctions: Sex, Gender, and the Social Order.* New Haven, CT: Yale University Press.

Erickson, Bonnie, and Rochelle R. Cote. 2009. "Social Capitals and Inequality: The Reproduction of Gender and Occupational Prestige Differences Through Individual Social Networks." Paper presented at American Sociological Association Annual Meetings, Social Capital Regular Session, August 7–11, San Francisco.

Erikson, Kai T. 1976. *Everything in Its Path.* New York: Simon and Schuster.

Erol, Ruth Yasemin, and Ulrich Orth. 2011. "Self-Esteem Development from Age 14 to 30 Years: A Longitudinal Study." *Journal of Personality and Social Psychology* 101 (3): 607–619.

Eskridge, William, and Philip Frickey. 1995. *Cases and Materials on Legislation: Statutes and the Creation of Public Policy.* St. Paul, MN: West Publishing Co.

Esping-Andersen, Gøsta. 2014. "Welfare Regimes and Social Stratification." *Journal of European Social Policy* 25 (1): 124–134.

Evans, Elizabeth, and Prudence Chamberlain. 2015. "Critical Waves: Exploring Feminist Identity, Discourse and Praxis in Western Feminism." *Social Movement Studies* 14 (4): 396–409.

Evans, Lorraine, and Kimberly Davies. 2000. "No Sissy Boys Here: A Content Analysis of the Representation of Masculinity in Elementary School Reading Textbooks." *Sex Roles* 42 (3–4): 255–270.

Evans, M. D. R., Jonathan Kelley, and Clayton D. Peoples. 2010. "Justifications of Inequality: The Normative Basis of Pay Differentials in 31 Nations." *Social Science Quarterly* 91 (5): 1405–1431.

Evertsson, Marie, and Magnus Nermo. 2004. "Dependence within Families and the Division of Labor: Comparing Sweden and the United States." *Journal of Marriage and Family* 66 (5): 1272–1286.

Ezcurra, Roberto, and Andrés Rodríguez-Pose. 2013. "Does Economic Globalization Affect Regional Inequality? A Cross-Country Analysis." *World Development* 52 (December): 92–103.

Fairdosi, Amir Shawn, and Jon C. Rogowski. 2015. "Candidate Race, Partisanship, and Political Participation. When Do Black Candidates Increase Black Turnout?" *Political Research Quarterly* 68 (2): 337–349.

Fajnzylber, Pablo, Daniel Lederman, and Norman Loayza. 2002. "Inequality and Violent Crime." *The Journal of Law and Economics* 45 (1): 1–39.

Fallahi, Firouz, Hamed Pourtaghi, and Gabriel Rodríguez. 2012. "The Unemployment Rate, Unemployment Volatility, and Crime." *International Journal of Social Economics* 39 (6): 440–448.

Fanger, Suzanne Marie, Leslie Ann Frankel, and Nancy Hazen. 2012. "Peer Exclusion in Preschool Children's Play: Naturalistic Observations in a Playground Setting." *Merrill-Palmer Quarterly* 58 (2): 224–254.

Fanon, Frantz. 1963. *The Wretched of the Earth.* New York: Grove Press.

Farber, Henry S., and Robert G. Valletta. 2013. "Do Extended Unemployment Benefits Lengthen Unemployment Spells? Evidence from Recent Cycles in the US Labor Market." Cambridge, MA: National Bureau of Economic Research. Available at http://www.nber.org/papers/w19048.

Farley, John E. 1988. *Majority-Minority Relations.* Englewood Cliffs, NJ: Prentice Hall.

Farley, John E., and Gregory D. Squires. 2005. "Fences and Neighbors: Segregation in 21st-Century America." *Contexts* 4 (1): 33–39.

Farough, Steven D. 2004. "The Social Geographies of White Masculinities." *Critical Sociology* 30 (2): 241–264.

Farrell, Chad R. 2008. "Bifurcation, Fragmentation or Integration? The Racial and Geographical Structure of US Metropolitan Segregation, 1990–2000." *Urban Studies* 45 (3): 467–499.

Fausto-Sterling, Anne. 2000. *Sexing the Body: Gender Politics and the Construction of Sexuality.* New York: Basic Books.

Faux, Jeff. 2003. "Corporate Control of North America." *The American Prospect* 3 (4): 24–28.

FBI. 2013. "Expanded Homicide Data Table 6." FBI. Available at https://www.fbi.gov/about-us/cjis/ucr/crime-in-the-u.s/2013/crime-in-the-u.s.-2013/offenses-known-to-law-enforcement/expanded-homicide/expanded_homicide_data_table_6_murder_race_and_sex_of_victm_by_race_and_sex_of_offender_2013.xls.

FBI. 2015. "Profits Over Safety." FBI, May 8. Available at https://www.fbi.gov/news/stories/2015/may/profits-over-safety/profits-over-safety.

Feagin, Joe R. 2006. *Systemic Racism: A Theory of Oppression*. New York: Routledge.

Feagin, Joe R., and Sean Elias. 2013. "Rethinking Racial Formation Theory: A Systemic Racism Critique." *Ethnic and Racial Studies* 36 (6): 931–960.

Featherman, David L., and Robert Mason Hauser. 1978. *Opportunity and Change*. New York: Academic Press.

Federal Election Commission. 2014. "FEC Summarizes Campaign Activity of the 2011–2012 Election Cycle." Available at http://www.fec.gov/press/press2013/pdf/20130419release.pdf.

Federal Election Commission. 2015. "Campaign Finance Statistics." Available at http://www.fec.gov/press/campaign_finance_statistics.shtml.

Federal Interagency Forum on Aging-Related Statistics. 2012. "Older Americans 2012: Key Indicators of Well-Being." Washington, D.C.: Federal Interagency Forum on Aging-Related Statistics. Available at http://www.agingstats.gov/main_site/data/2012_documents/docs/entirechartbook.pdf.

Feisthamel, Kevin, and Robert Schwartz. 2009. "Differences in Mental Health Counselors' Diagnoses Based on Client Race: An Investigation of Adjustment, Childhood, and Substance-Related Disorders." *Journal of Mental Health Counseling* 31 (1): 47–59.

Feldstein, Stanley, ed. 1972. *The Poisoned Tongue: A Documentary History of American Racism and Prejudice*. New York: William Morrow.

Fellner, Jamie. 2009. "Race, Drugs, and Law Enforcement in the United States." *Stanford Law and Policy Review* 20 (2): 257–292.

Fenton, Steve. 1984. *Durkheim and Modern Sociology*. New York: CUP Archive.

Ferguson, Ronald F. 2003. "Teachers' Perceptions and Expectations and the Black-White Test Score Gap." *Urban Education* 38 (4): 460–507.

Ferretti, Christine. 2015. "For Detroit Retirees, Pension Cuts Become Reality." *Detroit News*, February 27. Available at http://www.detroitnews.com/story/news/local/wayne-county/2015/02/27/detroit-retirees-pension-cuts-become-reality/24156301.

Fertig, Beth. 2014. "Why NYC Is Afraid of Free Lunch for All." NPR. June 9. Available at http://www.npr.org/sections/ed/2014/06/09/319558542/why-nyc-is-afraid-of-free-lunch-for-all.

File, Thom. 2013. "Young-Adult Voting: An Analysis of Presidential Elections, 1964–2012." United States Census Bureau (April 2014). Available at https://census.gov/content/dam/Census/library/publications/2014/demo/p20-573.pdf.

Finn, Patrick J. 2012. "Preparing for Power in Elite Boarding Schools and in Working-Class Schools." *Theory Into Practice* 51 (1): 57–63.

Firebaugh, Glenn. 2000. "The Trend in Between-Nation Income Inequality." *Annual Review of Sociology* 26: 323–339.

Firebaugh, Glenn, and Brian Goesling. 2004. "Accounting for the Recent Decline in Global Income Inequality." *American Journal of Sociology* 110 (2): 283–312.

Firebaugh, Glenn, and Matthew B. Schroeder. 2009. "Does Your Neighbor's Income Affect Your Happiness?" *American Journal of Sociology* 115 (3): 805–831.

Fishel, Leslie H., and Benjamin Quarles. 1967. *The Negro American: A Documentary History*. Glenview, IL: William Morrow.

Fisher, Max. 2013. "Map: How 35 Countries Compare on Child Poverty (the U.S. Is Ranked 34th)." *Washington Post*, April 15. Available at https://www.washingtonpost.com/news/worldviews/wp/2013/04/15/map-how-35-countries-compare-on-child-poverty-the-u-s-is-ranked-34th.

Fitzpatrick Bettencourt, Kathryn E., Tammi Vacha-Haase, and Zinta S. Byrne. 2011. "Older and Younger Adults' Attitudes toward Feminism: The Influence of Religiosity, Political Orientation, Gender, Education, and Family." *Sex Roles* 64 (11–12): 863–874.

Flanagan, Constance A., Bernadette Campbell, Luba Botcheva, Jennifer Bowes, Beno Csapo,

Petr Macek, and Elena Sheblanova. 2003. "Social Class and Adolescents' Beliefs about Justice in Different Social Orders." *Journal of Social Issues* 59 (4): 711–732.

Flippen, Chenoa A. 2014. "Intersectionality at Work: Determinants of Labor Supply among Immigrant Latinas." *Gender & Society* 28 (3): 404–434.

Flores, Glenda M., and Pierrette Hondagneu-Sotelo. 2014. "The Social Dynamics Channelling Latina College Graduates into the Teaching Profession." *Gender, Work & Organization* 21 (6): 491–515.

Floyd, Ife, and Lizz Schott. 2015. "TANF Cash Benefits Have Fallen by More Than 20 Percent in Most States and Continue to Erode." Washington, D.C.: Center on Budget and Policy Priorities. Available at http://www.cbpp.org/research/family-income-support/tanf-cash-benefits-have-fallen-by-more-than-20-percent-in-most-states.

Foner, Philip S. 1979. *Women and the American Labor Movement.* Vol. 1. New York: The Free Press.

Forbes. 2015. "Forbes 400." Available at http://www.forbes.com/forbes-400.

Ford, Jason A., and Jana L. Jasinski. 2006. "Sexual Orientation and Substance Use among College Students." *Addictive Behaviors* 31 (3): 404–13.

Foster, Ann C., and William R. Hawk. 2013. "Spending Patterns of Families Receiving Means-Tested Government Assistance." *Beyond the Numbers* 2 (26). Washington, D.C.: U.S. Bureau of Labor Statistics. Available at http://www.bls.gov/opub/btn/volume-2/spending-patterns-of-families-receiving-means-tested-government-assistance.htm.

Foster, George McClelland. 1973. *Traditional Societies and Technological Change.* New York: HarperCollins.

Fox, Mary Frank, and Sharlene Hesse-Biber. 1984. *Women at Work.* Palo Alto, CA: Mayfield.

France, Mike, and Dan Carney. 2002. "Why Corporate Crooks Are Tough to Nail." *Business Week*, July 1.

Francia, Peter L. 2007. "Reassessing Organized Labor's Political Power." *International Journal of Organization Theory and Behavior* 10: 188–212.

Frank, Andre Gunder. 1969. *Latin America and Underdevelopment.* New York: Monthly Review Press.

Frankenberg, Ruth. 1997. *Displacing Whiteness.* Durham, NC: Duke University Press.

Franklin, Cortney A., and Noelle E. Fearn. 2008. "Gender, Race, and Formal Court Decision-Making Outcomes: Chivalry/Paternalism, Conflict Theory or Gender Conflict?" *Journal of Criminal Justice* 36 (3): 279–290.

Franklin, John Hope. 1980. *From Slavery to Freedom: A History of Negro Americans.* 5th ed. New York: Knopf.

Frankovic, Kathy. 2014. "Feminism Today: What Does It Mean?" YouGov, August 1. Available at https://today.yougov.com/news/2014/08/01/feminism-today-what-does-it-mean.

Frazier, E. Franklin. 1937. "Negro Harlem: An Ecological Study." *American Journal of Sociology* 43: 72–88.

Fredrickson, George M. 1981. *White Supremacy: A Comparative Study in American and South African History.* New York: Oxford University Press.

Freeman, Jo. 1975a. "The Women's Liberation Movement: Its Origins, Structures, Impact, and Ideas." In *Women: A Feminist Perspective,* edited by Jo Freeman, 448–460. Palo Alto, CA: Mayfield.

Freeman, Jo., ed. 1975b. *Women: A Feminist Perspective.* Palo Alto, CA: Mayfield.

Freiburger, Tina L. 2009. "The Effects of Gender, Family Status, and Race on Sentencing Decisions." *Behavioral Sciences & the Law* 28: 378–395.

Freire, Paulo. 1986. *Pedagogy of the Oppressed.* New York: Continuum.

Freitag, Peter J. 1975. "The Cabinet and Big Business: A Study of Interlocks." *Social Problems* 23 (2): 137–152.

French, John R. P., and Bertram Raven. 1959. "The Bases of Social Power." In *Studies in Social Power,* edited by Dorwin Cartwright, 150–167. Ann Arbor, MI: Institute for Social Research.

Friedberg, Leora, and Michael Owyang. 2004. "Explaining the Evolution of Pension Structure and Job Tenure." Cambridge, MA: National Bureau of Economic Research. Available at http://www.nber.org/papers/w10714.

Friedman, M. Reuel, Brian Dodge, Vanessa Schick, Debby Herbenick, Randolph D. Hubach, Jessamyn Bowling, Gabriel Goncalves, Sarah Krier, and Michael Reece. 2014. "From Bias to Bisexual Health Disparities: Attitudes toward

Bisexual Men and Women in the United States." *LGBT Health* 1 (4): 309–318.

Friedman, Samantha, Angela Reynolds, Susan Scovill, Florence R. Brassier, Ron Campbell, and McKenzie Ballou. 2013. "An Estimate of Housing Discrimination against Same-Sex Couples." Washington, D.C.: U.S. Department of Housing and Urban Development, Office of Policy Development and Research. Available at http://papers.ssrn.com/sol3/papers.cfm?abstract_id=2284243.

Frith, Katherine, Ping Shaw, and Hong Cheng. 2005. "The Construction of Beauty: A Cross-Cultural Analysis of Women's Magazine Advertising." *Journal of Communication* 55 (1): 56–70.

Frongillo, Edward A., Eliza Fishbein, Maryah Fram, and Edward Frongillo. 2013. "Assessment and Surveillance of Child Food Insecurity and Hunger." Paper presented at the Workshop on Research Gaps and Opportunities on the Causes and Consequences of Child Hunger. Washington, D.C., April 8–9. Available at http://sites.nationalacademies.org/cs/groups/dbassesite/documents/webpage/dbasse_084307.pdf.

Fry, Richard, and Rakesh Kochhar. 2014. "America's Wealth Gap between Middle-Income and Upper-Income Families Is Widest on Record." Pew Research Center. December 17. Available at http://www.pewresearch.org/fact-tank/2014/12/17/wealth-gap-upper-middle-income.

Fujimura, Joan H. 2015. "A Different Kind of Association between Socio-Histories and Health." *The British Journal of Sociology* 66 (1): 58–67.

Fullerton, Andrew S., and Jeffrey C. Dixon. 2009. "Racialization, Asymmetry, and the Context of Welfare Attitudes in the American States." *Journal of Political and Military Sociology* 37 (1): 95–120.

Fuwa, Makiko. 2004. "Macro-Level Gender Inequality and the Division of Household Labor in 22 Countries." *American Sociological Review* 69 (6): 751–767.

Gallup. 2014. "Immigration." Gallup.com. Available at http://www.gallup.com/poll/1660/Immigration.aspx.

Gallup. 2015. "Gay and Lesbian Rights." Gallup.com. Available at http://www.gallup.com/poll/1651/Gay-Lesbian-Rights.aspx.

Galster, George C. 2012. "The Mechanism(s) of Neighbourhood Effects: Theory, Evidence, and Policy Implications." In *Neighbourhood Effects Research: New Perspectives*, edited by Maarten van Ham, David Manley, Nick Bailey, Ludi Simpson, and Duncan Maclennan, 23–56. Dordrecht: Springer Netherlands.

Galster, George, Jackie Cutsinger, and Jason C. Booza. 2006. "Where Did They Go? The Decline of Middle Income Neighborhoods in Metropolitan America." Washington, D.C.: Brookings Institution.

Galster, George, and A. Santiago. 2015. "Neighbourhood Ethnic Composition and Outcomes for Low-Income Latino and African American Children." *Urban Studies*, July.

Gamson, Joshua, and Dawne Moon. 2004. "The Sociology of Sexualities: Queer and Beyond." *Annual Review of Sociology* 30: 47–64.

Gangl, Markus, and Andrea Ziefle. 2009. "Motherhood, Labor Force Behavior, and Women's Careers: An Empirical Assessment of the Wage Penalty for Motherhood in Britain, Germany, and the United States." *Demography* 46 (2): 341–69.

Gans, Herbert J. 1995. *The War against the Poor: The Underclass and Antipoverty Policy*. New York: Basic Books.

Gans, Herbert J. 1996. "From 'Underclass' to 'Undercaste': Some Observations About the Future of the Post-Industrial Economy and Its Major Victims." In *Urban Poverty and the Underclass*, edited by Enzo Mingione. Cambridge, MA: Blackwell.

GAO. 2013a. "Corporate Income Tax: Effective Tax Rates Can Differ Significantly from the Statutory Rate." GAO-13-520. Government Accountability Office. Available at http://www.gao.gov/assets/660/654957.pdf.

GAO. 2013b. "Immigrant Detention." Report to Congressional Requesters GAO-14-38. Washington, D.C. Available at http://www.gao.gov/assets/660/659145.pdf.

Gao, George. 2015. "How Do Americans Stand Out from the Rest of the World?" Pew Research Center. March 12. Available at http://www.pewresearch.org/fact-tank/2015/03/12/how-do-americans-stand-out-from-the-rest-of-the-world.

Gapen, Mark, Dorthie Cross, Kile Ortigo, Allen Graham, Eboni Johnson, Mark Evces, Kerry Ressler, and Bekh Bradley. 2011. "Perceived Neighborhood Disorder, Community Cohesion and PTSD Symptoms among Low-Income African Americans in an Urban Health Setting." *American Journal of Orthopsychiatry* 81 (1): 31–37.

Garbarino, Merwyn S. 1976. *American Indian Heritage*. Boston: Little, Brown.

Garcia-Navarro, Lourdes, Tyler Fisher, Kainaz Amaria, and Lauren Migaki. 2015. "Why Deforestation Happens (And Why It's Hard To Stop)." National Public Radio. Available at http://apps.npr.org/lookatthis/posts/brazil.

Garfield, Rachel, and Anthony Damico. 2016. "The Coverage Gap: Uninsured Poor Adults in States That Do Not Expand Medicaid—An Update." The Henry J. Kaiser Family Foundation, October 23. Available at http://kff.org/health-reform/issue-brief/the-coverage-gap-uninsured-poor-adults-in-states-that-do-not-expand-medicaid-an-update.

Gartrell, Nanette, and Henny Bos. 2010. "US National Longitudinal Lesbian Family Study: Psychological Adjustment of 17-Year-Old Adolescents." *Pediatrics* 126 (1): 28–36.

Garza, Alicia. 2015. "A Herstory of the #BlackLivesMatter Movement." Black Lives Matter. Available at http://blacklivesmatter.com/herstory.

Gates, Gary J. 2011. "How Many People Are Lesbian, Gay, Bisexual and Transgender?" Los Angeles, CA: The Williams Institute. Available at https://escholarship.org/uc/item/09h684x2.pdf.

Gates, Gary J., and Frank Newport. 2012. "Special Report: 3.4% of U.S. Adults Identify as LGBT." Gallup.com, October 18. Available at http://www.gallup.com/poll/158066/special-report-adults-identify-lgbt.aspx.

Gauchat, Gordon, Maura Kelly, and Michael Wallace. 2012. "Occupational Gender Segregation, Globalization, and Gender Earnings Inequality in U.S. Metropolitan Areas." *Gender & Society* 26 (5): 718–747.

Gaventa, John. 1984. "Land Ownership, Power, and Powerlessness in the Appalachian Highlands." In *Cultural Adaptation to Mountain Environments*, edited by Patricia Beaver and Burton Purrington, 142–155. Athens: University of Georgia Press.

Gaztambide-Fernandez, Rubén A. 2009. *The Best of the Best: Becoming Elite at an American Boarding School*. Cambridge, MA: Harvard University Press.

Gazzola, Stephanie Beryl, and Melanie Ann Morrison. 2014. "Cultural and Personally Endorsed Stereotypes of Transgender Men and Transgender Women: Notable Correspondence or Disjunction?" *International Journal of Transgenderism* 15 (2): 76–99.

Gebeloff, Robert, and Shaila Dewan. 2012. "Measuring the Top 1% by Wealth, Not Income." Economix Blog, January 17. Available at http://economix.blogs.nytimes.com/2012/01/17/measuring-the-top-1-by-wealth-not-income.

Gecewicz, Claire, and Michael Lipka. 2014. "Blacks Are Lukewarm to Gay Marriage, but Most Say Businesses Must Provide Wedding Services to Gay Couples." Pew Research Center, October 7. Available at http://www.pewresearch.org/fact-tank/2014/10/07/blacks-are-lukewarm-to-gay-marriage-but-most-say-businesses-must-provide-wedding-services-to-gay-couples.

Geiger, Wendy, Jake Harwood, and Mary Lee Hummert. 2006. "College Students' Multiple Stereotypes of Lesbians: A Cognitive Perspective." *Journal of Homosexuality* 51 (3): 165–182.

Gengler, Amanda. 2012. "Defying (Dis)Empowerment in a Battered Women's Shelter: Moral Rhetorics, Intersectionality, and Processes of Control and Resistance." *Social Problems* 59 (4): 501–521.

Gensler, Howard. 1997. "Welfare and the Family Size Decision of Low-Income, Two-Parent Families." *Applied Economics Letters* 4 (10): 607–610.

George, Linda K., and Scott M. Lynch. 2003. "Race Differences in Depressive Symptoms: A Dynamic Perspective on Stress Exposure and Vulnerability." *Journal of Health and Social Behavior* 44 (3): 353–369.

George, Molly. 2013. "Seeking Legitimacy: The Professionalization of Life Coaching." *Sociological Inquiry* 83 (2): 179–208.

Gerhards, Jürgen, Silke Hans, and Michael Mutz. 2012. "Social Class and Highbrow Lifestyle—A Cross-National Analysis." Working Paper 24. Berlin Studies on the Sociology of Europe. Berlin: Freie Universität. Available at http://papers.ssrn.com/sol3/papers.cfm?abstract_id=2144700.

Gerhart, Ann. 2005. "And Now We Are in Hell." *Washington Post*, September 1. Available at http://www.washingtonpost.com/wp-dyn/content/article/2005/08/31/AR2005083102801.html.

Gerstel, Naomi, and Dan Clawson. 2014. "Class Advantage and the Gender Divide: Flexibility on the Job and at Home." *American Journal of Sociology* 120 (2): 395–431.

Gerstle, Gary, and Steve Fraser. 2005. "Coda: Democracy in America." In *Ruling America: A History of Wealth and Power in a Democracy*, edited by Steve Fraser and Gary Gerstle, 286–292. Cambridge, MA: Harvard University Press.

Gerth, Hans H., and C. Wright Mills, eds. 1962. *From Max Weber: Essays in Sociology*. New York: Oxford University Press.

Giddens, Anthony. 1973. *The Class Structure of the Advanced Societies*. New York: Harper and Row.

Giddens, Anthony. 1978. *Émile Durkheim*. New York: Penguin Books.

Giddens, Anthony. 1982. *Sociology: A Brief but Critical Introduction*. New York: Macmillan.

Giddens, Anthony. 1984. *The Constitution of Society: Outline of the Theory of Structuration*. Berkeley: University of California Press.

Giddings, Paula. 1984. *When and Where I Enter: The Impact of Black Women on Race and Sex in America*. New York: Bantam.

Gilbert, Dennis L. 2014. *The American Class Structure in an Age of Growing Inequality*. 9th ed. Los Angeles, CA: Sage.

Gilens, Martin. 2003. "How the Poor Became Black: The Racialization of American Poverty in the Mass Media." In *Race and the Politics of Welfare Reform*, by Sanford Schram, Joe Soss, and Richard C. Fording, 101–130. Ann Arbor: University of Michigan Press.

Gilens, Martin, and Benjamin I. Page. 2014. "Testing Theories of American Politics: Elites, Interest Groups, and Average Citizens." *Perspectives on Politics* 12 (3): 564–581.

Gimenez, Martha E. 2005. "Capitalism and the Oppression of Women: Marx Revisited." *Science & Society* 69: 11–32.

Ginzberg, Eli, and Hyman Berman. 1967. *The American Worker in the Twentieth Century: A History through Autobiographies*. New York: Free Press.

Giroux, Henry A. 1983. *Theory and Resistance in Education: A Pedagogy for the Opposition*. South Hadley, MA: Bergin & Garvey.

GLAAD. 2012. "Victims or Villains: Examining Ten Years of Transgender Images on Television." GLAAD. Available at https://www.glaad.org/publications/victims-or-villains-examining-ten-years-transgender-images-television.

Glenn, Evelyn Nakano. 2008. "Yearning for Lightness: Transnational Circuits in the Marketing and Consumption of Skin Lighteners." *Gender & Society* 22: 281–302.

Glenn, Evelyn Nakano. 2011. "Constructing Citizenship: Exclusion, Subordination, and Resistance." *American Sociological Review* 76 (1): 1–24.

GLSEN. 2013. "Out Online: The Experiences of Lesbian, Gay, Bisexual and Transgender Youth on the Internet." New York: Gay, Lesbian and Straight Educator's Network. Available at http://www.glsen.org/sites/default/files/Out%20Online%20FINAL.pdf.

Gneezy, Uri, Muriel Niederle, and Aldo Rustichini. 2001. "Performance in Competitive Environments: Gender Differences." Cambridge, MA: National Bureau of Economic Research. Available at http://users.nber.org/~rosenbla/econ311-05/syllabus/murielgender.pdf.

Goesling, Brian. 2001. "Changing Income Inequalities within and between Nations: New Evidence." *American Sociological Review* 66: 745–761.

Goffman, Erving. 1959. *The Presentation of Self in Everyday Life*. Garden City, NY: Doubleday.

Goffman, Erving. 1961. *Asylums: Essays on the Social Situation of Mental Patients and Other Inmates*. Garden City, NY: Double Day Anchor Books.

Goffman, Erving. 1967. *Interaction Ritual: Essays on Face-to-Face Interaction*. Garden City, NY: Anchor Books, Doubleday.

Goldsmith, P. R. 2009. "Schools or Neighborhoods or Both? Race and Ethnic Segregation and Educational Attainment." *Social Forces* 87 (4): 1913–1941.

Gordon, David M. 1972. *Theories of Poverty and Underemployment*. Lexington, MA: D.C. Heath.

Gore, Susan, and Robert H. Aseltine, Jr. 2003. "Race and Ethnic Differences in Depressed Mood Following the Transition from High School." *Journal of Health and Social Behavior* 44: 370–389.

Gorman, Elizabeth H. 2005. "Gender Stereotypes, Same-Gender Preferences, and Organizational Variation in the Hiring of Women: Evidence from Law Firms." *American Sociological Review* 70 (4): 702–728.

Gorman, Elizabeth H., and Julie A. Kmec. 2009. "Hierarchical Rank and Women's Organizational

Mobility: Glass Ceilings in Corporate Law Firms." *American Journal of Sociology* 114 (5): 1428–1474.

Gottfried, Heidi. 2004. "Gendering Globalization Discourses." *Critical Sociology* 30 (1): 9–16.

Gould, Roger V. 2002. "The Origins of Status Hierarchies: A Formal Theory and Empirical Test." *American Journal of Sociology* 107: 1143–1178.

Grabb, Edward G. 1984. *Social Inequality: Classical and Contemporary Theorists*. Toronto: Holt Rinehart & Winston.

Graham, David A. 2016. "What Did the Governor Know about Flint's Water, and When Did He Know It?" *Atlantic*, January 9. Available at http://www.theatlantic.com/politics/archive/2016/01/what-did-the-governor-know-about-flints-water-and-when-did-he-know-it/423342.

Gramsci, Antonio. 1971. *Selections from the Prison Notebooks*. Translated and Edited by Quintin Hoare and Geoffrey Nowell Smith. London: Lawrence and Wishart.

Grant, Jaime M., Lisa A. Mottet, J. D. Justin Tanis, and D. Min. 2011. "Injustice at Every Turn: A Report of the National Transgender Discrimination Survey." Washington, D.C.: National Center for Transgender Equality and National Gay and Lesbian Task Force. Available at http://endtransdiscrimination.org/PDFs/NTDS_Report.pdf.

Gray, Jeremy. 2015. "'A Lot of People Are Hurting': 1,100 Laid off US Steel Employees Face Uncertainty, Hard Times." AL.com, October 26. Available at http://www.al.com/news/index.ssf/2015/10/for_us_steel_employees_facing.html.

Gray, Kelsey Farson, and Esa Eslami. 2014. "Characteristics of Supplemental Nutrition Assistance Program Households: Fiscal Year 2012." U.S. Department of Agriculture, and Food and Nutrition Service, Nutrition Assistance Program Series.

Gray, Mary L. 2009. *Out in the Country: Youth, Media, and Queer Visibility in Rural America. Intersections: Transdisciplinary Perspectives on Genders and Sexualities*. New York: New York University Press.

Green, James R. 1980. *The World of the Worker*. New York: Hill and Wang.

Green, Alexander R., Dana R. Carney, Daniel J. Pallin, Long H. Ngo, Kristal L. Raymond, Lisa I.

Iezzoni, and Mahzarin R. Banaji. 2007. "Implicit Bias among Physicians and Its Prediction of Thrombolysis Decisions for Black and White Patients." *Journal of General Internal Medicine* 22 (9): 1231–1238.

Greenberg, Greg A., and Robert A. Rosenheck. 2008a. "Homelessness in the State and Federal Prison Population." *Criminal Behaviour and Mental Health* 18 (2): 88–103.

Greenberg, Greg A., and Robert A. Rosenheck. 2008b. "Jail Incarceration, Homelessness, and Mental Health: A National Study." *Psychiatric Services* 59 (2): 170–177.

Greenberg, Mark, and Jared Bernstein. 2004. "Holes Starting to Open in Welfare Reform." *Akron Beacon Journal*, B2, December 6.

Greenman, Emily, and Yu Xie. 2008. "Double Jeopardy? The Interaction of Gender and Race on Earnings in the United States." *Social Forces* 86 (3): 1217–1244.

Greenwood, Dara N., and Sonya Dal Cin. 2012. "Ethnicity and Body Consciousness: Black and White American Women's Negotiation of Media Ideals and Others' Approval." *Psychology of Popular Media Culture* 1 (4): 220–235.

Griffin, Larry J., and Kenneth A. Bollen. 2009. "What Do These Memories Do? Civil Rights Remembrance and Racial Attitudes." *American Sociological Review* 74 (4): 594–614.

Griffin, Larry J., Michael E. Wallace, and Beth A. Rubin. 1986. "Capitalist Resistance to the Organization of Labor before the New Deal: Why? How? Success?" *American Sociological Review* 51: 147–167.

Grimsley, Edwin. 2012. "What Wrongful Convictions Teach Us About Racial Inequality." Innocence Project. September 26. Available at http://www.innocenceproject.org/news-events-exonerations/what-wrongful-convictions-teach-us-about-racial-inequality.

Grodsky, Eric, John Robert Warren, and Erika Felts. 2008. "Testing and Social Stratification in American Education." *Annual Review of Sociology* 34: 385–404.

Gross, Neil. 2009. "A Pragmatist Theory of Social Mechanisms." *American Sociological Review* 74 (3): 358–379.

Grossmann, Matt. 2012. "Interest Group Influence on US Policy Change: An Assessment Based on Policy History." *Interest Groups & Advocacy* 1 (2): 171–192.

Gruberg, Sharita. 2013. "Dignity Denied: LGBT Immigrants in U.S. Detention." Washington, D.C.: Center for American Progress.

GSS. 2015. "SDA—GSS 1972–2014 Cumulative Datafile." Available at http://sda.berkeley.edu/sdaweb/analysis/?dataset=gss14.

Guetzkow, Joshua. 2010. "Beyond Deservingness: Congressional Discourse on Poverty, 1964–1996." *The Annals of the American Academy of Political and Social Science* 629 (1): 173–197.

Gunderson, Elizabeth A., Gerardo Ramirez, Susan C. Levine, and Sian L. Beilock. 2012. "The Role of Parents and Teachers in the Development of Gender-Related Math Attitudes." *Sex Roles* 66 (3–4): 153–166.

Guvenen, Fatih, Greg Kaplan, and Jae Song. 2014. "The Glass Ceiling and the Paper Floor: Gender Differences among Top Earners, 1981–2012." Cambridge, MA: National Bureau of Economic Research. Available at http://www.nber.org/papers/w20560.

Haaretz. 2014. "Ad in New York Times Sparks Debate over Israeli 'Pinkwashing.'" *Haaretz,* December 25. Available at http://www.haaretz.com/jewish/news/1.633659.

Haas, Ann P., Mickey Eliason, Vickie M. Mays, Robin M. Mathy, Susan D. Cochran, Anthony R. D'Augelli, Morton M. Silverman, et al. 2010. "Suicide and Suicide Risk in Lesbian, Gay, Bisexual, and Transgender Populations: Review and Recommendations." *Journal of Homosexuality* 58 (1): 10–51.

Haas, Steven. 2008. "Trajectories of Functional Health: The 'Long Arm' of Childhood Health and Socioeconomic Factors." *Social Science & Medicine* 66 (4): 849–861.

Hadjar, Andreas, Dirk Baier, Klaus Boehnke, and John Hagan. 2007. "Juvenile Delinquency and Gender Revisited: The Family and Power-Control Theory Reconceived." *European Journal of Criminology* 4 (1): 33–58.

Haelermans, Carla, and Lex Borghans. 2012. "Wage Effects of On-the-Job Training: A Meta-Analysis." *British Journal of Industrial Relations* 50 (3): 502–528.

Hagan, John, A. Ronald Gillis, and John Simpson. 1985. "The Class Structure of Gender and Delinquency: Toward a Power-Control Theory of Common Delinquent Behavior." *American Journal of Sociology* 90: 1151–1178.

Hagan, John, John Simpson, and A. Ronald Gillis. 1987. "Class in the Household: A Power-Control Theory of Gender and Delinquency." *American Journal of Sociology* 92: 788–816.

Hahl, Oliver, and Ezra W. Zuckerman. 2014. "The Denigration of Heroes? How the Status Attainment Process Shapes Attributions of Considerateness and Authenticity." *American Journal of Sociology* 120 (2): 504–554.

Haider-Markel, Donald P., and Mark R. Joslyn. 2008. "Beliefs about the Origins of Homosexuality and Support for Gay Rights." *Public Opinion Quarterly* 72: 291–310.

Hajnal, Zoltan L. 2007. "Black Class Exceptionalism Insights from Direct Democracy on the Race Versus Class Debate." *Public Opinion Quarterly* 71 (4): 560–587.

Hall, Diane, and Howard Stevenson. 2007. "Double Jeopardy: Being African-American and 'Doing Diversity' in Independent Schools." *The Teachers College Record* 109 (1): 1–23.

Haller, Archibald O., and Alejandro Portes. 1973. "Status Attainment Processes." *Sociology of Education* 46: 51–91.

Halloran, Liz. 2015. "Survey Shows Striking Increase in Americans Who Know and Support Transgender People." Human Rights Campaign. April 24. Available at http://www.hrc.org/blog/entry/survey-shows-striking-increase-in-americans-who-know-and-support-transgende.

Hamel, Liz, Jamie Firth, and Mollyann Brodie. 2015. "New Orleans Residents Are Optimistic and Rate Recovery Efforts Positively." 8763 New Orleans Ten Years After The Storm: The Kaiser Family Foundation Katrina Survey Project. Menlo Park, CA: Henry J. Kaiser Family Foundation. Available at http://kff.org/report-section/new-orleans-ten-years-after-the-storm-section-1-new-orleans-residents-are-optimistic-and-rate-recovery-efforts-positively.

Hamermesh, Daniel. 2011. *Beauty Pays: Why Attractive People Are More Successful.* Princeton, NJ: Princeton University Press.

Hamilton, Darrick, Algernon Austin, and William Darity, Jr. 2011. "Whiter Jobs, Higher Wages Occupational Segregation and the Lower Wages of Black Men." Briefing Paper. Washington, D.C.: Economic Policy Institute.

Hanagan, Michael. 2000. "States and Capital: Globalizations Past and Present." In *The Ends of Globalization: Bringing Society Back In* edited by Don Kalb, Marco van der Land, Richard Staring, Bart van Steenbergen, and Nico Wilterdink, 67–86. Lanham, MD: Rowman & Littlefield.

Hannon, Lance. 2015. "White Colorism." *Social Currents* 2 (1): 13–21.

Hannon, Lance, Robert DeFina, and Sarah Bruch. 2013. "The Relationship between Skin Tone and School Suspension for African Americans." *Race and Social Problems* 5 (4): 281–295.

Hanson, Sandra L., and John Zogby. 2010. "The Polls—Trends: Attitudes About the American Dream." *Public Opinion Quarterly* 74 (3): 570–584.

Hao, Lingxin. 2003. "Immigration and Wealth Inequality in the US." Working Paper 202. New York: Russell Sage Foundation.

Hardaway, Cecily R., and Vonnie C. McLoyd. 2009. "Escaping Poverty and Securing Middle Class Status: How Race and Socioeconomic Status Shape Mobility Prospects for African Americans during the Transition to Adulthood." *Journal of Youth and Adolescence* 38 (2): 242–256.

Hardoon, Deborah. 2015. "Wealth: Having It All and Wanting More." Issue Brief. Oxford: Oxfam.

Harrington, Michael. 1969. *The Other America: Poverty in the United States*. New York: MacMillan.

Harris, Alexes, Heather Evans, and Katherine Beckett. 2010. "Drawing Blood from Stones: Legal Debt and Social Inequality in the Contemporary United States." *American Journal of Sociology* 115 (6): 1753–1799.

Harris, Benjamin Cerf. 2015. "Likely Transgender Individuals in U.S. Federal Administrative Records and the 2010 Census." Washington, D.C.: U.S. Census Bureau. Available at http://www.census.gov/srd/carra/15_03_Likely_Transgender_Individuals_in_ARs_and_2010Census.pdf.

Harris, Hamil R. 2012. "Prominent Black Clergy Support Maryland Same-Sex Marriage." OnFaith. September 22. Available at http://www.faithstreet.com/onfaith/2012/09/22/prominent-black-clergy-support-maryland-same-sex-marriage/10815.

Harris Polls. 2014. "Doctors, Military Officers, Firefighters, and Scientists Seen as Among America's Most Prestigious Occupations." Harris: A Nielson Company. Available at http://www.theharrispoll.com/politics/Doctors__Military_Officers__Firefighters__and_Scientists_Seen_as_Among_America_s_Most_Prestigious_Occupations.html.

Harris, Richard J., Juanita M. Firestone, and William A. Vega. 2005. "The Interaction of Country of Origin, Acculturation, and Gender Role Ideology on Wife Abuse." *Social Science Quarterly* 86 (2): 463–483.

Hartmann, Douglas, Joseph Gerteis, and Paul R. Croll. 2009. "An Empirical Assessment of Whiteness Theory: Hidden from How Many?" *Social Problems* 56 (3): 403–424.

Hartmann, Heidi I. 1976. "Capitalism, Patriarchy, and Job Segregation by Sex." *Signs* 1 (3): 137–169.

Hartmann, Heidi I. 1979. "The Unhappy Marriage of Marxism and Feminism: Towards a More Progressive Union." *Capital & Class* 3 (2): 1–33.

Haskins, Ron. 2015. "TANF at Age 20: Work Still Works." *Journal of Policy Analysis and Management* 35 (1): 224–231.

Hatch, Stephani L., and Bruce P. Dohrenwend. 2007. "Distribution of Traumatic and Other Stressful Life Events by Race/Ethnicity, Gender, SES and Age: A Review of the Research." *American Journal of Community Psychology* 40 (3–4): 313–332.

Haveman, Heather A., and Lauren. S. Beresford. 2012. "If You're So Smart, Why Aren't You the Boss? Explaining the Persistent Vertical Gender Gap in Management." *The Annals of the American Academy of Political and Social Science* 639 (1): 114–130.

Haveman, Robert, Rebecca Blank, Robert A. Moffitt, Timothy Smeeding, and Geoffrey Wallace. 2015. "The War on Poverty: Measurement, Trends, and Policy." *Journal of Policy Analysis and Management* 34 (3): 593–638.

Hay, Carter, Edward N. Fortson, Dusten R. Hollist, Irshad Altheimer, and Lonnie M. Schaible. 2007. "Compounded Risk: The Implications for Delinquency of Coming from a Poor Family That Lives in a Poor Community." *Journal of Youth and Adolescence* 36 (5): 593–605.

Haynes, Norris M. 1995. "How Skewed Is 'The Bell Curve'?" *Journal of Black Psychology* 21: 275–292.

Hays, Sharon. 2003. *Flat Broke with Children: Women in the Age of Welfare Reform*. New York: Oxford University Press.

Healy, Patrick. 2015. "Hillary Clinton to Offer Plan on Paying College Tuition Without Needing Loans." *New York Times*, August 10. Available at http://www.nytimes.com/2015/08/10/us/politics/hillary-clinton-to-offer-plan-on-paying-college-tuition-without-needing-loans.html.

Hechter, Michael. 2004. "From Class to Culture." *American Journal of Sociology* 110 (2): 400–445.

Hedström, Peter, and Petri Ylikoski. 2010. "Causal Mechanisms in the Social Sciences." *Annual Review of Sociology* 36: 49–67.

Hegewisch, Ariane, and Hannah Liepmann. 2013. "Occupational Segregation and the Gender Wage Gap in the US." In *Handbook of Research on Gender and Economic Life*, edited by Deborah M. Figart and Tonia L. Warnecke. Northamptom, MA: Edward Elgar.

Hehir, J. Bryan. 1981. "The Bishops Speak on El Salvador." *Commonwealth*, April 10, pp. 199, 223.

Helfat, Constance E., Dawn Harris, and Paul J. Wolfson. 2006. "The Pipeline to the Top: Women and Men in the Top Executive Ranks of U.S. Corporations." *Academy of Management Perspectives* 20 (4):42–64.

Helleringer, Stephane, and Andrew Noymer. 2015. "Assessing the Direct Effects of the Ebola Outbreak on Life Expectancy in Liberia, Sierra Leone and Guinea." *PLOS Currents*, February 19. Available at http://currents.plos.org/outbreaks/article/assessing-the-direct-effects-of-the-ebola-outbreak-on-life-expectancy-in-liberia-sierra-leone-and-guinea.

Henderson, Debra A., and Ann R. Tickamyer. 2008. "Lost in Appalachia: The Unexpected Impact of Welfare Reform on Older Women in Rural Communities." *Journal of Sociology and Social Welfare* 35: 153–171.

Hennessy, Judith. 2009. "Morality and Work-Family Conflict in the Lives of Poor and Low-Income Women." *The Sociological Quarterly* 50 (4): 557–580.

Hennessy, Kathleen. 2010. "Tough-Talking Candidates Using Sexual Stereotypes." *Akron Beacon Journal*, November 17, p. A3.

Henning, Peter J. 2014. "The Year in White-Collar Crime." DealBook. December 29. Available at http://dealbook.nytimes.com/2014/12/29/the-year-in-white-collar-crime.

Henry, P. J., Christine Reyna, and Bernard Weiner. 2004. "Hate Welfare But Help the Poor: How the Attributional Content of Stereotypes Explains the Paradox of Reactions to the Destitute in America." *Journal of Applied Social Psychology* 34 (1): 34–58.

Herdt, Gilbert H. 1997. *Same Sex, Different Cultures: Gays and Lesbians across Cultures.* Boulder, CO: Westview Press.

Herek, Gregory M. 2002. "Gender Gaps in Public Opinion about Lesbians and Gay Men." *Public Opinion Quarterly* 66 (1): 40–66.

Herek, Gregory M. 2013. "Facts about Homosexuality and Child Molestation." Professor Herek's Blog. Available at http://psc.dss.ucdavis.edu/rainbow/HTML/facts_molestation.html.

Hergenrather, Kenneth C., Robert J. Zeglin, Maureen McGuire-Kuletz, and Scott D. Rhode. 2015. "Employment as a Social Determinant of Health: A Systematic Review of Longitudinal Studies Exploring the Relationship Between Employment Status and Physical Health." *Rehabilitation Research, Policy, and Education* 29 (1): 2–26.

Herkenrath, Mark, Claudia König, Hanno Scholt and Thomas Volken. 2005. "Convergence and Divergence in the Contemporary World System: An Introduction." *International Journal Comparative Sociology* 46 (5–6): 363–382.

Herring, Cedric. 2004. "Skin Deep: Race and Complexion in the 'Color-Blind' Era." In *Skin Deep: How Race and Complexion Matter the "Color-Blind" Era*, edited by C. Herring, Keith, and H. D. Horton, 1–21. Chicago: University of Illinois.

Herrnstein, Richard J., and Charles Murray. 199 *Bell Curve: Intelligence and Class Structure American Life.* New York: Free Press.

Hertz, Tom. 2005. "Rags, Riches and Race: T Intergenerational Economic Mobility of Bla and White Families in the United States." *Unequal Chances: Family Background a Economic Success*, edited by Samuel Bowl Herbert Gintis, and M. O. Groves, 165–19 New York: Russell Sage and Princeton Univsity Press.

Hess, Beth B., and Myra Marx Ferree. 1985. *Co troversy and Coalition: The New Femin Movement.* Boston: Twayne.

Higley, John, and Gwen Moore. 1981. "Elite In gration in the United States and Australi *American Political Science Review* 75 (581–597.

Hill, Mark E. 2000. "Color Differences in the Socio-economic Status of African American Men: Results of a Longitudinal Study." *Social Forces* 78 (4): 1437–1460.

Hill, Mark E. 2002. "Race of the Interviewer and Perception of Skin Color: Evidence from the Multi-City Study of Urban Inequality." *American Sociological Review* 67: 99–108.

Hipp, John R. 2007. "Income Inequality, Race, and Place: Does the Distribution of Race and Class within Neighborhoods Affect Crime Rates?" *Criminology* 45 (3): 665–697.

Hirsh, C. Elizabeth, and Sabino Kornrich. 2008. "The Context of Discrimination: Workplace Conditions, Institutional Environments, and Sex and Race Discrimination Charges." *American Journal of Sociology* 113: 1394–1432.

Hirshfield, Laura E., and Tiffany D. Joseph. 2012. "'We Need a Woman, We Need a Black Woman': Gender, Race, and Identity Taxation in the Academy." *Gender and Education* 24 (2): 213–227.

Hirschfield, Paul J. 2015. "Lethal Policing: Making Sense of American Exceptionalism." *Sociological Forum* 30 (4): 1109–1117.

Koch, Charles. 1987. "A Brief History of the Homeless Problem in the United States." In *Brief History of the Homeless Problem in the United States*, edited by R. D. Bingham, R. E. Green, and S. B. White, 16–32. Newbury Park, CA: Sage.

Hochschild, Jennifer L. 1981. *What's Fair? American Beliefs about Distributive Justice*. Cambridge, MA: Harvard University Press.

Hochschild, Jennifer L. 2003. "Social Class in Public Schools." *Journal of Social Issues* 59 (4): 821–840.

Hochschild, Jennifer L., and Vesla Weaver. 2007. "The Skin Color Paradox and the American Racial Order." *Social Forces* 86 (2): 643–670.

Hodge, Robert W., Paul M. Siegel, and Peter H. Rossi. 1964. "Occupational Prestige in the United States, 1925–63." *American Journal of Sociology* 70: 286–302.

Hodson, Randy, and Robert L. Kaufman. 1982. "Economic Dualism: A Critical Review." *American Sociological Review* 47: 727–739.

Hogler, Raymond L. 2015. *The End of American Labor Unions: The Right-to-Work Movement and the Erosion of Collective Bargaining*. Santa Barbara, CA: Praeger.

Hogler, Raymond L., Herbert G. Hunt, and Stephan Weiler. 2015. "Killing Unions with Culture: Institutions, Inequality, and the Effects of Labor's Decline in the United States." *Employee Responsibilities and Rights Journal* 27 (1): 63–79.

Hojnacki, Marie, David C. Kimball, Frank R. Baumgartner, Jeffrey M. Berry, and Beth L. Leech. 2012. "Studying Organizational Advocacy and Influence: Reexamining Interest Group Research." *Annual Review of Political Science* 15 (1): 379–399.

Hole, Judith, and Ellen Levine. 1975. "The First Feminists." In *Women: A Feminist Perspective*, edited by Jo Freeman, 436–447. Palo Alto, CA: Mayfield.

Holmes, Malcolm D., and Judith A. Antell. 2001. "The Social Construction of American Indian Drinking: Perceptions of American Indian and White Officials." *Sociological Quarterly* 42 (2): 151–173.

Holmes, William C., and Gail B. Slap. 1998. "Sexual Abuse of Boys: Definition, Prevalence, Correlates, Sequelae, and Management." *Jama* 280 (21): 1855–1862.

Holtfreter, Kristy, Shanna Van Slyke, Jason Bratton, and Marc Gertz. 2008. "Public Perceptions of White-Collar Crime and Punishment." *Journal of Criminal Justice* 36 (1): 50–60.

Hoobler, Jenny M., Grace Lemmon, and Sandy J. Wayne. 2014. "Women's Managerial Aspirations: An Organizational Development Perspective." *Journal of Management* 40 (3): 703–730.

hooks, bell. 1981. *Ain't I a Woman: Black Women and Feminism*. Boston: South End Press.

Hooks, Janet Montgomery. 1947. *Women's Occupations through Seven Decades*. Washington, D.C.: U.S. Government Printing Office.

Hopkins, Daniel J. 2009. "Partisan Reinforcement and the Poor: The Impact of Context on Explanations for Poverty." Social Science Quarterly 90 (3): 744–764.

Horowitz, Juliana Menasce. 2013. "Americans Less Accepting of Homosexuality than Other Westerners— Religion May Be One Reason." Pew Research Center. June 12. Available at http://www.pewresearch.org/fact-tank/2013/06/12/americans-are-less-accepting-of-homosexuality-than-canadians-western-europeans-and-religion-may-be-one-explanation.

Horrigan, Michael W., and Steven E. Haugen. 1988. "Declining Middle-Class Thesis: A Sensitivity Analysis." *Monthly Labor Review* 111: 3.

Horwitz, Suzanne R., Kristin Shutts, and Kristina R. Olson. 2014. "Social Class Differences Produce Social Group Preferences." *Developmental Science* 17 (6): 991–1002.

Hout, Michael. 1986. "Opportunity and the Minority Middle Class: A Comparison of Blacks in the United States and Catholics in Northern Ireland." *American Sociological Review* 51: 214–223.

Hout, Michael. 1988. "More Universalism, Less Structural Mobility: The American Occupational Structure in the 1980s." *American Journal of Sociology* 93: 1358–1400.

Hout, Michael. 2007. "How Class Works: Objective and Subjective Aspects of Class since the 1970s." Berkeley, CA: Survey Research Center.

Howard, Adam. 2008. *Learning Privilege: Lessons of Power and Identity in Affluent Schooling.* New York: Routledge.

Howell, Babe. 2009. "Broken Lives from Broken Windows: The Hidden Costs of Aggressive Order-Maintenance Policing." *New York University Review of Law & Social Change* 33: 271–329.

Hoynes, Hilary W. 2014. "A Revolution in Poverty Policy." *Pathways* Summer: 23–27.

Huber, Joan. 1982. "Toward a Sociotechnological Theory of the Women's Movement." In *Women and Work: Problems and Perspectives*, edited by Rachel Kahn-Hut, Arlene Kaplan Daniels, and Richard Colvard, 24–38. New York: Oxford University Press.

Huber, Joan. 1988. "From Sugar and Spice to Professor." In *Down to Earth Sociology: Introductory Readings*, edited by J. M. Henslin, 92–101. New York: The Free Press.

HUD. 2011. "American Healthy Homes Survey: Lead and Arsenic Findings." Washington, D.C.: U.S. Department of Housing and Urban Development, Office of Healthy Homes and Lead Hazard Control.

Huddleston, Tom. 2015. "5 Pope Francis Quotes on Capitalism, Inequality, Poverty." *Fortune.* September 14. Available at http://fortune.com/2015/09/14/pope-francis-capitalism-inequality.

Huddy, Leonie, Francis K. Neely, and Marilyn R. Lafay. 2000. "The Polls—Trends: Support for the Women's Movement." *Public Opinion Quarterly* 64: 309–350.

Hudson, Darrell L., H. W. Neighbors, A. T. Geronimus, and J. S. Jackson. 2012. "The Relationship between Socioeconomic Position and Depression among a U.S. Nationally Representative Sample of African Americans." *Social Psychiatry and Psychiatric Epidemiology* 47 (3): 373–381.

Hudson, Kenneth. 2007. "The New Labor Market Segmentation: Labor Market Dualism in the New Economy." *Social Science Research* 36 (1): 286–312.

Huff, Daniel D., and David A. Johnson. 1993. "Phantom Welfare: Public Relief for Corporate America." *Social Work* 38 (3): 311–316.

Hughes, Melissa K. 2003. "Through the Looking Glass: Racial Jokes, Social Context, and the Reasonable Person in Hostile Work Environment Analysis." *Southern California Law Review* 76: 1437.

Hughes, Michael, K. Jill Kiecolt, Verna M. Keith, and David H. Demo. 2015. "Racial Identity and Well-Being among African Americans." *Social Psychology Quarterly* 78 (1): 25–48.

Huguet, Nathalie, Mark S. Kaplan, and David Feeny. 2008. "Socioeconomic Status and Health-Related Quality of Life among Elderly People: Results from the Joint Canada/United States Survey of Health." *Social Science & Medicine* 66 (4): 803–810.

Hull, Kathleen E., and Robert L. Nelson. 2000. "Assimilation, Choice, or Constraint? Testing Theories of Gender Differences in the Careers of Lawyers." *Social Forces* 79 (1): 229–264.

Human Rights Campaign. 2015a. "An Overview of Federal Rights Granted to Married Couples." Human Rights Campaign. Available at http://www.hrc.org/resources/an-overview-of-federal-rights-and-protections-granted-to-married-couples.

Human Rights Campaign. 2015b. "Maps of State Laws and Policies." Human Rights Campaign. Available at http://www.hrc.org/state_maps.

Human Rights Watch. 2011. "Historic Decision at the United Nations." Human Rights Watch. June 17. Available at https://www.hrw.org/news/2011/06/17/historic-decision-united-nations.

Hunnicutt, Gwen, and Gary LaFree. 2008. "Reassessing the Structural Covariates of Cross-National Infant Homicide Victimization." *Homicide Studies* 12 (1): 46–66.

Hunt, Matthew O. 2002. "Religion, Race/Ethnicity, and Beliefs about Poverty." *Social Science Quarterly* 83 (3): 810–831.

Hunt, Matthew O. 2004. "Race/Ethnicity and Beliefs about Wealth and Poverty." *Social Science Quarterly* 85 (3): 827–853.

Hunt, Matthew O. 2007. "African American, Hispanic, and White Beliefs about Black/White Inequality, 1977–2004." *American Sociological Review* 72 (3): 390–415.

Hurst, Charles E., and David L. McConnell. 2010. *An Amish Paradox: Diversity and Change in the World's Largest Amish Community*. Baltimore: John Hopkins University.

Hutchinson, Darren Lenard. 2001. "Identity Crisis: Intersectionality, Multidimensionality, and the Development of an Adequate Theory of Subordination." *Michigan Journal of Race and Law* 6: 285.

Hyman, Paula E. 2009. "Eastern European Immigrants in the United States." Jewish Women: A Comprehensive Historical Encyclopedia. Brookline, MA: Jewish Women's Archive. Available at http://jwa.org/encyclopedia/article/eastern-european-immigrants-in-united-states.

Ibarra, Peter R., and John I. Kitsuse. 2003. "Claims-Making Discourse and Vernacular Resources." In *Challenges and Choices: Constructionist Perspectives on Social Problems*, edited by J. A. Hostein and G. Miller, 17–50. Hawthorne, NY: Aldine de Gruyter.

Iceland, John, Gregory Sharp, and Jeffrey M. Timberlake. 2013. "Sun Belt Rising: Regional Population Change and the Decline in Black Residential Segregation, 1970–2009." *Demography* 50 (1): 97–123.

IHEP. 2011. "Portraits: Initial College Attendance of Low-Income Young Adults." Washington, D.C.: Institute for Higher Education Policy. Available at http://www.ihep.org/sites/default/files/uploads/docs/pubs/portraits-low-income_young_adults_attendance_brief_final_june_2011.pdf.

Ingraham, Christopher. 2015. "Anti-Muslim Hate Crimes Are Still Five Times More Common Today Than before 9/11." *Washington Post*, February 11. Available at http://www.washingtonpost.com/news/wonkblog/wp/2015/02/11/anti-muslim-hate-crimes-are-still-five-times-more-common-today-than-before-911.

Ingraham, Christopher. 2016. "This Is How Toxic Flint's Water Really Is." *Washington Post*, January 15. Available at https://www.washingtonpost.com/news/wonk/wp/2016/01/15/this-is-how-toxic-flints-water-really-is/?tid=sm_fb.

Inkeles, Alex, and David H. Smith. 1974. *Becoming Modern: Individual Change in Six Developing Countries*. Cambridge, MA: Harvard University Press.

Institute for Policy Studies. 2015. "Facts and Figures in 99 to 1." Inequality.org: A Project of the Institute for Policy Studies. Available at http://inequality.org/99to1/facts-figures.

IRS. 2012. "IRS Releases New Tax Gap Estimates; Compliance Rates Remain Statistically Unchanged From Previous Study." Internal Revenue Service. https://www.irs.gov/uac/IRS-Releases-New-Tax-Gap-Estimates%3B-Compliance-Rates-Remain-Statistically-Unchanged-From-Previous-Study.

Irvine, Martha. 2005. "Youth Still Pushing Boundaries of Gender." *Akron Beacon Journal*, October 2, p. A5.

Isaac, Larry. 2008. "Movement of Movements: Culture Moves in the Long Civil Rights Struggle." *Social Forces* 87 (1): 33–63.

Isaacs, Julia B., Isabel V. Sawhill, and Ron Haskins. 2008. "Getting Ahead or Losing Ground: Economic Mobility in America." Washington, D.C.: Brookings Institution.

Jackall, Robert. 1988. "Moral Mazes: The World of Corporate Managers." *International Journal of Politics, Culture, and Society* 1 (4): 598–614.

Jackman, Mary R., and Robert W. Jackman. 1983. *Class Awareness in the United States*. University of California Press.

Jackson, Elton F., and Harry J. Crockett Jr. 1964. "Occupational Mobility in the United States: A Point Estimate and Trend Comparison." *American Sociological Review* 29: 5–15.

Jackson, Peter A. 2009. "Capitalism and Global Queering: National Markets, Parallels among Sexual Cultures, and Multiple Queer Modernities." *GLQ: A Journal of Lesbian and Gay Studies* 15 (3): 357–395.

Jacobs, David, and Amber M. Richardson. 2008. "Economic Inequality and Homicide in the Developed Nations from 1975 to 1995." *Homicide Studies* 12 (1): 28–45.

Jacobs, David, Zhenchao Qian, Jason T. Carmichael, and Stephanie L. Kent. 2007. "Who

Survives on Death Row? An Individual and Contextual Analysis." *American Sociological Review* 72: 610–632.

Jahoda, Andrew, Alastair Wilson, Kirsten Stalker, and Anja Cairney. 2010. "Living with Stigma and the Self-Perceptions of People with Mild Intellectual Disabilities." *Journal of Social Issues* 66 (3): 521–534.

Jaumotte, Florence, Subir Lall, and Chris Papageorgiou. 2013. "Rising Income Inequality: Technology, or Trade and Financial Globalization" *IMF Economic Review* 61 (2): 271–309.

Jencks, Christopher. 1992. *Rethinking Social Policy: Race, Poverty, and the Underclass*. Cambridge, MA: Harvard University Press.

Jenkins, J. Craig, and Craig M. Eckert. 1986. "Channeling Black Insurgency: Elite Patronage and Professional Social Movement Organizations in the Development of the Black Movement." *American Sociological Review* 51: 812–829.

Jenny, Carole, Thomas A. Roesler, and Kimberly L. Poyer. 1994. "Are Children at Risk for Sexual Abuse by Homosexuals?" *Pediatrics* 94 (1): 41–44.

Johns, Andrew, and Joel Slemrod. 2010. "The Distribution of Income Tax Noncompliance." *National Tax Journal* 63 (3): 397–418.

Johnson, Carey V., Matthew J. Mimiaga, and Judith Bradford. 2008. "Health Care Issues among Lesbian, Gay, Bisexual, Transgender and Intersex (LGBTI) Populations in the United States: Introduction." *Journal of Homosexuality* 54 (3): 213–224.

Johnson, Jennifer. 2002. *Getting By on the Minimum: The Lives of Working Class Women*. New York: Routledge.

Johnston, Angus. 2016. "American Student Protest Timeline, 2014–15." Available at http://studentactivism.net/2014/12/04/american-student-protest-timeline-2014-15/.

Jones, Jeffrey M. 2015a. "Majority in U.S. Now Say Gays and Lesbians Born, Not Made." Gallup.com. May 20. Available at http://www.gallup.com/poll/183332/majority-say-gays-lesbians-born-not-made.aspx.

Jones, Jeffrey M. 2015b. "In U.S., Confidence in Police Lowest in 22 Years." Gallup.com. June 19. Available at http://www.gallup.com/poll/183704/confidence-police-lowest-years.aspx.

Jones, Woodrow, Jr., and K. Robert Keiser. 1987. "Issue Visibility and the Effects of PAC Money." *Social Science Quarterly* 68: 170–176.

Jong-Sung, You, and Sanjeev Khagram. 2005. "A Comparative Study of Inequality and Corruption." *American Sociological Review* 70 (1): 136–157.

Jonsson, Jan O., David B. Grusky, Matthew D Carlo, Reinhard Pollak, and Mary C. Brinton. 2009. "Microclass Mobility: Social Reproduction in Four Countries." *American Journal o Sociology* 114 (4): 977–1036.

Jordahl, Henrick. 2007. *Inequality and Trust*. IFI Working Paper. No. 715. Stockholm: Research Institute of Industrial Economics.

Journal of Blacks in Higher Education. 2006. "Black Student College Graduation Rate Remain Low, But Modest Progress Begin to Show." Available at http://www.jbhe. com/features/50_blackstudent_gradrate. html.

Jurs, Mike. 2015. "How Much Is the Right t Marry Worth When It Comes to Social Security?" Financial Engines. June 9. Available http://blog.financialengines.com/2015/06/0 marriage-equality-and-social-security.

Kabeer, Naila. 2004. "Globalization, Labor Standards, and Women's Rights: Dilemmas of Collective (in) Action in an Interdependent World Feminist Economics 10 (1): 3–35.

Kahlenberg, Richard. 2010. "Elite Colleges, Colleges for the Elite?" *New York Times*, September 30, p. A39.

Kahn, Joan R., and Leonard I. Pearlin. 2006. "Financial Strain over the Life Course and Heal among Older Adults." *Journal of Health ar Social Behavior* 47 (1): 17–31.

Kaiser Family Foundation. 2015a. "Mortality Rat in the U.S. Compared to Other Countri Slideshow." The Henry J. Kaiser Family Fou dation. Available at http://kff.org/slidesho mortality-rates-in-the-u-s-compared-to-othe countries-slideshow.

Kaiser Family Foundation. 2015b. "Key Facts abo the Uninsured Population." The Henry J. Ka ser Family Foundation, October 5. Available http://kff.org/uninsured/fact-sheet/ke facts-about-the-uninsured-population.

Kalev, Alexandra. 2009. "Cracking the Gla Cages? Restructuring and Ascriptive Inequa ity at Work." *American Journal of Sociolo* 114 (6): 1591–1643.

Kallick, David Dyssegaard. 1994. "Toward a N Unionism." *Social Policy* 25: 2–6.

Kalogeras, Steven, and Marc Mauer. 2003. *Annotated Bibliography: Racial Disparities in the Criminal Justice System.* Washington, D.C.: Sentencing Project.

Kane, Emily W. 2006. "'No Way My Boys Are Going to Be Like That!' Parents' Responses to Children's Gender Nonconformity." *Gender & Society* 20 (2): 149–176.

Kansal, Tushar, and Marc Mauer. 2005. *Racial Disparity in Sentencing: A Review of the Literature.* Washington, D.C.: Sentencing Project.

Kanter, Rosabeth Moss. 1977a. *Men and Women of the Corporation.* New York: Basic Books.

Kanter, Rosabeth Moss. 1977b. "Some Effects of Proportions on Group Life: Skewed Sex Ratios and Responses to Token Women." *American Journal of Sociology* 82: 965–990.

Kantor, Jodi. 2006. "On the Job, Nursing Mothers Find a 2-Class System." *New York Times*, p. 1.

Karpoff, Jonathan M., D. Scott Lee, and Gerald S. Martin. 2008. "The Cost to Firms of Cooking the Books." *Journal of Financial and Quantitative Analysis* 43 (3): 581–612.

Katz, Jonathan Ned. 2004. "'Homosexual' and 'Heterosexual.'" In *Sexualities: Identities, Behaviors, and Society*, edited by M. S. Kimmel and R. F. Plante, 44–46. New York: Oxford University Press.

Katz, Michael B. 1996. *In the Shadow of the Poorhouse: A Social History of Welfare in America.* New York: Basic Books.

Katz, Michael B. 2013. *The Undeserving Poor: America's Enduring Confrontation With Poverty.* 2nd ed. New York: Oxford University Press.

Katz, Vikki. 2014. "Children as Brokers of Their Immigrant Families' Health-Care Connections." *Social Problems* 61 (2): 194–215.

Kaya, Yunus. 2010. "Globalization and Industrialization in 64 Developing Countries, 1980–2003." *Social Forces* 88 (3): 1153–1182.

Kaye, H. Stephen. 2010. "The Impact of the 2007–09 Recession on Workers with Disabilities." *Monthly Labor Review* 133 (10): 19–30.

Kearney, Melissa Schettini, and Phillip B. Levine. 2012. "Why Is the Teen Birth Rate in the United States so High and Why Does It Matter?" National Bureau of Economic Research. Available at http://www.nber.org/papers/w17965.

Keister, Lisa A. 2014. "The One Percent." *Annual Review of Sociology* 40 (1): 347–367.

Keister, Lisa A., and Stephanie Moller. 2000. "Wealth Inequality in the United States." *Annual Review of Sociology* 26: 63–81.

Keller, Suzanne. 1987. "Social Differentiation and Social Stratification: The Special Case of Gender." In *Structured Social Inequality*, edited by Celia S. Heller, 329–349. New York: MacMillan.

Kelley, Jonathan, and Mariah D. R. Evans. 1993. "The Legitimation of Inequality: Occupational Earnings in Nine Nations." *American Journal of Sociology* 99: 75–125.

Kelling, George L., and James Q. Wilson. 1982. "Broken Windows: The Police and Neighborhood Safety." *Atlantic* 249 (3): 29–38.

Kelly, Erin L., Phyllis Moen, J. Michael Oakes, Wen Fan, Cassandra Okechukwu, Kelly D. Davis, Leslie B. Hammer, Ellen Ernst Kossek, Rosalind Berkowitz King, and Ginger C. Hanson. 2014. "Changing Work and Work-Family Conflict Evidence from the Work, Family, and Health Network." *American Sociological Review* 79 (3): 485–516.

Kelly, Maura. 2010. "Regulating the Reproduction and Mothering of Poor Women: The Controlling Image of the Welfare Mother in Television News Coverage of Welfare Reform." *Journal of Poverty* 14 (1): 76–96.

Kendall, Diana Elizabeth. 2002. *The Power of Good Deeds: Privileged Women and the Social Reproduction of the Upper Class.* Lanham, MD: Rowman & Littlefield.

Kendall, Diana Elizabeth. 2011. *Framing Class: Media Representations of Wealth and Poverty in America.* Lanham, MD: Rowman & Littlefield.

Kentor, Jeffrey. 1998. "The Long-Term Effects of Foreign Investment Dependence on Economic Growth, 1940–1990." *American Journal of Sociology* 103 (4): 1024–1046.

Kenworthy, Lane. 2009. "Tax Myths." *Contexts* 8 (3): 28–32.

Kerbo, Harold R. 1983. *Social Stratification and Inequality.* New York: McGraw-Hill.

Kerrissey, Jasmine, and Evan Schofer. 2013. "Union Membership and Political Participation in the United States." *Social Forces* 91 (3): 895–928.

Kessler Foundation. 2015. "National Employment and Disability Survey: Report of Main Findings." West Orange, NJ: Kessler Foundation.

Kessler-Harris, Alice. 2003. *Out to Work: A History of Wage-Earning Women in the United States.* New York: Oxford University Press.

Khan, Shamus Rhaman. 2012. "The Sociology of Elites." *Annual Review of Sociology* 38 (1): 361–377.

Kiely, Ray. 2004. "The World Bank and 'Global Poverty Reduction': Good Policies or Bad Data?" *Journal of Contemporary Asia* 34 (1): 3–20.

Kim, ChangHwan, and Arthur Sakamoto. 2014. "The Earnings of Less Educated Asian American Men: Educational Selectivity and the Model Minority Image." *Social Problems* 61 (2): 283–304.

King, Brayden G., and Marie Cornwall. 2007. "The Gender Logic of Executive Compensation." Paper presented at Annual Meeting of American Sociological Association, August 11–14, New York.

King, C. Richard, and Charles Fruehling Springwood, eds. 2001. *Team Spirits: The Native American Mascots Controversy.* Lincoln: University of Nebraska Press.

King, Deborah K. 1988. "Multiple Jeopardy, Multiple Consciousness: The Context of a Black Feminist Ideology." *Signs* 14: 42–72.

King, Martin Luther, Jr. 1958. *Stride toward Freedom: The Montgomery Story.* New York: Harper & Row.

King, Michael, Joanna Semlyen, Sharon S. Tai, Helen Killaspy, David Osborn, Dmitri Popelyuk, and Irwin Nazareth. 2008. "A Systematic Review of Mental Disorder, Suicide, and Deliberate Self Harm in Lesbian, Gay and Bisexual People." *BMC Psychiatry* 8 (1): 70.

King, Ryan D., Steven F. Messner, and Robert D. Baller. 2009. "Contemporary Hate Crimes, Law Enforcement, and the Legacy of Racial Violence." *American Sociological Review* 74 (2): 291–315.

Kirby, James B., and Toshiko Kaneda. 2005. "Neighborhood Socioeconomic Disadvantage and Access to Health Care." *Journal of Health and Social Behavior* 46 (1): 15–31.

Kirby, Vicki. 2006. *Judith Butler: Live Theory.* New York: Continuum.

Kite, Mary E., and Bernard E. Whitley Jr. 1998. "Do Heterosexual Women and Men Differ in Their Attitudes toward Homosexuality? A Conceptual and Methodological Analysis." In *Psychological Perspectives on Lesbians and Gay Issues: Stigma and Sexual Orientation,* edited by G. Herek, 39–61. Thousand Oaks, CA: Sage.

Klawitter, Marieka M., and Victor Flatt. 1998. "The Effects of State and Local Antidiscrimination Policies on Earnings for Gays and Lesbians." *Journal of Policy Analysis and Management* 17 (4): 658–686.

Klein, Rebecca. 2013. "Brothers Kicked Out of School After Becoming Homeless." *Huffington Post.* December 17. Available at http://www.huffingtonpost.com/2013/12/17/homeless-students-easton-schools_n_4459026.html.

Kleiner, Sibyl, and Eliza K. Pavalko. 2014. "Double Time: Is Health Affected by a Spouse's Time at Work?" *Social Forces* 92 (3): 983–1007.

Kliff, Sarah. 2015. "Only 18 Percent of Americans Consider Themselves Feminists." Vox. April 8. Available at http://www.vox.com/2015/4/8/8372417/feminist-gender-equality-poll.

Kluegel, James R., and Eliot R. Smith. 1986. *Beliefs about Inequality: Americans' Views of What Is and What Ought to Be.* New York: Transaction

Kmec, Julie A. 2003. "Minority Job Concentration and Wages." *Social Problems* 50 (1): 38–59.

Knight, Kyle. 2015. "Dispatches: A Blueprint for Transgender Rights in Asia." Human Rights Watch. October 8. Available at https://www.hrw.org/news/ 2015/10/08/dispatches-blueprint-transgender- rights-asia.

Kochel, Tammy Rinehart, David B. Wilson, and Stephen D. Mastrofski. 2011. "Effect of Suspect Race on Officers' Arrest Decisions." *Criminology* 49 (2): 473–512.

Kochhar, Rakesh, and Richard Fry. 2014. "Wealth Inequality Has Widened along Racial, Ethnic Lines since End of Great Recession." Pew Research Center. December 12. Available a http://www.pewresearch.org/fact-tank/2014 12/12/racial-wealth-gaps-great-recession.

Kochhar, Rakesh, Richard Fry, and Paul Taylor. 2011 "Wealth Gaps Rise to Record Highs between Whites, Blacks, Hispanics." Pew Research Center's Social & Demographic Trends Project. July 26. Available at http://www.pewsocialtrends org/2011/07/26/wealth-gaps-rise-to-record highs-between-whites-blacks-hispanics.

Kofman, Eleonore, and Parvati Raghuram. 2015 *Gendered Migrations and Global Social Reproduction.* New York: Palgrave Macmillan

Kolenda, Pauline. 1985. *Caste in Contemporary India: Beyond Organic Solidarity*. Reissued. Prospect Heights, IL: Waveland.

Kolhatkar, Sheelah. 2015. "Has It Become Impossible to Prosecute White-Collar Crime?" *Bloomberg.com*. October 21. Available at http://www.bloomberg.com/news/articles/2015-10-21/has-it-become-impossible-to-prosecute-white-collar-crime-.

Kosciw, Joseph G., Emily A. Greytak, Neal A. Palmer, and Madelyn J. Boesen. 2014. "2013 National School Climate Survey: The Experiences of Lesbian, Gay, Bisexual and Transgender Youth in Our Nation's Schools." New York: GLSEN.

Kotkin, Joel. 2010. "Ready Set Grow." *Smithsonian Magazine*, August.

Kposowa, Augustine J., Kevin D. Breault, and Beatrice M. Harrison. 1995. "Reassessing the Structural Covariates of Violent and Property Crimes in the USA: A County Level Analysis." *British Journal of Sociology* 46: 79–105.

Kraus, Michael W., Stéphane Côté, and Dacher Keltner. 2010. "Social Class, Contextualism, and Empathic Accuracy." *Psychological Science* 21 (11): 1716–1723.

Kraus, Michael W., Paul K. Piff, and Dacher Keltner. 2011. "Social Class as Culture: The Convergence of Resources and Rank in the Social Realm." *Current Directions in Psychological Science* 20 (4): 246–250.

Kreidl, Martin. 2000. "What Makes Inequalities Legitimate? An International Comparison." *Czech Sociological Review*, no. 8: 9–54.

Kriesberg, Louis. 1979. *Social Inequality*. Englewood Cliffs, NJ: Prentice-Hall.

Krogstad, Jens Manuel, and Ana Gonzalez-Barrera. 2014. "Hispanics Split on How to Address Surge in Central American Child Migrants." Pew Research Center. July 29. Available at http://www.pewresearch.org/fact-tank/2014/07/29/hispanics-split-on-how-to-address-surge-in-central-american-child-migrants.

Krogstad, Jens Manuel, and Richard Fry. 2014. "More Hispanics, Blacks Enrolling in College, but Lag in Bachelor's Degrees." Pew Research Center. April 24. Available at http://www.pewresearch.org/fact-tank/2014/04/24/more-hispanics-blacks-enrolling-in-college-but-lag-in-bachelors-degrees.

Krogstad, Jens Manuel, and Mark Hugo Lopez. 2014. "Hispanic Nativity Shift." Pew Research Center's Hispanic Trends Project, April 29. Available at http://www.pewhispanic.org/2014/04/29/hispanic-nativity-shift.

Krogstad, Jens Manuel, and Jeffrey S. Passel. 2015. "5 Facts about Illegal Immigration in the U.S." Pew Research Center, November 19. Available at http://www.pewresearch.org/fact-tank/2014/11/18/5-facts-about-illegal-immigration-in-the-u-s.

Kromm, Jane E. 1994. "The Feminization of Madness in Visual Representation." *Feminist Studies* 20 (3): 507–535.

Krugman, Paul, and Anthony J. Venables. 1995. "Globalization and the Inequality of Nations." Cambridge, MA: National Bureau of Economic Research.

Krymkowski, Daniel H., and Beth Mintz. 2008. "What Types of Occupations Are Women Entering? Determinants of Changes in Female Representation: 1970–2000." *Research in Social Stratification and Mobility* 26 (1): 1–14.

Kubrin, Charis E., and Tim Wadsworth. 2009. "Explaining Suicide Among Blacks and Whites: How Socioeconomic Factors and Gun Availability Affect Race-Specific Suicide Rates." *Social Science Quarterly* 90 (5): 1203–1227.

Kurgan, Laura, and Eric Cadora. 2006. "Million Dollar Blocks." Spacial Information Design Lab, Columbia University. Available at http://spatialinformationdesignlab.org/projects/million-dollar-blocks.

Kusserow, Adrie. 2012. "When Hard and Soft Clash: Class-Based Individualisms in Manhattan and Queens." In *Facing Social Class: How Societal Rank Influences Interaction*, edited by Susan T. Fiske and Hazel Rose Markus, 195–215. New York: Russell Sage Foundation.

Kutner, Jenny. 2015. "Transgender Teen Leelah Alcorn's Death Ruled a Suicide—Mother Threw Away Handwritten Note." *Salon*. April 30. Available at http://www.salon.com/2015/04/30/transgender_teen_leelah_alcorns_death_ruled_a_suicide_mother_threw_away_handwritten_note.

Kwon, Hyun Soo. 2014. "Economic Theories of Low-Wage Work." *Journal of Human Behavior in the Social Environment* 24 (1): 61–70.

Lahood, Grant. 2012. *Intersexion—A Feature Documentary*. Documentary. Ponsonby Productions Limited. Available at http://www.intersexionfilm.com.

Lambda Legal. 2015. "FAQ about Identity Documents." Lambda Legal: Know Your Rights. Available at http://www.lambdalegal.org/know-your-rights/transgender/identity-document-faq.

Lamont, Michèle. 2001. "The Dignity of Working Men: Morality and the Boundaries of Race, Class, and Immigration." *Symbolic Interaction* 24 (4): 505–508.

LaMontagne, Christina. 2014. "NerdWallet Health Finds Medical Bankruptcy Accounts for Majority of Personal Bankruptcies," *NerdWallet*. March 26. Available at http://www.nerdwallet.com/blog/health/2014/03/26/medical-bankruptcy.

Landry, Bart, and Kris Marsh. 2011. "The Evolution of the New Black Middle Class." *Annual Review of Sociology* 37 (1): 373–394.

Lareau, Annette. 2003. *Unequal Childhoods*. Berkeley: University of California Press.

Laserna, Charlyn M., Yi-Tai Seih, and James W. Pennebaker. 2014. "Um... Who Like Says You Know: Filler Word Use as a Function of Age, Gender, and Personality." *Journal of Language and Social Psychology* 33 (3): 328–338.

Laslett, John H. M. 1987. "The American Tradition of Labor Theory and Its Relevance to the Contemporary Working Class." In *Theories of the Labor Movement*, edited by S. Larson and B. Nissen, 359–378. Detroit, MI: Wayne State University Press.

Latimer, Melissa. 2008. "A View from the Bottom: Former Welfare Recipients Evaluate the System." *Journal of Poverty* 12 (1): 77–101.

Latkin, Carl A., and Aaron D. Curry. 2003. "Stressful Neighborhoods and Depression: A Prospective Study of the Impact of Neighborhood Disorder." *Journal of Health and Social Behavior* 44: 34–44.

Lau, Holning, and Rebecca L. Stotzer. 2011. "Employment Discrimination Based on Sexual Orientation: A Hong Kong Study." *Employee Responsibilities and Rights Journal* 23 (1): 17–35.

Laufer, William S. 2014. "Where Is the Moral Indignation Over Corporate Crime?" In *Regulating Corporate Criminal Liability*, edited by Dominik Brodowski, Manuel Espinoza de los Monteros de la Parr, Klaus Tiedemann, and Joachim Vogel, 19–31. Cham, Switzerland: Springer International. Available at http://link.springer.com/10.1007/978-3-319-05993-8_3.

Leaf, Clifton. 2002. "White-Collar Criminals: They Lie, They Cheat, They Steal, and They've Been Getting Away with It for Too Long." *Fortune*, March 18.

Leaper, Campbell, and Diana M. Arias. 2011. "College Women's Feminist Identity: A Multidimensional Analysis with Implications for Coping with Sexism." *Sex Roles* 64 (7–8): 475–490.

Lee, Barrett A., and Meredith J. Greif. 2008. "Homelessness and Hunger." *Journal of Health and Social Behavior* 49 (1): 3–19.

Lee, Barrett A., Kimberly A. Tyler, and James D. Wright. 2010. "The New Homelessness Revisited." *Annual Review of Sociology* 36: 501–521.

Lee, Cheol-Sung, Francois Nielsen, and Arthur S. Alderson. 2007. "Income Inequality, Global Economy and the State." *Social Forces* 86 (1): 77–111.

Lee, Jennifer, and Frank D. Bean. 2004. "America's Changing Color Lines: Immigration, Race/Ethnicity, and Multiracial Identification." *Annual Review of Sociology* 30: 221–242.

Lee, Matthew R., and Tim Slack. 2008. "Labor Market Conditions and Violent Crime across the Metro–Nonmetro Divide." *Social Science Research* 37 (3): 753–768.

Leftwich, Richard H., and David M. Gordon. 1977. "Personal Income and Marginal Productivity." In *Problems in Political Economy: An Urban Perspective*, edited by David M. Gordon, 78–81. Lexington, MA: D.C. Heath.

Lehmann, Jennifer M. 1995. "The Question of Caste in Modern Society: Durkheim's Contradictory Theories of Race, Class, and Sex." *American Sociological Review* 60: 566–585.

Leibbrandt, Andreas, and John A. List. 2015. "Do Women Avoid Salary Negotiations? Evidence from a Large-Scale Natural Field Experiment." *Management Science* 61 (9): 2016–2024.

Leicht, Kevin, and Scott T. Fitzgerald. 2006. *Postindustrial Peasants: The Illusion of Middle-Class Prosperity*. New York: Worth.

Lengermann, Patricia Madoo, and Jill Niebrugge Brantley. 1988. "Contemporary Feminist Theory." In *Contemporary Sociological Theory*, edited by George Ritzer, 282–325. New York: Knopf.

Lens, Vicki. 2002. "TANF: What Went Wrong and What to Do Next." *Social Work* 47 (3): 279–290.

Lenski, Gerhard. 1988. "Rethinking Macrosociological Theory." *American Sociological Review* 53: 163–171.

Lensmire, Timothy, Shannon McManimon, Jessica Dockter Tierney, Mary Lee-Nichols, Zachary Casey, Audrey Lensmire, and Bryan Davis. 2013. "McIntosh as Synecdoche: How Teacher Education's Focus on White Privilege Undermines Antiracism." *Harvard Educational Review* 83 (3): 410–431.

Leslie, Sarah-Jane, Andrei Cimpian, Meredith Meyer, and Edward Freeland. 2015. "Expectations of Brilliance Underlie Gender Distributions across Academic Disciplines." *Science* 347 (6219): 262–265.

Lester, James P., David W. Allen, and Kelly M. Hill. 2001. *Environmental Injustice in the United States: Myths and Realities*. Boulder, CO: Westview Press.

Levine, Steven B. 1980. "The Rise of American Boarding Schools and the Development of a National Upper Class." *Social Problems* 28: 63–94.

Levy, Jenna. 2015. "In U.S., Uninsured Rate Dips to 11.9% in First Quarter." Gallup.com. April 13. Available at http://www.gallup.com/poll/182348/uninsured-rate-dips-first-quarter.aspx.

Lewis, Amanda E. 2004. "What Group? Studying Whites and Whiteness in the Era of' Color-Blindness." *Sociological Theory* 22: 623–646.

Lewis, Gregory B., and Jonathan L. Edelson. 2000. "DOMA and ENDA: Congress Votes on Gay Rights." In *The Politics of Gay Rights*, edited by C. A. Rimmerman, D. Wald, and C. Wilcox, 193–216. Chicago: University of Chicago Press.

Lewis, Jamie M., Nancy Bates, and Matthew Streeter. 2015. "Measuring Same-Sex Couples: The What and Who of Misreporting on Relationship and Sex." SEHSD Working Paper 2015-12. Washington, D.C.: Census Bureau.

Lewis, Krystal M., Devin A. Byrd, and Thomas H. Ollendick. 2012. "Anxiety Symptoms in African-American and Caucasian Youth: Relations to Negative Life Events, Social Support, and Coping." *Journal of Anxiety Disorders* 26 (1): 32–39.

Library of Congress. n/d. "Irish—Joining the Workforce" Immigration. Webpage. Teacher Resources. Available at http://www.loc.gov/teachers/classroommaterials/presentationsandactivities/presentations/immigration/irish4.html.

Lichter, Daniel T., and Rukamalie Jayakody. 2002. "Welfare Reform: How Do We Measure Success?" *Annual Review of Sociology* 28: 117–141.

Light, Donald, Suzanne Keller, and Craig Calhoun. 1989. *Sociology*. New York: Alfred A. Knopf.

Lim, Lucy, Allyson Clarke, Frank Ross, and Jean Wells. 2015. "Mentoring Experiences, Perceived Benefits, and Impact on Current Job Positions of African American Accountants." *Advancing Women in Leadership* 35: 193–203.

Lin, Ann Chih, and David R. Harris. 2009. "The Colors of Poverty: Why Racial & Ethnic Disparities Persist." National Poverty Center Policy Brief #16. Available at http://policylinkcontent.s3.amazonaws.com/PolicyBrief16%20-%20The%20Colors%20of%20Poverty.pdf.

Lindert, Peter H., and Jeffrey G. Williamson. 2012. "American Incomes 1774–1860." Cambridge, MA: National Bureau of Economic Research. Available at http://www.nber.org/papers/w18396.

Linneman, T. J. 2013. "Gender in Jeopardy!: Intonation Variation on a Television Game Show." *Gender & Society* 27 (1): 82–105.

Lino, Mark, and U.S. Department of Agriculture, Center for Nutrition Policy and Promotion. 2014. "Expenditures on Children by Families, 2013." Miscellaneous Publication 1528-2013. http://www.cnpp.usda.gov/sites/default/files/expenditures_on_children_by_families/crc2013.pdf.

Lipka, Michael. 2015. "5 Key Findings about the Changing U.S. Religious Landscape." Pew Research Center, May 12. Available at http://www.pewresearch.org/fact-tank/2015/05/12/5-key-findings-u-s-religious-landscape.

Lips, Hilary M. 2013. "The Gender Pay Gap: Challenging the Rationalizations. Perceived Equity, Discrimination, and the Limits of Human Capital Models." *Sex Roles* 68 (3–4): 169–185.

Lipset, Seymour. 1971. "Trade Unionism and the American Social Order." In *The American Labor Movement*, edited by David Brody, 7–29. New York: Harper & Row.

Lloyd, Moya. 2007. *Judith Butler: From Norms to Politics*. Vol. 20. Malden, MA: Polity.

Lobao, Linda M., Gregory Hooks, and Ann R. Tickamyer. 2007. *The Sociology of Spatial Inequality*. Albany, NY: SUNY Press.

Loftus, Jeni. 2001. "America's Liberalization in Attitudes toward Homosexuality, 1973 to 1998." *American Sociological Review* 66: 762–782.

Logan, John R., Jennifer Darrah, and Sookhee Oh. 2012. "The Impact of Race and Ethnicity, Immigration and Political Context on Participation in American Electoral Politics." *Social Forces* 90 (3): 993–1022.

Lombardi, Kristen. 2015. "Thirty Miles from Selma, a Different Kind of Civil Rights Struggle." Center for Public Integrity. August 5. Available at http://www.publicintegrity.org/2015/08/05/17703/thirty-miles-selma-different-kind-civil-rights-struggle.

Lopreato, Joseph, and Lawrence E. Hazelrigg. 1972. *Class, Conflict, and Mobility: Theories and Studies of Class Structure*. Corte Madera, CA: Chandler House Press.

Loprest, Pamela. 2011. "Disconnected Families and TANF." Brief 2. Washington, D.C.: Urban Institute. Available at http://www.acf.hhs.gov/sites/default/files/opre/disconnected.pdf.

Lorber, Judith. 1994. *Paradoxes of Gender*. New Haven, CT: Yale University Press.

Lorber, Judith. 1996. "Beyond the Binaries: Depolarizing the Categories of Sex, Sexuality, and Gender." *Sociological Inquiry* 66 (2): 143–160.

Lorber, Judith. 2001. *Gender Inequality*. Los Angeles, CA: Roxbury.

Loury, Linda Datcher. 2006. "Some Contacts Are More Equal than Others: Informal Networks, Job Tenure, and Wages." *Journal of Labor Economics* 24 (2): 299–318.

Lovasi, Gina S., Malo A. Hutson, Monica Guerra, and Kathryn M. Neckerman. 2009. "Built Environments and Obesity in Disadvantaged Populations." *Epidemiologic Reviews* 31 (1): 7–20.

Loveman, Mara, and Jeronimo O. Muniz. 2007. "How Puerto Rico Became White: Boundary Dynamics and Intercensus Racial Reclassification." *American Sociological Review* 72 (6): 915–939.

Lucal, Betsy. 1996. "Oppression and Privilege: Toward a Relational Conceptualization of Race." *Teaching Sociology* 24: 245–255.

Ludwig, Jens, Lisa Sanbonmatsu, Lisa Gennetian, Emma Adam, Greg J. Duncan, Lawrence F. Katz, Ronald C. Kessler, Jeffrey R. Kling, Stacy Tessler Lindau, and Robert C. Whitaker. 2011. "Neighborhoods, Obesity, and Diabetes—a Randomized Social Experiment." *New England Journal of Medicine* 365 (16): 1509–1519.

Luibheid, Eithne. 1998. "'Looking like a Lesbian': The Organization of Sexual Monitoring at the United States-Mexican Border." *Journal of the History of Sexuality* 8: 477–506.

Luo, Michael. 2009. "A Parent's Unemployment Stress Trickles Down to the Children." *New York Times*, November 11. Available at http://www.nytimes.com/2009/11/12/us/12families.html.

Lurie, Alison. 1987. "Fashion and Status." In *The Social World*, edited by Ian Robertson, 3rd ed., 124–130. New York: Worth.

Lurie, Nancy Oestreich. 1982. "The American Indian: Historical Background." In *Majority and Minority: The Dynamics of Race and Ethnicity in American Life*, edited by Norman R. Yetman and C. Hoy Steele, 3rd ed, 131–144. Boston: Allyn & Bacon.

Lyons, Daniel. 2002. "Bad Boys." *Forbes*, July 22.

MacInnis, Cara C., and Gordon Hodson. 2012. "Intergroup Bias toward 'Group X': Evidence of Prejudice, Dehumanization, Avoidance, and Discrimination against Asexuals." *Group Processes & Intergroup Relations* 15 (6): 725–743.

MacLeod, Jay. 2008. *Ain't No Makin' It: Aspirations and Attainment in a Low-Income Neighborhood*, 3rd ed. Boulder, CO: Westview Press.

Madden, Janice Fanning. 2012. "Performance-Support Bias and the Gender Pay Gap among Stockbrokers." *Gender & Society* 26 (3): 488–518.

Maddow, Rachel. 2015. "Snyder Admin Allowed Flint to Drink Toxic Water despite Warnings." *The Rachel Maddow Show*. MSNBC. Available at http://www.msnbc.com/rachel-maddow/watch/snyder-admin-knew-flint-water-toxicity-mails-590489667731.

Madon, Stephanie. 1997. "What Do People Believe about Gay Males? A Study of Stereotype Content and Strength." *Sex Roles* 37 (9–10): 663–685.

Mahler, Vincent A. 2004. "Economic Globalization, Domestic Politics, and Income Inequality in the Developed Countries: A Cross-National Study." *Comparative Political Studies* 37 (9): 1025–1053.

Majority Committee Staff Report. 2014. "Fulfilling the Promise: Overcoming Persistent Barriers to Economic Self-Sufficiency for People with Disabilities." United States Senate: Committee on Health, Education, Labor and Pensions. Available at http://www.help.senate.gov/imo/media/doc/HELP%20Committee%20Disability%20and%20Poverty%20Report.pdf.

Maldonado, Marta Maria. 2009. "'It Is Their Nature to do Menial Labor': The Racialization of 'Latino/a Workers' by Agricultural Employers." *Ethnic & Racial Studies* 32: 1017–1036.

Maloney, Carolyn B., and Charles E. Schumer. 2010. "Income Inequality and the Great Recession." In *Report by the U.S., Congress Joint Economic Committee*, pp. 1–13. Available at http://www.colorado.edu/AmStudies/lewis/ecology/decliningIncomes.pdf.

Mammen, Sheila, Elizabeth Dolan, and Sharon B. Seiling. 2015. "Explaining the Poverty Dynamics of Rural Families Using an Economic Well-Being Continuum." *Journal of Family and Economic Issues* 36: 434–450.

Manley, John F. 1983. "Neo-Pluralism: A Class Analysis of Pluralism I and Pluralism II." *American Political Science Review* 77 (2): 368–383.

Manning, Jennifer E. 2015. "Membership of the 114th Congress: A Profile." Congressional Research Service. Available at https://www.fas.org/sgp/crs/misc/R43869.pdf.

Mantovani, Richard, Eric Sean Williams, and Jacqueline Pflieger. 2013. "The Extent of Trafficking in the Supplemental Nutrition Assistance Program: 2009–2011." Washington, D.C.: U.S. Department of Agriculture, Food and Nutrition Service. Available at http://www.fns.usda.gov/sites/default/files/Trafficking2009.pdf.

Mantsios, Gregory. 2004. "Class in America." In *Race, Class, and Gender in the United States: An Integrated Study*, edited by Paula S. Rothenberg, 193–207. New York: Worth.

Marden, Charles F., and Gladys Meyer. 1973. *Minorities in American Society*. New York: Van Nostrand.

Marger, Martin N. 1997. *Race and Ethnic Relations: American and Global Definitions*. Belmont, CA: Wadsworth.

Mark, Noah P., Lynn Smith-Lovin, and Cecilia L. Ridgeway. 2009. "Why Do Nominal Characteristics Acquire Status Value? A Minimal Explanation for Status Construction." *American Journal of Sociology* 115 (3): 832–862.

Marsh, Kris, William A. Darity, Philip N. Cohen, Lynne M. Casper, and Danielle Salters. 2007. "The Emerging Black Middle Class: Single and Living Alone." *Social Forces* 86 (2): 735–762.

Marshall, Gordon, Adam Swift, and Stephen Roberts. 1997. *Against the Odds? Social Class and Social Justice in Industrial Societies*. New York: Oxford University Press.

Marshall, Ray, and Beth Paulin. 1987. "Employment and Earnings of Women: Historical Perspective." In *Working Women: Past, Present, Future*, edited by Karen S. Koziara, Michael H. Moscow, and Lucretia D. Tanner, 1–36. Washington, D.C.: Bureau of National Affairs.

Martin, Andrew W. 2008. "Resources for Success: Social Movements, Strategic Resource Allocation, and Union Organizing Outcomes." *Social Problems* 55 (4): 501–524.

Martin, Andrew W., and Marc Dixon. 2010. "Changing to Win? Threat, Resistance, and the Role of Unions in Strikes, 1984–2002." *American Journal of Sociology* 116 (1): 93–129.

Martin, Andrew W., Thomas Maher, Lisa Williams, and John McCarthy. 2009. "Whither the Civil Rights Movement? Towards an Empirical Model of Movement Decline." Paper delivered at American Sociological Society Annual Meeting, August 8, San Francisco.

Martin, Carol Lynn, Olga Kornienko, David R. Schaefer, Laura D. Hanish, Richard A. Fabes, and Priscilla Goble. 2013. "The Role of Sex of Peers and Gender-Typed Activities in Young Children's Peer Affiliative Networks: A Longitudinal Analysis of Selection and Influence." *Child Development* 84 (3): 921–937.

Martin, Sandra L., Neepa Ray, Daniela Sotres-Alvarez, Lawrence L. Kupper, Kathryn E. Moracco, Pamela A. Dickens, Donna Scandlin, and Ziya Gizlice. 2006. "Physical and Sexual Assault of Women With Disabilities." *Violence Against Women* 12 (9): 823–837.

Marx, Karl. 1967. *Capital*. Translated by Samuel Moore and Edward Aveling. Vol. 1. New York: International.

Marx, Karl, and Friedrich Engels. 1969 and 1970. *Selected Works*. Vols. 1, 2, and 3. Moscow: Progress.

Maskin, Eric. 2014. "Why Haven't Global Markets Reduced Inequality?" In *Annual Conference* on *Development Economics*. Washington, D.C.: World Bank.

Massad, Joseph Andoni. 2002. "Re-Orienting Desire: The Gay International and the Arab World." *Public Culture* 14 (2): 361–385.

Massey, Douglas S. 1995. "Review Essay of the Bell Curve." *American Journal of Sociology* 101: 747–753.

Massey, Douglas S. 2007. *Categorically Unequal: The American Stratification System*. New York: Russell Sage Foundation.

Massey, Douglas S. 2009. "Globalization and Inequality: Explaining American Exceptionalism." *European Sociological Review* 25 (1): 9–23.

Massey, Douglas S., and Nancy A. Denton. 1993. *American Apartheid: Segregation and the Making of the Underclass*. Boston: Harvard University Press.

Massey, Douglas S., Jonathan Rothwell, and Thurston Domina. 2009. "The Changing Bases of Segregation in the United States." *The Annals of the American Academy of Political and Social Science* 626 (1): 74–90.

Masters, N. Tatiana, Taryn Lindhorst, and Marcia Meyers. 2014. "Jezebel at the Welfare Office: How Racialized Stereotypes of Poor Women's Reproductive Decisions and Relationships Shape Policy Implementation." *Journal of Poverty* 18 (2):109–129.

Mathews, T. J., and Marian F. MacDorman. 2013. "Infant Mortality Statistics from the 2009 Period Linked Birth/Infant Death Data Set." *National Vital Statistics Reports* 61 (8): 1–27. Available at http://www.cdc.gov/nchs/data/nvsr/nvsr61/nvsr61_08.pdf.

Matthews, Donald R. 1954. "United States Senators and the Class Structure." *Public Opinion Quarterly* 18: 5–22. Reprinted in *Social Stratification: A Reader*, edited by J. Lopreato and L. S. Lewis, 331–342. New York: Harper & Row.

Maume, David J., Jr. 2004. "Wage Discrimination over the Life Course: A Comparison of Explanations." *Social Problems* 51: 505–527.

Mazumder, Bhashkar. 2005. "Fortunate Sons: New Estimates of Intergenerational Mobility in the United States Using Social Security Earnings Data." *Review of Economics and Statistics* 87 (2): 235–255.

McAdam, Doug. 2010. *Political Process and the Development of Black Insurgency, 1930–1970*. Chicago: University of Chicago Press.

McBride, Anne, Gail Hebson, and Jane Holgate. 2015. "Intersectionality: Are We Taking Enough Notice in the Field of Work and Employment Relations?" *Work, Employment & Society* 29 (2): 331–341.

McCabe, Kristen. 2012. "Foreign-Born Health Care Workers in the United States." Migration Policy Institute. June 27. Available at http://www.migrationpolicy.org/article/foreign-born-health-care-workers-united-states.

McCabe, Sean Esteban, Wendy B. Bostwick, Tonda L. Hughes, Brady T. West, and Carol J. Boyd. 2010. "The Relationship between Discrimination and Substance Use Disorders among Lesbian, Gay, and Bisexual Adults in the United States." *American Journal of Public Health* 100 (10): 1946–1952.

McCall, Leslie. 2005. "The Complexity of Intersectionality." *Signs: Journal of Women in Culture and Society* 30 (3): 1771–1800.

McCall, Leslie. 2014. "The Political Meanings of Social Class Inequality." *Social Currents* 1 (1): 25–34.

McCall, Leslie, and Christine Percheski. 2010. "Income Inequality: New Trends and Research Directions." *Annual Review of Sociology* 36 (1): 329–347.

McCall, Phil. 2008. "'We Had to Stick Together': Individual Preferences, Collective Struggle, and the Formation of Social Consciousness." *Science & Society* 72: 147–81.

McCann, Allison. 2015. "Here's What the Gender Pay Gap Looks Like by Income Level." FiveThirtyEightEconomics, April 14. Available at http://fivethirtyeight.com/datalab/heres-what-the-gender-pay-gap-looks-like-by-income-level.

McClellan, Frank M., Augustus A. White, Ramon L. Jimenez, and Sherin Fahmy. 2012. "Do Poor People Sue Doctors More Frequently? Confronting Unconscious Bias and the Role of Cultural Competency." *Clinical Orthopaedics and Related Research* 470 (5): 1393–1397.

McClelland, David C. 1961. *The Achieving Society*. New York: The Free Press.

McDonald, Steve. 2009. "Right Place, Right Time: Serendipity and Informal Job Matching." *Socio-Economic Review* 8 (2): 307–331.

McDonald, Steve. 2011. "What's in the 'Old Boys' Network? Accessing Social Capital in Gendered and Racialized Networks." *Social Networks* 33 (4): 317–30.

McDonald, Steve, Nan Lin, and Dan Ao. 2009. "Networks of Opportunity: Gender, Race, and Job Leads." *Social Problems* 56 (3): 385–402.

McDonough, Peggy, David R. Williams, James S. House, and Greg J. Duncan. 1999. "Gender and the Socioeconomic Gradient in Mortality." *Journal of Health and Social Behavior* 40: 17–31.

McFate, Katherine. 1987. "Defining the Underclass." *Focus* 15: 8–12.

McIntosh, Peggy. 1988. "White Privilege and Male Privilege: A Personal Account of Coming to See Correspondences through Work in Women's Studies." Working Paper 189. Wellesley, MA: Center for Research on Women.

McKernan, Signe-Mary, Caroline Ratcliffe, Margaret Simms, and Sisi Zhang. 2012. "Do Financial Support and Inheritance Contribute to the Racial Wealth Gap?" *Opportunity and Ownership Facts* 26. Washington, D.C.: Urban Institute. Available at http://www.urban.org/sites/default/files/alfresco/publication-pdfs/412644-Do-Financial-Support-and-Inheritance-Contribute-to-the-Racial-Wealth-Gap-.PDF.

McKinnon, John D., and Damian Paletta. 2014. "Obama Administration Issues New Rules to Combat Tax Inversions." *Wall Street Journal*, September 23. Available at http://www.wsj.com/articles/treasury-to-unveil-measures-to-combat-tax-inversions-1411421056.

McLanahan, Sara. 2009. "Fragile Families and the Reproduction of Poverty." *The Annals of the American Academy of Political and Social Science* 621 (1): 111–131.

McLanahan, Sara, and Christine Percheski. 2008. "Family Structure and the Reproduction of Inequalities." *Annual Review of Sociology* 34: 257–276.

McManus, Doyle. 2010. "The Long Shadow of the Great Recession." *Akron Beacon Journal*, July 22, p. A11.

McNamee, Stephen J., and Robert K. Miller Jr. 2013. *The Meritocracy Myth*. Lanham, MD: Rowman & Littlefield.

McQuillan, Julia, Arthur L. Greil, Karina M. Shreffler, and Veronica Tichenor. 2008. "The Importance of Motherhood among Women in the Contemporary United States." *Gender & Society* 22: 477–496.

McRuer, Robert. 2006. *Crip Theory: Cultural Signs of Queerness and Disability*. New York: NYU Press.

McVeigh, Rory. 2006. "Structural Influences on Activism and Crime: Identifying the Social Structure of Discontent." *American Journal of Sociology* 112 (2): 510–566.

Meiksins, Peter F. 1988. "A Critique of Wright's Theory of Contradictory Class Locations." *Critical Sociology* 15 (1): 73–82.

Melin, Anders. 2015. "How Companies Justify Big Pay Raises for CEOs." *Bloomberg*, June 4. Available at http://www.bloomberg.com/graphics/2015-executive-pay-peer-groups.

Meltzer, H., P. Bebbington, T. Brugha, R. Jenkins, S. McManus, and S. Stansfeld. 2010. "Job Insecurity, Socio-Economic Circumstances and Depression." *Psychological Medicine* 40 (8): 1401–1407.

Memmi, Albert. 1965. *The Colonizer and the Colonized*, Translated by Howard Greenfield. New York: Orion Press.

Mendes, Elizabeth, Lydia Saad, and Kyley McGeeney. 2012. "Stay-at-Home Moms Report More Depression, Sadness, Anger." Gallup.com. May 16. Available at http://www.gallup.com/poll/154685/Stay-Home-Moms-Report-Depression-Sadness-Anger.aspx.

Merikangas, Kathleen Ries, Jian-ping He, Marcy Burstein, Sonja A. Swanson, Shelli Avenevoli, Lihong Cui, Corina Benjet, Katholiki Georgiades, and Joel Swendsen. 2010. "Lifetime Prevalence of Mental Disorders in US Adolescents: Results from the National Comorbidity Survey Replication–Adolescent Supplement (NCS-A)." *Journal of the American Academy of Child & Adolescent Psychiatry* 49 (10): 980–989.

Merluzzi, Jennifer, and Stanislav D. Dobrev. 2015. "Unequal on Top: Gender Profiling and the Income Gap among High Earner Male and Female Professionals." *Social Science Research* 53 (September): 45–58.

Merten, Don E. 1997. "The Meaning of Meanness: Popularity, Competition, and Conflict among Junior High School Girls." *Sociology of Education* 70: 175–191.

Merullo, Roland. 2002. "The Challenge of First-Generation College Students." *Chronicle of Higher Education*, June 14. Available at http://chronicle.com/article/The-Challenge-of/12507.

Messerschmidt, James W. 1993. *Masculinities and Crime: Critique and Reconceptualization of Theory*. Lanham, MD: Rowman & Littlefield.

Messner, Steven F. 1989. "Economic Discrimination and Societal Homicide Rates: Further Evidence on the Cost of Inequality." *American Sociological Review* 54: 597–611.

Messner, Steven F., and Richard Rosenfeld. 2012. *Crime and the American Dream*. Boston: Cengage Learning.

Meyer, Ilan H., Jessica Dietrich, and Sharon Schwartz. 2008. "Lifetime Prevalence of Mental Disorders and Suicide Attempts in Diverse Lesbian, Gay, and Bisexual Populations." *American Journal of Public Health* 98 (6): 1004–1006.

Meyer, Lisa B. 2003. "Economic Globalization and Women's Status in the Labor Market." *Sociological Quarterly* 44 (3): 351–383.

Mian, Atif, and Amir Sufi. 2014. "How High Debt Leads to Income Inequality." Capital Ideas, June 17. Available at http://www.chicagobooth.edu/capideas/magazine/summer-2014/how-high-debt-leads-to-income-inequality.

Miliband, Ralph. 1977. *Marxism and Politics*. New York: Oxford University Press.

Miller, Brandon, and Jennifer Lewallen. 2015. "The Effects of Portrayals of Gay Men on Homonegativity and the Attribution of Gender-Based Descriptors." *Communication Studies* 66 (3): 358–377.

Miller, Lisa. 2010. "Divided We Eat: What Food Says about Class in America and How to Bridge the Gap." *Newsweek*, November 22.

Miller, Mark. 2014. "What Retirees Need to Know about the New Federal Pension Rules." *Time*, December 18. Available at http://time.com/money/3640006/pension-new-federal-rules-retirees.

Miller, Mark. 2015. "Pushing Aside 401(k)'s for Mandatory Savings Plans." *New York Times*, December 11. Available at http://www.nytimes.com/2015/12/12/your-money/pushing-aside-401-k-s-for-mandatory-savings-plans.html.

Miller, Susan M. 1963. *Max Weber: Selections from His Work*. New York: Thomas Y. Crowell.

Miller, William Lee. 1977. *Welfare and Values in America: A Review of Attitudes toward Welfare and Welfare Policies in the Light of American History and Culture*. Durham, NC: Institute of Policy Sciences and Public Affairs of Duke University.

Mills, C. Wright. 1956. *The Power Elite*. New York: Oxford University Press.

Mills, C. Wright. 1959. *The Sociological Imagination*. New York: Oxford University Press.

Mills, C. Wright. 1962. *The Marxists*. New York: Dell.

Mills, Mary Beth. 2003. "Gender and Inequality in the Global Labor Force." *Annual Review of Anthropology*, edited by W. H. Durham, J. Comaroff, and J. Hill, 41–62. Palo Alto, CA: Annual Reviews.

Mills, Melinda. 2009. "Globalization and Inequality." *European Sociological Review* 25 (1): 1–8.

Milner, Murray. 2016. *Freaks, Geeks, and Cool Kids: Teenagers in an Era of Consumerism, Standardized Tests, and Social Media*. New York: Routledge.

Mintz, Beth. 1975. "The President's Cabinet, 1891–1912: A Contribution to the Power Structure Debate." *Critical Sociology* 5 (3): 131–148.

Mirowsky, John, and Catherine E. Ross. 1983. "Paranoia and the Structure of Powerlessness." *American Sociological Review* 48 (2): 228–239.

Mirowsky, John, and Catherine E. Ross. 1986. "Social Pattern of Distress." *Annual Review of Sociology* 12: 23–45.

Mirowsky, John, and Catherine E. Ross. 2003. *Social Causes of Psychological Distress*. 2nd ed. New Brunswick, NJ: Aldine.

Mirowsky, John, and Catherine E. Ross. 2007. "Life Course Trajectories of Perceived Control and Their Relationship to Education." *American Journal of Sociology* 112 (5): 1339–1382.

Mishel, Lawrence R., Jared Bernstein, and Sylvia Allegretto. 2007. *The State of Working America 2006/2007*. Cornell, NY: Cornell University Press.

Mishel, Lawrence R., Jared Bernstein, and John Schmitt. 2001. *The State of Working America 2000–2001*. Ithaca, NY: Cornell University Press.

Mishel, Lawrence R., Jared Bernstein, and Heidi Shierholz. 2009. *The State of Working America: 2008–2009*. Ithaca, NY: ILR Press.

Mishel, Lawrence R., Joel Bivens, Elise Gould, and Heidi Shierholz. 2012. *The State of Working America*. 12th ed. Ithaca, NY: ILR Press.

Mishel, Lawrence R., and Alyssa Davis. 2015. "Top CEOs Make 300 Times More than Typical Workers: Pay Growth Surpasses Stock Gains and Wage Growth of Top 0.1 Percent." Economic

Policy Institute. June 21. Available at http://www.epi.org/publication/top-ceos-make-300-times-more-than-workers-pay-growth-surpasses-market-gains-and-the-rest-of-the-0-1-percent.

Mistry, Rashmita S., Christia S. Brown, Elizabeth S. White, Kirby A. Chow, and Cari Gillen-O'Neel. 2015. "Elementary School Children's Reasoning About Social Class: A Mixed-Methods Study." *Child Development* 86 (5): 1653–1671.

Mitzman, Arthur. 1970. *The Iron Cage: An Historical Interpretation of Max Weber.* New York: Transaction.

Mizruchi, Mark S. 1989. "Similarity of Political Behavior Among Large American Corporations." *American Journal of Sociology* 95 (2): 401–424.

Mizruchi, Mark S. 2013. *The Fracturing of the American Corporate Elite.* Cambridge, MA: Harvard University Press.

Mizruchi, Mark S., and David Bunting. 1981. "Influence in Corporate Networks: An Examination of Four Measures." *Administrative Science Quarterly* 26 (3): 475–489.

Mizruchi, Mark S., and Linda Brewster Stearns. 2001. "Getting Deals Done: The Use of Social Networks in Bank Decision-Making." *American Sociological Review* 66 (4): 647–671.

Moffitt, Robert A. 2015a. "The U.S. Safety Net and Work Incentives: The Great Recession and Beyond." *Journal of Policy Analysis and Management* 34 (2).

Moffitt, Robert A. 2015b. "The Deserving Poor, the Family, and the U.S. Welfare System." *Demography* 52 (3): 729–749.

Moffitt, Robert A., Brian J. Phelan, and Anne E. Winkler. 2015. "Welfare Rules, Incentives, and Family Structure." National Bureau of Economic Research. Available at http://www.nber.org/papers/w21257.

Mohai, Paul, Paula M. Lantz, Jeffrey Morenoff, James S. House, and Richard P. Mero. 2008. "Racial and Socioeconomic Disparities in Residential Proximity to Polluting Industrial Facilities: Evidence from the Americans Changing Lives Study." Paper delivered at Annual Meeting of American Sociological Association, August 2008.

Mohanty, Chandra Talpade. 1988. "Under Western Eyes: Feminist Scholarship and Colonial Discourses." *Feminist Review* 30: 61–88.

Monk Jr., Ellis P. 2014. "Skin Tone Stratification among Black Americans, 2001–2003." *Social Forces* 92 (4): 1313–1337.

Moore, Wilbert E. 1970. "But Some Are More Equal Than Others." In *The Logic of Social Hierarchies,* edited by Edward Otto Laumann, Paul M. Siegel, and Robert William Hodge, 143–148. Skokie, IL: Markham.

Mora, G. Cristina. 2014. "Cross-Field Effects and Ethnic Classification: The Institutionalization of Hispanic Panethnicity, 1965 to 1990." *American Sociological Review* 79 (2): 183–210.

Morris, Aldon D. 1986. *Origins of the Civil Rights Movements: Black Communities Organizing for Change.* New York: Simon and Schuster.

Morris, Michael, and John B. Williamson. 1986. *Poverty and Public Policy: An Analysis of Federal Intervention Efforts.* Vol. 3. New York: Praeger.

Morrissey, Monique. 2014. "How Do U.S. Retirees Compare with Those in Other Countries?" Economic Policy Institute, October 3. Available at http://www.epi.org/blog/retirees-compare-countries.

Mouw, Ted, and Arne L. Kalleberg. 2010. "Occupations and the Structure of Wage Inequality in the United States, 1980s to 2000s." *American Sociological Review* 75 (3): 402–431.

Murray, Charles. 1984. *Losing Ground: American Social Policy 1950–1980.* New York: Basic Books.

Murray, Stephen O. 1996. *American Gay.* Chicago: University of Chicago Press.

Mustanski, Brian, and Richard T. Liu. 2013. "A Longitudinal Study of Predictors of Suicide Attempts among Lesbian, Gay, Bisexual, and Transgender Youth." *Archives of Sexual Behavior* 42 (3): 437–448.

Myers, Amanda Lee. 2015. "Honda Settles Discrimination Claims with Justice Department." Associated Press, July 14. Available at http://bigstory.ap.org/article/af5af93f286244bc82a82eb713f3a67b/honda-settles-discrimination-claims-justice-department.

Myers Jr., Lewis A. 2014. "Globalization, Corporate Social Responsibility, and Ethical Considerations." *Journal of Management* 2 (2): 45–61.

Myles, John. 2003. "Where Have All the Sociologists Gone? Explaining Economic Inequality." *Canadian Journal of Sociology* 28: 551–559.

Nachescu, Voichita. 2008. "Radical Feminism and the Nation." *Journal for the Study of Radicalism* 3: 29–54.

Nadal, Kevin L., Kristin C. Davidoff, Lindsey S. Davis, Yinglee Wong, David Marshall, and Victoria McKenzie. 2015. "A Qualitative Approach to Intersectional Microaggressions: Understanding Influences of Race, Ethnicity, Gender, Sexuality, and Religion." *Qualitative Psychology* 2 (2): 147–163.

Nadal, Kevin L., Katie E. Griffin, Sahran Hamit, Jayleen Leon, Michael Tobio, and David P. Rivera. 2012. "Subtle and Overt Forms of Islamophobia: Microaggressions toward Muslim Americans." *Journal of Muslim Mental Health* 6 (2). Available at http://quod.lib.umich.edu/j/jmmh/10381607.0006.203?rgn=main;view=fulltext.

Nadal, Kevin L., Silvia L. Mazzula, David P. Rivera, and Whitney Fujii-Doe. 2014. "Microaggressions and Latina/o Americans: An Analysis of Nativity, Gender, and Ethnicity." *Journal of Latina/o Psychology* 2 (2): 67–78.

Nam, Yunju. 2004. "Is America Becoming More Equal for Children? Changes in the Intergenerational Transmission of Low- and High-Income Status." *Social Science Research* 33 (2): 187–205.

Nathans, Stephen J. 2001. "Twelve Years after Price Waterhouse and Still No Success for Hopkins in Drag: The Lack of Protection for the Male Victim of Gender Stereotyping under Title VII." *Villanova Law Review* 46: 713.

National Academies of Sciences, Engineering, and Medicine. 2015. "New Report Examines Implications of Growing Gap in Life Span by Income for Entitlement Programs." National Academies of Sciences, Engineering and Medicine. Office of News and Public Information, September 17. Available at http://www8.nationalacademies.org/onpinews/newsitem.aspx?RecordID=19015.

National Alliance to End Homelessness. 2015. "The State of Homelessness in America." Washington, D.C.: National Alliance to End Homelessness. Available at http://www.endhomelessness.org/library/entry/the-state-of-homelessness-in-america-2015.

National Alliance to End Homelessness. 2016. "Snapshot of Homelessness." Washington, D.C.: National Alliance to End Homelessness. Available at http://www.endhomelessness.org/pages/snapshot_of_homelessness.

National Center for Education Statistics. 2012. "Degrees Conferred by Sex and Race." Fast Facts: National Center for Education Statistics. Available at https://nces.ed.gov/fastfacts/display.asp?id=72.

National Center for Education Statistics. 2015. "Full-Time Faculty in Degree-Granting Postsecondary Institutions, by Race/Ethnicity, Sex, and Academic Rank: Fall 2009, Fall 2011, and Fall 2013." Washington, D.C.: U.S. Department of Education. Available at http://nces.ed.gov/programs/digest/d14/tables/dt14_315.20.asp.

National Center for Health Statistics. 2010. "Health, United States, 2009." Hyattsville, MD: U.S. Department of Health and Human Services.

National Center for Transgender Equality. 2015a. "Military & Veterans." Available at http://www.transequality.org/issues/military-veterans.

National Center for Transgender Equality. 2015b. "Passports." Available at http://www.transequality.org/know-your-rights/passports.

National Governors' Association Center for Best Practices. 1999. "Round Two Summary of Selected Elements of State Programs for Temporary Assistance for Needy Families." Washington, D.C.: National Governers' Association.

National Institute of Mental Health. 2015. "Any Mental Illness (AMI) Among Adults." Available at http://www.nimh.nih.gov/health/statistics/prevalence/any-mental-illness-ami-among-us-adults.shtml.

National Law Center on Homelessness and Poverty. 2014. "No Safe Place: The Criminalization of Homelessness in U.S. Cities." Washington, D.C.: National Law Center on Homelessness and Poverty.

National Low Income Housing Coalition. 2012. "Who Lives in Federally Assisted Housing?" *Housing Spotlight* 2 (2): 1–6.

National Low Income Housing Coalition. 2015. "Out of Reach 2015." Washington, D.C.: National Low Income Housing Coalition. Available at http://nlihc.org/sites/default/files/oor/OOR_2015_FULL.pdf.

National Public Radio. 2012. "Why Some Homeless Choose the Streets over Shelters." Talk of the Nation, December 6. Available at http://www.npr.org/2012/12/06/166666265/why-some-homeless-choose-the-streets-over-shelters.

National Rural Health Association. 2015. "NRHA: What's Different about Rural Health Care?" National Rural Health Association. Available http://www.ruralhealthweb.org/go/left/about-rural-health/what-s-different-about-rural-health-care.

National Women's Law Center. 2015. "The Schedules That Work Act: Giving Workers the Tools They Need to Succeed." Fact Sheet. National Women's Law Center. Available at http://www.nwlc.org/sites/default/files/pdfs/stwa_giving_workers_the_tools_fact_sheet_june_2015.pdf.

Nelson, Alan R., Brian D. Smedley, and Adrienne Y. Stith. 2002. Unequal Treatment: Confronting Racial and Ethnic Disparities in Health Care. Washington, D.C.: National Academies Press.

Neuman, Scott. 2015. "Obama: Katrina a 'Man-Made' Disaster Caused by Government Failure." The Two-Way: Breaking News from NPR. National Public Radio. Available at http://www.npr.org/sections/thetwo-way/2015/08/27/435258344/obama-katrina-a-man-made-disaster-caused-by-government-failure.

New, Jake. 2015. "A Common Sign." Inside Higher Education, August 28, Available at https://www.insidehighered.com/news/2015/08/28/sexist-banners-old-dominion-point-practice-many-campuses.

Newman, Katherine S., and Margaret M. Chin. 2003. "High Stakes: Time Poverty, Testing, and the Children of the Working Poor." Qualitative Sociology 26 (1): 3–34.

Newport, Frank. 2007. "Americans Split on Redistributing Wealth by Taxing the Rich." Princeton, NJ: Gallup Polls.

Newport, Frank. 2015a. "Religion, Same-Sex Relationships and Politics in Indiana and Arkansas." Gallup.com, April 3. Available at http://www.gallup.com/opinion/polling-matters/182300/religion-sex-relationships-politics-indiana-arkansas.aspx.

Newport, Frank. 2015b. "Americans Continue to Say U.S. Wealth Distribution Is Unfair." Gallup.com, May 4. Available at http://www.gallup.com/poll/182987/americans-continue-say-wealth-distribution-unfair.aspx.

Newport, Frank, and Gary J. Gates. 2015. "San Francisco Metro Area Ranks Highest in LGBT Percentage." Gallup.com, March 20. Available at http://www.gallup.com/poll/182051/san-francisco-metro-area-ranks-highest-lgbt-percentage.aspx.

Newsweek. 2009. "The People Speak: 'Yes, He Can,'" January 26.

Nicholson, Linda J. 1984. "Making Our Marx." The Women's Review of Books 1: 8–9.

Nielsen. 2013. "Upscale Latinos: America's New Baby Boomers." Nielsen Newswire. Available at http://www.nielsen.com/us/en/insights/news/2013/upscale-latinos--americas-new-baby-boomers.html.

Nivette, Amy E. 2011. "Cross-National Predictors of Crime: A Meta-Analysis." Homicide Studies 15 (2): 103–131.

Noel, Donald L. 1968. "A Theory of the Origin of Ethnic Stratification." Social Problems 16 (2): 157–172.

Norris, Floyd. 2013. "U.S. Companies Thrive as Workers Fall Behind." New York Times, August 9. Available at http://www.nytimes.com/2013/08/10/business/economy/us-companies-thrive-as-workers-fall-behind.html.

Norton, Michael I., and Dan Ariely. 2011. "Building a Better America—One Wealth Quintile at a Time." Perspectives on Psychological Science 6 (1): 9–12.

Oberschall, Anthony. 1973. Social Conflict and Social Movements. Englewood Cliffs, NJ: Prentice Hall.

O'Brien, Ellen O., Ke Bin Wu, and David Baer. 2010. "Older Americans in Poverty: A Snapshot." Chartbook 2010-03. Washington, D.C.: American Association of Retired Persons.

O'Brien, Kathleen. 2015. "Who Will Treat the Flood of Obamacare Medicaid Patients?" NJ.com, February 5. Available at http://www.nj.com/healthfit/index.ssf/2015/02/where_will_400k_new_nj_medicaid_patients_get_care.html.

O'Connor, James. 1973. The Fiscal Crisis of the State. New York: St. Martin's Press.

OECD. 2014. "United States: Tackling High Inequalities, Creating Opportunities for All." Paris: Organisation for Economic Co-operation and Development. Available at http://www.oecd.org/unitedstates/Tackling-high-inequalities.pdf.

Office of Unemployment Insurance. 2015. "Unemployment Insurance Data Summary." Washington, D.C.: Division of Fiscal and Actuarial Services, U.S. Department of Labor.

O'Hare, William P. 1987. America's Welfare Population: Who Gets What? Publication No. 13. Washington, D.C.: Population Reference Bureau.

Ohlemacher, Stephen. February 26, 2007. "Welfare Numbers Growing, Despite Efforts." *Akron Beacon Journal*, A1, A3.

Okun, Arthur M. 1977. *Equality and Efficiency: The Big Tradeoff*. Washington, D.C.: Brookings Institution.

Oliver, Melvin L., and Thomas M. Shapiro. 2006. *Black Wealth, White Wealth: A New Perspective on Racial Inequality*. New York: Taylor & Francis.

Ollman, Bertell. 1968. "Marx's Use of 'Class.'" *American Journal of Sociology* 73: 573–580.

Omi, Michael, and Howard Winant. 1994. *Racial Formation in the United States: From the 1960s to the 1990s*. 2nd ed. New York: Routledge.

Omi, Michael, and Howard Winant. 2005. "Racial Formation." In *Great Divides*, edited by T. M. Shapiro, 193–199. Boston: McGraw-Hill.

Onishi, Norimitsu. 2015. "U.S. Support of Gay Rights in Africa May Have Done More Harm Than Good." *New York Times*, December 20. Available at http://www.nytimes.com/2015/12/21/world/africa/us-support-of-gay-rights-in-africa-may-have-done-more-harm-than-good.html.

Orr, Andrea. 2010. *At the Top: Soaring Incomes, Falling Tax Rates*. Washington, D.C.: Economic Policy Institute.

Ortiz, Susan Y., and Vincent J. Roscigno. 2009. "Discrimination, Women, and Work: Processes and Variations by Race and Class." *Sociological Quarterly* 50: 336–359.

Osberg, Lars, and Timothy Smeeding. 2006. "'Fair' Inequality? Attitudes toward Pay Differentials: The United States in Comparative Perspective." *American Sociological Review* 71 (3): 450–473.

OSHA. 2015. "Commonly Used Statistics." U.S. Department of Labor: Occupational Safety and Health Administration. Available at https://www.osha.gov/oshstats/commonstats.html.

Ostrander, Susan. 1983. *Women of the Upper Class*. Philadelphia: Temple University Press.

O'Sullivan, Katherine, and William J. Wilson. 1988. "Race and Ethnicity." In *Handbook of Sociology*, edited by Neil J. Smelser, 223–242. Newbury Park, CA: Sage.

Otsubo, Shigeru, ed. 2015. *Globalization and Development*. Vol. 1. New York: Routledge.

Padavic, Irene, and Barbara F. Reskin. 2002. *Women and Men at Work*. Thousand Oaks, CA: Pine Forge Press.

Padilla, Amado M. 1994. "Ethnic Minority Scholars, Research, and Mentoring: Current and Future Issues." *Educational Researcher* 23 (4): 24–27.

Page, Benjamin I., and Lawrence R. Jacobs. 2009. *Class War? What Americans Really Think about Economic Inequality*. Chicago: University of Chicago Press.

Pager, Devah. 2003. "The Mark of a Criminal Record." *American Journal of Sociology* 108 (5): 937–975.

Pager, Devah, Bruce Western, and Bart Bonikowski. 2009. "Discrimination in a Low-Wage Labor Market: A Field Experiment." *American Sociological Review* 74 (5): 777–799.

Palmer, Barbara, and Dennis Simon. 2010. *Breaking the Political Glass Ceiling: Women and Congressional Elections*. New York: Routledge.

Palmer, Neal A., Joseph G. Kosciw, and Mark J. Bartkiewicz. 2013. "Strengths and Silences: The Experiences of Lesbian, Gay, Bisexual and Transgender Students in Rural and Small Town Schools." New York: GLSEN.

Pampel, Fred C., Patrick M. Krueger, and Justin T. Denney. 2010. "Socioeconomic Disparities in Health Behaviors." *Annual Review of Sociology* 36: 349–370.

Panagopoulos, Costas, and Peter L. Francia. 2008. "The Polls—Trends: Labor Unions in the United States." *Public Opinion Quarterly* 72 (1): 134–159.

Paradise, Julia. 2015. "Medicaid Moving Forward." The Henry J. Kaiser Family Foundation, March 9. Available at http://kff.org/health-reform/issue-brief/medicaid-moving-forward.

Parenti, Michael. 1970. "Power and Pluralism: A View from the Bottom." *The Journal of Politics* 32 (3): 501–530.

Parisi, Domenico, Daniel T. Lichter, and Michael C. Taquino. 2011. "Multi-Scale Residential Segregation: Black Exceptionalism and America's Changing Color Line." *Social Forces* 89 (3): 829–852.

Park, Haeyoun. 2015. "Which States Make Life Easier or Harder for Illegal Immigrants?" *New York Times*, March 29. Available at http://www.nytimes.com/interactive/2015/03/30/us/laws-affecting-unauthorized-immigrants.html.

Parkin, Frank. 1971. *Class Inequality and Political Order*. New York: Holt, Rhinehart, Winston.

Parkin, Frank. 1979. *Marxism and Class Theory: A Bourgeois Critique*. London: Tavistock.

Parreñas, Rhacel. 2015. *Servants of Globalization.* 2nd ed. Stanford, CA: Stanford University Press.

Patten, Eileen. 2013. "The Black-White and Urban-Rural Divides in Perceptions of Racial Fairness." Pew Research Center, August 28. Available at http://www.pewresearch.org/fact-tank/2013/08/28/the-black-white-and-urban-rural-divides-in-perceptions-of-racial-fairness.

Pattillo-McCoy, Mary E. 1999. *Black Picket Fences: Privilege and Peril among the Black Middle Class.* Chicago: University of Chicago Press.

Paxton, Pamela, Melanie M. Hughes, and Jennifer L. Green. 2006. "The International Women's Movement and Women's Political Representation, 1893–2003." *American Sociological Review* 71 (6): 898–920.

Peoples, Clayton D. 2008. "Uncovering Political Influence by Using Network Analyses and Exploring Contribution/Party Interactions: The Case of Ohio Legislative Voting." *Sociological Focus* 41 (4): 301–318.

Peoples, Clayton D., and Michael Gortari. 2008. "The Impact of Campaign Contributions of Policymaking in the US and Canada: Theoretical and Public Policy Implications." *Politics and Public Policy* 17: 43–64.

Peri, Giovanni. 2014. "Does Immigration Hurt the Poor?" *Pathways* Summer: 15–18.

Perlman, Selig, and Philip Taft. 1935. *History of Labor in the United States, 1896–1932.* Vol. IV. New York: Macmillan.

Perry, Barbara. 2001. *In the Name of Hate: Understanding Hate Crimes.* New York: Psychology Press.

Persell, Caroline Hodges. 1997. "The Interdependence of Social Justice and Civil Society." *Sociological Forum* 12: 149–172.

Pessen, Edward. 1973. *Riches, Class, and Power before the Civil War.* Lexington, MA: DC Heath.

Petersen, Trond, and Ishak Saporta. 2004. "The Opportunity Structure for Discrimination." *American Journal of Sociology* 109 (4): 852–901.

Petersen, Trond, Vemund Snartland, and Eva M. Meyersson Milgrom. 2007. "Are Female Workers Less Productive than Male Workers?" *Research in Social Stratification and Mobility* 25 (1): 13–37.

Peterson, Ruth D., and Lauren J. Krivo. 2009. "Segregated Spatial Locations, Race-Ethnic Composition, and Neighborhood Violent Crime." *Annals of the American Academy of Political and Social Science* 623 (1): 93–107.

Pettigrew, Thomas F., and Linda R. Tropp. 2006. "A Meta-Analytic Test of Intergroup Contact Theory." *Journal of Personality and Social Psychology* 90 (5): 751.

Pew. 2003. "Religious Beliefs Underpin Opposition to Homosexuality." Pew Research Center for the People and the Press, November 18. Available at http://www.people-press.org/2003/11/18/religious-beliefs-underpin-opposition-to-homosexuality.

Pew. 2007. "Blacks See Growing Values Gap between Poor and Middle Class." Washington, D.C.: Pew Research Center.

Pew. 2009a. "Views of Islam and Violence." Pew Research Center's Religion & Public Life Project, September 9. Available at http://www.pewforum.org/2009/09/09/publicationpage-aspxid1398-3.

Pew. 2009b. "Current Decade Rates as Worst in 50 Years." Pew Research Center for the People and the Press, December 21. Available at http://www.people-press.org/2009/12/21/current-decade-rates-as-worst-in-50-years.

Pew. 2010. "Support For Same-Sex Marriage Edges Upward." Pew Research Center for the People and the Press, October 6. Available at http://www.people-press.org/2010/10/06/support-for-same-sex-marriage-edges-upward.

Pew. 2011a. "Muslim Americans: No Signs of Growth in Alienation or Support for Extremism." Pew Research Center for the People and the Press, August 20. Available at http://www.people-press.org/2011/08/30/muslim-americans-no-signs-of-growth-in-alienation-or-support-for-extremism.

Pew. 2011b. "Section 1: A Demographic Portrait of Muslim Americans." Pew Research Center for the People and the Press, August 30. Available at http://www.people-press.org/2011/08/30/section-1-a-demographic-portrait-of-muslim-americans.

Pew. 2012. "For the Public, It's Not about Class Warfare, But Fairness." Pew Research Center Poll Analysis. Pew Research Center for the People and the Press, March 2. Available at http://www.people-press.org/2012/03/02/for-the-public-its-not-about-class-warfare-but-fairness.

Pew. 2013. "The Rise of Asian Americans." Pew Research Center's Social & Demographic Trends Project, April 4. Available at http://www.pewsocialtrends.org/2012/06/19/the-rise-of-asian-americans.

Pew. 2014a. "Emerging Nations Embrace Internet, Mobile Technology." Pew Research Center's Global Attitudes Project, February 13. Available at http://www.pewglobal.org/2014/02/13/emerging-nations-embrace-internet-mobile-technology.

Pew. 2014b. "Section 3: Fairness of the Economic System, Views of the Poor and the Social Safety Net." Pew Research Center for the People and the Press, June 26. Available at http://www.people-press.org/2014/06/26/section-3-fairness-of-the-economic-system-views-of-the-poor-and-the-social-safety-net.

Pew. 2014c. "Views of Job Market Tick Up, No Rise in Economic Optimism." Pew Research Center for the People and the Press, September 4. Available at http://www.people-press.org/2014/09/04/views-of-job-market-tick-up-no-rise-in-economic-optimism.

Pew. 2015a. "Global Computer Ownership." Pew Research Center's Global Attitudes Project, March 18. Available at http://www.pewglobal.org/2015/03/19/internet-seen-as-positive-influence-on-education-but-negative-influence-on-morality-in-emerging-and-developing-nations/technology-report-15.

Pew. 2015b. "Chapter 7: The Many Dimensions of Hispanic Racial Identity." Pew Research Center's Social & Demographic Trends Project, June 11. Available at http://www.pewsocialtrends.org/2015/06/11/chapter-7-the-many-dimensions-of-hispanic-racial-identity.

Pew. 2015c. "Multiracial in America." Pew Research Center's Social & Demographic Trends Project, June 11. Available at http://www.pewsocialtrends.org/2015/06/11/multiracial-in-america.

Pew. 2015d. "Changing Attitudes on Gay Marriage." Pew Research Center's Religion & Public Life Project, July 29. Available at http://www.pewforum.org/2015/07/29/graphics-slideshow-changing-attitudes-on-gay-marriage.

Pew. 2015e. "The American Middle Class Is Losing Ground." Pew Research Center's Social & Demographic Trends Project, December 9. Available at http://www.pewsocialtrends.org/2015/12/09/the-american-middle-class-is-losing-ground.

Pew. 2015f. "Parenting in America." Pew Research Center, December 15. Available at http://www.pewsocialtrends.org/2015/12/17/parenting-in-america.

Pew Charitable Trusts. 2012. "Pursuing the American Dream: Economic Mobility across Generations." Washington, D.C.: The Pew Charitable Trusts. Available at http://www.pewtrusts.org/~/media/legacy/uploadedfiles/pcs_assets/2012/pursuingamericandreampdf.pdf.

Pfeffer, Fabian T., Sheldon Danziger, and Robert F. Schoeni. 2013. "Wealth Disparities Before and After the Great Recession." *The Annals of the American Academy of Political and Social Science* 650 (1): 98–123.

Phelan, Jo, Bruce G. Link, Robert E. Moore, and Ann Stueve. 1997. "The Stigma of Homelessness: The Impact of the Label 'Homeless' on Attitudes toward Poor Persons." *Social Psychology Quarterly* 60: 323–337.

Phelan, Shane. 2001. *Sexual Strangers: Gays, Lesbians, and Dilemmas of Citizenship*. Philadelphia: Temple University Press.

Phelps, Linda. 1981. "Patriarchy and Capitalism." In *Building Feminist Theory: Essays from Quest*, edited by Charlotte Bunch, Jane Flax, Alexa Freeman, Nancy Hartsock, and Mary-Helen Manther, 161–173. New York: Longman.

Phelps, Timothy. 2015. "Next Frontier for Gays Is Employment and Housing Discrimination." *Los Angeles Times*, June 26. Available at http://www.latimes.com/nation/la-na-gays-employment-20150626-story.html.

Philipson, Ilene J., and Karen V. Hansen. 1990. "Women, Class, and the Feminist Imagination: An Introduction." In *Women, Class, and the Feminist Imagination: A Socialist-Feminist Reader*, edited by Karen V. Hansen and Ilene J. Philipson, 3–40. Philadelphia: Temple University Press.

Phillips, Julie, and Kenneth C. Land. 2012. "The Link between Unemployment and Crime Rate Fluctuations: An Analysis at the County, State, and National Levels." *Social Science Research* 41 (3): 681–694.

Phillips, Roxine Denise. 2015. "Lived Experiences of Women Over 50 Who Have Experienced Involuntary Job Loss." Dissertation. Minneapolis, MN: Walden University. Available at http://scholarworks.waldenu.edu/dissertations/1742.

Phillips, Scott. 2009. "Status Disparities in the Capital of Capital Punishment." *Law & Society Review* 43: 807–838.

Pickett, Justin T., Ted Chiricos, Kristin M. Golden, and Marc Gertz. 2012. "Reconsidering the Relationship between Perceived Neighborhood Racial Composition and Whites' Perceptions of Victimization Risk: Do Racial Stereotypes Matter?" *Criminology* 50 (1): 145–186.

Piff, Paul K., Michael W. Kraus, Stéphane Côté, Bonnie Hayden Cheng, and Dacher Keltner. 2010. "Having Less, Giving More: The Influence of Social Class on Prosocial Behavior." *Journal of Personality and Social Psychology* 99 (5): 771–784.

Piketty, Thomas. 2014. *Capital in the Twenty-First Century*. Translated by Arthur Goldhammer. Cambridge, MA: Belknap Press of Harvard University Press.

Piontak, Joy R., and Michael D. Schulman. 2014. "Food Insecurity in Rural America." *Contexts* 13 (3): 75–77.

Piori, Michael J. 1977. "The Dual Labor Market: Theory and Implications." In *Problems in Political Economy: An Urban Perspective*, edited by David M. Gordon, 93–97. Lexington, MA: Heath.

Piven, Frances Fox, and Richard Cloward. 1979. *Poor People's Movements: Why They Succeed, How They Fail*. New York: Vintage Books.

Piven, Frances Fox, and Richard Cloward. 1982. *The New Class War: Reagan's Attack on the Welfare State and Its Consequences*. New York: Pantheon.

Piven, Frances Fox, and Richard Cloward. 2012. *Regulating the Poor: The Functions of Public Welfare*. New York: Vintage.

Plumer, Brad. 2012. "Who Doesn't Pay Taxes, in Eight Charts." *Washington Post*, September 18. Available at http://www.washingtonpost.com/news/wonkblog/wp/2012/09/18/who-doesnt-pay-taxes-in-charts.

Podgor, Ellen S. 2007. "The Challenge of White Collar Sentencing." *The Journal of Criminal Law and Criminology* 97: 731–759.

Pollard, Kelvin, and Linda A. Jacobsen. 2011. "The Appalachian Region in 2010: A Census Data Overview Chartbook." Washington, D.C.: Appalachian Regional Commission. Available at http://www.igwg.org/pdf12/appalachia-census-chartbook-2011.pdf.

Pontell, Henry N., and Gilbert Geis. 2014. "The Trajectory of White-Collar Crime Following the Great Economic Meltdown." *Journal of Contemporary Criminal Justice* 30 (1): 70–82.

Porter, James N. 1974. "Race, Socialization and Mobility in Educational and Early Occupational Attainment." *American Sociological Review* 39: 303–316.

Portes, Alejandro, and Ruben G. Rumbaut. 2005. "Not Everyone Is Chosen." In *Great Divides: Readings in Social Inequality in the United States*, edited by Thomas M. Shapiro, 3rd ed. Boston: McGraw-Hill.

Portes, Alejandro, and Kenneth L. Wilson. 1976. "Black-White Differences in Educational Attainment." *American Sociological Review* 41: 414–431.

Powell. G. Bingham. 1986. "American Voter Turnout in Comparative Perspective." *American Political Science Review* 80 (1): 17–43.

Pratt, Travis C., and Timothy W. Godsey. 2003. "Social Support, Inequality, and Homicide: A Cross-National Test of an Integrated Theoretical Model." *Criminology* 41 (3): 611–644.

Pressman, Steven. 2007. "The Decline of the Middle Class: An International Perspective." *Journal of Economic Issues* 41: 181–200.

Prewitt, Kenneth, and Alan Stone. 1973. *The Ruling Elites: Elite Theory, Power, and American Democracy*. Harper & Row.

Price Waterhouse v. Hopkins. 1989. No. 87-1167. Supreme Court of the United States. 490 U.S. 228: 231–295.

Principe, Connor P., and Judith H. Langlois. 2013. "Children and Adults Use Attractiveness as a Social Cue in Real People and Avatars." *Journal of Experimental Child Psychology* 115 (3): 590–597.

Pryor, Frederic L. 2010. "American Crime from an International Perspective." *Society* 47 (3): 175–177.

Purtell, Kelly M., Elizabeth T. Gershoff, and J. Lawrence Aber. 2012. "Low Income Families' Utilization of the Federal 'Safety Net': Individual and State-Level Predictors of TANF and Food Stamp Receipt." *Children and Youth Services Review* 34 (4): 713–724.

Pyke, Karen, and Tran Dang. 2003. "'FOB' and 'whitewashed': Identity and Internalized Racism among Second Generation Asian Americans." *Qualitative Sociology* 26 (2): 147–172.

Rabito, Felicia A., Shahed Iqbal, Sara Perry, Whitney Arroyave, and Janet C. Rice. 2012. "Environmental Lead after Hurricane Katrina: Implications for Future Populations." *Environmental Health Perspectives* 120 (2): 180–184.

Rafferty, Anthony. 2012. "Ethnic Penalties in Graduate Level Over-Education, Unemployment and Wages: Evidence from Britain." *Work, Employment & Society* 26 (6): 987–1006.

Ragins, Belle Rose, and Doan E. Winkel. 2011. "Gender, Emotion and Power in Work Relationships." *Human Resource Management Review* 21 (4): 377–393.

Rampell, Catherine. 2015. "The Bizarre War against AP U.S. History Courses." *Washington Post*, February 19. Available at https://www.washingtonpost.com/opinions/an-unflattering-history-lesson/2015/02/19/3be9cb0c-b878-11e4-a200-c008a01a6692_story.html.

Raphael, Dennis. 2009. "Reducing Social and Health Inequalities Requires Building Social and Political Movements." *Humanity & Society* 33 (1–2): 145–165.

Raven, Betram H. 1965. "Social Influence and Power." In *Current Studies in Social Psychology*, edited by Ivan D. Steiner and Martin Fishbein, 399–444. New York: Holt, Rinehart and Winston.

Ray, Rashawn. 2014. "Stalled Desegregation and the myth of Racial Equality in the U.S. Labor Market." *Du Bois Review: Social Science Research on Race* 11 (2): 477–487.

Read, Jen'nan Ghazal, and Bridget K. Gorman. 2010. "Gender and Health Inequality." *Annual Review of Sociology* 36: 371–386.

Read, John. 2010. "Can Poverty Drive You Mad? Schizophrenia, Socio-Economic Status and the Case for Primary Prevention." *New Zealand Journal of Psychology* 39 (2): 7–19.

Reddy, Chandan. 2011. *Freedom with Violence: Race, Sexuality, and the US State (Perverse Modernities)*. Durham, NC: Duke University Press.

Reeves, Richard V., and Joanna Venator. 2014. "Women and Social Mobility: Six Key Facts." Brookings Institution, April 3. Available at http://www.brookings.edu/blogs/social-mobility-memos/posts/2014/04/03-women-social-mobility-six-key-facts-reeves.

Reich, Michael. 1977. "The Economics of Racism." In *Problems in Political Economy: An Urban Perspective*, edited by David M. Gordon, 183–188. Lexington, MA: D. C. Heath.

Reid, Pamela Trotman. 1984. "Feminism versus Minority Group Identity: Not for Black Woman Only." *Sex Roles* 10 (3–4): 247–255.

Reiman, Jeffrey H., and Paul Leighton. 2012. *The Rich Get Richer and the Poor Get Prison: Ideology, Class, and Criminal Justice*. 10th ed. New York: Routledge.

Reiss, Franziska. 2013. "Socioeconomic Inequalities and Mental Health Problems in Children and Adolescents: A Systematic Review." *Social Science & Medicine* 90 (August): 24–31.

Reskin, Barbara F. 2003. "Including Mechanisms in Our Models of Ascriptive Inequality." *American Sociological Review* 68 (1): 1–21.

Reskin, Barbara F., and Debra Branch McBrier. 2000. "Why Not Ascription? Organizations' Employment of Male and Female Managers." *American Sociological Review* 65: 210–233.

Resnick, Stephen, and Richard Wolff. 2003. "The Diversity of Class Analyses: A Critique of Erik Olin Wright and Beyond." *Critical Sociology* 29 (1): 7–27.

Reuters. 2015. "South Carolina: Trial Delayed in Church Massacre." *New York Times*, October 1. Available at http://www.nytimes.com/2015/10/02/us/south-carolina-trial-delayed-in-church-massacre-dylann-roof.html.

Reuveny, Rafael, and Quan Li. 2003. "Economic Openness, Democracy, and Income Inequality: An Empirical Analysis." *Comparative Political Studies* 36 (5): 575–601.

Rhode, Deborah L. 2010. *The Beauty Bias: The Injustice of Appearance in Life and Law*. New York: Oxford University Press.

Rhode, Deborah L. 2014. *What Women Want: An Agenda for the Women's Movement*. New York: Oxford University Press.

Riahi-Belkaoui, Ahmed. 2003. *Accounting—by Principle or Design?* Westport, CT: Praeger.

Rich, Adrienne. 1979. "Disloyal to Civilization: Feminism, Racism, Gynephobia." In *On Lies, Secrets, and Silence: Selected Prose 1966–1978*, 275–310. New York: W.W. Norton & Company.

Rich, Adrienne. 1980. "Compulsory Heterosexuality and Lesbian Existence." *Signs*, 631–660.

Ridgeway, Cecilia L. 2011. *Framed by Gender: How Gender Inequality Persists in the Modern World*. Cambridge, MA: Oxford University Press.

Ridgeway, Cecilia L. 2013. "Why Status Matters for Inequality." *American Sociological Review* 79 (1): 1–16.

Ridgeway, Cecilia L., Kristen Backor, Yan E. Li, Justine E. Tinkler, and Kristan G. Erickson. 2009. "How Easily Does a Social Difference Become a Status Distinction? Gender Matters." *American Sociological Review* 74 (1): 44–62.

Ridgeway, Cecilia L., Elizabeth Heger Boyle, Kathy J. Kuipers, and Dawn T. Robinson. 1998. "How Do Status Beliefs Develop? The Role of Resources and Interactional Experience." *American Sociological Review* 63: 331–350.

Ridgeway, Cecilia L., and T. Kricheli-Katz. 2013. "Intersecting Cultural Beliefs in Social Relations: Gender, Race, and Class Binds and Freedoms." *Gender & Society* 27 (3): 294–318.

Riegle-Crumb, Catherine, and Melissa Humphries. 2012. "Exploring Bias in Math Teachers' Perceptions of Students' Ability by Gender and Race/Ethnicity." *Gender & Society* 26 (2): 290–322.

Rigney, Daniel. 2001. *The Metaphorical Society: An Invitation to Social Theory*. Lanham, MD: Rowman & Littlefield.

Riis, Jacob. 1890. *How the Other Half Lives*. Williamstown, MA: Corner House.

Ringquist, Evan J. 1997. "Equity and the Distribution of Environmental Risk: The Case of TRI Facilities." *Social Science Quarterly* 78: 811–829.

Ringquist, Evan J. 2000. "Environmental Justice: Normative Concerns and Empirical Evidence." In *Environmental Policy*, edited by N. J. Vig and M. E. Kraft, 232–256. Washington, D.C.: CQ Press.

Rischin, Moses. 1965. *The American Gospel of Success: Individualism and Beyond*. Vol. 54. New York; Chicago: Quadrangle Books.

Risman, Barbara J. 2004. "Gender as a Social Structure: Theory Wrestling with Activism." *Gender & Society* 18 (4): 429–450.

Risman, Barbara J., and G. Davis. 2013. "From Sex Roles to Gender Structure." *Current Sociology* 61 (5–6): 733–755.

Ritzer, George. 2008. *Sociological Theory*. New York: Tata McGraw-Hill Education.

Rivera, David P., Erin E. Forquer, and Rebecca Rangel. 2010. "Microaggressions and the Life Experience of Latina/o Americans." In *Microaggressions and Marginality: Manifestation, Dynamics, and Impact*, edited by Derald W. Sue, 59–83. Hoboken, NJ: John Wiley & Sons.

Rivers, Daniel. 2010. "'In the Best Interests of the Child': Lesbian and Gay Parenting Custody Cases, 1967–1985." *Journal of Social History* 43 (4): 917–943.

Robbins, Alexandra. 2004. *Pledged: The Secret Life of Sororities*. New York: Hyperion.

Robinson, James W. 2009. "American Poverty Cause Beliefs and Structured Inequality Legitimation." *Sociological Spectrum* 29 (4): 489–518.

Robinson, Robert V., and Wendell Bell. 1978. "Equality, Success, and Social Justice in England and the United States." *American Sociological Review* 43: 125–143.

Rode, Joseph C., Marne L. Arthaud-Day, Christine H. Mooney, Janet P. Near, and Timothy T. Baldwin. 2008. "Ability and Personality Predictors of Salary, Perceived Job Success, and Perceived Career Success in the Initial Career Stage." *International Journal of Selection and Assessment* 16 (3): 292–299.

Rodriguez, S. Fernando, Theodore R. Curry, and Gang Lee. 2006. "Gender Differences in Criminal Sentencing: Do Effects Vary Across Violent, Property, and Drug Offenses?" *Social Science Quarterly* 87 (2): 318–339.

Rogin, Michael. 1971. "Voluntarism: The Political Functions of an Antipolitical Doctrine." In *The American Labor Movement*, edited by David Brody, 521–535. New York: Harper & Row.

Rollins, Judith. 1986. "Part of a Whole: The Interdependence of the Civil Rights Movement and Other Social Movements." *Phylon* 47: 61–70.

Roper Center. 2013. "Infographic: The Public and Transgendered People, by the Numbers." Roper Center. Available at http://www.ropercenter.uconn.edu/infographic-the-public-and-transgendered-people-by-the-numbers/.

Roscigno, Vincent J., Steven H. Lopez, and Randy Hodson. 2009. "Supervisory Bullying, Status Inequalities and Organizational Context." *Social Forces* 87 (3): 1561–1589.

Rose, Max, and Frank R. Baumgartner. 2013. "Framing the Poor: Media Coverage and US Poverty Policy, 1960–2008." *Policy Studies Journal* 41 (1): 22–53.

Rosen, Ruth. 2006. *The World Split Open: How the Modern Women's Movement Changed America*. Revised. New York: Penguin Books.

Rosenfeld, Dana. 2009. "Heteronormativity and Homonormativity as Practical and Moral Resources: The Case of Lesbian and Gay Elders." *Gender & Society* 23: 617–638.

Rosenfeld, Jake. 2010. "Economic Determinants of Voting in an Era of Union Decline." *Social Science Quarterly* 91 (2): 379–395.

Rosenfeld, Rachel A. 1992. "Job Mobility and Career Processes." *Annual Review of Sociology* 18: 39–61.

Rosenthal, Elisabeth. 2014. "How the High Cost of Medical Care Is Affecting Americans." *New York Times*, December 18. Available at http://www.nytimes.com/interactive/2014/12/18/health/cost-of-health-care-poll.html.

Rosenthal, Lisa, Amy Carroll-Scott, Valerie A. Earnshaw, Alycia Santilli, and Jeannette R. Ickovics. 2012. "The Importance of Full-Time Work for Urban Adults' Mental and Physical Health." *Social Science & Medicine* 75 (9): 1692–1696.

Rospenda, Kathleen M., Judith A. Richman, and Stephanie J. Nawyn. 1998. "Doing Power: The Confluence of Gender, Race, and Class in Contrapower Sexual Harassment." *Gender & Society* 12 (1): 40–60.

Ross, Catherine E., and John Mirowsky. 2002. "Age and the Gender Gap in the Sense of Personal Control." *Social Psychology Quarterly* 65 (2): 125–145.

Ross, Catherine E., John R. Reynolds, and Karlyn J. Geis. 2000. "The Contingent Meaning of Neighborhood Stability for Residents' Psychological Well-Being." *American Sociological Review* 65: 581–597.

Ross, Janell. 2015. "The Remarkable Racial Divide in the Days after Hurricane Katrina." *Washington Post*, August 28. Available at https://www.washingtonpost.com/news/the-fix/wp/2015/08/28/the-remarkable-racial-divide-in-the-days-after-hurricane-katrina.

Rostker, Bernard D., Susan D. Hosek, and Mary E. Vaiana. 2011. "Gays in the Military." Santa Monica, CA: RAND Corporation. Available at http://www.rand.org/pubs/periodicals/rand-review/issues/2011/spring/gays.html.

Rostow, Walt W. 1960. *The Stages of Economic Growth*. Cambridge, UK: Cambridge University Press.

Roth, Louise Marie. 2004a. "Bringing Clients Back In: Homophily Preferences and Inequality on Wall Street." *Sociological Quarterly* 45 (4): 613–635.

Roth, Louise Marie. 2004b. "Engendering Inequality: Processes of Sex-Segregation on Wall Street." *Sociological Forum* 19 (2): 203–228.

Roth, Max, and Max Wittich, eds. 1968. *Economy and Society: An Outline of Interpretive Sociology*. New York: Bedminster Press.

Roth, Wendy D. 2005. "The End of the One-Drop Rule? Labeling of Multiracial Children in Black Intermarriages." *Sociological Forum* 20: 35–67.

Roth, Wendy D. 2013. "Creating a 'Latino' Race." The Society Pages. Available at http://thesocietypages.org/papers/creating-a-latino-race.

Rothenberg, Paula S. 2008. *White Privilege*. New York: Worth.

Rothstein, Bo, and Eric M. Uslaner. 2005. "All for All: Equality, Corruption, and Social Trust." *World Politics* 58 (1): 41–72.

Rouse, Stella M., Betina Cutaia Wilkinson, and James C. Garand. 2010. "Divided Loyalties? Understanding Variation in Latino Attitudes Toward Immigration." *Social Science Quarterly* 91 (3): 856–882.

Roy, Siddhartha. 2015. "Our Sampling of 252 Homes Demonstrates a High Lead in Water Risk: Flint Should Be Failing to Meet the EPA Lead and Copper Rule." Flint Water Study Updates. September 8. Available at http://flintwaterstudy.org/2015/09/our-sampling-of-252-homes-demonstrates-a-high-lead-in-water-risk-flint-should-be-failing-to-meet-the-epa-lead-and-copper-rule.

Roy, Siddhartha. 2016a. "Research Update: Corrosivity of Flint Water to Iron Pipes in the City — A Costly Problem." Flint Water Study Updates. Available at http://flintwaterstudy.org/2015/09/research-update-corrosivity-of-flint-water-to-iron-pipes-in-the-city-a-costly-problem.

Roy, Siddhartha. 2016b. "The Surreal Flint Experience: 2014–2015 Water Crisis." Flint Water Study Updates. Available at http://flintwaterstudy.org/2015/12/the-surreal-flint-experience-2014-2015-water-crisis-video-of-resident-getting-arrested-for-questioning-safety-of-water.

Rubenstein, Ruth. 2001. *Dress Codes: Meanings and Messages in American Culture*. Boulder, CO: Westview Press.

Rubin, Marcie S., Cynthia G. Colen, and Bruce G. Link. 2010. "Examination of Inequalities in HIV/AIDS Mortality in the United States from a Fundamental Cause Perspective." *American Journal of Public Health* 100 (6): 1053–1059.

Ruderman, Marian N., Patricia J. Ohlott, Kate Panzer, and Sara N. King. 2002. "Benefits of Multiple Roles for Managerial Women." *Academy of Management Journal* 45 (2): 369–386.

Rudra, Nita. 2004. "Openness, Welfare Spending, and Inequality in the Developing World." *International Studies Quarterly* 48 (3): 683–709.

Ruggles, Steven. 2015. "Patriarchy, Power, and Pay: The Transformation of American Families, 1800–2015." *Demography* 52 (6): 1797–1823.

Rupp, Leila J. 1985. "The Women's Community in the National Woman's Party, 1945 to the 1960s." *Signs* 10 (4): 715–740.

Ryan, Caitlin, David Huebner, Rafael Diaz, and Jorge Sanchez. 2009. "Family Rejection as a Predictor of Negative Health Outcomes in White and Latino Lesbian, Gay, and Bisexual Young Adults." *Pediatrics* 123 (1): 346–352.

Ryan, William. 1981. *Equality*. New York: Random House.

Ryff, Carol D., Corey L. M. Keyes, and Diane L. Hughes. 2003. "Status Inequalities, Perceived Discrimination, and Eudaimonic Well-Being: Do the Challenges of Minority Life Hone Purpose and Growth?" *Journal of Health and Social Behavior* 44 (3): 275–291.

Rytina, Steven. 2000. "Is Occupational Mobility Declining in the US?" *Social Forces* 78 (4): 1227–1276.

Saad, Lydia. 2010. "Americans Acceptance of Gay Relations Crosses 50% Threshold." *Gallup Poll Briefing*, May 25, p. 1.

Saad, Lydia. 2012. "U.S. Acceptance of Gay/Lesbian Relations Is the New Normal." Gallup.com, May 14. Available at http://www.gallup.com/poll/154634/Acceptance-Gay-Lesbian-Relations-New-Normal.aspx.

Saad, Lydia. 2015. "Americans' Support for Labor Unions Continues to Recover." Gallup.com, August 17. Available at http://www.gallup.com/poll/184622/americans-support-labor-unions-continues-recover.aspx.

Sabol, Steven. 2012. "Comparing American and Russian Internal Colonization: The 'Touch of Civilisation' on the Sioux and Kazakhs." *Western Historical Quarterly* 43 (1): 29–51.

Sacks, Karen. 1975. "Engels Revisited: Women, the Organization of Production, and Private Property." In *Toward an Anthropology of Women*, edited by R.R. Reiter, 211–234. New York: Monthly Review Press.

Sacks, Meghan, Vincenzo A. Sainato, and Alissa R. Ackerman. 2015. "Sentenced to Pretrial Detention: A Study of Bail Decisions and Outcomes." *American Journal of Criminal Justice* 40 (3): 661–681.

Saez, Emmanuel. 2014. "U.S. Income Inequality Persists amid Overall Growth in 2014." Washington Center for Equitable Growth. Available at http://equitablegrowth.org/research/u-s-income-inequality-persists-amid-overall-growth-2014.

Sahlins, Marshall D. 1968. *Tribesman*. Englewood Cliffs, NJ: Prentice Hall.

Salin, Denise. 2003. "Ways of Explaining Workplace Bullying: A Review of Enabling, Motivating and Precipitating Structures and Processes in the Work Environment." *Human Relations* 56 (10): 1213–1232.

SAMHSA. 2015. "Results from the 2014 National Survey on Drug Use and Health: Mental Health Tables, SAMHSA, CBHSQ." National Survey on Drug Use and Health 2013 and 2014. Substance Abuse and Mental Health Services Administration, Center for Behavioral Health Statistics and Quality. Available at http://www.samhsa.gov/data/sites/default/files/NSDUH-MHDetTabs2014/NSDUH-MHDetTabs2014.htm#tab1-42a.

Sampson, Robert J. 2008. "Moving to Inequality: Neighborhood Effects and Experiments Meet Structure." *American Journal of Sociology* 114 (11): 189–231.

Sampson, Robert J, and Patrick Sharkey. 2008. "Neighborhood Selection and the Social Reproduction of Concentrated Racial Inequality." *Demography* 45 (1): 1–29.

Sampson, Robert J., and William Julius Wilson. 1995. "Toward a Theory of Race, Crime, and Urban Inequality." In *Race, Crime, and Justice: A Reader*, edited by John Hagan and Ruth D. Peterson, 177–190. Stanford, CA: Stanford University Press.

Samuels, Ellen. 2014. *Fantasies of Identification: Disability, Gender, Race*. New York: NYU Press.

Sanday, Peggy Reeves. 1981. *Female Power and Male Dominance: On the Origins of Sexual Inequality*. Cambridge, MA: Cambridge University Press.

Sandberg, Jonathan G., James M. Harper, E. Jeffrey Hill, Richard B. Miller, Jeremy B. Yorgason, and Randal D. Day. 2013. "'What Happens at Home Does Not Necessarily Stay at Home': The Relationship of Observed Negative Couple Interaction with Physical Health, Mental Health, and Work Satisfaction." *Journal of Marriage and Family* 75 (4): 808–821.

Sandberg, Sheryl. 2013. *Lean In: Women, Work, and the Will to Lead*. New York: Alfred A. Knopf.

Sanderson, Stephen K. 2005. "World-Systems Analysis after Thirty Years: Should It Rest in Peace?" *International Journal of Comparative Sociology* 46 (3): 179–213.

Sandler, Bernice R., and Roberta M. Hall. 1986. *The Campus Climate Revisited: Chilly for Women Faculty, Administrators, and Graduate Students*. Washington, D.C.: Association of American Colleges.

Santiago, Anna Maria. 2015. "Fifty Years Later: From a War on Poverty to a War on the Poor." *Social Problems* 62 (1): 2–14.

Saperstein, Aliya, and Andrew M. Penner. 2012. "Racial Fluidity and Inequality in the United States." *American Journal of Sociology* 118 (3): 676–727.

Sassen, Saskia. 2000. "The State and the New Geography of Power." In *The Ends of Globalization: Bringing Society Back In*, edited by Don Kalb, Marco van der Land, Richard Staring, Bart van Steenbergen, and Nico Wilterdink, 49–65. Lanham, MD: Rowman & Littlefield.

Saunders, Laura. 2015. "Top 20% of Earners Pay 84% of Income Tax." *Wall Street Journal*, April 10. Available at http://www.wsj.com/articles/top-20-of-earners-pay-84-of-income-tax-1428674384.

Savage, Charlie. 2012. "Wells Fargo to Settle Mortgage Bias Charges." *New York Times*, July 12. Available at http://www.nytimes.com/2012/07/13/business/wells-fargo-to-settle-mortgage-discrimination-charges.html.

Save the Children. 2015. "The Urban Disadvantage: State of the World's Mothers." Fairfield, CT: Save the Children Federation, Inc. Available at http://www.savethechildren.org/atf/cf/%7B9def2ebe-10ae-432c-9bd0-df91d2eba74a%7D/SOWM_2015.PDF.

Sawhill, Isabel V. 1988. "Poverty in the US: Why Is It so Persistent?" *Journal of Economic Literature* 26: 1073–1119.

Sawhill, Isabel V. 2008. "Spending America into Fiscal Collapse." *Akron Beacon Journal*, May 27, sec. A.

Scanlan, Stephen. 2009. "Coal Sludge, Toxics, and Trash: Facility Siting, Inequality, and Environmental Justice in Appalachia." Paper presented at Annual Meeting of American Sociological Association, August 2008.

Schaefer, Richard T. 2015. *Racial and Ethnic Groups*. 14th ed. Boston: Pearson.

Schauer, Edward J., and Elizabeth M. Wheaton. 2006. "Sex Trafficking into the United States: A Literature Review." *Criminal Justice Review* 31 (2): 146–169.

Schervish, Paul G., Platon E. Coutsoukis, and Ethan Lewis. 1994. *Gospels of Wealth: How the Rich Portray Their Lives*. Westport, CT: Praeger.

Schieman, Scott, and Jong Hyun Jung. 2012. "'Practical Divine Influence': Socioeconomic Status and Belief in the Prosperity Gospel." *Journal for the Scientific Study of Religion* 51 (4): 738–756.

Schieman, Scott, and Gabriele Plickert. 2008. "How Knowledge Is Power: Education and the Sense of Control." *Social Forces* 87 (1): 153–183.

Schilt, Kristen, and Laurel Westbrook. 2015. "Bathroom Battlegrounds and Penis Panics." *Contexts* 14 (3): 26–31.

Schlozman, Kay L., Sidney Verba, and Henry E. Brady. 2012. *The Unheavenly Chorus: Unequal Political Voice and the Broken Promise of American Democracy*. Princeton, NJ: Princeton University Press.

Schnittker, Jason. 2007. "Working More and Feeling Better: Women's Health, Employment, and Family Life, 1974–2004." *American Sociological Review* 72 (2): 221–238.

Schnittker, Jason, Bernice A. Pescosolido, and Thomas W. Croghan. 2005. "Are African Americans Really Less Willing to Use Health Care?" *Social Problems* 52 (2): 255–271.

Schooler, Carmi, Mesfin Samuel Mulatu, and Gary Oates. 2004. "Occupational Self-Direction, Intellectual Functioning, and Self-Directed Orientation in Older Workers: Findings and Implications for Individuals and Societies." *American Journal of Sociology* 110 (1): 161–197.

Schott, Liz, LaDonna Pavetti, and Ife Floyd. 2015. "How States Use Federal and State Funds Under the TANF Block Grant." Washington, D.C.: Center on Budget and Policy Priorities.

Schram, Sanford F., and Joe Soss. 2001. "Success Stories: Welfare Reform, Policy Discourse, and the Politics of Research." *The Annals of the*

American Academy of Political and Social Science 577 (1): 49–65.

Schuck, Amie, and Christine Martin. 2013. "Residents' Perceptions of Procedural Injustice during Encounters with the Police." *Journal of Ethnicity in Criminal Justice* 11 (4): 219–237.

Schulz, Amy J., Shannon N. Zenk, Barbara A. Israel, Graciela Mentz, Carmen Stokes, and Sandro Galea. 2008. "Do Neighborhood Economic Characteristics, Racial Composition, and Residential Stability Predict Perceptions of Stress Associated with the Physical and Social Environment? Findings from a Multilevel Analysis in Detroit." *Journal of Urban Health* 85 (5): 642–661.

Schwalbe, Michael. 2008. *Rigging the Game: How Inequality Is Reproduced in Everyday Life.* New York: Oxford University Press.

Schwalbe, Michael, Sandra Godwin, Daphne Holden, Douglas Schrock, Shealy Thompson, and Michele Wolkomir. 2000. "Generic Processes in the Reproduction of Inequality: An Interactionist Analysis." *Social Forces* 79 (2): 419–452.

Schwartz, Christine R. 2010. "Earnings Inequality and the Changing Association between Spouses' Earnings." *American Journal of Sociology* 115 (5): 1524–1557.

Schwartz, Michael. 1987. *The Structure of Power in America: The Corporate Elite as a Ruling Class.* New York: Holmes & Meier.

Schwartz, Nelson D. 2016. "Economists Take Aim at Wealth Inequality." *New York Times*, January 3. Available at http://www.nytimes.com/2016/01/04/business/economy/economists-take-aim-at-wealth-inequality.html.

Schwartz, Robert C., and David M. Blankenship. 2014. "Racial Disparities in Psychotic Disorder Diagnosis: A Review of Empirical Literature." *World Journal of Psychiatry* 4 (4): 133–140.

Scott, Janny, and David Leonhardt. 2005. "Class in America: Shadowy Lines That Still Divide." *New York Times*, May 15, pp. A1, A16.

Scott, Robert E. 2015. "The Manufacturing Footprint and the Importance of U.S. Manufacturing Jobs." Washington, D.C.: Economic Policy Institute. Available at http://www.epi.org/publication/the-manufacturing-footprint-and-the-importance-of-u-s-manufacturing-jobs.

Scott, Susie, and M. Dawson. 2015. "Rethinking Asexuality: A Symbolic Interactionist Account." *Sexualities* 18 (1–2): 3–19.

Sedgwick, Eve Kosofsky. 1998. "What's Queer?" In *Gender Inequality*, edited by Judith Lorber, 183–187. Los Angeles: Roxbury.

Seligman, Hilary K., Barbara A. Laraia, and Margot B. Kushel. 2010. "Food Insecurity Is Associated with Chronic Disease among Low-Income NHANES Participants." *Journal of Nutrition* 140 (2): 304–310.

Sellers, Robert M., Cleopatra H. Caldwell, Karen H. Schmeelk-Cone, and Marc A. Zimmerman. 2003. "Racial Identity, Racial Discrimination, Perceived Stress, and Psychological Distress among African American Young Adults." *Journal of Health and Social Behavior* 44 (3): 302–317.

Sennett, Richard, and Jonathan Cobb. 1973. *The Hidden Injuries of Class.* New York: Vintage Books.

Sentencing Project. 2014. "Felony Disenfranchisement and the 2014 Midterm Elections." The Sentencing Project News. October 2. Available at http://www.sentencingproject.org/detail/news.cfm?news_id=1877.

Sentencing Project. 2015a. "Incarceration." The Sentencing Project News. Available at http://www.sentencingproject.org/template/page.cfm?id=107.

Sentencing Project. 2015b. "Felony Disenfranchisement: A Primer." Washington, D.C.: The Sentencing Project. Available at http://sentencingproject.org/doc/publications/fd_Felony%20Disenfranchisement%20Primer.pdf.

Sernau, Scott. 2006. *Worlds Apart: Social Inequalities in a Global Economy.* 2nd ed. Thousand Oaks, CA: Pine Forge Press.

Seshanna, Shubhasree, and Stéphane Decornez. 2003. "Income Polarization and Inequality across Countries: An Empirical Study." *Journal of Policy Modeling* 25 (4): 335–358.

Sevak, Purvi, and Lucie Schmidt. 2014. "Immigrants and Retirement Resources." *Social Security Bulletin* 74 (1). Available at http://www.ssa.gov/policy/docs/ssb/v74n1/v74n1p27.html.

Sewell, William Hamilton, Archibald O. Haller, and George W. Ohlendorf. 1970. "The Educational and Early Occupational Status Attainment Process: Replication and Revision." *American Sociological Review* 35: 1014–1027.

Sewell, William Hamilton, and Robert Mason Hauser. 1976. "Recent Developments in the Wisconsin Study of Social and Psychological

Factors in Socioeconomic Achievement." Working Paper 76-11. Madison: Center for Demography and Ecology, University of Wisconsin.

Sewell, William Hamilton, and Vimal P. Shah. 1967. "Socioeconomic Status, Intelligence, and the Attainment of Higher Education." *Sociology of Education* 40: 1–23.

Shaefer, H. Luke, and Kathryn Edin. 2014. "The Rise of Extreme Poverty in the United States." *Pathways* Summer: 28–32.

Shamir, Ronen. 2005. "Without Borders? Notes on Globalization as a Mobility Regime." *Sociological Theory* 23 (2): 197–217.

Shams, Tahseen. 2015. "The Declining Significance of Race or the Persistent Racialization of Blacks? A Conceptual, Empirical, and Methodological Review of Today's Race Debate in America." *Journal of Black Studies* 46 (3): 282–296.

Shanahan, Michael J., Richard A. Miech, and Glen H. Elder. 1998. "Changing Pathways to Attainment in Men's Lives: Historical Patterns of School, Work, and Social Class." *Social Forces* 77 (1): 231–256.

Shapiro, Joseph. 2015. "Jail Time for Unpaid Court Fines and Fees Can Create Cycle of Poverty." National Public Radio. February 9. Available at http://www.npr.org/sections/codeswitch/2015/02/09/384968360/jail-time-for-unpaid-court-fines-and-fees-can-create-cycle-of-poverty.

Shapiro, Thomas M. 2004. *The Hidden Cost of Being African American: How Wealth Perpetuates Inequality.* New York: Oxford University Press.

Shapiro, Thomas, Tatjana Meschede, and Sam Osoro. 2013. "The Roots of the Widening Racial Wealth Gap: Explaining the Black-White Economic Divide." Research and Policy Brief February. Brandeis University, Waltham MA: Institute on Assets and Social Policy. Available at http://www.naacpldf.org/files/case_issue/Shapiro%20racialwealthgapbrief.pdf.

Shattuck, Rachel M., and Rose M. Kreider. 2013. "Social and Economic Characteristics of Currently Unmarried Women with a Recent Birth: 2011." ACS-21. American Community Survey Reports. Washington, D.C.: U.S. Department of Commerce Economics and Statistics Administration, U.S. Census Bureau.

Shepelak, Norma J. 1987. "The Role of Self-Explanations and Self-Evaluations in Legitimating Inequality." *American Sociological Review* 52 495–503.

Shepelak, Norma J., and Duane F. Alwin. 1986 "Beliefs about Inequality and Perceptions o Distributive Justice." *American Sociologica Review* 51: 30–46.

Shifman, Pamela. 2003. "Trafficking and Women' Human Rights in a Globalised World." *Gende & Development* 11 (1): 125–132.

Shihadeh, Edward S., and Raymond E. Barranco 2010. "Latino Employment and Black Vio lence: The Unintended Consequence of U Immigration Policy." *Social Forces* 88 (3 1393–1420.

Shils, Edward A. 1970. "Deference." In *The Log of Social Hierarchies*, edited by Edward (Laumann, Paul M. Siegel, and Robert V Hodge, 420–428. Chicago: Markham.

Shor, Francis. 2015. "'Black Lives Matter': Con structing a New Civil Rights and Black Freedo Movement." *New Politics* 15 (3): 28–32.

Shostak, Sara, Jeremy Freese, Bruce G. Link, and J C. Phelan. 2009. "The Politics of the Gen Social Status and Beliefs about Genetics f Individual Outcomes." *Social Psycholo Quarterly* 72 (1): 77–93.

Silverman, Arielle M., and Geoffrey L. Cohe 2014. "Stereotypes as Stumbling-Blocks: Ho Coping with Stereotype Threat Affects Li Outcomes for People with Physical Disabilities *Personality and Social Psychology Bulle* 40 (10): 1330–1340.

Silverstein, Sara. 2014. "These Animated Char Tell You Everything About Uber Prices in Cities." Business Insider. October 16. Availab at http://www.businessinsider.com/uber-vs-ta pricing-by-city-2014-10.

Simon, Donald. 2009. "Corporate Accountabili A Summary of the Sarbanes-Oxley Ac Legalzoom.com. December. Available at https www.legalzoom.com/articles/corporat accountability-a-summary-of-the-sarbane oxley-act.

Simon, Lawrence H. 1994. *Selected Writings: K Marx.* Indianapolis, IN: Hackett.

Simpson, Sally S. 2013. "White-Collar Crime: Review of Recent Developments and Prom ing Directions for Future Research." *Ann Review of Sociology* 39 (1): 309–331.

Sitkoff, Harvard. 1981. *The Black Struggle Equality, 1954–1980.* New York: Hill and Wa

Skocpol, Theda. 2007. "Government Activism and the Reorganization of American Civic Democracy." In *The Transformation of American Politics: Activist Government and the Rise of Conservatism*, edited by Theda Skocpol and Paul Pierson, 39–67. Princeton, NJ: Princeton University Press.

Smeeding, Timothy M. 2005. "Public Policy, Economic Inequality, and Poverty: The United States in Comparative Perspective." *Social Science Quarterly* 86: 955–983.

Smeeding, Timothy M. 2009. "Differences in Higher Education: Investments, Costs, and Outcomes." *LaFollette Policy Report* 18: 1–4.

Smeeding, Timothy M. 2012. "Income, Wealth, and Debt and the Great Recession." The Russell Sage Foundation and the Stanford Center on Poverty and Inequality. Available at http://web.stanford.edu/group/recessiontrends-dev/cgi-bin/web/sites/all/themes/barron/pdf/Income-WealthDebt_fact_sheet.pdf.

Smith, Aaron. 2015. "U.S. Smartphone Use in 2015." Pew Research Center: Internet, Science & Tech. April 1. Available at http://www.pewinternet.org/2015/04/01/us-smartphone-use-in-2015.

Smith, Dorothy E. 1987. *The Everyday World as Problematic: A Feminist Sociology*. Boston: Northeastern University Press.

Smith, Dorothy E. 2009. "Categories Are Not Enough." *Gender and Society* 23 (1): 76–80.

Smith, James D. 1987. "Recent Trends in the Distribution of Wealth in the US: Data, Research Problems, and Prospects." International Comparisons of the Distribution of Household Wealth, 72–90.

Smith, James P., and Barry Edmonston, eds. 1997. *The New Americans: Economic, Demographic, and Fiscal Effects of Immigration*. Washington, D.C.: National Academic Press.

Smith, Kristin, and Andrew Schaefer. 2012. "Who Cares for the Sick Kids? Parents' Access to Paid Time to Care for a Sick Child." Paper 171. Durham, NC: The Carsey School of Public Policy at the Scholars' Repository. Available at http://scholars.unh.edu/carsey/171/?utm_source=scholars.unh.edu%2Fcarsey%2F171&utm_medium=PDF&utm_campaign=PDFCoverPages.

Smith, Sandra Susan. 2010. "Race and Trust." *Annual Review of Sociology* 36: 453–475.

Smith, Sara J., Amber M. Axelton, and Donald A. Saucier. 2009. "The Effects of Contact on Sexual Prejudice: A Meta-Analysis." *Sex Roles* 61 (3–4): 178–191.

Snell, Tracy. 2014. "Capital Punishment, 2013—Statistical Tables." Statistical Tables NCJ248448. Washington, D.C.: U.S. Department of Justice, Bureau of Justice Statistics. Available at http://www.bjs.gov/content/pub/pdf/cp13st.pdf.

Snipp, C. Matthew. 2003. "Racial Measurement in the American Census: Past Practices and Implications for the Future." *Annual Review of Sociology* 29: 563–588.

Snyder, Eloise C., ed. 1979. *The Study of Women: Enlarging Perspectives of Social Reality*. New York: Harper and Row.

Snyder, Mary Gail. 2005. "It Didn't Begin with Katrina." National Housing Institute: Shelterforce Online, no. 143, October. Available at http://www.nhi.org/online/issues/143/beforekatrina.html.

Snyder, R. Claire. 2008. "What Is Third-Wave Feminism? A New Directions Essay." *Signs: Journal of Women in Culture and Society* 34 (1): 175–196.

Sobolewski, Juliana M., and Paul R. Amato. 2005. "Economic Hardship in the Family of Origin and Children's Psychological Well-Being in Adulthood." *Journal of Marriage and Family* 67 (1): 141–156.

Solari, Claudia D., Alvaro Cortes, Meghan Henry, Natalie Matthews, Sean Morris, Jill Khadduri, and Dennis P. Culhane. 2014. "The 2013 Annual Homeless Assessment Report (AHAR) to Congress." Available at http://works.bepress.com/dennis_culhane/143.

Solt, Frederick. 2008. "Economic Inequality and Democratic Political Engagement." *American Journal of Political Science* 52 (1): 48–60.

Soltow, Lee. 1975. *Men and Wealth in the United States, 1850–1870*. New Haven, CT: Yale University Press.

Sontag, Susan. 1973. "The Third World of Women." *Partisan Review* 60: 201–203.

Sørensen, Aage B. 2000. "Toward a Sounder Basis for Class Analysis." *American Journal of Sociology* 105 (6): 1523–1558.

Spain, Daphne. 1992. *Gendered Spaces*. Chapel Hill: University of North Carolina Press.

Spector, Malcom, and John I. Kitsuse. 1977. *Constructing Social Problems*. Menlo Park, CA: Cummings.

Spencer, Herbert. 1892. *The Man versus the State.* Caldwell, ID: Caxton.

Spencer, Herbert. 1897. *The Principles of Ethics.* Vol. 2. New York: D. Appleton.

Spencer, Herbert. 1909. *The Principles of Sociology.* Vol. 2. New York: D. Appleton.

Spencer, Herbert. 1961. *The Study of Sociology.* Ann Arbor: University of Michigan Press.

Spilerman, Seymour. 2000. "Wealth and Stratification Processes." *Annual Review of Sociology* 26: 497–524.

Springer, Kimberly. 2002. "Third Wave Black Feminism?" *Signs: Journal of Women in Culture and Society* 27 (4): 1059–1082.

Srinivasan, U. Thara, Susan P. Carey, Eric Hallstein, Paul A. T. Higgins, Amber C. Kerr, Laura E. Koteen, Adam B. Smith, Reg Watson, John Harte, and Richard B. Norgaard. 2008. "The Debt of Nations and the Distribution of Ecological Impacts from Human Activities." *Proceedings of the National Academy of Sciences* 105 (5): 1768–1773.

Stack, Steven, and Delore Zimmerman. 1982. "The Effect of World Economy on Income Inequality: A Reassessment." *Sociological Quarterly* 23: 345–358.

Staff, Jeremy, and Christopher Uggen. 2003. "The Fruits of Good Work: Early Work Experiences and Adolescent Deviance." *Journal of Research in Crime and Delinquency* 40 (3): 263–290.

Stainback, Kevin, and Donald Tomaskovic-Devey. 2012. *Documenting Desegregation: Racial and Gender Segregation in Private Sector Employment Since the Civil Rights Act.* New York City: Russell Sage Foundation.

Stainback, Kevin, Donald Tomaskovic-Devey, and Sheryl Skaggs. 2010. "Organizational Approaches to Inequality: Inertia, Relative Power, and Environments." *Annual Review of Sociology* 36 (1): 225–247.

Stanczyk, Alexandra. 2009. "Low-Income Working Families: Updated Facts and Figures." *LIWF Fact Sheet.* Washington, D.C.: The Urban Institute.

Staples, Brent. 2007. "How 'Black' Is Barack Obama?" *Akron Beacon Journal*, February 15, A13.

Starr, Sonja B. 2012. "Estimating Gender Disparities in Federal Criminal Cases." *SSRN Scholarly Paper ID 2144002*. Rochester, NY: Social Science Research Network. Available at http://papers.ssrn.com/abstract=2144002.

Steen, Sara, Rodney L. Engen, and Randy R. Gainey. 2005. "Images of Danger and Culpability: Racial Stereotyping, Case Processing, and Criminal Sentencing." *Criminology* 43: 435–468.

Steensland, Brian. 2006. "Cultural Categories and the American Welfare State: The Case of Guaranteed Income Policy." *American Journal of Sociology* 111 (5): 1273–1326.

Steffensmeier, Darrell, and Stephen Demuth. 2000. "Ethnicity and Sentencing Outcomes in US Federal Courts: Who Is Punished More Harshly?" *American Sociological Review* 65: 705–729.

Steffensmeier, Darrell, and Chris Hebert. 1999. "Women and Men Policymakers: Does the Judge's Gender Affect the Sentencing of Criminal Defendants?" *Social Forces* 77 (3): 1163–1196.

Steffensmeier, Darrell, Jeffrey T. Ulmer, Ben Feldmeyer, and Casey T. Harris. 2010. "Scope and Conceptual Issues in Testing the Race-Crime Invariance Thesis: Black, White, and Hispanic Comparisons." *Criminology: An Interdisciplinary Journal* 48 (4): 1133–1169.

Steiker, Carol S. 2013. "Lessons from Two Failures: Sentencing for Cocaine and Child Pornography under the Federal Sentencing Guidelines in the United States." *Law and Contemporary Problems* 76: 27–52.

Stellar, Jennifer E., Vida M. Manzo, Michael W. Kraus, and Dacher Keltner. 2012. "Class and Compassion: Socioeconomic Factors Predict Responses to Suffering." *Emotion* 12 (3): 449–459.

Stephens, Nicole M., Hazel Rose Markus, and L. Taylor Phillips. 2014. "Social Class Culture Cycles: How Three Gateway Contexts Shape Selves and Fuel Inequality." *Annual Review of Psychology* 65 (1): 611–634.

Stephenson, Charles, and Robert Asher. 1986. *Life and Labor: Dimensions of American Working-Class History.* Albany, NY: SUNY Press.

Stern, Michael Joseph. 2010. "Inequality in the Internet Age: A Twenty-First Century Dilemma." *Sociological Inquiry* 80 (1): 28–33.

Stern, Mark Joseph. January 12, 2015. "Oklahoma Republican Proposes Bill Banning Hoodies in Public." *Slate.* Available at http://www.slate.com/blogs/the_slatest/2015/01/12/hoodie_ban_oklahoma_republican_proposes_bill_to_outlaw_wearing_hoods_in.html.

Stern, Philip M. 1988. *The Best Congress Money Can Buy*. New York: Pantheon.

Stevenson, Betsey, and Justin Wolfers. 2013. "Subjective Well-Being and Income: Is There Any Evidence of Satiation?" Cambridge, MA: National Bureau of Economic Research. Available at http://www.nber.org/papers/w18992.

Stokes, Allyson. 2015. "The Glass Runway: How Gender and Sexuality Shape the Spotlight in Fashion Design." *Gender & Society* 29 (2): 219–243.

Stoll, Michael A., and Kenya Covington. 2012. "Explaining Racial/Ethnic Gaps in Spatial Mismatch in the US: The Primacy of Racial Segregation." *Urban Studies* 49 (11): 2501–2521.

Stolte, John F. 1983. "The Legitimation of Structural Inequality: Reformulation and Test of the Self-Evaluation Argument." *American Sociological Review* 48: 331–342.

Stolte, John F. 1987. "The Formation of Justice Norms." *American Sociological Review* 52: 774–784.

Stolzenberg, Lisa, Stewart J. D'Alessio, and David J. Eitle. 2013. "Race and Cumulative Discrimination in the Prosecution of Criminal Defendants." *Race and Justice* 3 (4): 275–299.

Stoops, Michael. 2014. "Vulnerable to Hate: A Survey of Hate Crimes and Violence Committed against Homeless People in 2013." Washington, D.C.: National Coalition for the Homeless.

Streib, Jessi. 2015. *The Power of the Past: Understanding Cross-Class Marriages*. New York: Oxford University Press.

Strolovitch, Dara, Dorian Warren, and Paul Frymer. 2006. "Katrina's Political Roots and Divisions: Race, Class, and Federalism in American Politics." Brooklyn, NY: Social Science Research Council. Available at http://understandingkatrina. ssrc.org/FrymerStrolovitchWarren.

Stroshine, Meghan S., and Steven G. Brandl. 2011. "Race, Gender, and Tokenism in Policing: An Empirical Elaboration." *Police Quarterly* 14 (4): 344–365.

Sturm, James Lester. 1977. *Investing in the United States, 1798–1893: Upper Wealth-Holders in a Market Economy*. New York: Arno Press.

Sue, Derald Wing. 2010. *Microaggressions and Marginality: Manifestation, Dynamics, and Impact*. Hoboken, NJ: John Wiley & Sons.

Suicide Prevention Resource Center. 2008. "Suicide Risk and Prevention for Lesbian, Gay, Bisexual, and Transgender Youth." Newton, MA: Education Development Center, Inc. Available at http://www.sprc.org/sites/sprc.org/files/library/SPRC_LGBT_Youth.pdf.

Supeli, Abas, and Peter. A. Creed. 2015. "The Longitudinal Relationship between Protean Career Orientation and Job Satisfaction, Organizational Commitment, and Intention-to-Quit." *Journal of Career Development* 43 (1): 66–80.

Sutphin, Suzanne Taylor, and Brent Simpson. 2009. "The Role of Self-Evaluations in Legitimizing Social Inequality." *Social Science Research* 38 (3): 609–621.

Swanson, Guy E. 1964. *The Birth of the Gods*. Ann Arbor: University of Michigan Press.

Swartz, Teresa Toguchi. 2009. "Intergenerational Family Relations in Adulthood: Patterns, Variations, and Implications in the Contemporary United States." *Annual Review of Sociology* 35: 191–212.

Sweet, Elizabeth. 2014. "Toys Are More Divided by Gender Now Than They Were 50 Years Ago." *Atlantic*, December 9. Available at http://www.theatlantic.com/business/archive/2014/12/toys-are-more-divided-by-gender-now-than-they-were-50-years-ago/383556.

Swift, Adam. 2004. "Would Perfect Mobility Be Perfect?" *European Sociological Review* 20 (1): 1–11.

Swim, Janet K., Robyn Mallett, and Charles Stangor. 2004. "Understanding Subtle Sexism: Detection and Use of Sexist Language." *Sex Roles* 51 (3–4): 117–128.

Sykes, Jennifer, Katrin Križ, Kathryn Edin, and Sarah Halpern-Meekin. 2015. "Dignity and Dreams: What the Earned Income Tax Credit (EITC) Means to Low-Income Families." *American Sociological Review* 80 (2): 243–267.

Syracuse University. 2015. "Federal White Collar Crime Prosecutions at 20-Year Low." Trac Reports. Available at http://trac.syr.edu/tracreports/crim/398.

Szafran, Robert F. 1982. "What Kinds of Firms Hire and Promote Women and Blacks? A Review of the Literature." *Sociological Quarterly* 23: 171–190.

Szasz, Andrew, and Michael Meuser. 1997. "Environmental Inequalities: Literature Review and Proposals for New Directions in Research and Theory." *Current Sociology* 45 (3): 99–120.

Szymanski, Albert. 1978. *The Capitalist State and the Politics of Class*. Cambridge, MA: Winthrop.

Tannehill, Brynn. February 25, 2013. "Why 'LGB' and 'T' Belong Together." *Huffington Post*. Available at http://www.huffingtonpost.com/brynn-tannehill/why-lgb-and-t-belong-together_b_2746616.html.

Tapia, Michael. 2010. "Untangling Race and Class Effects on Juvenile Arrests." *Journal of Criminal Justice* 38 (3): 255–265.

Tax Policy Center. 2008. "What Is the Tax Gap?" Tax Policy Center: A Joint Project of the Urban Institute and Brookings Institution. Available at http://www.taxpolicycenter.org/briefing-book/background/tax-gap/what-is.cfm.

Taylor, Catherine J. 2010. "Occupational Sex Composition and the Gendered Availability of Workplace Support." *Gender & Society* 24 (2): 189–212.

Taylor, Timothy. 2002. "The Truth about Globalization." *Public Interest* 147: 24–44.

Taylor, Verta. 1989. "Social Movement Continuity: The Women's Movement in Abeyance." *American Sociological Review* 54: 761–775.

Teachman, Jay, and Lucky M. Tedrow. 2004. "Wages, Earnings, and Occupational Status: Did World War II Veterans Receive a Premium?" *Social Science Research* 33 (4): 581–605.

Thébaud, Sarah. 2010. "Masculinity, Bargaining, and Breadwinning: Understanding Men's Housework in the Cultural Context of Paid Work." *Gender & Society* 24 (3): 330–354.

Thoits, Peggy A. 1983. "Multiple Identities and Psychological Well-Being: A Reformulation and Test of the Social Isolation Hypothesis." *American Sociological Review* 48 (2): 174–187.

Thompson, Erik S. 2015. "Compromising Equality: An Analysis of the Religious Exemption in the Employment Non-Discrimination Act and Its Impact on LGBT Workers." *Boston College Journal of Law and Social Justice* 35: 284–319.

Thompson, Melissa. 2010. "Race, Gender, and the Social Construction of Mental Illness in the Criminal Justice System." *Sociological Perspectives* 53 (1): 99–126.

Thorpe, Roland J., Caryn N. Bell, Alene Kennedy-Hendricks, Jelani Harvey, Jenny R. Smolen, Janice V. Bowie, and Thomas A. LaVeist. 2015. "Disentangling Race and Social Context in Understanding Disparities in Chronic Conditions among Men." *Journal of Urban Health: Bulletin of the New York Academy of Medicine* 92 (1): 83–92.

Thurow, Lester C. 1969. *Poverty and Discrimination*. Washington, D.C.: Brookings Institution.

Tilcsik, András, Michel Anteby, and Carly R. Knight. 2015. "Concealable Stigma and Occupational Segregation: Toward a Theory of Gay and Lesbian Occupations." *Administrative Science Quarterly* 60 (3): 446–481.

Tilly, Charles. 1998. *Durable Inequalities*. Berkeley: University of California Press.

Tilly, Charles. 2003. "Changing Forms of Inequality." *Sociological Theory* 21 (1): 31–36.

Tiwari, Krittika, and Sarvesh Bandhu. 2014. "Impact of Globalisation on Caste System: An Econometric Analysis." *Indian Streams Research Journal* 4 (6). Available at http://isrj.org/ColorArticles/4821.pdf.

Tocqueville de, Alexis. 1966. *Democracy in America*. Edited by Max Lerner and Jacob Peter Mayer. Translated by George Lawrence. New York: Harper & Row.

Tomaskovic-Devey, Donald, Dustin Avent-Holt, Catherine Zimmer, and Sandra Harding. 2009. "The Categorical Generation of Organizational Inequality: A Comparative Test of Tilly's Durable Inequality." *Research in Social Stratification and Mobility* 27 (3): 128–142.

Tomaskovic-Devey, Donald, Catherine Zimmer, Kevin Stainback, Corre Robinson, Tiffany Taylor, and Tricia McTague. 2006. "Documenting Desegregation: Segregation in American Workplaces by Race, Ethnicity, and Sex 1966–2003." *American Sociological Review* 71: 565–588.

Törnblom, Kjell Y., and Riël Vermunt. 1999. "An Integrative Perspective on Social Justice Distributive and Procedural Fairness Evaluations of Positive and Negative Outcome Allocations." *Social Justice Research* 12 (1): 39–64.

Trei, Lisa. 2006. "'Black' Features Can Sway in Favor Death Penalty, according to Study." *Stanford News Service*. May 3. Available at http://news.stanford.edu/news/2006/may3/deathworthy-050306.html.

Tropman, John E. 1989. *American Values and Social Welfare: Cultural Contradictions in the Welfare State*. Englewood Cliffs, NJ: Prentice Hall.

Troshynski, Emily I., and Jennifer K. Blank. 2008. "Sex Trafficking: An Exploratory Study Interviewing Traffickers." *Trends in Organized Crime* 11 (1): 30–41.

Tumin, Melvin M. 1953. "Some Principles of Stratification: A Critical Analysis." *American Sociological Review* 18: 387–394.

Turner, Bryan S. 1986. *Equality (Key Ideas)*. New York: Methuen.

Turner, Jonathan H. 1985. *Herbert Spencer: A Renewed Appreciation*. Beverly Hills, CA: Sage.

Turner, Jonathan H., Royce Singleton, and David Musick. 1984. *Oppression: A Socio-History of Black–White Relations in America*. Chicago: Nelson Hall.

Tyler, Melissa, and Laurie Cohen. 2010. "Spaces That Matter: Gender Performativity and Organizational Space." *Organization Studies* 31 (2): 175–198.

Uchegbu, Amaka. 2015. "Homeless Women Find Sexual Violence Part of Life on the Street." *Pittsburgh Post-Gazette*. August 18. Available at http://www.post-gazette.com/news/health/2015/08/18/Homeless-women-find-sexual-violence-part-of-life-on-the-street/stories/201507130149.

Ueno, Koji, Teresa Roach, and Abráham E. Peña-Talamantes. 2013. "Sexual Orientation and Gender Typicality of the Occupation in Young Adulthood." *Social Forces* 92 (1): 81–108.

Uggen, Christopher. 1999. "Ex-Offenders and the Conformist Alternative: A Job Quality Model of Work and Crime." *Social Problems* 46 (1): 127–151.

Uggen, Christopher, and Amy Blackstone. 2004. "Sexual Harassment as a Gendered Expression of Power." *American Sociological Review* 69 (1): 64–92.

UNICEF Innocenti Research Centre. 2012. "Measuring Child Poverty: New League Tables of Child Poverty in the World's Richest Countries." Innocenti Report Card 10. Florence, Italy: UNICEF Innocenti Research Centre. Available at http://www.unicef-irc.org/publications/pdf/rc10_eng.pdf.

United Church of Christ. 1987. *Toxic Wastes and Race: A National Report on the Racial and Socio-Economic Characteristics of Communities with Hazardous Waste Sites*. New York: United Church of Christ.

United Nations. 1998. "Human Development Report 1998." New York: Oxford University Press.

United Nations, ed. 2010. *The World's Women 2010: Trends and Statistics*. Social Statistics and Indicators Series K 19. New York: United Nations.

United Nations. 2015. "Facts and Figures: Leadership and Political Participation." UN Women. September. Available at http://www.unwomen.org/en/what-we-do/leadership-and-political-participation/facts-and-figures.

United Nations Development Programme. 2015. "Human Development Report 2015: Statistical Annex." New York: United Nations. Available at http://hdr.undp.org/sites/default/files/hdr_2015_statistical_annex.pdf.

United States Attorney Southern District of New York. 2008. "Former Goldman Sachs Associate Sentenced to 57 Months in Prison for Engineering Massive, International Insider Trading Scheme." New York: United States Attorney. Available at http://www.justice.gov/archive/usao/nys/pressreleases/January08/plotkinsentencingpr.pdf.

United States Sentencing Commission. 2015. "Amendments to the Sentencing Guidelines." Washington, D.C.: United States Sentencing Commission. Available at http://heinonline-backup.com/hol-cgi-bin/get_pdf.cgi?handle=hein.journals/aktax15&section=4.

Unnever, James D. 2016. "The Racial Invariance Thesis Revisited: Testing an African American Theory of Offending." *Journal of Contemporary Criminal Justice* 32 (1): 7–26.

Unnever, James D., and Francis T. Cullen. 2012. "White Perceptions of Whether African Americans and Hispanics Are Prone to Violence and Support for the Death Penalty." *Journal of Research in Crime and Delinquency* 49 (4): 519–544.

U.N. World Food Programme. 2015. "Who Are the Hungry?" Available at https://www.wfp.org/hunger/who-are.

U.S. Attorneys. 2014. "United States Attorneys' Annual Statistical Report Fiscal Year 2014." Washington, D.C.: U.S. Department of Justice Executive Office for United States Attorneys.

U.S. Bureau of Labor Statistics. 2012. "Occupational Employment by Race and Ethnicity, 2011." TED: The Economics Daily. October 26. Available at http://www.bls.gov/opub/ted/2012/ted_20121026.htm.

U.S. Bureau of Labor Statistics. 2014. "Current Population Survey, 2014 Annual Report." Washington, D.C.: U.S. Bureau of Labor Statistics.

U.S. Bureau of Labor Statistics. 2015a. "Fastest Growing Occupations." *Occupational Outlook Handbook*. http://www.bls.gov/ooh/fastest-growing.htm.

U.S. Bureau of Labor Statistics. 2015b. "Union Members." News Release. Washington, D.C.: U.S. Department of Labor.

U.S. Bureau of Labor Statistics. 2015c. "1988–2014 Annual Social and Economic Supplements to the Current Population Survey (CPS)." Washington, D.C.: U.S. Bureau of Labor Statistics.

U.S. Bureau of Labor Statistics. 2015d. "Foreign Trade: Data." United States Census Bureau. August. Available at https://www.census.gov/foreign-trade/statistics/highlights/toppartners.html.

U.S. Census Bureau. 1979. "The Social and Economic Status of the Black Population in the United States: An Historical View, 1790–1978." Series P-21, No. 80. Current Population Reports. Washington, D.C.: U.S. Government Printing Office.

U.S. Census Bureau. 2012a. "Monthly Child Support Payments Report 2010." June 29. Available at https://www.census.gov/newsroom/releases/archives/children/cb12-109.html.

U.S. Census Bureau. 2012b. "The American Indian and Alaska Native Population: 2010." 2010 Census Briefs C2010BR-10. Washington, D.C.: U.S. Census Bureau.

U.S. Census Bureau. 2013a. "How Do We Know? America's Foreign Born in the Last 50 Years." U.S. Census Bureau. Available at http://www.census.gov/library/infographics/foreign_born.html.

U.S. Census Bureau. 2013b. "Frequently Asked Questions about Same-Sex Couple Households." Washington, D.C.: U.S. Census Bureau. Available at http://www.census.gov/hhes/samesex/files/SScplfactsheet_final.pdf.

U.S. Census Bureau. 2014a. "ACS Demographic and Housing Estimates—Flint, Michigan." American FactFinder. Available at http://factfinder.census.gov/faces/tableservices/jsf/pages/productview.xhtml?src=CF.

U.S. Census Bureau. 2014b. "Income." Available at http://www.census.gov/hhes/www/income/data/historical/household/.

U.S. Census Bureau. 2014c. "People in Poverty by Selected Characteristics: 2013 and 2014." Table 3. Available at https://www.census.gov/hhes/www/poverty/data/incpovhlth/2014/table3.pdf.

U.S. Census Bureau. 2014d. "Wealth and Asset Ownership." Available at http://www.census.gov/people/wealth.

U.S. Census Bureau. 2015a. "Same Sex Couples." Table 1. Household Characteristics of Opposite-Sex and Same-Sex Couple Households ACS 2014. Washington, D.C.: U.S. Bureau of the Census. Available at http://www.census.gov/hhes/samesex.

U.S. Census Bureau. 2015b. "Supplemental Poverty Measure Overview." Poverty: Experimental Measures. U.S. Census. Available at http://www.census.gov/hhes/povmeas/methodology/supplemental/overview.html.

U.S. Census Bureau. 2015c. "Survey of Small Business Owners—2012 Results." American Fact Finder— Results. Available at https://www.census.gov/econ/sbo/getdata.html.

U.S. Census Bureau. 2015d. "Income, Poverty and Health Insurance Coverage in the United States: 2014." News Release. Washington, D.C.: U.S. Census Bureau. Available at http://census.gov/newsroom/press-releases/2015/cb15-157.html.

U.S. Census Office. 1903. Statistical Atlas of the United States, 1900. Washington, D.C.: U.S. Government Printing Office.

U.S. Conference of Mayors. 2013. "Hunger and Homelessness Survey." Washington, D.C.: United States Conference of Mayors. Available at http://www.usmayors.org/pressreleases/uploads/2013/1210-report-HH.pdf.

U.S. Department of Commerce and Labor. 1911. Statistical Abstract of the United States. Washington, D.C.: U.S. Government Printing Office.

U.S. Department of Health and Human Services. 2015. "Characteristics and Financial Circumstances of TANF Recipients: Fiscal Year 2013." Available at http://www.acf.hhs.gov/sites/default/files/ofa/tanf_characteristics_fy2013.pdf.

Useem, Michael. 1984. *The Inner Circle Large Corporations and the Rise of Business Political Activity in the U.S. and U.K.* New York: Oxford University Press.

U.S. General Accounting Office. 1983. *Siting of Hazardous Waste Landfills and Their Correlations with Racial and Economic Status of Surrounding Communities*. Washington, D.C.: U.S. Government Printing Office.

U.S. Social Security Administration. 2014. "SSI Annual Statistical Report, 2013." Available at https://www.ssa.gov/policy/docs/statcomps/ssi_asr.

Valdes, Francisco. 1995. "Queers, Sissies, Dykes, and Tomboys: Deconstructing the Conflation of 'Sex,' 'Gender,' and 'Sexual Orientation' in Euro-American Law and Society." *California Law Review* 83: 129–204.

Van Apeldoorn, Bastiaan, and Nana De Graaff. 2014. "Corporate Elite Networks and US Post-Cold War Grand Strategies from Clinton to Obama." *European Journal of International Relations* 20 (1): 1–27.

Van den Berghe, Pierre L. 1985. "Review of JS Chafetz's Sex and Advantage." *American Journal of Sociology* 90: 1350.

Van der Toorn, Jojanneke, Mihály Berkics, and John T. Jost. 2010. "System Justification, Satisfaction, and Perceptions of Fairness and Typicality at Work: A Cross-System Comparison Involving the US and Hungary." *Social Justice Research* 23 (2–3): 189–210.

Van Doorn, Bas W. 2015. "Pre-and Post-Welfare Reform Media Portrayals of Poverty in the United States: The Continuing Importance of Race and Ethnicity." *Politics & Policy* 43 (1): 142–162.

Van Leeuwen, Marco H. D., and Ineke Maas. 2010. "Historical Studies of Social Mobility and Stratification." *Annual Review of Sociology* 36: 429–451.

Van Slyke, Shanna R., and William D. Bales. 2013. "Gender Dynamics in the Sentencing of White-Collar Offenders." *Criminal Justice Studies* 26 (2): 168–196.

Vaught, Sabina E., and Angelina E. Castagno. 2008. "'I Don't Think I'm a Racist': Critical Race Theory, Teacher Attitudes, and Structural Racism." *Race Ethnicity and Education* 11 (2): 95–113.

Veblen, Thorstein. 1953. *The Theory of the Leisure Class*. New York: New American Library.

Venkatesh, Sudhir Alladi. 1994. "Getting Ahead: Social Mobility among the Urban Poor." *Sociological Perspectives* 37 (2): 157–182.

Verba, Sidney, Nancy Burns, and Kay Lehman Schlozman. 2003. "Unequal at the Starting Line: Creating Participatory Inequalities across Generations and among Groups." *American Sociologist* 34 (1–2): 45–69.

Viglione, Jill, Lance Hannon, and Robert DeFina. 2011. "The Impact of Light Skin on Prison Time for Black Female Offenders." *Social Science Journal* 48 (1): 250–258.

Vincent, Wilson, John L. Peterson, and Dominic J. Parrott. 2009. "Differences in African American and White Women's Attitudes toward Lesbians and Gay Men." *Sex Roles* 61 (9–10): 599–606.

Vogel, Lise. 1983. *Marxism and the Oppression of Women*. New Brunswick, NJ: Rutgers University Press.

Volgy, Thomas J., John E. Schwarz, and Lawrence E. Imwalle. 1996. "In Search of Economic Well-Being: Worker Power and the Effects of Productivity, Inflation, Unemployment and Global Trade on Wages in Ten Wealthy Countries." *American Journal of Political Science* 40: 1233–1252.

Wacquant, Loïc. 2007. *Urban Outcasts: A Comparative Sociology of Advanced Marginality*. Cambridge, MA: Polity Press.

Wacquant, Loïc. 2009. *Prisons of Poverty*. Minneapolis: University of Minnesota Press.

Wade, Robert Hunter. 2004. "Is Globalization Reducing Poverty and Inequality?" *World Development* z32 (4): 567–589.

Wadhwa, Vivek, AnnaLee Saxenian, and Francis Daniel Siciliano. 2012. "Then and Now: America's New Immigrant Entrepreneurs, Part VII." Kansas City, MO: Ewing Marion Kauffman Foundation Research Paper. Available at http://papers.ssrn.com/sol3/papers.cfm?abstract_id=2159875.

Wakefield, Sara, and Christopher Uggen. 2010. "Incarceration and Stratification." *Annual Review of Sociology* 36: 387–406.

Walasek, Lukasz, and Gordon D. A. Brown. 2015. "Income Inequality and Status Seeking: Searching for Positional Goods in Unequal U.S. States." *Psychological Science* 26 (4): 527–533.

Wallace, Michael. 1997. "Revisiting Broom and Cushing's 'Modest Test of an Immodest Theory'." *Research in Social Stratification Mobility* 15: 239–253.

Wallerstein, Immanuel. 1974. *The Modern World System I: Capitalist Agriculture and the Origins of the European World Economy.* New York: Academic Press.

Wallerstein, Immanuel. 1979. *The Capitalist World-Economy.* Vol. 2. Cambridge, UK: Cambridge University Press.

Wang, Jennifer. 2015. "The Youngest Moneymakers on the Forbes 400: 17 Under 40." *Forbes,* September 29. Available at http://www.forbes.com/sites/jenniferwang/2015/09/29/the-youngest-moneymakers-on-the-forbes-400-17-under-40.

Wang, Qingfang. 2008. "Race/Ethnicity, Gender and Job Earnings across Metropolitan Areas in the United States: A Multilevel Analysis." *Urban Studies* 45 (4): 825–843.

Ward, Brian W., J. S. Schiller, Gulnur Freeman, and J. A. Peregoy. 2015. "Early Release of Selected Estimates Based on Data from the January–September 2012 National Health Interview Survey." Washington, D.C.: US Department of Health and Human Services, Centers for Disease Control, National Center for Health Statistics. Available at http://www.cdc.gov/nchs/data/nhis/earlyrelease/earlyrelease201503.pdf.

Ward, Kathryn B. 1993. "Reconceptualizing World System Theory to Include Women." In *Theory on Gender/Feminism on Theory,* edited by Paula England, 43–68. New York: Aldine de Gruyter.

Warren, John Robert. 2009. "Socioeconomic Status and Health across the Life Course: A Test of the Social Causation and Health Selection Hypotheses." *Social Forces* 87 (4): 2125–2153.

Warren, Patricia, Ted Chiricos, and William Bales. 2012. "The Imprisonment Penalty for Young Black and Hispanic Males: A Crime-Specific Analysis." *Journal of Research in Crime and Delinquency* 49 (1): 56–80.

Waters, Mary C., Philip Kasinitz, and Asad L. Asad. 2014. "Immigrants and African Americans." *Annual Review of Sociology* 40 (1): 369–390.

Watkins, Nicole L., Theresa L. LaBarrie, and Lauren M. Appio. 2010. "Black Undergraduates' Experience with Perceived Racial Microaggressions in Predominantly White Colleges and Universities." In *Microaggressions and Marginality: Manifestation, Dynamics, and Impact,* edited by Derald W. Sue, 25–58. Hoboken, NJ: John Wiley & Sons.

Weaver, Jay. 2010. "Medicare Fraud: Defying Justice." *AARP Bulletin* 51: 12–14.

Webb, Janette. 2009. "Gender and Occupation in Market Economies: Change and Restructuring Since the 1980s." *Social Politics: International Studies in Gender, State & Society* 16 (1): 82–110.

Webb, Jennifer B., Jan Warren-Findlow, Ying-Yi Chou, and Lauren Adams. 2013. "Do You See What I See? An Exploration of Inter-Ethnic Ideal Body Size Comparisons among College Women." *Body Image* 10 (3): 369–379.

Weber, Max. 1947. *The Theory of Social and Economic Organization.* Edited by Talcott Parsons. Translated by A. M. Henderson. New York: Free Press.

Weber, Max. 1964. *The Theory of Social and Economic Organization.* Edited by Talcott Parsons. Translated by A.M. Henderson. New York: Free Press.

Weber, Ryan. 2014. "After Suicide, Gay Teen's Eye Donation Rejected." *Washington Post,* August 15. Available at http://www.washingtonpost.com/news/morning-mix/wp/2014/08/15/gay-teens-organ-donation-rejected.

Wednesday, Jennifer Erickson. 2014. "The Middle Class Squeeze." Center for American Progress, September 24. Available at https://www.americanprogress.org/issues/economy/report/2014/09/24/96903/the-middle-class-squeeze.

Weede, Erich. 2008. "Globalization and Inequality." *Comparative Sociology* 7 (4): 415–433.

Weeden, Jason, Michael J. Abrams, Melanie C. Green, and John Sabini. 2006. "Do High Status People Really Have Fewer Children?" *Human Nature* 17 (4): 377–392.

Weeden, Kim A. 2002. "Why Do Some Occupations Pay More than Others? Social Closure and Earnings Inequality in the United States." *American Journal of Sociology* 108 (1): 55–101.

Weinberg, Richard A. 1989. "Intelligence and IQ: Landmark Issues and Great Debates." *American Psychologist* 44 (2): 98.

Weinfeld, Nancy S., Gregory Mills, Christine Borger, Maeve Gearing, Theodore Macaluso, Jill Montaquila, and Sheila Zedlewski. 2014. "Hunger in America 2014." Chicago: Feeding America. Available at http://www.resourcelibrary.gcyf.org/sites/gcyf.org/files/resources/2014/hunger-in-america-2014-full-report.pdf.

Weisshaar, Katherine. 2014. "Earnings Equality and Relationship Stability for Same-Sex and Heterosexual Couples." *Social Forces* 93 (1): 93–123.

Weiss, Jillian Todd. 2003. "GL vs. BT: The Archaeology of Biphobia and Transphobia within the US Gay and Lesbian Community." *Journal of Bisexuality* 3 (3–4): 25–55.

Weiss, Michael J. 1988. *Clustering of America*. New York: Harper & Row.

Weissman, Jordan. 2013. Census: Medical Expenses Put 10.6 Million Americans in Poverty. *Atlantic*, November 7. Available at http://www.theatlantic.com/business/archive/2013/11/census-medical-expenses-put-106-million-americans-in-poverty/281256.

Weissman, Judith, Laura A. Pratt, Eric A. Miller, and Jennifer D. Parker. 2015. "Serious Psychological Distress among Adults: United States, 2009–2013." NCHS Data Brief 203. Washington, D.C.: U.S. Department of Health and Human Services. Available at http://www.cdc.gov/nchs/data/databriefs/db203.htm.

Weitzer, Ronald, and Steven A. Tuch. 2004. "Race and Perceptions of Police Misconduct." *Social Problems* 51: 305–325.

West, Candace, and Sarah Fenstermaker. 1995. "Doing Difference." *Gender & Society* 9 (1): 8–37.

West, Candace, and Don H. Zimmerman. 1987. "Doing Gender." *Gender & Society* 1 (2): 125–151.

Westbrook, Laurel, and Kristen Schilt. 2014. "Doing Gender, Determining Gender: Transgender People, Gender Panics, and the Maintenance of the Sex/Gender/Sexuality System." *Gender & Society* 28 (1): 32–57.

Western, Bruce. 1993. "Postwar Unionization in Eighteen Advanced Capitalist Countries." *American Sociological Review* 58: 266–282.

Western, Bruce, and Becky Pettit. 2010. "Collateral Costs." Washington, D.C.: The Pew Charitable Trusts. Available at https://csgjusticecenter.org/wp-content/uploads/2010/09/2010-Pew.pdf.

Western, Bruce, and Jake Rosenfeld. 2011. "Unions, Norms, and the Rise in US Wage Inequality." *American Sociological Review* 76 (4): 513–537.

Western, Mark, and Erik Olin Wright. 1994. "The Permeability of Class Boundaries to Intergenerational Mobility among Men in the United States, Canada, Norway and Sweden." *American Sociological Review* 59: 606–629.

Weston, William. 2010. "The Power Elite and the Philadelphia Gentlemen." *Society* 47 (2): 138–146.

West Virginia State Archives. 2015. "West Virginia's Mine Wars." West Virginia Division of Culture and History. Available at http://www.wvculture.org/history/minewars.html.

Wheeler, Stanton, David Weisburd, and Nancy Bode. 1982. "Sentencing the White-Collar Offender: Rhetoric and Reality." *American Sociological Review* 47: 641–659.

Wheelock, Darren, Christopher Uggen, David Harris, and Ann Chih Lin. 2008. "Race, Poverty and Punishment: The Impact of Criminal Sanctions on Racial, Ethnic, and Socioeconomic Inequality." In *The Colors of Poverty: Why Racial and Ethnic Disparities Persist*, edited by Ann Chih Linn and David R. Harris, 261–292. New York: Russell Sage.

White, Jack E. 1997. "I'm Just Who I Am." *Time*, May 5: 34.

Wiersma, Jenneke E., Patricia van Oppen, Digna J. F. van Schaik, A. J. Willem van der Does, Aartjan T. F. Beekman, and Brenda W. J. H. Penninx. 2011. "Psychological Characteristics of Chronic Depression: A Longitudinal Cohort Study." *The Journal of Clinical Psychiatry* 72 (3): 288–294.

Wildeman, Christopher, and Bruce Western. 2010. "Incarceration in Fragile Families." *The Future of Children* 20 (2): 157–177.

Wilkinson, Richard G, and Kate E. Pickett. 2009. "Income Inequality and Social Dysfunction." *Annual Review of Sociology* 35: 493–511.

Wilks, Stephen. 2013. *The Political Power of the Business Corporation*. Northamptom, MA: Elgar Publishing.

Williams, Christine. L. 2013. "The Glass Escalator, Revisited: Gender Inequality in Neoliberal Times, SWS Feminist Lecturer." *Gender & Society* 27 (5): 609–629.

Williams, Christine. L., Chandra Muller, and Kristine Kilanski. 2012. "Gendered Organizations in the New Economy." *Gender & Society* 26 (4): 549–573.

Williams, Kirk R. 1984. "Economic Sources of Homicide: Reestimating the Effects of Poverty and Inequality." *American Sociological Review* 49: 283–289.

Williams, Kirk R., and Robert L. Flewelling. 1988. "The Social Production of Criminal Homicide: A Comparative Study of Disaggregated Rates in American Cities." *American Sociological Review* 53: 421–431.

Williams, Roberton. 2010. "Why Nearly Half of Americans Pay No Federal Income Tax." Tax Notes. Washington, DC: Tax Policy Center.

Williams, Robin Murphy. 1970. *American Society: A Sociological Interpretation.* New York: Knopf.

Willson, Andrea E. 2003. "Race and Women's Income Trajectories: Employment, Marriage, and Income Security over the Life Course." *Social Problems* 50 (1): 87–110.

Wilson, Denis. 2012. "The History of the Hoodie." *Rolling Stone,* April 3. Available at http://www.rollingstone.com/culture/news/the-history-of-the-hoodie-20120403.

Wilson, George, and Vincent J. Roscigno. 2010. "Race and Downward Mobility from Privileged Occupations: African American/White Dynamics across the Early Work-Career." *Social Science Research* 39 (1): 67–77.

Wilson, George, Vincent J. Roscigno, and Matt L. Huffman. 2013. "Public Sector Transformation, Racial Inequality and Downward Occupational Mobility." *Social Forces* 91 (3): 975–1006.

Wilson, George, Vincent Roscigno, and Matt Huffman. 2015. "Racial Income Inequality and Public Sector Privatization." *Social Problems* 62 (2): 163–185.

Wilson, William Julius. 1970. "Race Relations Models and Explanations of Ghetto Behavior." Paper presented at the Seventh World Congress of Sociology of the International Sociological Association, September 14–19, Varna, Bulgaria.

Wilson, William Julius. 1982. "The Declining Significance of Race-Revisited But Not Revised." In *Majority and Minority: The Dynamics of Race and Ethnicity in American Life,* edited by Norman R. Yetman and C. Hoy Steele, 399–405. Boston: Allyn & Bacon.

Wilson, William Julius. 2012. *The Truly Disadvantaged: The Inner City, the Underclass, and Public Policy.* Chicago: University of Chicago Press.

Wiltz, Teresa. 2014. "Lobbying for a 'MENA' Category on U.S. Census." USA Today, October 7. Available at http://www.usatoday.com/story/news/nation/ 2014/08/13/stateline-census-mena-africa-mid-east/13999239/.

Wingfield, Adia Harvey. 2009. "Racializing the Glass Elevator: Reconsidering Men's Experiences with Women's Work." *Gender & Society* 23 (1): 5–26.

Winters, Jeffrey A., and Benjamin I. Page. 2009. "Oligarchy in the United States?" *Perspectives on Politics* 7 (4): 731–751.

Witko, Christopher. 2006. "PACs, Issue Context, and Congressional Decisionmaking." *Political Research Quarterly* 59 (2): 283–295.

Wolf, Naomi. 2002. *The Beauty Myth: How Images of Beauty Are Used against Women.* Reprint Edition. New York: Harper Perennial.

Wolfe, Barbara, Jessica Jakubowski, Robert Haveman, and Marissa Courey. 2012. "The Income and Health Effects of Tribal Casino Gaming on American Indians." *Demography* 49 (2): 499–524.

Wolff, Edward N. 1998. "Recent Trends in the Size Distribution of Household Wealth." *The Journal of Economic Perspectives* 12: 131–150.

Wolff, Edward N. 2000. "Recent Trends in Wealth Ownership, 1983–1998." Working Paper 300. Bard College, Annandale-on-Hudson, NY: Jerome Levy Economics Institute.

Wolff, Edward N. 2002. "Recent Trends in Living Standards in the United States." New York: New York University and the Jerome Levy Economics Institute. Available at http://www.econ.nyu.edu/user/wolffe/LevyLivingStandard May2002.pdf.

Wolff, Edward N. 2012. "The Asset Price Meltdown and the Wealth of the Middle Class." Cambridge, MA: National Bureau of Economic Research. Available at http://www.nber.org/papers/w18559.

Wolniak, Gregory C., Tricia A. Seifert, Eric J. Reed, and Ernest T. Pascarella. 2008. "College Major and Social Mobility." *Research in Social Stratification and Mobility* 26 (2): 123–139.

Wong, Alia. 2015. "The Renaissance of Student Activism." *Atlantic,* May 21. Available at http://www.theatlantic.com/education/archive/2015/05/the-renaissance-of-student activism/393749.

Wong, Alia, and Adrienne Green. 2016. "Campus Racial-Justice Protests Unfolding Across America: An Overview and Timeline." *Atlantic,* January 19. Available at http://www.theatlantic.com/education/archive/2016/01/campus protest-roundup/417570.

Wong, Raymond Sin-Kwok. 1994. "Postwar Mobility Trends in Advanced Industrial Societies." *Research in Social Stratification and Mobility* 13: 121–144.

Wood, Wendy, and Alice H. Eagly. 2002. "A Cross-Cultural Analysis of the Behavior of Women and Men: Implications for the Origins of Sex Differences." *Psychological Bulletin* 128 (5): 699–727.

Wood, Wendy, and Alice H. Eagly. 2015. "Two Traditions of Research on Gender Identity." *Sex Roles* 73 (11–12): 461–473.

Woodford, Michael R., Perry Silverschanz, Eric Swank, Kristin S. Scherrer, and Lisa Raiz. 2012. "Predictors of Heterosexual College Students' Attitudes toward LGBT People." *Journal of LGBT Youth* 9 (4): 297–320.

Wooldredge, John. 2012. "Distinguishing Race Effects on Pre-Trial Release and Sentencing Decisions." *Justice Quarterly* 29 (1): 41–75.

Workneh, Lilly. 2015. "#SayHerName: Why We Should Declare That Black Women and Girls Matter, Too." *Huff Post: Black Voices*, May 21. Available at http://www.huffingtonpost.com/2015/05/21/black-women-matter_n_7363064.html.

World Bank. 2012. "Investing in People to Fight Poverty in Haiti Overview." Washington, DC: World Bank Group and Republique D'Haiti. Available at http://www.worldbank.org/content/dam/Worldbank/document/Poverty%20documents/Haiti_PA_overview_web_EN.pdf.

World Bank. 2015a. "Health Expenditure, Total (% of GDP)." World Bank Data. Available at http://data.worldbank.org/indicator/SH.XPD.TOTL.ZS.

World Bank. 2015b. "Life Expectancy at Birth." World Bank Data. Available at http://data.worldbank.org/indicator/SP.DYN.LE00.IN.

World Bank. 2015c. "Mortality Rate, Infant (per 1,000 Live Births)." World Bank Data. Available at http://data.worldbank.org/indicator/SP.DYN.IMRT.IN?order=wbapi_data_value_2015+wbapi_data_value+wbapi_data_value-last&sort=asc.

World Health Organization. 2011. World Health Statistics 2011. Geneva, Switzerland: World Health Organization.

World Health Organization. 2014. "World Health Statistics 2014." News Release. Geneva, Switzerland: World Health Organization.

Available at http://www.who.int/mediacentre/news/releases/2014/world-health-statistics-2014/en.

World Health Organization. 2015. "Lead Poisoning and Health." Fact Sheet #379. WHO. August. Available at http://www.who.int/mediacentre/factsheets/fs379/en.

Worstall, Tim. 2014. "The US Treasury Would Not Lose $20 Billion from Corporate Tax Inversions." *Forbes*, August 3. Available at http://www.forbes.com/sites/timworstall/2014/08/03/the-us-treasury-would-not-lose-20-billion-from-corporate-tax-inversions.

Worts, Diana, Amanda Sacker, and Peggy McDonough. 2010. "Falling Short of the Promise: Poverty Vulnerability in the United States and Britain, 1993–2003." *American Journal of Sociology* 116 (1): 232–271.

Wright, Eric Olin. 2006. "Two Redistributive Proposals: Universal Basic Income and Stakeholder Grants." *Focus* 24 (2): 5–7.

Wright, Erik Olin, Janeen Baxter, and Gunn Elisabeth Birkelund. 1995. "The Gender Gap in Workplace Authority: A Cross-National Study." *American Sociological Review* 60: 407–435.

Wright, Erik Olin, and Donmoon Cho. 1992. "The Relative Permeability of Class Boundaries to Cross-Class Friendships: A Comparative Study of the United States, Canada, Sweden, and Norway." *American Sociological Review* 57: 85–102.

Wrong, Dennis H. 1959. "The Functional Theory of Stratification: Some Neglected Considerations." *American Sociological Review* 24: 772–782.

Wrye, Harriet Kimble. 2009. "The Fourth Wave of Feminism: Psychoanalytic Perspectives Introductory Remarks." *Studies in Gender and Sexuality* 10 (4): 185–189.

Xu, Jun, and Jennifer C. Lee. 2013. "The Marginalized 'Model' Minority: An Empirical Examination of the Racial Triangulation of Asian Americans." *Social Forces* 91 (4): 1363–1397.

Yamaguchi, Kazuo, and Yantao Wang. 2002. "Class Identification of Married Employed Women and Men in America." *American Journal of Sociology* 108 (2): 440–475.

Yang, Crystal S. 2014. "Have Interjudge Sentencing Disparities Increased in an Advisory Guidelines Regime-Evidence from Booker." *New York University Law Review* 89: 1268–1342.

Yavorsky, Jill E., Claire M. Kamp Dush, and Sarah J. Schoppe-Sullivan. 2015. "The Production of Inequality: The Gender Division of Labor across the Transition to Parenthood." *Journal of Marriage and Family* 77 (3): 662–679.

Ybarra, Vickie D., Lisa M. Sanchez, and Gabriel R. Sanchez. 2015. "Anti-Immigrant Anxieties in State Policy: The Great Recession and Punitive Immigration Policy in the American States, 2005–2012." *State Politics & Policy Quarterly*, September.

Yen, Iris. 2008. "Of Vice and Men: A New Approach to Eradicating Sex Trafficking by Reducing Male Demand through Educational Programs and Abolitionist Legislation." *Journal of Criminal Law and Criminology* 98: 653–686.

Yoo, Grace J. 2008. "Immigrants and Welfare: Policy Constructions of Deservingness." *Journal of Immigrant & Refugee Studies* 6 (4): 490–507.

YouGov. 2015. "One Third Think It Is Morally Wrong to Be Transgender." YouGov: What the World Thinks. Available at https://today.yougov.com/news/2015/06/05/transgender.

Young, Christobal. 2012. "Losing a Job: The Nonpecuniary Cost of Unemployment in the United States." *Social Forces* 91 (2): 609–634.

Zavodny, Madeline, and Marianne P. Bitler. 2010. "The Effect of Medicaid Eligibility Expansions on Fertility." *Social Science & Medicine* 71 (5): 918–924.

Zeitlin, Irving M. 1968. *Ideology and the Development of Sociological Theory*. Englewood Cliffs, NJ: Prentice-Hall.

Zhao, Na, Mingjie Zhao, Yuanyan Shi, and Jianxin Zhang. 2015. "Face Attractiveness in Building Trust: Evidence from Measurement." *Social Behavior and Personality* 43 (5): 855–866.

Zieger, Robert H. 1986. *American Workers, American Unions, 1920–1985*. Baltimore, MD: Johns Hopkins University Press.

Zillien, Nicole, and Eszter Hargittai. 2009. "Digital Distinction: Status-Specific Types of Internet Usage." *Social Science Quarterly* 90 (2): 274–291.

Zillow. 2015. "Black Applicants More than Twice as Likely as Whites to Be Denied Home Loans." Zillow. February 9. Available at http://zillowmediaroom.com/2015-02-09-Black-Applicants-More-Than-Twice-as-Likely-as-Whites-to-be-Denied-Home-Loans.

Zimmer, Michael J., Charles A. Sullivan, Deborah Calloway, and Richard Richards. 2000. *Case and Materials on Employment Discrimination* 5th ed. New York: Aspen Law & Business.

Zimmerman, Gregory M., and Steven F. Messner. 2010. "Neighborhood Context and the Gender Gap in Adolescent Violent Crime." *American Sociological Review* 75 (6): 958–980.

Zmerli, Sonja, and Ken Newton. 2008. "Social Trust and Attitudes toward Democracy." *Public Opinion Quarterly* 72 (4): 706–724.

Zuckerman, Mortimer B. 2006. "We're Not Playing Fair on Taxes." *US News and World Report* 140 (16): 64.

Zwerdling, Daniel. 2015. "Hospitals Fail to Protect Nursing Staff from Becoming Patients." National Public Radio, February 25. Available at http://www.npr.org/2015/02/04/382639199/hospitals-fail-to-protect-nursing-staff-from-becoming-patients.

INDEX

Page numbers in italic refer to figures. Page numbers in bold refer to tables.